Principles of Macroeconomics

AN ANALYTICAL APPROACH

Peter N. Hess
DAVIDSON COLLEGE

Clark G. Ross
DAVIDSON COLLEGE

WEST PUBLISHING COMPANY

Minneapolis/St. Paul   New York   Los Angeles   San Francisco

COPYEDITING	Margaret Jarpey
COMPOSITION	Graphic World
COVER DESIGN	David Farr, Imagesmythe
COVER IMAGE	Uniphoto
TEXT DESIGN	K. M. Weber
ARTWORK	Visual Graphic Systems
INDEX	Northwind Editorial Services

Production, printing, and binding by West Publishing Company.

WEST'S COMMITMENT TO THE ENVIRONMENT

In 1906, West Publishing Company began recycling materials left over from the production of books. This began a tradition of efficient and responsible use of resources. Today, up to 95 percent of our legal books and 70 percent of our college and school texts are printed on recycled, acid-free stock. West also recycles nearly 22 million pounds of scrap paper annually—the equivalent of 181,717 trees. Since the 1960s, West has devised ways to capture and recycle waste inks, solvents, oils, and vapors created in the printing process. We also recycle plastics of all kinds, wood, glass, corrugated cardboard, and batteries, and have eliminated the use of styrofoam book packaging. We at West are proud of the longevity and the scope of our commitment to the environment.

COPYRIGHT ©1993 By WEST PUBLISHING COMPANY
610 Opperman Drive
P.O. Box 64526
St. Paul, MN 55164-0526

All rights reserved

Printed in the United States of America

00 99 98 97 96 95 94 93   8 7 6 5 4 3 2 1 0

Library of Congress Cataloging-in-Publication Data

Hess, Peter N.
    Principles of macroeconomics : an analytical approach / Peter N. Hess, Clark G. Ross.
      p. cm.
    Includes index.
    ISBN 0-314-01258-3 (alk. paper)
    1. Macroeconomics.   I. Ross, Clark G.   II. Title.
HB172.5.H47 1993
339—dc20

93-9211
CIP

*To my mother, June,
whose love, humor, strength, and courage
endure and sustain,
I dedicate this work.*

Peter Hess

*To my parents, Helen and Nate,
whose love and concern
knew no bounds.*

Clark Ross

Contents

Preface xi

PART I
Introduction to Economics

CHAPTER 1
An Overview of Economics 2

Four Economic Questions 3
   Output Selection 3
   Production Technique 3
   Distribution 3
   Growth 4
Resolution of the Economic Questions 4
   Tradition 4
   Market Capitalism 4
   Socialism 5
   Mixed Economic Systems 5
Efficiency and Equity within an Economic System 6

CHAPTER 2
The Methodology of Economics 8

Overview of Modern Economy 9
Developing an Economic Model 12
   Hypothesis Testing 13
   Extending the Model 17

CHAPTER 3
Scarcity, Choice, and Opportunity Cost 23

Production Possibilities Boundary 24
   An Economy of One Individual 24

Trade-offs on the National Level 26
Implications of Present Resource Allocations 31

—CHAPTER 4—
COMPARATIVE ADVANTAGE: A BASIS FOR TRADE 36

Absolute Advantage 36
Comparative Advantage 39
Determining the Gains from Trade 40
Production and Consumption Possibilities Boundaries 42

PART II
DEMAND AND SUPPLY: FUNDAMENTALS OF THE MARKET MECHANISM

—CHAPTER 5—
MARKET EQUILIBRIUM: DEMAND AND SUPPLY 50

Demand Schedule 51
   Determinants of Demand Schedule 52
   Changes in Demand 53
Supply Schedule 56
   Determinants of Supply Schedule 58
   Changes in Supply 58
Determining Equilibrium Price and Quantity 60
Comparative Statics: Changes in Market Equilibrium 65

—CHAPTER 6—
ELASTICITY 71

Measurement of Elasticity 71
Price Elasticity of Demand 72
   Price Elasticity along a Linear Demand Schedule 75
   Relationship between Marginal Revenue and Price 76
   Total Revenues and Price Elasticity of Demand 77
Cross–Price Elasticity of Demand 79
Income Elasticity of Demand 80
Demand Elasticities for Electricity 82
Other Demand Elasticities 82
Price Elasticity of Supply 83

PART III
INTRODUCTION TO AGGREGATE ANALYSIS

CHAPTER 7
MACROECONOMIC CONCEPTS 88

Unemployment 89
Inflation 91
Real Growth in National Output 98
Introduction to Aggregate Demand and Aggregate Supply 99
Equilibrium Real National Output and Aggregate Price Level 103

CHAPTER 8
NATIONAL INCOME ACCOUNTING 107

Value Added 108
Measurement of Gross Domestic Product 109
   Output-Expenditure Approach 109
   Gross Domestic Product and Gross National Product 113
   Factor-Payments Approach 113
Other National Income Statistics 116
   Net National Product 116
   Net Investment 116
   Disposable Personal Income 116
Basic Macroeconomic Identity 117
Gross National Product and Welfare 119

PART IV
NATIONAL INCOME DETERMINATION

CHAPTER 9
A SIMPLE KEYNESIAN MODEL OF NATIONAL INCOME DETERMINATION 126

Components of Desired Aggregate Expenditures 127
   Consumption Function 128
   Consumption Expenditures 131
   Investment Expenditures 131
   Other Components of Desired Aggregate Expenditures 133
Solving the Simple Keynesian Model 133
   Keynesian Cross Diagram 135
   Numerical Example for Simple Keynesian Model 137
Comparative Statics and the Multiplier 140

CHAPTER 10
The Demand for Money 148

Functions of Money 148
Types of Money 150
Aggregate Measures of Money 152
Determinants of Money Demand 153
   Transactions Demand 154
   Precautionary Demand 158
   Speculative Demand 158
Portfolio Management 158
Liquidity Preference 161

CHAPTER 11
The Banking System and the Money Supply 166

Federal Reserve System 167
Commercial Banks 168
   Liabilities 169
   Assets 169
   Capital Account 171
Deposit Expansion 171
   Required Reserves 172
   Excess Reserves 174
   Cash Withdrawals 175
The Fed's Influence on the Money Supply 178
Money Market Equilibrium 182

CHAPTER 12
Aggregate Demand and Aggregate Supply 186

Interest-Sensitive Expenditures 187
Aggregate Demand Curve 188
Shifts in Aggregate Demand Curve 192
Aggregate Supply Curve 194
Shifts in Aggregate Supply Curve 195
Aggregate Demand and Aggregate Supply: Comparative Statics 199
   Shifts in Aggregate Demand 199
   Shifts in Aggregate Supply 202
Business Cycles 203

PART V
MACROECONOMIC POLICY

CHAPTER 13
THE CONDUCT OF FISCAL POLICY 212

Keynes and Demand-Management Policy in a Depressed Economy 213
Fiscal Policy Options 215
   Change in Government Spending 217
   Change in Net Lump-Sum Taxes 218
Effectiveness of Fiscal Policy 221
   Aggregate Supply Constraints 221
   Interest-Sensitivities and the Monetarist Position 222
   Lags in Policymaking 223
Built-in Stabilizers 226
National Debt and Federal Budget Deficits 227
   Momentum of the National Debt 229
   Financing Federal Budget Deficits 229
   Budget Deficits and the Macroeconomic Identity 230
Balanced Budget Amendment 232

CHAPTER 14
THE CONDUCT OF MONETARY POLICY 237

Instruments of Monetary Policy 238
Effectiveness of Monetary Policy 240
Inflation and Contractionary Monetary Policy 242
Monetary Policy and Demand Management 244
   Lags in Policymaking 245
   Uncertain Multiplier Effects 245
Monetary Policy Targets 248
   Monetarist Monetary Rule 249
Comparing Monetary and Fiscal Policy 253

CHAPTER 15
SUPPLY-SIDE POLICY 260

Taxes and Incentives 262
   Labor Supply 262
   Personal Saving 266
   Business Investment 269
Reaganomics and the 1980s 270
An Assessment of Reaganomics 273

— CHAPTER 16 —
Unemployment and Inflation: Trade-offs 280

Phillips Curve 280
Unemployment 283
    Types of Unemployment 284
    Other Dimensions of Unemployment 286
Inflation 287
    Causes of Inflation 288
    Consequences of Inflation 289
Natural Rate of Unemployment 292
Neutrality of Money Hypothesis 296
Rational Expectations 298

PART VI
The International Economy

— CHAPTER 17 —
Balance of Payments and Exchange Rates 304

Balance of Payments Account 305
    Current Account 307
    Capital Account 308
    Official Settlements Account 309
Exchange Rates and Demand and Supply of Foreign Exchange 311
    Demand Curve for Foreign Exchange 312
    Supply Curve of Foreign Exchange 314
    Equilibrium Exchange Rate 315
Changes in the Exchange Rate 317
    Determinants of Exchange Rate Changes 317
    Consequences of Exchange Rate Changes 319

— CHAPTER 18 —
Exchange Rate Systems 323

Flexible Exchange Rates 324
Fixed Exchange Rates 329
Adjustable Peg Exchange Rates 332
Demise of Bretton Woods System 335
Managed Float 336
Demand-Management Policy and External Balance 336
Exchange Value of Dollar After Bretton Woods 337

CHAPTER 19
Economic Growth and Development 345

Country Classification 346
Growth and Development 351
Growth Model Approach 351
Basic Needs Approach 354
Trade and Economic Development 357
  Import Substitution 357
  Export Expansion 358
Emergence of the External Debt Problem 359
Radical School's Critique 362
An Agenda for Development 363

CHAPTER 20
Socialism and the Transformation to Market Capitalism 368

Marx and His Critique of Capitalism 368
Theory of Socialism 370
  Centralized Socialism 371
  Decentralized Socialism 372
Soviet Economy 373
  Historical Perspective 373
  Soviet Economy under Stalin 374
  Gorbachev Reform Process and Demise of the USSR 378
  Transition from Command Socialism 379

Glossary 385
Index 400

Preface

After more than twenty years of experience in teaching economic principles, we are convinced that a crisp, challenging, and focused text can significantly enhance the quality of an introductory economics course. Finding current offerings inadequate and concerned with what we perceived as the prevailing trend in principles texts, we decided to write *Principles of Economics: An Analytical Approach*.

A RIGOROUS, STREAMLINED TREATMENT

Our approach to the teaching of economics is straightforward. We set out the theoretical framework, carefully defining the variables and the underlying assumptions, and then develop concepts, illustrate applications, and discuss policy implications. Verbal description is complemented by algebraic formulation, graphical analysis, and, where possible, numerical example. The development of the material should be accessible to all college students, who, with a basic competence in high school algebra, are willing to put forth a fair effort.

We seek to present the core of economic principles in an efficient, careful, and rigorous manner. Unifying concepts like opportunity cost, decision-making on the margin, adjustment to disequilibria, and policy tradeoffs in the political economy integrate the text. The emphasis at all times is on economic reasoning.

The text is concisely written. We depart from the conventional encyclopedic approach, where exhaustive attempts to sample subjects come at the expense of focus and analysis. We believe that the otherwise worthy objective of being "reader friendly" has unfortunately fostered cumbersome, overly conversational writing styles, with material presented in bite-size segments and an undue emphasis on vocabulary. Difficult material is often regulated to appendices, especially when algebra is involved—the implicit message being that it is all right to skip over any analysis which requires extra effort. As is typical of the video age, illustrations in three, four, or more colors are used to dazzle the reader. The overall result is that students, overwhelmed by the volume of reading and distracted by the bells and whistles, revert to skimming the chapters and memorizing the highlights. We believe these volumes serve to jade students to the excitement of learning and applying economics.

On the other hand, the cursory coverage and superficiality of analysis in the shorter texts expressly designed for one-semester principles courses tend to be well below what competent and motivated college students deserve.

Instead we seek to stimulate learning with a diligent presentation of the material. We believe that one or two colors provide the greatest clarity in illustrations. Key terms are presented in the natural progression of analysis, with formal definitions found in the glossary. The development of topics flows logically within and across chapters. Challenging concepts are integrated within the chapters, not buried in appendices. We believe that important yet difficult material, such as multiplier effects in an open Keynesian model of national income determination, can and should be incorporated into a first course in economics. Students are not asked to accept results on faith; rather, they are shown how the results are derived. The end-of-chapter exercises bolster understanding by allowing students to work through the theoretical models.

We do not pretend that reading an economics text will be as easy as reading a novel. Working through some of the chapters may well require pencil and paper. The effort put forth, however, will pay rich dividends in comprehension and economic reasoning.

INTERNATIONAL EMPHASIS

As a review of the table of contents will show, international economics is emphasized throughout the text. Of the 20 chapters, five are international, including an early chapter on comparative advantage. International topics addressed in other chapters include national security (chapter 3), the incorporation of foreign trade in the Simple Keynesian macroeconomic model (chapter 9), and the relationship between the federal budget deficits and current account deficits of the United States (chapter 13).

POLICY ORIENTATION

Throughout the text we stress the political-economic dynamics of policy making including: examining the macroeconomic debate over the efficacy of demand-management policy; contrasting the discipline required by fixed exchange rates to the automatic adjustment of flexible exchange rates; and comparing the growth model approach to the basic needs orientation in economic development. Excerpts from the *Wall Street Journal* and other periodicals are used to illustrate the relevance of theories and to encourage students to find their own confirmations of economic principles in practice.

For the students using our text, we seek to provide a sense of how the discipline works and why economics as a mode of inquiry is important. For those students continuing on with economics, our text offers a solid foundation in the fundamentals of macroeconomic analysis. As one of our reviewers said,

> [the text] provides many more useful examples of real world policy debate which would enable students to intelligently discuss policy issues in other settings beside class. It also focuses on economic methodology and thinking in a way that no other text I know of does.

In sum, we believe that the current attention to excellence in education, the renewed interest in math and science in the curriculum, and the challenge to compete in the international marketplace all suggest that the time is right for a streamlined, analytical text in economic principles.

ORGANIZATION OF THE MACROECONOMICS TEXT

The text begins with an introduction to the methodology of economics: the issues addressed by economists and the process of testing economic theories. The key concept of opportunity cost is emphasized early—in chapter 3 with the production possibilities boundary and in chapter 4 with international specialization. In the first four chapters, which comprise Part I of the text, we provide in-depth examples of economics analysis, including an empirical model (the determinants of residential construction) and two theoretical models. In one, the trade-off between national security and the standard of living is conveyed through graphical analysis. In the second, the basis for international trade is conveyed through an extended numerical example.

Part II, consisting of chapters 5 and 6, covers the fundamentals of demand and supply in competitive markets and the concept of elasticity. After developing the market mechanism, we turn in Part III to aggregate economic analysis, with the introduction of macroeconomic concepts (unemployment, inflation, economic growth, aggregate demand, and aggregate supply) in chapter 7 and national income accounting in chapter 8. Part IV of the text concerns national income determination. In chapter 9, as a first exercise in macroeconomic model-building, we present a Simple Keynesian model. We then extend the analysis to the money market (money demand in chapter 10 and money supply in chapter 11). In chapter 12 supply constraints are incorporated into the macro model and the aggregate demand-aggregate supply framework is further developed.

Chapters on the conduct of macroeconomic policy (fiscal policy in chapter 13, monetary policy in chapter 14, and supply-side policy in chapter 15) set up the analysis of the inflation-unemployment trade-offs in chapter 16. After working through these four chapters in Part V, students should understand why economists (Keynesians, monetarists, New Classicals, and supply-siders) disagree on the efficacy of demand-management macroeconomic policy.

In Part VI we turn to the international economy. In chapters 17 and 18 the macroeconomics of the open economy, with balance of payments and exchange rate adjustments, add another dimension to the analysis. We discuss the concerns of economically less developed nations in chapter 19 and the transformation from socialism to market capitalism in chapter 20.

SUPPLEMENTS

We have written the *Instructor's Manual,* which includes options for course outlines, the purpose of each chapter, summaries of the main points in each chapter, teaching notes, and answers to questions found in the text at the end of each chapter. The manual also contains more than 50 transparency masters of key figures from the text.

The *Study Guide* for students, written by Professor David Cleeton of Oberlin College, includes a section on how to read graphs, a brief review of the relevant mathematics, a summary of the logic underlying the organization of the text, problems, and hints on analysis.

The *Test Bank,* prepared by Professor Stephen Marks of Pomona College, includes multiple-choice questions, a sample test for each chapter, problems, and discussion questions.

West Publishing Company offers *WesTest 3.0 Computerized Testing,* a program run on IBM PCs and compatible on Macintoshes, which allows instructors to create, edit, store, and print exams. An *Economic Videodisc,* where economic illustrations and footage from the Economics U$A series by Annenberg/CPB can be accessed, and *Macroeconomics$/Microeconomics$ Study Wizard Software* are also available to adopters.

ACKNOWLEDGMENTS

Needless to say, writing an economics principles text is a major undertaking; one which reflects the contributions of many individuals. We consider ourselves fortunate to have worked with the team at West Publishing Company. We are indebted to Richard Fenton, senior economics editor, for believing with us that there is a need for a streamlined, analytically rigorous treatment of economic principles, and for having the confidence in us to write such a text. We have enjoyed working with Nancy Hill-Whilton, developmental editor, whose guidance and encouragement throughout the entire process significantly improved our efforts. Maggie Jarpey was terrific in her copyediting of the manuscript. We are grateful to Laura Evans, who professionally handled the production of our book, and Mary Steiner, for her skill in marketing our book. We realize that many others, with whom we did not come in contact, were instrumental in producing this text, and we take this opportunity to thank them too.

The success of a text reflects in no small measure the contributions of the reviewers. We benefitted from their insights and suggestions. Every comment received on the manuscript during the review process was carefully evaluated, and whether or not it was incorporated into the text, served to improve the final product. To our reviewers, listed below, we say thanks.

David Denslow, University of Florida
Paul M. Taube, University of Texas–Pan America
Frank P. Stafford, University of Michigan
Stephen V. Marks, Pomona College
Gary J. Krueger, Macalester College
Dereka Rushbrook, University of Texas–Austin
Peter Gordon, University of Southern California
Carol A. M. Clark, Guilford College
Gerald D. Toland, Jr., Southwest State University
Robert A. Margo, Vanderbilt University
James A. Wilde, University of North Carolina–Chapel Hill
Daniel Barbezat, Amherst College
George H. Lamson, Carleton College

Klaus G. Becker, Texas Tech University
Charles D. DeLorme, Jr., University of Georgia
C. Richard Long, Georgia State University
Christine Rider, St. John's University
Larry G. Sgontz, University of Iowa
Jan Palmer, Ohio University
Duncan P. Mann, Williams College
Werner Baer, University of Illinois–Urbana/Champaign
Royall Whitaker, U.S. Naval Academy

We are most fortunate in having fine colleagues and good students at Davidson College, who inspire us to strive for excellence in teaching. We especially wish to thank Professors Dennis Appleyard, David Martin, and Charles Ratliff, Jr., for reading drafts of manuscript chapters. As always their counsel is well taken.

Finally, we wish to acknowledge those students who will study principles of economics with our text. We trust you will find the text challenging and your efforts worthwhile. Most of all, we hope you will be encouraged to continue your study of economics.

Peter Hess and Clark Ross

Boo, Jamie, and Joey Hess, with their love and understanding, continually help me appreciate the meaning of life. This text would not have been possible without them.

PNH

PART

I

INTRODUCTION TO ECONOMICS

CHAPTERS

— 1 —
AN OVERVIEW OF ECONOMICS

— 2 —
THE METHODOLOGY OF ECONOMICS

— 3 —
SCARCITY, CHOICE,
AND OPPORTUNITY COST

— 4 —
COMPARATIVE ADVANTAGE:
A BASIS FOR TRADE

CHAPTER

1

AN OVERVIEW OF ECONOMICS

The term economics has assimilated so many connotations that it would be misleading to put a rigid meaning upon it by a single crisp definition.[1]

While necessarily general, definitions of economics have been offered, and certain themes have seemed to garner consensus. A sample: Economics is...

the science or study of wealth (welfare) and its production, applicable either to the individual, the family, the state, or in the widest sense, the world.[2]

mainly concerned with . . . such human activities as are directed towards the production, appropriation, and application of the material means of satisfying human desires, so far as such means are capable of being exchanged.[3]

the study of the allocation of scarce resources among unlimited and competing uses. It is the social science that deals with the ways in which men and societies seek to satisfy their material needs and desires, since the means at their disposal do not permit them to do so completely.[4]

A common theme that links these definitions is **scarcity.** The quantities of goods and services available are less than the total wants of society. Insofar as any member of the society desires to have more of any good or service than currently consumed, scarcity exists. In a general sense, economics is the study of the choices that must be made as a result of scarcity.

---

[1] Albert Gailord Hart in *Encyclopedia of Economics,* edited by Douglas Greenwald (New York: McGraw-Hill, 1982), p. 322.
[2] William Albert Samuel Hewins in *The Encyclopedia Britannica,* 11th ed. vol. III (Cambridge, England: The University Press, 1910), p. 899.
[3] Henry Sidgwick in *The New Palgrave: A Dictionary of Economics,* vol. 2, edited by John Eatwell, Murray Milgate, and Peter Newman (London: The Macmillan Press Limited, 1987), p. 59; reprinted from *Palgrave's Dictionary of Political Economy,* vol. 1, edited by Henry Higgs (London: Macmillan and Company Limited, 1926), p. 679.
[4] Albert Rees in *International Encyclopedia of the Social Sciences,* vol. 4, edited by David Sills (The Macmillan Company and the Free Press, 1968), p. 472.

No society has ever escaped this economic predicament. Goods have always been scarce. In any period of time there are limited amounts of resources or *inputs* (labor, capital, or machines, land, and raw materials) available for producing *output*.

FOUR ECONOMIC QUESTIONS

The economic choices that scarcity imposes on any society relate to the

1. Selection of goods and services to produce (what to produce).
2. Selection of production techniques to use (how to produce).
3. Distribution of the available output (for whom to produce).
4. Growth in the capacity to produce future output (how to enhance future production).

Output Selection

Given the available resources and the existing technology, there are different combinations of goods and services possible in a society. For example, broadly defined, there are *civilian goods* (for example, plowshares) and *military goods* (for example, swords). There cannot be enough production of both types of goods to satisfy completely all the individuals in the society. Thus, some output combination must be chosen, recognizing that as more of one good (swords) is produced, there can be less produced of the other good (plowshares). A more rigorous development of this question follows in Chapter 3, where the production possibilities boundary for a society is introduced.

Production Technique

Assume that a society is going to produce a certain number of plowshares. There will likely be different input combinations for the given state of technology that will yield the desired quantity. For instance, the quantity of plowshares could be produced largely by machines, that is, by using little labor and much capital; or the same quantity could be produced with less capital (machine time) but a more intensive use of labor. Choosing between these two input combinations to produce the desired number of plowshares is a question addressed by economics.

Distribution

Given that the output of the society will be limited relative to the total desires of the population, choices concerning the distribution of the output must be made. For instance, should each individual receive the same quantity of output? Or should the amount received by each be based on need? Or should each receive according to the ability to produce? Obviously, the question of distribution can be a particularly contentious one in any society.

Growth

The primary consequence of economic growth is increased production of goods and services in the future. Growth in output occurs as a result of increases in the quantities and qualities of resources available and advances in technology. A society influences the potential for future economic growth with its current decisions. Generally speaking, reducing the amount of present consumption in order to devote resources to enhance future consumption is the process by which economic growth occurs. For instance, in agrarian societies, eating less corn today in order to have more seed for the next planting would increase the potential corn harvests of the future.

A contemporary concern is with generating **sustainable growth,** or economic growth that will not impair the natural environment for future generations. Economic growth accompanied by irreparable pollution of the air, water, and land or the extinction of species would not be considered sustainable.

RESOLUTION OF THE ECONOMIC QUESTIONS

Three types of economic systems have evolved from societies' attempts to resolve these economic questions: tradition, market capitalism, and socialism.

Tradition

As applied to an economic system, **tradition** refers to methods of production, distribution, and consumption established in the past and perpetuated by custom. While it would be impossible to resolve the economic questions of a modern society solely by tradition, in primitive societies tradition has played a major role. For instance, meat might be produced only by male hunters and grain crops produced only by females. Tradition could determine that adult males first eat to their satisfaction, with women and children eating later. Once economic activity has progressed to involve specialization of labor (such as factory work) and exchanges of goods among individuals, tradition no longer provides a satisfactory basis for the resolution of the economic questions—though it may still provide some influence.

Market Capitalism

Market capitalism is predicated on the notion that the means of production (labor, machines, land, and raw materials) are privately owned by individuals. The presumption is that individuals seek to maximize their self-interest in making decisions concerning the disposition of the inputs. Using labor, natural resources, and machines to produce output generates *income* that can be used to acquire other goods and services. Through this process, illustrated in the next chapter as the *circular flow of economic activity,* the preceding economic questions can be resolved. The demands for output by those who have the income to purchase the output determine the output mix, or combination, produced. In a sense, consumers vote with their dollars, seeking to make those expenditures that will yield them the most satisfaction.

Optimal (or *least-cost*) input combinations for producing the goods and services will be chosen by producers who are trying to maximize economic profits. Under market capitalism the distribution of output is essentially determined by the distribution of income, which in turn flows from the ownership and use of the inputs.

Elements of capitalism have always existed. However, historians of economic thought credit the Scottish economist Adam Smith with providing the first complete description of market capitalism in his 1776 publication of *An Inquiry into the Nature and Causes of the Wealth of Nations*. Smith's view of small economic agents (buyers and sellers) maximizing their self-interest in competitive markets, with minimal government intervention, is called **laissez-faire capitalism.**

Socialism

The critique of capitalism offered by Karl Marx in the mid-eighteenth century was instrumental in advancing **socialism,** wherein the means of production are collectively, not individually, owned. The individual decision making characteristic of capitalism is replaced, under the command variant of socialism, by the state, which through central planning resolves the economic questions. For instance, the state may direct firms to produce certain quantities of output using specified input combinations. It may set wage levels for different occupations and workers, thus addressing the distribution issue. The allocation of output between current consumption and investment for enhancing future consumption is similarly made by the state.

The Russian Revolution of 1917 and the rise to power of Vladimir Lenin marked the first significant experiment with a socialist economic system. The command elements of socialism appeared in the 1920s; by the mid-1930s a full command economy had been instituted under the direction of Joseph Stalin.

It is possible to relax the role of the state in a socialist economy and move from a command to a more decentralized economic system, for example, one using markets to determine prices and granting individual firms more autonomy in their production and input decisions. The republics of the former Soviet Union and the East European socialist countries are experimenting with such decentralization.

Mixed Economic Systems

At this point, it is important to understand that the economic systems found in practice are **mixed.** For instance, the economy of the United States, while predominately capitalist, contains elements of socialism and tradition. Government regulation of business, agricultural price supports, the social security system, and subsidized medical care represent departures from laissez-faire capitalism. The summer school recess has been traditional, originating with the need for children to help with their family farms. The U.S. military's exclusion of women from some aspects of combat is another example of tradition within a contemporary economic system.

The former Soviet Union (USSR), while predominantly socialist, had elements of capitalism in its economy. Farmers growing vegetables on a plot of land assigned for their individual usage and selling the harvest in free markets was clearly a capitalist feature of that economy. So was the practice of plumbers and other tradesmen doing work for profit on hours off from their state assignment.

Economists are careful to distinguish the theoretical models from the actual economic systems. This text is primarily devoted to explaining the theory that underlies market capitalism. The economic insights developed can be applied to other economic systems. Socialism and the transformation to a market economy of the former Soviet Union are discussed in the final chapter.

EFFICIENCY AND EQUITY WITHIN AN ECONOMIC SYSTEM

The two most widely used criteria to judge the desirability of an economic system are **efficiency** and **equity**. To the economist, an *efficient* situation is one in which it is impossible to enhance the well-being of one party without reducing the well-being of another. For instance, if more plowshares and fewer swords were desired by consumers, an efficient economic system would respond to this desire and alter the production mix. As will be seen in the study of markets, *competitive capitalism* responds to the consumers' tastes. In contrast, *monopoly capitalism* yields inefficient restrictions on output.

Another aspect of efficiency concerns the allocation of inputs across the different goods produced. When inputs are not efficiently allocated, it is possible to rearrange input usage to produce more goods, clearly making some (or all) people better off without reducing the well-being of others. A competitive market system, which leads profit-maximizing producers to minimize the cost of each output level, will tend toward efficiency in production.

The economic efficiency of socialism was challenged in the former command economies of the Soviet Union and Eastern Europe. Difficulties in responding to consumer wants and in producing at minimum cost have encouraged economic reform, a complicated process, in these countries.

Economists tend to place a high priority on the efficiency of an economic system. In our study of economic principles, there will be many references to economic efficiency. We will illustrate how international trade can generate efficiencies for the trading partners. We will discuss how price controls (such as minimum wages and agricultural price supports) tend to reduce efficiency; yet, we will also show circumstances where such price controls enhance economic efficiency.

A second important criteria used by economists is *equity,* for which a definition is rather subjective. Essentially, an equitable economic result is one viewed as fair or just. No universally accepted standard for equity exists. The equity assessment is most often applied to the distribution of output, or income, in a society. In a democratic society, the voters or their representatives must address the question of equity when determining taxes and government outlays.

A discussion of equity often raises important questions for economists, political scientists, and philosophers. For example, does market capitalism with its reliance on individual self-interest and market-generated incomes tend toward unacceptable inequities? Also, is it possible to pursue simultaneously both economic efficiency and equity? Or is there a trade-off between efficiency and equity? Some argue that transferring income to help the poor will reduce the total amount of income available, leading to a less efficient result. Others argue that income redistribution can be designed to minimize the efficiency loss.

Moreover, the gain in equity can offset a loss of total output. In studying economics it is not only important to be aware of such broad questions, but to realize that all the particular topics of economics fit into a larger context affecting all members of society.

For example, two important economic issues related to the performance of the national economy are unemployment and inflation. Both have implications for efficiency and equity. For one, unemployment and economic efficiency are incompatible. When an input, in this case labor, is not fully utilized, the amount of output produced is less than the potential output of the economy. Moreover, unemployment tends to generate poverty and greater inequalities in income.

In the next chapter, we continue our study of economics with an overview of the economy and with an illustration of how economic theory can be tested.

KEY TERMS

scarcity
sustainable growth
tradition
market capitalism
laissez-faire capitalism

socialism
mixed economic system
efficiency
equity

QUESTIONS

1. What are the three most important ideas or lessons in this chapter? Discuss why each is important.
2. Does the concept of scarcity have the same relevance in a developed economy like that of the United States as it does in a poorer country like India?
3. Imagine two prisoners being given the same allocations of two goods, ten pieces of candy and four oranges. Explain how this initial allocation of goods could be inefficient and how the prisoners could improve the efficiency of the allocation.
4. Compare and discuss the implications for economic growth and equity of the following methods for distributing income.
   a. Each individual receives the same income.
   b. Each individual receives an income based on his or her need.
   c. Each individual receives an income based on his or her contribution to production.
5. How might the distribution of incomes differ in a traditional economy, a capitalist economy, and a socialist economy? Which type of economic system would likely be the most equitable? Why? Which type of economic system would likely be the most efficient? Why?

CHAPTER

2

THE METHODOLOGY OF ECONOMICS

ECONOMICS, AS A **social science,** is concerned with human behavior and social institutions. Unlike the natural sciences (biology, chemistry, physics), economics allows few possibilities for controlled laboratory experimentation.[1] Thus, in studying human behavior, economists must rely on uncontrolled experiments, basically observations of actual events.

Human behavior, especially on an individual basis, is difficult to predict. It is often possible, however, to observe certain tendencies or common patterns in behavior. For example, other things being equal, an increase in the price of beef would likely result in a decrease in the quantities of beef purchased—as most individuals would substitute less expensive forms of meat or protein for beef. This is not to say that all individuals would behave in this way. Some, deriving satisfaction from "going against the crowd"—and being able to afford more of the higher priced commodities—might actually increase their consumption of beef. But economists do not attempt to account for all the possibilities in human behavior. Instead economic theories are based on representative or typical behavior. The goal is to illuminate the key relationships among selected economic phenomena. To be useful, a theory must abstract from reality—offering a condensed, yet insightful, explanation of the behavior in question.

---

[1] Some controlled laboratory experimentation has been done by economists, measuring the responses of both human and animal subjects to economic stimuli, but far more numerous are experiments outside the laboratory environment—for example, those that attempt to assess the responses of households and firms to tax incentives and transfer programs.

OVERVIEW OF MODERN ECONOMY

An overview of the economist's laboratory—a modern economy—is provided in Figure 2.1. This diagram looks rather complex now. By the end of a first course in economics, however, a diligent student will have studied each of the components represented—separately and as part of the larger system—and will have a fundamental understanding of the social science known as economics. (Indeed, you will want to refer to Figure 2.1 as you progress through this text.)

The task of the economist is to make sense of the myriad of activities found in an economic system. To begin, economists discern three major groups of decision makers in the economy. **Households** constitute one group. Each household is considered to be a single economic unit that seeks to maximize its "satisfaction" through the consumption of final goods and services.[2] This is not to suggest that all the satisfaction households derive comes from goods and services. Recall that economics deals with the "material means of satisfying human desires."

Members of households receive income from supplying their scarce factor services for the production of final goods and services. Primarily labor services are exchanged for wages and salaries. Not all of the income received by

---

[2] A **service** refers to the performance of a task: for example, barbers cut hair, bankers manage money, teachers provide instruction, and doctors dispense health care.

FIGURE 2.1
OVERVIEW OF THE ECONOMY

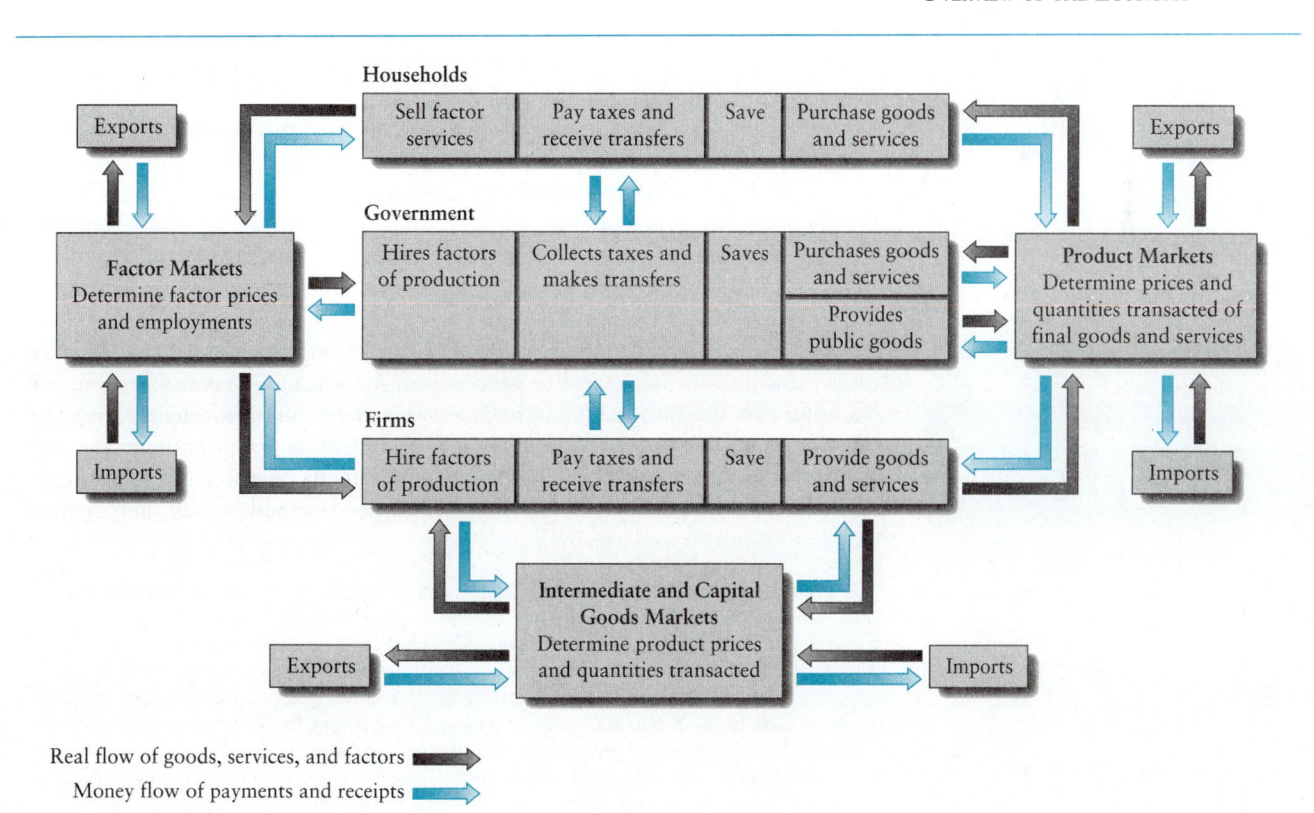

households is used for present consumption. Some of the income may be set aside as savings, which may be made available (through banks and other financial intermediaries) to others for spending in the economy. Households receive income (interest and dividends) on the savings made available for loans and investment.

Firms make up the second group. Economists assume that firms seek to maximize **profits,** defined as the difference between the revenues received from the sale of their output and the costs of making the output. In the process of producing goods and services, firms hire labor, rent land, extract resources from nature, and borrow money to purchase **physical capital** (plant, equipment, and machinery). Firms may set aside, or *save,* some of their profits for future expansion in physical capital.[3]

Very simple models of the economy include only these two groups of economic agents. Focusing for the moment on households and firms, we can identify the **basic circular flows of economic activity** as shown in Figure 2.2. Firms (which are ultimately owned by households) use labor (supplied by households), with physical capital (the purchases of which are financed in part from the saving of households), land, and natural resources to produce goods and services that are then sold to households. In a clockwise direction is a counterflow, where money earned by households is used for expenditures on the final goods and services produced by firms.

Two sets of markets have been identified: **factor markets,** where households supply the factor services demanded by firms, and **product markets,** where firms supply the final goods and services demanded by households. Examples of factor markets would include the markets for computer programmers, farmland, and credit. Product markets would include the markets for personal computers, breakfast cereal, and entertainment.

As illustrated in Figure 2.1, the economy is considerably more complex than suggested by our discussion of factor and product markets. Firms not only buy factor services from households, firms also buy goods from each other. We have already noted one type. **Capital goods** are the plant, equipment, and machinery used by firms to produce their final goods and services. An automobile manufacturer's purchases of a forklift and a spray gun for paint are expenditures on capital goods that add to the productive capacity of the automaker. **Intermediate goods** are the final products of one firm that are used as inputs by other firms into further stages of production. An automobile manufacturer, for example, uses the intermediate goods of steel, paint, tires, and ballbearings to produce cars.

Without going into great detail at this point, we will mention the third major actor in the economy, the **government** (also referred to as the **central**

---

[3] Even in this overview, we should be clear on the difference between **financial capital** (money funds) and **physical capital** (plant, equipment, and machinery used by firms in the production of goods and services). Physical capital (along with labor, land, and natural resources) is a primary factor of production. Financial capital, while not a primary factor of production, provides a factor service and represents purchasing power over the primary factors of production. Firms can raise financial capital in several ways, including issuing stock, or shares of ownership, in the firm, issuing bonds, or instruments of debt, and borrowing money directly from banks. Firms need to raise financial capital initially to purchase the physical capital required to begin production. Later, if successful, firms may want to raise additional capital to expand their productive capacities.

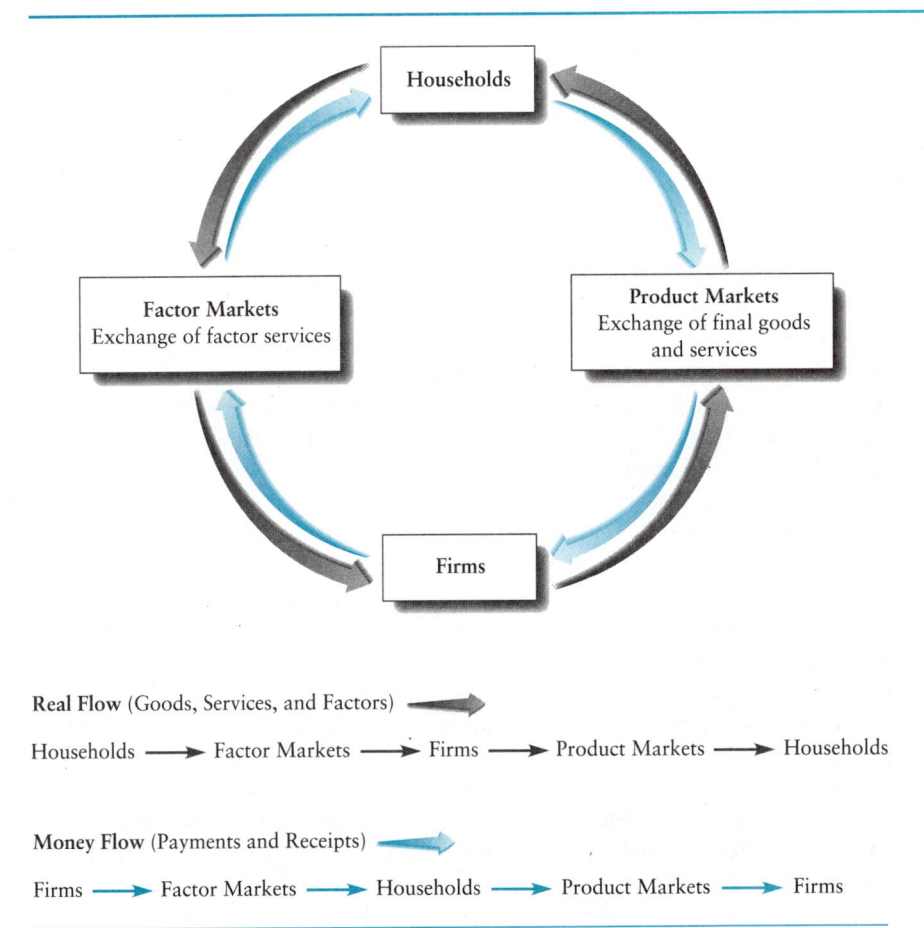

FIGURE 2.2
Basic Circular Flows in the Economy

Real Flow (Goods, Services, and Factors) →

Households → Factor Markets → Firms → Product Markets → Households

Money Flow (Payments and Receipts) →

Firms → Factor Markets → Households → Product Markets → Firms

---

authorities). The government includes the public officials and civil servants at the local, state, and federal levels. Government enters the factor markets as a demander of factor services. Labor is hired, land and natural resources may be purchased, and money is borrowed. Government enters the product markets as the producer of final goods and services (for example, national defense, the judiciary system, and public education) and as the demander of final goods and services (for example, tanks and airplanes from defense industries and the services of highway construction firms). User fees, such as tolls on interstate highways, and taxes are collected to pay for the activities of the government. Some of the tax revenues are used to make **transfer payments,** payments for which no services are rendered or output produced. Social security checks and unemployment compensation are examples of *income transfers*. Public housing for low-income families and food stamps are examples of *in-kind transfers*. Transfer payments serve to redistribute income.

If the government spends less than it receives in user fees and tax revenues, a *surplus* in the government budget results. This is equivalent to government saving. On the other hand, if the government spends more on goods and services, salaries, and transfers than it receives, a *deficit* results. Budget deficits are usually financed by borrowing.

For an economy isolated from the rest of the world, this introduction would be complete. Some of the goods and services purchased by residents of one nation, however, are not produced domestically. Similarly, some of the goods and services produced in the domestic economy are consumed by residents of other nations. For instance, if a resident of Maine buys a Volvo, this is considered to be a U.S. **import** of a good (and a Swedish **export**). If a Japanese family spends a weekend at Disney World in Orlando, their expenditures on entertainment, food, and lodging are considered to be U.S. exports (Japanese imports) of services. If a farmer in Texas hires Mexican migrants at harvest time, this is a U.S. import of a factor service (labor). If a Canadian insurance company buys a bond issued by a U.S. firm, this is an import of a factor service (financial capital) by the United States in exchange for an asset (the bond). Thus, the rest of the world may participate in one nation's domestic economy in its markets for factor services, intermediate and capital goods, and final goods and services.

This chapter presents only an overview of the economy; in later chapters we will fill in the details. One final observation: the type of economic system reflects the relative influence of the government in determining the allocation of resources. As noted in the first chapter, in practice all economies are **mixed,** operating somewhere on the continuum from socialism to market capitalism. Decentralized decision making prevails in a **market economy.** The actions of households and firms largely determine the prices and quantities transacted in the economy. Even so, the government will be involved in market economies, not only as a participant in the factor and product markets, but in the regulation of business and the redistribution of income. In a **command economy** the central authorities dictate official prices and quantities for goods and services. Nevertheless, households and firms still influence—if sometimes illegally, and then only marginally—the prices and quantities of the output actually produced. The Western industrialized nations are basically market economies, while nations under communist influence tend toward command systems. In the 1980s the Soviet Union and the nations of Eastern Europe began reforms designed to integrate more market features into their command economies. In the 1990s, with the democratic movements in Eastern Europe and the dissolution of the Soviet Union, communism itself was widely rejected as a viable political-economic system.

DEVELOPING AN ECONOMIC MODEL

Economics is concerned with how resources are allocated. Questions addressed by economists include (1) how households allocate expenditures to achieve maximum satisfaction, (2) how firms determine the optimal amount of labor to hire, and (3) how government budget deficits affect the economy. In order to focus on the key relationships, or to attempt to "control the experiment," economists frequently employ the technique of **partial equilibrium analysis,** in which factors other than the ones being studied are assumed to hold constant—even though it is understood that in real life they might change. To make clear the conditional nature of the experiment, the Latin phrase **ceteris**

paribus, meaning "other things being equal," is used. For example: "Ceteris paribus, a rise in the price of movie tickets will lead to a decrease in the number of movie tickets sold." This statement is conditional on all other influences on movie attendance being held constant. Change in the average level of income, the population of potential movie-goers, the prices of other forms of entertainment, or the perceived quality of the movies would each have an impact on movie attendance—whatever the price of movie tickets. But to isolate the relationship between price and the quantity of tickets sold, we "control" the analysis by assuming that other pertinent factors do not change.

Another example would be, "Ceteris paribus, the federal government should be required to balance its budget every year." We may want to condition this statement by allowing for unbalanced budgets, particularly deficits, during times of war. Others would go further and maintain that the federal government should regularly run an unbalanced budget in order to offset the business cycle.

There is an important difference underlying these two examples. The first, regarding movie attendance, illustrates a **positive statement** concerning "what is," or "what will be." It can be tested or resolved by observation, experience, or factual evidence. In contrast, the second, regarding the federal budget, illustrates a **normative statement** expressing an opinion or value judgment and concerning "what ought to be."

"Lower interest rates will ease the foreign debt burden of developing nations," is a positive statement. "Interest rates should be lowered to help the developing nations," is a normative statement.

"Raising import barriers will save American jobs," is a positive statement that may or may not be supported by the evidence. "Eliminating all import barriers is desirable," is a normative statement that will evoke agreement and disagreement but whose validity cannot be determined.

Theories are constructed using positive statements. Specific propositions that can be tested are set forth. If confirmed by the evidence, theories can form the basis for *policy,* which refers to the most appropriate way of achieving certain goals. However, differences in policy recommendations may reflect not only differences in the assumptions underlying theories, but differences in opinion and values.

Hypothesis Testing

To illustrate the testing of economic theory, assume an economist is interested in the determinants of residential construction. She begins her investigation by formulating the following **hypothesis,** which is a statement expressing a possible relationship between the variables under investigation: "Residential construction is directly related to income." Intuitively it would seem that as household incomes rise, expenditures on goods and services, including new housing, would also rise.

The next step for our economist is to define carefully the terms used. For the measure of residential construction, she selects the real value of residential fixed investment during a given period of time. **Residential fixed investment** is defined as the private expenditures for the construction of residential units, including new houses, apartments, and condominiums plus renovations and additions to existing housing units. *Real value* refers to the money value (dollars) adjusted for changes in the price level. For the measure of income, the economist selects real **disposable personal income,** or the real income available to households after taxes are paid and transfers are received.

A simple economic model has been set forth with the direction of causality specified as disposable income affecting residential fixed investment. An **endogenous variable** is a variable to be explained by the model (in this case, real residential fixed investment) and is assumed to be dependent upon the **exogenous variable,** which in turn is assumed to be determined by factors outside the scope of the model. In other words, for the purpose of the analysis, the values of the exogenous variable are regarded as given. Thus, the exogenous variable influences the endogenous variable, but itself is assumed not to be influenced by the endogenous variable.[4] Real disposable income is the exogenous variable in this model.

To test the hypothesis, evidence must be assembled. The economist would collect data for the variables in the model. Suppose she wanted to test the hypothesis for the U.S. economy. A good source for aggregate data on the U.S. economy is the *Economic Report of the President* (an annual report from the president and the Council of Economic Advisers). Further suppose that the 26-year period from 1965 to 1990 is selected as a representative sample of recent years for the U.S. economy. Let

RFI_t = real residential fixed investment in the U.S. economy in year t (in billions of 1987 dollars).

DI_t = real disposable personal income in the U.S. economy in year t (in billions of 1987 dollars).

Note that the variables are expressed in real terms, or constant dollars, with 1987 as the reference year. Essentially, using real values adjusts for the effect of *inflation* (the general tendency for prices to rise over time) and allows for a clearer assessment of the hypothesized relationship between residential construction and disposable income. The hypothesized positive relationship (indicated by the plus sign above the explanatory variable) can be represented consisely by the following equation:

$$RFI = f(\overset{+}{DI})$$

In Table 2.1 the 26 annual observations are presented. To get a quick idea of the relationship, the observations can be plotted as ordered pairs on a **scatter diagram** as shown in Figure 2.3. Note that the dependent variable *RFI* is represented on the vertical axis and the explanatory variable *DI* on the horizontal axis. The scatter diagram appears to show a positive relationship—with higher (lower) values of real disposable income associated with higher (lower) values of real residential fixed investment.[5]

Regression analysis, the subject of a course in statistics, can be used to obtain a quantitative measure of this relationship. While the mechanics of regression

---

[4] You may wonder why causality does not run in both directions, that is, why residential fixed investment (residential construction) does not also affect disposable personal income. Actually, residential fixed investment does affect disposable personal income, as we will see with macroeconomic analysis, where a more comprehensive model of the economy is developed. For our purposes here, however, a single equation model with disposable income assumed to be exogenous is useful.

[5] Note that if there were no relationship between the two variables in the sample, the scatter plot would appear as a series of randomly dispersed points.

TABLE 2.1
Data for the Economic Model, Hypothesis $RFI = f(DI)$

Observation t	RFI_t	DI_t	$MORT_t$
1965	137.3	1653.5	5.81
1966	124.5	1734.3	6.25
1967	120.2	1811.4	6.46
1968	136.4	1886.8	6.97
1969	140.1	1947.4	7.81
1970	131.8	2025.3	8.45
1971	168.1	2099.9	7.74
1972	198.0	2186.2	7.60
1973	196.6	2334.1	7.96
1974	155.6	2317.0	8.92
1975	134.7	2355.4	9.00
1976	166.4	2440.9	9.00
1977	201.9	2512.6	9.02
1978	214.5	2638.4	9.56
1979	207.4	2710.1	10.78
1980	164.8	2733.6	12.66
1981	151.6	2795.8	14.70
1982	124.1	2820.4	15.14
1983	174.2	2893.6	12.57
1984	199.3	3080.1	12.38
1985	202.0	3162.1	11.55
1986	226.2	3261.9	10.17
1987	225.2	3289.6	9.31
1988	222.7	3404.3	9.19
1989	214.2	3471.2	10.13
1990	195.5	3538.3	10.05

RFI_t = real residential fixed investment in the U.S. economy in year t (in billions of 1987 dollars).

DI_t = real disposable personal income in the U.S. economy in year t (in billions of 1987 dollars).

$MORT_t$ = new home mortgage yields (%) in the U.S. economy in year t. This is the effective rate (in the primary market) on conventional mortgages, reflecting fees and charges as well as contract rate and assuming, on average, repayment at the end of 10 years.

SOURCE: *Economic Report of the President 1992* (Washington, DC: Government Printing Office, 1992), Table B-2, B-25, B-69.

analysis need not detain us here, we know from it that a straight line can be fitted to the data in a way that best represents the observations in the sample.[6] It turns out that, using the most basic type of regression technique, the estimated equation for this sample of 26 annual observations on *RFI* and *DI* is

---

[6] Formally, the **line of best fit** is the line that minimizes the sum of the squares of the vertical distances between the plotted observations and the fitted line. We would not expect all of the plotted points to fall on the line of best fit even for a valid theory, since (1) the theoretical relationship may be nonlinear (the linear assumption is frequently made for analytical convenience when it does not appear to be at great odds with the evidence), (2) there may be errors of measurement in the variables, and (3) other relevant influences on residential construction may have been omitted from the analysis.

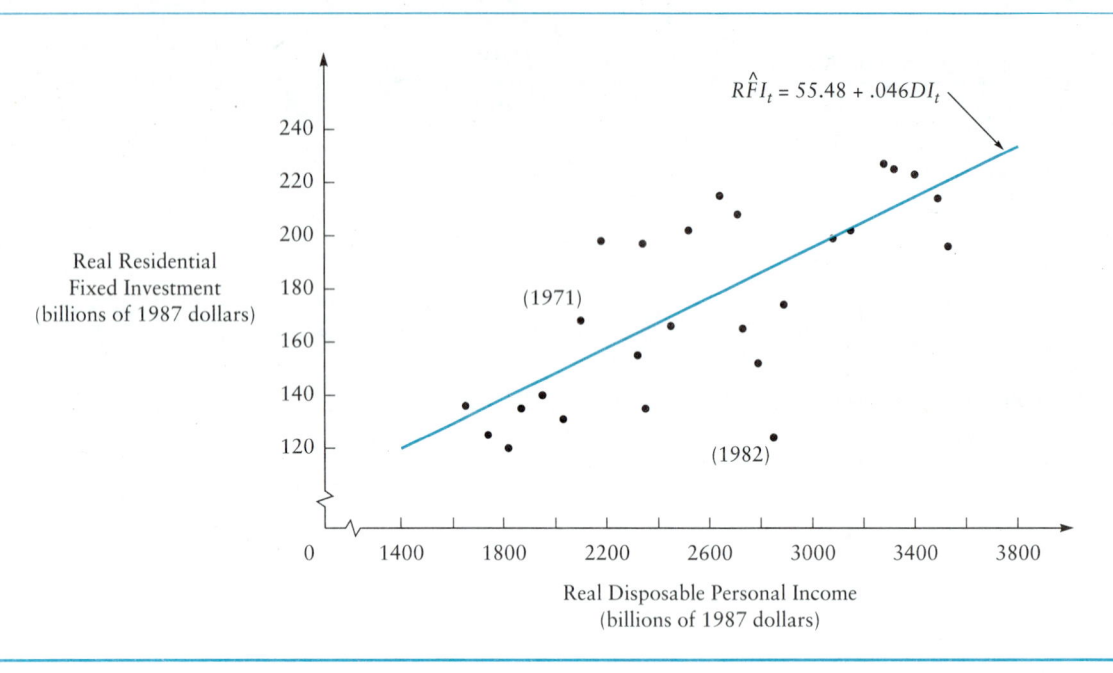

FIGURE 2.3

SCATTER DIAGRAM

This scatter diagram represents the plotted ordered pairs for real residential fixed investment *(RFI)* and real disposable personal income *(DI)* from Table 2.1. For example, the point labeled (1971) represents the ordered pair for the year 1971:

$$DI_{1971} = 2099.9 \text{ and}$$
$$RFI_{1971} = 168.1$$

The point labeled (1982) represents the ordered pair for the year 1982:

$$DI_{1982} = 2820.4 \text{ and}$$
$$RFI_{1982} = 124.1$$

The equation for the "line of best fit" is

$$\hat{RFI}_t = 55.48 + .046DI_t$$

$$\hat{RFI}_t = 55.48 + .046DI_t$$

where $\hat{RFI}_t$ (with the "hat") refers to the value of real residential fixed investment predicted for year t by the regression line.[7] Consistent with the hypothesis, the estimated slope of the regression line is positive (.046) and indicates that, ceteris paribus, an increase of $1 billion in real disposable personal income would be associated with an increase of $.046 billion ($46 million) in real residential fixed investment in any given year.

Additional statistical measures can be used to assess the strength of this relationship, that is, how much confidence can be placed in the estimated line

---

[7] For example, the actual (reported) value for real residential fixed investment in 1990 is $195.5 billion ($RFI_{1990} = 195.5$). Given the actual value of real disposable income in 1990 of $3538.3 billion ($DI_{1990} = 3538.3$), then the predicted value for real residential fixed investment in 1990 ($\hat{RFI}_{1990}$) can be found using the estimated regression line:

$$\hat{RFI}_{1990} = 55.48 + .046DI_{1990}$$
$$\hat{RFI}_{1990} = 55.48 + .046(3538.3)$$
$$\hat{RFI}_{1990} = 55.48 + 162.76$$
$$\hat{RFI}_{1990} = 218.24$$

For any observation, the **prediction error** is the difference between the actual and predicted values for the dependent variable. For 1990 the prediction error equals -22.7 (billion dollars).

$$RFI_{1990} - \hat{RFI}_{1990} = 195.5 - 218.2 = -22.7$$

That is, the estimated regression line overpredicts the actual value of real residential fixed investment in 1990. The plotted observation for 1990 lies below the regression line. In some years (for example, 1988) the estimated regression line underpredicts the actual value—giving a positive prediction error. You should confirm that the prediction error in this example for 1988 equals 10.6 (billion dollars).

of best fit and how statistically significant is the influence of income on residential construction. For this example, it can be shown that 54 percent of the total variation in (or changes in the annual values of) real residential fixed investment over the period 1965–1990 can be accounted for by variation in real disposable personal income.[8]

Extending the Model

Additional hypotheses to the primary one in our example can be tested as follows. This is called *extending the model*. For example, the cost of credit would be expected to affect residential construction. Most home construction is financed through bank loans to the builder, and most home purchases involve mortgages. Increases in interest rates add to the financing costs of construction and home mortgages, and therefore decrease the incentives to build and purchase housing. It follows that residential fixed investment should be inversely related to the cost of credit.

To capture this influence, the economist adds a second exogenous variable to the model representing the cost of credit. Let

$MORT_t$ = the average interest rate on new home mortgages in the U.S. economy in year t (in percentage points).

The model can now be succintly written as

$$RFI = f(\overset{+}{DI}, \overset{-}{MORT})$$

where the plus and minus signs over the explanatory variables indicate their hypothesized influences on real residential fixed investment. Annual observations for the mortgage rate variable are also given in Table 2.1. A scatter diagram for residential fixed investment and the mortgage rate similar to Figure 2.3 could be drawn. A three-dimensional graph, however, would be required to represent the annual observations (ordered triplets) for *RFI*, *DI*, and *MORT*. Fortunately, regression analysis can easily handle the dimensional extension.[9]

The new estimated equation for residential fixed investment over the period 1965–1990 is

$$\hat{RFI}_t = 73.60 + .065 DI_t - 7.06 MORT_t$$

---

[8] Here 54 percent refers to the value of the **coefficient of determination**. This statistic indicates the percentage of the variation in the dependent variable *(RFI)* that can be attributed to the variation in the explanatory variable *(DI)*. If all the prediction errors were equal to zero, then the plotted scatter points would all lie on the line of best fit. The regression model would "perfectly" explain or account for the variation in the values of the dependent variable (real residential fixed investment) over the sample period. In this case the coefficient of determination would be equal to 100 percent. With the regression technique used in the preceding example, the line of best fit minimizes the sum of the squares of the prediction errors (which, it so happens, is the same as maximizing the coefficient of determination.)

[9] Adding the second explanatory variable essentially means that the task of finding the line of best fit is replaced by finding the plane of best fit. The estimated regression equation takes the form

$$\hat{RFI}_t = a + bDI_t + cMORT_t$$

where *a*, *b*, and *c* are the coefficients to be estimated.

As hypothesized, the influence of the mortgage rate of interest on residential fixed investment is negative. Controlling for the influence of real disposable income, a 1 percentage point increase in the average interest rate on new home mortgages would be associated with a decrease of $7.06 billion in annual real residential fixed investment. Adding the cost-of-credit variable does improve the explanatory power of the model, though. The total variation in real residential fixed investment accounted for by the model increases to 68 percent (from 54 percent with just real disposable income as the explanatory variable). Note that adding the mortgage rate of interest changes the estimated coefficient for disposable income (from .046 to .065). Thus, a more accurate estimate of the influence of disposable income on residential fixed investment would be that, ceteris paribus, an increase of $1 billion in real disposable personal income is associated with an increase of $.065 billion ($65 million) in real residential fixed investment.[10]

If the hypotheses are accepted as confirmed by the evidence, then the estimated equation may be used for prediction. For example, if the levels for real disposable income and mortgage rates in 1993 are expected to be

$$DI_{1993} = \$3700 \text{ billion}$$
$$MORT_{1993} = 8.50\%$$

then the predicted value for real residential fixed investment in 1993 would be

$$\hat{RFI}_{1993} = 73.60 + .065(3700) - 7.06(8.50) = 254.1$$

The actual value for real residential fixed investment in 1993 will likely differ from the value predicted from the regression equation. For one, the actual values for disposable income and the mortgage rate will differ from the anticipated values used above. Moreover, the estimated regression line accounts for only 68 percent of the total variation in annual real residential fixed investment over the period 1965–1990. Other factors that affect residential construction, such as the costs of construction, population shifts, and marriage and divorce rates, are not included in the model. Exogenous shocks such as unusually severe weather (for example, Hurricane Andrew in Florida) would have an impact on residential construction as well. Finally, even if all the relevant influences could be accurately measured and incorporated into the model, the "unpredictability" or "randomness" of human behavior would almost ensure that the actual value for residential fixed investment in 1993 will be different from the predicted value.

The inability of the model to predict the future with precision does not mean that the exercise is futile. The alternative to formulating and testing behavioral models such as this may be simply extrapolating the past—an alternative likely to have even less predictive power. More important is that empirically

---

[10] We should caution that the estimated effects of changes in the explanatory variables (here DI and $MORT$) on the dependent variable *(RFI)* should be regarded as only approximate magnitudes. In this example, we can say with a high degree of confidence that the estimated coefficient for $MORT$ (which gives the estimated effect of a one percentage point increase in the mortgage rate of interest on real residential fixed investment, ceteris paribus), would fall in the range of -5 to -9. Similarly, we can show that the estimated coefficient for DI (which gives the estimated effect of an increase of $1 billion in real disposable personal income on real residential fixed investment, ceteris paribus) would very likely fall between .055 and .075. Technically, we can set such *confidence intervals* around the point estimates.

supported theories can form the basis for policy. For example, if the construction industry is in a slump, then monetary policy could be used to lower the cost of credit, which would tend to stimulate residential construction. Expansionary fiscal policy in the form of a cut in income tax rates could be used to boost disposable personal income.

Before an economic theory is used for policy, however, it should be well tested. In this example, other time periods for the U.S. economy or regions within the country may provide additional samples with which to test the hypothesized relationships. If the theory is consistently confirmed by the evidence, then confidence in the theory grows. As noted earlier, unlike controlled experiments in the natural sciences, behavioral theories in economics cannot be rigorously proven. Even widely accepted economic theories are subject to reinterpretation and revision according to differing basic assumptions about human behavior.

Furthermore, finding occasional counterexamples to an economic theory does not disprove or invalidate the theory. For instance, perusing the data in Table 2.1, we can see that from 1974 to 1975 annual real residential fixed investment declined by over 13 percent—as real disposable personal income rose and the yield on new home mortgages only slightly increased. From 1984 to 1985 real residential fixed investment barely increased (by less than 1.5 percent)—despite rapid growth in real disposable personal income (6.4 percent) and a drop of nearly a percentage point on the average mortgage yield. It bears repeating that other relevant influences on residential construction have been omitted from the model.

CONCLUDING NOTE

The model constructed here is very simple. Only one type of expenditure (residential fixed investment) in the economy was analyzed, and only two explanatory variables (disposable personal income and the yield on new home mortgages) were used. Most economic models are more complicated, using numerous equations and variables. Nevertheless, the simple model depicted here illustrates the point: economists, like other scientists, attempt to develop theories, or coherent explanations of reality, that, when confirmed by the evidence, can provide insight into the complexities of the human behaviors observed.

In the next chapter we construct another kind of economic model to illustrate a dilemma facing every nation—the tradeoff between the standard of living and national defense.

KEY TERMS

social science
households
service
firms
profits
physical capital
financial capital
basic circular flows of economic activity
factor markets

product markets
capital goods
intermediate goods
government (central authorities)
transfer payments
import
export
mixed economy
market economy
command economy
partial equilibrium analysis
ceteris paribus
positive statement

normative statement
hypothesis
residential fixed investment
disposable personal income
endogenous variable
exogenous variable
scatter diagram
line of best fit
prediction error
coefficient of determination
consumer durables
prime rate of interest

QUESTIONS

1. What are the three most important ideas or lessons in this chapter? Discuss why each is important.

2. Assume a simple economy consisting of farm households that are entirely self-sufficient except for the services offered by a doctor. No money is used in this economy. The doctor barters his services for farm produce. Diagram the circular flow of economic activity for this simple barter economy.

   Now add a village, where other services are provided (for example, a boarding house, a blacksmith, a schoolteacher). Suppose that the exchange of money replaces the bartering of goods and services. The farm households sell their surplus produce in the village market. Diagram the circular flow of economic activity for this economy.

3. Consider the following two statements: "Individual incomes are directly related to educational attainment," and, "The best investment in the future that a nation can make is to educate its children." Which is the positive statement? Which is the normative statement? Explain.

   Now discuss how you would test the positive statement. What are some of the other exogenous variables you may want to include in your analysis? Why?

4. Suppose you are interested in the determinants of spending on new **consumer durables** (consumer goods that are expected to last at least three years, such as automobiles, appliances, and furniture) in the U.S. economy. You hypothesize that consumer expenditures on durable goods are directly related to (that is, a positive function of) household income. To measure household income you select *disposable personal income*, which is the income (after taxes and transfers) available to the households for spending. Specifically, the selected variables for the model are

CD_t = real personal consumption expenditures on durable goods in year t (in billions of 1987 dollars).

DI_t = real disposable personal income in year t (in billions of 1987 dollars).

The hypothesis can be consisely written as $CD_t = f(\overset{+}{DI_t})$.

A sample of 21 annual observations for the period 1970–1990 on the two variables (*CD* and *DI*) follows, along with another variable *(PR)* to be used later:

Year	CD	DI	PR
1970	183.7	2025.3	7.91
1971	201.4	2099.9	5.72
1972	225.2	2186.2	5.25
1973	246.6	2334.1	8.03
1974	227.2	2317.0	10.81
1975	226.8	2355.4	7.86
1976	256.4	2440.9	6.84
1977	280.0	2512.6	6.83
1978	292.9	2638.4	9.06
1979	289.0	2710.1	12.67
1980	262.7	2733.6	15.27
1981	264.6	2795.8	18.87
1982	262.5	2820.4	14.86
1983	297.7	2893.6	10.79
1984	338.5	3080.1	12.04
1985	370.1	3162.1	9.93
1986	402.0	3261.9	8.33
1987	403.7	3289.6	8.21
1988	428.7	3404.3	9.32
1989	440.8	3471.2	10.87
1990	438.9	3538.3	10.01

Note that the variables *CD* and *DI* are expressed in constant (1987) dollars in order to assess better the underlying behavioral relationship. The data are from the *Economic Report of the President 1992* (Tables B-2 and B-25).

a. Plot the scatter diagram, placing the endogenous variable on the vertical axis and the exogenous variable on the horizontal axis. Does the scatter plot of points seem to support the hypothesis?

Using regression analysis we can fit a line through the data points that best represents the evidence from the sample. The estimated line of best fit is $\hat{CD}_t = -161.73 + .17 DI_t$, where $\hat{CD}_t$ is the real value of consumer durable spending in the U.S. economy in year t predicted by the estimated regression equation.

It turns out that a very high percentage (93 percent) of the variation in real consumer durable spending over the 20 year sample period is accounted for (or explained by) the variation in real disposable personal income.

b. Ceteris paribus, what is the estimated effect of an increase of $1 billion in real disposable personal income on real consumer spending on durable goods?

c. Calculate the prediction error for 1988, that is, the difference between the actual value for real consumer durable spending in 1988, CD_{1988}, and the predicted value for real consumer durable spending in 1988, $\hat{CD}_{1988}$. What could account for this prediction error?

d. Specifically, what other factors might influence real consumer spending on durable goods in the economy? Set up other hypotheses to test.

Suppose we extend the model to add the cost of credit as an explanatory variable. Many consumer durables are expensive and must be purchased on credit or financed through consumer loans. (State the implied hypothesis.) To measure the cost of credit we select the **prime rate of interest,** which is the rate of interest commercial banks charge on loans to their best corporate customers. The prime rate of interest is a benchmark interest rate. Households would be charged more than the prime rate of interest for consumer loans. Thus, let

$$PR_t = \text{prime rate of interest (average) for the U.S. economy in year } t \text{ in percentage points.}$$

The annual values for the prime rate of interest (presented earlier with those for CD and DI) are also drawn from the *Economic Report of the President 1992* (Table B-69). Adding the prime rate of interest as an explanatory variable does improve the fit of the model—98 percent of the variation in the values of real consumer durable spending over the period from 1970 through 1990 is accounted for now by the regression equation. The new estimated regression line is

$$\hat{CD}_t = -139.70 + .18DI_t - 5.84PR_t$$

e. Ceteris paribus, what is the estimated impact of an increase of $1 billion in real disposable personal income on real spending on consumer durables? And what is the estimated effect of an increase of 1 percent in the prime rate of interest on real spending on consumer durables?

f. Using the estimated regression line from part "e" of this question, and assuming the following values for 1993 for the exogenous variables, real disposable personal income and the prime rate of interest,

$$DI_{1993} = \$3700 \text{ billion}$$
$$PR_{1993} = 9.0$$

calculate the predicted value in 1993 for real personal consumption expenditures on durable goods, $\hat{CD}_{1993}$.

CHAPTER

3

SCARCITY, CHOICE, AND OPPORTUNITY COST

A THEME UNDERLYING the study of economics is the allocation of resources for the satisfaction of human wants. There are great disparities in standards of living, both across nations and within societies. There is also a growing awareness of environmental thresholds and the finiteness of the earth's resources. Economics addresses a fundamental conflict of human existence. Human wants, which are essentially limitless, are confronted by a world of limits. With growing populations and rising affluence, material aspirations tend to expand faster than the capacities for producing goods and services; thus, choices must be made. Associated with such choices are **opportunity costs,** or what must be forgone in the sense of wants not met or possibilities not realized in order to meet other wants or realize other possibilities.

The opportunity cost of using resources for a given endeavor is measured by the best alternative use of the same resources. This is a more comprehensive measure of cost than is typically encountered. For example, the opportunity cost of attending college includes not only the direct costs of tuition and the related educational expenses (such as book costs), but also the income sacrificed while studying and going to classes rather than being employed. Individuals choose to pursue a college education when the perceived benefits (that is, the college experience and the prospect of enhanced future earnings) outweigh the direct college expenses and the forgone income.

Another example is the opportunity cost of carrying cash. This is measured by the interest that the money could have earned if placed in an interest-bearing account like a savings deposit. Individuals who carry cash accept the "lost" interest income for the convenience of liquidity, that is, immediate purchasing power.

PRODUCTION POSSIBILITIES BOUNDARY

Economists frequently employ graphs to aid in the explanation of theory. While helpful, graphical analysis is limited to conveying two, or at most three, dimensions. Here we set forth two economic models, one on the individual level and the second on the national level, which use the graphical device of a **production possibilites boundary** to illustrate this central theme in economics:

$$\text{scarcity} \xrightarrow{\text{(implies)}} \text{choice} \xrightarrow{\text{(results in)}} \text{opportunity cost}$$

An Economy of One Individual

Consider an individual, Defoe, the sole survivor of a shipwreck, who finds himself washed ashore on a deserted tropical island. For food, Defoe must either fish (the fish being plentiful in the many ponds on the island) or hunt rabbits (the rabbits running wild in abundance over the island). After a few days, Defoe determines that with the long pointed stick he has discovered, he requires an average of four hours to spear a rabbit and two hours to spear a fish. Given the sixteen hours of daylight on the island, Defoe calculates that spending all day fishing would yield eight fish, while spending all day hunting would yield four rabbits. Other possible combinations of fish and rabbits are plotted and listed in Figure 3.1. If we connect these output combinations, we obtain Defoe's

FIGURE 3.1

PRODUCTION POSSIBILITIES BOUNDARY FOR DEFOE: RABBITS AND FISH CAUGHT PER DAY

Defoe's production possibilities boundary *(ae)* represents the combinations of rabbits and fish Defoe could catch each day using the available resources fully and efficiently. The combination represented by point *s* is not attainable. The combination represented by point *u,* while attainable, implies an inefficient use or an underutilization of the resources available.

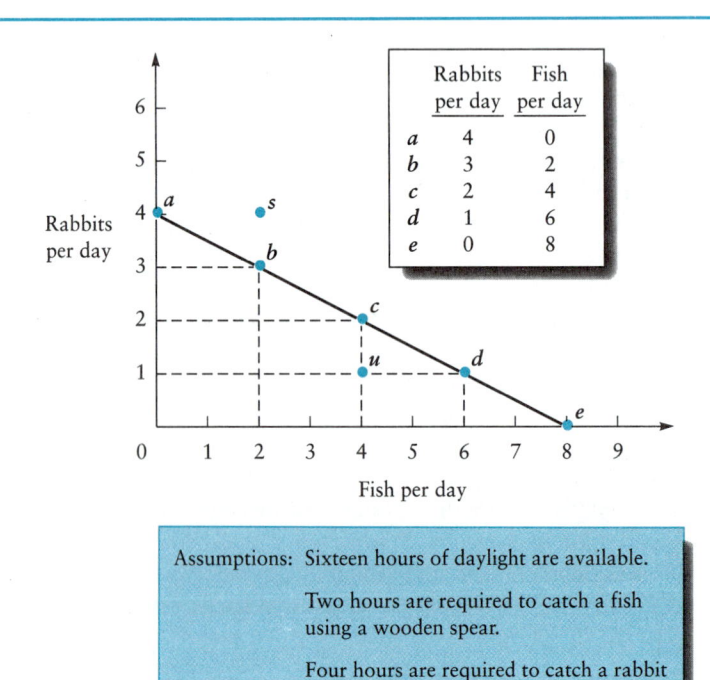

	Rabbits per day	Fish per day
a	4	0
b	3	2
c	2	4
d	1	6
e	0	8

Assumptions: Sixteen hours of daylight are available.

Two hours are required to catch a fish using a wooden spear.

Four hours are required to catch a rabbit using a wooden spear.

production possibilities boundary, which depicts the maximum combinations of fish and rabbits Defoe could catch given the resources available—the sixteen hours of daylight, the fish and the rabbits on the island, the wooden spear, and his labor—and the technique of spearing.

Scarcity is illustrated by the fact that combinations to the right of the production possibilities boundary (for example, point s, indicating a catch of four rabbits and two fish) are unattainable, given the resources available and the spearing technique used. Combinations inside the production possibilites boundary (for example, point u, indicating a catch of one rabbit and four fish), while attainable, imply that Defoe is either not using all of the available resources or not using the resources efficiently. For instance, he may not be using the full sixteen hours of daylight to hunt and fish due to fatigue, illness, or other activities. Poor weather may impair his hunting, or he may not be working as efficiently as possible if his coughing and sneezing, brought on by a cold, scare off the rabbits and fish he is attempting to catch.

Each day Defoe must decide how to allocate the available sixteen hours of daylight. Depending upon his preference for eating fish versus rabbit, he will divide his time between fishing and hunting. For example, he may spend Mondays fishing for eight hours (producing four fish) and hunting for eight hours (producing two rabbits). See point c on Defoe's production possibilites boundary. Suppose that on Tuesdays he switches to twelve hours of fishing (producing six fish) and four hours of hunting (producing one rabbit). See point d on the production possibilites boundary. The opportunity cost of catching an additional two fish would be the one rabbit that he would not catch. Suppose instead that on Tuesdays Defoe spends twelve hours hunting (producing three rabbits) and only four hours fishing (producing two fish). See point b on the boundary. Here the opportunity cost of using another four hours to hunt for rabbits (yielding an increase of one rabbit) would be the two fish that could have been caught if the time had been spent fishing. We note that Defoe's opportunity cost is constant at two fish for one rabbit, since both activities require four hours of labor.

If Defoe were to sacrifice some of his leisure time each day after sunset, building a simple snare for rabbits and a net for fishing, he should be able to improve his daily output. The rabbit snare and the fish net, considered, like the wooden spear, to be *capital goods*, would augment Defoe's production possibilities. Supposing that with the snare he can trap a rabbit in only two hours, then the maximum catch during the sixteen hours of daylight would be eight rabbits. Similarly, if using the fish net reduces the time it takes Defoe to catch a fish from two hours to only forty minutes (or two-thirds of an hour), then during the daylight he could catch as many as twenty-four fish. The production possibilites boundary thus shifts to the right, from the line ae to the line $a'e'$ (see Figure 3.2). Note that the opportunity cost changes from one rabbit for two fish to one rabbit for three fish.

Other factors could contribute to growth in Defoe's island production possibilities. Another shipwrecked individual could wash ashore and join Defoe on the island. Defoe could make more rabbit snares and fish nets, adding further to the *capital stock*. Defoe could even develop an improved rabbit snare or fish net—another form of technological progress in this simple island economy, just as was the switch in production technique from spearing to snaring (rabbits) and netting (fish). Finally, Defoe could learn from experience that the morning hours are better for fishing and the afternoon hours are better for hunting. If so, then

FIGURE 3.2

SHIFT IN DEFOE'S PRODUCTION POSSIBILITIES BOUNDARY

A rightward shift in Defoe's production possibilities boundary (from ae to $a'e'$) results from an increase in the resources available for catching rabbits and fish and/or improvements in the technology of rabbit hunting and fishing.

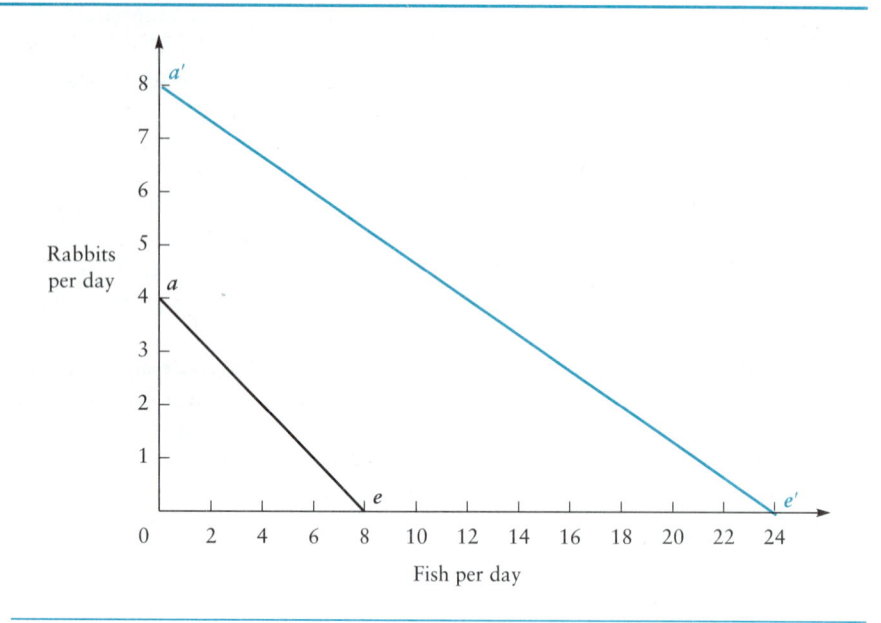

he could enhance the productivity of his day by rearranging his labor hours accordingly.

As this simple example of the island economy of Defoe illustrates, economic growth (evidenced by the expansion of the production possibilites boundary) allows for the consumption of commodity combinations previously unattainable. Economic growth, however, does not eliminate the problem of resource scarcity, nor the need for choice imposed by limited resources, nor the opportunity costs that arise from the choices made when the resources are allocated.

Trade-offs on the National Level

Just as individuals are faced with decisions arising from the need to allocate scarce resources—for example, choosing among several desired expenditures or selecting the best use of a given block of time—so too are communities and nations confronted with choices and opportunity costs. Let us consider the "guns versus butter" or "swords versus plowshares" decision facing every nation.

Assume that the welfare or general well-being of a nation, call it Atlantica, depends on the average standard of living within the nation and the perceived national security. With the available resources—the land and raw materials, the capital stock, and labor—and the known technologies, Atlantica is able to produce both civilian goods (C goods) and military goods (M goods). Civilian goods, that is, nonmilitary goods, are those goods and services that contribute to the national welfare by increasing the average standard of living. Basically these civilian goods include the personal consumption expenditures of households, social services, and those capital goods designed to augment the future production of civilian goods. Military goods are those expenditures that are intended to enhance the security of the nation.

At any point in time *(T)*, Atlantica's welfare can be written as a positive function of its stocks of civilian goods and military goods:

$$W_T = f(\overset{+}{C}_T, \overset{+}{M}_T)$$

where

W_T = the level of national welfare in Atlantica at time T.
C_T = the stock of civilian goods in Atlantica at time T.
M_T = the stock of military goods in Atlantica at time T.

The plus signs over the variables in the function indicate that national welfare is directly related to the stocks of civilian and military goods.

Specifically, the stock of civilian goods includes the dwellings, consumer goods, schools, hospitals, factories, machines, and the existing skills and accumulated knowledge of a nonmilitary nature. Derived from the use of the stock of civilian goods are the goods and services that contribute to the standard of living. For example, houses provide shelter, cars provide transportation, and television and books provide entertainment. A nation uses its hospitals and schools in the provision of health care and education. Factories and machinery are used to produce other civilian goods and services. In contrast, the stock of military goods includes the military bases and equipment, the arsenals, and the military skills and knowledge used in the production of national defense.[1]

Over any period of time the nation will allocate resources for the production of civilian and military goods. Some of the resources will be used to produce civilian goods and services (such as food, gasoline, entertainment) and military goods and services (such as food, gasoline, the guarding of the nation's borders) that are consumed during the current period. Other resources will be devoted to production that adds to the existing stocks of civilian goods (such as new factories for manufacturing passenger cars and public education in the schools) and military goods (such as fighter jets and training for fighter jet pilots), which carry over into future periods.

The production of a good refers to a **flow**, or a change in the **stock** of the good. For instance, if c_t refers to the production (flow) of civilian goods in the nation during a period of duration t, then C_{T+t} would be the stock of civilian goods in the nation at time $T + t$.[2]

---

[1] Implicitly we are making the assumption that all goods (and services) can be classified strictly as either civilian or military. This twofold classification is necessary for graphing the production possibilities boundary. In reality, of course, the distinction made here between C goods and M goods is not as clear-cut. Some of a nation's military expenditures (e.g., military base housing and military pensions) contribute to the average standard of living; and some of civilian expenditures (e.g., education, health care, and highways) enhance national security. Similarly, the stock of human knowledge cannot be neatly divided into civilian and military. Nevertheless, this simple model proves useful in illustrating the trade-offs nations make with respect to national security and the standard of living.

[2] We should note that we are really considering *net production,* i.e., gross or total output less the output needed to replace the loss in current stocks due to depreciation. For example, suppose that every year 1 million automobiles wear out and have to be junked. If at the beginning of the current year there are 30 million automobiles on hand, and if during the year the total production of new automobiles is 1.2 million, then the net production of automobiles for the year would be .2 million. Thus, at the beginning of the next period the stock of automobiles on hand would be 30.2 million, i.e., 30.2 = 30 + (1.2 − 1).

$$C_{T+t} = C_T + c_t$$

Thus, flows have an associated time dimension, while stocks refer to levels at a point in time.

For any given time period, it would theoretically be possible to chart the nation's production possibilities boundary, which would represent all the possible combinations of C goods and M goods that the nation could produce with the known technology and using all the available resources fully and efficiently. Atlantica's production possibilities boundary is illustrated in Figure 3.3 by the curve az. Here the flow of civilian goods, measured in physical units, is represented on the vertical axis, while the flow of military goods, also measured in physical units, is represented on the horizontal axis.

The combination of goods represented by point a would result if Atlantica devoted all of its resources during the given period to the production of civilian goods. In this case, there would be the maximum addition to the stock of civilian goods and the greatest gain in the average standard of living. Conversely, point z represents the maximum production of military goods by Atlantica during the given period.

As in our earlier example of a simple island economy of one man, the concept of scarcity can be illustrated with the production possibilities boundary. Combinations to the right of the az curve (for example, point s) are not attainable given the available resources and known technologies. Over time, however, the presently unattainable combinations of C goods and M goods may become possible with increases in the labor force, net additions to the capital stock, the discovery of new resources, and technological progress. This real growth in the nation's production possibilities can be shown by an outward shift in the boundary from az to $a'z'$ (see Figure 3.4).

Combinations of output within the curve az, while presently attainable, are less desirable. Operating within the production possibilites boundary (for example, point u in Figure 3.3) would imply either the unemployment of resources or inefficiencies in production and distribution (such as the

FIGURE 3.3

PRODUCTION POSSIBILITIES BOUNDARY FOR NATION

The production possibilities boundary *(az)* represents the combinations of the two goods (civilian goods and military goods) that the nation could produce using all of its available resources fully and efficiently. The combination represented by point *s* is not attainable, given the available resources and known technologies. The combination represented by point *u*, while attainable, indicates an underutilization of resources or inefficiencies in production.

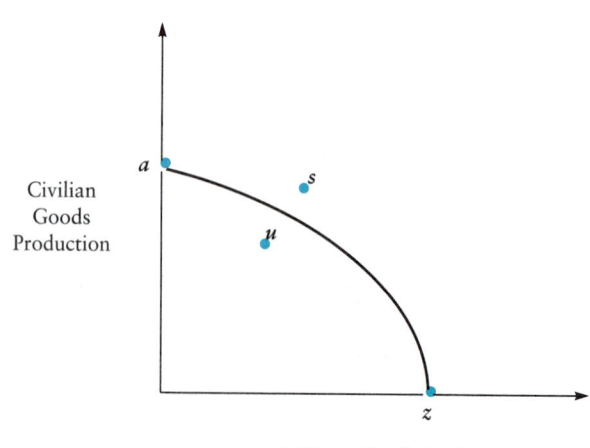

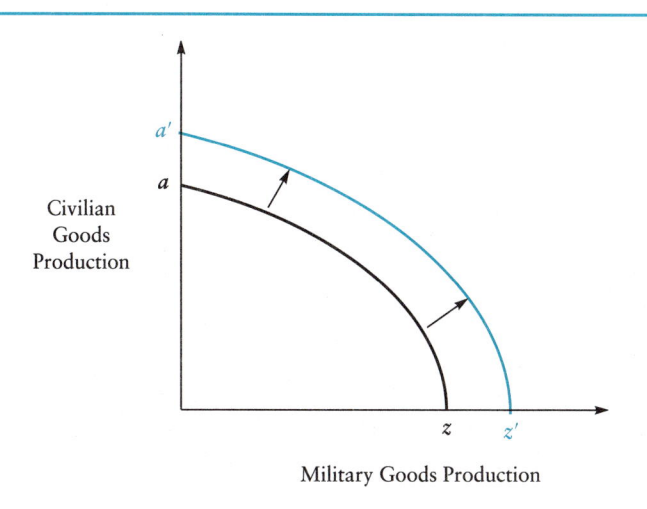

FIGURE 3.4

REAL GROWTH IN NATION'S PRODUCTION POSSIBILITIES

Rightward shifts in the production possibilities boundary (from az to $a'z'$) indicate economic growth due to increases in the quantity or quality of the available resources or technological progress.

misuse of technology or an inappropriate combination of the available resources).[3]

In any given period a nation must choose how to allocate the available resources. Atlantica, desiring both a higher standard of living and enhanced security, must select some output combination of C goods and M goods. Preferably, this combination would lie on the production possibilites boundary and not within it.

The allocation of resources within a nation will reflect not only the general trade-off between material well-being and national security, but the type of political-economic system in place. Recall that in market-oriented economies the resource allocation reflects the aggregate decisions of households (as consumers, taxpayers, and voters), firms, and government officials. In command economies, the central authorities have the dominant role in the allocation of resources. Moreover, a nation's security is also affected by other nations' military capabilities—which are usually not known with certainty.

Suppose Atlantica had selected the combination of outputs labeled e_0 on the production possibilities boundary in Figure 3.5. This would determine the present allocation of resources between the production of civilian and military goods. If Atlantica, however, felt relatively vulnerable, due perhaps to a perceived military buildup by an unfriendly nation, it might opt for increasing its production of military goods. This would entail shifting resources away from producing civilian goods and incurring some sacrifice in the standard of living in the current period for the sake of maintaining national security. This shift is represented by the movement from e_0 to e_1 on the production possibilities

---

[3] During the Great Depression in the 1930s the United States and many other nations were operating well within their production possibilites boundaries—with 10 percent or more of the labor forces unemployed and much of the plant, equipment, and machinery lying idle. Similarly, inefficiencies in production and distribution due to excessive bureaucracies and poor worker motivation have pulled command economies well within their production possibilites boundaries—despite basically full employment of the resources. Such inefficiencies were perhaps the major reason for the reforms of the command economies of the former Soviet Union and Eastern Europe into more market-oriented systems.

FIGURE 3.5

CHOICES FOR NATION ON THE PRODUCTION POSSIBILITIES BOUNDARY

Given a full and efficient use of the available resources, the combinations of civilian goods and military goods from among which the nation chooses will lie on the production possibilites boundary *(az)*. Opportunity cost is represented by the slope of the production possibilities boundary.

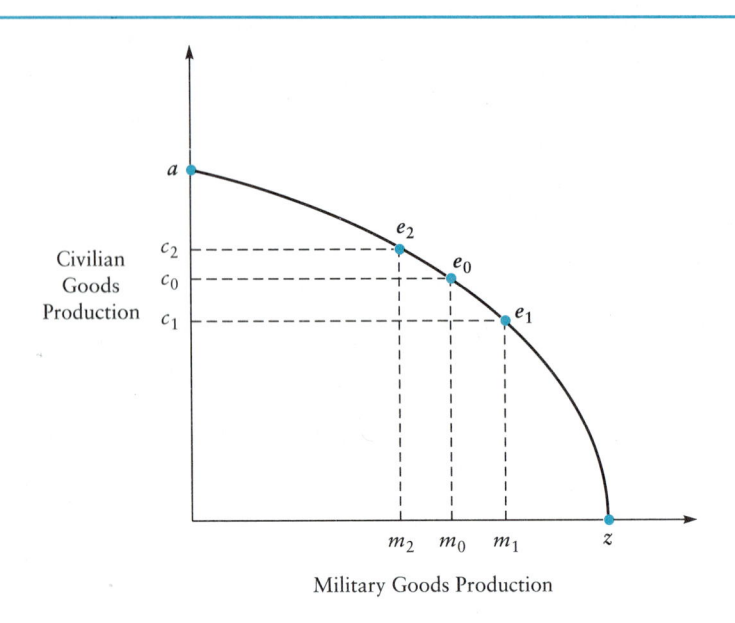

boundary. The opportunity cost of producing an additional $(m_1 - m_0)$ military goods is measured by the $(c_0 - c_1)$ civilian goods that could have been produced with the same resources during the period.

In contrast, in the case of a recently negotiated arms control agreement, Atlantica might decide to devote more resources to the production of civilian goods. Starting again at combination e_0, the opportunity cost of $(c_2 - c_0)$ civilian goods would be a drop in the current production of military goods of $(m_0 - m_2)$.

In general, opportunity cost is reflected in the slope of the production possibilities boundary. The negative slope denotes a trade-off between C goods production and M goods production. If Atlantica desired to produce more of one type of good during a given period of time, resources would have to be transferred from the production of the other type of good. Furthermore, the production possibilities boundary az is concave—meaning that the slope of the curve becomes steeper (more negative) moving left to right.[4] The economic interpretation of the concave curvature of the production possibilites boundary is **increasing opportunity costs**. This can be shown in Figure 3.5 in the movement from e_2 to e_0 to e_1. As drawn here, the gain in military goods production going from point e_2 to point e_0 and then from e_0 to e_1 is the same, that is, $(m_0 - m_2) = (m_1 - m_0)$. The loss in civilian goods production, however, increases, that is, $(c_0 - c_1) > (c_2 - c_0)$.

Increasing opportunity cost will occur whenever resources are not perfect substitutes. That is, if not all resources (or factors of production) are equally

---

[4] The slope of a curve at any point is given by the slope of the tangent line to the curve at that point. As you move down the production possibilites boundary from a to z in Figure 3.5, you can see that the slope of any line tangent to the curve is increasingly steeper. Thus, the production possibilities boundary is (strictly) concave.

well-suited for both types of production, then increasing opportunity costs will characterize changes in production. Suppose Atlantica had originally selected the output combination represented by point e_2. If greater production of military goods in this period were then desired, the nation would want to transfer those resources (labor, capital, and raw materials) best suited for military goods production first.

For example, it might be relatively easy to convert automobile workers and production facilities from manufacturing civilian jeeps to manufacturing military jeeps, or to use steel intended for refrigerators for producing tanks. As the resource transfers continue, however, factors relatively ill-suited for the production of military goods (and better suited for civilian goods) would increasingly have to be shifted to producing military goods. Therefore, the loss in civilian goods production per unit gain in military goods would rise.

Of course, increasing opportunity cost works in both directions. For some factors of production, conversion from military to civilian use would be rather easy. Military hospitals could readily be converted to civilian hospitals. Many of the skills acquired in the military are in demand in the civilian goods sectors. Other conversions, though, such as the decommissioning of submarines, the dismantling of weapons, and the retraining of tank commanders, are more difficult.

IMPLICATIONS OF PRESENT RESOURCE ALLOCATIONS

An important decision for any nation is determining the appropriate production of civilian and military goods, and this varies according to national priorities and political-economic systems. For example, for the period 1980–1985, the average percentage of national output for military expenditures in the Soviet Union was an estimated 12.9 percent. For the United States, the counterpart superpower nation, the average was 6.1 percent. For Switzerland, a nation with a tradition of neutrality, it was only 2.4 percent.[5]

To some extent, a nation determines its future production possibilities with its present allocation of resources. Does current research favor the development of civilian or military technologies? Does investment in new plants, equipment, and machinery enhance more the future production of civilian or of military goods and services? Do long-term contracts for weapons systems lock a nation into increased future production of military goods? Does social legislation providing for health care restrict the future possibilities for producing military goods?

Consider two possible scenarios for the nation Atlantica.
Let

- az = the present production possibilities boundary.
- $a'z'$ = the future production possibilities boundary when present investment and research and development expenditures favor military applications.

---

[5] The averages are calculated from statistics presented in *World Military Expenditures and Arms Transfers 1989*, U.S. Arms Control and Disarmament Agency, Washington, DC, October 1990.

$a''z''$ = the future production possibilities boundary when present investment and research and development expenditures favor civilian applications.

The production possibilites boundaries are illustrated in Figure 3.6. To facilitate the comparison, suppose Atlantica is at point f at some time in the future—where point f is the intersection of the two potential production possibilities boundaries. At this point of intersection, earlier investment and research and development expenditures are neutral, meaning they do not affect the nation's future standard of living and national security. If however, at that point in the future, Atlantica decided to step up the production of military goods (perhaps in response to heightened international tensions), then the prior resource commitments would affect the prevailing opportunity costs.

Suppose the new desired production of military goods is m^*. Then, if the relevant production possibilities boundary is $a'z'$ (military-biased growth), the opportunity cost of producing the additional $d'h'$ of military goods is the decrease in the production of fd' civilian goods. On the other hand, if the nation found itself on the production possibilities boundary $a''z''$ (civilian-biased

FIGURE 3.6

FUTURE PRODUCTION POSSIBILITIES

If the nation is producing the combination of civilian goods and military goods represented by point f, then the opportunity cost of increasing the production of military goods to m^* would be fd' of civilian goods when the production possibilites boundary is $a'z'$. The opportunity cost of increasing the production of military goods to m^* would be fd'' of civilian goods, however, when the production possibilities boundary is $a''z''$.

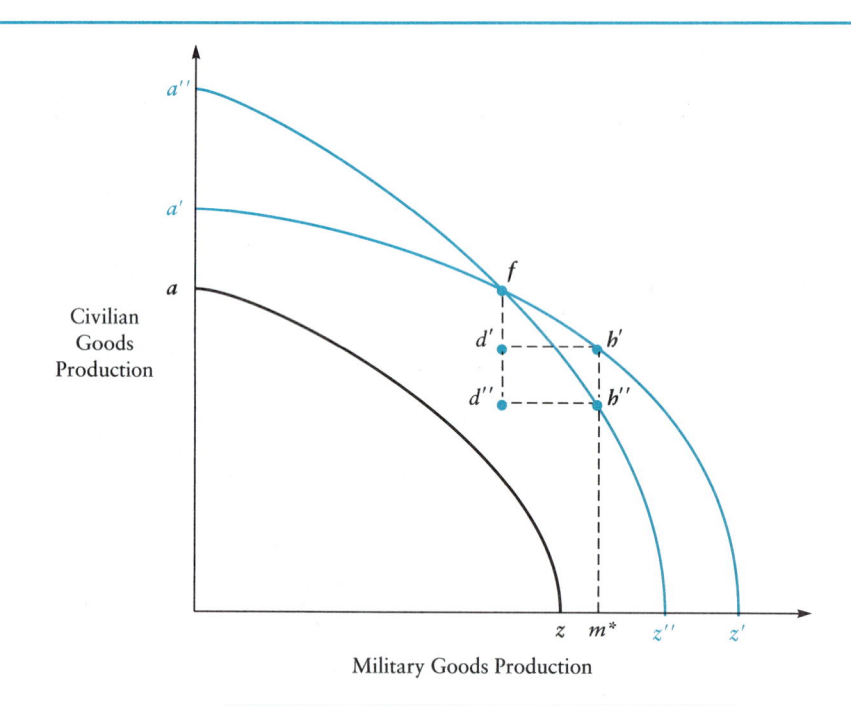

az = present production possibilities boundary.

$a'z'$ = future production possibilities boundary with military-biased investment and technology.

$a''z''$ = future production possibilities boundary with civilian-biased investment and technology.

growth), the opportunity cost of producing the additional $d'h'$ (equals $d''h''$) of military goods would be greater—a sacrifice of fd'' in the production of civilian goods. Therefore, in this case, where the nation has to gear up military production in the future, a more military-oriented growth would have been advantageous.

Conversely, if at some time in the future there is a more stable international environment, as in the event of a comprehensive arms agreement, then an earlier emphasis on civilian-oriented research and development would permit a higher standard of living for the nation for any given cutback in military goods production. The point to be emphasized is that current resource allocations will have longer run consequences.

CONCLUDING NOTE

During the two Reagan administrations the share of expenditures on national defense in the national output of the United States increased by nearly a full percentage point over the two previous administrations—from 5.3 percent for 1973–1980 to 6.2 percent for 1981–1988 (statistics derived from the *Economic Report of the President 1992,* Table B-1). Moreover, there was a shift in federal research and development funding in favor of military technologies, such as the Strategic Defense Initiative, or "Star Wars." Whether this shift in priorities was desirable is a normative question. Proponents might argue that national security concerns justified the expansion in military-oriented research and development. Opponents might emphasize the opportunity costs of such resource shifts. It is important to recall that opportunity cost refers to the "best alternative use of resources." Often what is "best" is a matter of opinion.

Indeed, with the recent nuclear arms treaties, the jettisoning of communism by the nations of Eastern Europe, and the dissolution of the Soviet Union, the four decade–long Cold War appears to have ended. In the United States, the end of the superpower confrontation brings a so-called "peace dividend"—the ability to reduce the allocation of resources toward military goods production without any sacrifice in national security. However, this situation brings forth other questions. For example, if the U.S. government cuts $20 billion annually from the military budget, should social spending be increased by $20 billion? Or should the "released" $20 billion go toward reducing the federal budget deficit? Or should personal income taxes be cut by $20 billion? Or perhaps a combination of the above options might be desirable. Recall the distinction between positive and normative. Using economics, we can estimate the economic costs and consequences of the various policy options. We can also calculate the most efficient or productive use of given resources. Unfortunately, we cannot determine the ranking of the various states of social welfare associated with the policy options. The science of economics will take us only so far.

In the next chapter we will illustrate how international trade allows a nation to consume commodity combinations lying beyond its production possibilities boundary. The underlying concept, comparative advantage, is directly related to opportunity cost.

KEY TERMS

opportunity costs
production possibilities boundary
flow
stock
increasing opportunity costs

QUESTIONS

1. What are the three most important ideas in this chapter? Discuss why each is important.
2. Assume that a nation, Pacifica, using all the available resources in the most efficient manner, can produce the following combinations of civilian and military goods in 1993.

Combination	Civilian Goods (in millions)	Military Goods (in millions)
a	100	0
b	98	10
c	92	20
d	82	30
e	68	40
f	50	50
g	28	60
h	0	70

   a. Sketch Pacifica's production possibilities boundary. Select appropriate scales for the two axes and place civilian goods on the vertical axis.
   b. Can Pacifica produce 80 million units of civilian goods and 40 million units of military goods in 1993? If not, what are the constraints?
   c. If Pacifica actually produces 35 million units of military goods and 60 million units of civilian goods in 1993, what are the economic implications?
   d. If Pacifica increased military goods production in 1993, the opportunity cost of military goods would rise. Find the opportunity costs of increasing military goods production from 10 to 20, from 20 to 30, and from 30 to 40 million units, respectively.
   e. Suppose instead that the opportunity cost of military goods is always constant at 1 military good = 1 civilian good. Assuming that combination a were still feasible, draw the new production possibilites boundary. Which assumption about opportunity cost (increasing or constant) seems more realistic? Why?
3. During "Operation Desert Shield" and "Operation Desert Storm," the United States called into active duty thousands of reservists. Discuss the opportunity cost for the nation of using the military reserves.
4. In an article in the *Atlantic Monthly* ("A Post-Cold War Budget," February 1990, pp. 74, 76, 80–81) Jack Beatty offered some alternatives for government spending, including

   [B]uild the stealth bomber . . . at nearly $600 million per plane.

Currently only 451,000 of the country's 1.7 million poor children are enrolled in Head Start [a program of enriched learning for pre-schoolers]. For about $1.2 billion more a year Head Start could be expanded to cover all eligible children for at least one year.

Currently 7.3 million women are eligible for food and medical care under the income criteria of WIC [the supplemental food program for women, infants, and children], but only 4.4 million are served by it.... WIC now costs $2.1 billion; for about a billion more, it could be expanded to serve all the women eligible for it.

Using these examples, state the opportunity cost of another stealth bomber in terms of Head Start enrollment or WIC coverage. Which groups in the United States would favor more spending on national defense (e.g., stealth bombers), and which groups would favor more spending on social programs (e.g., Head Start and WIC)? Why?

CHAPTER

4

COMPARATIVE ADVANTAGE: A BASIS FOR TRADE

As we discussed in Chapter 3, opportunity cost is one of the key insights in economics. In this chapter, we will apply this concept to *international trade,* the exchange of commodities across national borders, which promotes a more efficient allocation of the world's resources. In general, nations participating in international trade are able to consume commodity combinations that lie beyond their production possibilities boundaries.

Let us use a simple model of two countries and two commodities to convey the basis for international trade and to introduce the principles of absolute advantage and comparative advantage.[1] Then we will extend the model to incorporate the production and consumption possibilities boundaries for a nation engaging in trade in order to show more clearly the gains from trade. Finally, we will note how the theoretical advantages of trade hold not only for nations, but for geographical regions within a nation and even across individuals.

ABSOLUTE ADVANTAGE

Let us begin with two countries, call them Gaul and Sumer, and two commodities, say cloth and wine. Assume that with one unit of resources (where a unit of resources refers to a given physical combination of land, labor, and capital, such as r acres of land, l hours of labor, and k units of capital), Gaul and Sumer can each produce the following amounts of cloth or wine:

---

[1] The concepts of absolute and comparative advantages date back two centuries to the classical economists Adam Smith (1723–1790) and David Ricardo (1772–1823).

EXAMPLE 1
Output per Unit of Resources

	Cloth	Wine
Gaul	10 Units	2 units
Sumer	8 units	4 units

That is, with each unit of resources, the nation Gaul could produce either ten units of cloth ($10c$) or two units of wine ($2w$). If the additional assumption of **constant costs of production** is made, then no matter how much cloth or wine Gaul has already produced, it still takes one unit of resources to produce another ten units of cloth or two units of wine.[2] Similarly, with one unit of resources (the same physical amounts of land, labor, and capital), the nation Sumer could produce either eight units of cloth or four units of wine. This ratio, too, is assumed to hold regardless of the levels of cloth and wine production.

In this example, each nation has an **absolute advantage** in the production of a commodity. Gaul is absolutely superior in the production of cloth: with one unit of resources, Gaul can produce ten units of cloth and Sumer only eight. Sumer is absolutely superior in the production of wine: with one unit of resources, Sumer can produce four units of wine and Gaul only two. The differences in output might be due to differences in climate, technology, or the quality of the land, labor, and capital in the countries.

From the information provided, it is possible to derive the opportunity costs of production and the pre-trade exchange ratios in the two countries. In Gaul, since either ten units of cloth or two units of wine can be produced with one unit of resources, the opportunity cost of ten units of cloth is two units of wine. (Implicitly we are assuming full employment of resources.) Therefore, ten units of cloth are equivalent in value to, and thus should exchange for, two units of wine. In terms of unit production, in Gaul the opportunity cost of one additional unit of wine would be five units of cloth. Alternatively, the opportunity cost of producing another unit of cloth in Gaul is one-fifth of a unit of wine.

In Sumer, eight units of cloth should exchange for four units of wine—since both embody one unit of resources. In terms of unit production, the opportunity cost of producing another unit of wine in Sumer would be two fewer units of cloth. We can show the opportunity costs in the two countries as follows:

EXAMPLE 2
Output per Unit of Resources

	Cloth	Wine	Opportunity Costs
Gaul	10 Units	2 units	$5c = 1w$, or $1c = \frac{1}{5}w$
Sumer	8 units	4 units	$2c = 1w$, or $1c = \frac{1}{2}w$

The opportunity costs in the two nations determine the pre-trade exchange ratios. Now, if you were traveling from Gaul to Sumer, which commodity would

---

[2] In other words, the unit cost of production (here the amounts of the resources required to produce one unit of output) does not vary with the rate of production (the amount of the output produced).

you take to trade? (Note: We are assuming no qualitative differences in wine or cloth between the two countries.)

If you take one unit of wine, then in Sumer you can exchange one unit of wine for two units of cloth. Returning to Gaul with two units of cloth and exchanging back into wine would yield two-fifths (²⁄₅) of a unit of wine [²⁄₅ = (2) (¹⁄₅)], for a net loss of three-fifths (³⁄₅) of a unit of wine. On the other hand, if you selected cloth to take from Gaul to Sumer, then one unit of cloth exchanges for one-half (½) of a unit of wine in Sumer, which back in Gaul would be worth ⁵⁄₂ units of cloth. This series of exchanges would result in a net gain of ³⁄₂ units of cloth.

Schematically, the sequence of exchanges would be as follows for a traveler from Gaul to Sumer and back to Gaul:

$$1w \to 2c \to \tfrac{2}{5}w = \text{(net loss of } \tfrac{3}{5}w)$$
$$1c \to \tfrac{1}{2}w \to \tfrac{5}{2}c = \text{(net gain of } \tfrac{3}{2}c)$$

For a traveler from Sumer to Gaul, it would be advantageous to bring wine to trade. In this example, one unit of wine could be exchanged for five units of cloth in Gaul. The five units of cloth could then be traded back in Sumer for ⁵⁄₂ units of wine for a net gain of ³⁄₂ units of wine. There would be a net loss if the traveler took cloth to Gaul to trade. Schematically, for a traveler from Sumer to Gaul and back to Sumer:

$$1w \to 5c \to \tfrac{5}{2}w = \text{(net gain of } \tfrac{3}{2}w)$$
$$1c \to \tfrac{1}{5}w \to \tfrac{2}{5}c = \text{(net loss of } \tfrac{3}{5}c)$$

The traveler's choice of commodities to take to trade depends on a comparison of the exchange ratios in the nations. In Sumer, one unit of wine exchanges for only two units of cloth. In Gaul, one unit of wine exchanges for five units of cloth. Clearly, the incentive exists for a traveler from Sumer to take wine to Gaul, where it commands more cloth.

If this sequence of trades works for one traveler, it should work for others. Indeed, in this example, trade would be mutually beneficial. Gaul would export cloth to Sumer in return for wine.

Allowing nations to trade results in a more efficient allocation of resources and greater global output. To illustrate this, suppose Gaul cuts back the production of wine by one unit. Gaul could then produce another five units of cloth. To keep the global output of wine constant, Sumer would have to increase its production of wine by one unit. The opportunity cost for Sumer of increasing wine production by one unit is two fewer units of cloth production. If this reorientation of production and reallocation of resources took place, the global production of cloth would increase by three units, while the total output of wine would be unchanged. These are the gains from international specialization. The greater global output can be divided between the two nations so that both benefit. Schematically:

Gaul	$\Delta w = -1$	$\Delta c = +5$
Sumer	$\Delta w = +1$	$\Delta c = -2$
World	$\Delta w = 0$	$\Delta c = +3$

where Δ denotes the "change in" the quantity.

COMPARATIVE ADVANTAGE

Suppose now that Sumer improves its technology of cloth production so that one unit of resources in Sumer can now produce twelve units of cloth, as shown:

EXAMPLE 3
Output per Unit of Resources

	Cloth	Wine	Opportunity Costs
Gaul	10 Units	2 units	$5c = 1w$, or $1c = 1/5 w$
Sumer	12 units	4 units	$3c = 1w$, or $1c = 1/3 w$

Sumer now has the absolute advantage in both commodities, since one unit of resources in Sumer can produce more of either cloth or wine than in Gaul. Note that the opportunity costs in Sumer have also changed. Is trade still mutually advantageous? In particular, would Sumer have any incentive to trade with Gaul?

Return to the heuristic device of the traveler. If a traveler from Sumer took one unit of wine to Gaul to trade for five units of cloth, upon returning to Sumer, the traveler could exchange the five units of cloth for $5/3$ units of wine. So, just as before, it is profitable for Sumer to export wine to Gaul, since wine has a higher exchange value in Gaul. On the other hand, if the traveler took one unit of cloth to Gaul to trade for wine and then exchanged the wine back into cloth in Sumer, there would be a net loss in cloth. For a traveler from Sumer to Gaul and back to Sumer:

$$1w \to 5c \to 5/3 w = \text{(net gain of } 2/3 w\text{)}$$
$$1c \to 1/5 w \to 3/5 c = \text{(net loss of } 2/5 c\text{)}$$

So even though Sumer has an absolute advantage in the production of both commodities, trade is still mutually beneficial. (You can show that a traveler from Gaul would still benefit from trading cloth for wine in Sumer.) In fact, it is **comparative advantage**, or relative efficiency, rather than absolute advantage that is required for trade. To see this, consider an example where absolute advantage exists, but comparative advantage does not:

EXAMPLE 4
Output per Unit of Resources

	Cloth	Wine	Opportunity Costs
Gaul	10 Units	2 units	$5c = 1w$, or $1c = 1/5 w$
Sumer	20 units	4 units	$5c = 1w$, or $1c = 1/5 w$

For a traveler from Sumer to Gaul and back to Sumer:

$$1w \to 5c \to 1w = \text{(no gain)}$$
$$1c \to 1/5 w \to 1c = \text{(no gain)}$$

It is the difference in opportunity costs between nations that indicates comparative advantage. In Example 4, Sumer is 100 percent more productive in both cloth and wine. The opportunity cost in each country is the same despite Sumer's absolute advantages. In Example 3, Sumer also has the absolute advantages in cloth and wine, but its greater advantage, that is, its comparative advantage, is in wine production. Sumer is 100 percent more productive than Gaul in wine [(4 − 2)/2] and only 20 percent more productive in cloth [12 − 10)/10]. Sumer is therefore said to have a comparative disadvantage in cloth production. Gaul is said to have a comparative advantage in cloth production and a comparative disadvantage in wine production.

The device of the traveler was useful for indicating the direction of trade. But comparative advantage can be discerned more quickly on the basis of opportunity costs. A country will have the comparative advantage when its opportunity cost is lower. Referring to Example 3, note that the opportunity cost of one unit of wine is five units of cloth in Gaul, but only three units of cloth in Sumer. Thus, Sumer has the comparative advantage in wine production and would export wine to Gaul. Conversely, the opportunity cost for cloth is one-fifth of a unit of wine in Gaul, but one-third of a unit of wine in Sumer. Gaul, with the lower opportunity cost for cloth, would export cloth in exchange for wine.

Again, international specialization would increase global output. Here, Sumer would shift resources out of cloth production and into wine production, and Gaul would transfer resources in the opposite direction. Allowing countries to produce according to comparative advantages leads to a more efficient allocation of the world's resources.

To illustrate, suppose Sumer shifted resources and increased wine production by one unit. The opportunity cost of doing so would be three fewer units of cloth production. To keep the global production of wine constant, Gaul could cut back wine production by one unit, freeing up enough resources in the process to produce another five units of cloth. As a result of these internal resource transfers, the global production of wine would be unchanged, but the global production of cloth would increase by two units. The greater global output reflects a more efficient allocation of resources, since each nation is producing more of its comparative-advantage commodity.

Schematically:

Sumer	$\Delta w = +1$	$\Delta c = -3$
Gaul	$\Delta w = -1$	$\Delta c = +5$
World	$\Delta w = 0$	$\Delta c = +2$

This additional output could be distributed between the two countries so that both benefit.

DETERMINING THE GAINS FROM TRADE

To repeat, the device of the traveler was useful for illustrating the direction of trade. To determine the exact gains from trade accruing to each country, however, we need to know the **international terms of trade,** or the rate at which one commodity can actually be exchanged for another in the world market. Consider Example 3 reproduced as follows:

EXAMPLE 5
Output per Unit of Resources

	Cloth	Wine	Opportunity Costs
Gaul	10 Units	2 units	$5c = 1w$, or $1c = \frac{1}{5}w$
Sumer	12 units	4 units	$3c = 1w$, or $1c = \frac{1}{3}w$

With the opening of trade between the two countries, Sumer will produce more wine for export to Gaul. In turn, Gaul will shift resources into the production of cloth for export to Sumer. On net, then, wine will flow into Gaul and cloth will flow into Sumer. Before trade, one unit of wine exchanged for three units of cloth in Sumer. Now, with trade, and more cloth available in Sumer, one unit of wine will exchange for more than three units of cloth. In Gaul, where one unit of cloth exchanged for one-fifth of a unit of wine before trade, now, with trade and wine relatively more plentiful, one unit of cloth will exchange for more than one-fifth of a unit of wine. The exact international exchange ratio, or terms of trade, will fall between the opportunity costs or pre-trade exchange ratios for the two nations (here between $1w = 3c$ and $1w = 5c$).[3]

Assume that the international terms of trade are one unit of wine for four units of cloth ($1w = 4c$, or $\frac{1}{4}w = 1c$). To illustrate the gains from trade, note that Sumer could either (1) produce directly twelve units of cloth with one unit of resources or (2) keep that unit of resources in wine production, produce four units of wine, and trade with Gaul at the international exchange ratio for sixteen units of cloth. Thus, by indirectly producing cloth, that is, by producing wine and trading for cloth, Sumer gains four units of cloth ($16 - 12$) per unit of resources kept in wine production and used for trade.

In the same way, Gaul could shift one unit of resources out of cloth production and produce directly two units of wine. Or Gaul could keep the unit of resources in cloth production—where it enjoys the comparative advantage—and produce ten units of cloth, which could be traded for $\frac{5}{2}$ units of wine. Doing the latter yields a net gain of one-half ($\frac{1}{2}$) of a unit of wine ($\frac{5}{2} - 2$) per unit of resources left in cloth production. To reiterate, the basis for trade is comparative advantage, which is reflected in different opportunity costs for a commodity across countries.

---

[3] If the international terms of trade coincided with the pre-trade exchange ratio and opportunity cost in a country, then that country would have no incentive to engage in international trade. For example, if the international terms of trade were equal to Sumer's pre-trade exchange ratio of $1w = 3c$, then despite a comparative advantage in wine, Sumer would not receive any more units of cloth in exchange for a unit of wine through international trade than could be received domestically.

If the international terms of trade were outside the opportunity costs of the two nations, then there would be no common basis for international trade. For example, if the international terms of trade were $1w = 2c$, (alternatively $\frac{1}{2}w = 1c$), then both countries would have an incentive to export cloth—a unit of cloth commanding more wine in international trade than in either country. With both countries trying to export cloth, a surplus of cloth would result on the international market (and a shortage of wine) until the international terms of trade adjusted (the cloth price of a unit of wine rose) and both goods were again offered in trade.

PRODUCTION AND CONSUMPTION POSSIBILITIES BOUNDARIES

With one additional piece of information for each country we can extend the analysis. Recall that constant costs of production are assumed for both nations. From Example 5 we know that one unit of resources can produce ten units of cloth or two units of wine in Gaul, and twelve units of cloth or four units of wine in Sumer. All that is needed to derive the production possibilities boundaries (PPBs) are the number of resource units in each country.

Suppose that Sumer has 75 resource units and Gaul has 60 resource units. Then the PPBs would be as illustrated in Figures 4.1 and 4.2. Sumer's PPB is given by the line az; Gaul's by the line $a'z'$. If Sumer devoted all of its resources to just cloth production, then it could produce 900 units of cloth (point a). At the other extreme, Sumer's maximum production of wine in this example would be 300 units (point z). Gaul has maximum possible outputs of 600 units of cloth (point a') and 120 units of wine (point z'). Note, as expected, the slopes of the two production possibilities boundaries are constant and reflect the different opportunity costs in the two nations:

$$\text{Sumer: } \Delta c/\Delta w = -3$$
$$\text{Gaul: } \Delta c/\Delta w = -5$$

Suppose that without trade Sumer is producing (and consuming) 200 units of wine and 300 units of cloth. Sumer's pre-trade position is point e on its PPB in

FIGURE 4.1
PRODUCTION POSSIBILITIES BOUNDARY FOR SUMER

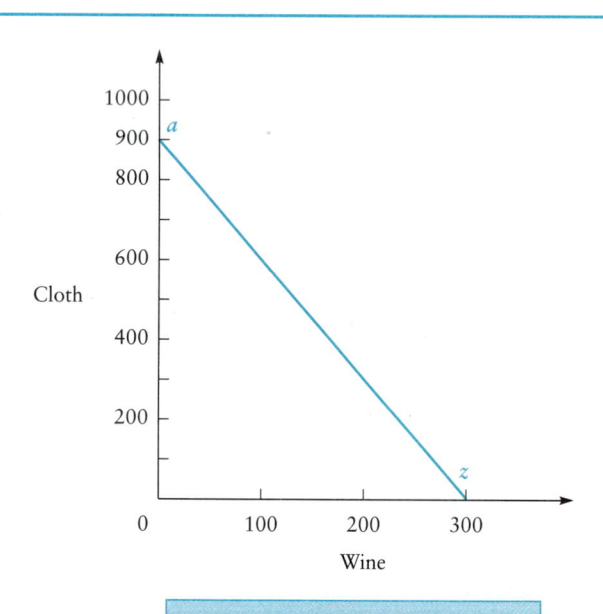

Sumer has 75 resource units. One unit of resources can produce either 4 units of wine or 12 units of cloth.

CHAPTER 4 COMPARATIVE ADVANTAGE: A BASIS FOR TRADE

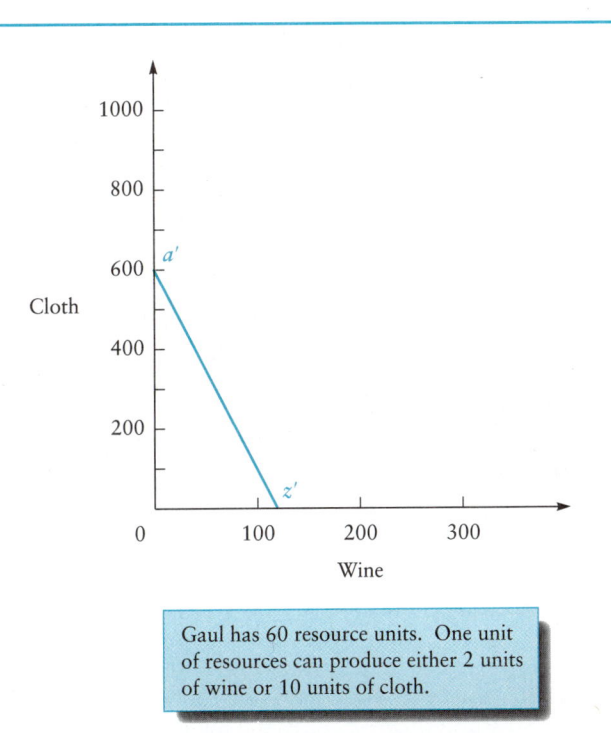

FIGURE 4.2

PRODUCTION POSSIBILITIES BOUNDARY FOR GAUL

Gaul has 60 resource units. One unit of resources can produce either 2 units of wine or 10 units of cloth.

Figure 4.3. Further suppose that Gaul's pre-trade production (and consumption) combination is 80 units of wine and 200 units of cloth (point e' on Gaul's PPB in Figure 4.4). Both nations are using all the available resources efficiently (that is, they are on their respective PPBs); however, without the benefit of international trade, their consumption possibilities must coincide with their production possibilities.

Now let the nations trade. As before, assume that the international terms of trade are one unit of wine for four units of cloth. Assume also that with trade, both nations completely specialize in the production of their comparative advantage goods. This would place Sumer at point z and Gaul at point a' on their PPBs. As an example, if Sumer arranged to exchange 90 units of wine for 360 units of cloth with Gaul, then Sumer would end up consuming 210 units of wine (300 − 90) and 360 units of cloth (all imported from Gaul). This combination lies beyond Sumer's PPB. (See point f in Figure 4.3). In fact, the combination represented by point f lies on Sumer's **consumption possibilities boundary** (CPB). The CPB represents all the combinations of the commodities the nation could consume given its PPB and the international terms of trade. In *autarky*, that is, without international trade, the consumption possibilities of a nation are restricted by—in fact, coincide with—the production possibilities. In the extreme, Sumer could trade 300 units of wine for 1200 units of cloth.[4] Sumer's

---

[4] Actually, in this numerical example, the maximum possible output of cloth in Gaul would be 600 units. (See point a' on Gaul's PPB.) Therefore, the maximum output of wine Sumer would export at the international terms of trade of $4c = 1w$ would be 150 wine. In effect, the CPB for Sumer, the larger economy, is given by the line segment zh in Figure 4.3.

CPB is given by the line *zt*. Note that the slope of Sumer's CPB is given by the international terms of trade: $\triangle c/\triangle w = -4$.

Gaul, with complete specialization in cloth, would be producing at *a'*. In the extreme, Gaul could trade 600 units of cloth for 150 units of wine at the international terms of trade. Gaul's CPB is given by the line *a't'*, the slope of which also equals the international terms of trade. In this example, Gaul imports 90 units of wine in exchange for 360 units of cloth. This exchange places Gaul at the point *f'* on its CPB with 90 units of wine and 240 units of cloth (240 = 600 − 360).

The gains from trade for each nation can be represented by the difference between the post-trade and pre-trade consumption positions. For Sumer, the gains from trade are 10 units of wine and 60 units of cloth. For Gaul, the gains from trade are 10 units of wine and 40 units of cloth. Thus, in this example, international specialization resulted in an increase in global output of 20 units of wine and 100 units of cloth. International trade based on each nation producing according to its comparative advantage can allow each nation to

FIGURE 4.3
GAINS FROM TRADE IN SUMER

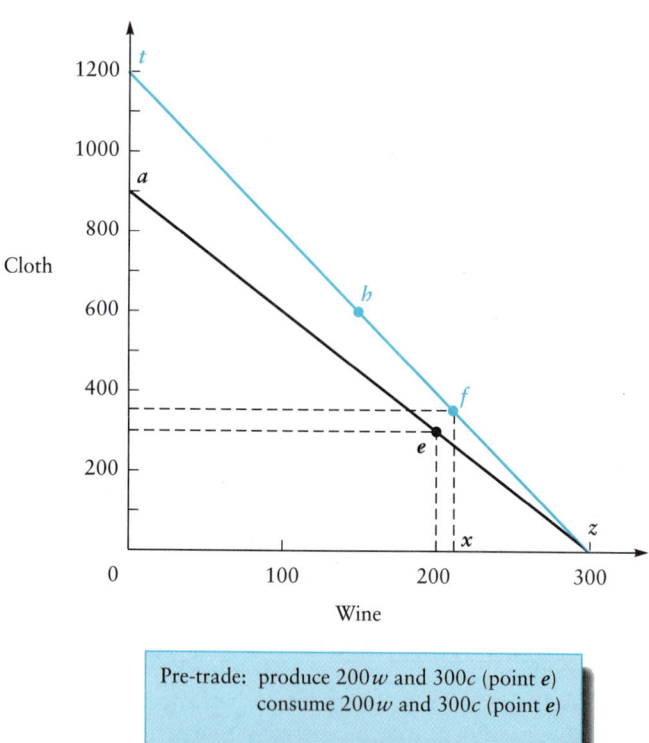

Pre-trade: produce 200*w* and 300*c* (point *e*)
consume 200*w* and 300*c* (point *e*)

Post-trade: produce 300*w* and 0*c* (point *z*)
consume 210*w* and 360*c* (point *f*)

export 90*w* (*zx*)
import 360*c* (*fx*)

Gains from trade: 10*w* and 60*c*

FIGURE 4.4
Gains from Trade in Gaul

Pre-trade: produce 80*w* and 200*c* (point *e'*)
consume 80*w* and 200*c* (point *e'*)

Post-trade: produce 0*w* and 600*c* (point *a'*)
consume 90*w* and 240*c* (point *f'*)

export 360*c* (*a'x'*)
import 90*w* (*x'f'*)

Gains from trade: 10*w* and 40*c*

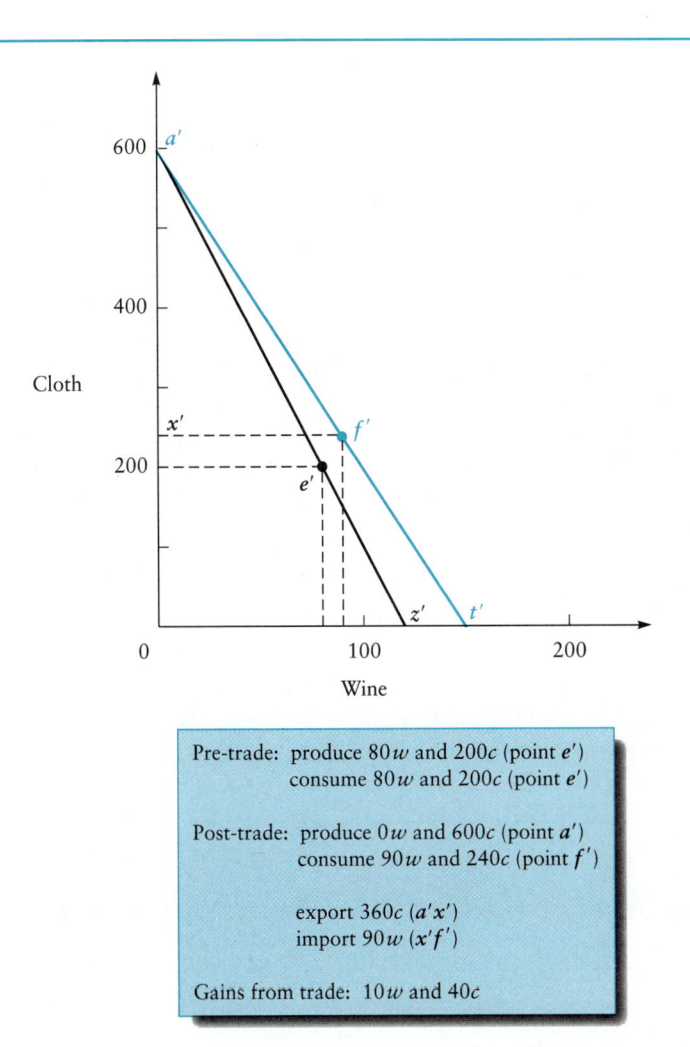

consume beyond its production possibilities boundary. In other words, international trade can relax the constraint imposed by the scarcity of resources. This is a powerful theoretical argument for international trade.

CONCLUDING NOTE

In this chapter we used a simple model and an extended numerical example to illustrate the concept of opportunity cost as applied to international trade. Realism could be added to the model by considering more than two countries and two goods, by incorporating transportation costs, and by replacing the assumption of constant opportunity costs (linear PPBs) with the more valid one of increasing opportunity costs (concave PPBs). Furthermore, the barter system of trade implicit in this model could be modified to allow for exchange based on money prices—although this extension would necessitate a discussion of exchange rates. Nevertheless, despite the abstractions from reality, the model proves useful for illustrating the benefits of international trade. International trade, whereby production is based upon comparative advantage, results in a more efficient allocation of resources and consequently greater global output. In sum, the world wins, and all the nations participating in trade win. However, this is not the entire story. While many people do "win" from international trade, some people "lose." Barriers to trade exist, with justifications including national security and protection of domestic labor from "unfair" foreign competition.

The principle of comparative advantage holds in contexts other than international trade. Free trade based on comparative advantage naturally takes place within a nation. Due to variations in geography, natural-resource endowments, and climate, regions within a nation will have different opportunity costs for producing commodities. For example, in the United States cotton is produced in the southern states and wheat is produced in the plains states of the Midwest. Across individuals, differences in aptitudes and skills mean there are gains from labor specialization—individuals specialize in (and within) different occupations (medicine, farming, carpentry), becoming more proficient with training and experience. Thus, on the international, national, and individual levels, significant gains in output derive from specialization and production according to comparative advantages.

KEY TERMS

constant costs of production
absolute advantage
comparative advantage

international terms of trade
consumption possibilities boundary

QUESTIONS

1. What are the three most important ideas in this chapter? Discuss why each is important.
2. Given two countries, Norte and Sierra, and two commodities, apples and cotton, assume constant costs of production. Now assume that a unit of resources can produce the following amounts of apples and cotton:

	Apples	Cotton
Norte	10 units	4 units
Sierra	20 units	16 units

a. Which country has the absolute advantage in producing apples? In producing cotton?
b. Why is it beneficial for the countries to trade with each other? Which commodity would Norte export? Why? Give an numerical example

where trade would not occur between these two countries. Explain why.
   c. What are the potential gains from international specialization—in terms of increased cotton production with no change in the total amount of apple production?
   d. If the international terms of trade were 2 apples = 1 cotton, what are the gains from trade for Norte—in terms of additional units of its import commodity per unit of its export commodity?
   e. If Norte has 50 units of resources and Sierra has 40 units of resources, then on separate graphs, sketch the production possibilities boundary for each nation. Can Norte produce the output combination of 400 units of apples and 50 units of cotton? Explain why or why not.
   f. For the international terms of trade of 2 apples = 1 cotton, sketch the consumption possibilities boundary for each nation on the same graphs as the production possibilities boundaries. With trade can Norte consume the output combination of 400 units of apples and 50 units of cotton? Explain why or why not.
3. Suppose Jamie can earn $25 an hour as a carpenter. What is the cost to Jamie of taking eight hours off from work to paint his fence, when he could hire a painter to paint his fence for $120? (Assume the painter takes six hours to paint Jamie's fence.)

   Suppose Joey can earn $20 an hour as a painter. What is the cost to Joey of taking eight hours off from work to build a house for his dog, when he could hire a carpenter to build the dog house for $125? (Assume the carpenter takes five hours to build the doghouse.)

   Show how it would be more efficient for Jamie to hire Joey to paint the fence and for Joey to hire Jamie to build the doghouse.

   How would your answer change if it takes the painter (Joey) nine hours to paint Jamie's fence?

PART

II

DEMAND AND SUPPLY: FUNDAMENTALS OF THE MARKET MECHANISM

CHAPTERS

— 5 —

MARKET EQUILIBRIUM: DEMAND AND SUPPLY

— 6 —

ELASTICITY

CHAPTER

5

MARKET EQUILIBRIUM: DEMAND AND SUPPLY

AN EQUILIBRIUM STATE can be thought of as a situation in which all of the acting forces in the economic system are counterbalanced. Unless something changes to disturb this balance, the equilibrium persists. This working definition of equilibrium, necessarily vague at this point, can be illustrated in the context of a market.

As discussed in Chapter 2, economists study markets. A fundamental question of economic analysis concerns how the prices and quantities transacted in the markets are determined. Equilibrium states serve as reference points in such economic analysis.

To begin, a **market** is any arrangement by which buyers and sellers exchange a well-defined product. Examples abound. There are local markets for goods like eggs, lumber, and flowers, and for services like haircuts, auto repair, and landscaping. There are regional markets for electricity and banking. There are national markets for college education and magazines. Many markets are international—for example, foreign exchange, wheat, and petroleum. Markets can be formal, with specific rules for trading, like the New York Stock Exchange, or they can be informal and characterized by considerable flexibility and autonomy, such as the market for babysitting services in a small town or the weekend farmers' market for local produce. Markets can be legal or illegal (for example, illicit drugs or prostitution). Whatever the case, there are two sides to a market: the buyers, or the **demanders** of the good or service, and the sellers, or the **suppliers** of the good or service.

What follows is a discussion of how a competitive market operates. In a competitive market there are many buyers and sellers of a commodity and no one buyer or seller is able to exert any significant influence over the market price. Alternative market structures, in which small groups, or even individual buyers or sellers, are able to influence the market outcomes will not be examined in this chapter.

DEMAND SCHEDULE

As in any model, the variables used should be carefully defined. Consider the market for commodity j, a good or a service. Let

$$Q_j^d = \text{quantity demanded of commodity } j.$$

The **quantity demanded** refers to the total physical amount of commodity j that all buyers are willing to purchase over a specific time period. Note that the quantity demanded is a *flow*. It has a time dimension. Note also that the quantity demanded will not necessarily be the same as the quantity *transacted*, meaning the amount actually exchanged.

The quantity demanded of commodity j depends on the price of commodity j, P_j. Ceteris paribus, a rise in the price of commodity j would probably cause demanders to shift to a less expensive alternative commodity that meets a similar need. A rise in the price of commodity j also would reduce the *purchasing power* of a given income (that is, the quantitites of commodities in general that could be purchased with the income)—because more of the income would have to go to commodity j, leaving less for other commodities. This would likely further decrease the quantity demanded of commodity j. Conversely, a fall in the price of commodity j, by itself, should lead to an increase in the quantity demanded. We hypothesize, then, that the quantity demanded of a commodity is inversely related to its own price.[1]

The relationship between the quantity demanded of a commodity and its unit price is known as the **demand schedule** and can be written concisely as

$$Q_j^d = d(\bar{P_j})$$

where the minus sign over the price variable reminds us of the hypothesized inverse relationship. The graphical analog of a demand schedule is a **demand curve**. (See the curve labeled D_j in Figure 5.1.) When graphing the demand curve, economists traditionally place the price of the commodity on the vertical axis and the quantity on the horizontal axis.[2]

When we speak of the demand for commodity j, we refer to the entire demand schedule, $Q_j^d = d(P_j)$, and the entire demand curve, D_j. When we speak of the quantity demanded of commodity j, however, it is with reference to a specific price for commodity j. For example, in Figure 5.1, the quantity demanded of

---

[1] In their study of consumer behavior, economists have formally developed a theory to explain the **law of demand,** or the hypothesized inverse relationship between the price of a commodity and the quantity demanded of it.

[2] This graphical orientation runs counter to the standard practice in mathematics of placing the dependent variable (here the quantity demanded) on the vertical axis. The reason follows from a blending of two historical approaches to market analysis. In one approach, represented by the French economist, Leon Walras (1834–1910), the quantity demanded of commodity j is written as a function of the price of commodity j, much as we have presented it here. In the other approach, represented by the English economist, Alfred Marshall (1842–1924), the demand price of commodity j (P_j^d) is written as a function of the quantity of commodity j. That is,

$$P_j^d = d(Q_j)$$

where the demand price is the unit price the buyers are willing to pay for a given quantity of the commodity. The switch in axes occurred because economists have tended to use Walras's mathematical version with the graphical orientation compatible with Marshall's specification.

FIGURE 5.1

A Demand Curve

A demand curve illustrates the relationship between the price of a commodity and the quantity demanded of it.

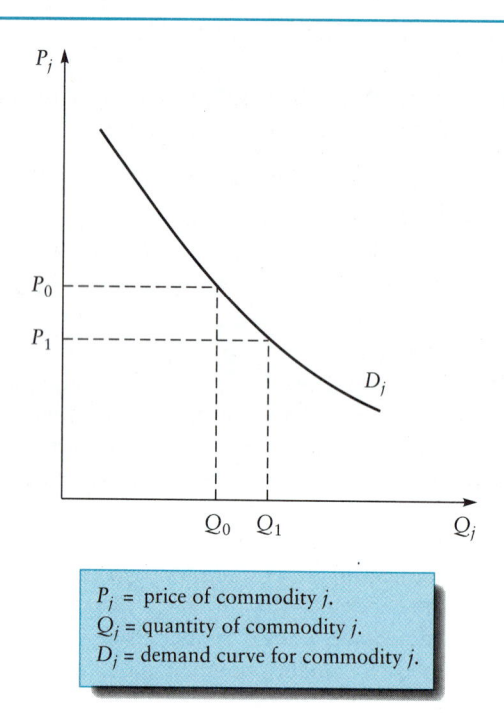

P_j = price of commodity j.
Q_j = quantity of commodity j.
D_j = demand curve for commodity j.

commodity j is Q_0 when the price of commodity j is P_0. The quantity demanded is Q_1 when the price is P_1. Assuming there is an inverse relationship between the quantity demanded and price of the commodity, if $P_1 < P_0$, then $Q_1 > Q_0$.

Determinants of Demand Schedule

The demand for a commodity is influenced by a number of exogenous factors, particularly

- Average income of the demanders of the commodity.
- Number of demanders of the commodity.
- Tastes and preferences of the demanders of the commodity.
- Prices of related commodities.

For most goods and services, a rise in the average income of the demanders would be associated with an increase in demand. A rise in income, ceteris paribus, corresponds to an increase in purchasing power, which allows for increased purchases of goods and services in general. Conversely, a fall in the average income of the demanders of the commodity would be associated with a decrease in demand for the commodity. Commodities that exhibit this positive (or direct) relationship between income and demand are called **normal.** Some commodities are **inferior,** meaning an increase (decrease) in the average level of income results in a decrease (increase) in the demand for the commodity. An example may be Spam, a processed product that serves as an inexpensive substitute for ham.[3] With increases in income, most people would be less likely to satisfy their desire for ham with Spam, so demand for Spam would fall.

Clearly, the demand for a commodity is directly related to the number of demanders. For any price of commodity j, therefore, an increase in the number of buyers, ceteris paribus, would increase the quantity demanded.

Changes in tastes and preferences, often shaped by advertising, can be influential. Fads and styles come and go. If tastes change in favor of commodity j, then demand increases.

Finally, the prices of related commodities may be important determinants of the demand for a given commodity. Suppose commodity j refers to golf balls. What would be the effect on the demand for golf balls of an increase in the price of greens fees? What would be the effect on the demand for golf balls of an increase in the price of tennis lessons? Why would there be a difference in effect?

In the first case, a rise in the price of greens fees would, ceteris paribus, reduce the incidence of golf playing and thus the need for golf balls—regardless of their price. The demand for golf balls would fall. Playing golf and golf balls are **complementary commodities,** that is, commodities that tend to be used jointly. With complementary commodities an inverse relationship exists between the price of one and the demand for the other. Cameras and film, fishing rods and tackle, cars and gasoline are pairs of complementary goods.

In the second case, a rise in the price of tennis lessons would reduce the incidence of tennis playing and perhaps induce people to play more golf, causing the demand for golf balls to increase. Golf balls and tennis lessons are **substitute commodities,** which tend to be consumed independently. Golf and tennis are alternative forms of recreation. Coffee and tea, movies and concerts, neckties and bow ties are pairs of substitute goods.

Most commodities, however, are not closely related, so changes in the price of one usually has an insignificant effect on the demand for others.

The four determinants of demand discussed here (the average income and number of demanders of commodity j, tastes and preferences, and prices of related goods), while important, do not exhaust all the influences on the demand for a commodity. You may be able to think of others.

Changes in Demand

The demand curve, which illustrates the relationship between the quantity demanded of a commodity and its price, is drawn holding constant all the other influences on the demand for the commodity. It is important to be clear on the difference between a change in demand and a change in the quantity demanded.

A **change in demand** refers to a change in the entire demand schedule—and graphically to a shift in the demand curve. In Figure 5.2 an increase in demand is indicated by a rightward shift in the demand curve from D_j to D'_j. For every price of commodity j there is an increase in the quantity demanded (for example,

---

[3] To avoid offending Spam fans, it should be noted that what might be an inferior good for some will not be for others. Furthermore, at some levels of income a good might be considered *normal* that at higher levels would be considered *inferior* (e.g., subcompact economy cars).

FIGURE 5.2
INCREASE IN DEMAND VERSUS INCREASE IN QUANTITY DEMANDED

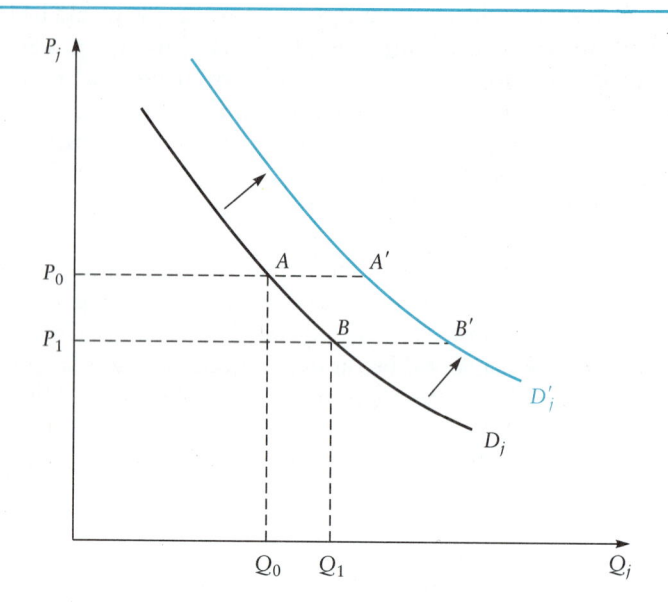

The shift in the demand curve from D_j to D'_j indicates an increase in demand. The movement from A to B (or A' to B') indicates an increase in the quantity demanded of commodity j due to a fall in its price. The movement from A to A' (or B to B') indicates an increase in the quantity demanded of commodity j due to an increase in demand for it.

point A to point A' and point B to point B'). Such an increase in the demand for commodity j might result from

1. An increase in the average income of the demanders of commodity j (assuming that commodity j is normal).
2. An increase in the number of demanders of commodity j.
3. A shift in tastes and preferences in favor of commodity j.
4. An increase in the price of a substitute commodity or a decrease in the price of a complementary commodity.

A **change in quantity demanded** refers to a movement along a given demand schedule caused by a change in the price of the commodity. For instance, in Figure 5.2 the movement from point A to point B represents an increase in the quantity demanded of commodity j (from Q_0 to Q_1) due to a decrease in the price of commodity j (from P_0 to P_1). Also, as implied, with a change in the demand for commodity j (that is, a shift in the demand curve), there will be changes in the quantities demanded of commodity j over the entire range of prices for the commodity.

In sum, a change in demand means a change in the entire relationship between the quantity demanded and price of the commodity and is reflected in a shift in the demand curve. A change in the quantity demanded refers to the response of the quantity demanded to a change in the price of the commodity (a

CHAPTER 5 MARKET EQUILIBRIUM: DEMAND AND SUPPLY

movement along a given demand curve) or, holding the price of the commodity constant, the response of the quantity demanded to a change in the demand for the commodity (a horizontal movement between two demand curves).

To make this theoretical discussion more concrete, consider the following example. Suppose an economics consulting firm, after research and data collection, estimates the demand schedule for premium unleaded gasoline in the Charlotte, North Carolina, market to be

$$Q_g^d = 90 - 40P_g$$

where

Q_g^d = quantity demanded of premium unleaded gasoline in Charlotte (in thousands of gallons per week).
P_g = the price (in dollars) of a gallon of premium unleaded gasoline.

Based on this quantitative relation, a demand curve can be sketched.[4] To derive ordered pairs of price and quantity demanded, simply select a price, substitute it into the demand equation, and calculate the associated quantity demanded. The only economic restrictions are that the price and quantity demanded should not be negative. For example, if the price of a gallon of premium unleaded gasoline is $.75, then according to the demand schedule, the quantity demanded would be 60 (thousand) gallons per week. Other combinations of P_g and Q_g^d could be similarly derived. In Figure 5.3 we illustrate the demand curve. In general, the estimated demand equation indicates that for every increase of $.10 (ten cents) in the price of premium unleaded gasoline, the quantity demanded per week in the Charlotte market would decrease by 4 thousand gallons.

This demand curve is drawn holding constant all the other relevant influences on the demand for premium unleaded gasoline in the Charlotte market. If any of these factors change, then the entire relationship between the price and quantity demanded will be affected. Possible conditions that could increase the demand for premium unleaded gasoline in this example include

1. An increase in the population of Charlotte (in particular, an increase in the number of registered vehicles in the Charlotte area).
2. A rise in the average income level of households in Charlotte (which may be reflected in not only increased driving but in an increase in the demand for premium (as opposed to regular) unleaded gasoline.
3. A rise in the price of city bus tickets, which induces some individuals to shift to private means of transportation (constituting a rise in the price of a substitute commodity).
4. A change in tastes in favor of larger, less fuel-efficient automobiles prompted by increased concerns with safety (believed to be greater with larger automobiles in the event of an accident).

---

[4] For ease of exposition, the demand schedule is a linear function. The assumption of linearity is frequently made throughout this text. Recall from Chapter 2 that the estimated line of best fit is unlikely to represent perfectly the relationship between the variables under analysis (here the quantity demanded and price of premium unleaded gasoline). For the following example we will ignore the estimation problems and assume that the given demand schedule accurately portrays the demand for premium unleaded gasoline in the Charlotte market.

FIGURE 5.3
DEMAND CURVE FOR PREMIUM UNLEADED GASOLINE IN CHARLOTTE

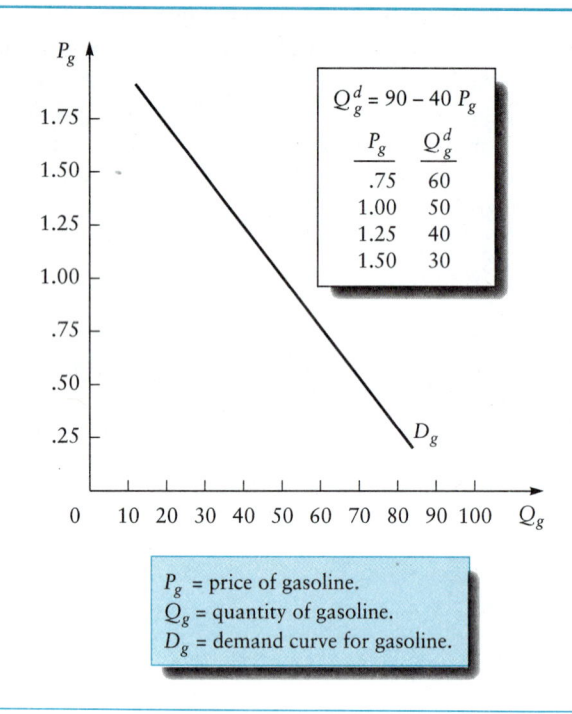

$Q_g^d = 90 - 40 P_g$

P_g	Q_g^d
.75	60
1.00	50
1.25	40
1.50	30

P_g = price of gasoline.
Q_g = quantity of gasoline.
D_g = demand curve for gasoline.

In each case the demand curve for premium unleaded gasoline would shift to the right—indicating that at any price the quantity demanded has increased.

A fall in demand (that is, a leftward shift in the demand curve), meaning fewer gallons of premium unleaded gasoline would be demanded per week at any price, could be due to decreases in the population or average income level of the households in Charlotte, an increase in car pooling arising from concern about air pollution, or a fall in the price of regular unleaded gasoline (a substitute good).

These examples of *changes in the demand* can be contrasted with *changes in the quantity demanded* that result from a change in the price of premium unleaded gasoline. For instance, if the price of a gallon of premium unleaded gasoline fell from $1.25 to $1.00, then the quantity demanded would increase from 40 to 50 (thousand) gallons per week—a movement down the demand curve.

With just the demand schedule, however, we are unable to determine the market price and quantity transacted. Supply, the other side of the market, must be considered.

SUPPLY SCHEDULE

The discussion of supply will parallel that for demand. Let

$$Q_j^s = \text{quantity supplied of commodity } j.$$

The **quantity supplied** refers to the total physical amount of a commodity that is offered by all sellers over a specified period of time. Like quantity demanded, quantity supplied is a flow. And the quantity supplied is not always the same as the quantity transacted.

The quantity supplied of a commodity depends on its own price. Other things being equal, a rise in the price of commodity *j*, by increasing the gain or incentive in selling commodity *j*, would result in an increase in the quantity supplied. Thus, a positive relationship between the quantity supplied and the price of a commodity is hypothesized.[5]

This relationship between the quantity supplied of a commodity and its own price is known as the **supply schedule** and can be concisely written as

$$Q_j^s = s(\overset{+}{P_j})$$

where the plus sign over the price variable reminds us of the hypothesized positive relationship.

The graphical representation of a supply schedule is a **supply curve.** (See the supply curve S_j illustrated in Figure 5.4.) The **supply** of commodity *j* refers to the entire supply schedule, $Q_j^s = s(P_j)$, and the entire supply curve, S_j. The quantity supplied is in reference to a particular price for commodity *j*. For example, in Figure 5.4 the quantity supplied of commodity *j* when the price is P_0 is Q_0. Assuming there is a positive relationship between the quantity supplied and the price, then the quantity supplied will rise when the price increases ($Q_1 > Q_0$ if $P_1 > P_0$).

---

[5] In their study of the behavior of firms, economists have formally developed the theory underlying the positive relationship between the price and quantity supplied of a commodity, known as the **law of supply**.

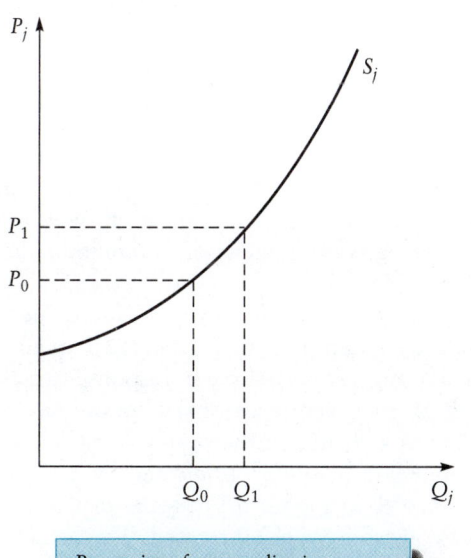

FIGURE 5.4

A Supply Curve

A supply curve illustrates the relationship between the price of a commodity and the quantity supplied of it.

P_j = price of commodity *j*.
Q_j = quantity of commodity *j*.
S_j = supply curve for commodity *j*.

Determinants of Supply Schedule

The supply of a commodity is determined by factors such as

- Number of suppliers.
- Prices of the inputs used to produce a unit of the commodity.
- State of technology used to produce the commodity.
- Effects of government regulations (including taxes) on the suppliers of the commodity.

Again, this list is not exhaustive, but representative of the most important determinants of the supply of a commodity.

We would expect that as the number of suppliers in the market increases, ceteris paribus, the supply of the commodity, that is, the quantities supplied for all prices of that commodity, would increase.

The prices of the inputs used to make the commodity should be inversely related to the supply. An increase in the prices of the inputs, ceteris paribus, would make it less profitable to produce and sell the commodity.

The state of technology affects the amount of output that can be produced per unit of inputs. Technological advances, including the adoption of more efficient production techniques, increase the amount of output produced from a given amount of inputs. Thus, improved technologies should increase the supply of a commodity.

Government regulations on the suppliers of a commodity, whether for environmental, safety, or health reasons, tend to reduce the efficiency with which the commodity can be produced. The added costs of conforming with the government regulations reduce the profitability of supplying the affected commodity, hence reduce the supply of the commodity.

Changes in Supply

The supply curve, which depicts the relationship between the quantity supplied and the price of the commodity, is drawn conditional on the underlying determinants of supply, including those just noted: the number of suppliers, input prices, technology, and government regulation. We should emphasize the difference between a change in the *supply* of a commodity and a change in the *quantity supplied*.

A **change in supply** reflects a shift in the supply curve due to a change in one (or more) of the underlying determinants. A **change in quantity supplied** refers to either a movement along a supply curve in response to a change in the price of the commodity or, for a given price of the commodity, the change in the quantity supplied due to a change in the supply of the commodity.

For example, an increase in supply (indicated by a rightward shift in the supply curve from S_j to S'_j in Figure 5.5) means that at any price level, the quantity supplied of commodity j has increased. This increase in supply could be due to an increase in the number of suppliers in the market, lower input prices, improved technology, or a relaxation of government regulations.

An increase in the quantity supplied of commodity j could result from a rise in its price (in Figure 5.5 the upward movement along the supply curve from point A to point B), or from an increase in the supply of commodity j, holding

FIGURE 5.5

INCREASE IN SUPPLY VERSUS INCREASE IN QUANTITY SUPPLIED

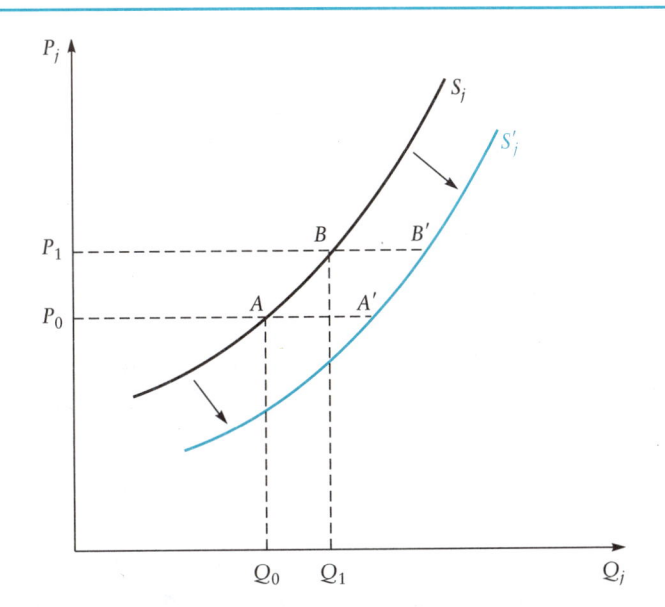

The shift in the supply curve from S_j to S'_j indicates an increase in supply. The movement from A to B (or A' to B') indicates an increase in the quantity supplied of commodity j due to a rise in its price. The movement from A to A' (or B to B') indicates an increase in the quantity supplied of commodity j due to an increase in the supply of it.

constant its price (in Figure 5.5 the rightward movement from point A to point A' for the price of P_0).

Returning to the example of gasoline, suppose that the supply schedule for premium unleaded gasoline in the Charlotte market is estimated to be

$$Q_g^s = -30 + 60 P_g$$

where

Q_g^s = quantity supplied of premium unleaded gasoline in Charlotte (in thousands of gallons per week).

P_g = price (in dollars) of a gallon of premium unleaded gasoline.

This schedule can be plotted as a supply curve in a similar manner as for the demand curve. Note the negative horizontal intercept of the supply curve (here equal to -30). Together with the positive coefficient for price (here equal to 60), the implication is that the price for premium unleaded gasoline has to exceed a minimum level before any will be offered for sale on the market. In this example the minimum supply price for premium unleaded gasoline is $.50. The supply curve is shown in Figure 5.6. According to the supply schedule, for every increase of $.10 in the price of premium unleaded gasoline, the quantity supplied per week in the Charlotte market is estimated to rise by 6 (thousand) gallons.

FIGURE 5.6

Supply Curve for Premium Unleaded Gasoline in Charlotte

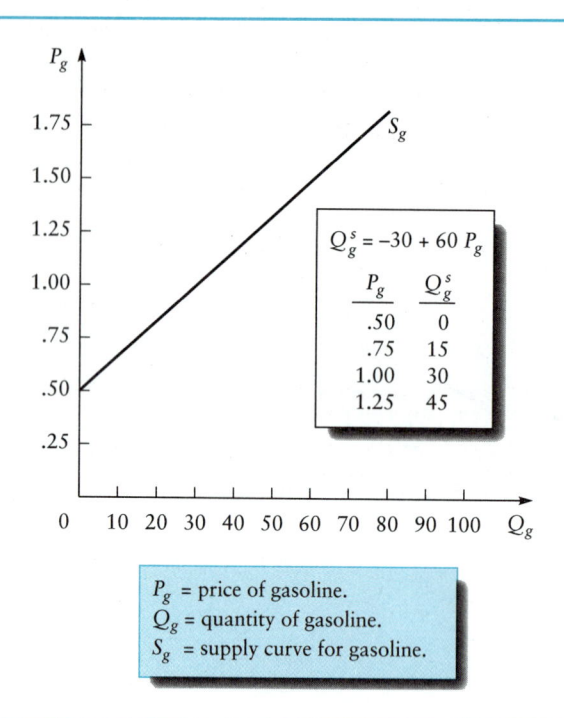

$Q_g^s = -30 + 60 P_g$

P_g	Q_g^s
.50	0
.75	15
1.00	30
1.25	45

P_g = price of gasoline.
Q_g = quantity of gasoline.
S_g = supply curve for gasoline.

DETERMINING EQUILIBRIUM PRICE AND QUANTITY

Recall the working definition of equilibrium offered at the beginning of the chapter: a situation in which all of the acting forces in the system are counterbalanced. Here the acting forces in the system are represented by the buyers and sellers of the commodity in question. When the quantity demanded by the buyers is exactly offset by the quantity supplied by the sellers, an equilibrium is reached.

For commodity j the system can be written concisely in the form of three equations:

$$\text{Demand Schedule: } Q_j^d = d(P_j)$$
$$\text{Supply Schedule: } Q_j^s = s(P_j)$$
$$\text{Equilibrium Condition: } Q_j^d \stackrel{e}{=} Q_j^s$$

The first two equations are the demand and supply schedules, respectively conditional on all of the factors underlying the demand and supply of commodity j. The third equation is the equilibrium condition, where an "e" is placed over the equals sign for emphasis. In equilibrium the quantity demanded of commodity j by all the buyers must equal the quantity supplied of commodity j from all the sellers. The **equilibrium price** is the price that equates the quantity demanded with the quantity supplied over the given period of time. In other

CHAPTER 5 MARKET EQUILIBRIUM: DEMAND AND SUPPLY

words, the equilibrium price "clears" the market, with zero excess quantity demanded.[6]

Combining Figures 5.1 and 5.4 gives the market situation for commodity j shown in Figure 5.7. Graphically the equilibrium price occurs at the intersection of the demand and supply curves (point E in Figure 5.7). Here the equilibrium price for commodity j is P_0. To find the equilibrium quantity or the quantity transacted, simply drop a perpendicular line from the point of intersection of the demand and supply curves to the quantity axis. Here Q_0 is the equilibrium quantity.

Note the different units of measurement. Price is measured in terms of money value (dollars and cents). Quantity is measured in physical units (gallons of gasoline). If the equilibrium price (P_0) is multiplied by the equilibrium quantity (Q_0), then we obtain the total expenditures (TE).

$$TE = P_0 \cdot Q_0$$

Total expenditures, also measured in money terms, refer to the value of the total spending by the buyers for the quantity purchased. Graphically, total expenditures can be measured as the area formed by the rectangle P_0EQ_00 (which is the same as the product of P_0 and Q_0). **Total revenues** refer to the total

---

[6] The system of three equations can be collapsed into the equilibrium condition and rearranged to indicate that at the equilibrium price the excess quantity demanded is equal to zero.

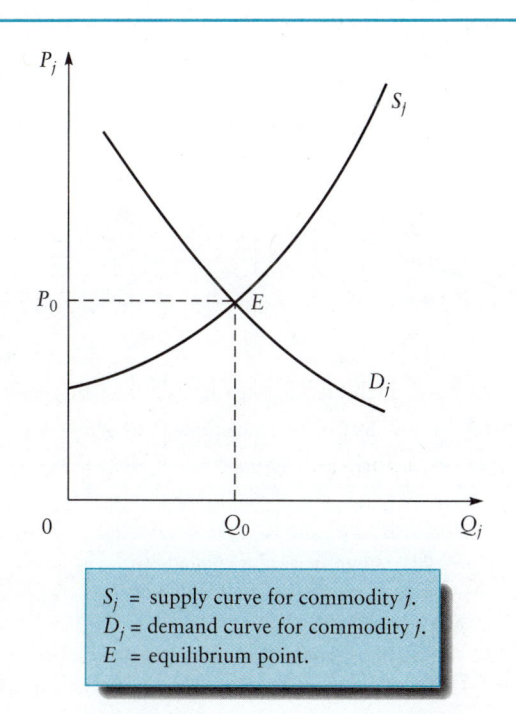

$$Q_j^d(P_j) - Q_j^s(P_j) \stackrel{e}{=} 0$$

FIGURE 5.7

EQUILIBRIUM IN THE MARKET

The market equilibrium price (P_0) and quantity transacted (Q_0) are found where the quantity demanded equals the quantity supplied—or at the intersection of the demand and supply curves.

S_j = supply curve for commodity j.
D_j = demand curve for commodity j.
E = equilibrium point.

receipts of the sellers for the quantity sold. In this example, where there are no taxes or other market distortions, total expenditures equal total revenues.

The market system is said to be self-regulating, meaning that there are inherent forces in the system that push any price toward the equilibrium, or market-clearing, price. Consider a price that is below the market equilibrium, such as P_1 in Figure 5.8. At this price the quantity buyers desire to purchase (the quantity demanded) is equal to Q_1^d, while the quantity offered on the market (the quantity supplied) is equal to Q_1^s. Therefore, at this low price there is an excess quantity demanded equal to $Q_1^d - Q_1^s$ (also indicated by the dashed-line segment GF). With an excess quantity demanded there is a **shortage** of the commodity on the market. Some of the buyers are frustrated since they are not able to purchase the commodity in the desired amounts. The frustrated buyers would pay more than the current market price of P_1 for the commodity. Consequently, to obtain some of the limited quantity on the market, frustrated buyers bid up the price of the commodity. Suppliers may also react to the disequilibrium situation by directly raising the selling price. As the market price of the commodity rises, there are two responses:

1. The quantity supplied increases as the incentive to sell is greater (indicated in Figure 5.8 by the movement up the supply curve from G to E).

FIGURE 5.8

Disequilibrium Prices in the Market

At the price P_2 (above the market equilibrium price), there is an excess quantity supplied. The surplus would be eliminated by a fall in the market price to P_0. At the price P_1 (below the market equilibrium price), there is an excess quantity demanded. The shortage would be eliminated by a rise in the market price to P_0.

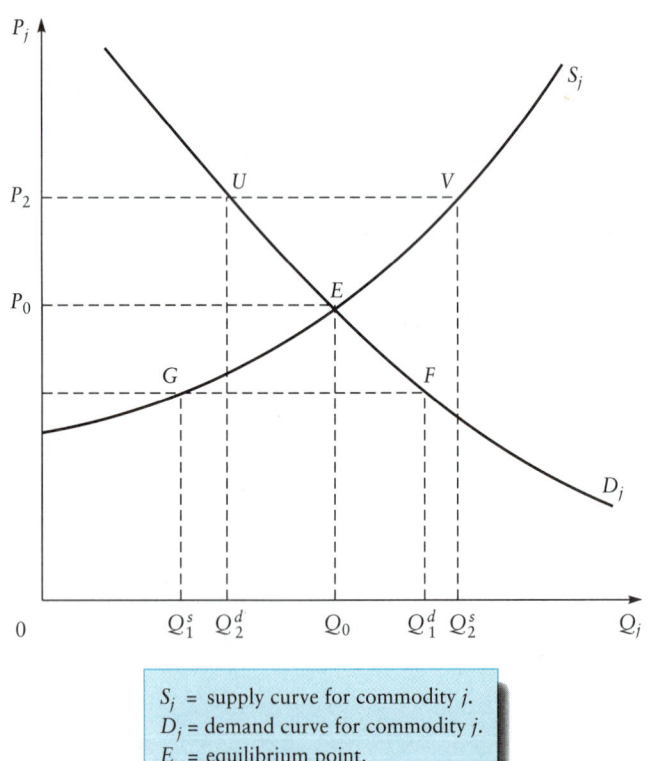

S_j = supply curve for commodity j.
D_j = demand curve for commodity j.
E = equilibrium point.

2. The quantity demanded falls as some buyers now find the price is too high to justify purchasing the commodity (indicated in Figure 5.8 by the movement back up the demand curve from F to E).

That is, as the price rises, the excess quantity demanded decreases. The market price will continue to rise until it reaches P_0, where the quantity supplied has increased by enough to meet the reduced quantity demanded. At P_0 there is a balance between the desired transactions of the buyers and sellers of the commodity for this period.

Conversely, if the market price were too high, for example, P_2 in Figure 5.8, there would be an excess quantity supplied (that is, a negative excess quantity demanded) equal to $Q_2^s - Q_2^d$ (or the dashed-line segment UV). With the **surplus** of the commodity on the market, the sellers find their inventories of the unsold commodity rising. In order to reduce the excess inventories (which are expensive to hold) and stimulate sales in this period, some of the sellers would accept prices lower than P_2. Buyers who perceive the surplus on the market also may bid down the price. With the decline in market price, quantity demanded increases (indicated by the movement down the demand curve from U to E) as the commodity becomes more affordable. Concurrently, the quantity supplied decreases (from V to E along the supply curve) as suppliers are less willing to offer so much on the market in this period. The market price would fall to P_0, where the quantities demanded and supplied are equal. This self-regulating feature, whereby forces in the market (the actions of the demanders and suppliers of the commodity) respond to restore the equilibrium price, is known as the **market mechanism.**

To summarize, under the market mechanism, an excess quantity demanded (shortage) would result in a price increase, while an excess quantity supplied (surplus) would result in a price decrease. In each case the price level would adjust to clear the market in that period.

We can illustrate using the example of the market for premium unleaded gasoline in Charlotte. To the demand and supply schedules used earlier we add the equilibrium condition.

$$\text{Demand Schedule: } Q_g^d = 90 - 40 P_g$$
$$\text{Supply Schedule: } Q_g^s = -30 + 60 P_g$$
$$\text{Equilibrium Condition: } Q_g^d \stackrel{e}{=} Q_g^s$$

Graphically, the demand and supply schedules are shown in Figure 5.9.

Reading from the graph, the equilibrium price and quantity transacted are approximately $1.25 and 40 (thousand) gallons per week. In this example, given the estimated equations for the demand and supply schedules, we can be more precise by solving the model algebraically.

The algebraic equivalent to finding the point of intersection of the demand and supply curves is to set the demand schedule equal to the supply schedule and solve for the common price. Substituting the demand and supply schedules into the equilibrium condition yields

$$Q_g^d = 90 - 40 P_g \stackrel{e}{=} -30 + 60 P_g = Q_g^s$$

FIGURE 5.9

EQUILIBRIUM IN THE CHARLOTTE MARKET FOR PREMIUM UNLEADED GASOLINE

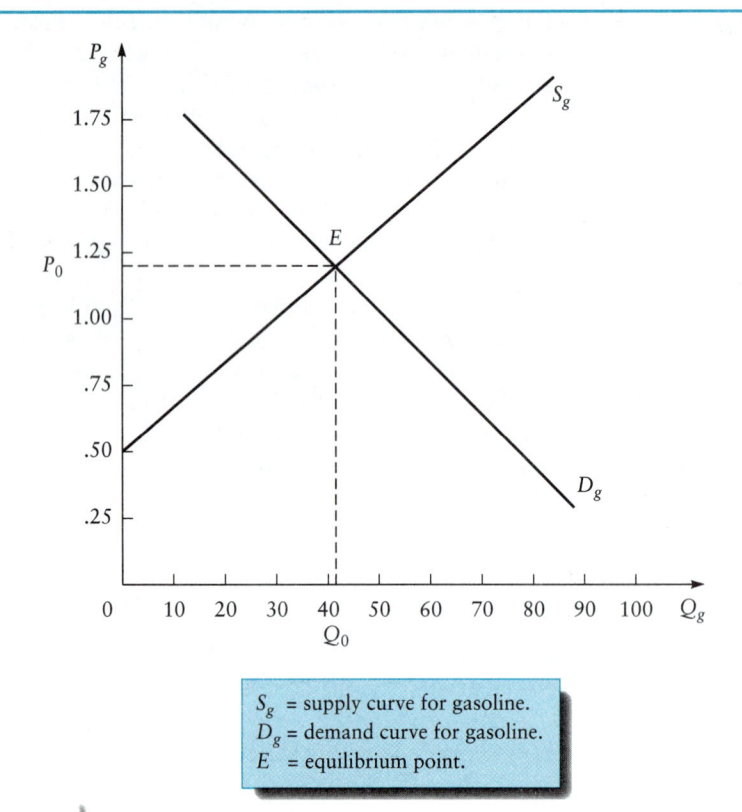

S_g = supply curve for gasoline.
D_g = demand curve for gasoline.
E = equilibrium point.

Now with one equation and one unknown (P_g), we can solve

$$90 - 40P_g \stackrel{e}{=} -30 + 60P_g$$
$$120 \stackrel{e}{=} 100P_g$$
$$1.2 \stackrel{e}{=} P_g$$

or

$$\$1.20 = P_0$$

Therefore, in this example, the equilibrium price for premium unleaded gasoline in the Charlotte market is $1.20.

To determine the quantity transacted, the equilibrium price of $P_0 = 1.20$ can be substituted back into either the demand or supply schedule. (Why does it not matter in this case?)

$$Q_g^d = 90 - 40(1.20) = 42 = -30 + 60(1.20) = Q_g^s = Q_0$$

Therefore, the equilibrium quantity or the quantity transacted is

$Q_0 = 42$ (thousand) gallons of premium unleaded gasoline per week.

Finally, total expenditures (*TE*) and total revenues (*TR*) can be calculated.

$$TE = \$1.2 \cdot 42 = \$50.4 \text{ (thousand) per week} = TR$$

You can verify that any price other than $P_0 = \$1.20$ would not clear the market. For instance, if the price were $P_1 = \$1.00$, then there would be an excess quantity demanded of 20 (thousand) gallons per week. Suppliers would perceive the shortage (long lines of frustrated buyers), and the price would rise back up toward the equilibrium level. In contrast, if the price were initially set too high, for example, $P_2 = \$1.50$, then there would be a surplus of unsold gasoline each week equal to 30 (thousand) gallons. The burden of unwanted inventories would tend to force the price back to a market-clearing level. There would be no need for the government or central authorities to intervene to lower the market price. Automatically, there are forces operating in the market to restore the equilibrium.

COMPARATIVE STATICS: CHANGES IN MARKET EQUILIBRIUM

Understanding how equilibrium in a market is attained allows us to analyze changes in market conditions. Recall that the demand curves are drawn holding constant the average income of the demanders, the number of demanders, tastes and preferences, and the prices of related goods (as well as other influences on the demand for the commodity). A change in any one of these factors would shift the demand curve and upset the equilibrium in the system. Similarly, the supply curves are drawn conditional on the number of suppliers in the market, the prices of the inputs used to produce the commodity, the state of technology, and government regulations (as well as other influences on the supply of the commodity). A change in any one of these factors will shift the supply curve and also upset any initial balance in the system.

Comparative statics refers to a method of analysis whereby two or more equilibrium states of a system are compared. We begin with the system in equilibrium. Then the value of one of the exogenous, or conditional, factors is allowed to change. A new equilibrium is determined and then contrasted with the initial equilibrium. The difference in the two equilibrium states can be attributed to the exogenous change that altered the original balance. To illustrate, consider the initial equilibrium shown below in the market for commodity j. See point E_0 in Figure 5.10 where P_0 and Q_0 are the initial equilibrium price and quantity.

Suppose there is a decrease in the demand for commodity j caused by, for example, a fall in the average income of the demanders of commodity j (assuming commodity j is a normal commodity) or a rise in the price of a complementary good. The decrease in demand would be reflected in a leftward shift in the demand curve to D'_j. At the original equilibrium price of P_0, there would now be an excess quantity supplied equal to $Q_0 - Q'$ or FE_0. The surplus of the good and the consequent building of inventories would prompt a fall in the price until an equilibrium is reestablished at P_1 and Q_1. Thus, the decrease in demand results in a fall in the equilibrium price and quantity transacted. Comparative statics involves contrasting the equilibrium positions represented by E_0 and E_1.

As another example, consider the impact of a new technology that allows commodity j to be manufactured with cheaper materials and in less time. In

FIGURE 5.10

IMPACT OF A FALL IN DEMAND ON MARKET EQUILIBRIUM

A decrease in the demand for commodity j results in a surplus of the commodity at the original equilibrium price P_0. The excess quantity supplied is eliminated by a fall in the market price to P_1.

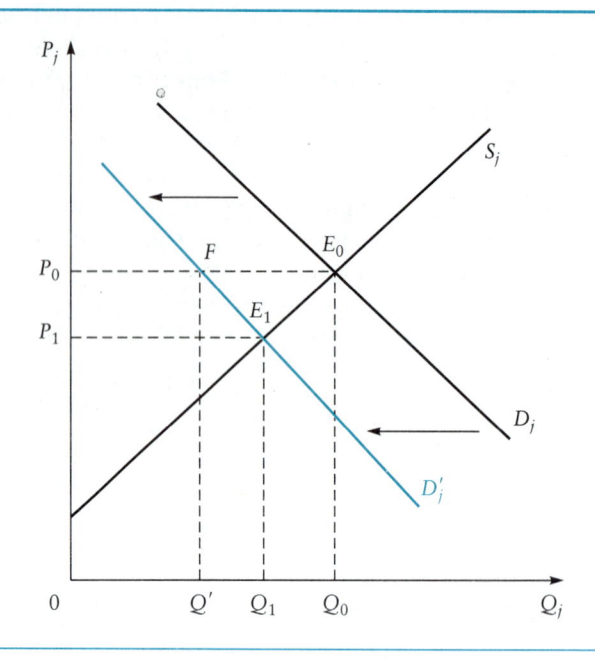

FIGURE 5.11

IMPACT OF TECHNOLOGICAL CHANGE ON MARKET EQUILIBRIUM

An increase in the supply of commodity j due to technological change results in a surplus of the commodity at the original equilibrium price P_0. The excess quantity supplied is eliminated by a fall in the market price to P_1.

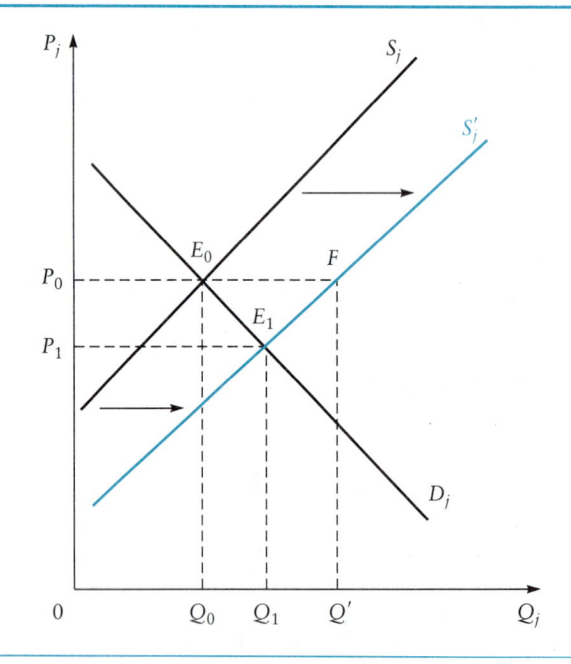

Figure 5.11 the shift in the supply curve from S_j to S'_j due to the technological change is illustrated. At the original equilibrium price of P_0, there would now be a surplus of commodity j equal to $Q' - Q_0$, or E_0F. Consequently, the market price would fall until the market cleared, with zero excess quantity

demanded at E_1 with P_1 and Q_1. The new technology results in a lower equilibrium price and increased quantity transacted.

As a final illustration, return to the numerical example of premium unleaded gasoline:

$$Q_g^d = 90 - 40P_g$$
$$Q_g^s = -30 + 60P_g$$

with $P_0 = \$1.20$ and $Q_0 = 42$ (thousand). Suppose now there was an increase in the price of petroleum—as occurred in late 1973 when the Organization of Petroleum Exporting Countries (OPEC) exercised its considerable influence in the world market for petroleum. Predict the impact of this change on the market equilibrium price and quantity transacted of premium unleaded gasoline.

If you are thinking like an economist, you would visualize an initial equilibrium at an intersection of a supply curve and demand curve. You would then determine which curve would be affected by the price increase for petroleum.

The rise in the price of petroleum, a key input in the production of gasoline, would increase the cost of supplying a gallon of premium unleaded gasoline (as well as all other grades of gasoline). Thus, for any given market price for premium unleaded gasoline, the suppliers would be less willing to offer a gallon for sale. The supply curve for premium unleaded gasoline would shift left. Alternatively, the suppliers would try to pass along the increased costs of production to the buyers by raising the selling price for any quantity of premium unleaded gasoline supplied. The supply curve for premium unleaded gasoline would shift up. From either perspective, the decrease in the supply of premium unleaded gasoline results in an increased market price and reduced quantity demanded and transacted.

If the new supply schedule is given by

$$Q_g^{s'} = -45 + 60P_g$$

then the new equilibrium price would be $P_1 = \$1.35$, and the new quantity transacted would be $Q_1 = 36$ (thousand) gallons per week. The new total expenditures of the buyers of premium unleaded gasoline in the Charlotte area would be $48.6 (thousand) per week. (You should check the math yourself.) As a further exercise, you should sketch the new supply schedule on the same graph as the original supply and demand curves and confirm the impact of the increased input price on the market equilibrium.[7]

---

[7] Implicitly we are assuming there is no change in the relative prices of regular and premium unleaded gasoline. How would your answer change if the increase in the price of petroleum also resulted in a relative decrease (although still an absolute increase) in the price of regular unleaded gasoline?

Here the leftward shift in the supply curve for premium unleaded gasoline would be accompanied by a fall (leftward shift) in the demand for premium unleaded gasoline—due to the decrease in the price of a substitute good. The net effect of the decreases in both supply and demand is clearly a reduction in the quantity transacted of premium unleaded gasoline. (Why?) The net effect on the market price of premium unleaded gasoline, however, depends on the magnitudes of the supply and demand shifts. (Why?) If, as is likely in this example, the increase in the price of petroleum results in a greater fall (leftward shift) in the supply than in the demand for premium unleaded gasoline, then the net effect will be to increase the equilibrium price. (You should graphically illustrate this result.)

CONCLUDING NOTE

In this chapter we have investigated the rudiments of demand, supply, and the market mechanism. From the insight gained, you should be able to predict, for example, the effect of an increase in the wage rate for automobile workers on the price and quantity transacted of new cars, ceteris paribus, or the effect of a fall in the price of videocassette recorders (VCRs) on the price and quantity transacted of videos, ceteris paribus.

We have seen that the market mechanism is self-regulating. The market price level adjusts to equilibrate the quantity demanded and the quantity supplied. In later chapters we will see what happens when the adjustment of the market price is restricted. First we will introduce another key concept in economics, elasticity, which is the subject of Chapter 6.

KEY TERMS

equilibrium state
market
demanders
suppliers
quantity demanded
law of demand
demand schedule
demand curve
normal commodities
inferior commodities
complementary commodities
substitute commodities
change in demand
change in quantity demanded

quantity supplied
law of supply
supply schedule
supply curve
supply
change in supply
change in quantity supplied
equilibrium price
total expenditures
total revenues
shortage
surplus
market mechanism
comparative statics

QUESTIONS

1. What are the three most important ideas in this chapter? Discuss why each is important.
2. Assume the demand and supply schedules for apples are

$$Q_a^d = 20 - 5P_a$$

and

$$Q_a^s = -2 + 1P_a$$

where

Q_a^d = quantity demanded of apples (in thousand bushels per day).

Q_a^s = quantity supplied of apples (in thousand bushels per day).

P_a = price (in dollars) of a bushel of apples.

a. Using a large graph and an appropriate scale for the axes, plot the demand and supply curve for apples. Find the equilibrium price and quantity transacted, first graphically, then algebraically. Calculate the total expenditures on apples.
b. If the suppliers of apples initially set a price of $3.80 for a bushel of apples, what would they find? Would the situation likely persist? Explain.
c. Predict the effects on the equilibrium price and quantity transacted of the following events. Briefly explain your answer, carefully distinguishing between changes in demand (supply) and changes in the quantity demanded (supplied). (You will find graphical illustrations to be helpful.)
- A severe drought decimates the apple crop.
- Scientific evidence is presented on the adverse health effects of alar, a chemical used to treat apples.
- The price of pears decreases.
- A new fertilizer is developed that increases the yield per acre of apples.

3. Assume the world demand and supply schedules for bauxite are

$$Q_b^d = 50 - 2P_b$$

and

$$Q_b^s = -10 + 3P_b$$

where Q_b^d and Q_b^s refer to the quantities demanded and supplied of bauxite (in millions of tons per month), and P_b is the price of a ton of bauxite.
a. Find the equilibrium price and quantity transacted for bauxite—graphically and algebraically. Calculate the total revenues of the suppliers.
b. Assume that because of a world recession, the demand for bauxite fell to

$$Q_b^{d'} = 45 - 2P_b$$

Find the new equilibrium price, quantity transacted, and total revenues of the suppliers.
c. Suppose that the suppliers of bauxite attempted to keep the price of bauxite constant at the initial equilibrium price (found in part "a"). In order to do this when the demand for bauxite falls to $Q_b^{d'}$ (as in part "b"), how much bauxite would have to be supplied on the world market?

4. Suppose that for the month of January the market equilibrium price and quantity transacted of videocassette recorders (VCRs) in the Daytona Beach, Florida, market were $250 and 6000 units, respectively. For February, the new market equilibrium price and quantity transacted were $200 and 5000 units, respectively. Should you conclude that the law of demand (the hypothesized inverse relationship between the quantity demanded of a commodity and its own price) does not hold for VCRs in this market? Discuss.

5. Consider the demand and supply for chocolate ice cream (in thousands of gallons per week) in Portland, Maine. What could cause the following results in the market? In each case, first identify the likely source of the disturbance to market equilibrium—that is, a change in demand or supply—then note possible underlying reasons for the change.
a. An increase in the market equilibrium price and a decrease in the quantity transacted.

b. A decrease in the market equilibrium price and a decrease in the quantity transacted.
c. A decrease in the market equilibrium price and an increase in the quantity transacted.
d. An increase in the market equilibrium price and an increase in the quantity transacted.
e. An increase in the market equilibrium price with no change in the quantity transacted.
f. A decrease in the quantity transacted with no change in the market equilibrium price.

CHAPTER 6

ELASTICITY

IN CHAPTER 5 we discussed the process by which market equilibrium is attained for given supply and demand schedules. Further, in that chapter the concept of comparative statics was introduced. For a given change in a determinant of demand or supply, it was explained how the equilibrium price and quantity transacted would be affected. For instance, if income increased, the demand curve would shift to the right for a normal good, and both the equilibrium price and quantity would increase. The *degree* of change, however, was not discussed. It was not indicated whether the demand would shift significantly or very little with the change in income. This degree of responsiveness of demand or supply to a change in an underlying determinant is called **elasticity**. It can be defined as the responsiveness of a dependent variable to a change in a related variable. Clearly it is important. Firms selling a product, for example, would certainly like to know how much sales would increase following an increase in average consumer income.

MEASUREMENT OF ELASTICITY

The most general measure of elasticity is percentage change in a dependent variable (Y) divided by the percentage change in a related variable (X), or

$$E_{Y,X} = \frac{\text{Percent Change in } Y}{\text{Percent Change in } X}$$

This equation provides a standardized measure of the responsiveness of one variable to a change in a second variable.

A more specific measure of elasticity, applicable to a discrete change, is **arc elasticity**, which is derived as follows.[1] Given a general relationship, $Y = f(X)$,

---

[1] As the change in the underlying influence, ΔX, approaches zero, the elasticity calculation captures the impact of an instantaneous change and is called a **point elasticity**. For students of calculus, the point elasticity is calculated as $(dY/Y)/(dX/X)$, where d is the derivative operator.

where Y is the dependent variable and X is a determinant of Y, the arc elasticity of Y with respect to X can be written as

$$E_{Y,X} = \frac{\Delta Y/.5(Y_1 + Y_0)}{\Delta X/.5(X_1 + X_0)}$$

$$= \frac{\text{Percent Change in } Y}{\text{Percent Change in } X}$$

The percentage change in a variable refers to the absolute change in the value of the variable, $\Delta Y = (Y_1 - Y_0)$, divided by the average of the values of the variable before (Y_0) and after (Y_1) the change.[2] Simply using a comparison of absolute changes would be inappropriate. A fifty-dollar ($50) change in the price of a new automobile would have little impact on the quantity demanded of new automobiles, whereas a fifty-cent ($.50) change in the price of a gallon of gasoline would have a significant effect on the quantity demanded of gasoline.

If a variable is explicitly a function of more than one determinant, then the appropriate measure is a **partial elasticity**, where the assumption is that only one of the influences changes and that all other determinants of the dependent variable are held constant. For example, if $Y = f(X, Z)$, then

$$E_{Y,X} = \frac{\Delta Y/.5(Y_1 + Y_0)}{\Delta X/.5(X_1 + X_0)}$$

$$= \text{Partial elasticity of } Y \text{ with respect to } X$$

$$E_{Y,Z} = \frac{\Delta Y/.5(Y_1 + Y_0)}{\Delta Z/.5(Z_1 + Z_0)}$$

$$= \text{Partial elasticity of } Y \text{ with respect to } Z$$

In the calculation of each partial elasticity, the assumption is that all other influences on the dependent variable are held constant.

PRICE ELASTICITY OF DEMAND

We begin with the demand schedule, which gives the relationship between the quantity demanded of a commodity and the price of the commodity.

$$Q^d = d(P)$$

Recall that the demand schedule is conditional upon given values for the determinants of the demand for the commodity: the average income and the number of demanders, their tastes and preferences, and the price of related commodities. We will assume that the price of the commodity varies but that all the other influences on demand are held constant. The **price elasticity of demand** is a measure of the responsiveness of the quantity demanded of a commodity to a change in its price. The formula is

---

[2] The advantage of using the average of the two values, the base and the final value, for X and Y, is that the calculation will be identical for a decrease or for an increase of equal magnitude in the related influence, X.

$$E_p^d = \frac{\Delta Q^d/.5(Q_1^d + Q_0^d)}{\Delta P/.5(P_1 + P_0)}$$

$$= \frac{\Delta Q^d/\text{Average } Q^d}{\Delta P/\text{Average } P}$$

$$= \frac{\text{Percent Change in Quantity Demanded}}{\text{Percent Change in Price}}$$

where Q_0^d and P_0 are the initial values for the quantity demanded and price, and Q_1^d and P_1 are the corresponding new values. To illustrate, let us return to the example for premium unleaded gasoline used in the previous chapter. If Q_g^d is the quantity demanded of gasoline, then

$$Q_g^d = 90 - 40P_g$$

Four points, labeled A, B, C, and D, are shown for that demand schedule in Table 6.1 and on the demand curve in Figure 6.1. Given that only the price of the good, premium unleaded gas, varies along the demand curve, the price elasticity of demand can be calculated using the price-quantity combinations shown.

For example, between A and B, the price elasticity of demand is

$$E_p^d = \frac{(40 - 30)/35}{(1.25 - 1.50)/1.375} = -1.57$$

Note that the price elasticity of demand is negative. As the price falls, the quantity demanded increases. Therefore, given a negatively sloped demand curve, the main interest is in the magnitude of the price elasticity of demand.

If the value is between 0 and -1, the demand for the commodity is **price inelastic;** the percentage change in quantity demanded is less (in absolute value) than the percentage change in price (for example, a 10 percent increase in price reduces the quantity demanded by less than 10 percent). In that case, quantity demanded is not highly responsive to a change in price. Goods such as salt and ordinary bath soap, for which there are few substitutes, are examples of goods that are price inelastic. If the value is equal to -1, the demand for the good is **unitary price elastic;** the percentage change in quantity demanded is just equal to the percentage change in price. Finally, if the value is less than -1, the demand for the good is **price elastic;** the percentage change in quantity demanded exceeds the percentage change in price (for example, a 10 percent increase in price reduces the quantity demanded by more than 10 percent). Examples of such elastic goods are different brands of soft drinks or other commodities with close substitutes.

TABLE 6.1
Price Elasticity of Demand

	Q_g^d	P_g	E_p^d
A	30	1.50	
B	40	1.25	-1.57
C	50	1.00	-1.00
D	60	.75	$-.64$

FIGURE 6.1

CHANGE IN QUANTITY DEMANDED WITH CHANGE IN PRICE OF GASOLINE

Points A, B, C, and D represent four distinct price-quantity combinations on this linear demand curve.

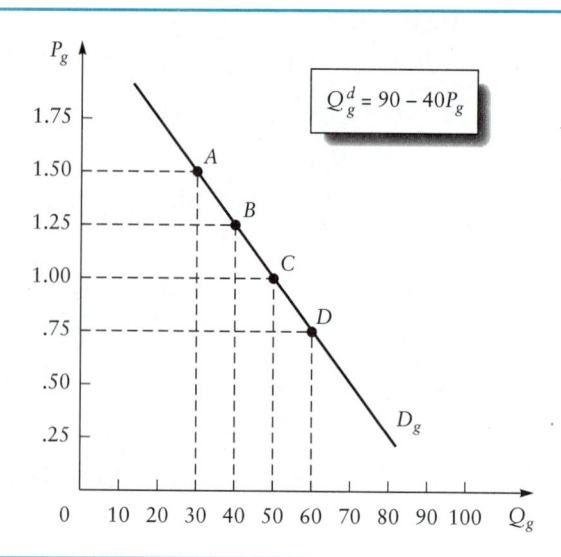

$$Q_g^d = 90 - 40P_g$$

At any point on a demand curve it is possible to calculate the total expenditures by consumers. As explained in Chapter 5, total expenditures (*TE*) are the product of the equilibrium price and quantity transacted. When there are no taxes or other market distortions, total expenditures by consumers equal the total revenues (*TR*) of the producers.

Average revenue (*AR*) refers to the total revenues per unit of output. Since total revenues divided by quantity transacted is the price per unit, then average revenue and price are the same.

$$AR = \frac{TR}{Q}$$
$$= \frac{P \cdot Q}{Q}$$
$$= P$$

Economics is concerned with decision making on the margin. An important concept related to demand is **marginal revenue** (*MR*), which measures the change in total revenues per unit change in output and is calculated as

$$MR = \frac{\Delta TR}{\Delta Q}$$

Table 6.2 shows price, quantity demanded, total revenues, average revenue, marginal revenue, and price elasticity of demand for the example of premium unleaded gasoline.

There are important relationships between the price elasticity of demand, total revenues, and marginal revenue, as follows:

1. The price elasticity of demand varies along a negatively sloped, linear demand curve. As the price falls, the (absolute) value of the price elasticity of demand decreases.

2. Marginal revenue is less than or equal to price.
3. Total revenues rise when marginal revenue is positive. Total revenues fall when marginal revenue is negative.
4. When the demand is price inelastic, total revenues vary directly with price changes. When the demand is price elastic, total revenues vary inversely with price changes.

Price Elasticity along a Linear Demand Schedule

With two exceptions, when the slope of the demand curve, $(\Delta P/\Delta Q^d)$ is constant, the price elasticity of demand varies continuously along the demand curve. Rewriting the price elasticity of demand formula will make this assertion clearer.

$$E_p^d = \frac{\Delta Q^d/.5(Q_1^d + Q_0^d)}{\Delta P/.5(P_1 + P_0)}$$

$$= \frac{\Delta Q^d/\text{Average Quantity}}{\Delta P/\text{Average Price}}$$

$$= \frac{\Delta Q^d/\Delta P}{\text{Average Quantity/Average Price}}$$

As price falls and quantity demanded increases, the demand becomes less elastic (or more inelastic). (Note the term $\Delta Q^d/\Delta P$, which for a linear demand schedule is constant and equal to the reciprocal of the slope of the demand curve.) Equal decreases in price elicit proportionately smaller increases in quantity. In fact, the upper half of a negatively sloped, linear demand curve is the price-elastic region. The lower half of the linear demand curve is the price-inelastic region. Refer to Table 6.2 and Figure 6.2. Here the slope of the demand curve, $\Delta P/\Delta Q^d$, is $-.025$ (that is, $-1/40$), and as the price falls so does the value of the price elasticity of demand. (We will discuss Figure 6.2 again under the next heading, "Relationship between Marginal Revenue and Price.")

The two exceptions to the varying price elasticity of demand for a linear demand schedule are the perfectly elastic and the perfectly inelastic demand schedules. In Figure 6.3 we illustrate both exceptions. When demand is *perfectly price elastic,* the demand curve is horizontal. Here additional units of output can be sold with no reduction in the unit price. In such a case, marginal revenue coincides with price (and average revenue), and total revenues vary proportionally with quantity. The perfectly elastic demand schedule plays a role in the economic theory of perfect competition. For instance, a small wheat

TABLE 6.2

Selected Price and Quantity Demanded Combinations, $Q_g^d = 90 - 40P_g$

	Price	Quantity Demanded	Total Revenues	Average Revenue	Marginal Revenue	Price Elasticity
A	$1.50	30	$45	$1.50		−1.57 (Elastic)
B	$1.25	40	50	1.25	$ .50	−1.00 (Unitary)
C	$1.00	50	50	1.00	0	−.64 (Inelastic)
D	$ .75	60	45	.75	−.50	

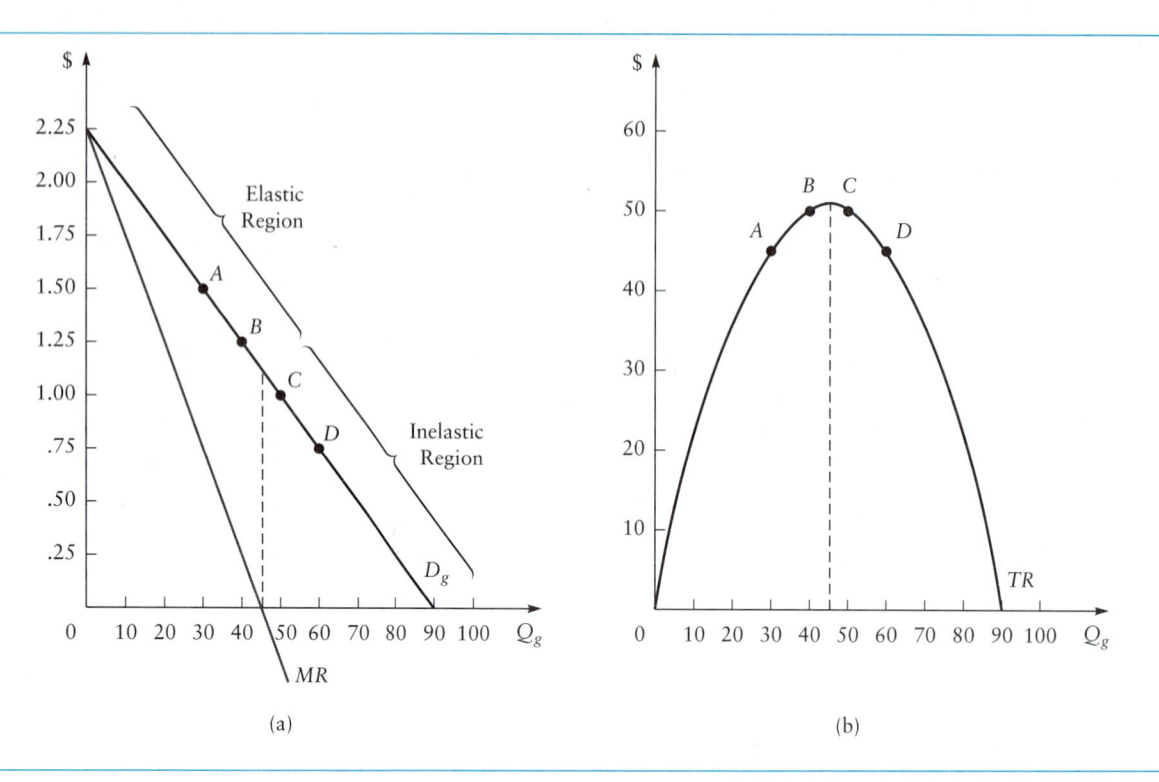

FIGURE 6.2

DEMAND, MARGINAL REVENUE, AND TOTAL REVENUES

Moving down a linear demand curve, the commodity's own price elasticity will become less elastic and eventually will become inelastic. The marginal revenue (*MR*) curve lies below the demand curve, falling twice as rapidly as demand. *MR* is negative when demand is price inelastic. Total revenues (*TR*) increase with quantity when demand is elastic, reach a maximum when demand is unitary elastic, and fall with quantity when demand is inelastic.

farmer will view the wheat price as given and presume to face a perfectly elastic demand for wheat.

When demand is *perfectly price inelastic,* the demand curve is vertical. Here the quantity demanded is constant regardless of the price. Thus, the price elasticity of demand is zero. An example might be the demand for heart transplants in the case of otherwise critically ill patients.

Relationship between Marginal Revenue and Price

For a downward-sloping demand curve, marginal revenue is less than price (see Table 6.2 and Figure 6.2). In order to sell additional units of output in any period, the price on all units must be decreased. For example, moving from combination *A* to combination *B* along the demand curve, the change in total revenues associated with a drop in the price from $1.50 to $1.25 is $5.00. At combination *A*, 30 gallons of gasoline are sold at a price of $1.50 per gallon for total revenues of $45.00 while at combination *B*, 40 gallons are sold at a price of $1.25 for total revenues of $50.00. An additional 10 gallons of gasoline would be sold at $1.25 per gallon, yielding an additional $12.50 in revenues. The 30 gallons that could previously be sold at $1.50 per gallon, however, must now be sold at $1.25 per gallon, which reduces potential revenues by $7.50 (30 gallons times $.25). The incremental revenue, then, is only $5.00, which when divided by the change in quantity of 10 gallons yields a marginal revenue of $.50.

Between combinations *C* and *D,* the marginal revenue is actually negative, the gain from additional sales is $7.50 (10 gallons times $.75), but the reduction in potential revenues is $12.50 (50 gallons times −$.25), yielding an incremental revenue of −$5.00 and a marginal revenue of −$.50.[3]

Total Revenues and Price Elasticity of Demand

In Figure 6.2 we illustrate the relationship between total revenues (total expenditures), marginal revenue, and the price elasticity of demand.[4] Observe the total revenue function. At a critically high price, where quantity demanded is zero, total revenues, $(P)(Q)$, will clearly be zero, because Q is equal to zero. Thereafter, as price falls and quantity demanded increases, total revenues rise. At some point, however, total revenues reach a maximum and then begin falling. There is a quantity demanded associated with a price of zero; at that quantity total revenues will again be zero, since P is equal to zero.

---

[3] It can be shown that for a linear demand schedule, the marginal revenue schedule has the same vertical intercept and twice the slope as the demand or average revenue schedule. Let

$$Q_j^d = a - bP_j$$

where $a > 0$ and $b > 0$, be a linear demand schedule. Rearranging and solving for P_j yields

$$P_j = a/b - (1/b)Q_j$$

The slope equals $-1/b$. Total revenues equal

$$(P)(Q) = [a/b - (1/b)Q_j]Q_j$$
$$TR = (a/b)Q_j - (1/b)Q_j^2$$

Using calculus, marginal revenue is just the first derivative of total revenues with respect to quantity.

$$MR = dTR/dQ_j = a/b - (2/b)Q_j$$

The slope equals $-2/b$.

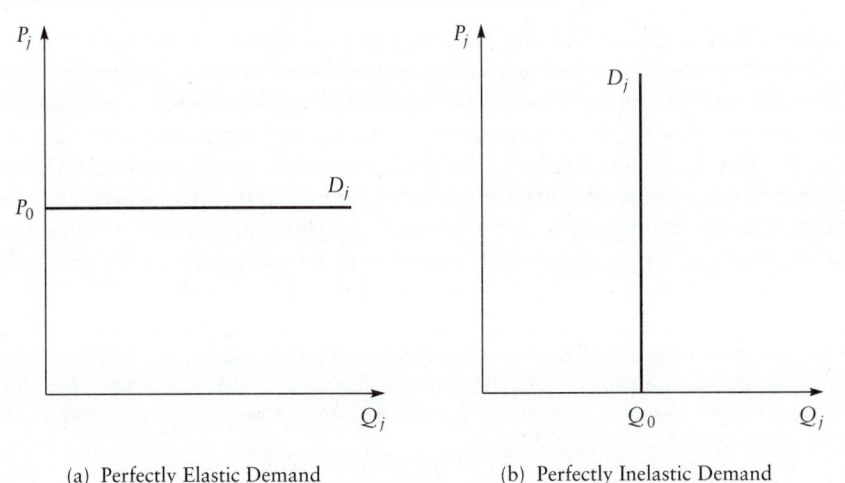

[4] Recall that if there are no market distortions (e.g., unit taxes), total revenues equal total expenditures.

FIGURE 6.3

PERFECTLY ELASTIC AND PERFECTLY INELASTIC DEMAND CURVES

The perfectly elastic demand curve is horizontal, drawn for a given price. The perfectly inelastic demand curve is vertical, indicating no change in quantity demanded as price varies.

(a) Perfectly Elastic Demand

(b) Perfectly Inelastic Demand

The key point in this discussion is to recognize the relationship between the behavior of total revenues and price elasticity. When the demand is price elastic, a decrease in price (and increase in quantity) leads to an increase in total revenues. Why? Because with a price-elastic demand, the percentage change in quantity demanded exceeds the percentage change in price; so a decrease in price leads to a greater than proportionate increase in quantity demanded and an increase in total revenues. Analogously, if the demand is price elastic, an increase in price leads to a more than proportionate decrease in quantity and a decrease in total revenues.

If demand is price inelastic, then a decrease in price induces a less than proportionate increase in quantity demanded and, consequently, a reduction in total revenues. With the inelastic demand, an increase in price will increase total revenues.

Finally, if demand is unitary elastic, a change in price will lead to a change in quantity demanded that is proportionately equal (but opposite in sign) to the change in price; total revenues will not change. For instance, a 10 percent increase in price that leads to a 10 percent decrease in quantity demanded, that is, a price elasticity of -1, would not change the total revenues of producers or the total expenditures of consumers.[5]

In the elastic range of the demand schedule, marginal revenue is positive, so lower prices increase total revenues. In the inelastic range, marginal revenue is negative, so lower prices reduce total revenues. Total revenues are maximized when marginal revenue is zero and the price elasticity of demand is unitary.

As suggested earlier, a primary determinant of the price elasticity of demand for a commodity is the availability of substitutes. Generally, for goods with elastic demands there are other goods that are considered close substitutes. Conversely, for commodities with price-inelastic demands (such as cigarettes for smokers) there are no close substitutes readily available.[6]

When the price of gasoline more than doubled with the oil embargo engineered by OPEC (Organization of Petroleum Exporting Countries) in late 1973, total expenditures on gasoline rose. That is, the quantities demanded of gasoline fell, but not nearly enough to offset the much higher prices. This reflected a price-inelastic demand for gasoline—at least in the short run. In the longer run, when consumers have time to adjust fully (for example, by switching to more fuel-efficient cars), the price elasticity of demand is greater.

The price elasticity of demand for a commodity is also influenced by the share of total expenditures represented by the commodity. As a commodity accounts for a smaller percentage of a consumer's total expenditures, it can be expected that its demand will be less price elastic. For a middle-income consumer in the United States, the demand for tissue paper may not be highly sensitive to price, since the commodity does not represent a significant portion of total expenditures. For a commodity such as an automobile, the price of which would

---

[5] An example of a demand relationship that is everywhere unitary elastic is $Q^d = k/P$, where k is a constant greater than zero ($k > 0$). Any percentage change in P will lead to an equal but offsetting percentage change in Q; total revenues, PQ, will always equal k. When graphed, this demand function is a rectangular hyperbola.

[6] The degree of responsiveness to a price change will be related to the definition of the commodity. For instance, the demand for a particular brand of cigarettes (e.g., Camels) may be price elastic, while the overall demand for cigarettes is price inelastic.

represent a significant portion of total expenditures, demand will be more price elastic.

CROSS–PRICE ELASTICITY OF DEMAND

The **cross–price elasticity of demand** measures the responsiveness of the demand of one good to a change in the price of another good. For instance, assuming that hamburger and chicken are substitutes, if the price of hamburger increases, ceteris paribus, consumers will likely purchase less hamburger and more chicken. Alternatively, assuming that cameras and film are complements, a decrease in the price of cameras would induce an increase in the demand for film.

The cross–price elasticity calculation measures the degree of sensitivity of the demand for one good to the price of another good. The actual value of the arc cross–price elasticity is calculated as

$$E_{j,i}^d = \frac{\Delta Q_j^d / .5(Q_{j1}^d + Q_{j0}^d)}{\Delta P_i / .5(P_{i1} + P_{i0})}$$

$$= \frac{\text{Percent Change in Quantity Demanded of Commodity } j}{\text{Percent Change in Price of Commodity } i}$$

Suppose that an increase in the price of commodity i from \$5 to \$7, ceteris paribus, increases the quantity demanded of commodity j (holding constant the price of commodity j) from 16 to 20 units. That is, following the increase in the price of commodity i, the demand curve for commodity j has shifted to the right. The cross–price elasticity of demand is

$$E_{j,i}^d = \frac{(20 - 16)/.5(20 + 16)}{(7 - 5)/.5(7 + 5)}$$

$$= \frac{+4/18}{+2/6}$$

$$= {}^+.67$$

A positive value for the cross–price elasticity indicates that the goods are **substitutes.** In fact, the larger the calculated elasticity, the more substitutable are the products. For instance, Coca-Cola and Pepsi-Cola have a very high cross–price elasticity of demand, while coffee and tea have a lower one.

Suppose that, ceteris paribus, an increase in the price of commodity k from \$4 to \$6 reduces the quantity demanded of commodity m (holding constant the price of commodity m) from 100 to 80 units. The cross–price elasticity of demand in this case is

$$E_{k,m}^d = \frac{-20/90}{+2/5} = -.56$$

The negative value indicates that the goods are **complements** (like tennis racquets and tennis balls). The more negative is the calculated cross–price elasticity, the more complementarity there is between the two goods.

INCOME ELASTICITY OF DEMAND

Consider now the concept of **income elasticity of demand,** the sensitivity of the demand for a commodity to a change in the average income of the demanders. Observe the demand curves for commodity j drawn in Figure 6.4. The demand curve D_0 represents the original curve for an average income of $100. For each of the other demand curves (D_1, D_2, and D_3) there is a different response to a given increase in income from $100 to $200. These responses are listed in Table 6.3 as Case 1, Case 2, and Case 3. Assume that initially the price of commodity j is P_0 and the quantity demanded (Q_0^d) is 50 units. All other factors influencing demand are held constant.

The income elasticity of demand can be measured for each of the three cases. Remember that the measurement occurs at a common price of good j. The income-elasticity calculation captures only the impact on demand from a change in income.

The formula for the arc income-elasticity of demand is similar to the other elasticities formulas.

$$E_I^d = \frac{\Delta Q^d / .5(Q_1^d + Q_0^d)}{\Delta I / .5(I_1 + I_0)}$$

$$= \frac{\text{Percent Change in Quantity Demanded}}{\text{Percentage Change in Income}}$$

where I_0 and I_1 are the initial and new levels of income respectively.

FIGURE 6.4

SHIFTS IN DEMAND WITH CHANGES IN INCOME

Given the initial demand curve D_0, if an increase in income shifts demand to D_1, then demand is income inelastic; to D_2, then demand is income elastic; to D_3, then the commodity is inferior and the income elasticity of demand is negative.

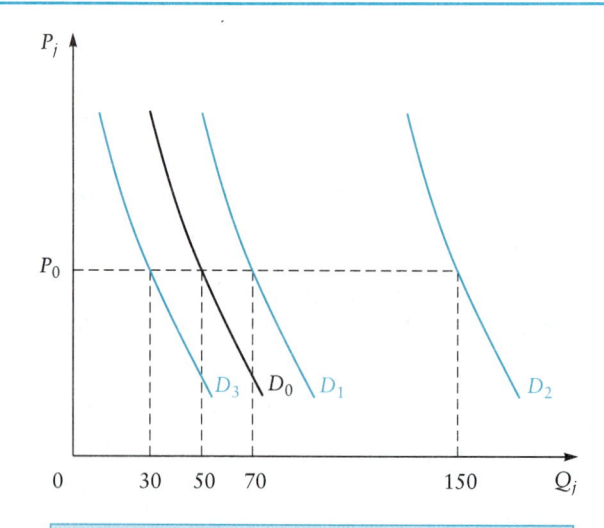

ΔIncome = +100
D_0 = original demand curve.
D_1 = new demand curve with income inelastic demand.
D_2 = new demand curve with income elastic demand.
D_3 = new demand curve for inferior good.

TABLE 6.3
Income Elasticities

		Income	Quantity Demanded	Income Elasticity
CASE 1	Initial	$100	50	.50
	New	200	70	
CASE 2	Initial	100	50	1.50
	New	200	150	
CASE 3	Initial	100	50	−.75
	New	200	30	

The value for the income elasticity of demand in Case 1, while positive, is less than 1; the percentage change in income exceeds the percentage change in the quantity demanded.

$$E_1^d = \frac{(70 - 50)/.5(70 + 50)}{(200 - 100)/.5(200 + 100)}$$

$$= \frac{20/60}{100/150}$$

$$= .50$$

Demand was not highly responsive to the change in income in Case 1. Economists would say that the demand for the good is **income inelastic**. Necessities like bread and milk are examples of goods that are income inelastic.

The value of the income elasticity is greater than 1 in Case 2. The percentage change in the quantity demanded exceeds the percentage change in income.

$$E_2^d = \frac{(150 - 50)/.5(150 + 50)}{(200 - 100)/.5(200 + 100)}$$

$$= \frac{100/100}{100/150}$$

$$= 1.50$$

Demand was very responsive to the change in income, meaning it was **income elastic**. Luxury items like stereos or designer clothing are examples of goods that are income elastic.

The value of the income elasticity for Case 3 is negative. As income increases, the demand for the commodity falls.

$$E_3^d = \frac{(30 - 50)/.5(30 + 50)}{(200 - 100)/.5(200 + 100)}$$

$$= \frac{-20/40}{100/150}$$

$$= -.75$$

Some goods, such as used clothing or very low-quality food items, are inferior goods, meaning that as income increases, individuals tend to substitute a higher-quality good for the lower-quality good—actually reducing demand for the lower-quality good.

Knowing the income elasticity of demand can assist in predicting the impact on demand for a particular good following a change in consumer income.

DEMAND ELASTICITIES FOR ELECTRICITY

The residential demand for electricity should be negatively related to the price of electricity, positively related to income (since electricity is presumed to be a normal good), and positively related to the price of a substitute commodity such as natural gas. In fact, these predictions received empirical support in an earlier investigation of electricity consumption.[7] Using data from 1946 to 1971, the following elasticities of residential demand for electricity were found:

Price elasticity of demand	−1.30
Income elasticity of demand	+0.30
Cross–price elasticity of demand with the price of natural gas	+0.15

Thus, the residential demand for electricity seems to be price elastic with a calculated elasticity of −1.3. An increase in the price of electricity will lead to a more than proportionate decrease in residential electricity usage. Given that this elasticity is calculated over an extended time frame—that is, a long-run elasticity—the result should not be surprising. Consumers have the option of responding to an increase in the price of electricity by using more energy-efficient appliances and taking other steps (such as adding insulation) to reduce electricity consumption in their residences. In the shorter term, the response to an increase in price will be more muted, as consumers do not have the flexibility to reduce significantly electricity consumption in response to a price increase. Electricity demand in the short run may well be price inelastic.

The income elasticity of +0.3 suggests that the residential demand for electricity is income inelastic. For instance, an increase in income will generate a less than proportionate increase in electricity demand. The cross–price elasticity of electricity demand with respect to the price of natural gas has an estimated value of +0.15. This value suggests that natural gas and electricity are substitutes. An increase in the price of natural gas will increase the demand for electricity, as residential users substitute electricity for natural gas.

OTHER DEMAND ELASTICITIES

For any measurable or quantifiable influence on demand, there is an associated elasticity. The elasticity can be calculated as the percentage change in the quantity demanded divided by the percentage change in the value of the related variable, holding all other influences constant.

---

[7] Duane Chapman, Timothy Tyrrell, and Timothy Mount, "Electricity Demand Growth and the Energy Crisis," *Science* 178 (November 17, 1972): 703–708. The sample is comprised of annual average observations from each of the 50 states. While somewhat dated, this empirical evidence is still relevant to energy market conditions.

Consider the demand for an illegal drug, which would be a function of the price of the drug, the demanders' incomes, the price of substitute drugs, and the penalty for purchase or use if the demanders are caught and convicted. Suppose that, to reduce the consumption of this drug and mitigate its negative impact on society, penalties for drug use are increased, decreasing the demand for the drug. The penalty elasticity of demand would measure the extent to which the demand for the drug would change following a change in the penalty for possession, holding all other factors constant. Consider the following example:

Penalty for Possession	Quantity Demanded
8 months in jail	160 units
12 months in jail	140 units

The penalty elasticity of demand would be calculated like any other demand elasticity. In this example the value would be:

$$E^d_{penalty} = \frac{(160-140)/150}{(8-12)/10} = -.33$$

The negative sign indicates that an increase in the penalty for possession will lead to a decrease in the demand. The value of $-.33$ shows that the percentage change in the quantity demanded is roughly one-third of the percentage change in penalty. In such a case, one would question a sole reliance on increased penalties to reduce significantly the demand for this drug. Other measures aimed at decreasing demand or supply might be needed to complement the increased penalties.

PRICE ELASTICITY OF SUPPLY

The elasticity of supply is calculated in a manner analogous to the calculation of the elasticity of demand. In this case the quantity supplied is the dependent variable, and for each related influence, there will be an associated elasticity of supply. Here we will only discuss the **price elasticity of supply,** the degree of responsiveness of the quantity supplied of a commodity to a change in the price of the commodity.

Given a supply schedule of $Q^s = s(P)$, the calculation of the arc price elasticity of supply is

$$E^s_p = \frac{\Delta Q^s / .5(Q^s_1 + Q^s_0)}{\Delta P / .5(P_1 + P_0)}$$

Again, we can return to the example from Chapter 5 of a simple supply schedule where the quantity of premium unleaded gasoline supplied (Q^s_g) in the Charlotte market was a function of the price of premium unleaded gasoline (P_g).

$$Q^s_g = -30 + 60P_g$$

The price and quantity combinations in Table 6.4 are from that supply relationship.

Clearly, as the unit price of gasoline increases, the quantity of gasoline supplied also increases. Between points A and B the elasticity calculation yields 1.80; between points B and C the elasticity is 1.57. Given the positive

TABLE 6.4
Price Elasticities of Supply

	Price of Gas	Quantity Supplied of Gas	Price Elasticity of Supply
A	$1.00	30 units	
B	$1.25	45 units	1.80
C	$1.50	60 units	1.57

relationship assumed between the price of the good and the quantity supplied, the elasticity of supply should be positive. A value greater than 1 indicates that the percentage change in quantity supplied exceeds the percentage change in price. In such a case, supply is elastic. A value between 0 and 1 indicates that the percentage change in price exceeds the percentage change in the quantity supplied. In this case the quantity supplied is less responsive to a change in price; thus, supply is considered to be price inelastic.

CONCLUDING NOTE

Elasticity is an important concept in economics. Knowledge of the price elasticity of demand is valuable for firms, since this determines whether the total expenditures (total revenues) will increase or decrease with a rise in the price of the product. Similarly, knowledge of cross–price elasticities is useful for firms in assessing the impacts of changes in the prices of related goods on the demands for their products. With rising standards of living, the share of income spent on food declines while the share of income going for leisure activities rises—reflecting the respective income elasticities. With respect to supply, the ability of firms to increase production in response to an increase in demand depends on the price elasticities of supply.

In our study of economics we will see numerous applications of elasticity. For example, the relative burden of a sales tax between producers and consumers depends on the price elasticity of demand. Basic agricultural commodities like wheat and corn present an interesting application of elasticity, since both the demand and supply of these goods tend to be price inelastic. In *macroeconomics*, or the analysis of the aggregate economy, the relative effectiveness of monetary and fiscal policies depends on interest elasticities. In the market for foreign exchange, if the underlying foreign demand for a nation's goods and services is price inelastic, the supply curve of foreign exchange to the nation may actually be negatively sloped.

KEY TERMS

elasticity
arc elasticity
point elasticity
partial elasticity
price elasticity of demand

price inelastic
unitary price elastic
price elastic
average revenue
marginal revenue

cross–price elasticity of demand
substitutes
complements
income elasticity of demand

income inelastic
income elastic
price elasticity of supply

QUESTIONS

1. What are the three most important ideas in this chapter? Discuss why each is important.
2. Assume that the demand and supply schedules for commodity j are given by

$$Q_j^d = 30 - 3P_j$$

and

$$Q_j^s = -2 + 5P_j$$

   a. Plot the curves and determine the equilibrium price and quantity transacted graphically and algebraically.
   b. Assuming the supply decreases to

$$Q_j^{s'} = -5 + 4P_j$$

   plot the new supply curve on the same graph. Determine the new equilibrium price and quantity transacted.
   c. Find the value of the price elasticity of demand between the initial and the new equilibrium points.
   d. Find the change in total expenditures (total revenues) between the initial and new equilibrium points. Relate the change in total expenditures to the price elasticity of demand.
3. Assume that an increase in the average income of households from $9,600 to $10,400 is associated with an increase in the purchases of oatmeal from 450,000 to 460,000 boxes per week. Calculate the income elasticity of oatmeal. Is oatmeal, based on the evidence here, an inferior good?
4. Calculate the cross–price elasticity between commodities j and k when an increase in the price of commodity k from $4 to $5 results in a drop in the quantity demanded of commodity j from 90 to 88 units per day. Are commodities j and k likely to be substitutes or complements?
5. Suppose that you were appointed as an economic consultant to the board of directors for the local symphony orchestra. The board is considering changing the price for a concert ticket as a means to increase total ticket revenues. To achieve that objective, would you recommend an increase or a decrease in the ticket price? Explain your reasoning.

PART

III

Introduction to Aggregate Analysis

CHAPTERS

— 7 —
MACROECONOMIC CONCEPTS

— 8 —
NATIONAL INCOME ACCOUNTING

CHAPTER

7

Macroeconomic Concepts

The fundamental difference between microeconomics and macroeconomics is scale. **Microeconomics** is concerned with the determination of prices and outputs in individual markets. It also addresses the behavior of households and firms. For households the economic decisions include how much to work and how to allocate the income available to obtain the most satisfaction. For firms the decisions include what and how much to produce and the optimal means of production. Relative prices, the allocation of resources, and the distribution of output and income are the domain of microeconomics.

In **macroeconomics** the unit of analysis is the national economy. The absolute price level rather than the relative prices of commodities, the national level of employment rather than the number of employees in a given firm or industry, and growth in national output rather than growth in the sales of a particular commodity fall within the realm of macroeconomics. Microeconomics and macroeconomics are complements to each other; indeed, microeconomics forms the foundation of macroeconomic analysis.

This chapter serves as an introduction to aggregate economic analysis, or macroeconomics. To measure the performance of the national economy, three macroeconomic indicators are widely reported: the unemployment rate, the inflation rate, and the growth rate in real national output. While related, these three indicators capture different dimensions of the macroeconomy. The unemployment rate provides a measure of the underutilization of the available labor in the nation. The inflation rate measures the rate of change in the average level of prices. The growth rate in real national output indicates the pace at which the economy is producing goods and services.

The appropriate interpretation and use of these macroeconomic statistics requires an understanding of the assumptions underlying their calculations. Thus, we begin with the construction of each of these measures. Data from the U.S. economy are used to illustrate. Then we introduce the concepts of aggregate demand and aggregate supply. Finally, within the aggregate demand–

aggregate supply framework, we show how the unemployment, inflation, and growth rates are related.

UNEMPLOYMENT

Each month the Bureau of Labor Statistics surveys nearly 60,000 households on employment status.[1] To be counted as **employed** an individual must be at least 16 years of age and must currently have a job: either self-employed, as a paid employee, or as an unpaid worker of at least 15 hours per week in a family-operated enterprise. Individuals working less than 35 hours per week are counted as employed, part-time workers.

To be counted as **unemployed,** an individual must be currently out of work and (1) actively looking for work within the past month, (2) waiting to be recalled to work after being laid-off, or (3) waiting to report to a new job within the month. An individual is not counted as unemployed if under 16 years of age or if voluntarily not working in a job (as in the case of full-time students in school, homemakers providing primary care for their children, and retirees), or if physically or mentally incapable of work.

The **unemployment rate** in any month is the ratio of the unemployed to the labor force. That is,

$$\text{Unemployment Rate} = \frac{\text{Unemployed}}{\text{Labor Force}}$$

where the **labor force** is the sum of the employed and unemployed. The size of the labor force is determined by the population in the labor force years (16 years of age and older) and by the labor force participation rates (the percentage of each age group that is economically active—either currently working or searching for work).

The official unemployment rate may understate the unemployment problem due to the omission of the discouraged workers. The **discouraged worker** is one who would like to work, but is not working, and has given up actively looking for work in the belief that no suitable jobs exist. Consider the following hypothetical example. Suppose there are officially 94 million employed workers and 6 million unemployed. The unemployment rate is then 6 percent.

$$\text{Unemployment Rate} = \frac{6}{94 + 6} = \frac{6}{100} = .06 = 6.0\%$$

If in the next month, .5 million of the unemployed drop out of the labor force, dispirited by the poor job prospects, then the official unemployment rate declines to 5.53 percent, although the employment conditions in the economy have not improved.

$$\text{New Unemployment Rate} = \frac{5.5}{94 + 5.5} = \frac{5.5}{99.5} = .0553 = 5.53\%$$

---

[1] For a useful summary of the measurement of the unemployment rate, see Roy Webb and William Whelpley, "Labor Market Data," *Macroeconomic Data: A User's Guide,* Federal Reserve Bank of Richmond, 1990. See also the discussion in *Economic Report of the President 1992,* 249–253.

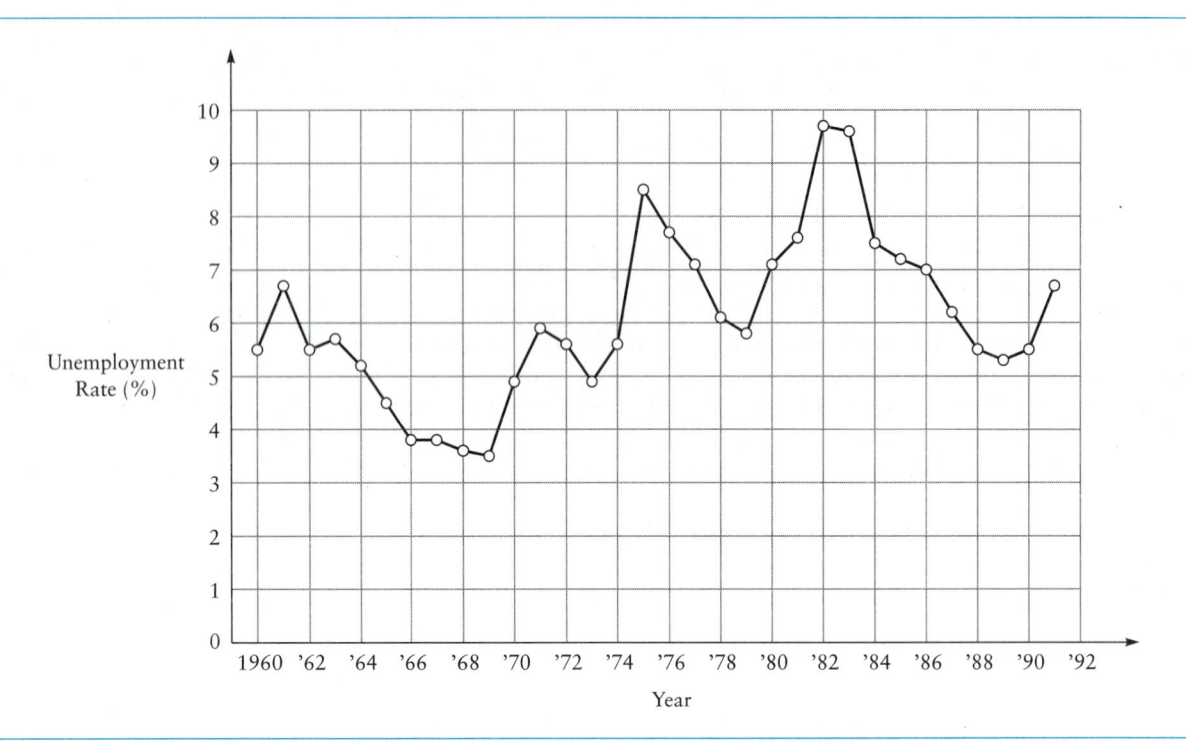

FIGURE 7.1

U.S. CIVILIAN UNEMPLOYMENT RATE: ANNUAL AVERAGES FOR 1960–1991

SOURCE: *Economic Report of the President, 1992*, Table B-37.

For example, the U.S. unemployment rate averaged 7 percent over the last three months of 1991. Including the estimates of the discouraged workers in the nation would have added approximately .7 percent to the unemployment rate.[2]

In Figure 7.1 we plot the annual civilian unemployment rates for the United States for the 1960–1991 period.[3] The U.S. civilian unemployment rate averaged 4.8 percent for the 1960s, 6.2 percent for the 1970s, and 7.3 percent for the 1980s—a disturbing upward trend that reflects both economic conditions and demographic factors (such as population growth rates and labor force participation rates).

It is possible to have both national employment and the unemployment rate increase simultaneously. To illustrate, over the 1970s total U.S. civilian employment increased by more than 20 million, yet the unemployment rate went from 4.9 percent in 1970 to 5.8 percent in 1979. Two factors primarily account for this phenomenon. First, the U.S. population of working age expanded dramatically with the entrance into the labor force of the baby boomers (those individuals born in the two decades following World War II). From 1970 to 1979 the U.S. population age 16 years and older increased by more than 26 million, largely due to the earlier baby boom, although immigration to the United States was also a factor. Second, the labor force participation rates for females increased. In 1970 the female labor force

---

[2] *Economic Report of the President 1992*, 104, and Tables B-31, B-37.
[3] Actually there are two national unemployment rates calculated—one for all workers (including resident armed forces) and one for civilian workers. The latter, the civilian unemployment rate, has tended to be one- to two-tenths of a percentage point higher than the all worker unemployment rate, since the resident armed forces are considered to be fully employed.

participation rate was 43.3 percent, and it steadily rose to 50.9 percent by 1979.

In fact, compared to the next decade, the U.S. economy was relatively successful in absorbing the large increase in the labor supply during the 1970s. Over the 1980s, the female labor force participation rates continued to rise (from 51.5 percent in 1980 to 57.4 percent in 1989), but the U.S. population aged 16 years and older increased by "only" 19 million.[4] Low birth rates in the 1970s and 1980s, unless compensated for by further increases in female labor force participation rates and greater immigration to the United States imply a continuing tightening of the U.S. labor supply in the 1990s and early part of the next century.

A degree of unemployment is inevitable due to the natural turnover of the labor force. Examples include the worker who has moved to a different region of the country and is between jobs, the student seeking employment after graduation, the parent reentering the labor force after an absence for child care, and the individual who has quit a present job to look for better employment.[5]

Moreover, in a dynamic economy characterized by technological change, shifts in consumer tastes and preferences, and increased foreign competition, unemployment will occur whenever the labor released from the contracting industries is not readily absorbed into the expanding industries. Consider the telephone operator replaced by a computerized answering machine, the cowboy no longer needed to herd cattle when a cholesterol-conscious public reduces its consumption of beef, or the steelworker laid off as foreign steel producers capture a larger share of the domestic steel market. Which of these workers would likely be immediately qualified for an opening as a health care attendant in a nursing home?

The major swings in the unemployment rate, however, tend to mirror the general health of the economy. At times the national economy will slow down, business conditions will deteriorate, and workers will be laid off as sales and production decline. For example, the U.S. unemployment rate averaged nearly 10 percent in 1982 (a post–World War II high, but still far below the 25 percent recorded in 1933 in the depths of the Great Depression). Roughly half of the unemployment in 1982 could be accounted for by the severe economic recession that began in the summer of 1981.

To conclude this introduction, we note that the unemployment rate, by itself, gives only a partial picture of the employment conditions in the nation. We return to this theme in Chapter 16, when the causes and consequences of unemployment are addressed.

INFLATION

Inflation refers to an increase in the average level of prices. A decrease in the average level of prices is known as **deflation**. Inflation erodes the purchasing power of a given nominal or money income. And, as we will discuss in the

---

[4] Over these two decades the male labor force participation rate declined slightly, from 79.7 percent in 1970 to 77.4 percent in 1980 to 76.4 percent in 1989. (See *Economic Report of the President 1992*, Table B-34.)

[5] The Bureau of Labor Statistics adjusts the unemployment rate for seasonal variations, e.g., the increased employment during Christmas holidays and summer vacation.

following chapters, inflation also affects the distribution of income and the allocation of resources.

To measure the inflation rate, a price index is required. Formally, if INF_t represents the inflation rate in period t, then

$$INF_t = \frac{P_t - P_{t-1}}{P_{t-1}}$$

where

P_t = the value of an aggregate price index in period t.
P_{t-1} = the value of the same aggregate price index in period $t-1$, the previous period.

The **Consumer Price Index (CPI)** is widely used as a measure of inflation.[6] It measures the changes in the cost of a fixed *market basket*, or representative sample, of goods and services purchased by the average urban household according to a calculation that is rather involved. First, a *base period* must be selected to serve as a reference point for comparing price changes over time. The three-year period of 1982–1984 currently is used. By definition, the value of the CPI in the base period is set equal to 100. (Actually the annual values of the CPI for 1982, 1983, and 1984 are averaged together to give 100.)

Second, a market basket of goods and services must be chosen, representing commodities typically purchased by the average household. Third, the items in the market basket must be weighted to reflect their relative importance in overall consumer expenditures.

Based on consumer expenditure patterns recorded for the 1982–1984 period, the Bureau of Labor Statistics determined the market basket and expenditure weights for urban households in the United States. Every month each of the items in the market basket is priced and the cost of the market basket is calculated. Seven major expenditure categories are identified: food and beverages, housing, apparel and upkeep, transportation, medical care, entertainment, and other goods and services.[7]

Specifically, the formula for the CPI in time period t is

$$CPI_t = 100 \sum_{i=1}^{n} \left(\frac{\overline{C}_i}{\overline{C}} \right) \times CPI_{it}$$

where

$\overline{C}_i$ = the consumption expenditures on category i by the average household.

---

[6] For an account of the construction of the Consumer Price Index and other price indexes, see Roy Webb and Rob Willemse, "Macroeconomic Price Indexes," *Macroeconomic Data: A User's Guide,* Federal Reserve Bank of Richmond, 1990. See also the discussion in the *Economic Report of the President 1992,* 253–257.

[7] The percentage weights for the expenditure categories are currently: food and beverages (17.8%), housing (42.6%), apparel and upkeep (6.5%), transportation (18.7%), medical care (4.8%), entertainment (4.4%), and other goods and services (5.2%). The consumer expenditure survey from which the market basket and expenditure weights are determined need not be for the same period as the base period (in which the CPI is set equal to 100). Prior to 1982–1984 the base period was 1967 and the consumer expenditure survey was in the 1972–1973 period.

$\overline{C}$ = total consumption expenditures by the average household.
CPI_{it} = the value of the Consumer Price Index for expenditure category i in period t.
n = the number of expenditure categories ($i = 1 \ldots n$).

In effect, then, the CPI is a weighted average of price changes for consumer goods and services. For expenditure category i, it is relative to a base period. The weights ($\overline{C}_i/\overline{C}$) are the percentages of total consumption expenditures on category i by the average household (recorded from an earlier consumer expenditure survey). The convention is to express the CPI (and most price indexes) as a multiple of 100.

To illustrate, we will construct a simple CPI. Assume that consumption expenditures can be broken down into four major categories: food, shelter, other goods, and other services. Based on surveys of household expenditure patterns, assume further that the percentages of total expenditures accounted for by each of the four categories are 30 percent, 35 percent, 20 percent, and 15 percent, respectively. A sample of items from each expenditure category (a weekly market basket) would be chosen and priced in the base period. The same market baskets would be again priced in period t. The ratio of the market basket costs for each expenditure category would be calculated. The resulting CPIs for the individual expenditure categories would then be weighted to obtain the overall CPI.

In Table 7.1 we present the weights for the expenditure categories, $\overline{C}_i/\overline{C}$ (in column 2), the costs of the market baskets for the expenditure categories in the base period, X_{i0} and in period t, X_{it} (in columns 3 and 4), and the calculated price indexes, CPI_{it} (in column 5). For example, in Table 7.1 we see that the food market basket costs 34 percent more in period t than in the base period. That is, to purchase the food items that cost \$35.20 in the base period would require

TABLE 7.1
Construction of a Hypothetical Consumer Price Index

Expenditure Category i	Percent of Total Household Expenditures $\overline{C}_i/\overline{C}$	Costs of Market Baskets for Expenditure Category i Base Period, X_{i0}	Period t, X_{it}	Consumer Price Index for Expenditure Category i CPI_{it}
Food	30%	$35.20	$47.20	1.34
Shelter	35	40.00	64.00	1.60
Other Goods	20	24.00	36.00	1.50
Other Services	15	18.00	24.00	1.33
	100%			
(1)	(2)	(3)	(4)	(5)

$$CPI_t = 100 \sum_{i=1}^{n} \frac{\overline{C}_i}{\overline{C}} \times \frac{X_{it}}{X_{i0}} = 100 \sum_{i=1}^{n} \frac{\overline{C}_i}{\overline{C}} \times CPI_{it}$$

$CPI_t = 100[(.30)(1.34) + (.35)(1.60) + (.20)(1.50) + (.15)(1.33)] = 146$

$47.20 in period t, a 34 percent increase. Similarly, the cost of the market basket of items related to shelter (such as rent or mortgage payments, home heating oil, insurance, repairs) has risen by 60 percent, from $40.00 to $64.00.

The overall CPI for period t is calculated as the weighted average of the CPIs for the designated expenditure categories.

$$\text{CPI}_t = 100 \times [(.30)(1.34) + (.35)(1.60) + (.20)(1.50) + (.15)(1.33)] = 146$$

Compared to the base period, it costs the average household 46 percent more money in period t to purchase the same quantities of commodities. In other words, on average, consumer prices have increased by 46 percent: what cost $1.00 in the base period, will cost $1.46 t periods later. In terms of the purchasing power of the consumer's dollar, $1.00 in period t is therefore "worth" only 68 cents (.68 = 1.00/1.46) compared to the base period. Roughly this is what happened to the American consumer's purchasing power from 1981 to 1990 when the CPI rose from 90.9 to 130.7.

This hypothetical construction of a CPI needs to be explained a bit further. In particular, the calculation of the price indexes of the individual expenditure categories should be illustrated, since this step actually precedes the calculation of the overall CPI.

TABLE 7.2
Construction of Price Index for Food Expenditure Category

Item j	Quantity q_j	$(p_j)_0$	$(p_j)_t$
Milk	5 gallons	$3.00	$4.00 (per gallon)
Bread	3 loaves	$ .60	$1.00 (per loaf)
Hamburger	4 pounds	$1.80	$2.70 (per pound)
Eggs	2 dozen	$1.20	$1.60 (per dozen)
Potatoes	2 10-lb. bags	$2.40	$2.00 (per bag)
Ice cream	1 gallon	$2.40	$3.00 (per gallon)
Apples	10 apples	$ .16	$ .32 (per apple)

$$X_0 = \sum_j (p_j)_0 \times (q_j)$$

$$X_0 = 5(3.00) + 3(.60) + 4(1.80) + 2(1.20) + 2(2.40) + 1(2.40) + 10(.16)$$

$$X_0 = \$35.20$$

$$X_t = \sum_j (p_j)_t \times (q_j)$$

$$X_t = 5(4.00) + 3(1.00) + 4(2.70) + 2(1.60) + 2(2.00) + 1(3.00) + 10(.32)$$

$$X_t = \$47.20$$

$$\text{CPI}_{\text{Food}} = 100 \times \frac{X_t}{X_0} = 100 \times \frac{47.20}{35.20} = 134$$

Consider the market basket for the first expenditure category of food. Suppose that the seven items and associated quantities shown in Table 7.2 were selected as representative of the typical household's weekly purchases of food. That is, the food market basket consists of 5 gallons of milk, 3 loaves of bread, 4 pounds of hamburger, 2 dozen eggs, 2 ten-pound bags of potatoes, 1 gallon of ice cream, and 10 apples. (Actually the market baskets are more precisely defined—for example, 5 gallons of whole milk, 3 sixteen-ounce loaves of wheat bread.) Of course, this would not constitute all of the food expenditures by an average household for a particular week; rather, the selected market basket is intended to be characteristic of consumer food purchases.

Each item j in the market basket for food would be priced in the base period $(p_j)_0$. The total cost of the market basket in the base period (X_0) is the sum of the products of unit prices and quantities. In this example, the cost of the food market basket in the base period is $35.20. In period t, the same market basket would be priced. For instance, a gallon of milk increased from $3.00 to $4.00 compared to the base period. The price of a bag of potatoes actually fell from $2.40 to $2.00, due perhaps to a bumper crop of potatoes. In period t, the same market basket costs $47.20. Thus, the value of the CPI for food in period t is 134.

$$\text{CPI}_{\text{Food}} = 100 \times \frac{X_t}{X_0} = 100 \times \frac{47.20}{35.20} = 134$$

Checking back to Table 7.1 we find the corresponding entries used for the calculation of the overall CPI. Similarly, market baskets for the other expenditure categories must be constructed and the respective price indexes tabulated before the value of the overall CPI can be determined. In this hypothetical example, food prices have increased since the base period, but proportionally less than the prices of shelter and other goods.

In 1991 the actual CPI for the United States stood at 136.2. Compared to the base period of 1982–1984, the purchasing power of the consumer's dollar in 1990 was only 73.4 cents (.734 = 1.00/1.362). Table 7.3 presents the values of the price indexes for the seven major expenditure categories in 1991. The rapidly rising cost of medical care stands out among the major expenditure categories.

TABLE 7.3
Consumer Price Indexes by Expenditure Category: 1991

EXPENDITURE CATEGORY	1991 CPI (ANNUAL AVERAGE)
Food and Beverages	136.8
Housing	133.6
Apparel and Upkeep	128.7
Transportation	123.8
Medical Care	177.0
Entertainment	138.4
Other Goods and Services	171.6
ALL ITEMS	136.2

NOTE: For 1982-1984, CPI = 100.
SOURCE: *Economic Report of the President 1992*, Table B-56.

The percentage change in the CPI is one useful measure of inflation.[8] In order for the CPI to be interpreted properly, however, we need to be clear on the assumptions underlying its construction. Foremost is the assumption that the market basket and expenditure weights are fixed according to the consumption patterns of a sample period. The market basket that is relevant for the average household, however, will change over time with changes in tastes and preferences and with the introduction of new consumer goods and services. Also, fixing the quantities purchased of the commodities does not allow for substitution away from relatively expensive items. For instance, during the energy crises of the 1970s, households responded to the sharply higher prices of gasoline and home heating oil by driving less (and switching to more fuel-efficient automobiles) and turning down thermostats (and adding to the insulation of their homes). The calculation of the CPI would not incorporate these adjustments in consumer behavior but would instead assume that the same items would be purchased in the same quantities in each period. Thus, the CPI may tend to overstate the effective impact of inflation on the purchasing power of the consumer's dollar.

Moreover, although an attempt is made to compare prices of the same items over time, and where possible, adjustments for qualitative improvements are made (such as for more fuel-efficient automobiles), some of the price increases may reflect superior products, as in the case of more powerful computers or better health care. For these reasons, the market basket and weights of the CPI should periodically be revised to reflect changes in consumer spending patterns.

Changes in the CPI should not be regarded as necessarily indicative of changes in any one household's welfare or standard of living. To the extent that an individual household's expenditure pattern deviates from that of the hypothetical average urban consumer represented in the sample, the CPI is less relevant for that household. For example, tuition is a major expenditure for many families putting children through college. Health care costs are a significant concern for older people. Each of these cases is a deviation from the average consumer's spending patterns.

Also important is that the CPI accounts only for price changes. Households are more interested in real income. Consider the following example. Suppose that the value of the CPI in year t is 125 and that the *nominal*, or money, income of the Smith household is $10,000. Relative to the base year, the *real income* (or the purchasing power of the money income) of the Smith household is $8000 ($8000 = $10,000/1.25). In the next year, if the CPI rises to 130 while the nominal income of the Smith household increases to $10,500, would the Smith household be financially better off? To answer this question, start with the fact that the annual inflation rate (*INF*) is 4 percent.

---

[8] Two other price indexes used to measure inflation are the Producer Price Index and the Implicit Price Deflator for Gross Domestic Product. Like the CPI, the **Producer Price Index (PPI)** is a Laspeyres price index, where quantities fixed from an earlier period weight the price changes. The PPI measures price changes for goods (services are not included) at different stages of production: crude materials, intermediate goods, and finished goods. Changes in the PPI often forecast later changes in the CPI, which includes only final consumer goods and services. The Implicit Price Deflator for Gross Domestic Product is an example of a Paasche price index, where current quantities weight the price changes. The Implicit Price Deflator for Gross Domestic Product will be discussed later.

$$INF = \frac{130 - 125}{125} = .04 = 4 \text{ percent}$$

The gain in nominal income (%ΔI) for the Smith household is 5 percent.

$$\%\Delta I = \frac{\$10,500 - \$10,000}{\$10,000} = .05 = 5 \text{ percent}$$

So the Smiths have kept ahead of inflation, if just barely, and their annual real income has increased to $8077 ($8077 = $10,500/1.30).

In Figure 7.2 we plot the annual rates of inflation based on the Consumer Price Index for the period from 1960 to 1991. The annual inflation rates averaged 2.4 percent for the 1960s, 7.1 percent for the 1970s, and 5.6 percent for the 1980s. Explaining the variations in inflation and unemployment rates is one of the main objectives of macroeconomics.

Knowledge of the inflation rate is important for households seeking to preserve, if not enhance, the purchasing power of their money incomes. In many labor contracts, money wages are indexed to the rate of inflation. Some government transfer payments, like social security, are also automatically adjusted for inflation. In Chapter 16 we will discuss the consequences of inflation and how expectations of inflation can influence the effectiveness of macroeconomic policy.

FIGURE 7.2

INFLATION RATE IN THE U.S. ECONOMY: PERCENTAGE CHANGES IN THE CONSUMER PRICE INDEX FOR 1960–1991

SOURCE: *Economic Report of the President 1992*, Table B-59.

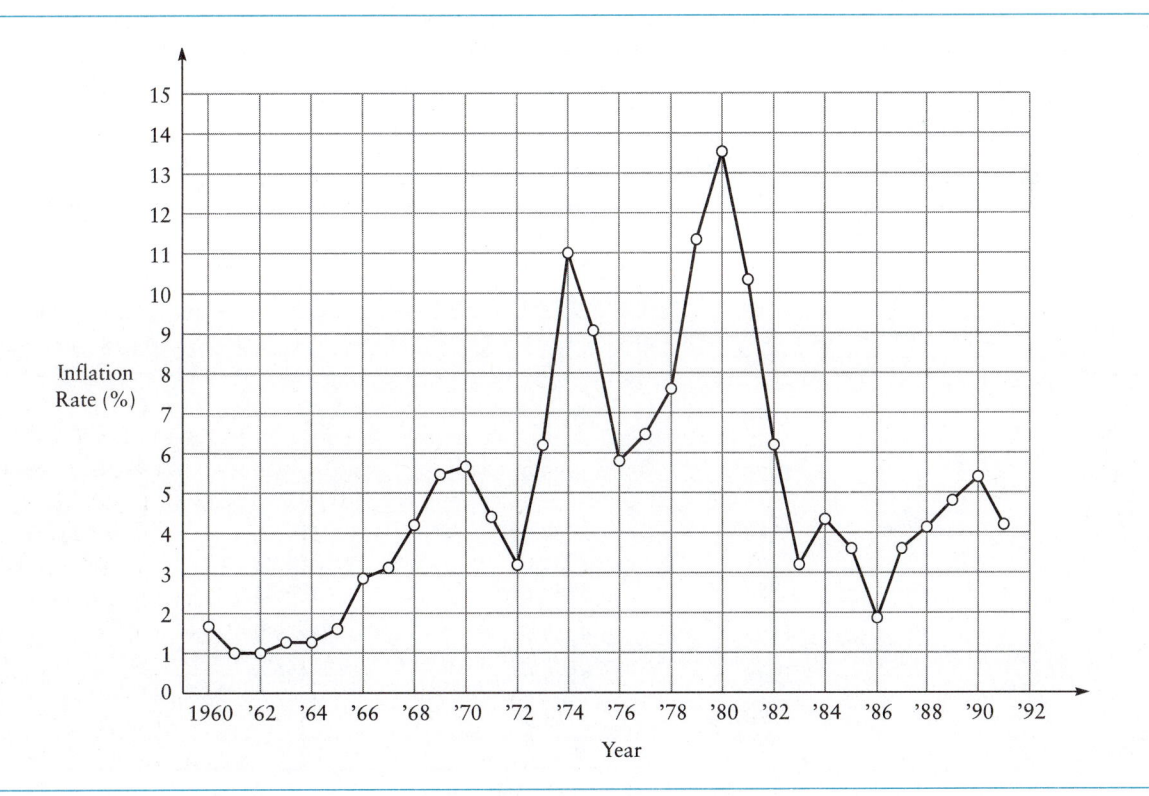

REAL GROWTH IN NATIONAL OUTPUT

As noted in the introduction to this chapter, macroeconomics is also concerned with economic growth, or changes in real national output. The most widely used measure of national output now is **Gross Domestic Product (GDP)**, the market value of all final goods and services produced in an economy during a year.[9] In the next chapter we will discuss in detail the measurement of GDP. For the present, it will be sufficient to distinguish between nominal GDP and real GDP. The difference is in the valuation of the national output of final goods and services. If the output is valued at the prices prevailing at the time, then GDP is said to be measured in current dollars as **nominal GDP**. If the output is valued at prices prevailing in some base period, it is said to be measured in constant dollars as **real GDP**. Increases in nominal GDP may reflect inflation, growth in real output, or both. Growth in real GDP measures the ability of the economy to produce more goods and services during a year and abstracts from price changes. In Table 7.4 nominal and real GDPs for the United States for selected years since 1960 are given.

From the data on nominal GDP, we see that U.S. output of final goods and services measured in current dollars has increased by nearly 1000 percent from 1960 to 1990, or from $513.4 billion to $5513.8 billion. Most of the increase in nominal GDP, however, reflects inflation, as a comparison of the correspond-

---

[9] Until 1992 the most frequently cited measure of national output for the United States was Gross National Product (GNP). In 1992 the U.S. Government shifted to Gross Domestic Product (GDP). In the next chapter we will discuss the difference (which is relatively slight for the United States) between these two measures of aggregate output.

TABLE 7.4
NOMINAL AND REAL GROSS DOMESTIC PRODUCTS FOR THE UNITED STATES

YEAR	NOMINAL GDP (BILLIONS OF CURRENT DOLLARS)	REAL GDP (BILLIONS OF 1987 CONSTANT DOLLARS)	IMPLICIT PRICE DEFLATOR FOR GDP (1987 = 100)
1960	513.4	1973.2	26.0
1965	702.7	2473.5	28.4
1970	1010.7	2875.8	35.1
1975	1585.9	3221.7	49.2
1980	2708.0	3776.3	71.7
1981	3030.6	3843.1	78.9
1982	3149.6	3760.3	83.8
1985	4038.7	4279.8	94.4
1987	4539.9	4539.9	100.0
1990	5513.8	4884.9	112.9
1991[a]	5671.8	4848.4	117.0

[a]Preliminary estimates.
SOURCE: *Economic Report of the President 1992*, Tables B-1, B-2, B-3.

ing real GDP totals will show. In constant dollars (that is, using 1987 prices), the nation's output has increased a more modest, but still impressive, 150 percent from 1960 to 1990.

Nominal GDP may rise even as real GDP falls, which happened from 1981 to 1982. The fall in real national output of 2.2 percent was surpassed by the rise in the aggregate price level of 6.2 percent. In 1982 negative real growth coexisted with positive nominal growth in GDP. A similar situation characterized the 1990–1991 period. (Compare the preliminary estimates for nominal and real GDP for 1991 with the estimates for 1990 in the table.) In contrast, during the depths of the Great Depression from 1929 to 1933, both real output and the aggregate price level fell, so nominal GDP declined proportionally more than real GDP. Deflation accompanied the Great Depression.

Another measure of inflation is given by the percentage change in the **implicit price deflator for GDP,** defined as the ratio of nominal GDP to real GDP (see the third column in Table 7.4). As is the convention, the implicit price deflator is expressed as an index with a base value of 100. The current base year for the GDP deflator is 1987. For example, in 1990 the value of the nation's output of final goods and services expressed in the prices prevailing in 1990 is estimated to be $5513.8 billion. The value of the 1990 output of final goods and services expressed in 1987 constant dollars—that is, using the prices prevailing in 1987—is estimated to be $4884.9 billion. The value of the implicit price deflator for GDP in 1990 is 112.9 (or 5513.8/4884.9).

Compared to the Consumer Price Index, the Implicit Price Deflator for GDP yields a more comprehensive measure of inflation, since the GDP price deflator encompasses all types of expenditures on final goods and services, and not just consumption expenditures.[10]

INTRODUCTION TO AGGREGATE DEMAND AND AGGREGATE SUPPLY

The macroeconomic performance measures of inflation, growth in real output, and implicitly, the unemployment rate, can be related conceptually within the framework of the aggregate demand and aggregate supply schedules.

The **aggregate demand schedule** represents the relationship between the total amount of national output that is demanded—by domestic households, firms, and the government, and by foreigners—and the aggregate price level. The graphical analog of the aggregate demand schedule is the **aggregate demand curve.** Letting P represent the average level of prices in the nation, or specifically, the implicit price deflator for Gross Domestic Product, and letting Y represent real national output or real GDP, we illustrate a hypothetical aggregate demand curve, AD, in Figure 7.3. Notice that it is downward sloping. From our knowledge of microeconomic theory, quantity demanded is expected to be

---

[10] Due to the differences in construction between the Implicit Price Deflator for GDP and the Consumer Price Index—namely, the GDP price deflator includes all final goods and services and is based on current quantities purchased—we would not expect the estimates of inflation using the CPI and the GDP price deflator to be identical. The CPI is actually the more widely used price index since it is calculated on a monthly basis. The GDP price deflator is available only on a quarterly basis (every three months).

FIGURE 7.3

AGGREGATE DEMAND CURVE

The aggregate demand curve *(AD)* illustrates the relationship between the total quantity of national output demanded and the aggregate price level.

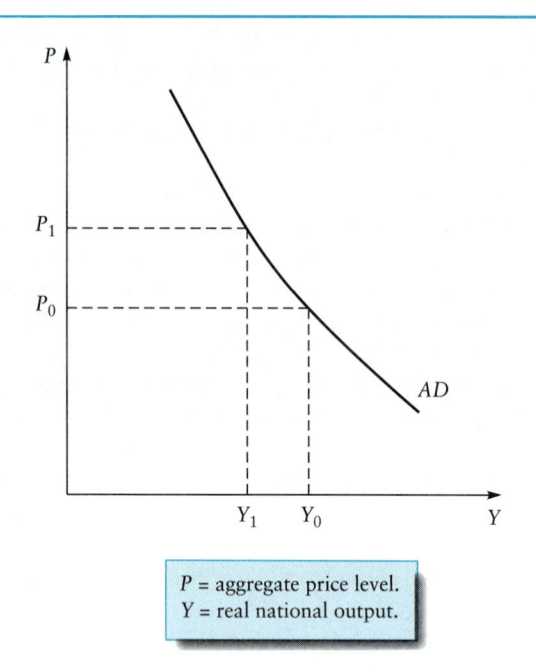

P = aggregate price level.
Y = real national output.

inversely related to the price level. The underlying reasons in macroeconomics, however, are not the same as those derived for a single commodity. Recall, in microeconomics, if the price of commodity *j* falls, ceteris paribus, commodity *j* will become more attractive to consumers (compared to other substitute commodities); hence the quantity demanded of commodity *j* will rise.[11] In macroeconomics the concern is with the aggregate price level, not the relative prices of commodities, and the quantity demanded is in terms of the national output, not a single commodity. One of the most important reasons for the negative slope of the aggregate demand curve involves the user cost of money.

To illustrate, let P_0 and Y_0 represent the initial aggregate price level and real national output, respectively. If the aggregate price level rises to P_1, then households, firms, and the government will need more money in order to make the same real purchases, since the purchasing power of any given nominal income will be less.[12] As a consequence, the demand for money balances will increase, and for a given money supply, the user cost of money (that is, the interest rate) will rise. The higher interest rate would make interest-sensitive expenditures (expensive commodities typically purchased with credit) more costly. The quantities demanded of consumer durables, capital goods, and residential construction will fall as the cost of credit increases. The

---

[11] Recall also that a fall in the price of commodity *j* would enhance the purchasing power of a given money income and allow more of all commodities (including *j*) to be purchased.
[12] In Chapters 10 and 11 the demand and supply of money will be discussed in detail. For the purposes of this introduction to the subject of the aggregate demand curve, think of money as cash balances and funds in checking accounts that are immediately available for spending.

end result of the initial rise in the aggregate price level (from P_0 to P_1) is a decrease in the aggregate quantity of national output demanded (from Y_0 to Y_1).[13]

Conversely, if the aggregate price level decreases, then households, firms, and the government will need to hold less money to make the same real purchases of goods and services. The demand for money balances will fall, and for a given supply of money, the user cost of money will tend to decline. Interest-sensitive expenditures will be stimulated and the aggregate quantity demanded of national output will rise.

In Chapter 12 we will develop more carefully the negatively sloped aggregate demand curve. Also in that chapter, factors that shift the aggregate demand curve will be examined in detail. By itself, aggregate demand cannot determine real national output or the level of prices. Aggregate supply is also needed.

The **aggregate supply schedule** represents the relationship between the total amount of national output produced and the aggregate price level associated with the output. The graphical counterpart of the aggregate supply schedule is the **aggregate supply curve.** In Figure 7.4 we illustrate a hypothetical aggregate

---

[13] Another consequence of a rise in the domestic price level is that for a given set of exchange rates between the domestic currency and foreign currencies, the national output of goods and services would become relatively expensive compared to foreign output. Thus, the quantity demanded of national output by foreigners (exports) would decrease and the quantity demanded of foreign output (imports) by domestic households, firms, and the government would increase. (Exchange rates will be discussed in Chapters 17 and 18.)

A third reason for the negatively sloped aggregate demand curve is that the real value of assets with fixed nominal yields (such as dividends from stocks and interest from bonds) would decrease with inflation. The resulting decline in wealth reduces the quantity demanded of national output.

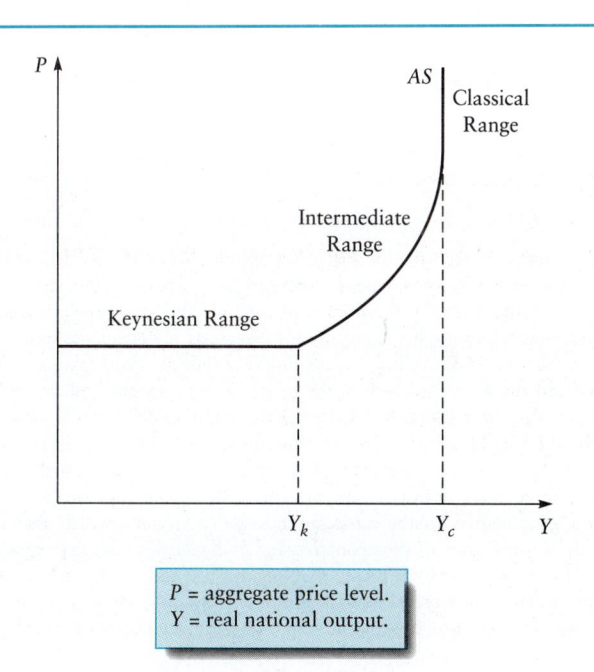

FIGURE 7.4

AGGREGATE SUPPLY CURVE

The aggregate supply curve *(AS)* illustrates the relationship between the total quantity of national output produced and the aggregate price level.

P = aggregate price level.
Y = real national output.

supply curve *(AS)*. Like the production possibilities boundary discussed in Chapter 3, the aggregate supply curve is drawn for a given size and quality of the labor force, size and quality of the capital stock, availability of natural resources, and state of technology. Also held constant when the aggregate supply curve is drawn are the schedules of input prices.

Three ranges of the aggregate supply curve are usually distinguished. The **Keynesian range** includes all levels of real national output along the perfectly elastic or flat portion of the aggregate supply curve (here up to Y_k).[14] In the Keynesian range increases in real national output can be realized without any upward pressure on the aggregate price level. This condition implies that there is considerable underutilization of resources in the economy. In other words, in the Keynesian range the economy is operating well within the nation's production possibilities boundary—and there is significant excess capacity and unemployed labor in the economy that can be drawn upon to increase output.

As real national output increases and the economy moves rightward along the aggregate supply curve, the abilities of industries to expand production will differ, since the elasticities of supply vary across industries. Specifically, as firms increase output and employment and move out along their short-run cost curves, diminishing returns set in, capacity constraints are met, and unit costs of production rise. Consequently, the aggregate price level associated with producing the national output rises. Thus, in the **intermediate range** of the aggregate supply curve (shown in Figure 7.4 as the region between Y_k and Y_c), increases in real national output are accompanied by inflation or increases in the aggregate price level.

Eventually the economy would move into the **classical range,** or the vertical (perfectly inelastic) portion of the aggregate supply curve.[15] Here the economy is operating at maximum factor utilization and simply cannot increase the rate of production any further. Attempts to increase the rate production would only result in inflation.

Factors that shift the aggregate supply curve will also be examined in detail in Chapter 12. It is useful now, however, to introduce the subject of how aggregate supply and aggregate demand jointly determine real national output and the aggregate price level.

---

[14] The Keynesian range is named for the English economist John Maynard Keynes (1883–1946). His most famous work, *The General Theory of Employment, Interest, and Money* (1936), written during the Great Depression, contained insights that revolutionized macroeconomic theory and policy. Despite his death some 45 years ago, Keynes's influence lives on. His advocacy of active government intervention through expenditures and taxes to moderate the business cycle formed the basis for much of the demand-management policies in the United States in the post–World War II era. In Chapter 9 we will develop a simple version of the Keynesian model. We should add that not all economists are Keynesians. In fact, many economists disagree with the Keynesian macroeconomic model and have developed alternative models. In later chapters we will discuss some of these alternative approaches.

[15] The classical range is named for the classical school of economics, which assumed full employment to be the natural state of the economy. In the classical model the aggregate supply curve is perfectly inelastic at the level of real national output consistent with full employment of the labor force. Keynes criticized the classical model, which clearly was at variance with the reality of the persistent double-digit unemployment rates during the Great Depression of the 1930s.

EQUILIBRIUM REAL NATIONAL OUTPUT AND AGGREGATE PRICE LEVEL

Equilibrium real national output and the aggregate price level are found at that level of output where the aggregate quantity demanded of national output is equal to the aggregate quantity supplied. Graphically, equilibrium occurs at the intersection of the aggregate demand (*AD*) and aggregate supply (*AS*) curves—as shown in Figure 7.5 by the point E_0 (with Y_0 and P_0).

The effect of a change in aggregate demand on the aggregate price level and real national output depends on both the magnitude of the change in aggregate demand and the economy's position on the aggregate supply curve. For example, if the economy were on the Keynesian range, a change in aggregate demand (a shift in the *AD* curve) would result in a change in real output only. In the classical range of the aggregate supply, a change in aggregate demand would affect only the aggregate price level.

The aggregate supply curve, like the production possibilities boundary, shifts to the right with (1) growth in the labor force (due to increases in the population of working age, higher labor force participation rates, and improvement in the quality of labor with gains in the average levels of education and nutrition), (2) growth in the capital stock (due to more and better plant, equipment, and machinery), (3) the discovery and recovery of additional raw materials, and (4) technological progress (leading to inventions and innovations that allow more output per unit of factor inputs).

A simple explanation for inflation (a rise in the aggregate price level) is that it occurs when increases in aggregate demand exceed increases in aggregate supply. In Figure 7.6, assume the economy begins at E_0 with Y_0 and P_0. If the

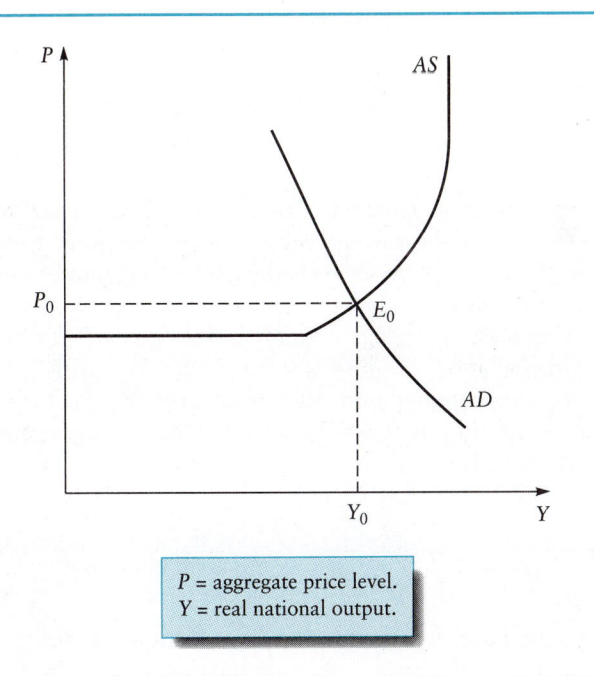

FIGURE 7.5

EQUILIBRIUM REAL NATIONAL OUTPUT AND THE AGGREGATE PRICE LEVEL

Equilibrium real national output and the aggregate price level are determined at the level of real national output where aggregate demand equals aggregate supply.

P = aggregate price level.
Y = real national output.

FIGURE 7.6

INFLATIONARY VERSUS NONINFLATIONARY GROWTH

Equal increases in aggregate demand and aggregate supply (AD to AD' and AS to AS') produce noninflationary growth (Y_0 to Y_1 with P_0). If aggregate demand increases relative to aggregate supply (e.g., AD to AD' for a given AS), then inflation (indicated by an increase in the aggregate price level from P_0 to P_1) would accompany the growth in real output (Y_0 to Y_2). If aggregate supply increases relative to aggregate demand (e.g., AS to AS' for a given AD), then deflation (indicated by a decrease in the aggregate price level from P_0 to P_2) would accompany the growth in real output (Y_0 to Y_2).

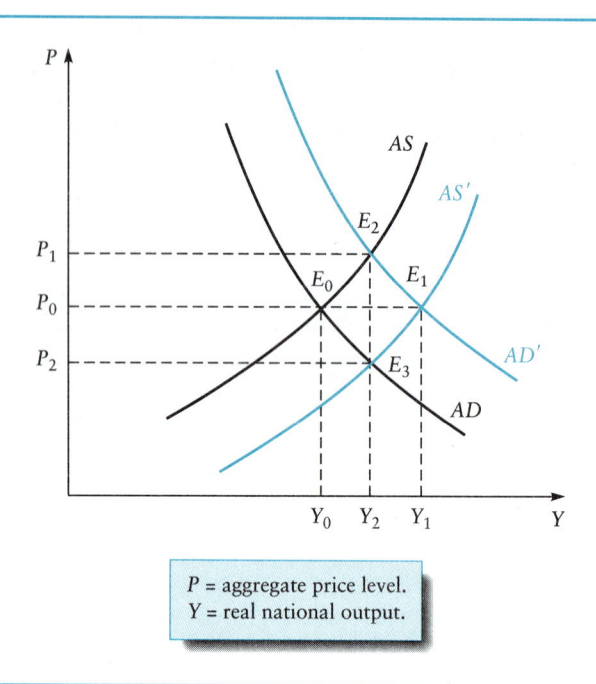

P = aggregate price level.
Y = real national output.

---

demand for goods and services produced by the domestic economy increases at the same rate as the supply, then noninflationary real growth with rising employment is possible—illustrated by the rightward shifts in the AD and AS curves (to AD' and AS') and the change in real national output to Y_1 with a stable price level of P_0. Employment would rise with the growth in real national output. In Figure 7.6 the increase in nominal output is from $(P_0)(Y_0)$ to $(P_0)(Y_1)$ and proportional to the increase in real output. Whether this rate of output growth is sufficient to reduce, or even maintain, the national unemployment rate depends on whether the employment generated by the growth is sufficient to absorb any increase in the labor force.

For a relative increase in aggregate demand (AD shifts to AD' for the given AS), real growth with inflation would result. The proportional gain in nominal output from $(P_0)(Y_0)$ to $(P_1)(Y_2)$ exceeds the gain in real output due to the rise in the aggregate price level.

For a relative increase in aggregate supply (AS shifts to AS' for the given AD), real growth with deflation would result. In Figure 7.6, with the increase in supply the proportional gain in nominal output from $(P_0)(Y_0)$ to $(P_2)(Y_2)$ is less than the gain in real output (from Y_0 to Y_2) since the aggregate price level decreased (from P_0 to P_2).

CONCLUDING NOTE

In this chapter we have provided a brief introduction to aggregate demand and aggregate supply and the macroeconomic indicators of the unemployment rate, the inflation rate, and the growth rate in real national output. The primary goals of macroeconomic policy are full employment, price stability, and a healthy rate of economic growth. As will become evident in our study of macroeconomics, these goals often conflict, which makes for difficult policy choices. Indeed, we will see that there is considerable disagreement among economists over macroeconomic policy.

In the next chapter we discuss national income accounting, the established procedures for measuring the national output of the economy. Then, in Chapter 9, we develop a simple model of the economy. In subsequent chapters the analysis will be extended to include the money market, exchange rates, and the balance of international payments.

KEY TERMS

microeconomics
macroeconomics
employed
unemployed
unemployment rate
labor force
discouraged worker
inflation
deflation
Consumer Price Index
Producer Price Index

Gross Domestic Product
nominal GDP
real GDP
implicit price deflator for GDP
aggregate demand schedule
aggregate demand curve
aggregate supply schedule
aggregate supply curve
Keynesian range
intermediate range
classical range

QUESTIONS

1. What are the three most important ideas in this chapter? Discuss why each is important.
2. Suppose that a 1985 survey of college students across the nation found a representative market basket of snack food in a typical week to be as follows:

		UNIT PRICE	
ITEM	QUANTITY	1985	1993
Soft drinks	2 six-packs	$1.60	$2.40
Cheeseburgers	5 (regular)	.75	.90
Potato chips	3 eight-ounce bags	.50	.80
Pizza	2 medium (plain)	4.00	6.00
Orange juice	1 gallon	1.20	1.50
Cookies	1 sixteen-ounce bag	.90	1.20

In an attempt to construct a college student snack food price index (CSSFPI) the snack food market basket was priced in 1985 and in 1993.
   a. Calculate the CSSFPI for 1993 using 1985 as the base year.
   b. What is the purchasing power of the college student's snack food dollar in 1993?
   c. What assumptions are made in calculating this price index?

3. The three primary macroeconomic goals are full employment, price stability, and a healthy rate of economic growth. Which of these three goals do you think should be the most important? Which should be the least important? Why? What are some other macroeconomic goals that are important? Discuss.
4. Given the following data for the U.S. economy:

Year	Nominal GDP (billions of current dollars)	Real GDP (billions of 1987 dollars)	Civilian Labor Force (millions)	Civilian Employment (millions)
1972	1207.0	3107.1	87.0	82.2
1973	1349.6	3268.6	89.4	85.1
1974	1458.6	3248.1	91.9	86.8
1975	1585.9	3221.7	93.8	85.8
1976	1768.4	3380.8	96.2	88.8

SOURCE: *Economic Report of the President 1992*, Tables B-1, B-2, B-30.

   a. Calculate the annual inflation rates for 1973 through 1976 using the Implicit Price Deflator for Gross Domestic Product.
   b. Calculate the annual unemployment rates for 1972 through 1976.
   c. From 1974 to 1975 the inflation rate and the unemployment rate both increased. How could you illustrate this using the aggregate demand–aggregate supply framework?
5. Given the following data for the U.S. economy:

Year	Nominal GDP (billions of current dollars)	Real GDP (billions of 1987 dollars)	Civilian Labor Force (millions)	Civilian Employment (millions)
1981	3030.6	3843.1	108.7	100.4
1982	3149.6	3760.3	110.2	99.5
1983	3405.0	3906.6	111.6	100.8
1984	3777.2	4148.5	113.5	105.0
1985	4038.7	4279.8	115.5	107.2

SOURCE: *Economic Report of the President 1992*, Tables B-1, B-2, B-30.

   a. Calculate the annual inflation rates for 1982 through 1985 using the Implicit Price Deflator for Gross Domestic Product.
   b. Calculate the annual unemployment rates for 1981 through 1985.
   c. From 1984 to 1985 the inflation rate and unemployment rate both declined. How could you illustrate this using the aggregate demand–aggregate supply framework?

CHAPTER

8

NATIONAL INCOME ACCOUNTING

NATIONAL INCOME ACCOUNTING provides a set of consistent guidelines for measuring aggregate income and production in a nation. Accurate income and production data are not only necessary for assessing the present condition of the economy, but are essential input for the models used to formulate economic policy and forecast economic trends.

The summary measure of national output is **Gross Domestic Product (GDP)**, which you will recall from Chapter 7 is defined as the total market value of all final goods and services produced in an economy during a year. Several points should be made at the outset. First, GDP refers to a flow of current output. Sales of previously produced goods and the exchange of assets are not counted in GDP. Second, the output is restricted to final goods and services. The value of the intermediate goods used as inputs in further stages of production is included in the value of the final output. Third, the output is valued at market prices, including sales taxes. Production that does not enter the market (such as barter activity or do-it-yourself projects around the home) is not counted in GDP. Fourth, GDP can be obtained also from the sum of the values added or the sum of the factor incomes earned in producing the national output of final goods and services.

The measurement of GDP and its components is developed in this chapter. Recent data for the U.S. economy are used to illustrate. Other national income statistics of importance are also defined. We conclude the chapter with a discussion of the limitations of using national output as an indicator of national welfare.

VALUE ADDED

Intuitively we know that the *market value* of a commodity should encompass the factor incomes earned in producing the commodity, which in turn, reflect the *values added* in production. Consider the following example.

Suppose Firm 1, a timber company, cuts down some trees on land it owns. The logs are sold to Firm 2, a sawmill, for $100. Firm 2 processes the logs into a semi-finished state of rough lumber, which is sold to Firm 3, a lumber company, for $165. The lumber company cuts the rough lumber into standardized sizes and pressure treats and dries the boards. The finished boards are sold to Firm 4, a retail outlet, for $250. Firm 4, incurring the costs of operating the store, advertising, and sales personnel, sells the finished boards to a homeowner for $320, before tax. With an ad valorem sales tax of 5 percent on the sale of the final good, the market price becomes $336. The homeowner uses the boards to build a small deck on her home.

On the basis of this series of transactions, how much has the nation's GDP increased? Adding up the sales inclusive of the tax gives $851. As illustrated in Table 8.1, however, summing the sales involves multiple counting: the contribution of Firm 1 ($100) is counted four times (see the column of $100s under Firm 1 which sums to $400), the contribution of Firm 2 ($65) is counted three times, the contribution of Firm 3 ($85) is counted twice, and the contribution of Firm 4 ($70) is counted once.

In order to get the market value of the output (or the contribution to GDP), the values added by the firms should be summed. A firm's **value added** is the difference between the value of the output sold by the firm and the value of inputs purchased from other firms and used to produce the output. Firm 1, assumed to be the owner of the land and trees, contributes the original $100 of value, which equals the intrinsic value of the trees and the value attributed to

TABLE 8.1
Example of Value Added in the Production of Boards

Sales		Firm's Contributions to the Value of Output Sold			
		Firm 1	Firm 2	Firm 3	Firm 4
$100	=	$100			
+ $165	=	($100) +	$ 65		
+ $250	=	($100) +	($ 65) +	$ 85	
+ $320	=	($100) +	($ 65) +	($ 85) +	$70 = sum of values added
= $835	=	$400 +	$195 +	$170 +	$70 = sum of sales
+ 16		(sales tax)			
= $851	=	sum of sales including sales tax			

Firm 1 sells logs to Firm 2 for $100.
Firm 2 processes the logs and sells rough lumber to Firm 3 for $165.
Firm 3 finishes the rough lumber into boards and sells to Firm 4 for $250.
Firm 4, a retail outlet, sells the finished boards to consumer for $320.
Consumer pays $336, the sales price of $320 plus the 5% sales tax of $16.

The market price of the final product is $336, which equals the sum of the values added by the four firms' $320 ($100 + $65 + $85 + 70) and the 5% sales tax of $16.

the labor and equipment used by Firm 1 to harvest the trees. Firm 2 adds $65 in value to this product, or the difference between the value of the output sold to Firm 3 in a semi-finished state and the value of the intermediate goods (logs) purchased from Firm 1. Similarly, the $85 and $70 are the values added by Firms 3 and 4, respectively. The sales tax of $16 is added to give the market value of final output. While not directly involved in this production process, the government does provide services such as national defense, fire and police protection, courts, highways, and public education, which are funded by taxes (excise, sales, income, and property) and are important for the operation of the economy.

The values added by firms are equivalent to the payments made to the factors of production employed by the firms. Labor receives wages and benefits. Investors receive returns (profits) on the capital invested. Owners of land and natural resources receive rent. Firms pay interest to creditors on the borrowed funds. The value of the services rendered during production by the physical capital owned by the firm is credited to depreciation or capital consumption (as will be discussed).

MEASUREMENT OF GROSS DOMESTIC PRODUCT

Two alternative approaches to measuring Gross Domestic Product follow from the relationship between the market value of output and the factor payments that result from the production of the output. The underlying idea is that for every dollar of expenditures on final goods and services produced in the economy, there is a dollar's worth of income generated. Thus, tabulating GDP from the incomes of the factors used to produce the output should be equivalent to measuring the market value of the output.

Output-Expenditure Approach

The **output-expenditure approach** involves adding up the expenditures required to purchase the nation's current output of final goods and services. The expenditures can be broken down into four major components: personal consumption, investment, government purchases, and net exports of goods and services.

Personal consumption expenditures (C) are the largest component of GDP. With the exception of new home purchases, expenditures of households on final goods and services comprise C. Consumption expenditures can be broken down into expenditures on durable goods (new automobiles and appliances, for example), nondurable goods (food and clothing), and services (shelter, medical care and college tuition.)

Gross private domestic investment (I) encompasses *business fixed investment* (*BFI*), or business expenditures on new plant, equipment, and machinery; *residential fixed investment* (*RFI*), or the value of residential construction during the period—which was excluded from personal consumption expenditures; and the *change in business inventories* (ΔINV).

Business inventories (*INV*) are the stocks of raw materials, intermediate goods, semi-finished and finished goods held by firms in reserve to smooth over possible short-run fluctuations in the supply of inputs and the demand for output. Firms seek to reduce their vulnerability to input supply interruptions (like a labor strike at the factory of a supplier of a key input in production). Firms also want to retain the flexibility to increase their rate of production quickly, without waiting for suppliers to fill the additional orders for the required inputs. On the other hand, businesses want to be able to meet unexpected surges in demand by drawing down the inventories of finished goods. Often the change in inventories is unplanned; for example, if actual sales fall short of expected sales, there may be unintended inventory investment ($\Delta INV > 0$).

Like GDP, the change in business inventories is a flow. In the aggregate, if the change in inventories is positive, $\Delta INV > 0$, then some of the national output currently produced is not being sold; that is, gross production exceeds gross expenditures. Conversely, if the change in inventories is negative, $\Delta INV < 0$, then gross expenditures are outpacing gross production and some of the output being sold was produced in an earlier period. As we will discuss in the following chapter, the change in business inventories, whether positive or negative, may be either planned or unplanned.

Government purchases of goods and services, G, refers to purchases of goods (such as tanks and buildings) and services (such as the labor of civil servants and public schoolteachers) by all levels of government. Government purchases of goods and services, however, are not the same as *government outlays,* which also include government transfers and interest on government debt. **Transfers** are payments to individuals for which no current services are rendered in return—as a result, no output is currently produced. Examples of *government transfers* to households are social security payments to the elderly, welfare assistance, and unemployment compensation. The subsidies to farmers and to firms that export are examples of government transfers to business. The foreign aid provided by the federal government to other nations is an *international transfer*.

Including government transfers in government purchases of goods and services (G) would involve considerable double-counting. For example, households receiving transfers use the income for personal consumption expenditures, which are counted in C in the output-expenditure approach to GDP. By convention, government interest payments are considered like transfers and not included in the output-expenditure approach to Gross Domestic Product.

So far we have accounted for the expenditures on national output of domestic households (C), firms (I), and government (G). What about foreign expenditures on the nation's output? **Exports of goods and services** (X) are commodities produced domestically and purchased by foreign households, firms, and governments. On the other hand, not all of the expenditures by domestic households, firms, and government are for domestically produced goods and services. Americans consume French wine, purchase videocassette recorders made in Korea, and fly on British Airways. Therefore, **imports of goods and services** (M), the expenditures on goods and services produced in foreign countries, must be subtracted out of personal consumption expenditures, gross private domestic investment, government purchases, and exports to yield those expenditures on domestically produced goods and services.

Combining all the major expenditure categories gives the GDP identity.

$$C + I + G + X - M \equiv GDP$$

where

C = personal consumption expenditures.
I = gross private domestic investment.
G = government purchases of goods and services.
X = exports of goods and services.
M = imports of goods and services.
GDP = Gross Domestic Product.

The GDP identity holds that for the accounting period in question (usually a year), the nation's output of final goods and services can be allocated across the expenditure categories of personal consumption, private investment, government purchases, and exports—with the expenditures on imports of goods and services subtracted out.

The output-expenditure approach to GDP is illustrated in Table 8.2 with data for the U.S. economy for 1990. In the United States, personal consumption expenditures typically account for between 60 and 65 percent of GDP; although in recent years the share of personal consumption has increased to two out of every three dollars of spending on national output. Gross private domestic investment, while a rather volatile component of aggregate spending, averages roughly 15 percent of GDP. It so happens that in 1990, inventory investment or the change in business inventories was equal to zero. Government purchases of goods and services largely account for the remaining 20 percent. For most of the post–World War II era, U.S. exports, on average, were offset by imports, so that net exports of goods and services were a small percentage of GDP. In

TABLE 8.2
U.S. GROSS DOMESTIC PRODUCT IN 1990: OUTPUT-EXPENDITURE APPROACH

		AMOUNT IN BILLIONS OF DOLLARS				PERCENTAGE OF GDP
C	=	3742.6	=	Personal consumption expenditures		(67.9%)
				durable goods	465.9	
				nondurable goods	1217.7	
				services	2059.0	
+ I	=	802.6	=	Gross private domestic investment		(14.6)
				business fixed investment	587.0	
				residential fixed investment	215.7	
				change in business inventories	.0	
+ G	=	1042.9	=	Government purchases of goods and services		(18.9)
				federal	424.9	
				state and local	618.0	
+ X	=	550.4	=	**Exports of goods and services**		(10.0)
− M	=	624.8	=	**Imports of goods and services**		(11.3)
= GDP	=	5513.8	=	**Gross Domestic Product**		

NOTE: Totals may not sum exactly due to rounding error. Figures in parentheses represent percentages of GDP.
SOURCE: *Survey of Current Business*, November 1991, Table 1.1.

the 1980s the United States consistently ran large balance-of-trade deficits. By 1990, however, the trade gap had narrowed, although imports of goods and services still exceeded exports by 1.3 percent of GDP.

Along with fixed investment expenditures (business purchases of new plant and equipment and residential construction), spending on consumer durables tends to be a rather cyclical component of GDP. These expenditures are sensitive to credit conditions and to swings in consumer and business confidence. In Chapter 12 we will address the business cycle in more depth. For now, with Figure 8.1 we can compare changes in these volatile expenditures with the steadier components of GDP for the U.S. economy over the last two decades. Although consumer durables and fixed investment account for roughly only one out of every four dollars of spending on national output, these cyclical expenditures contribute disproportionately to the variability in real GDP—especially during economic downturns (in 1974–1975, 1980, 1982, and most recently in 1991).

FIGURE 8.1

VOLATILITY IN REAL AGGREGATE EXPENDITURES ON NATIONAL OUTPUT: 1970–1991

Volatile expenditures include personal consumption expenditures on durable goods, business fixed investment, and residential fixed investment. All expenditures are in billions of constant 1987 dollars.

SOURCE: *Economic Report of the President 1992*, Table B-2.

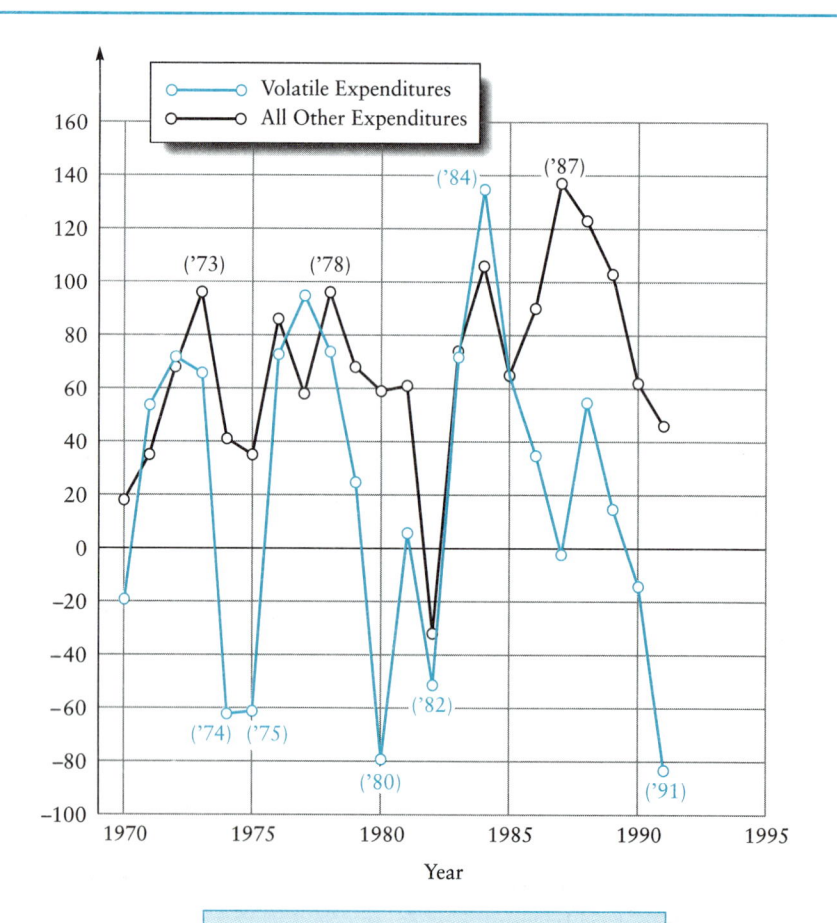

$ = annual change in real aggregate expenditures (billions of 1987 dollars).

Gross Domestic Product and Gross National Product

Before 1992, the most widely reported statistic for aggregate output in the United States was Gross National Product. In 1992 the U.S. government shifted to reporting Gross Domestic Product as a better indicator of the aggregate level of production in the nation. Let's compare the two.

Gross National Product (GNP) is the market value of all final goods and services produced by the residents of the nation—whether or not the output is produced within the borders of the nation.[1] In contrast, Gross Domestic Product (GDP) is the market value of all final goods and services produced within the nation's borders—whether or not the output is produced by the residents of the nation. The difference between GNP and GDP is **net factor income.** From the perspective of the United States, the factor income earned using the labor and capital supplied by U.S. residents on the goods and services produced abroad would add to U.S. GNP, but not to U.S. GDP. For example, if a U.S. construction company is hired to build a factory in Spain, then U.S. Gross National Product would increase by the wages earned by U.S. labor employed on the project and the returns on U.S. capital invested in the project.

Conversely, the income earned by residents of foreign countries on goods and services produced in the United States would contribute to U.S. GDP, but not to U.S. GNP. For example, the wages earned by a Mexican migrant working in California and the interest received by a resident of Toronto, Canada, on a bond issued by a Boston corporation would be included in U.S. Gross Domestic Product.

For the United States, the difference between factor income payments to foreigners (included in GDP) and factor income receipts from foreigners (included in GNP) has been relatively small, so that the values of GNP and GDP have been roughly equal. In fact, over the 1980s the excess of GNP over GDP steadily declined. In 1990 U.S. GDP was estimated to be $5513.8 billion, and U.S. GNP to be $5524.5 billion (or only 100.2 percent of GDP).

Factor-Payments Approach

The second approach to measuring GDP is through the factor payments generated in the production of national output. In Table 8.3 we illustrate the **factor-payments approach** for the U.S. economy for 1990. Not surprisingly, the major factor payment is for labor. **Compensation of employees** includes all payments to and on behalf of employees (wages, salaries, and benefits) before any deductions for income taxes, social security taxes, or pension fund contributions. In 1990 the compensation of employees accounted for nearly 60 percent of GDP.

Proprietors' income encompasses the income of unincorporated enterprises (single proprietorships, partnerships, and family-owned farms). **Rental income of persons** comprises rents and royalties received by persons. In national income accounting for the United States, an imputed rental value for owner-occupied housing—that is, an estimate of the services provided by housing or the value of the shelter to the homeowner—is included in rental income, which in turn

---

[1] Residents of a nation include the individuals, firms, and government agencies who make the nation their legal domicile.

TABLE 8.3
U.S. Gross Domestic Product in 1990: Factor-Payments Approach

AMOUNT IN BILLIONS OF DOLLARS		
3290.3	=	Compensation of employees
+ 373.2	=	Proprietors' income
+ −12.9	=	Rental income of persons
+ 490.1	=	Net interest
+ 319.0	=	Corporate profits
= 4459.6		**National income**
+ 439.2	=	Indirect business taxes
+ 31.0	=	Other items
= 4929.8	=	**Net National Product (NNP)**
+ 594.8	=	Capital consumption (CC)
= 5524.5	=	**Gross National Product (GNP)**
− 10.7	=	Net receipts of factor income from the rest of the world
= 5513.8	=	**Gross Domestic Product (GDP)**

NOTE: Other items include business transfer payments (27.7), current surplus less subsidies of government enterprises (−4.8), and a statistical discrepancy (+8.1). Totals may not sum exactly due to rounding error.

SOURCE: *Survey of Current Business,* November 1991, Tables 1.9, 1.14.

is included in C, personal consumption expenditures, in the output-expenditure approach to GDP. Rental income is negative in 1990 because the capital consumption adjustment for rental units (an adjustment for the estimated loss in value due to depreciation) exceeded the rental income earned (and imputed).

Net interest refers to interest paid by business less interest received by business. By convention, excluded from net interest are interest on the government debt (considered to be like a government transfer payment) and the interest paid on consumer debt (other than interest on mortgage and home improvement loans).

The last major category is **corporate profits.** These are gross profits of corporations, measured before corporate profits taxes are paid and corporate dividends are distributed. In 1990 corporate profits accounted for less than 6 percent of U.S. GDP.

Summing the factor payments of employee compensation, proprietors' income, rental income of persons, net interest, and corporate profits gives the **national income,** a measure of the value of national output at factor costs. (In contrast, GDP is a measure of the value of national output at market prices.) In 1990 national income was 81 percent of GDP. To account for the remainder of GDP, several items are added to national income, and some other adjustments are necessary.

Recall from the example of value added how sales taxes could drive a wedge between factor payments and market prices. **Indirect business taxes** are the taxes collected by the government on the production and sale of national output—primarily sales, excise, and property taxes. The government also collects direct taxes on factor income (personal income taxes from individuals and profits taxes from corporations). These direct taxes, however, are included in national income.

"Other items" in Table 8.3 comprise business transfer payments, current surplus less subsidies of government enterprises, and the statistical discrepancy. **Business transfer payments** include gifts to nonprofit institutions and the write-off of bad consumer debts. Such transfers by business are part of the market value of the output produced, but are not retained by business for payment to the owners of the factors of production.

Similarly, **current surplus less subsidies of government enterprises** must be counted. If government enterprises (for example, state liquor stores and the Tennessee Valley Authority) generate "profits" (an excess of revenues over operating costs), then the value of the output produced exceeds the value of the factor payments made. The surplus of the government enterprise is counted like tax revenue and added to national income. On the other hand, if government enterprises require subsidies to cover operating losses, then the value of the output produced by the enterprises is less than the factor payments made. Correspondingly, the subsidies should be subtracted from national income in the calculation of GDP.

A significant component of Gross Domestic Product is **capital consumption** (CC), an estimate of the depreciation or the loss in value of the nation's capital stock (including residential structures) over the accounting period in question. The loss in value due to physical wear in production and technological obsolescence is a measure of the contribution of the capital stock to national output. Since capital consumption is not paid out as factor income, it is not included in national income. In 1990 it was nearly 11 percent of U.S. GDP.

Adding business transfer payments, current surplus less subsidies of government enterprises, indirect business taxes, and capital consumption to national income should yield the Gross National Product from the factor-payments approach. To obtain Gross Domestic Product from Gross National Product, we need to subtract net receipts of factor income from the rest of the world. Recall, some of the factor income generated in the production of output in the United States is paid to residents of other countries—and counted in U.S. GDP but not U.S. GNP. On the other hand, some of the factor income received by residents of the United States is earned in the production of foreign goods and services—thus counted in U.S. GNP but not in U.S. GDP. In 1990, U.S. receipts of factor income from the rest of the world ($147.7 billion) exceeded U.S. payments of factor income to the rest of the world ($137.0 billion). Subtracting the difference of $10.7 billion from U.S. Gross National Product gives the U.S. Gross Domestic Product of $5513.8 billion.

Due to the inevitable measurement errors in the various components, only by chance would the calculations of Gross Domestic Product by the factor-payments and output-expenditure approaches yield exactly the same value for GDP. Therefore, a **statistical discrepancy** item—the allowance for the measurement incongruity between the two approaches—is included to reconcile them. For 1990 the statistical discrepancy (incorporated in the factor-payments approach as "other items") is equal to $8.1 billion. In other words, the estimate of GDP by the output-expenditure approach (considered to be the more reliable measurement) exceeded the estimate of GDP by the factor-payments approach by $8.1 billion.

OTHER NATIONAL INCOME STATISTICS

At this point we should note other National Income statistics frequently reported: Net National Product, net investment, and disposable personal income.

Net National Product

Net National Product (NNP) is the net output of final goods and services after subtracting from GNP the output required to replace the capital stock that has depreciated. That is, NNP is equal to the difference between GNP and capital consumption (*CC*). Capital consumption can be regarded as that part of the national output needed to maintain the nation's productive capacity or the capital stock intact.

Net Investment

A similar relationship is found between gross private domestic investment (*I*) and **net private domestic investment** (*NI*), the difference being again the capital consumption ($NI = I - CC$). Abstracting from the change in business inventories, we see that **net private domestic fixed investment** (*NFI*) equals gross private domestic fixed investment (*GFI*) less capital consumption ($NFI = GFI - CC$). Over the accounting period, net investment can be positive, negative, or equal to zero. If *NFI* is positive, then the value of the nation's capital stock (plant, equipment, machinery, residential and nonresidential structures) will increase. From 1942 to 1945 the annual values for net private domestic fixed investment for the U.S. economy were negative. With the need to direct resources toward the war effort, the nation's capital stock wore out faster than it could be replaced.

Disposable Personal Income

If all the income earned but not received by individuals (for example, due to social security taxes, corporate profits taxes, and undistributed corporate profits) is subtracted from national income, and all the income received but not currently earned by individuals (for example, from government and business transfers) is added to National Income, a measure called **personal income** is derived—essentially the current income received from all sources by individuals. In 1990 personal income in the U.S. economy was $4679.8 billion.[2]

Subtracting personal taxes (primarily income and personal property taxes) from personal income yields **disposable personal income** ($4058.8 in 1990), which is the income available to persons for spending or saving. In 1990, $3742.6 billion (or slightly over 92 percent) of disposable personal income were used for personal consumption expenditures (*C* in the calculation of GDP from the output-expenditure approach). Subtracting personal consumption expenditures, interest payments on consumer debt ($107.5 billion), and net personal

---

[2] *Survey of Current Business,* November 1991, Table 2.1.

transfer payments to foreigners ($2.1 billion) from disposable personal income gives **personal saving** ($206.6 billion in 1990).

BASIC MACROECONOMIC IDENTITY

From the output-expenditure approach we obtained the identity

$$C + I + G + X - M \equiv GDP$$

which shows how the national output of final goods and services (GDP) is allocated across the types of expenditures—by households (C), firms (I), government (G), and foreigners (X), with the expenditures on foreign produced goods and services (M) subtracted out.

We can also account for the disposition or uses of the income generated in the production of the national output.

$$GDP \equiv C + S + T + R + F$$

where

S = Gross private saving.
T = Net taxes (i.e., tax receipts less government transfer payments and net interest payments of the government).
R = Net unilateral transfers to foreigners.
F = Net payments of factor income to foreigners.

In effect, after subtracting net taxes from Gross Domestic Product, the remaining income can be used for personal consumption expenditures (C), gross private saving (S), net unilateral transfers to foreigners (R), and net payments of factor income to foreigners (F).

The **basic macroeconomic identity** is formed by equating the sum of the expenditures on national output $(C + I + G + X - M)$ with the sum of the uses of the income earned in the production of the national output $(C + S + T + R + F)$. In Table 8.4 we illustrate the basic macroeconomic identity for the United States in 1990.

$$C + I + G + X - M = GDP = C + S + T + R + F$$

Gross private saving can be divided into personal saving and gross business saving. Recall, personal saving is calculated as the residual income after personal consumption expenditures, interest payments on consumer debt, and net personal transfers to foreigners are subtracted from disposable personal income. Gross business saving includes undistributed corporate profits (that is, corporate profits after corporate profit taxes and dividends), and capital consumption.

The components of net taxes, net unilateral transfers to foreigners, and net factor payments to foreigners are also given in Table 8.4. "Contributions for social insurance" basically refers to social security taxes paid by employers and employees.

We can rearrange the basic macroeconomic identity and solve for the government budget balance $(T - G)$, as follows:

TABLE 8.4
Basic Macroeconomic Identity for the U.S. Economy in 1990

$$C + I + G + X - M = \text{GDP} = C + S + T + R + F$$

				Amount in Billions of Dollars
	C	=	Personal consumption expenditures	+ 3742.6
+	I	=	Gross private domestic investment	+ 802.6
+	G	=	Government purchases of goods and services	+ 1042.9
+	X	=	Exports of goods and services	+ 550.4
−	M	=	Imports of goods and services	− 624.8
=	GDP	=	Gross Domestic product	= 5513.8
+	C	=	Personal consumption expenditures	+ 3742.6
+	S	=	Gross private saving	+ 859.4
+	T	=	Net taxes	+ 903.3
+	R	=	Net unilateral transfers to foreigners	+ 19.2
+	F	=	Net payments of factor income to foreigners	+ −10.7

S = gross private saving = 859.4.
   = personal saving (206.6) + gross business saving (652.8).

Gross business saving = 652.8
   = capital consumption (594.8)
   + undistributed corporate profits (49.9)
   + statistical discrepancy (8.1)

T = Net Taxes = 903.3
   = Taxes (1697.2) − Government Transfers (793.9)

Taxes = 1697.2
   = Personal Taxes (621.0)
   + Corporate Profits Taxes (135.3)
   + Indirect Business Taxes (439.2)
   + Contributions for Social Insurance (501.7)

Government Transfers = 793.9
   = Government Transfers to Persons (661.7)
   + Government Transfers to Foreigners (12.6)
   + Subsidies less Current Surplus of Government Enterprises (4.8)
   + Government Net Interest Payments (114.8)

R = Net Unilateral Transfers to Foreigners = 19.2
   = Net Personal Transfer Payments to Foreigners (2.1)
   + Net Government Transfer Payments to Foreigners (12.6)
   + Net Business Transfer Payments to Foreigners (4.5)

F = Net Payments of Factor Income to Foreigners = −10.7
   = Payments of Factor Income to the Rest of the World (137.0)
   − Receipts of Factor Income from the Rest of the World (147.7)

Totals may not sum exactly due to rounding error.
SOURCE: *Survey of Current Business* November 1991, Tables 1.1, 2.1, 3.2, 3.3, 5.1.

$$C + I + G + X - M = C + S + T + R + F$$

Subtracting C from both sides and solving for $T - G$, we obtain

$$(T - G) = (I - S) + (X - M - R - F)$$

Government Budget Balance = Private Domestic Investment-Saving Balance + Current Account Balance on the Balance of International Payments

If government purchases of goods and services (G) equal net taxes (T), which is equivalent to government outlays equaling tax receipts, then the government's budget is balanced. If net taxes exceed government purchases, then the government budget balance is in surplus, which implies positive public saving. Finally, if government purchases exceed net taxes, then the government budget balance is in deficit, which implies negative public saving.

A government budget deficit must be covered by an overall deficit in the private domestic investment-saving balance and current account balance. A current account deficit ($X - M - R - F < 0$), is referred to as *net foreign saving*. (In later chapters we will discuss the financing of a government budget deficit and the constructs of the current account balance and the balance of international payments.)

For the purpose at hand here, we will simply illustrate the identity with the 1990 data for the U.S. economy. In 1990 the budget balance for all levels of government equaled − $139.6 billion. Offsetting the budget deficit of the government were deficits of $56.8 billion and $82.9 billion in the private domestic investment-saving balance and current account balance, respectively. In other words, the excess of government spending over receipts was covered by an excess of private domestic saving over private domestic investment and net foreign saving. The calculations follow:

$$(T - G) = (I - S) + (X - M - R - F)$$
$$(903.3 - 1042.9) = (802.6 - 859.4) + [550.4 - 624.8 - 19.2 - (-10.7)]$$
$$-139.6 = -56.8 + -82.9$$
$$-139.6 = -139.7$$

allowing for rounding error.

GROSS NATIONAL PRODUCT AND WELFARE

Often comparisons of Gross National Product *per capita* (i.e., GNP divided by the total population of a nation) are used to infer relative standards of living across nations. GNP is preferable to GDP as a measure of aggregate income because it includes the net factor income received by residents of the nation from the rest of the world.[3] In Table 8.5 we present estimates of per capita GNPs in 1990 for a half-dozen nations, including the United States, at different stages

---

[3] For some nations, often a significant portion of factor income received is earned in other countries—due to residents working abroad and remitting part of their incomes to families at home or to the receipt of interest and dividends from foreign investments. On the other hand, for nations that have a large number of foreign (nonresident) workers or substantial investment by foreigners, GDP may significantly exceed GNP.

TABLE 8.5
Per Capita Gross National Products and Infant Mortality Rates

COUNTRY	GNP PER CAPITA 1990	INFANT MORTALITY RATE 1990
India	$ 350	92
China	370	29
Brazil	2,680	57
United States	21,790	9
Sweden	23,660	6
Japan	25,430	5

NOTE: The infant mortality rate is the number of infant deaths (below age one) per thousand live births in a year.
SOURCE: Adapted from *World Development Report 1992*, Tables 1, 28. Copyright © 1992 by The International Bank for Reconstruction and Development/The World Bank. Reprinted by permission of Oxford University Press, Inc.

of economic development. Cross-country comparisons require not only estimates of national incomes and populations, but the conversion of national incomes to a common currency with exchange rates. If the exchange rates used are not market equilibrium exchange rates—and for many developing nations the official exchange rate is not the market equilibrium exchange rate—then international comparisons will be biased.[4]

On the other hand, prices will vary across nations, especially for nontraded commodities. For example, as shown in Table 8.5, India's estimated per capita GNP in 1990 of $350 is less than 2 percent of the estimated per capita GNP for the United States of $21,790. Adjusting for relative purchasing power (because many goods and services in India are much less expensive than in the United States) increases the effective per capita income in India to nearly 5 percent of the U.S. level.[5]

Per capita GNP, moreover, may be a misleading measure of the average standard of living, especially for nations with very different economic systems. Recall that GNP excludes nonmarket activity. Thus, the economic value of the labor services provided by homemakers is not included in GNP. For instance, in the earlier illustration of value added, if the homeowner hires a carpenter for $150 to build the deck with the purchased lumber, GNP would rise by the value of the output produced by the carpenter ($150). If the homeowner builds the deck herself, the value of the output produced is not included in GNP. Yet, in either case the deck is built and output has been generated. In less developed countries much of the economic activity never enters the formal market—for example, subsistence agriculture and the bartering of services. In all economies illegal activities such as drug trafficking and evasion of tax liabilities mean that

---

[4] In Chapters 17 and 18 we will study exchange rates, and in Chapter 19 we will discuss why developing nations may prefer to operate with overvalued currencies. Conversion of national incomes using overvalued exchange rates will inflate the resulting per capita dollar figures. For example, suppose the official exchange rate in India is 15 Indian rupees to 1 U.S. dollar. If per capita GNP in India is estimated to be 6000 rupees, then using the official exchange rate gives a per capita GNP of $400 for India. If the market equilibrium exchange rate is instead 20 Indian rupees to the dollar, then the Indian per capita GNP of 6000 rupees converts to only $300.
[5] World Bank, *World Development Report 1992*, 298–301 and Table 30.

some of the income generated is either not measured at all or significantly underreported.

GNP per capita is an aggregate statistic that does not reflect the composition of national output. For example, to achieve superpower status, the Soviet Union in the post–World War II era channeled resources into the production of military goods. The production of civilian goods was relatively slighted. Thus, using GNP per capita would likely have overstated the standard of living for the average Soviet citizen (and understated the national security) compared to a citizen of another nation with the same per capita GNP but less of a military burden.

GNP per capita does not reflect the distribution of income and output. In some nations, wealth and income are highly concentrated, so while per capita GNP may be relatively high, the majority of the population is poor. A more accurate measure of the average standard of living might be the **infant mortality rate** (the number of infants who die before reaching one year of age per thousand live births in a year). The infant mortality rate captures not only the average level of income, but the distribution of income and popular access to basic amenities and health care. In Table 8.5 we can compare per capita GNPs and infant mortality rates for the selected nations.

Although in 1990 per capita GNPs were approximately equal in the United States and Sweden, the infant mortality rate was significantly lower in Sweden. In the United States many individuals do not receive adequate health care. Sweden, with more of a welfare-state orientation, appears to be comparatively more successful in providing for the basic health needs of its population. For the less developed countries of Brazil and China, the contrast is even more dramatic. In 1990, with more than six times the per capita GNP, Brazil had nearly twice the infant mortality rate of China. In the postwar era Brazil placed its policy emphasis on economic growth, and the resulting distribution of income is very unequal. China, on the other hand, has been very effective in providing for the primary health care needs of its population, but less successful in generating economic growth.

Too much about national policies should not be inferred from these selected examples. In general, there is a positive relationship between per capita GNP and the average standard of living as indicated by the national infant mortality rate; however, as discussed here, there are exceptions.

Like GDP, GNP measures the costs of producing the nation's output, which may very well exceed the benefits derived. For instance, the costs of cleaning up the environment from industrial pollution add to GNP. If a chemical company produces $100 million worth of herbicides in a year, but improperly disposes of the chemical waste, which in turn requires $2 million worth of cleanup, GNP increases by $102 million. Perhaps a more accurate measure of the gain in national output would be just the $100 million (or maybe just the $98 million?).

Lester Brown, President of Worldwatch Institute, writes,

> GNP includes depreciation of plant and equipment, but it does not take into account the depreciation of natural capital, including nonrenewable resources such as oil or renewable resources such as forests.
>
> This shortcoming can produce a misleading sense of national economic health. According to the conventional approach, for example, countries that overcut forests actually do better in the short run than those that manage forests on a

sustained-yield basis: the trees cut down are counted as income but no subtraction is made to account for depletion of the forest, a natural asset.[6]

One of the features of an affluent society is additional leisure time. GNP could be increased, ceteris paribus, if the population worked longer hours or commuted greater distances to work, but would the average quality of life increase? We can see from Table 8.5 that per capita GNP in Japan in 1990 was estimated to be over $3500 higher than in the United States. On the other hand, the cost of living in Japan (especially the cost of housing) is much higher than in the United States, and there is widespread concern in Japan about the stressful lifestyle of long working hours, few vacations, and extensive commuting times.[7]

In sum, due to the difficulties in converting national incomes to a common base, measuring market activity, and accounting for differences in the composition of output and distribution of income, per capita GNP is at best an imperfect measure of average economic welfare. When we add considerations of the quality of life as reflected in the enjoyment of leisure and the preservation of a clean and healthy natural environment, the limitations of using per capita GNP (or per capita GDP) as an indicator of the average standard of living become even more apparent.

CONCLUDING NOTE

We should not conclude that GDP, GNP, and the associated national income and expenditure measures are simply accounting measures of little practical use. The consistent process for measuring national output and income offered by national income accounting aids in the formulation of macroeconomic policy. The consolidation of the multitude of economic activities into summary measures provides the statistical input for the macromodels used to understand and forecast the trends in the economy. For example, if the national unemployment rate is rising, knowing which components of aggregate expenditures on national output are primarily responsible is important.

Declines in residential fixed investment may elicit a different policy response than declines in exports of goods and services. To a large degree, the success of economic policy depends on the relevancy, accuracy, and immediacy of the underlying economic data. By the same token, we need to continue to develop more relevant, accurate, and current measures of economic progress and social welfare.

In the following chapters simple macroeconomic models will be constructed, and the rudiments of macroeconomic policy will be discussed. We begin in Chapter 9 with the Simple Keynesian model of national income determination.

---

[6] Lester Brown, "The Illusion of Progress," *State of the World 1990* (New York: W. W. Norton and Company, 1990), 8.

[7] In fact, when the higher cost of living in Japan is taken into consideration, the purchasing power of Japan's per capita income is estimated to be less than 80 percent that of the United States. Similarly, when Sweden's per capita GNP in 1990 of $23,660 is adjusted for the relatively higher cost of living in Sweden—compared to the United States—the purchasing power of Sweden's per capita income is less than 75 percent of that for the United States. (See World Bank, *World Development Report 1992,* Table 30.)

KEY TERMS

Gross Domestic Product
value added
output-expenditure approach
personal consumption expenditures
gross private domestic investment
business inventories
government purchases of goods and services
transfers
exports of goods and services
imports of goods and services
Gross National Product
net factor income
factor-payments approach
compensation of employees
proprietors' income
rental income of persons
net interest

corporate profits
national income
indirect business taxes
business transfer payments
current surplus less subsidies of government enterprises
capital consumption
statistical discrepancy
net national product
net private domestic investment
net private domestic fixed investment
personal income
disposable personal income
personal saving
basic macroeconomic identity
infant mortality rate

QUESTIONS

1. What are the three most important ideas in this chapter? Discuss why each is important.
2. Assume that a mining company sells copper to a processing firm for $10,000. The processing firm refines the copper into copper sheets and sells the copper sheets to a weather vane company for $14,000. The weather vane company manufacturers 1,000 pure copper weather vanes which are sold to a department store for $21,000. The department store lists the copper weather vanes for a unit price of $30.00. The final price to consumers (with the 5 percent sales tax) is $31.50. Given the following series of transactions, Find the change in GDP by summing the values added by each firm in the production process. Why is there a discrepancy between the market price paid by consumers for the final product and the sum of the values added?
3. Is it possible for the value added by a firm to be negative? What would a negative value added imply? Give an example.
4. In 1990 Sri Lanka's per capita GNP was estimated to be $470, while Mexico's was estimated at $2490. Yet Sri Lanka's infant mortality rate in 1990 of 19 (deaths to infants under age one year per thousand live births) was half Mexico's rate of 39. (*World Development Report 1992*, Tables 1, 28.) What could account for Sri Lanka's lower infant mortality rate despite its much lower per capita income?
5. What adjustments would you make in per capita GNP to obtain a better measure of the average standard of living in a nation? Discuss.
6. Using the following data from *Survey of Current Business,* November 1991, Tables 1.1, 1.9, 1.14, 5.1, on the U.S. economy for 1988 (in billions of dollars),

a. Find the value of GDP by using first the output-expenditure approach and then the factor-payments approach. What is the value of the statistical discrepancy?
b. Confirm that the basic macroeconomic identity holds.
c. Rearrange the basic macroeconomic identity to solve for the government budget balance. Show how the government budget balance was covered for the United States in 1988.

Business transfer payments = 26
Capital consumption = 534
Compensation of employees = 2921
Corporate profits = 365
Current surplus less subsidies of government enterprises = −11
Exports of goods and services = 444
Government purchases of goods and services = 919
Gross private domestic investment = 793
Gross private saving = 774
Imports of goods and services = 552
Indirect business taxes = 385
Net interest = 388
Net receipts of factor income from the rest of the world = 8
Net taxes = 821
Net unilateral transfers to foreigners = 17
Personal consumption expenditures = 3296
Proprietors' income = 324
Rental income of persons = 4

PART

IV

NATIONAL INCOME DETERMINATION

CHAPTERS

— 9 —
A SIMPLE KEYNESIAN MODEL OF
NATIONAL INCOME DETERMINATION

— 10 —
THE DEMAND FOR MONEY

— 11 —
THE BANKING SYSTEM
AND THE MONEY SUPPLY

— 12 —
AGGREGATE DEMAND
AND AGGREGATE SUPPLY

CHAPTER 9

A Simple Keynesian Model of National Income Determination

From the last chapter we saw that *national income accounting* is concerned with the conventions used to measure Gross Domestic Product (GDP) and its components. Associated with national income accounting is the GDP identity,

$$\text{GDP} \equiv C + I + G + X - M$$

which states that for the accounting period in question, the value of the expenditures on national output by domestic households, firms, and government and by foreigners must sum to the value of national output actually produced. The "≡" notation is often used to accent the definitional nature of the equation. National income accounting is *ex post*—a tally of a nation's economic performance after the fact and according to established procedures.

National income determination, on the other hand, involves the construction of a behavioral macroeconomic model that explains how the equilibrium level of national output is attained. The concern here is with solving for the level of national output whereby the income produced will generate desired aggregate expenditures just sufficient to purchase that output. For national income determination, the condition analogous to the GDP identity of national income accounting is the equilibrium condition,

$$\text{GDP} \stackrel{e}{=} C + I + G + X - M.$$

The "e" over the equals sign emphasizes that the equation represents an equilibrium condition.

Why are macroeconomic models needed? When the president and Congress draw up the federal government's budget for the next year, they have in mind not only a set of national expenditure priorities, but also a macro model of the economy. Disagreement within and between the executive and legislative branches of the federal government can reflect both different expenditure priorities and different macroeconomic models. In any case, how much the federal government allocates for expenditures depends on how much revenue it expects to receive from taxes and how much of a deficit (or surplus) it is willing to run. The tax revenues received will depend upon the tax system in place and the performance of the national economy. The nation's economic performance, in turn, partly depends upon how much the federal government spends and the tax system in place. The circularity and simultaneity of the macroeconomic process should be clear.

Macroeconomic models are developed to make the process more tractable. Such models may be very simple, with only a few variables and equations easily solved with pencil and paper, or highly complex, with many variables and equations that must be solved by computer. The insights and projections of these macroeconomic models are used to formulate the nation's economic policies. Businesses also employ economists to forecast whether market conditions warrant new ventures and investments. Even some of the decisions of households, such as whether to purchase a new house or search for a new job, depend on assessments of the economic climate.

We start with a very basic macroeconomic model of national income determination known as the *Simple Keynesian model*.[1] As the analysis proceeds in subsequent chapters, we will extend the model, making it more realistic—and more complex.

COMPONENTS OF DESIRED AGGREGATE EXPENDITURES

To begin, we make the following assumptions:

1. The aggregate price level (P) does not change. Essentially we will restrict the analysis to an economy operating on the Keynesian range (perfectly elastic portion) of the aggregate supply curve. The implicit assumption is that the economy is well below full employment. The magnitudes discussed—that is, output and expenditures—will be in real terms.
2. All taxes are assumed to be personal income taxes. Real disposable personal income (Y_d) is equal to real national income (Y) less real net taxes (T). That is, $Y_d = Y - T$. Recall that net taxes are tax revenues less government transfer payments. We will assume further that there are no government transfer payments; so here T can be regarded simply as real taxes.
3. Net unilateral transfers to foreigners are assumed to equal zero.
4. Net payments of factor income to foreigners are assumed to equal zero.
5. In addition to assuming no indirect business taxes, we will ignore capital consumption. Consequently, real national income, real national output, and

---

[1] The distinguishing feature of the Simple Keynesian model, named after the British economist John Maynard Keynes, is its emphasis on aggregate demand in determining equilibrium real national output and employment. The Simple Keynesian model is the most basic version of the *Keynesian model*.

real GDP will be used interchangeably and will be designated by the variable Y.

We define desired aggregate expenditures (A) as

$$A = C + I + G + X - M$$

where

C = personal consumption expenditures.
I = investment expenditures.
G = government purchases of goods and services.
X = exports of goods and services.
M = imports of goods and services.

and all expenditures are in real terms.

In the following discussion we will make certain assumptions about these expenditure components. While the assumptions may seem to be overly simplistic, they are useful abstractions for a first exercise in macroeconomic model building.

Consumption Function

As we discussed in Chapter 8, personal consumption expenditures (C) constitute the majority of the aggregate expenditures on national output. The behavioral relationship of most interest is between consumption and disposable income. Restricting the analysis to a linear consumption function gives

$$C = C_0 + cY_d$$

where

$$0 < c < 1.$$

Real personal consumption expenditures are directly related to real disposable personal income by the parameter c. Assuming c to be a positive fraction less than 1 means that while consumption expenditures rise with disposable income, not all of the increase in disposable income will be used for consumption. Some of any increase in disposable income will be saved. The intercept term C_0 is referred to as **autonomous consumption** and accounts for all other influences on aggregate consumption expenditures. For example, a change in population (such as an increase in the population under age 15), a change in real wealth (such as a stock market boom), or a change in the cost of credit (due to lower interest rates that make big-ticket items like automobiles less expensive) would each affect aggregate personal consumption expenditures at any given level of real disposable income. If we assume that the parameter c is fixed by income distribution and saving habits, then in this model each of the preceding examples would tend to increase C by raising C_0.

Two terms associated with the aggregate consumption function are

$$APC_{Y_d} = \frac{C}{Y_d} = \text{Average Propensity to Consume out of Disposable Income}$$

and

$$MPC_{Y_d} = \frac{\Delta C}{\Delta Y_d} \quad \text{Marginal Propensity to Consume out of Disposable Income}$$

The **average propensity to consume** is the share of personal consumption expenditures in disposable income. The **marginal propensity to consume** is the proportion of any increment to disposable income that is used for consumption. Consider the numerical example illustrated in Table 9.1 and Figure 9.1. Assuming that autonomous consumption is 30 ($C_0 = 30$) and the coefficient of disposable income (c) is .9, the aggregate consumption function can be written as

$$C = 30 + .9Y_d$$

If arbitrary values for real disposable personal income are selected and substituted into the consumption function, associated values for real personal consumption expenditures are generated. From these ordered pairs the average and marginal propensities to consume can be derived. For example, if real disposable income were zero in a given period (an unrealistic but useful starting point), real consumption expenditures would be 30, the level of autonomous consumption. If real disposable income were 100, then real consumption expenditures would be 120; that is, $120 = 30 + .9(100)$. If real disposable income rises by another 100, aggregate consumption would again increase by 90. In this example, the overall share of real disposable income used for consumption,

$$APC_{Y_d}$$

declines as income rises, but the proportion of the next dollar of real disposable income going for consumption expenditures,

$$MPC_{Y_d}$$

TABLE 9.1

EXAMPLE OF LINEAR CONSUMPTION AND SAVING FUNCTIONS

Consumption: $C = C_0 + cY_d = 30 + .9Y_d$

Saving: $S = -C_0 + (1 - c)Y_d = -30 + .1Y_d$

Y_d	C	APC_{Y_d}	MPC_{Y_d}	S	APS_{Y_d}	MPS_{Y_d}
0	30	—		−30	—	
100	120	1.20	.9	−20	−.20	.1
200	210	1.05	.9	−10	−.05	.1
300	300	1.00	.9	0	.00	.1
400	390	.975	.9	10	.025	.1
500	480	.96	.9	20	.04	.1
600	570	.95	.9	30	.05	.1
700	660	.943	.9	40	.057	.1
800	750	.9375	.9	50	.0625	.1

$MPC_{Y_d} + MPS_{Y_d} = 1$

i.e., $.9 + .1 = 1$

$APC_{Y_d} + APS_{Y_d} = 1$

FIGURE 9.1

GRAPH OF THE CONSUMPTION AND SAVING FUNCTIONS

The slope of the consumption function is given by the marginal propensity to consume out of disposable personal income (here equal to .9). The slope of the personal saving function is given by the marginal propensity to save out of disposable personal income (here equal to .1).

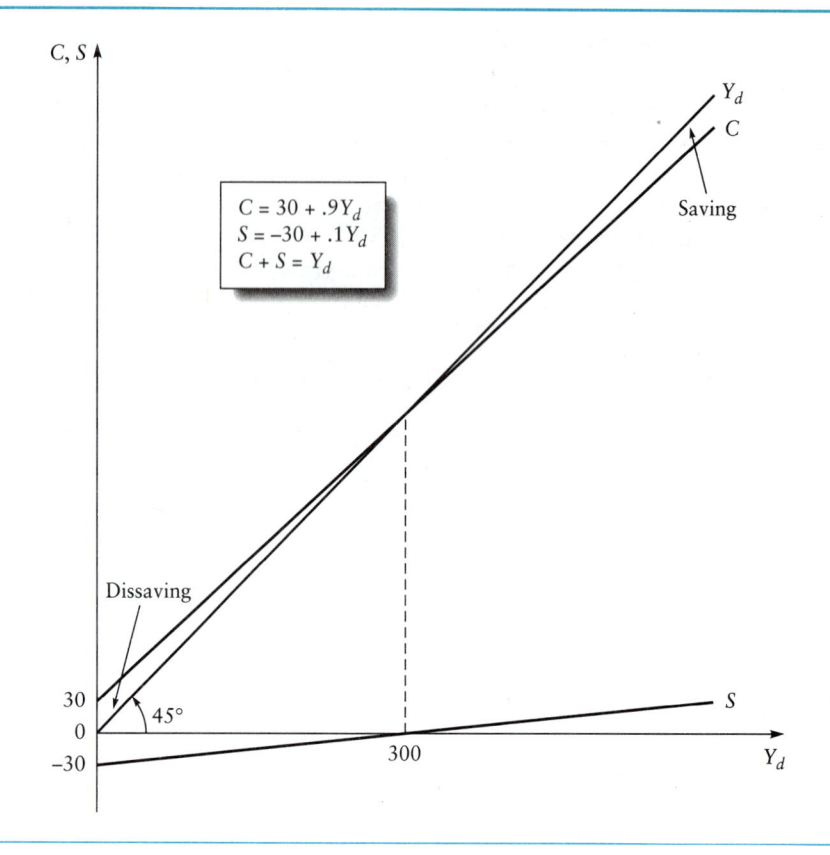

$C = 30 + .9Y_d$
$S = -30 + .1Y_d$
$C + S = Y_d$

---

remains constant at .9. In fact, the marginal propensity to consume out of disposable income is represented by the parameter c, the coefficient of Y_d in the consumption function. Graphically, the marginal propensity to consume is the slope of the consumption function (see Figure 9.1).

Given the linear consumption function, $C = C_0 + cY_d$, it is quick work to derive the personal saving function. Recall that disposable personal income can either be consumed or saved.

$$Y_d = C + S$$

where S = real personal saving. It follows that

$$S = Y_d - C$$

and substituting in the behavioral equation for C yields

$$S = Y_d - C_0 - cY_d$$
$$S = -C_0 + (1 - c)Y_d$$

In Table 9.1 the saving function is represented in the last three columns. The **average propensity to save**,

$$APS_{Y_d}$$

is the share of real disposable personal income that is saved. The **marginal propensity to save** out of disposable personal income,

$$MPS_{Y_d}$$

is the proportion of the next dollar of real disposable income that is saved. Note that the marginal propensity to save is the coefficient of real disposable income in the linear savings function. The sum of the marginal propensities to consume and save out of disposable income equals 1. The same is true for the average propensities. With respect to the preceding numerical example, the saving function is

$$S = -30 + .1Y_d$$

One final point is worth making. Note that aggregate saving is negative over a range of disposable income. Negative saving is called **dissaving.** On an individual basis dissaving occurs regularly. Individual households spend beyond their present incomes by drawing on the savings accumulated in the past or by incurring debt.

Consumption Expenditures

Recall that in this model we have assumed that all taxes are personal income taxes, that there are no government transfer payments, and that disposable personal income is equal to national income less taxes. Real taxes (T), however, are assumed to depend on real national income (Y). Specifically, we assume

$$T = tY$$

where $0 < t < 1$, and t is the given **income tax rate,** that is, the percentage of income that is taxed.

Real disposable personal income can now be written in terms of real national income:

$$Y_d = Y - T = Y - tY = (1 - t)Y$$

That is, real disposable personal income is proportional to real national income. Consequently, real personal consumption expenditures and real personal saving can be written in terms of real national income. For consumption expenditures, substituting in the expression for real disposable income yields

$$C = C_0 + cY_d = C_0 + c(1 - t)Y$$

For personal saving,

$$S = -C_0 + (1 - c)Y_d = -C_0 + (1 - c)(1 - t)Y$$

Investment Expenditures

The next major expenditure component is investment. Recall that Gross Private Domestic Investment in the national income accounts is disaggregated into business fixed investment (*BFI*), residential fixed investment (*RFI*), and the change in business inventories (ΔINV).

For the model constructed here, the following assumptions are made. Based on expected future sales, current profits, and the cost of credit, firms decide at the beginning of the period on the amount they will invest in new plant, equipment, and machinery. We regard these decisions as given, so business fixed investment is modeled as exogenous: $BFI = BFI_0$.

Similarly, we model residential fixed investment as exogenous: $RFI = RFI_0$. Residential construction depends on, among other factors, the cost of credit, the cost of building materials, and demographic factors (marriage rates, birth rates, migration rates, and so on).

With respect to the change in business inventories, ΔINV, we will assume that firms desire to keep a certain level of inventories on hand at all times. The decision on inventories is made at the beginning of the period. The desire by firms for a stable level of inventories is an important behavioral assumption of this Simple Keynesian model.[2] The change in inventories plays a role in the adjustment of the model to disequilibrium situations. The immediate consequence of the assumption of a constant level of inventories is that over the period of analysis, the desired change in inventories is zero. That is, **planned inventory investment**, ΔINV^p, is zero. Consequently, any change in the level of business inventories over the period would be **unplanned inventory investment**, ΔINV^u.

For example, if actual sales fell short of output and expected sales, then unplanned inventories would increase ($\Delta INV^u > 0$). Firms would respond to the unwanted addition to inventories by cutting back on current production. On the other hand, an unexpected surge in sales may initially be met by depleting inventories ($\Delta INV^u < 0$). Under the assumption of desired stability in the level of inventories, firms would respond by increasing the rate of output produced in order to replenish the inventories. In sum, firms maintain the current rate of production only when $\Delta INV^u = 0$.

Bringing together the three components of investment expenditures, the simplifying assumptions of this model mean

$$I = BFI_0 + RFI_0 + \Delta INV$$

where

$$\Delta INV = \Delta INV^p + \Delta INV^u$$

and

$$\Delta INV^p = 0$$

Therefore, desired investment expenditures can be regarded as *exogenous*, and in the notation adopted, autonomous investment expenditures are written as

$$I = I_0.$$

---

[2] It is not necessary to assume that desired or planned inventory investment is zero. All that is required is that, at the beginning of the period, firms set a desired level of inventories that they wish to reach by the end of the period. That is, firms base production on expected sales and planned inventory investment. Planned inventory investment (ΔINV^p) may be positive or negative depending on the difference between the level of inventories desired by the end of the period and the level of inventories that exist at the beginning of the period. If the actual sales of firms differ from expected sales, then the firms will experience unplanned inventory investment ($\Delta INV^u > 0$) or disinvestment ($\Delta INV^u < 0$). The assumption that planned inventory investment is zero is made to simplify the model.

Other Components of Desired Aggregate Expenditures

Real government purchases of goods and services are assumed to be exogenous. Based on prior budget deliberations, purchases by the government are assumed to be set at the beginning of the period: $G = G_0$.

Real exports of goods and services are determined by, among other factors, foreign incomes and foreign tastes and preferences, trade barriers, and the exchange rate. Real exports are assumed to be exogenous in this model: $X = X_0$.

It is important to stress that modeling investment, government purchases, and exports as exogenous does not imply that these components of desired aggregate expenditures are unimportant or never change. Rather, simplifying assumptions are made for these expenditure components for the exposition of a basic model. Once we understand this Simple Keynesian model, we can extend the analysis by relaxing some of these initial assumptions.

The final item in the aggregate expenditure function is M, real imports of goods and services. Part of the expenditures by households on consumption, by firms for investment, and by government will be for foreign goods and services. In other words, there are import components in the C, I, and G expenditures. Even some of the goods exported by a nation may contain imported inputs. To determine desired aggregate expenditures on national output, imports must be netted out of total expenditures.

In this model, we will assume that all induced imports are for personal consumption.[3] Therefore, real imports of goods and services will be written as a linear function of real disposable personal income.

$$M = M_0 + mY_d$$

where $0 < m < 1$, and M_0 refers to **autonomous imports** and mY_d to induced imports. Autonomous imports are affected by domestic tastes and preferences, the exchange rate, and barriers to trade, among other factors. Induced imports, where m is the **marginal propensity to import,** depend positively on the level of real disposable personal income (Y_d). Converting imports into a function of national income yields

$$M = M_0 + mY_d = M_0 + m(1 - t)Y$$

SOLVING THE SIMPLE KEYNESIAN MODEL

Substituting in the behavioral expressions for the components of desired aggregate expenditures (A) gives

$$A = C + I + G + X - M$$
$$A = C_0 + c(1 - t)Y + I_0 + G_0 + X_0 - M_0 - m(1 - t)Y$$

---

[3] In our model, real personal consumption (C) is the only other component of desired aggregate expenditures that is endogenous. Real personal consumption expenditures depend on real disposable personal income. Similarly, writing real imports of goods and services (M) as a function of real disposable personal income seems to be a consistent, if not the only reasonable, approach for this initial exposition of the Simple Keynesian model. Actually, when we turn to the comparative static analysis of the model, there is considerable flexibility. For example, we can evaluate the effect on the equilibrium level of real national income from an increase of $N in real autonomous investment expenditures ($\Delta I_0 = N$), of which $V ($V \leq N$) are for imported capital goods ($\Delta M_0 = V$).

where the subscript of zero indicates an autonomous level of spending. In equilibrium, desired aggregate expenditures (A) must equal the national output produced (Y), so the economy "clears" with no change in inventories. (Recall the assumption that firms desire a stable level of inventories.)

The solution to the Simple Keynesian model involves finding the level of real national output (Y) whereby the real income earned (Y) in producing the output generates an equal amount of desired aggregate expenditures (A).

Rewriting the desired aggregate expenditure function by combining like terms gives

$$A = C_0 + c(1 - t)Y + I_0 + G_0 + X_0 - M_0 - m(1 - t)Y$$
$$A = C_0 + I_0 + G_0 + X_0 - M_0 + (c - m)(1 - t)Y$$

Simplifying, we obtain

$$A = A_0 + aY$$

where

A_0 = desired real autonomous expenditures on national output.
$A_0 = C_0 + I_0 + G_0 + X_0 - M_0$

and

a = marginal propensity to spend on national output
$a = c(1 - t) - m(1 - t) = (c - m)(1 - t)$

That is, desired aggregate expenditures on real national output have an autonomous component (A_0), which is affected by factors exogenous to the model, and an induced component (aY), which is directly related to real national output and income. The coefficient a, the **marginal propensity to spend** on national output, is the slope of the aggregate expenditure schedule. It is reasonable to expect that a would be a positive fraction less than 1. If real national output increases by $1, then induced spending on national output would rise by less than $1. Intuitively, we know that if a $1 increase in national output induces a $1 or more increase in spending on national output, then the production of output would never catch up with the desired spending on output. Given a positive level of real autonomous expenditures, $A_0 > 0$, the model of national income determination would never reach an equilibrium. In particular, the marginal propensity to spend is equal to

$$(c - m)(1 - t)$$

As long as the marginal propensity to consume is greater than the marginal propensity to import, that is, as long as $0 < m < c < 1$, then given an income tax rate of less than 100 percent ($0 < t < 1$), the marginal propensity to spend will be positive and less than 1.

The equilibrium condition for the Simple Keynesian model—that desired aggregate expenditures on national output equal national output, thus unplanned inventory investment equals zero—reduces to

$$A \stackrel{e}{=} Y$$

where $\Delta INV^u = 0$, or

$$A_0 + aY \stackrel{e}{=} Y$$

In short, the model reduces to one equation, the equilibrium condition, in one variable, Y, real national output (real national income). Solving for the equilibrium level of real national output gives

$$A_0 + aY \stackrel{e}{=} Y$$

$$A_0 \stackrel{e}{=} Y - aY$$

$$A_0 \stackrel{e}{=} (1-a)Y$$

$$\bar{Y}_0 = \frac{A_0}{1-a}$$

In sum, the equilibrium real national output and real national income, $\bar{Y}_0$, is a function of the desired real autonomous expenditures on national output, A_0, and the marginal propensity to spend on national output, a.

To make economic sense, the equilibrium level of real national output $\bar{Y}_0$, should be positive. This condition will be met as long as desired real autonomous expenditures on national output are positive and the marginal propensity to spend on national output is a positive fraction less than 1. In Table 9.2 a summary of the Simple Keynesian model is given.

Keynesian Cross Diagram

Graphically we can illustrate the equilibrium of the model. In Figure 9.2 we place A, desired aggregate expenditures on real national output, on the vertical axis, and Y, real national output, on the horizontal axis. We draw a line with

TABLE 9.2
SUMMARY OF SIMPLE KEYNESIAN MODEL

$C = C_0 + cY_d$	Personal consumption expenditures
$I = I_0$	Investment expenditures
$G = G_0$	Government purchases of goods and services
$X = X_0$	Exports of goods and services
$M = M_0 + mY_d$	Imports of goods and services
$T = tY$	Taxes
$Y_d = Y - T$	Disposable income
$A = C + I + G + X - M$	Desired aggregate expenditures on national output
$A \stackrel{e}{=} Y$	Equilibrium condition (where $\Delta INV^u = 0$)
Solution:	
$A = A_0 + aY$	Desired aggregate expenditure schedule
$A_0 + aY \stackrel{e}{=} Y$	Equilibrium condition
$\bar{Y}_0 = A_0/(1-a)$	Equilibrium value for national output (income)
where	
$A_0 = C_0 + I_0 + G_0 + X_0 - M_0$	Desired autonomous expenditures
$a = (c - m)(1 - t)$	Marginal propensity to spend
	$0 < m < c < 1$

FIGURE 9.2

GRAPHICAL SOLUTION TO SIMPLE KEYNESIAN MODEL

Equilibrium in the Simple Keynesian model is found in the Keynesian cross diagram where the desired aggregate expenditure schedule ($A = A_0 + aY$) intersects the 45 degree line from the origin ($A = Y$). The equilibrium is stable. If desired aggregate expenditures exceed national output, or $A(Y'') > Y''$, the run-down in inventories will prompt an increase in national output. If desired aggregate expenditures fall short of national output, or $A(Y') < Y'$, the buildup in inventories will prompt a decrease in national output. In equilibrium, desired aggregate expenditures on national output equal the production of national output, here $A(\bar{Y}_0) = \bar{Y}_0$, and unplanned inventory investment equals zero ($\Delta INV^u = 0$).

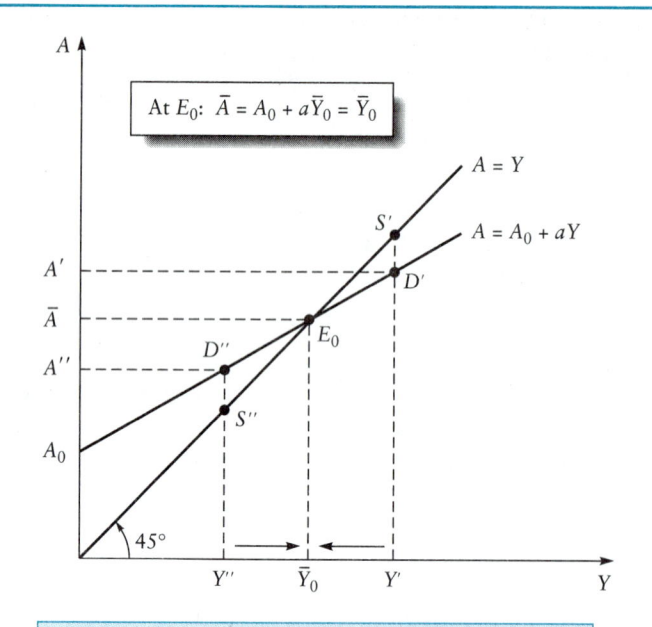

At E_0: $\bar{A} = A_0 + a\bar{Y}_0 = \bar{Y}_0$

A = desired aggregate expenditures on real national output.
Y = real national output (real national income).

---

a slope equal to 1, that is, a line with a 45 degree angle, from the origin. Any point on this *equilibrium line* satisfies the condition that $A = Y$.[4]

The aggregate expenditure schedule can be graphed. The vertical intercept is A_0, where $A_0 > 0$, and the slope of the aggregate expenditure schedule is a, where $0 < a < 1$, so there should be an intersection with the 45 degree line from the origin. (Note: Graphically if $a = 1$ or $a > 1$, there will be no point of intersection.) The intersection will occur at the level of real national output and income (Y) where desired aggregate expenditures equal output. That is, $A(\bar{Y}_0) = A_0 + a\bar{Y}_0 = \bar{Y}_0$ (see point E_0 in Figure 9.2).

Figure 9.2, known as the **Keynesian cross diagram,** also proves useful for illustrating the stability of the model. There are natural tendencies for the macroeconomic system to adjust to disequilibria. Consider a level of real national output that is greater than the equilibrium level of $\bar{Y}_0$. At Y', desired aggregate expenditures on national output equal A' ($A' = A_0 + aY'$), which is less than the national output produced by the amount $S' - D'$. Business inventories would accumulate, since some of the national output produced is not sold—unplanned inventory investment occurs ($\Delta INV^u > 0$). Since a key assumption of the model is that firms desire a constant level of inventories, the unwelcome increase in inventories would prompt firms to cut back on current production. Workers would be laid off, and wage income would decrease. Real

---
[4] The coordinates of any point on a 45 degree line from the origin will be equal. In this example, the value of desired real expenditures (A) will equal the value of real national output (Y).

national output and income would fall back to the equilibrium rate, given by $\bar{Y}_0$, where again $\Delta INV'' = 0$.

On the other hand, if the initial level of real national output were too low, as in Y'', a state of excess aggregate demand (equal to $D'' - S''$) would exist. Desired aggregate expenditures at the level of real national income, A'', would exceed real national output, Y''. Firms would find their sales outpacing current production, and inventories would be drawn on to meet the excess demand ($\Delta INV'' < 0$). The decline in inventories would then induce firms to increase the rate of production in order to restore the initial desired level of inventories. Additional labor would be employed, and wage income would increase. Real national output and income would rise until $\bar{Y}_0$ was reached, where again desired aggregate expenditures would be matched by current production (and $\Delta INV'' = 0$).

It is important to recall the assumption of a constant price level, that is, the economy is assumed to be operating on the Keynesian range of the aggregate supply curve. Therefore, the equilibrating mechanism works not through changes in the price level, but through changes in real output and income triggered by unplanned changes in the level of business inventories. In the following chapters we will extend the model to allow for variation in the aggregate price level. The Simple Keynesian model, the subject of this chapter, is based on income and output adjustments.

Numerical Example for Simple Keynesian Model

Given the following Simple Keynesian model, solve for the equilibrium level of national income.

$$C = 30 + .9Y_d$$
$$I_0 = 80$$
$$G_0 = 120$$
$$X_0 = 50$$
$$M = 10 + .167Y_d$$
$$T = .25Y$$

The first step is to write the desired aggregate expenditure function in terms of real national income. The marginal propensities to consume and save out of disposable personal income are .9 and .1, respectively. The marginal propensity to import out of disposable personal income is .167 (one-sixth, or .1666 rounded off). The income tax rate is .25 (or 25 percent). Thus, real disposable personal income is equal to 75 percent of national income:

$$Y_d = Y - T = Y - .25Y = .75Y$$

Converting the consumption and import functions gives

$$C = 30 + .9Y_d = 30 + .9(.75Y) = 30 + .675Y$$
$$M = 10 + .167Y = 10 + .167(.75Y) = 10 + .125Y$$

The desired aggregate expenditure function becomes

$$A = C + I + G + X - M$$
$$= 30 + .675Y + 80 + 120 + 50 - (10 + .125Y)$$
$$= 270 + .55Y$$

Thus, desired aggregate expenditures on real national output are equal to 270 (e.g., $270 billion) plus 55 percent of the level of real national income. The marginal propensity to spend on national output, a, is equal to .55. Graphically, we can solve the model by plotting the aggregate expenditure schedule and finding the intersection with the equilibrium line ($A = Y$) (see Figure 9.3).

Algebraically, we use the equilibrium condition, setting desired aggregate expenditures equal to national output and solving for Y.

$$A = 270 + .55Y = Y$$
$$270 = .45Y$$
$$\bar{Y}_0 = \frac{270}{.45} = 600$$

With the equilibrium level of real national output and income, the equilibrium levels of the endogenous components of aggregate expenditures can be found. For instance,

$$\bar{Y}_d = .75(600) = 450$$

FIGURE 9.3
GRAPHICAL SOLUTION TO NUMERICAL EXAMPLE OF SIMPLE KEYNESIAN MODEL

The equilibrium level of national output and national income is equal to $\bar{Y}_0 = 600$. At this level of national output, desired aggregate expenditures equal the rate of national output produced, $\bar{A} = A(\bar{Y}_0) = \bar{Y}_0$.

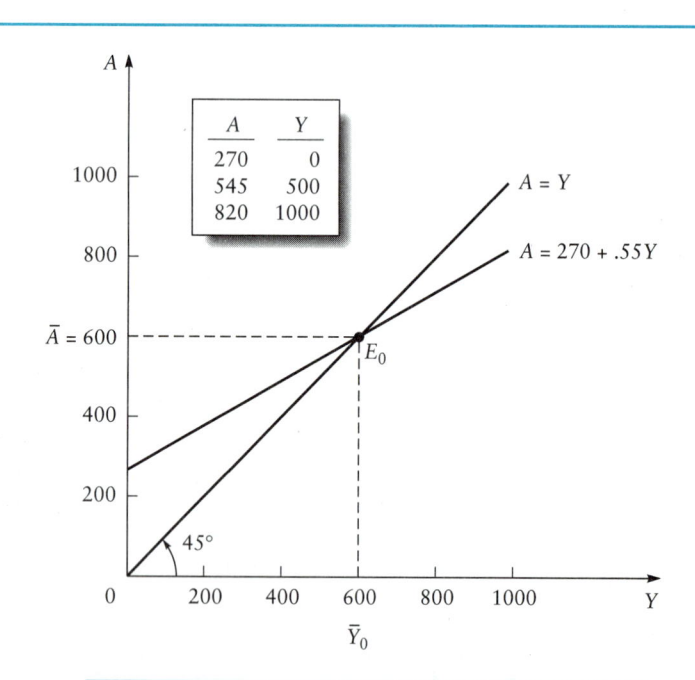

A	Y
270	0
545	500
820	1000

A = desired aggregate expenditures on real national output.
Y = real national output (real national income).

$$\overline{C} = 30 + .9\overline{Y}_d = 30 + .9(450) = 435 = 30 + .675\overline{Y} = 30 + .675(600)$$
$$\overline{M} = 10 + .167\overline{Y}_d = 10 + .167(450) = 85 = 10 + .125\overline{Y} = 10 + .125(600)$$
$$\overline{T} = .25\overline{Y} = .25(600) = 150$$
$$\overline{S} = -30 + .1\overline{Y}_d = -30 + .1(450) = 15 = \overline{Y}_d - \overline{C} = 450 - 435$$

At this point it is a good idea to check the results—in particular, we need to confirm that $A(\overline{Y}_0) = \overline{Y}_0$. Substituting into the aggregate expenditure schedule the equilibrium values gives

$$\overline{A} = \overline{C} + I_0 + G_0 + X_0 - \overline{M}$$
$$= 435 + 80 + 120 + 50 - 85 = 600 = \overline{Y}$$

(It checks.)

Note that in equilibrium, it is not necessary that private investment expenditures (I) equal personal saving (S), or that government purchases (G) equal net taxes (T), or that exports (X) equal imports, (M). In this example,

$I = 80$ and $\overline{S} = 15$ (an excess of private investment equal to 65).

$G = 120$ and $\overline{T} = 150$ (an overall government budget surplus of 30).

$X = 50$ and $\overline{M} = 85$ (a balance-of-trade deficit of 35).

What is required for equilibrium, however, is that the injections into the expenditure stream (from investment, government purchases, and exports) equal the withdrawals from the national expenditure stream (from saving, taxes, and imports). In fact, an alternative equilibrium condition can be derived. From the definition of disposable income, we have

$$Y_d = Y - T = C + S$$

Disposable income is national income less net taxes, and disposable income can either be consumed or saved. It follows that

$$Y = C + S + T$$

National income can be broken down into personal consumption expenditures, personal saving, and taxes. Therefore, we combine the two approaches to national income as follows:

$$C + I + G + X - M = Y = C + S + T$$

Then we subtract consumption expenditures from both sides,

$$I + G + X - M = S + T$$

and add imports of goods and services to both sides,

$$I + G + X = S + T + M$$

which is the *injections equal withdrawals* approach to national income determination. In this numerical example,

$$I + G + X = S + T + M$$
$$80 + 120 + 50 = 15 + 150 + 85$$
$$250 = 250$$

An intuitive illustration of the injections-equal-withdrawals condition might involve a bucket of water. The level of water in the bucket represents the level of real national output (income). Into the bucket one pipe is running with the expenditure flows of investment, government purchases, and exports. Out of the bottom of the bucket is another pipe where leaking occurs from national income in the form of saving, net taxes, and imports. If inflows (injections) are greater than outflows (withdrawals), then the level of water (real national output) will rise. Only when the inflow of injections is matched by the outflow of withdrawals will the water level remain stable.

COMPARATIVE STATICS AND THE MULTIPLIER

As discussed and illustrated in the Keynesian cross diagram, the Simple Keynesian model is stable. Once the equilibrium level of real national output (income) is determined, ceteris paribus, there is no tendency for the rate of national output to be altered. Unplanned inventory investment equals zero. Changes in any of the underlying exogenous variables, however, will upset the equilibrium. The economy will adjust to the disequilibrium and eventually return to a new equilibrium level of national output. We will now investigate the impact on equilibrium national output of changes in desired autonomous expenditures.

Return to the numerical example where

$$C = 30 + .9Y_d = 30 + .675Y$$

$$I_0 = 80$$

$$G_0 = 120$$

$$X_0 = 50$$

$$M = 10 + .167Y_d = 10 + .125Y$$

$$T = .25Y$$

Recall that we found that $A = 270 + .55Y$ and the equilibrium income is $\overline{Y}_0 = 600$. Now suppose the government decides to spend $130 billion instead of $120 billion (perhaps new legislation passes Congress authorizing an additional $10 billion annually for water projects and pollution control). The federal government may elect to increase spending in order to stimulate the economy. The question we want to address with our model is, assuming the entire $10 billion increase in government purchases is for national output, how much will national income increase? By the full $10 billion, by more than $10 billion, or by less?

It is a straightforward process to solve the model again. The new aggregate expenditure schedule is

$$A' = 270 + (10) + .55Y = 280 + .55Y$$

since autonomous expenditures on national output have increased by 10. Setting the new desired aggregate expenditure schedule equal to national output and solving gives

$$A' = 280 + .55Y = Y$$
$$280 = .45Y$$
$$\bar{Y}_1 = 622.2$$

Thus, an increase in government purchases of $10 billion results in an increase in equilibrium national output and income of $22.2 billion.

Now instead of an increase in government purchases of $10 billion, suppose firms decided to step up investment spending by $5 billion. The new autonomous level of investment in the period becomes 85. The new desired aggregate expenditure schedule is

$$A'' = 270 + (5) + .55Y = 275 + .55Y$$

Solving this numerical version of the model yields a new equilibrium level of national output of $611.1 billion. So an increase in autonomous investment of $5 billion generates an increase in equilibrium national output and income of $11.1 billion.

One last example should confirm the relationship. Instead of increased government purchases or investment spending, suppose autonomous imports rise from $10 billion to $30 billion, (perhaps the result of an increase in the value of the U.S. dollar). Then the aggregate expenditure schedule becomes

$$A''' = 270 + (-20) + .55Y = 250 + .55Y$$

Recall that imports are a withdrawal from the national expenditure stream. An increase in autonomous imports, ceteris paribus, reduces spending on national output. Solving this third case gives a new equilibrium level of national income of $555.6 billion. To summarize:

G_0 increases by 10, and $\bar{Y}$ increases by 22.2.

I_0 increases by 5, and $\bar{Y}$ increases by 11.1.

M_0 increases by 20, and $\bar{Y}$ decreases by 44.4.

Generalizing, a $1 billion change in autonomous expenditures on national output has a greater than $1 billion effect on equilibrium national income. In this particular numerical example, a $1 billion increase in real autonomous expenditures results in an increase of $2.22 billion in equilibrium real national income. The additional spending reflects the *multiplier effect*.

The **autonomous expenditure multiplier** is the ratio of the change in equilibrium national income to the initiating change in autonomous expenditures.

$$K_{A_0} = \frac{\Delta \bar{Y}}{\Delta A_0} = \text{Autonomous Expenditure Multiplier}$$

The autonomous expenditure multiplier is greater than 1 in the Simple Keynesian model due to the additional spending that is induced by the change in autonomous expenditures. In this example, the value of the autonomous expenditure multiplier is 2.22.

To develop this concept further, consider the following scenario: U.S. exports rise by $4 million when a German company places an annual order for $4 million worth of computers with a U.S. computer manufacturer. Although desired aggregate expenditures on national output (autonomous exports) therefore increase by $4 million, this is not the final increase in U.S. national output or income. There will be additional rounds of spending on U.S. output generated from the increased sales of $4 million worth of computers.

The first-round effect on real national output is the gain of $4 million. Assume the American computer company initially sells the $4 million worth of computers out of stock, and then steps up the rate of production to replace the loss in inventories. The resulting expansion of production creates $4 million in factor incomes such as wages and profits. Additional labor may be hired or the existing labor works overtime. The computer company may enjoy an increased level of profits. The increase of $4 million in factor incomes then involves the following events:

1. *Income taxes are withdrawn.* In this model, the income tax rate is .25. Thus, tax revenues in the United States rise by $1 million.

$$\Delta T = .25 \Delta Y = .25(4) = 1$$

This means that disposable income increases by $3 million. Given the marginal propensity to consume of .9, personal consumption expenditures will increase by $2.7 billion.

$$\Delta C = .9 \Delta Y_d = .9(3) = 2.7$$

2. *Personal saving increases.* The increase in disposable income not used for consumption will be saved.

$$\Delta S = \Delta Y_d - \Delta C = 3 - 2.7 = .3 = .1 \Delta Y_d = .1(3)$$

3. *Imports of goods and services increase.* Not all of the increase in personal consumption expenditures will be for domestically produced goods and services. With an assumed marginal propensity to import out of disposable income of .167, there will be an induced increase in imports in this second round of $.5 million.

$$\Delta M = .167 \Delta Y_d = .167(3) = .5$$

In all, from the $4 million increase in national income created in round 1 by the sale of computers to the German company, $2.2 million in additional spending on national output is generated in round 2. Induced spending on national output in this second round is equal to the increase in personal consumption expenditures ($2.7 million) net of import purchases ($.5 million). From another perspective, the initial $4 million increase in national income is subject to three leakages, or withdrawals, totaling $1.8 million: the $1 million in income taxes, $.3 million in personal saving, and $.5 million in spending on imports. The remainder of $2.2 million is put back into the U.S. economy as increased spending on domestically produced goods and services. Thus, after two rounds, spending on national output has increased by $6.2 million—the initial $4 million plus an induced $2.2 million.

A similar sequence of events occurs in a third round. The $2.2 million increase in expenditures on national output from the second round will run down inventories in the affected industries, thereby prompting firms to increase production. The increased production generates $2.2 million in additional factor income. With the induced rise in national income of $2.2 million, net tax revenues go up by $.55,

$$\Delta T = .25(2.2) = .55$$

so disposable income rises by $1.65 million,

$$\Delta Y_d = \Delta Y - \Delta T = 2.2 - .55 = 1.65$$

Out of the increase of $1.65 million in disposable income, 90 percent, or $1.485 million, will be used for personal consumption expenditures.

$$\Delta C = .9(1.65) = 1.485$$

Ten percent, or $.165 million, will be withdrawn as personal saving.

$$\Delta S = .1(1.65) = .165$$

Out of the increased consumption expenditures, spending on imports in the third round will increase by $.275 million.

$$\Delta M = .167(1.65) = .275$$

Thus, from the increase of $2.2 million in spending on national output that is passed from the second to the third round in the multiplier process, $1.21 million will be passed on to the fourth round. (The $1.21 million equals the $1.485 million in consumption less the $.275 million on imports.)

So after three rounds of spending, real national output and income have increased by a cumulative amount of $7.41 million ($4 + 2.2 + 1.21). The final increase in real national income will approach $8.88 million, which is the product of the initial increase in autonomous expenditures of $4 million and the autonomous expenditure multiplier of 2.22. Note that after just three rounds, over 80 percent of the ultimate increase in national output has been realized. We should add that the multiplier process may take many months, even years, to be finally exhausted.

One quick multiplication can give the increase in national output and income induced in the fourth round. The increase would be $.6655 million. How did we obtain this amount? The infinite series of increases in expenditure and income can be written as

$$\Delta \bar{Y} = 4 + 2.2 + 1.21 + .6655 + \ldots$$
$$\Delta \bar{Y} = 4 + .55(4) + .55(2.2) + .55(1.21) + \ldots$$

That is, 55 percent of an increase in real national output and income will be passed on as increased spending on national output in the next round. Recall that in this example, the slope of the aggregate expenditure schedule, a, the marginal propensity to spend on national output, is .55. Each time real national output and income increase by $1, nearly half ($.45) will be "lost" to taxes, saving, and imports. The remainder (here $.55) will ripple through the economy, creating additional spending on national output. The amount passed through on each round decreases, so that after a half-dozen rounds only a few cents of every dollar of the initial increase will be left to induce further spending.

It should be emphasized that the exact value of the autonomous expenditure multiplier will vary according to the specification of the macro model. In particular, as will be shown in subsequent chapters, allowing the interest rate and the aggregate price level to change—that is, moving off the Keynesian range of the aggregate supply curve—reduces the size of the autonomous expenditure multiplier. Here, with a linear version of a Simple Keynesian model, a formula for the autonomous expenditure multiplier can be given.[5]

$$K_{A_0} = \frac{1}{1-a} = \frac{1}{1-(c-m)(1-t)}$$

For this particular numerical example,

$$K_{A_0} = \frac{1}{1-.55} = \frac{1}{1-(.9-.167)(1-.25)} = 2.22$$

The multiplier effect can also be shown graphically. Let $\bar{Y}_0$ be the initial equilibrium level of real national income in Figure 9.4. If autonomous expenditures on national output increase by ΔA_0 from A_0 to A'_0, the aggregate expenditure schedule would shift up in a parallel fashion by the amount ΔA_0, which is equal to $E_1 G$. The new level of equilibrium national output would be $\bar{Y}_1$. The equilibrium point moves from E_0 to E_1.

The change in equilibrium output of $\bar{Y}_1 - \bar{Y}_0$ equals the distance $E_0 F$, which in turn is equal to the line segment $E_1 F$ (since $E_0 F E_1$ forms a right triangle with two 45-degree angles). The line segment $E_1 F$ can be broken down into the line segment $E_1 G$ (which is equal to the initial change in autonomous expenditures) and the line segment GF (which is the induced spending brought on by the initial

---

[5] In the simple Keynesian model of national income determination, the change in equilibrium national output and income ($\Delta \bar{Y}$) will be greater than the initiating change in autonomous expenditures on national output, ΔA_0. We can derive the value of the autonomous expenditure multiplier as follows. Let $\Delta A_0 = N$ be the initial change in real autonomous expenditures. The sequence of induced changes in spending on national output can be written as expression

$$\Delta A = \Delta \bar{Y} = N + aN + a(aN) + a[a(aN)] + \ldots$$

(1)
$$\Delta A = \Delta \bar{Y} = N + aN + a^2 N + a^3 N + \ldots$$

That is, on each round of induced spending, the proportion a, the marginal propensity to spend on national output is passed on to the next round. If we multiply both sides of expression (1) by a, we obtain expression (2).

(2)
$$a \Delta \bar{Y} = aN + a^2 N + a^3 N + a^4 N + \ldots$$

Subtracting expression (2) from expression (1), both infinite series, yields

$$\Delta \bar{Y} - a \Delta \bar{Y} = N$$

or

$$\Delta \bar{Y}(1-a) = N$$

Dividing through by $(1-a)$ and replacing N with ΔA_0, we arrive at the expression for the cumulative change in equilibrium real national output.

$$\Delta \bar{Y} = \frac{\Delta A_0}{(1-a)} = K_{A_0} \Delta A_0$$

where

$$K_{A_0} = \frac{1}{(1-a)} = \text{Autonomous Expenditure Multiplier}$$

FIGURE 9.4

Autonomous Expenditure Multiplier

An increase in desired autonomous expenditures on national output ($\Delta A_0 > 0$) shifts the desired aggregate expenditure schedule up in a parallel fashion by the change in autonomous expenditures (represented by the line segment E_1G). The increase in equilibrium national output ($\Delta \bar{Y} = \bar{Y}_1 - \bar{Y}_0$, represented by the line segment E_0F) is a multiple of the increase in autonomous expenditures due to the additional spending on national output (represented by the line segment GF) induced by the increase in autonomous expenditures. (Note: The distance E_0F equals the distance E_1F due to the 45 degree right triangle formed by E_0FE_1.) In moving from the initial equilibrium rate of national output, $\bar{Y}_0$, to the new equilibrium rate of national output, $\bar{Y}_1$, the final change in desired aggregate spending on national output, E_1F, must equal the final change in national output produced, E_0F.

A = desired aggregate expenditures on real national output.
Y = real national output (real national income).

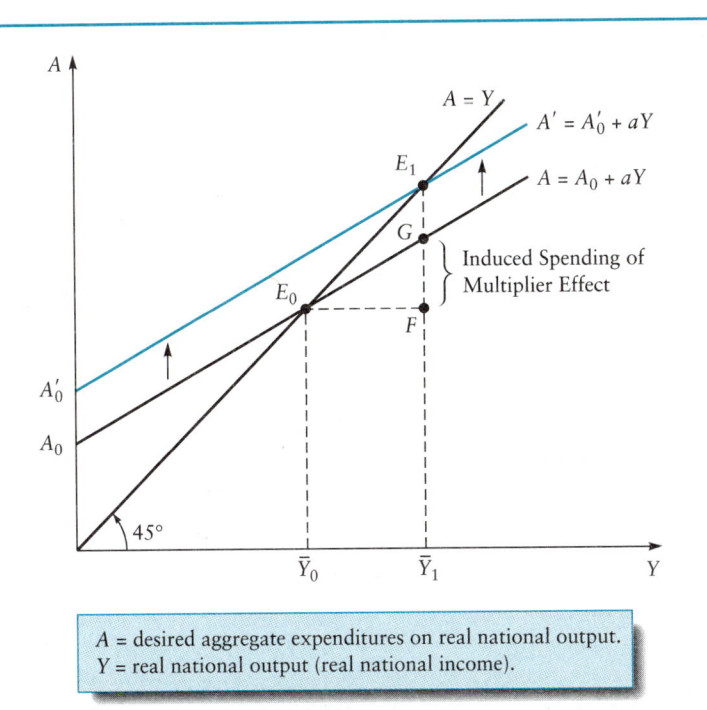

change in autonomous expenditures). Thus, the increase in equilibrium real national output exceeds the change in autonomous expenditures.

CONCLUDING NOTE

In this chapter, as a first exercise in macroeconomic model building, we introduced a Simple Keynesian model of national income determination. Real national output in the Simple Keynesian model is determined solely by aggregate demand. The economy is assumed to be operating on the Keynesian range (that is, the perfectly elastic portion) of the aggregate supply curve—well below full employment). As a consequence, the aggregate price level is assumed to be constant, and changes in aggregate demand induce equal changes in aggregate production. In short, the Simple Keynesian model relies entirely on quantity, or output, adjustments.

In this chapter we also introduced the concept of the autonomous expenditure multiplier. A second expenditure multiplier, the lump-sum tax multiplier, will be discussed in a later chapter on fiscal policy. Knowledge of the multiplier effects is crucial for macroeconomic policy. To reiterate, the estimated value for any multiplier depends upon the condition of the economy and the macroeconomic model specified. The absence of a consensus model among macroeconomists (there are several major schools of thought in macroeconomics) makes for a range of estimated values for each of the multipliers, even when there is agreement on the condition of the economy. The absence of a consensus macroeconomic model also means that different, even conflicting, policy prescriptions may be proposed for the same macroeconomic problem.

In order to extend the analysis to an economy operating beyond the Keynesian range of the aggregate supply curve, that is, an economy on the intermediate range of the aggregate supply curve where aggregate supply constraints must be taken into consideration, we need to develop further the concept of aggregate demand. To do this, we turn to the money market. In the next two chapters we discuss the demand and supply of money. Then in Chapter 12 we integrate the output and money markets with the aggregate demand-aggregate supply framework introduced in Chapter 7. From that point we are able to explore the controversies over the efficacy of macroeconomic policies designed to promote full employment, price stability, and economic growth.

KEY TERMS

autonomous consumption
average propensity to consume
marginal propensity to consume
average propensity to save
marginal propensity to save
dissaving
income tax rate

planned inventory investment
unplanned inventory investment
autonomous imports
marginal propensity to import
marginal propensity to spend
Keynesian cross diagram
autonomous expenditure multiplier

QUESTIONS

1. What are the three most important ideas in this chapter? Discuss why each is important.
2. Using the Simple Keynesian model summarized in Table 9.2 and the Keynesian cross diagram, and assuming an initial equilibrium level of real national output and income ($\bar{Y}_0$), where $A(\bar{Y}_0) = \bar{Y}_0$, discuss and illustrate the adjustment process to a new equilibrium level of real national output ($\bar{Y}_1$) if
    - the marginal propensity to consume out of disposable personal income increases ($\Delta c > 0$).
    - the marginal propensity to import increases ($\Delta m > 0$).
    - the income tax rate increases ($\Delta t > 0$).

    Discuss the effects of each of these changes on
    - the government budget balance ($T - G$).
    - the trade balance ($X - M$).
    - the value of the autonomous expenditure multiplier (K_{A_0}).
3. Given the following Simple Keynesian model

$C = 40 + .75Y_d$	Personal consumption expenditures
$I = 110$	Investment expenditures
$G = 180$	Government purchases of goods and services
$X = 100$	Exports of goods and services
$M = 10 + .25Y_d$	Imports of goods and services
$T = .20Y$	Taxes

$Y_d = Y - T$ Disposable income
$A = C + I + G + X - M$ Desired aggregate expenditures
$A \stackrel{e}{=} Y$ Equilibrium condition

a. Derive the desired aggregate expenditure schedule. What is the marginal propensity to spend on national output?
b. Graph the desired aggregate expenditure schedule by finding and plotting the values for desired aggregate expenditures when real national income equals 0, 500, and 1000. Plot the 45 degree equilibrium line from the origin.
c. Using the Keynesian cross diagram, find the equilibrium level of real national output and income. Why is $Y = 600$ not an equilibrium level of real national output and income? What would be the adjustments if $Y = 600$?
d. Algebraically solve for the equilibrium value of real national income using the equilibrium condition $A = Y$.
e. Calculate the equilibrium values for C (personal consumption), S (personal saving), M (imports) and T (net taxes).
f. Calculate the equilibrium value for the
   1. government budget balance $(T - G)$.
   2. trade balance $(X - M)$.
   3. personal saving–private investment balance $(S - I)$.
g. Confirm the equilibrium solution to the model by checking with the injections-equal-withdrawals condition.
h. Resolving the model, find the effects on equilibrium real national income of
   1. an increase in government purchases of 10, $(G' = 210)$.
   2. an increase in investment expenditures of 20, $(I' = 120)$.
   3. a decrease in autonomous consumption of 20, $(C' = 20 + .75Y_d)$.
i. Calculate directly the value of the autonomous expenditure multiplier, and compare with the results obtained in part "h."

CHAPTER

10

THE DEMAND FOR MONEY

ONE OF THE key markets studied in macroeconomics is the *money market*. Money, clearly, is important for the efficient operation of an economy. In this chapter the economic functions of money and the determinants of the demand for money are discussed. In the next chapter the banking system and the determinants of the supply of money will be examined. We can then develop the linkages between the product and the money markets—linkages that underlie the aggregate demand curve for real national output. In turn, the aggregate demand curve combined with the aggregate supply curve provide the general framework for macroeconomic analysis.

FUNCTIONS OF MONEY

Money serves three primary functions. As a **medium of exchange,** money facilitates the transaction of goods and services. Without a commonly accepted means of payment all exchanges would be reduced to *barter;* with barter there must be a "double coincidence of wants." That is, each of the parties involved in the transaction must have something of value that is acceptable to the other. For example, a dairy farmer who wished to acquire a kitchen table would have to find someone who was (1) willing to trade a kitchen table and (2) willing to accept milk or butter or something the dairy farmer had to offer in exchange. It would be cumbersome for the farmer, while searching for a trading partner, to carry along the goods to be offered in exchange. Even if there were a town market where many goods and services were bartered, it might take quite some time for the farmer to locate an accommodating seller and complete the transaction. In fact, it could be simpler and quicker for the farmer's family to build their own kitchen table, and grow their own vegetables, make their own clothes, and so on. Consequently, under a barter system households tend to be more self-sufficient.

In contrast, if gold coins, for example, were widely accepted as a means of payment, the dairy farmer could sell his milk and butter in the market for gold coins and then use the gold coins to purchase the desired kitchen table—and vegetables and clothes. The use of gold coins, a type of money, encourages *specialization,* which in turn increases labor *productivity.* The dairy farmer spends less time searching for willing partners in exchange and does not have to learn additional skills like table-making. Other individuals with talents and interests in table-making can concentrate on producing kitchen tables, knowing that the gold coins earned can be used to purchase other goods and services. With money as a medium of exchange, labor can specialize, transactions costs are reduced, and output is increased.

To serve as a suitable medium of exchange an asset should be

1. Readily acceptable as a means of payment.
2. Divisible into small units (in order to make change).
3. Easily transportable.
4. Difficult to counterfeit (or illegally reproduce).

Why would bricks fail as a medium of exchange? Why did cigarettes serve as a medium of exchange in prisoner of war camps?

The second function of money is as a **store of value.** Money, like any asset of value, represents a stock of purchasing power or potential command over goods and services. A distinguishing feature of money is its **liquidity,** meaning the ease with which it can be converted into a medium of exchange without a loss in value. A house, car, and gold ring also represent stores of value, but with less liquidity than money. While a house could be quickly converted into money, i.e., sold on very short notice, the greater the urgency, the more likely the house will be sold for less than full value.

The third primary function of money is as a **unit of account.** Money provides a standardized unit of measurement. For instance, in the United States value is measured in dollars and cents. By providing a unit of account, or common denominator, money allows a ready expression of relative values or opportunity costs. If a bushel of wheat costs $2, and a ton of steel costs $70, then 35 bushels of wheat are "worth" one ton of steel; or the *opportunity cost* of a ton of steel is 35 bushels of wheat.

Inflation erodes the store of value function of money. Hyperinflation can even impair the medium of exchange and unit of account functions of money. For example, over the 1980s Bolivia had the highest inflation of the 107 nations reported by the World Bank. For the period 1980–1988, Bolivia's annual rate of inflation averaged 390 percent; Argentina, with an annual average inflation rate of 335 percent, was a close second.[1] The situation at the height of inflation was described in an article in *The Wall Street Journal* as follows:

> Tons of paper money are printed to keep the country of 5.9 million inhabitants going. Planeloads of money arrive twice a week from printers in West Germany and Britain. Purchases of money cost Bolivia more than $20 million last year, making it the third-largest import, after wheat and mining equipment.

---

[1] World Bank, *World Development Report 1991,* Table 1.

The 1,000 peso bill, the most commonly used, costs more to print than it purchases. It buys one bag of tea. To purchase an average size television set with 1,000 peso bills, customers have to haul money weighing more than 68 pounds into the showroom. (The inflation makes use of credit cards impossible here, and the merchants generally don't take checks, either.) To ease the strain, the government in November came out with a new 100,000 peso note, worth $1. But there aren't enough in circulation to satisfy demand.... Food shortages abound, and fights break out as people try to squeeze into line to buy sugar at several times the official price. Some companies have resorted to barter.

The situation has upset all phases of life in Bolivia. Private banks were closed a few days ago because of worries about executive safety. Strikes frequently close the factories. Many shops have closed. Because pesos are practically worthless, dollars now are being demanded for big-ticket purchases. People get their dollars from the 800 or so street-side money vendors who line Avenida Camacho, long La Paz's Wall Street. Banking, in effect, has moved outside.[2]

TYPES OF MONEY

There are several types of money, differing mainly in their physical forms. Precious stones, pearls, gold jewelry, and cigarettes are examples of **commodity money,** which may be demanded for reasons other than as a medium of exchange, store of value, and unit of account. One drawback is that, unless standardized (e.g., gold bars or gold coins instead of gold nuggets), commodity money has limited usefulness as a medium of exchange and unit of account.

Coins or **metallic money** may be viewed, then, as standardized commodity money. The exchange value is clearly denominated on the face of the coin. Coins are also collected as a hobby and investment. Coins, moreover, have intrinsic value equal to the market value of the metals extracted when the coin is melted down.

With rare exception, all coins in circulation—that is, used as a medium of exchange—are **token coins.** With token coins, the face value is greater than the intrinsic value. In the United States silver dimes, quarters, half-dollars, and even silver dollars used to circulate widely. With inflation and increases in the market price of silver, the U.S. Treasury began in the mid-1960s minting *sandwich coins,* with other, less expensive metals in between two layers of silver. All-silver coins disappeared from circulation as individuals hoarded them and used the token coins for transactions. This is an example of *Gresham's Law,* which states that *debased money* (that is, money with lower intrinsic value for a given face value) will drive out of circulation undebased money.

Two recent examples of coins that have lost some of their allure might be noted. Due to a decrease in purchasing power over the years, the penny has become more of an inconvenience than an asset—as described in the following excerpts:

> [I]ndustries complain that pennies actually cost them—and consumers—money. The National Association of Convenience Stores estimated that workers waste 5.5 million hours a year counting pennies. Retailers are also irked by the six-cent bank service charge on each 50-penny roll, fees they say total $15 million annually.

---

[2] Reprinted by permission of the *Wall Street Journal,* © 1985 Dow Jones & Company, Inc. All Rights Reserved Worldwide.

In practice, Americans have little use for the cent: according to one survey, there are nearly 1,000 pennies lying unused in every U.S. household. ... But the public has a sentimental attachment to the cent. A recent Gallup poll found that 62 percent oppose dumping the coin.

That's good news for the zinc industry (pennies are now 97 percent zinc) and the U.S. Treasury. The penny's seigniorage—the difference between the cost of producing a coin and its face value—added $42 million to federal coffers last year. As they say at the mint, a penny made is a penny earned.[3]

The second example is the Susan B. Anthony dollar. First minted in 1979 as a tribute to an early leader of the women's rights campaign and as a durable substitute for the dollar bill, the Susan B. Anthony dollar coin quickly fell out of favor with the American public. Poorly designed, the new coin was too easily mistaken for a quarter. It was shunned by the public, and by the end of the 1980s, 425 million, or roughly half, of the Susan B. Anthony dollars were being held in storage by the federal government.

Fiat money, a type of money with no intrinsic value, is declared by law to be acceptable as a medium of exchange. *Paper currency* is the best example. Take a look at a dollar bill, the smallest denomination of paper currency issued by the *Federal Reserve,* the nation's central bank. At the top of the dollar bill (or *Federal Reserve Note*) is printed, "This note is legal tender for all debts public and private." Today the Federal Reserve Notes outstanding are not backed by or convertible into gold or any other precious metal. The notes are acceptable as a means of payment only because the U.S. government has so decreed. Since they have high value for their weight, especially the larger denominations, they are easily transportable. Coins and smaller denominations are used to make change. Extensive measures are taken to prevent the counterfeiting of the paper currency.

Demand deposits, or *checking accounts,* also qualify as money. These are accounts in banks from which money can be withdrawn "on demand" and funds transferred to designated parties through checks written on the accounts. Given sufficient funds in the accounts, banks promise to honor the checks when presented. (In the next chapter, how checks clear the banking system will be discussed.) Checks can be used as a medium of exchange, although personal identification may be required by the recipients of the checks. Banks usually charge fees for the checks themselves and for servicing the checking accounts, although under some circumstances the fees may be waived.

There are several advantages to paying by check. First, using checks makes it easier to keep track of transactions. Even if one does not make entries in the checkbook when each check is written, the cancelled checks aid in recordkeeping. By using checks for major purchases, you avoid the risk of carrying large amounts of cash, which, if lost or stolen, would be more difficult to recover. Finally, with the innovations in banking over the past 15 years, interest can be earned on some types of checkable deposits. At one time, to have the liquidity provided by money (in a traditional checking account), individuals had to sacrifice interest earnings. By the 1980s, however, new federal regulations

---

[3] "It's Raining Pennies—But Not from Heaven," *Newsweek,* January 7, 1991, 31. Note that in 1960 a first-class stamp cost four pennies. By 1990 it cost 25 cents, or a quarter. The most recent increase in the cost of a first-class stamp to 29 cents may have resurrected the penny—at least until the Postal Service raises the price to 30 cents.

allowed banks to create accounts that paid interest and on which checks could be written. *Automatic Transfer Service (ATS)* and *Negotiable Order of Withdrawal (NOW)* accounts combined liquidity with interest income.

Traveler's checks are a type of money favored by those traveling far from home. Traveler's checks are generally accepted around the world, and if lost or stolen, can usually be replaced on short notice. Purchasers often have to pay a service charge for the convenience and protection afforded by this type of money.

Before we define aggregate measures of the money supply, we should mention that credit cards do not qualify as money, but rather are considered a **money substitute**. That is, credit cards serve only as a temporary medium of exchange. With proper identification typically required, they can be used to make purchases, but they do not serve as a store of value or as an ultimate medium of exchange. Outstanding credit card balances and interest due at the end of the month must be paid with checks or cash—not with additional credit card charges. Nevertheless, to the extent individuals use credit cards to finance transactions, the need to hold large amounts of cash or maintain large balances in checking accounts throughout the month is reduced. Credit card companies usually charge an annual service fee to the holders of the credit cards in addition to relatively high interest rates on unpaid credit card balances.

AGGREGATE MEASURES OF MONEY

The most narrow definition of the *aggregate money supply*, known as **M1**, focuses on the medium of exchange function of money and is composed of currency in circulation (that is, outside the bank vaults), demand deposits, other checkable deposits (such as ATS and NOW accounts), and traveler's checks. In Table 10.1 the components of M1 are given for a selected time period (the month of June 1992).

TABLE 10.1
COMPONENTS OF THE M1 MONEY SUPPLY: JUNE 1992

COMPONENTS OF M1	BILLIONS OF DOLLARS (AVERAGE OF DAILY FIGURES)
CURRENCY IN CIRCULATION	276.2
DEMAND DEPOSITS	311.0
OTHER CHECKABLE DEPOSITS	357.0
TRAVELER'S CHECKS	7.9
TOTAL M1	952.1

NOTE: *Currency in circulation* refers to cash outside the U.S. Treasury, Federal Reserve Banks, and the vaults of depository institutions. *Other checkable deposits* consist of NOW and ATS balances at all depository institutions, credit union share draft balances, and demand deposits at thrift institutions. *Traveler's checks* include only U.S. dollar–denominated traveler's checks of nonbank issuers. Traveler's checks issued by depository institutions are included in *demand deposits*.

SOURCE: *Federal Reserve Bulletin* 78, no. 9 (September 1992): Table 1.21.

A broader measure of money, **M2,** includes less liquid assets that serve as a store of value but cannot (or are not) generally used as a medium of exchange. Included in M2 but not M1 are savings accounts, small time deposits (denominations under $100,000), money market deposit accounts, and money market mutual funds.

Savings accounts are deposits in banks and thrift institutions that pay a higher rate of interest than checkable deposits in return for restrictions on access to the accounts. That is, unlike checking accounts, monies placed in savings accounts may not be legally subject to withdrawal on demand. Advance notice may be required, or there may be a maximum number of withdrawals allowed per time period.[4]

Time deposits of under $100,000 are similar to savings accounts. They pay a higher rate of interest than can be earned on ATS and NOW accounts. Unlike savings accounts, though, they have an explicit maturity date before which withdrawals cannot be made without a substantial penalty. Time deposits cannot be directly used for transactions purposes. **Certificates of deposit (CDs)** are time deposits with minimum denominations. The large CDs (denominations of $100,000 or more) are negotiable and can be sold before the maturity date, but are not included in M2.

Money market deposit accounts (MMDAs), like ATS and NOW accounts, blur the distinction between M2 and M1. MMDAs are offered by banks, require minimum deposits, pay competitive rates of interest, and provide limited check-writing privileges. MMDAs are generally not used for transactions purposes, so are included in the M2 but not in the M1 aggregate.

Money market mutual funds (MMMFs) are issued by investment companies, which pool together investor funds to purchase government securities and large time deposits (minimum denomination of $100,000). While checks can be written on MMMF accounts, there are restrictions, such as a minimum amount for each check written, which effectively limit the medium of exchange function of these accounts.

In Table 10.2 the components of M2 are listed with the average amounts for June 1992. Over the last few years M2 has been roughly four times the level of M1.

One last aggregate measure of the money supply, **M3,** equals M2 plus large time deposits (denominations of $100,000 or more) and other longer-term money instruments. Over the last few years M3 has exceeded M2 by approximately 25 percent. Table 10.3 lists the components of M3 with the average amounts for June 1992.

DETERMINANTS OF MONEY DEMAND

In the following discussion of the determinants of the demand for money, we will adopt the most narrow definition of money, M1, currency in circulation plus checkable deposits. Three primary motives for holding money balances are for transactions, as a precaution, and for speculation. Each will be addressed.

---

[4] In some cases withdrawals may be made on demand; however, interest earnings may be forfeited if the withdrawals occur prior to the end of the month or the quarter.

TABLE 10.2
Components of the M2 Money Supply: June 1992

COMPONENTS OF M2	BILLIONS OF DOLLARS (AVERAGE OF DAILY FIGURES)
M1	952.1
Savings deposits	1127.1
Small time deposits	955.9
Money market mutual funds	353.3
Other	70.4
Total M2	3458.8

NOTE: *Small time deposits* are time deposits with denominations of less than $100,000. Money market deposit accounts are included here. *Money market mutual funds* in M2 refer to general-purpose and broker-dealer money market mutual funds. *Other* components of M2 include overnight repurchase agreements (i.e., overnight secured loans from firms to banks) and overnight Eurodollars (i.e., dollar deposits of U.S. residents at foreign branches of U.S. banks.)
SOURCE: *Federal Reserve Bulletin* 78, no. 9 (September 1992): Table 1.21.

TABLE 10.3
Components of the M3 Money Supply: June 1992

COMPONENTS OF M3	BILLIONS OF DOLLARS (AVERAGE OF DAILY FIGURES)
M2	3458.8
Large time deposits	396.2
Other	303.0
Total M3	4158.0

NOTE: *Large time deposits* are time deposits with minimum denominations of $100,000. *Other* components of M3 include term repurchase agreements and term Eurodollars held by U.S. residents at foreign branches of U.S. banks and institution-only money market mutual funds.
SOURCE: *Federal Reserve Bulletin* 78, no. 9 (September 1992): Table 1.21.

Transactions Demand

The **transactions demand** for money refers to the medium of exchange function. Since an individual household's or firm's expenditures will not exactly coincide with income receipts, *money balances* will be held. An individual receiving income (a check for wages, interest, or dividends) needs to decide in what forms to hold the income. If income is held as money balances, that is, as cash or on deposit in a checking account, liquidity is gained. Funds are readily available for spending. The opportunity cost of this liquidity, however, is the earnings that would have been obtained had the income been invested in stocks or bonds or placed in a savings account.

Individuals determine their desired balance between liquidity and earnings. While the opportunity cost of liquidity has been significantly reduced with innovations in banking like ATS and NOW accounts, it is still the case that any interest received on checkable deposits will be less than the expected return on less liquid assets.

To illustrate the determinants of the transactions demand for money, consider an individual, Paula, who receives a monthly salary of $2500. After taxes are taken out, the take-home pay of the check received at the end of the month is $2000. Assume that Paula's usual expenses during the month total $1500. Further assume that these expenses are incurred at a constant rate of $50 a day for a typical 30-day month. For simplicity, assume that Paula can hold her income as money balances, with no interest paid, or in a savings account paying a 6 percent annual rate of interest (or .5 percent on the average monthly balance in the savings account).

If she runs out of money balances, then it is necessary for Paula to go to the bank and transfer funds from the savings account into cash or the checking account. Assume that the cost of each trip to the bank is $1.50, which includes the gas to drive to the bank, the opportunity cost of Paula's time, and a transfer fee, if any, charged by the bank.

Under these assumptions, how much of the $2000 check received by Paula would be initially held as money balances, and how many trips to the bank during the month (including the initial trip to cash the check) would she make to minimize the cost of managing these money balances?

In Table 10.4, summaries of three options are given. For now we will assume that in each case Paula deposits $500 of the check directly in the savings account as savings, leaving $1500 to cover the expected expenditures over the month.

At one extreme, option A, Paula would make only this one trip to the bank, depositing the $500 in the savings account and holding $1500 as money balances—as cash and in her checking account. The average money balance would be $750. That is, the initial money balance of $1500 is steadily depleted by daily expenditures of $50 by the end of the month to zero. Therefore, the average size of money (M1) balances would be $750, or half of the initial balance of $1500. See Figure 10.1 for an illustration of the relationship between average money balances and the number of trips to the bank. This option would "cost" Paula $3.75 in forgone interest (an average monthly balance of $750 times a monthly interest rate of .5 percent). With the $1.50 cost of one transfer (one trip to the bank) added in, the total cost of managing the money balances is $5.25.

Option B entails a second trip to the bank halfway through the month. On the initial trip only $750 is held as money balances. In addition to the $500 of planned savings, Paula places $750 in the savings account to earn interest for 15 days. On the fifteenth day of the month, she will have exhausted the $750 in money balances (see Figure 10.1b), and so returns to the bank. The $750 placed temporarily in the savings account is shifted to money balances to cover the last half of the month's expenditures. In this option Paula reduces the interest cost of managing the money balances since more funds are earning interest in the savings account—an additional $750 for half of the month. With an average money balance of $375, the forgone interest is reduced to $1.875. The cost of the extra trip to the bank, however, adds to the total cost of managing the funds. Nevertheless, the reduction in interest costs (from $3.75 to $1.875) outweighs the increase in transfer costs ($1.50 to $3.00). Thus, option B, with two trips to the bank, is a lower cost method of managing money balances than option A, with only the initial trip.

More trips to the bank during the month would further decrease the interest cost. Option C involves three trips. On the initial trip to cash the $2000 check, Paula places $500 of planned savings and $1000 in future transactions balances in the savings account. This leaves $500 as money balances to cover

TABLE 10.4
Options for Managing Money Balances

ASSUMPTIONS

1. Individual (Paula) receives a check for $2000 in take-home pay on the last day of the month. Paula has a savings account and a checking account. She also can hold cash.
2. $500 is placed in a savings account as planned savings.
3. $1500 in expected expenditures over the month occur at a constant daily rate of $50 for 30 days.
4. The annual interest rate earned on funds in Paula's savings account is 6 percent (monthly rate of .5%). No interest is earned on funds in the checking account.
5. Each trip to the bank to make a deposit or transfer funds from the savings account to the checking account or cash costs $1.50.

OPTIONS	Interest Cost	Transfer Cost	Total Cost
A. *One trip to the bank:* $1500 kept as money balances to cover monthly expenditures (average money balances = $750).	$3.75	$1.50	$5.25
B. *Two trips to the bank:* $750 kept as money balances to cover expenditures for first half of month, and $750 added temporarily to savings account. Second trip to bank at midpoint of month to transfer $750 from savings account into money balances (average money balances = $375).	$1.875	$3.00	$4.875
C. *Three trips to the bank:* $500 kept as money balances cover expenditures for first third of month, and $1000 added temporarily to savings account. Second trip to bank after 10 days to transfer $500 from savings account into money balances. Third trip to bank after 20 days to transfer $500 from savings account into money balances (average money balances = $250).	$1.25	$4.50	$5.75

expenditures over the first third of the month. After ten days a second trip to the bank to transfer $500 from the savings account to money balances for the middle third of the month is made. Then, after the twentieth day, a third trip to the bank is necessary to withdraw the last $500 of transactions balances from the savings account. With three trips to the bank, the interest cost is the lowest yet. The average money balance is $250 and the total interest cost is $1.25 (.005 times $250). The transfer cost is the highest at $4.50 (three transfers at $1.50 per transfer). Overall at $5.75, option C has the highest cost of managing the money balances.

In this example, the least-cost option involved two trips to the bank. The marginal benefit of a third trip (an interest savings of $.625, that is, $1.875 − $1.25) is less than the marginal cost of a third trip ($1.50). Note that in any case the average money balance held is only a fraction of the income earned. The income earned by Paula for the month is $2500. With two trips to the bank, the average money balance is $375, or 15 percent of income earned.

Ceteris paribus, if the annual interest rate on savings fell from 6 percent to 2 percent (a decline in the monthly interest rate from .5 percent to .167 percent), the least-cost option for managing the money balances would be option A, with just the one trip to the bank. With the fall in the interest rate, the opportunity cost of holding money balances declines. At a monthly interest rate of .167 percent, the forgone interest from holding an average money balance of $750 is $1.25. A second trip to the bank in the middle of the month that reduces the average money balance for the month to $375 lowers the interest cost to $.625, which is not enough to offset the $1.50 transfer cost. Thus, a fall in the rate of interest tends to increase the quantity of money demanded, reflected in higher average money balances for a given nominal income.

The quantity of nominal money balances demanded is positively related to nominal income. As income rises, so do expenditures and the derived demand for money balances. In the preceding example, assuming the same ratios of consumption expenditures to disposable income (.75 = 1500/2000) and disposable income to personal income (.80 = 2000/2500), and for an annual interest rate of 6 percent on savings, an increase in monthly personal income from $2500 to $2750 would increase the optimal average money balances from $375 to $412.50. That is, even though the rise in income and average money balances held increases the possible interest earnings, two trips to the bank are still the least-cost option. With one, two, and three trips to the bank, the total costs of managing the money balances are $5.625, $5.0625, and $5.875, respectively.

While we cast the illustration of the transactions demand for money in terms of an individual, it is important to note that firms also need to manage their cash

FIGURE 10.1

AVERAGE MONEY BALANCES GRAPHED FOR THREE OPTIONS

In panel (a), with only the one trip to the bank, the initial money balances of $1500 are continuously depleted by expenditures over the month. In panel (b), the $750 that is initially held as money balances is depleted by the midpoint of the month (15 days). Paula then returns to the bank to transfer $750 from the savings account into money balances to cover the expenditures over the last half of the month. In panel (c), the $500 that is initially held as money balances is depleted after a third of the month (10 days). Paula returns to the bank twice, each time shifting $500 from the savings account into money balances to cover expenditures for a 10-day period.

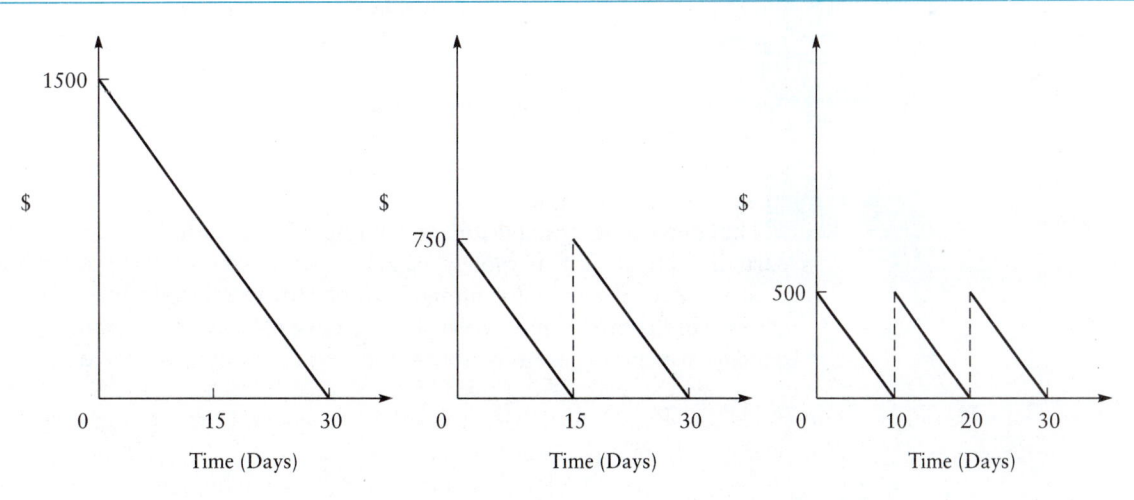

(a) One Trip to the Bank (average money balances = $750)

(b) Two Trips to the Bank (average money balances = $375)

(c) Three Trips to the Bank (average money balances = $250)

Assumptions: $1500 in planned expenditures over the 30-day month. Expenditures occur at a constant daily rate of $50.

balances. Whether dealing with thousands or millions of dollars in receipts and expenditures each week, firms clearly have an incentive to manage their money balances carefully.

Precautionary Demand

Up to now we have assumed that the individual's expenditures over the month were all expected and occurred at a constant daily rate. Unexpected expenditures also arise, however, such as car repairs, which may require immediate payment. Therefore, in addition to the transactions demand for money to cover the expected expenditures, there is a **precautionary demand** for money to cover unforeseen expenditures. Note that the use of credit cards will reduce both the transactions and precautionary demands for money.

Suppose that in our initial example Paula keeps an extra 10 percent of anticipated transactions balances on hand as precautionary money balances. With 6 percent annual interest on savings, two trips to the bank are still optimal. The extra cost of the average precautionary balances of $75 ($.375 in forgone interest) may be worth the peace of mind of a "rainy day fund."

Speculative Demand

A third motive for holding money balances is based on the theory of *portfolio management* and a desire to speculate. A **portfolio** consists of an arrangement of assets. Investors, be they households with savings, firms with retained earnings, or managers of pension funds, usually seek balanced portfolios with assets whose market values and returns tend to move in opposite directions—for example, common stocks and Treasury bonds, or gold and money market mutual funds. By *diversifying* their wealth in this manner, investors reduce their vulnerability to adverse movements in the value of any one asset. More simply put is the adage, "Don't put all your eggs in one basket." Goals of investors include *capital gains* (realized increases in the market value of assets), steady income flows (for example, interest and dividends), and safety (that is, a store of value).

The **speculative demand** for money refers to the desire of investors to keep part of their wealth as money balances—in excess of the transactions and precautionary demands for money—to be able to take advantage of expected changes in the market prices of assets. To develop the concept of the speculative demand for money, we turn to the topic of portfolio management.

PORTFOLIO MANAGEMENT

As discussed earlier, liquidity is gained with money balances; and some checkable deposits like ATS and NOW accounts combine interest with liquidity. Savings accounts and time deposits are less liquid than money balances but pay higher interest. Other financial assets like stocks and bonds have the potential for even greater returns than savings accounts and time deposits but are riskier.

Real assets such as property, gold, art, antiques, rare coins, and baseball card collections may directly provide pleasure as well as make up part of an investor's *portfolio*.

To elaborate, acquiring a savings account or time deposit is less risky than purchasing stocks, bonds, or other assets whose market values fluctuate. The initial and subsequent deposits in a savings account (the *principal*) can always be recovered—even if the bank fails, since in the United States bank deposits up to $100,000 are protected by federal insurance. Moreover, while inflation may erode the store of value sought in savings accounts, the owners of such accounts know in advance the interest rate to be earned. Money market deposit accounts and money market mutual funds can also be counted on to return the sums invested; however, the yields on these assets vary with market interest rates.

Stocks and bonds are purchased not only for the income flows of dividends and interest, but for speculative gains. Speculators live by the maxim, "Buy low and sell high." Speculators in stocks try to time their purchases for when the market prices are low—with the anticipation that the stocks will appreciate in value over time. If they are correct, a future rise in the market price of the stock will allow the sale of the stock for a *capital gain*. Speculators who guess wrong and purchase stock at a relatively high price suffer a *capital loss*: a *realized loss* if the stock is sold for a lower price, or a *paper loss* in the value of the stock portfolio when the stock is kept. The market value of a stock depends largely on the market's perception of the present strength and growth potential of the issuing company. Since speculators differ in their expectations for stocks, active trading of stocks occur.

A **bond** is a promise to repay a certain sum of money (the face value of the bond) with interest at a specified date in the future (the maturity date). Its market value is inversely related to the level of interest rates. Suppose you could purchase a bond with a face value of $1000 that is redeemable in one year. The holder of this bond (let's call it bond A), also receives $100 in interest in one year. If the market rate of interest is 10 percent when the bond is issued, the market price of the bond would be $1000 and the rate of interest on the bond would be 10 percent (.10 = 100/1000).

If halfway through the year the interest rate offered on a new series of similar one-year bonds (call them B bonds), also equals 10 percent, the market value of bond A would be $1047.62. That is, bond A would pay $1100 in six months, and at the current annual interest rate of 10 percent (or 5 percent for half a year) $1047.62 would increase to $1100. ($1047.62)(1.05) = $1100.

If instead, interest rates rose, and halfway through the year the newly issued bond B offered an annual interest rate of 11 percent (or $1110 at maturity), then the market value of bond A with an annualized yield of 10 percent would fall to $1042.65. That is, it would take only $1042.65 earning interest at 5.5 percent for half a year to yield $1100. Thus, when market interest rates rise, the present values or market prices of existing bonds with fixed interest payments fall.

On the other hand, if interest rates decline, and halfway through the year the newly issued bond B offers an annual interest rate of 9 percent (or a yield of $90 above the face value of $1000), then the market value of bond A (with an annualized yield of 10 percent) would rise to $1052.63. ($1052.63)(1.045) = $1100. So when market interest rates fall, the market prices or present values of existing bonds with fixed interest payments rise.

The formula for the market price of a bond with a one-year maturity and interest received at maturity along with the face value of the bond is

$$P_b = \frac{FV + INT}{1 + (d)(i)}$$

where

P_b = market price (present value) of the bond.
FV = face value of the bond (received when the bond matures).
INT = interest payment on the bond (received when the bond matures).
i = current annual market rate of interest on newly issued comparable bonds (i.e., same risk of default and term to maturity).
d = fraction of the year left before the bond matures.

Recall the example of bond A purchased for the face value of $1000 and paying $1100 in one year. If the market rates of interest six months after the bond was purchased were 9 percent, 10 percent, or 11 percent, the market prices of bond A would then be $1052.63, $1047.62, or $1042.65, respectively.

$$i = .09: P_b = \frac{1000 + 100}{1 + .5(.09)} = 1052.63$$

$$i = .10: P_b = \frac{1000 + 100}{1 + .5(.10)} = 1047.62$$

$$i = .11: P_b = \frac{1000 + 100}{1 + .5(.11)} = 1042.65$$

Note that as the bond approaches maturity (d nears zero), the market price approaches the final cash value of the bond (the sum of the face value and interest payment). For bonds with longer than one-year maturity or more than simple annual compounding of interest, the formula for the market price or present value of the bond is more complicated. Nevertheless, the basic relationship holds. The price of bonds is inversely related to the market rate of interest.

In particular, if an investor expects interest rates to rise, then speculative money balances may be held in anticipation of the fall in bond prices. Thus, an actual rise in interest rates would be associated with a reduction in the level of speculative balances held as investors shift their portfolios to bonds. Conversely, when interest rates fall, the market prices of existing bonds rise. Investors who expect that bond prices will rise no further may then sell their bonds (hopefully for capital gains) and replenish their speculative balances. An additional reason for the inverse relationship between the interest rate and the quantity demanded of money has been established. Speculative balances allow investors to reallocate their portfolios of assets quickly as financial conditions change.

Investors may opt to keep their speculative balances in money market deposit accounts and money market mutual funds rather than in ATS and NOW accounts. If so, the sensitivity of the demand for narrowly defined money balances (M1) to the interest rate will be reduced. The basic point, however, remains the same. A *diversified portfolio* can balance liquidity, income flows, the potential for capital gains, and risk. Consequently, there may be a demand for money balances (M1) in excess of the transactions and precautionary demands.

LIQUIDITY PREFERENCE

Liquidity preference refers to the desire to hold wealth in the most liquid form, as money balances. In the aggregate, the quantity demanded of nominal money balances, M1, is positively related to real national income and the aggregate price level, and negatively related to the interest rate.

$$M^d = M^d(\overset{+}{Y}, \overset{+}{P}, \overset{-}{i})$$

where

M^d = aggregate quantity of money balances demanded.
Y = real national income.
P = aggregate price level.
i = nominal interest rate.

Increases in real income allow individual households and firms to purchase more goods and services. Increases in the aggregate price level or inflation reduce the purchasing power of money by raising the cost of a given market basket of goods and services. Both real income gains and higher prices increase the transactions and precautionary demands for money. Increases in interest rates raise the opportunity cost of holding money balances. Higher interest rates also reduce the market prices of bonds, which can stimulate speculative bond purchases. For both reasons, an increase in interest rates reduces the quantity of money demanded.

The **liquidity preference schedule** relates the quantity of nominal money balances demanded to the interest rate. Illustrated in Figure 10.2, the money

FIGURE 10.2

LIQUIDITY PREFERENCE SCHEDULE

The liquidity preference schedule (money demand curve) is drawn holding constant real national income (Y) and the aggregate price level (P), among other factors.

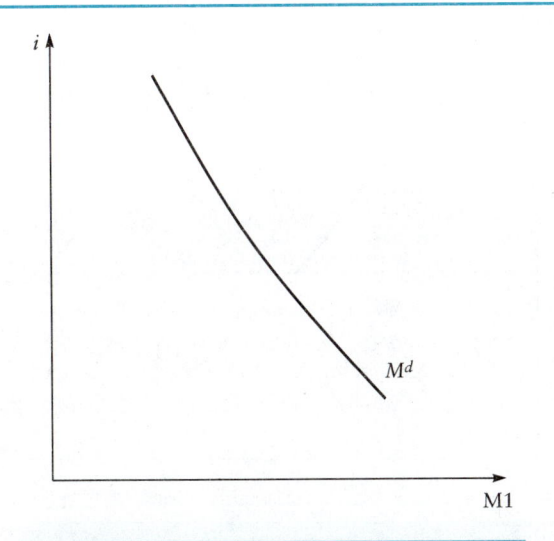

M1 = currency in circulation and checkable deposits.
M^d = demand for nominal money balances.
i = nominal interest rate.

demand curve representing the liquidity preference schedule is downward-sloping. The money demand curve is drawn holding constant, among other factors, real national income and the aggregate price level. Increases in the nominal demand for money, indicated by rightward shifts in the money demand curve, could be caused by increases in real national income or higher prices (see the shift from M^d to $M^{d'}$ in Figure 10.3). Recession and deflation would cause a decrease in the demand for money balances and leftward shifts in the money demand curve.

Increases in the quantity of nominal money balances demanded are indicated by movements down the money demand curve in response to declines in the interest rate (see the movement from A to B along the money demand curve M^d in Figure 10.3). In addition, increases in the quantity of nominal money balances demanded may reflect—holding the nominal interest rate constant—a rightward movement between two money demand curves in response to an increase in the demand for money (see the movement from A to A' in response to an increase in the demand for money from M^d to $M^{d'}$).

Innovations in banking and changes in payments habits may also cause shifts in money demand. For example, the introduction of ATS and NOW accounts, which combine liquidity (through check-writing) with interest earnings and count as M1 balances, would increase the demand for M1 money balances, ceteris paribus. Money market deposit accounts and money market mutual funds, which pay higher interest and offer limited check-writing privileges, and which count as M2 but not M1, would likely reduce the demand for M1 money balances. Greater use of credit cards may also reduce the demand for money balances, since many transactions can be bundled together with one payment

FIGURE 10.3

INCREASES IN DEMAND FOR MONEY VERSUS INCREASES IN QUANTITY OF MONEY DEMANDED

The shift in the money demand curve from M^d to $M^{d'}$ indicates an increase in the demand for money. The movement from A to B (or A' to B') indicates an increase in the quantity of money demanded due to a decrease in the nominal interest rate. The movement from A to A' (or B to B') indicates an increase in the quantity of money demanded due to an increase in the demand for money.

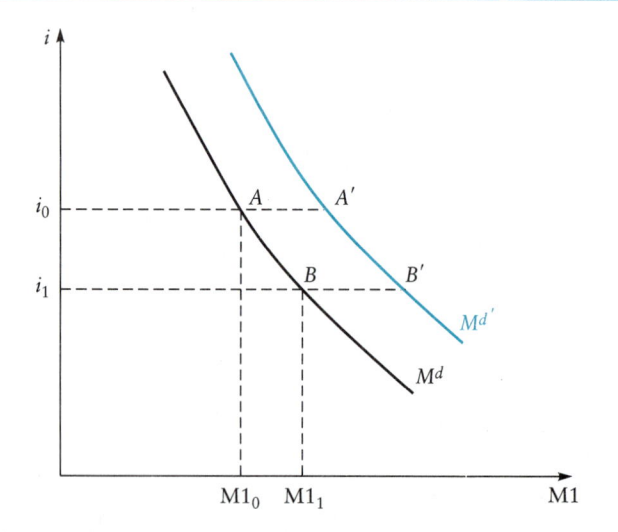

M1 = currency in circulation and checkable deposits.
M^d = demand for nominal money balances before increase.
$M^{d'}$ = demand for nominal money balances after increase.
i = nominal interest rate.

CHAPTER 10 THE DEMAND FOR MONEY

made at the end of the month, rather than individual payments made as the transactions occur over the month.

CONCLUDING NOTE

On the micro level, individuals, when arranging their assets, seek a desired balance among several objectives: liquidity, store of value, income generation, risk minimization. An important component in portfolio management is the determination of the quantity of money balances to hold.

On the macro level, the aggregate demand for money is an important component of the economy. The demand for and supply of money jointly determine the market rate of interest, which in turn affects desired aggregate expenditures on national output.

In the next chapter the banking system, the determinants of the money supply, and equilibrium in the money market will be analyzed. As will be shown in later chapters, the interest sensitivity of the demand for money is a key factor in the relative effectiveness of fiscal and monetary policies.

KEY TERMS

medium of exchange
store of value
liquidity
unit of account
commodity money
coins or metallic money
token coins
fiat money
demand deposits
traveler's checks
money substitute
M1
M2
savings accounts
time deposits
certificates of deposit
money market deposit accounts
money market mutual funds
M3
transactions demand
precautionary demand
portfolio
speculative demand
bond
liquidity preference
liquidity preference schedule

QUESTIONS

1. What are the three most important ideas in this chapter? Discuss why each is important.
2. From the information given below, determine the levels of the aggregate measures of the money supply, M1 and M2. (Figures are in billions of dollars.)

167.8	Currency in circulation
266.8	Demand deposits
437.0	Large time deposits ($100,000 minimum denomination)
513.0	Money market deposit accounts

177.2	Money market mutual funds
179.6	Other checkable deposits
301.2	Savings deposits
884.0	Small time deposits
5.9	Traveler's checks

3. Assume that Alan receives a check for $3000 in take-home pay (that is, after taxes) on the last day of each month. He has a savings account that pays an annual interest rate of 9 percent (or .75 percent on the average balance per month). Alan can hold his money balances either as cash or in a checking account that does not pay interest. He places $300 of his take-home pay in the savings account each month as planned saving, and expects to have expenditures of $2700 over the 30-day period at a constant rate of $90 per day. Assume that every trip Alan makes to the bank (whether to make a deposit or to transfer funds from the savings account to money balances) costs him $2.

Determine the optimal number of trips Alan would make to the bank (including the first trip with the check for $3000) in order to minimize the cost of managing his balances. Determine the minimum cost and the average money balance.

Discuss the consequences of the following changes on Alan's demand for money balances. Then determine the new optimal number of trips to the bank, the minimum cost, and the average money balance.

   a. Alan's take-home pay is increased to $3300 a month (after taxes) and his planned expenditures increase to $2970 a month at a constant daily rate of $99.

   b. Alan switches from a checking account that pays no interest to a checkable deposit (a NOW account) that pays an annual interest rate of 6 percent (or .5 percent on the average monthly balance). Assume that this checkable deposit has no required minimum balance or other service charges and that Alan writes checks for all the transactions he makes during the month. In practice, why might Alan still want to hold some cash that pays no interest?

   c. Alan acquires a credit card, which he uses to pay for $2100 of his $2700 of monthly expenditures by writing one check at the end of the month to the credit card company. His daily expenditures needing to be covered by money balances shrink to $20. Note: Alan would need to make a trip to the bank on the last day of the month to shift $2100 from his savings account to his checking account to cover the payment to the credit card company.

From the examples in these questions, what do you conclude about the determinants of the demand for money? What simplifying assumptions were made in these examples? Why would more realistic examples add to the complexity of determining the optimal number of trips to the bank and the average money balances?

4. Given a bond with a one-year maturity and a face value of $10,000, which pays $800 (or 8 percent interest) to the holder of the bond at maturity, what is the market price of the bond if the market rate of interest is also 8 percent? 7 percent? 9 percent?

   a. What is the market price of the bond if nine months before maturity the interest rate offered on a new series of similar bonds is 8 percent? 7 percent? 9 percent?

   b. What is the market price of the bond if three months before maturity the interest rate offered on a new series of similar bonds is 8 percent? 7 percent? 9 percent?

5. An innovation in banking that may revolutionize payment practices is *electronic funds transfer (EFT)*. Instead of using cash or checks as a medium of exchange and making trips to the bank to deposit and withdraw money balances, funds can be transferred immediately to designated accounts through a computer network linking banks and businesses. For example, employees may have their paychecks deposited directly into their bank accounts, and firms can gain immediate access to the receipts from their sales (as funds are transferred at the time of each sale from the purchaser's account to the seller's account).

   Discuss the advantages of EFT for households and firms. Why might households still prefer to use credit cards for major purchases? What is the likely impact of EFT on the demand for M1 money balances? Why?

CHAPTER

11

THE BANKING SYSTEM AND THE MONEY SUPPLY

BANKING AND THRIFT institutions in the United States experienced rapid change with the financial deregulation of the 1980s. The phasing out of interest rate ceilings increased the competition for deposits. The development of instruments such as NOW accounts and money market deposit accounts, while offering new options to depositors, blurred the distinction between M1 and M2, making it more difficult to supervise the depository institutions and regulate the money supply. Some of the more aggressive banks even began to expand across state lines through mergers and acquisitions of other banks.

Yet, despite the longest peacetime expansion in the U.S. economy (from 1983 into 1990), many banks and thrifts failed. Mismanagement, misfortune, lax regulatory oversight, and in some cases, fraud combined to produce the *savings and loan crisis*. The problem, however, was not confined to the thrift institutions.

> [T]he 1980s also generated the greatest number of commercial bank failures since the Great Depression. More than 200 banks failed each year from 1987 to 1989, and the annual average failure rate for the decade was almost nine times the average annual level between 1934 and 1979.[1]

Regionally, tough times in the farm belt in the mid-1980s contributed to an increase in delinquent loans and farm foreclosures. In the Southwest, the collapse of oil prices depressed the local and state economies (particularly in Texas), and, combined with a general overexpansion in commercial real estate development (for example, underutilized malls and office buildings), left many banks with *nonperforming assets,* that is, assets that were no longer generating

---

[1] These statistics are from Lynn Seballos and James Thomson, "Underlying Causes of Commercial Bank Failures in the 1980s," *Economic Commentary,* Federal Reserve Bank of Cleveland, September 1, 1990.

income. Internationally, the debt crisis of developing nations and the inability of some of the larger debtor nations (such as Mexico, Brazil, and Poland) to make scheduled loan repayments reduced the value of these assets for the involved commercial banks.

Moreover, as noted, the phasing out of interest rate ceilings on deposits increased the competition for funds. Thrifts locked into long-term mortgages issued earlier at relatively low fixed rates of interest found their profit margins squeezed by the higher rates required to retain and attract deposits. The probabilities and the ultimate magnitudes of failure increased when some banks and thrifts, relying on federal deposit insurance to safeguard the interests of their depositors, assumed greater risks in order to pursue higher-yielding loans. As a significant portion of these loans fell into default, the vulnerable banks and thrifts were hurt—some irreparably so. The ultimate cost to taxpayers of bailing out the failed depository institutions has been estimated to run in the hundreds of billions of dollars.

Sorting out the causes and assessing the consequences of the financial crisis that emerged in the United States during the 1980s, however, is not the intent of this chapter. Rather, in this chapter we will discuss the role of the Federal Reserve and the operation of the banking system in setting the nation's money supply. The supply and the demand for money jointly determine the equilibrium level of interest rates. Changes in the money market that result in changes in interest rates affect the real sector of the economy, with consequences for economic growth, inflation, and unemployment.

FEDERAL RESERVE SYSTEM

The **Federal Reserve System** (or the *Fed* as it is popularly called) was established in 1913 as the nation's central bank in order to consolidate control over the banking system. It is responsible for supervising and regulating the nation's depository institutions—primarily the commercial banks. Through its influence over the money supply, the Fed is also charged with implementing monetary policy consistent with the goals of full employment, price stability, and economic growth. Its other roles include providing the paper money (Federal Reserve Notes) for the U.S. economy, serving as bankers for the federal government, and promoting a stable foreign exchange value for the U.S. dollar.

At the top of the Federal Reserve System is the seven-member Board of Governors, headquartered in Washington, D.C. The members of the board are appointed by the president of the United States and confirmed by the Senate for terms of 14 years. Every two years one term expires. The president appoints one governor to serve as chair for a four-year term, with reappointment possible. Often the president must serve with a Federal Reserve Board chair appointed by his predecessor. For instance, Ronald Reagan "inherited" Chairman Paul Volcker from President Carter. President Reagan reappointed Volcker for a second term and then later selected Alan Greenspan to be the next chairman. Greenspan was in office when George Bush was elected in 1988. President Bush reappointed Greenspan to a second term.

The Federal Reserve System is set up with twelve district Federal Reserve Banks corresponding to regions of the nation. The district banks are located in Boston, New York City, Philadelphia, Cleveland, Richmond, Atlanta, Chicago,

St. Louis, Minneapolis, Kansas City, Dallas, and San Francisco. In addition, there are twenty-five branch Federal Reserve Banks. For example, in the Cleveland district, branch banks are in Cincinnati and Pittsburgh. The twelve Federal Reserve Banks supervise the other banks in their districts and operate as bankers to the member commercial banks—holding deposits, making loans, and serving as a clearinghouse for checks.

The **Federal Open Market Committee** (FOMC), composed of the seven members of the Board of Governors and the twelve presidents of the Federal Reserve Banks, meets every six weeks to review economic conditions and chart the nation's monetary policy. At any one time, however, there are only twelve voting members of the FOMC: the seven governors, the president of the New York Federal Reserve Bank, and the presidents of four other Federal Reserve Banks selected on a rotating basis. The president of the New York Fed is always on the FOMC since New York City is the nation's financial center. The Fed's open market operations (to be discussed in this chapter) are carried out through the New York branch.

COMMERCIAL BANKS

While there are differences between commercial banks, savings and loan associations, mutual savings banks, and credit unions, there is also considerable overlap in the function of these depository institutions. Consequently, we will restrict our discussion to *commercial banks,* the so-called "full-service" banks.[2]

Commercial banks are privately owned, profit-seeking institutions. Until recently, commercial banks were restricted to operating in single states. Interstate banking, however, is becoming more prevalent. Like all depository institutions, commercial banks serve as financial intermediaries, channeling the supply of loanable funds to the demanders of credit. Banks accept deposits and provide safekeeping services for monies (in checking accounts and savings accounts) and valuables (in safe deposit boxes). Moreover, in the case of checking accounts, banks agree to transfer funds to parties designated on the checks, thus facilitating the medium of exchange function of money.

Banks charge directly for some of the services provided. There are user fees for safe deposit boxes and checks, consultant fees for the management of trust funds, and commissions on foreign exchange transactions. Banks primarily earn income by investing a portion of the deposits placed on account. They purchase

---

[2] In the United States at the end of 1989 there were slightly over 12,700 insured commercial banks with cumulative assets of $3.3 trillion. Commercial banks range in size from the very small (total assets of under $5 million) to the very large (total assets of over $500 million). There were also nearly 3400 savings institutions, with cumulative assets of $1.5 trillion, and roughly 13,400 credit unions, with cumulative assets of $184 billion (*Statistical Abstract of the United States 1991* (Washington, DC: U.S. Government Printing Office, 1992, Table 802).

Commercial banks may be chartered by the federal government, in which case they are *national banks,* or by state governments. National banks by law must be members of the Federal Reserve System. Commercial banks chartered by state government may apply for membership in the Federal Reserve System. Member banks are required to purchase stock in the Federal Reserve Bank in their district. All commercial banks (whether members of the Federal Reserve System or not), savings and loan associations, savings banks, and credit unions fall under the jurisdiction of the Federal Reserve Board.

ASSETS		LIABILITIES	
Reserves	203.0	Checkable Deposits	665.7
U.S. Government Securities	586.8	Savings Deposits	704.1
Other Securities	158.0	Time Deposits	969.9
Loans	2237.6	Other Liabilities	807.9
Other Assets	317.3	Capital Account	355.1
Total Assets	3502.7	Total Liabilites	3502.7

NOTE: Figures are in billions of dollars.

SOURCE: *Federal Reserve Bulletin* 78, no. 9 (September 1992), Table 1.25.

FIGURE 11.1

SIMPLIFIED VERSION OF CONSOLIDATED BALANCE SHEET—ALL COMMERCIAL BANKS: JUNE 24, 1992

government securities and make loans to households and firms. Then they earn profits on the differences between the higher yields on these assets and the interest rates paid depositors (on savings accounts, time deposits, and checkable deposits like ATS and NOW accounts). If bank revenues (net of capital losses on asset holdings and write-offs of bad loans) exceed the costs incurred in operating the bank, then profits are earned. If bank expenses exceed the net income earned, the bank suffers an overall loss.

To understand better the operations of commercial banks, study the consolidated balance sheet shown in Figure 11.1. Consistent with accounting practices, there are two sides to the balance sheet: assets and liabilities. In general, *assets* are items of value and *liabilities* are financial obligations.

Liabilities

Banks hold deposits of all types, including demand deposits or simple checking accounts that pay no interest, NOW accounts that combine liquidity with modest interest rates, money market deposit accounts with market-determined rates of interest and limited check-writing privileges, and time deposits with specific maturities. While assets for the owners of the accounts, these deposits are liabilities for the bank. Deposits form a pool of funds from which the bank can make loans and purchase securities.

Assets

Banks are required to hold a certain percentage of deposits as **reserves**. Counted as reserves are cash in the vaults of banks and bank deposits at the Federal Reserve. The Federal Reserve sets the **required reserve ratio**. For all checkable deposits beyond a certain minimum level, the required reserve ratio is 10 percent.[3]

For example, a required reserve ratio of 10 percent on checkable deposits means that the bank must retain $10 of required reserves (as vault cash or on deposit with the Federal Reserve) for every $100 of checkable deposits.

---

[3] As of December 1991 the required reserve ratio on checkable deposits up to $42 million per bank was only 3 percent, and for those above $42 million, it was 12 percent. In April of 1992, however, the latter required reserve ratio became 10 percent.

Reserves held by banks beyond the minimum required are called **excess reserves**. In general,

$$ER = R - RR$$

where

ER = excess reserves.
RR = required reserves.
R = reserves (cash in the bank vault plus bank deposits at the Fed).

and

$$RR = rr \cdot CD$$

rr = required reserve ratio for checkable deposits.
CD = checkable deposits in the bank.

If the required reserve ratio were 100 percent, then banks would do little more than provide safekeeping services and transfer funds to the parties designated on the checks written by their depositors. With a required reserve ratio of less than 100 percent, however, it is not possible for all depositors to withdraw all of their funds at once. If a bank's depositors panic and rush to withdraw their money, the bank's reserves will be sufficient for covering only a fraction of the outstanding deposits. Indeed, during the Great Depression many depositors lost some or all of their savings when their banks failed in just this way. Deposits at banks now are protected by insurance. Moreover, the Fed stands ready, as a lender of last resort, to inject reserves into the banking system to head off any financial crisis. Nevertheless, *runs* (or massive withdrawals) on individual banks still occur when depositors lose confidence in the management of a bank.

On average, individuals (households, firms, institutions) hold only a fraction of their income as M1 money balances. Therefore, banks at any point in time have positive deposit balances. It follows that banks can use part of these deposits to generate income—through loans and asset purchases—and still satisfy the usual requests for withdrawals from the deposits on hand.

Because banks do not earn interest on reserves, they have a profit incentive to hold no excess reserves. On the other hand, banks cannot forecast with precision the net flow of deposits (that is, new deposits less withdrawals) over a given time period. Therefore, banks tend to hold some excess reserves as a precaution. And on certain days of the week (Fridays) and during certain times of the year (Christmas holidays), banks hold more excess reserves to accommodate the anticipated larger numbers of cash withdrawals and checks written.

Beyond holding required and excess reserves, banks seek a portfolio of assets that balances rate of return, liquidity, and risk. The main source of commercial bank income is the interest received on business and consumer loans. As shown in Figure 11.1, approximately two-thirds of the total assets of commercial banks consist of loans. Banks also purchase U.S. government securities (primarily short-term U.S. Treasury bills) and state and local government bonds (included as "Other Securities" on the balance sheet). Of the three groups of assets, loans carry the highest interest rates, but are generally the least liquid and the most risky. That is, the probability of *default,* or the failure of the borrower to make payments of interest and repayments of principal on time, is the highest for business and consumer loans. U.S. government securities are the most liquid of these assets (in fact, there is an active secondary market where previously issued Treasury bills are traded), and the least likely to be defaulted. Other securities, like state and local government bonds, tend to fall in between loans and U.S. government securities in terms of return, liquidity, and risk.

The most pertinent risk on a Treasury bill or government bond is the risk of capital loss from fluctuations in the market rate of interest. Recall from Chapter 10 that the market value of bonds is inversely related to the market rate of interest. Actually, with fixed rate, longer-term loans, banks are also vulnerable to fluctuations in interest rates. If a bank holds a 30-year mortgage with 10 years of payments remaining at a fixed interest rate of 7 percent, but then due to inflation and a general rise in nominal interest rates, the bank has to pay 8 percent on time deposits to attract new funds, it will be locked into an unprofitable investment—one that could only be sold for a loss.

Capital Account

Returning to the consolidated balance sheet of Figure 11.1, "Other Assets" on the left-hand side includes the value of bank premises and equipment and other properties owned by banks. "Other Liabilities" on the right-hand side include short-term loans to banks from other banks, the Federal Reserve, and corporations (for example, overnight repurchase agreements). The "Capital Account" is the residual category, which ensures the bottom-line identity of "Total Assets" and "Total Liabilities." **Bank capital**, equal to the difference between the value of total assets and total liabilities, is a measure of the **net worth** of a bank.

Bank capital is necessary to absorb income losses of the bank. When the value of a bank's liabilities exceeds the value of its assets, the bank is insolvent. While the bank may fail, individual depositors are protected; since 1933 the Federal Deposit Insurance Corporation (FDIC) has insured individual deposits at commercial banks. (Currently deposits up to $100,000 are legally protected.) Thrift institutions and credit unions can obtain similar insurance for their deposits.

DEPOSIT EXPANSION

Recall that banks are financial intermediaries. They bring together the suppliers of loanable funds—those with financial wealth and incomes greater than current expenditures—with the demanders of loanable funds—those wishing to spend beyond present financial wealth and incomes. When funds are placed in a bank, the bank's liabilities (deposits on the right-hand side of the balance sheet) and assets (reserves on the left-hand side of the balance sheet) increase by an equal amount. As explained, the bank must, by law, hold a minimum percentage of deposits as required reserves; and as a precaution, it may hold excess reserves. Reserves beyond the required and the desired excess reserves are invested. With loans to businesses and consumers and with purchases of government securities, banks are able to extend credit to the demanders of loanable funds.

As we illustrate how banks help determine the money supply, you will see that, as in the Simple Keynesian model of national income determination, there is a multiplier process at work. We begin with *bank loans*. When a bank makes a loan, it accepts a promise from the borrower to repay the loan plus interest. In exchange the borrower receives a demand deposit equal to the amount of the loan. Thus the asset side of the balance sheet is increased by the amount of the loan, and the liability side is increased by the equivalent demand deposit. Consider the following three scenarios.

Required Reserves

In the simplest scenario we assume

1. The required reserve ratio is .10 (10 percent).
2. Banks do not want to hold excess reserves; in other words, the excess reserve ratio desired by banks is 0 percent. Any reserves not required to be held are used to make loans.
3. Whenever any party receives a check, the entire amount of the check is placed in a demand deposit (or checking account). That is, there are no cash withdrawals.

Suppose Ms. Allen discovers $1000 hidden in a jar in an old house she has just purchased. She takes the $1000 down to First City Bank and deposits the entire amount in a checking account. The initial transaction for First City Bank is illustrated in Figure 11.2. First City's assets (reserves) and liabilities (demand deposits) increase by $1000—see the entries on the balance sheet followed by "(a)." With the required reserve ratio of 10 percent, First City Bank now has $900 in excess reserves. Under the simplifying assumptions for this scenario, $900 in new loans can be made. (Note: In practice, First City may want to invest part of the excess reserves in government securities.)

Suppose First City loans $900 to Mr. Burns. The bank's assets and liabilities each increase by $900—as Burns receives a demand deposit equal to the amount of the loan—see the entries followed by "(b)." Burns uses the loan to pay Costello for painting his house. Costello deposits the $900 check written by Burns on First City Bank in his checking account at Second City Bank. A Federal Reserve Bank, acting as a clearinghouse for checks, credits Second City's account at the Fed with $900 and debits First City's account by $900—see the entries followed by "(c)." First City Bank's liabilities (demand deposits held by Burns) and assets (reserves held in the form of deposits at the Fed) decrease by $900. Second City Bank's assets (reserves held at the Fed) and liabilities (demand deposits of Costello) increase by $900. First City Bank's final balance sheet changes are shown in the second column in Figure 11.2.

After the first round is completed, demand deposits in the system have increased by $1000. With a fractional reserve system, however, the deposit expansion process continues. Second City Bank now has new deposits and reserves of $900. Ten percent (or $90) of the $900 in demand deposits must be kept as required reserves. Assuming no excess reserves are desired, Second City Bank will make loans of $810. With the loans, new demand deposits are created—entries followed by "(b′)" on the balance sheet. (Note: Again the borrowers are assumed to receive the entire loan in the form of a demand deposit—no cash is received from the bank.) When the recipients of the

FIGURE 11.2
Changes in Bank Balance Sheets

- Initial change in reserves of $1000.
- Required reserve ratio of .10, no excess reserves.
- No cash withdrawals.

First City Bank (initial)

Assets		Liabilities	
Res.	+1000 (a)	Dem. Dep.	+1000 (a)
(RR	+100)		
(ER	+900)		+900 (b)
	−900 (c)		−900 (c)
Loans	+900 (b)		

First City Bank (final)

Assets		Liabilities	
Res.	+100	Dem. Dep.	+1000
(RR	+100)		
(ER	+ 0)		
Loans	+900		
	+1000		+1000

Second City Bank (initial)

Assets		Liabilities	
Res.	+900 (c)	Dem. Dep.	+900 (c)
(RR	+90)		
(ER	+810)		+810 (b′)
	−810 (c′)		−810 (c′)
Loans	+810 (b′)		

Second City Bank (final)

Assets		Liabilities	
Res.	+90	Dem. Dep.	+900
(RR	+90)		
(ER	+ 0)		
Loans	+810		
	+900		+900

Third City Bank (initial)

Assets		Liabilities	
Res.	+810 (c′)	Dem. Dep.	+810 (c′)
(RR	+81)		
(ER	+729)		+729 (b″)
	−729 (c″)		−729 (c″)
Loans	+729 (b″)		

Third City Bank (final)

Assets		Liabilities	
Res.	+81	Dem. Dep.	+810
(RR	+81)		
(ER	+ 0)		
Loans	+729		
	+810		+810

loans made by Second City Bank write checks to cover their expenditures, and the checks clear the banking system, the liabilities and assets of Second City Bank are reduced by $810—see entries followed by "(c′)." Another bank in the system, call it Third City Bank, will find its demand deposits and reserves increasing by $810 when parties deposit the checks drawn on Second City Bank into their accounts at Third City. Holding back the reserves ($81) required by the new deposits, Third City Bank can make new loans of $729.

In the second and third rounds, demand deposits would increase by $900 and $810, respectively. (See the final changes in the liabilities of the Second and Third City Banks in Figure 11.2.) The deposit multiplier process continues. The initial increase of $1000 in deposits and reserves sets off a sequence of new loans. Banks use the new deposits to create credit. In each round of the deposit expansion process, required reserves are withdrawn. If the process continued on indefinitely, the cumulative change in demand deposits would be

$$\Delta \text{ Demand Deposits} = +\$1000 + \$900 + \$810 + \$729 + \ldots$$
$$= \$10{,}000$$
$$= (1/.1)(\$1000)$$
$$= 10(\$1000)$$

In general, the change in demand deposits is a multiple (d) of the initial change in reserves (ΔX).

$$\Delta \text{ Demand Deposits} = d\Delta X$$

where

$$\Delta X = \text{initial change in reserves (here } \Delta X = +\$1000).$$
$$d = \text{deposit multiplier (here } d = 1/.1 = 10).$$

Note that in this example, where the required reserve ratio is .10 (10 percent), and there are no desired excess reserves or cash withdrawals, the **deposit multiplier** is equal to the reciprocal of the required reserve ratio. If we allow for the additional leakages of desired excess reserves and cash withdrawals, the value of the deposit multiplier will be less.

Excess Reserves

Consider a similar scenario of an initial deposit of $1000 discovered by Ms. Allen. Suppose that all banks desire to keep 5 percent of demand deposits as excess reserves, in addition to the 10 percent of required reserves.[4] First City Bank, with the increase of $1000 in deposits and reserves, would now want to make loans of $850, retaining $50 as excess reserves. As illustrated in Figure 11.3, Second City Bank would likewise pass on only 85 percent of the new demand deposits. Thus, with a desired excess reserve ratio of .05, less credit and fewer demand deposits are generated by the banking system. If the process continued to the end, the cumulative change in demand deposits would be

$$\Delta \text{ Demand Deposits} = +\$1000 + \$850 + \$722.50 + \$614.25 + \ldots$$
$$= \$6666.67$$
$$= \frac{1}{.10 + .05} \times \$1000$$
$$= (6.67)(\$1000)$$

Here the new deposit multiplier (6.67) is given by the reciprocal of the sum of the required reserve ratio and the excess reserve ratio. With the additional leakage of desired excess reserves, the deposit multiplier is reduced.

---

[4] In this example we assume that the common excess reserve ratio is a constant 5 percent of demand deposits. In practice, excess reserve ratios will vary across banks, depending on the particular circumstances and bank policies. The opportunity cost to a bank of holding a dollar of excess reserves is equal to the interest rate that could be earned if the dollar were invested by the bank—for example, as a loan or in the purchase of government securities. In general, then, the excess reserve ratio of a bank will vary inversely with the market rate of interest.

FIGURE 11.3
CHANGES IN BANK BALANCE SHEETS

- Initial change in reserves of $1000.
- Required reserve ratio of .10, excess reserve ratio of .05.
- No cash withdrawals.

First City Bank (initial)

Assets	Liabilities
Res. +1000 (a) (RR +100) (ER +900)	Dem. Dep. +1000 (a)
	+850 (b)
−850 (c)	−850 (c)
Loans +850 (b)	

First City Bank (final)

Assets	Liabilities
Res. +150 (RR +100) (ER +50)	Dem. Dep. +1000
Loans +850	
+1000	+1000

Second City Bank (initial)

Assets	Liabilities
Res. +850 (c) (RR +85) (ER +765)	Dem. Dep. +850 (c)
	+722.5 (b′)
−722.5 (c′)	−722.5 (c′)
Loans +722.5 (b′)	

Second City Bank (final)

Assets	Liabilities
Res. +127.5 (RR +85) (ER +42.5)	Dem. Dep. +850
Loans +722.5	
+850	+850

The deposit expansion process continues according to what is shown here. The Third City Bank would be willing to make loans of $614.125. After three rounds, the change in demand deposits would be

$$\Delta \text{ Demand Deposits} = +1000 + 850 + 722.5$$

If the deposit expansion process continues to the end, the cumulative change in demand deposits would be $6666.67.

$$\Delta \text{ Demand Deposits} = +1000/.15 = 6666.67$$

Cash Withdrawals

The final leakage from the deposit expansion process is due to cash withdrawals by the nonbank public (e.g., households, firms, government). If some of the deposits are withdrawn as cash, then banks have fewer reserves available to make loans. The deposit multiplier will consequently be lower. To illustrate, assume that the recipients of checks drawn on other banks, while still depositing the entire check, immediately withdraw 20 percent of the deposit as cash. This 20 percent cash withdrawal rate is equivalent to a currency-deposit ratio of 1 to 4, or 25 percent. That is, for every $1 of new deposits, 20 cents are withdrawn as cash and 80 cents are left on deposit. We will still assume a required reserve ratio of 10 percent and a desired excess reserve ratio of 5 percent.[5]

---

[5] Here too, for the sake of exposition we assume a constant currency-deposit ratio of 25 percent for all depositors. In practice the currency-deposit ratio may vary across depositors depending on income, portfolio preferences, and the interest rates, if any, offered on checkable deposits.

For First City Bank there would still be a net increase of $1000 in demand deposits with Ms. Allen's placement of $1000 in cash in the bank. Mr. Burns would still get a loan and demand deposit of $850. And, Mr. Costello would still initially deposit the check for $850 drawn on Burns's bank in his checking account in Second City Bank. (Note: Compared to the initial scenario, Costello agrees to paint Burns's house for less—$850 instead of $900—perhaps using a less expensive brand of paint.) The difference is that Costello withdraws $170 (or 20 percent of the $850 deposit) in cash, leaving Second City Bank with a net increase of $680 in deposits and reserves. The Fed, in its clearinghouse function, still debits First City Bank's account by $850 and credits Second City Bank's account by $850. Second City Bank loses $170 in reserves in the form of vault cash paid out to Mr. Costello. See Figure 11.4 and the entries followed by "(c)" and "(d)." Second City Bank gains, on net, $680 in reserves ($850 in deposits at the Fed less $170 in its vault cash) and $680 in demand deposits. Reserves equal to 10 percent and 5 percent of the demand deposits are held back as

FIGURE 11.4
CHANGES IN BANK BALANCE SHEETS

- Initial change in reserves of $1000.
- Required reserve ratio of .10, excess reserve ratio of .05.
- Cash withdrawal ratio of .20 (currency-deposit ratio of .25).

	First City Bank (initial)			First City Bank (final)	
	Assets	Liabilities		Assets	Liabilities
Res.	+1000 (a)	Dem. Dep. +1000 (a)	Res.	+150	Dem. Dep. +1000
(RR	+100)		(RR	+100)	
(ER	+900)	+850 (b)	(ER	+50)	
	−850 (c)	−850 (c)			
Loans	+850 (b)		Loans	+850	
				+1000	+1000

	Second City Bank (initial)			Second City Bank (final)	
	Assets	Liabilities		Assets	Liabilities
Res.	+850 (c)	Dem. Dep. +850 (c)	Res.	+102	Dem. Dep. +680
(RR	+68)	−170 (d)	(RR	+68)	
(ER	+612)	+578 (b′)	(ER	+34)	
	−170 (d)	−578 (c′)			
	−578 (c′)				
Loans	+578 (b′)		Loans	+578	
				+680	680

The deposit expansion process continues according to what is shown here. The Third City Bank would be willing to make loans of $393.04. If the deposit expansion process continues to the end, the cumulative change in demand deposits would be $2500.

$$\Delta \text{ Demand Deposits} = +1000/.40 = +2500$$

The cumulative change in currency held by the public would be $625.

$$\Delta \text{ Currency in Circulation} = .25(+2500) = +625$$

CHAPTER 11 THE BANKING SYSTEM AND THE MONEY SUPPLY

required and excess reserves, respectively. Second City Bank can now lend out only $578 ($850 − $170 − $68 − $34), or 68 percent of the initial deposit of $850.

So with the additional leakage of cash withdrawals, banks are less able to extend credit. If the deposit expansion process continued on to the end, the cumulative change in demand deposits would be

$$\Delta \text{ Demand Deposits} = +\$1000 + \$680 + \$462.40 + \ldots$$

$$= \$2500$$

$$= \frac{1}{.10 + .05 + .25}\$1000$$

$$= (2.5)(\$1000)$$

In this case the deposit multiplier (2.5) is given by the reciprocal of the sum of the required reserve ratio (.10), the excess reserve ratio (.05), and the currency-deposit ratio (.25).

$$d = \frac{1}{rr + er + cu_d} = \frac{1}{.10 + .05 + .25} = \frac{1}{.4} = 2.5$$

Note, however, that the change in the money supply, narrowly defined as M1, is not just the change in demand deposits. In this third scenario there has been an increase in currency in circulation, that is, currency held by the nonbank public.

$$\Delta \text{ Currency in Circulation} = +\$170 + \$115.6 + \$78.61 + \ldots$$

$$= \$625$$

$$= (.25)(\$2500)$$

$$= (cu_d)(\Delta \text{ Demand Deposits}).$$

where cu_d is the currency-deposit ratio (here for demand deposits). The change in M1 is the sum of the changes in demand deposits (or checkable deposits in general) and currency in circulation.

In general, assuming consistent behavior across banks (that is, a common excess reserve ratio and lending policy) and for the nonbank public (that is, a common currency-deposit ratio), the final changes in checkable deposits, currency in circulation, and the M1 money supply due to an initial change in reserves are given by the formulas

$$\Delta \text{Checkable Deposits} = \frac{1}{rr + er + cu_d} \Delta X = d \Delta X$$

$$\Delta \text{Currency in Circulation} = \frac{cu_d}{rr + er + cu_d} \Delta X$$

$$\Delta M1 = \Delta \text{Checkable Deposits} + \Delta \text{Currency in Ciruclation}$$

$$\Delta M1 = \frac{1 + cu_d}{rr + er + cu_d} \Delta X$$

where

ΔX = initial change in reserves.
rr = required reserve ratio on checkable deposits.
er = excess reserve ratio on checkable deposits.
cu_d = currency-deposit ratio.
d = deposit multiplier.

The important point to understand is that the deposit multiplier process depends on the actions of the Federal Reserve (which sets the required reserve ratio), the depository institutions in the system (which determine the excess reserve ratio), and the nonbank public (which selects the currency-deposit ratio). We should also note that the deposit multiplier process is not instantaneous, but unfolds over time. Moreover, as we will discuss further in Chapter 14 on monetary policy, the value of the deposit multiplier may change with the condition of the economy. In particular, the excess reserve ratio of banks and the currency-deposit ratio of the nonbank public may vary. Finally, we should mention that the deposit multiplier works in both directions. That is, an initial decrease in reserves will set off a deposit contraction process.

THE FED'S INFLUENCE ON THE MONEY SUPPLY

Although the actions of the Federal Reserve, depository institutions, and the nonbank public jointly determine the nation's money supply, the Fed plays the dominant role. In addition to setting the required reserve ratio, the Fed can indirectly influence the excess reserve ratios of banks through changes in the **discount rate,** the rate of interest the Fed charges member banks for the loan of reserves. If a bank's reserves fall below the required reserve ratio, the bank can ask to borrow reserves temporarily from the Fed at the discount rate; however, the Fed is not obliged to lend to the bank. A bank short of reserves does have other options. It can borrow excess reserves from other banks at the **federal funds rate,** the rate of interest charged on interbank loans. Unlike the discount rate that is set by the Fed, the federal funds rate is determined in the market according to the demand for and supply of excess reserves. The Fed, however, can also influence the federal funds rate through open market operations (to be discussed shortly).

In the short run, individual banks short of reserves can sell government securities from their asset portfolios and add the proceeds to their reserves. In the longer run, banks may bolster their reserve positions by cutting back on lending—opting to hold more excess reserves as a buffer against future shortfalls in required reserves.

By increasing the discount rate, the Fed sends a message to banks and the nonbank public. A higher discount rate suggests that banks should be more cautious in their lending, and perhaps increase the interest rates charged on loans. Banks may respond to an increase in the discount rate by increasing their excess reserve ratios. Moreover, a higher discount rate puts upward pressure on the federal funds rate. If it becomes more expensive to borrow from the Fed, then banks needing reserves will be more likely to borrow from each other.

Conversely, a fall in the discount rate is a signal from the Fed that banks should increase their lending. A lower discount rate would likely reduce bank excess reserve ratios and put downward pressure on the federal funds rate.

The Fed rarely changes the required reserve ratios and only periodically changes the discount rate.[6] By far, the Fed relies on open market operations to change the money supply. **Open market operations** refer to the Federal Reserve's purchases and sales of U.S. government securities in the *open market,* a secondary market where U.S. government securities that have not yet matured are traded. Through open market operations, the Fed can alter the **monetary base,** which is equal to the sum of reserves and currency in circulation (that is, currency held by the nonbank public).

$$\begin{aligned} \text{Monetary Base} &= \text{Reserves} + \text{Currency in Circulation} \\ &= \frac{\text{Bank Deposits at}}{\text{Federal Reserve Banks}} + \frac{\text{Currency in}}{\text{Bank Vaults}} + \frac{\text{Currency in}}{\text{Circulation}} \\ &= \text{Bank Deposits at Federal Reserve Banks} + \text{Currency} \end{aligned}$$

When the Fed purchases U.S. government securities in the open market it usually pays with a check—although it could print up Federal Reserve Notes and pay with cash. (As the nation's central bank, the Fed is unique in its ability to write checks on itself and print up new money.) The seller of the securities will deposit the check drawn on the Fed in a bank, and the bank will credit the recipient of the check with a deposit (increasing the bank's liabilities) and present the check to the Fed. The bank's reserves (assets) increase when the Fed adds the amount of the check to the bank's deposits at the Fed. As illustrated earlier (see Figure 11.3), the bank will need to hold a portion of the new deposits as required reserves and may want to hold an additional portion as excess reserves. The bank will then be in a position to make new loans. Consequently, through the deposit expansion process, the money supply will increase by a multiple of the initial open market purchase.

With an open market sale the Fed will withdraw reserves from the banking system, reducing the money supply. In Figure 11.5 the effects of an open market sale of $1000 worth of government securities are illustrated. Assume that all the banks in the system are satisfied with their portfolios—in particular, with the ratio of excess reserves to demand deposits. Suppose, as before, that the required reserve ratio is 10 percent and the desired excess reserve ratio is 5 percent. The buyer of the government securities sold by the Fed writes a check for $1000 on her account at First City Bank. The Fed deducts $1000 from First City Bank's deposits at a Federal Reserve Bank—see entries followed by "(a)" in Figure 11.5. First City Bank would need to sell $850 in government securities to meet its required reserve ratio and restore its desired excess reserve position. (Note: First City Bank does not have to sell $1000 in government securities with the decrease of $1000 in demand deposits and reserves, since its required reserves and desired excess reserves decrease by $100 and $50, respectively.)

---

[6] In April of 1992 the Federal Reserve reduced the required reserve ratio on checkable deposits from 12 percent to 10 percent in an attempt to boost bank profits and stimulate the economy. In December of 1990 it eliminated all remaining reserve requirements on time deposits. Prior to this, the last time the Fed altered the required reserve ratio was 1983. Also, during 1991, in attempts to restart an economy mired in recession, the Fed lowered the discount rate six times, usually by a half of a percentage point on each occasion. In Chapter 14 we will discuss the monetary policy options of the Federal Reserve.

FIGURE 11.5
Changes in Bank Balance Sheets

- Open market sale of $1000 of government securities by the Fed.
- Required reserve ratio of .10, excess reserve ratio of .05.

First City Bank (initial)			First City Bank (final)		
Assets		Liabilities	Assets		Liabilities
Res.	−1000 (a)	Dem. Dep. −1000 (a)	Res.	−150	Dem. Dep. −1000
(RR	−100)		(RR	−100)	
(ER	−900)		(ER	−50)	
	+850 (b)				
Gov. Sec.	−850 (b)		Gov. Sec.	−850	
			−1000		−1000

Second City Bank (initial)			Second City Bank (final)		
Assets		Liabilities	Assets		Liabilities
Res.	−850 (b)	Dem. Dep. −850 (b)	Res.	−127.5	Dem. Dep. −850
(RR	−85)		(RR	−85)	
(ER	−765)		(ER	−42.5)	
	+722.5 (c)				
Gov. Sec.	−722.5 (c)		Loans	−722.5	
			−850		−850

Cumulative changes if the process continues to the end would be as follows:

$$\Delta \text{ Demand Deposits} = -1000 - 850 - 722.5 - \ldots$$
$$= (1/.15)(-1000)$$
$$= -6666.67$$

$$\Delta \text{ Reserves} = -150 - 127.5 - 108.375 - \ldots$$
$$= (.10 + .05)(-6666.67)$$
$$= -1000$$

Changes in Fed's Balance Sheet

Assets	Liabilities
Gov. Sec. −1000 (a)	Reserves −1000 (a)

If First City Bank did not want to sell government securities to replenish its reserves, it could either try to borrow reserves from the Fed at the discount rate or from other banks at the federal funds rate. Suppose First City Bank does sell $850 in government securities; and the purchaser of the securities pays with a check drawn on his account at Second City Bank. When the check clears, the Fed transfers $850 from Second City's deposits at the Fed to First City's deposits—see entries followed by "(b)" in Figure 11.5. First City Bank is now square in terms of its reserve position. Second City Bank, on the other hand, is down $850 in deposits and reserves. Assuming a similar desire to maintain an excess reserve ratio of 5 percent, Second City Bank would itself need to sell $722.50 in government securities, with the proceeds from the sale added to its reserves—see entries followed by "(c)."

CHAPTER 11 THE BANKING SYSTEM AND THE MONEY SUPPLY

The deposit contraction process would continue. If all succeeding banks in the sequence sold government securities to meet any shortage of reserves, then the cumulative decrease in demand deposits in the system would equal $6667. Reserves in the system would decline by $1000, the amount of the Fed's open market sale. Again we see that a change in reserves has a multiplier effect on the money supply—a direct result of the fractional reserve nature of the banking system. Note that the decrease in the monetary base, equal to the decrease in reserves, is also equal to the amount of the Fed's open market sale. The decreases in reserves and the money supply would put upward pressure on interest rates.

In fact, the relationship between the money supply as measured by M1 and the monetary base reflects the fractional reserve basis of the banking system.

$$M1 = \text{Checkable Deposits} + \text{Currency in Circulation}$$

$$\text{Monetary Base} = \text{Reserves} + \text{Currency in Circulation}$$

$$M1 - \text{Monetary Base} = \text{Checkable Deposits} - \text{Reserves}$$

M1 is a multiple of the monetary base. The difference between checkable deposits and reserves essentially reflects the credit created by the banking system. See Table 11.1, where the annual averages for the monetary bases and money supplies are given for 1980–1991. Over the decade, the M1 money supply varied between a multiple of 2.75 and 3.15 of the monetary base.

The Fed sets the monetary base, the required reserve ratios, and the discount rate. Depository institutions, based on the required reserve ratios and their excess reserve policies, build upon the monetary base and extend credit through loans to consumers and businesses and purchases of government securities. The

TABLE 11.1
THE MONETARY BASE AND THE M1 MONEY SUPPLY: 1980–1991

	DAILY AVERAGES (IN BILLIONS OF DOLLARS)		
	M1[a]	Monetary Base[b]	Ratio of M1 to Monetary Base
December 1980	408.8	145.9	2.80
December 1981	436.4	153.0	2.85
December 1982	474.4	164.3	2.89
December 1983	521.2	179.9	2.90
December 1984	552.2	191.4	2.89
December 1985	619.9	208.6	2.97
December 1986	724.3	230.0	3.15
December 1987	749.7	246.3	3.04
December 1988	786.4	263.5	2.98
December 1989	793.6	274.2	2.89
December 1990	825.4	299.8	2.75
December 1991[c]	896.7	324.8	2.76

[a] M1 = currency in circulation + demand deposits + other checkable deposits + traveler's checks.
[b] Monetary Base = currency in circulation + reserves.
[c] preliminary estmiate
SOURCE: *Economic Report of the President 1992* (Washington, DC: U.S. Government Printing House, 1992) Tables B-65, B-67.

nonbank public chooses the ratio of currency to checkable deposits. From these interdependent decisions the M1 money supply is determined. A similar relationship exists between the monetary base and M2. The portfolio decisions of the nonbank public include not only the ratio of currency to checkable deposits, but also the ratio of checkable deposits to the less liquid assets included in M2, such as time deposits.

MONEY MARKET EQUILIBRIUM

With our understanding of the determinants of the demand and supply of money, we can analyze the equilibrium in the money market. Recall from the previous chapter that the aggregate quantity of nominal money balances demanded depends positively on real national income and the price level and negatively on the nominal interest rate. As just discussed in this chapter, the nominal supply of money is jointly determined by the actions of the Fed, depository institutions, and the nonbank public. In particular, the supply of money depends on the monetary base, the required reserve ratio, the excess reserve ratio, and the currency-deposit ratio. We will regard these determinants of the money supply as given, which means that the supply of money will be modeled as exogenous.[7]

The equations for the money market are

$$M^d = M^d(\overset{+}{Y}, \overset{+}{P}, \overset{-}{i})$$

$$M^s = M^s_0$$

$$M^d \overset{e}{=} M^s \qquad \text{(money market equilibrium condition)}$$

where

M^d = aggregate quantity demanded of nominal money balances.

Y = real national income.

P = aggregate price level.

i = nominal interest rate.

M^s = nominal money supply (M1).

The signs over the variables in the money demand equation indicate the hypothesized direction of influence on the quantity demanded of nominal

---

[7] The money supply, M1 (currency in circulation and checkable deposits) is perfectly interest inelastic for given values of the required reserve ratio, excess reserve ratio, and currency-deposit ratio. If the excess reserve ratio, however, is inversely related to the nominal interest rate (i.e., banks are less likely to hold excess reserves as the opportunity cost of excess reserves rises), then increases in the interest rate would reduce the excess reserve ratio and increase the value of the deposit multiplier. A higher interest rate may also reduce the currency-deposit ratio to the extent that the interest rate paid by banks on checkable deposits counted in M1 (e.g., NOW accounts) also would increase. Hence, for any monetary base, the money supply that could be supported would rise with the interest rate. In other words, the money supply curve would be upward-sloping (up to the point where the excess reserve ratio and currency-deposit ratio have been reduced to zero).

money balances. The nominal interest rate, i, can be thought of as either an index of interest rates in general, or as a specific, market-determined interest rate like the federal funds rate. For given levels of real national income and prices, equilibrium in the money market will be at that level of the interest rate where the quantity of money balances demanded equals the given money supply. In Figure 11.6 we illustrate the equilibrium in the money market. An increase in the equilibrium interest rate could be the result of either an increase in the demand for money or a decrease in the supply of money.

In Figure 11.7, an increase in the demand for money, caused by a rise in the price level or growth in real income, results in an excess quantity of money demanded at the original equilibrium interest rate (indicated by the line segment E_0F). Reflecting the excess demand for money, the interest rate rises. Higher interest rates reduce the quantities demanded of money balances in two ways. The opportunity cost of holding money balances increases, prompting individuals to conserve on transactions balances. Also, the price of bonds falls with an increase in the interest rate. The quantity of speculative money balances demanded is reduced as individuals shift into bonds. The interest rate rises until the excess quantity of money demanded is eliminated (indicated by the movement back along the money demand curve from F to E_1). (Note that the overall supply of money does not change here. The higher interest rate—and thus the lower price of bonds—is necessary to eliminate the excess demand for money due to the increase in nominal income.)

A decrease in the money supply, caused by open market sales by the Fed (a decrease in the monetary base), or an increase in the required reserve ratio, excess reserve ratio, or currency-deposit ratio, would also push up the

FIGURE 11.6

MONEY MARKET EQUILIBRIUM

The demand for M^d is drawn holding constant real national income and the aggregate price level. The nominal money supply, M^s, is drawn holding constant the monetary base, the required reserve ratio, the excess reserve ratio, and the currency-deposit ratio.

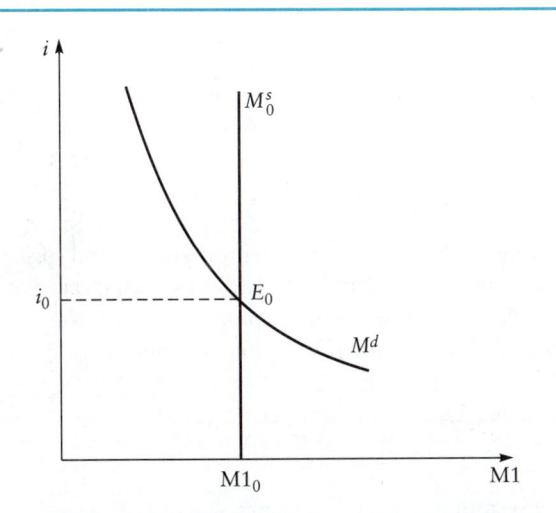

M1 = currency in circulation and checkable deposits.
M^d = demand for nominal money balances.
M^s_0 = nominal money supply (exogenous).
i = nominal interest rate.

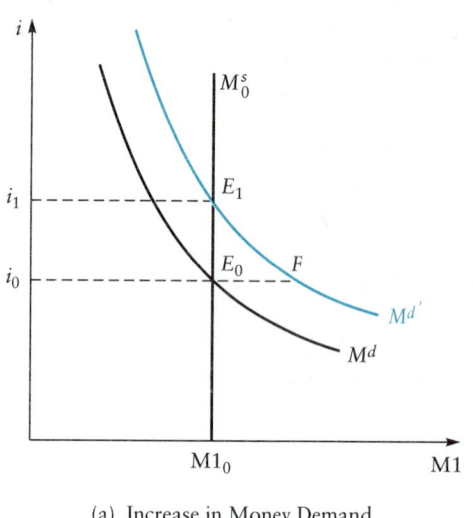

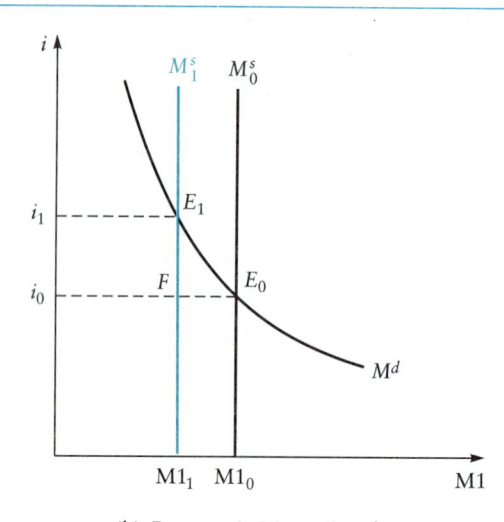

(a) Increase in Money Demand

(b) Decrease in Money Supply

FIGURE 11.7

INCREASES IN THE EQUILIBRIUM INTEREST RATE

An increase in the demand for money (from M^d to $M^{d'}$) results in an excess quantity of money demanded at the initial equilibrium interest rate. The equilibrium interest rate rises from i_0 to i_1 to clear the money market. Conversely, a decrease in the supply of money (from M^s_0 to M^s_1) results in an excess quantity of money demanded at the initial equilibrium interest rate. The equilibrium interest rate rises from i_0 to i_1 to clear the money market.

equilibrium interest rate. As shown in Figure 11.7, the excess quantity demanded of money (FE_0) will be eliminated by higher interest rates. (See the movement from E_0 to E_1 along the money demand curve.)

CONCLUDING NOTE

We now have the tools to analyze changes in the money market. For example, what could cause a decrease in the equilibrium interest rate? Or suppose we observed an increase in the money supply but no change in the equilibrium interest rate. What could explain this?

In the next chapter we return to the aggregate demand-aggregate supply framework introduced earlier and explicitly link the product and money markets. Understanding the mutual dependence of these two aggregate markets is crucial for understanding the operation of the macroeconomy. With this basic model set out, we then turn in Chapters 13 and 14 to the effectiveness of the fiscal and monetary policies designed to achieve full employment and price stability. In these two chapters we begin to explore some of the controversies in macroeconomics.

KEY TERMS

Federal Reserve System
Federal Open Market Committee
reserves
required reserve ratio
excess reserves
bank capital

net worth
deposit multiplier
discount rate
federal funds rate
open market operations
monetary base

QUESTIONS

1. What are the three most important ideas in this chapter? Discuss why each is important.
2. Compare the deposit multiplier process of the money supply with the autonomous expenditure multiplier process of the Simple Keynesian model of national income determination. Discuss the similarities. What could cause a decrease in the magnitude of the deposit multiplier? Explain why.
3. Assume that there are no excess reserves in the banking system. Mr. Smothers withdraws $400 in cash from his checking account at First City Bank. If the required reserve ratio is 10 percent, what amount of government securities would First City Bank need to sell from its asset portfolio to meet the reserve requirement? Illustrate the final changes in First City Bank's balance sheet from the cash withdrawal and resulting sale of government securities.

    Suppose the purchaser of the government securities sold by First City Bank, is a Ms. Tomlin, who pays with a check drawn on her account at Second City Bank. Discuss the clearinghouse function for checks provided by the Fed. What amount of government securities would Second City Bank need to sell to meet the reserve requirement of 10 percent? Illustrate the final changes in Second City Bank's balance sheet.

    If the process continued to the end, with each bank short of required reserves selling the necessary amount of government securities, what would be the final cumulative change in demand deposits in the banking system?
4. Redo the analysis of Question 3 assuming that in addition to the required reserve ratio of 10 percent, each bank in the system desires to keep 2 percent of deposits as excess reserves. Assume that initially all banks are just meeting the required reserve ratio and the desired excess reserve ratio.
5. Suppose the Federal Reserve purchases previously issued government bonds in the open market for $10,000 from Mr. Winters, who deposits the entire check written by the Fed in his checking account at First City Bank. Assuming First City Bank had been just meeting the required reserve ratio of 10 percent, what is the maximum amount of new loans First City Bank could now make? Illustrate the final changes in First City Bank's balance sheet after the (maximum) loans are made and the loaned funds spent.

    Under what conditions would the maximum increase in money supply be realized with this open market purchase of $10,000 by the Fed? What would this maximum increase be?
6. Predict and discuss the effect on the market equilibrium interest rate of each of the following, ceteris paribus:
    a. a decrease in the level of real income.
    b. an open market purchase of bonds by the Fed.
    c. a decrease in the required reserve ratio.
    d. an increase in the public's currency-deposit ratio.
    e. an increase in the desired excess reserve ratio of banks.
    f. an increase in the annual fees charged to credit card users.

CHAPTER

12

AGGREGATE DEMAND AND AGGREGATE SUPPLY

IN THE SIMPLE Keynesian model real national output and income are demand-determined. The economy is assumed to be operating on the Keynesian range, or the perfectly elastic portion of the aggregate supply curve—well below full employment and with much excess capacity. Changes in desired aggregate expenditures and aggregate demand result in changes in real output only. The aggregate price level is constant.

For example, an increase in aggregate demand (a shift from AD_0 to AD_1 in Figure 12.1) can be accommodated by rehiring the laid-off labor, using the idled plant and machinery, and stepping up the rate of production with no upward pressure on the unit costs of production or the aggregate price level. Implicitly, the marginal product of labor is constant as the amount of labor employed increases. In other words, diminishing returns to labor have not yet set in.

A decrease in aggregate demand (a shift from AD_0 to AD_2) is met by laying off additional workers and idling more of the plant and machinery. Prices and profit margins are already at low levels. Institutional rigidities (such as minimum wage laws and union wage contracts) may also contribute to downwardly inflexible wages and prices.

When the economy is in a depressed state, changes in interest rates have little effect on desired aggregate expenditures. With excess capacity, firms are unwilling to invest in additional plant and equipment, even when interest rates are low. With a high rate of unemployment and the associated uncertainties in household income, consumers are unlikely to borrow to purchase durable goods and new homes. Moreover, banks may be reluctant to lend given the lower return on the loans and the greater risk of default during an economic downturn.

Exactly such an economic depression had befallen the United States and other industrialized nations in the 1930s. In his work, *The General Theory of Employment, Interest and Money,* published in 1936, John Maynard Keynes

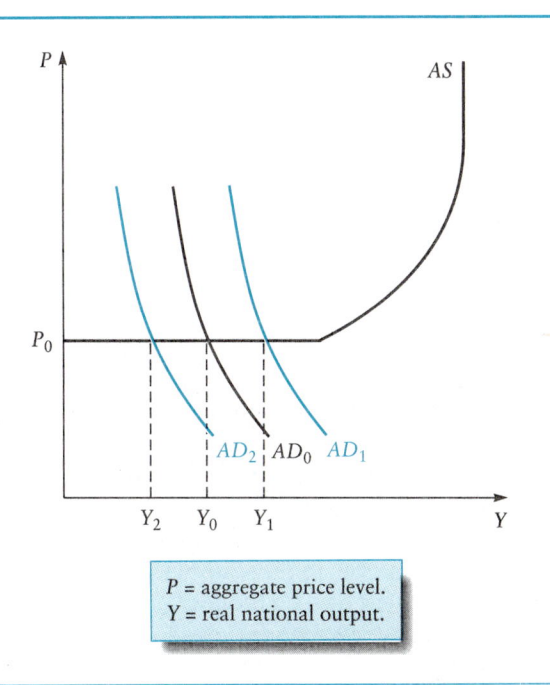

FIGURE 12.1

CHANGES IN AGGREGATE DEMAND ON THE KEYNESIAN RANGE OF THE AGGREGATE SUPPLY CURVE

On the Keynesian range of the aggregate supply curve, changes in aggregate demand result in changes in real national output only; the aggregate price level is constant.

P = aggregate price level.
Y = real national output.

---

addressed the problem of how to recharge an economy stalled in a low level equilibrium. In the next chapter on fiscal policy, we will discuss the Keynesian remedy.

The relevance of the Simple Keynesian model is limited largely to an economy in a depressed state. Usually economies operate in the intermediate region of the aggregate supply curve, where changes in aggregate demand elicit changes in both real output and the aggregate price level. In this chapter we extend the Simple Keynesian framework in three ways. We allow for changes in the interest rate to affect investment expenditures. We explicitly link the product and money markets. Finally, by incorporating aggregate supply constraints, we allow for variations in the aggregate price level.

INTEREST-SENSITIVE EXPENDITURES

With *interest-sensitive expenditures,* the cost of financing the transaction may be significant. By their nature, interest-sensitive expenditures are "big-ticket items," such as business investment in plant and machinery, residential construction, and household purchases of consumer durables, like automobiles and expensive appliances.

Since large amounts of money are involved, differences in the interest rate translate into marked differences in the overall cost of the item. For example, a major component of the overall cost of purchasing a house is the interest on the mortgage. A $100,000 loan for 30 years at an annual rate of interest of 12 percent carries monthly mortgage payments of $1028.61. In any year, the monthly mortgage payments would total $12,343.32. In comparison, a

$100,000 loan for 30 years at an annual rate of 11 percent carries a monthly mortgage payment of $952.32. In any year, the monthly mortgage payments would total $11,427.84. Thus, in this example, a one percentage point difference in the interest rate translates into an annual difference of $915.48 in mortgage payments. Clearly, all other factors considered, home buyers have an incentive to time their purchases for when interest rates are low.[1] The same logic holds for other consumer loans.

Business purchases of plant and machinery, whether financed by borrowing directly from banks, by issuing corporate bonds, or by drawing on retained earnings (with the associated opportunity costs), are also sensitive to the level of interest rates. Although other factors (capacity constraints, expectations of future demand, tax incentives, technological change) influence the decision to invest, firms tend to hold off on expansion plans when interest rates are high or credit is tight.

Thus, we hypothesize an inverse relationship between interest-sensitive expenditures and the rate of interest—noting that the strength of the relationship may vary with the state of the economy. To simplify the model that follows, we will restrict interest-sensitive expenditures to business fixed investment (*BFI*) and residential fixed investment (*RFI*), although, as we noted, expenditures on consumer durables are also affected by the cost of credit. We will continue to assume that planned inventory investment is zero ($\Delta INV^p = 0$). In short, desired investment spending is now explicitly dependent on the interest rate.

In Figure 12.2, desired investment expenditures by firms for new plant, equipment and machinery, and by households for residential construction are graphed against the nominal rate of interest. The demand curve for investment is drawn holding constant the other factors that influence *BFI* and *RFI*. A rightward shift in the investment demand curve (from I^d to $I^{d'}$ in Figure 12.2) reflects an increase in the demand for fixed investment—due to an increase in autonomous business investment (perhaps with optimism about the economy or the introduction of a cost-saving technology) or an increase in autonomous residential investment (perhaps with growth in population).

An increase in the quantity demanded of fixed investment is illustrated by the movement down the investment demand curve (from A to B on I^d in Figure 12.2) in response to a fall in the interest rate. An increase in the quantity demanded of fixed investment is also indicated by a rightward movement between two investment demand curves—holding constant the interest rate—in response to an increase in investment demand (see the movement from A to A' in the figure).

AGGREGATE DEMAND CURVE

Recall from Chapter 7 that the **aggregate demand schedule** describes the relationship between the total quantity of national output demanded and the aggregate price level. The **aggregate demand curve,** the graphical representation

---

[1] Recall from Chapter 2 the equation estimating real residential fixed investment for the U.S. economy over the 26-year period from 1965 to 1990. Controlling for the influence of real disposable income, we found that a one percentage point decrease in the nominal interest rate on new home mortgages was associated with an increase of approximately $7 billion in annual real residential fixed investment, ceteris paribus.

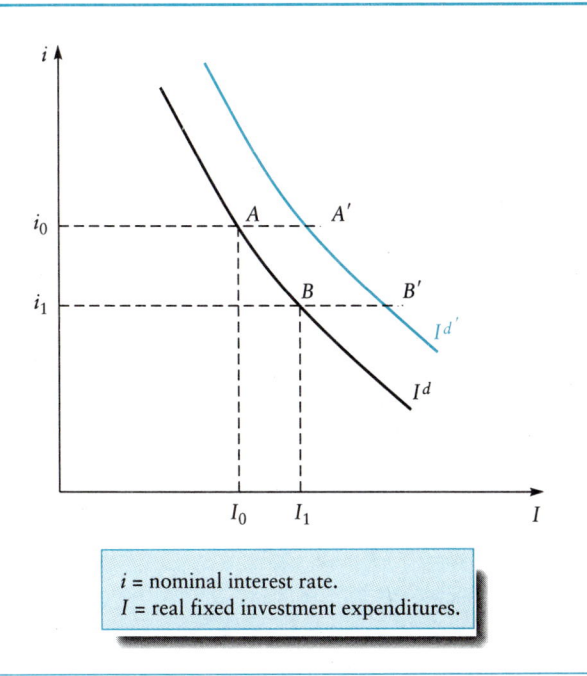

FIGURE 12.2

DEMAND FOR REAL FIXED INVESTMENT

A rightward shift in the investment demand curve from I^d to $I^{d'}$ indicates an increase in investment demand. The movement from A to B (or A' to B') indicates an increase in the quantity of fixed investment demanded due to a decrease in the nominal interest rate. The movement from A to A' (or B to B') indicates an increase in the quantity of fixed investment demanded due to an increase in investment demand from I^d to $I^{d'}$.

i = nominal interest rate.
I = real fixed investment expenditures.

---

of the aggregate demand schedule, is derived from the product and money markets. In Figure 12.3 we present a four panel diagram to illustrate why the aggregate demand curve is negatively sloped.

In panel (a) we depict the money market, which is assumed initially to be in equilibrium with a nominal money supply of $M1_0$ and a nominal interest rate of i_0. Recall that the money demand curve (M^d) is drawn holding constant, among other factors, real national income (Y) and the aggregate price level (P). The money supply curve (M^s) is drawn for given levels of the monetary base, required reserve ratio, excess reserve ratio, and currency-deposit ratio.

In panel (b) the investment demand curve (I^d) is illustrated. As just discussed, investment demand is drawn holding constant the factors (other than the nominal interest rate) that affect business and residential fixed investment. With an interest rate of i_0, desired fixed investment expenditures are I_0.

In panel (c) we have the Keynesian cross. The vertical intercept (A_0) of the desired aggregate expenditure curve ($A = A_0 + aY$) represents real desired autonomous expenditures, that is, any expenditures on national output by domestic households, firms, and government and by foreigners that are not dependent on real national income. In the Simple Keynesian model interest-sensitive expenditures are regarded as autonomous, so I_0 is included in A_0. The slope of the desired aggregate expenditure curve, a, is the marginal propensity to spend on national output. Y_0 is the initial level of equilibrium real national output and income, consistent with the equilibrium conditions in the money market (i_0 and $M1_0$).

Finally, in panel (d) we have the aggregate demand curve. The aggregate price level (P) is on the vertical axis, and real national output and income (Y) are on the horizontal axis. The point E_0 represents the initial general equilibrium in the model. That is, E_0 is the point on the aggregate demand curve consistent with

(a) Money Market

(c) Keynesian Cross

(b) Investment Expenditures

(d) Aggregate Demand

i = nominal interest rate.
I = real fixed investment expenditures.
A = desired real aggregate expenditures.
Y = real national output.
P = aggregate price level.

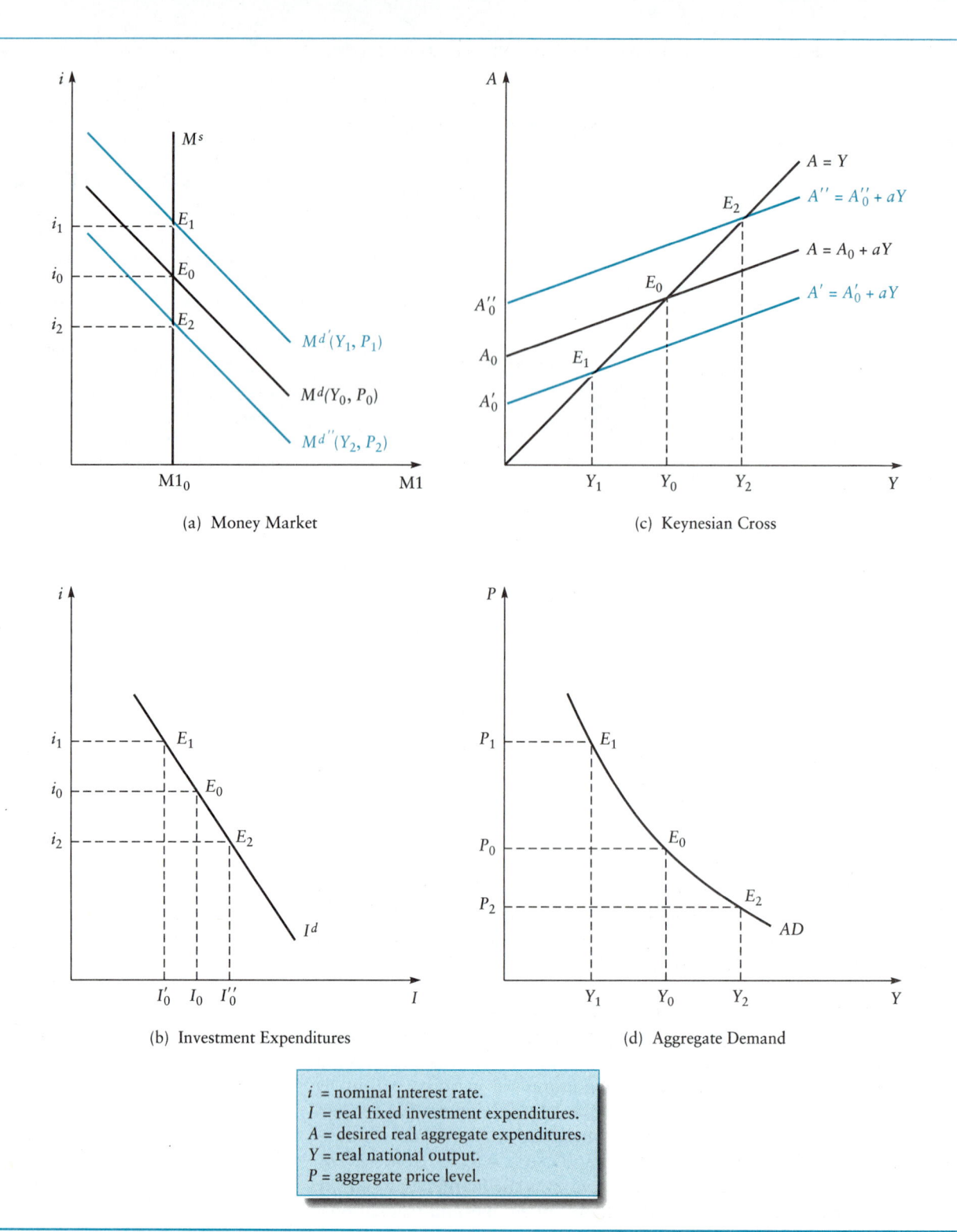

FIGURE 12.3

SLOPE OF THE AGGREGATE DEMAND CURVE

From the initial general equilibrium in the product and money markets (labeled E_0), an increase in the aggregate price level from P_0 to P_1 increases the demand for money resulting in economic adjustments and a transition to a new equilibrium (labeled E_1) with a higher nominal interest rate ($i_1 > i_0$) and a lower rate of real national output and income ($Y_1 < Y_0$). Conversely, from the initial general equilibrium of E_0, a fall in the aggregate price level from P_0 to P_2 reduces the demand for money and results in a new equilibrium (labeled E_2) with a lower nominal interest rate ($i_2 < i_0$) and a higher rate of real national output and income ($Y_2 > Y_0$).

the given money and product market equilibriums. The initial equilibrium price level (P_0) and real national output (Y_0) set the money demand curve (M^d). Note that nominal national income equals (P_0)(Y_0).

Now suppose there is a rise in the aggregate price level from P_0 to P_1 caused by a decrease in aggregate supply. The higher price level increases the demand for money balances. (The money demand curve shifts to the right.) Inflation, by reducing the purchasing power of money, increases the amount of money required to purchase a given market basket of goods and services. The resulting excess demand for money puts upward pressure on the interest rate. The increase in the interest rate reduces desired investment expenditures, which in the Simple Keynesian model is regarded as a fall in autonomous expenditures. The decrease in desired aggregate expenditures results in an excess supply of goods and unplanned increases in inventories. Consequently, firms cut back on the rate of production. Real national output and income fall. The decline in real national income, in turn, modifies the initial increase in money demand from the rise in the aggregate price level. (That is, the money demand curve shifts partially back toward the initial money demand curve, which diminishes the rise in the interest rate. The initial direct effect of the price increase on the demand for money is greater than the subsequent indirect effect of the decrease in real income. Thus, on net, nominal income and the demand for money increase.) The system adjusts to a new equilibrium, E_1, with a lower real national output and income ($Y_1 < Y_0$) and a higher nominal interest rate ($i_1 > i_0$), consistent with the higher aggregate price level ($P_1 > P_0$).

Graphically, in Figure 12.3, the net increase in the demand for money—caused by the rise in the nominal income, (P_1)(Y_1) > (P_0)(Y_0)—is shown by the new money demand curve $M^{d'}$ in panel (a). The increase in the equilibrium interest rate from i_0 to i_1 reduces the desired quantity of real fixed investment expenditures from I_0 to I'_0 in panel (b). The desired aggregate expenditure curve in panel (c) shifts downward with the decrease in investment expenditures. This new equilibrium, where again the product and money markets clear with zero excess quantities demanded, is represented by the point E_1 on the aggregate demand curve. Thus, a rise in the aggregate price level results in a decrease in desired aggregate expenditures on national output.[2]

Conversely, a fall in the aggregate price level from P_0 to P_2 reduces the demand for money balances. (The money demand curve shifts left.) The nominal interest rate falls, which induces a rise in the desired quantity of fixed investment expenditures. Inventories are run down to satisfy the increased spending on national output. Production and income rise, which increases money demand, in turn, partially offsetting the initial decline. (The money demand curve shifts partially back to the right and the fall in the interest rate is moderated. The initial direct effect on the demand for money from the decrease in the aggregate price level dominates the subsequent indirect effect

---

[2] There is a more elegant way to derive the aggregate demand curve, which involves varying the aggregate price level and solving simultaneously the product and money markets for the general equilibrium values for real national income and the nominal interest rate. That is, the points on the aggregate demand curve represent combinations of real national income and the aggregate price level where both the product and money markets are in equilibrium. This treatment, however, is better left to a course in intermediate macroeconomic theory.

from the increase in real national income.) The system converges to a new equilibrium, characterized by higher real national output and income ($Y_2 > Y_0$) and a lower nominal interest rate ($i_2 < i_0$), consistent with the lower aggregate price level ($P_2 < P_0$).

Graphically, in Figure 12.3 the net decrease in money demand—from M^d to $M^{d''}$ in panel (a) due to the decrease in nominal income, $(P_2)(Y_2) < (P_0)(Y_0)$—reduces the equilibrium interest rate (from i_0 to i_2), which increases the quantity demanded of real fixed investment (from I_0 to I_0'' in panel (b)). The increase in desired investment expenditures shifts up the desired aggregate expenditure curve in the Keynesian-cross diagram of panel (c) from A to A''. The new general equilibrium in the product and money markets is represented by E_2. Thus, a decrease in the aggregate price level results in an increase in desired aggregate expenditures on national output.

In sum, the aggregate quantity demanded of real national output is inversely related to the aggregate price level. The aggregate demand curve is downward-sloping as illustrated in panel (d) of Figure 12.3.

SHIFTS IN AGGREGATE DEMAND CURVE

We have established that the aggregate demand curve is negatively sloped. We now turn to shifts in the aggregate demand curve. First we should review the distinction between the desired aggregate expenditure schedule ($A = A_0 + aY$) and the aggregate demand schedule (AD).

The desired aggregate expenditure schedule (A) is from the Simple Keynesian model, where we assume that the aggregate price level and nominal interest rate are constant and that desired real fixed investment expenditures are autonomous. The desired aggregate expenditure schedule relates aggregate expenditures on real national output to real national income. When we graph the desired aggregate expenditure curve, we hold constant the level of real autonomous expenditures (A_0) and the marginal propensity to spend on real national output (a). In the Simple Keynesian model, equilibrium real national output is demand-determined. Desired aggregate expenditures on national output therefore determine the equilibrium level of production.

The aggregate demand schedule (AD) relates desired aggregate expenditures on real national output to the aggregate price level. The aggregate demand schedule incorporates the money market and allows for changes in the nominal interest rate to affect desired investment expenditures. The aggregate price level and the nominal interest rate along with real national output (income) are endogenous variables (whose values are to be solved for within the model). Moreover, desired real fixed investment expenditures are a function of the nominal interest rate. The aggregate demand schedule indicates those combinations of real national output and the aggregate price level for which the product and money markets simultaneously are in equilibrium.

The aggregate demand curve is drawn holding constant the nominal money supply, the marginal propensity to spend on real national output, and desired autonomous expenditures on real national output. Desired autonomous expenditures are defined in this case as those expenditures on real national output that are not dependent on the level of real national income or the aggregate price level. Changes in the nominal money supply, desired real autonomous expenditures, and the marginal propensity to spend on national output will produce shifts in the aggregate demand curve.

For example, an increase in the nominal money supply (due perhaps to open market purchases by the Fed) would reduce the nominal interest rate and stimulate investment spending. The increase in desired investment expenditures would initially be met by running down inventories. Firms would respond by stepping up the rate of production, increasing real national output and income. Thus, the increase in the nominal money supply increases the aggregate quantity demanded of national output for any aggregate price level, which is reflected in a rightward shift in the aggregate demand curve.[3]

Similarly, an increase in autonomous expenditures on national output (autonomous consumption, investment, government spending, or net exports) or an increase in the marginal propensity to spend on national output would produce an increase in aggregate demand and a rightward shift in the aggregate demand curve. Unlike an increase in the nominal money supply, which directly reduces the nominal interest rate, an increase in the level of autonomous spending or in the propensity to spend indirectly puts upward pressure on the interest rate. That is, the rise in real national output (and income) and the aggregate price level (assuming the economy is operating on the intermediate range of the aggregate supply curve) increases the demand for money. Thus, for a given supply of money, the equilibrium interest rate will rise.

A decrease in the aggregate demand for real national output (a leftward shift in the aggregate demand curve) can be caused by a decrease in the nominal money supply, a decrease in desired autonomous expenditures, or a decrease in the marginal propensity to spend on real national output. (You should be able to explain why.)

How much aggregate demand shifts with a given change in the money supply or desired autonomous expenditures depends on the associated multiplier effects—the deposit and expenditure multipliers—which we will discuss in some detail in the next two chapters. How much real national output and the aggregate price level change with a given shift in aggregate demand depends on the elasticity of the aggregate supply curve, or how close to the Classical range the economy is operating.

In Figure 12.4 we illustrate the distinction between an increase in aggregate demand and an increase in the aggregate quantity demanded of real national output. Rightward shifts in the aggregate demand curve (from AD to AD') indicate increases in aggregate demand resulting from increases in the nominal money supply, desired real autonomous expenditures on national output, or the marginal propensity to spend on real national output. Movements down the aggregate demand curve (for example, from E_0 to E_1) indicate increases in the aggregate quantity of national output demanded, resulting from a decrease in the aggregate price level. An increase in the aggregate quantity demanded of real national output may also be indicated by a rightward movement from one

---

[3] The potential impact of a given change in the nominal money supply on the equilibrium interest rate, and hence on desired real fixed investment expenditures and aggregate demand, tends to be greater the lower is the initial aggregate price level. For example, if the aggregate price level is $P_1 = 1.0$, then an increase in the nominal money supply of 10 (billion dollars) increases the real money supply by 10 (billion dollars): $\Delta M^s/P_1 = 10/1 = 10$. If, however, the aggregate price level is $P_2 = 2.0$, then an increase in the nominal money supply of 10 (billion dollars) increases the real money supply by only 5 (billion dollars): $\Delta M^s/P_2 = 10/2 = 5$.

FIGURE 12.4

INCREASE IN AGGREGATE DEMAND VERSUS INCREASE IN AGGREGATE QUANTITY DEMANDED OF REAL NATIONAL OUTPUT

An increase in aggregate demand (from AD to AD') is indicated by a rightward shift in the aggregate demand curve. An increase in the aggregate quantity demanded of real national output is indicated by a movement down an aggregate demand curve (e.g., from E_0 to E_1) in response to a decrease in the aggregate price level. An increase in the aggregate quantity demanded of real national output is indicated also by a rightward movement between two aggregate demand curves for a given price level (e.g., E_0 to E_0') in response to an increase in aggregate demand (e.g., from AD to AD').

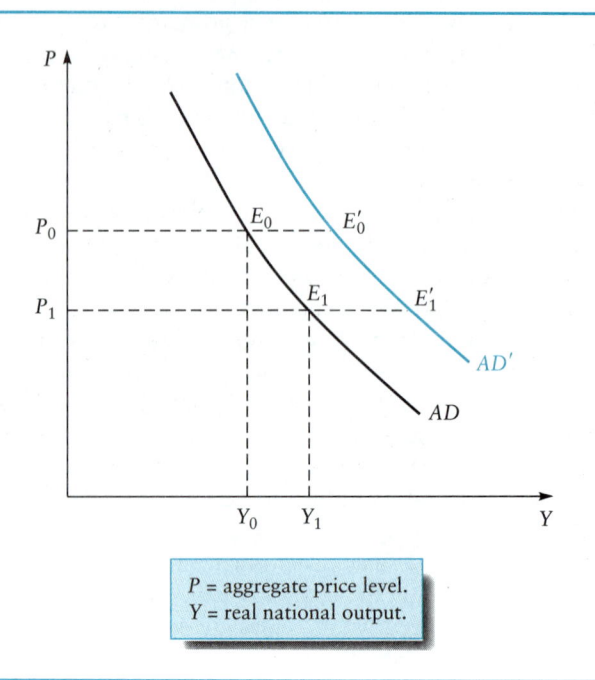

P = aggregate price level.
Y = real national output.

aggregate demand curve to another—holding the aggregate price level constant—resulting from an increase in aggregate demand (for example, from E_0 to E_0').

With just the aggregate demand schedule (or curve) we cannot determine the equilibrium real national output and the aggregate price level. The aggregate supply schedule (or curve) is also needed.

AGGREGATE SUPPLY CURVE

The **aggregate supply schedule** describes the relationship between the total quantity of national output produced and the aggregate price level. The **aggregate supply curve** is the graphical representation of the aggregate supply schedule. Introduced in Chapter 7 (see Figure 7.4), it is reproduced here in Figure 12.5. Real national output (Y) is on the horizontal axis, and the aggregate price level (P) is on the vertical axis. Recall that there are three ranges of the aggregate supply curve.

In the **Keynesian range** ($Y \leq Y_k$), the aggregate supply curve is perfectly elastic. Consistent with the Simple Keynesian model, the economy is operating well below its potential—with high rates of unemployment and excess capacity. In the Keynesian range there is no trade-off between unemployment and inflation. Unemployment can be reduced as real output expands without engendering inflation. That is, changes in aggregate demand affect only the rate of production, not the unit costs of production or the aggregate price level.

In the **intermediate range** ($Y_k < Y < Y_c$), the aggregate supply curve becomes less elastic. Increases in real output, responding to increases in aggregate demand, are accompanied by rising unit costs of production. As firms move out along their short-run cost curves, diminishing returns set in—the marginal products of labor decline and the marginal costs of production rise. Prices received by firms must also rise to induce the firms to supply more output. Thus, in the intermediate range, there is a short-run trade-off between inflation and unemployment. Increases in real output, which tend to reduce unemployment, put upward pressure on the aggregate price level. Moreover, as the economy continues to expand and move out along the aggregate supply curve, the increases in the unit costs of production accelerate. Capacity constraints become more binding. Labor, if required to work overtime, may receive higher overtime wages. To keep pace with demand, firms may employ additional workers, who, being less experienced, may also be less productive. In sum, real gains in output are harder to achieve.

Eventually, increases in aggregate demand can no longer be accommodated. In the **Classical range** ($Y = Y_c$), the economy is operating at maximum capacity. All the capital stock is being fully utilized, and unemployment has been reduced as far as possible. The trade-off between inflation and unemployment found in the intermediate range disappears. Increases in aggregate demand only fuel inflation. The aggregate supply curve is perfectly inelastic.

SHIFTS IN AGGREGATE SUPPLY CURVE

The aggregate supply curve illustrates the short-run relationship between real national output and the aggregate price level. Held constant when the aggregate supply curve is drawn are (1) the quantities and qualities of the available factors of production, (2) technology, (3) the schedules of factor prices, and (4) government regulation and taxes.

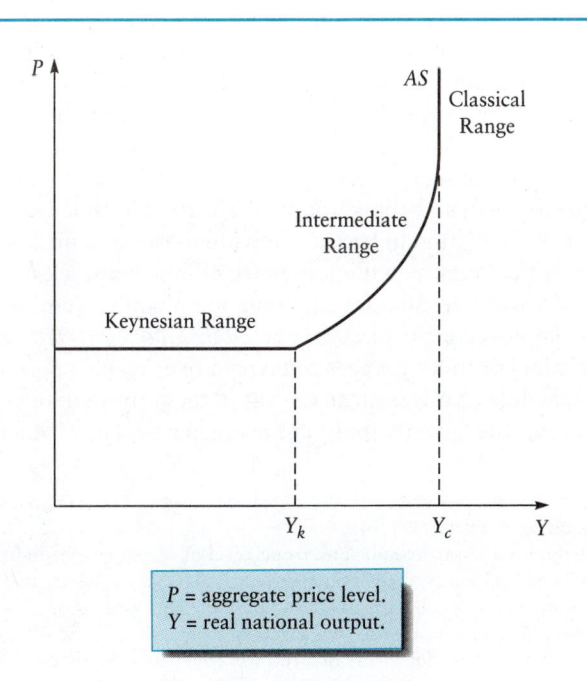

FIGURE 12.5

AGGREGATE SUPPLY CURVE

The aggregate supply curve illustrates the relationship between the aggregate price level (P) and the aggregate quantity of real national output produced (Y). In the Keynesian range, the curve is perfectly elastic. In the intermediate range, it becomes less elastic. Finally, in the Classical range, it is perfectly inelastic—the economy is operating at maximum capacity.

P = aggregate price level.
Y = real national output.

In the aggregate, the quantity of *labor* available is measured by the labor force, which in turn reflects the population of labor force age and the labor force participation rates. The quality of the labor force is reflected in the average levels of education, nutrition, health and work experience.

The quantity of *physical capital* is the capital stock of the nation—the plant, equipment and machinery, the residential and nonresidential structures, and the economic infrastructure of the transportation and communication systems. The physical capital stock increases with positive net fixed investment, that is, when gross fixed investment exceeds depreciation. The quality of the capital stock is indicated by the average productivity of a unit of capital. Technological change, much of which is embodied in new capital, as in the case of more energy-efficient machines and more powerful computers, increases the quality of the capital stock.

Natural resources include the land, forests, mineral deposits, and bodies of water available to a nation for use in production. The quality of the available resources reflects their intrinsic values in production. For example, some nations possess reserves of higher-grade petroleum than other nations. On the other hand, acid rain may result in a deterioration of a nation's forests. In general, environmental pollution diminishes the quality of natural resources.

Technological change also contributes to output growth. Advances in technology bring new products (such as semiconductors, which have been instrumental in the development of the computer industry) and new production techniques (as typified in the Green Revolution technology in agriculture with the high-yielding varieties of wheat and rice used in many developing nations). A nation can enhance technological progress by allocating resources to research and development.

The *schedule of factor prices* refers to the supply curves of the primary factors of production. Of these, labor is the most important; labor costs usually account for the majority of the factor costs of production. For the U.S. economy in 1990, employee compensation accounted for 74 percent of national income.[4]

Aggregate labor supply curves are upward-sloping. For any expected rate of inflation, individuals are generally willing to supply more hours of labor as the money wage rate rises. Given the finite number of hours in a week, however, more work implies less leisure time. Consumer theory suggests that the marginal utility of leisure increases as the amount of leisure consumed diminishes. To compensate for the reduction in leisure, individuals demand higher wages.[5] For instance, an individual may be willing to work 40 hours a week for $8 an hour, but unwilling to work overtime for anything less than $12 an hour.

Much of the employed labor force is covered by *labor contracts,* which set the schedule of nominal or money wages to be paid over a given period of time. A change in the schedule of wages means a shift in the supply curve of labor—not a movement along the given supply curve. In particular, an increase in the

---

[4] *Survey of Current Business,* November 1991, vol. 71, Number 11 (Washington, DC: U.S. Department of Commerce): Tables 1.9, 1.14.

[5] Assuming that leisure is a normal good, above some level of wage rates the individual's labor supply curve may bend backwards. If so, the positive income effect on leisure of a wage increase outweighs the negative substitution effect, and the higher wage elicits fewer hours of labor supplied. In macroeconomic analysis, we generally assume that the substitution effect dominates for the labor force, so for this reason the aggregate labor supply curve is upward-sloping.

schedule of wages indicates an upward (or leftward) shift in the labor supply curve (or a decrease in labor supply), indicating that a higher nominal wage would be required for any given quantity of labor supplied. For example, laborers would react to inflation, which diminishes the purchasing power of nominal wages, by demanding higher nominal wages. Ceteris paribus, an increase in the schedule of wages would increase the overall unit cost of production. This does not imply that all increases in the wage schedule are inflationary, though. The relevant concept is the **unit cost of labor,** which is equal to the ratio of the average cost of labor (the wage rate) to the average product of labor. To illustrate, suppose that the wage rate for a 40-hour week is $8 per hour and that the average product of labor is 10 units of output per hour. Then the unit cost of labor is $.80 per unit of output.

$$\text{Unit Cost of Labor} = \frac{\text{Average Cost of Labor}}{\text{Average Product of Labor}}$$

$$= \frac{\$8.00 \text{ per hour}}{10 \text{ units per hour}}$$

$$= \$.80 \text{ per unit of output}$$

That is, $.80 worth of labor is embodied in each unit of output. Now, if due to improved technology or more capital per worker, the average product of labor increases to 12 units of output per hour (a 20 percent gain in labor productivity), then the wage could increase by 20 percent to $9.60 per hour and still maintain the unit cost of labor at $.80. In short, wage increases that keep pace with productivity gains are not inflationary—that is, they do not contribute to upward shifts in firms' cost curves. If the percentage increase in the nominal wage, however, exceeds the percentage gain in labor productivity, then the unit cost of labor would rise, and the short-run average variable and average total cost curves of the output produced would shift up. For the economy, if the average cost of labor is rising faster than the average product of labor, the aggregate supply curve would shift up, ceteris paribus, and the price level associated with any rate of national output would rise.

A change in the schedule of natural resource prices would also shift the aggregate supply curve. For example, when OPEC engineered the quadrupling of the world price of oil in late 1973, the aggregate supply curves of all nations, particularly those dependent on oil imports, shifted upward, raising the costs of production and the aggregate price level associated with any rate of national output.

Similarly, a change in the profit margins or returns on invested capital sought by firms would affect the aggregate supply curve. Suppose firms widely used the *full-cost* pricing method, where the price charged for output is a percentage markup over the average cost of production at capacity. Firms seeking a greater profit margin would increase the percentage markup, which would increase the product prices and contribute to upward pressure on the aggregate price level.

Government regulations on business, whether for health, safety, or environmental reasons, tend to increase the costs of production. Usually firms are forced to use more expensive methods of production to comply with the government regulations. Finally, indirect taxes added onto the factor cost of production increase the market price of the output and shift up the aggregate supply curve.

FIGURE 12.6

INCREASE IN AGGREGATE SUPPLY VERSUS INCREASE IN AGGREGATE QUANTITY SUPPLIED OF REAL NATIONAL OUTPUT

An increase in aggregate supply (from AS to AS') is indicated by a rightward shift in the aggregate supply curve. An increase in the aggregate quantity supplied of real national output is indicated by a movement up an aggregate supply curve (e.g., from E_0 to E_1) in response to an increase in the aggregate price level. An increase in the aggregate quantity supplied of real national output is indicated also by a rightward movement between two aggregate supply curves for a given aggregate price level (e.g., from E_0 to E_0') in response to an increase in aggregate supply (e.g., from AS to AS').

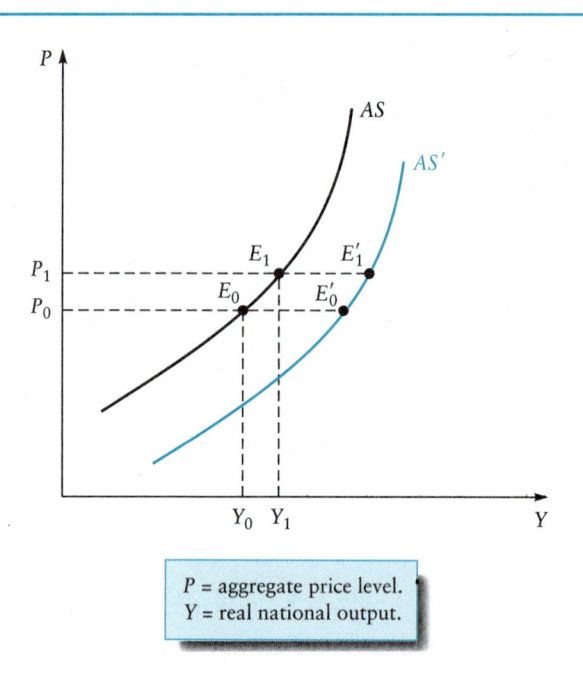

P = aggregate price level.
Y = real national output.

In Figure 12.6, to illustrate the distinction between an increase in aggregate supply and an increase in the aggregate quantity of national output supplied, we will focus on the intermediate range of the aggregate supply curve. An increase in aggregate supply is indicated by a rightward shift in the aggregate supply curve, which signifies that at any aggregate price level the quantity of real national output supplied is greater. (See the shift in the aggregate supply curve from AS to AS'.) Alternatively, an increase in aggregate supply can be viewed as a downward shift in the aggregate supply curve, signifying that the aggregate price level associated with any rate of real national production is lower. Increases in aggregate supply can be caused by increases in the quantity and quality of the factors of production, gains in technology, or reductions in the factor price schedules (rightward shifts in the factor supply curves).

Increases in the aggregate quantity supplied of real national output are indicated by movements to the right along a given aggregate supply curve in response to a rise in the aggregate price level. (See the movement to the right along the aggregate supply curve AS from E_0 to E_1.) That is, as the rate of production of real national output increases beyond the Keynesian range of the aggregate supply curve, unit costs of production rise—as the marginal products of labor fall and factor scarcities drive up the market-clearing prices of inputs. Therefore, increases in the aggregate price level are required to induce firms to increase their rates of production.[6]

---

[6] Note that the aggregate supply curve for the nation is not simply the horizontal summation of the supply curves of all the firms in the economy. Recall, for the perfectly competitive firm in the factor markets, an increase in the market-clearing price of an input would shift up the firm's cost curves. Suppose that the market demand (and price) for the input increases due to an increase in the market demand (and price) for the output of the firms. As long as the price of the

Increases in the aggregate quantity supplied of real national output also are indicated by a rightward movement between two aggregate supply curves—holding constant the aggregate price level. (See the movement from E_0 to E_0' in response to an increase in aggregate supply from AS to AS'.)

AGGREGATE DEMAND AND AGGREGATE SUPPLY: COMPARATIVE STATICS

Equilibrium in the macroeconomic model is found at the real national output (income) and aggregate price level where the quantity demanded of national output equals the quantity of national output supplied. Graphically the equilibrium occurs at the intersection of the aggregate demand and supply curves. In equilibrium, unplanned inventory investment is zero; consequently, there is no tendency for the rate of national output to be altered.

Changes in aggregate demand or aggregate supply will upset the equilibrium balance. The model is stable if any disequilibrium automatically sets in motion forces to restore the balance between supply and demand. Let us consider four comparative static results. In each case we assume the economy is initially in equilibrium (represented by the point E_0) on the intermediate range of the aggregate supply curve.

Shifts in Aggregate Demand

In Figure 12.7, we illustrate shifts in aggregate demand along the intermediate range of a given aggregate supply curve. An increase in aggregate demand (for example, due to an increase in desired autonomous expenditures on real national output) is shown by a rightward shift in the aggregate demand curve. At any aggregate price level, desired spending on real national output is higher. At the initial equilibrium price level, the excess quantity demanded of national output is represented by E_0E_0'. The increase in spending is initially met by

---

firms' output increases by more than the firm's unit cost of production, higher prices will elicit increased output.

Thus, increases in the rate of real national output produced (rightward movements along the aggregate supply curve in response to a rising aggregate price level with increases in aggregate demand) are consistent with increases in the market-clearing prices of the factors of production (rightward movements along the supply curves of the factors of production) and upward shifts in the cost curves of the firms in the economy.

Consider the case of labor. Increases in the rate of production of real national output will increase the demand for labor and—assuming there is no excess supply of labor—exert upward pressure on the market-clearing money wage. Firms have an incentive to hire more labor as long as the prices of their outputs are rising faster than their unit costs of labor. Reasons for the relatively sluggish response in the money wages of labor may include a delayed recognition by labor supply of the increase in the aggregate price level and the inability of labor bound by wage contracts to negotiate money wage increases that keep pace with the increase in the aggregate price level. (Note that as firms use more labor in the short run, eventually the marginal products of labor decline, which accelerates the increases in the unit cost of labor.) When workers recognize that the aggregate price level has increased, and when any existing wage contracts expire so labor is free to demand higher money wages for any quantity of labor supplied, then the labor supply curves will shift up and to the left, which, in turn, shifts up the aggregate supply curve.

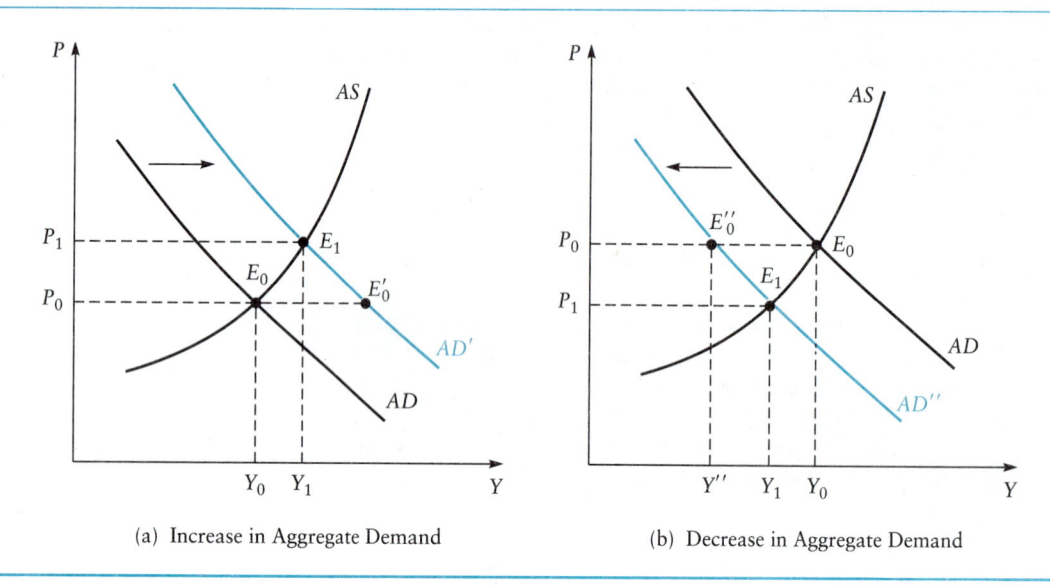

FIGURE 12.7

SHIFTS IN AGGREGATE DEMAND

In the intermediate range of the aggregate supply curve, an increase in aggregate demand from *AD* to *AD'* results in an increase in the aggregate price level and the rate of real national output produced. Also in the intermediate range of the aggregate supply curve, a decrease in aggregate demand from *AD* to *AD''* results in a decrease in the aggregate price level (assuming that prices are downwardly flexible) and a decrease in the rate of real national output produced.

drawing down inventories. As firms increase the rate of production, the unit costs of production rise. (Recall that diminishing returns to labor characterize the intermediate range of the aggregate supply curve.) The higher unit costs of production that accompany the expansion of output push up the aggregate price level. In the first panel of Figure 12.7 the economy moves from E_0 to E_1 along the aggregate supply curve. The rising real income and aggregate price level increase the demand for money. For a given money supply, the increased demand for money pushes up the interest rate. The higher interest rate reduces interest-sensitive expenditures (here business and residential fixed investment). Consequently, the aggregate quantity demanded of national output decreases (from E_0' to E_1 along the new aggregate demand curve). The economy converges to a new equilibrium at E_1. The increase in aggregate demand has increased real national output (from Y_0 to Y_1) and the aggregate price level (from P_0 to P_1).

A fall in aggregate demand (for example, due to a decrease in desired autonomous expenditures) is illustrated in the second panel of Figure 12.7 by a leftward shift in the aggregate demand curve. At the initial equilibrium price level, there is an excess supply of national output equal to $Y_0 - Y''$. As inventories build up, firms scale back production. Unit costs of production therefore fall. Assuming wages and prices are downwardly flexible, the aggregate price level falls as the economy contracts along the aggregate supply curve from E_0 to E_1. The lower real income and price level reduce the demand for money, which puts downward pressure on the interest rate. The drop in the interest rate will stimulate interest-sensitive expenditures so that the initial decline in aggregate demand (from E_0 to E_0'' with the shift from *AD* to *AD''*) is offset somewhat by an induced increase in the aggregate quantity demanded (from E_0'' to E_1 along the new aggregate demand curve). The economy eventually converges to a new equilibrium at E_1 with a lower national output ($Y_1 < Y_0$) and price level ($P_1 < P_0$).

Note, there is evidence that in the short run the aggregate price level may be downwardly inflexible. In not one year since 1960 has the implicit price deflator for GDP in the United States fallen. Economists speak of the *ratcheting effect* of the aggregate supply curve, meaning that once a price level is established, the aggregate supply curve, in effect, ratchets upward, becoming perfectly elastic at that price level. Labor contracts with automatic cost-of-living adjustments contribute to this ratcheting up.

For example, once P_0 is reached in the second panel of Figure 12.7, the aggregate supply curve AS becomes $P_0 E_0 AS$. Subsequent declines in aggregate demand (at least in the short run) produce the full contraction in national output consistent with the multiplier effect of the Simple Keynesian model. If prices do not adjust downward in the face of excess supply, and if interest-sensitive expenditures do not respond to a decline in the interest rate when national income and money demand fall, then a decline in aggregate demand from AD to AD'' will reduce real national output and income from Y_0 to Y''.

Explanations for the downward inflexibility in the aggregate price level include institutional rigidities like agricultural price supports, minimum wage laws, and money wages set in labor contracts. Also, if firms are reluctant to engage in price competition, and if workers covered by union funds and unemployment insurance prefer "temporary" layoffs over cuts in money wages, then prices in the short run will be sticky downward.[7]

Not all prices and wages, however, are downwardly inflexible. Even in the short run, raw material prices tend to fluctuate freely in both directions. And not all labor is covered by fixed money wage contracts. Moreover, if the economic downturn is severe enough, eventually even reluctant firms will cut profit margins and prices to sell off inventories, and unions may succumb to wage concessions. Nevertheless, the less flexible are prices and wages, the greater will be the burden of adjustment on output and employment.

In sum, shifts in aggregate demand produce the short-run trade-off between inflation and unemployment found on the intermediate range of the aggregate supply curve. Increases in aggregate demand will expand production, reduce unemployment, and increase the aggregate price level. Decreases in aggregate demand will contract production, increase unemployment, and reduce the aggregate price level—assuming prices are not completely inflexible downward.

---

[7] Even where workers are not covered by explicit labor contracts that detail the money wages to be paid and conditions of employment, labor markets may be characterized less by perfectly flexible, continuously equilibrating money wages than by institutionally set money wages, which are downwardly inflexible—at least in the short run. That is, in order to screen the job applicants, firms may find it advantageous to fix the money wage at a level somewhat above the level necessary to attract the desired number of workers. As long as there are more job applicants than openings, firms can choose from among the most promising applicants and thereby maintain the pressure on present employees to work hard. Moreover, even if the excess supply of labor increases (e.g., due to a fall in the demand for the outputs of the firms), firms may be reluctant to lower the set money wage—since to do so may not only risk morale problems (and work effort) among the employees, but result in the loss of the more productive of the employees. In sum, money wages may be downwardly inflexible in the short run in the face of an excess supply of labor. Note that for a given money wage, however, inflation reduces the real wage, so by holding the line on the money wage, firms may still realize reductions in the real wage paid.

On the other hand, if the money wage paid by firms falls below the level needed to fill the job openings, firms may have to increase it in order to retain present employees and hire the additional labor desired.

Shifts in Aggregate Supply

Shifts in aggregate supply, in contrast to shifts in aggregate demand, tend to move unemployment and inflation in the same direction. Increases in aggregate supply increase real output, increasing employment while exerting deflationary pressure. Decreases in aggregate supply result in higher prices and unemployment.

For example, in Figure 12.8 the increase in aggregate supply (due perhaps to technological change, growth in the labor force, or increases in the capital stock) increases the capacity for producing national output at each price level—alternatively, the increase in aggregate supply reduces the aggregate price level for any rate of national output. At the initial equilibrium price level of P_0, there will be an excess of production over expenditures, which causes a buildup in inventories. Firms then trim the rate of production, moving back down their new short-run cost curves, lowering the unit costs of production and the associated aggregate price level. (See the movement from E'_0 to E_1 along the new aggregate supply curve AS'.) The lower price level, in turn, reduces the demand for money, reducing the interest rate and stimulating interest-sensitive expenditures. Aggregate quantity demanded increases (from E_0 to E_1 along the aggregate demand curve). Thus, with an increase in aggregate supply the economy moves to a new equilibrium with higher rates of national output and employment and a lower aggregate price level. Whether or not the increase in aggregate supply actually reduces the unemployment rate depends on the source of the increase. For example, it is possible that an increase in aggregate supply due to growth in the labor force raises the unemployment rate even as the level of national employment increases. In the 1980s the declines in the price of petroleum helped shift the aggregate supply curve to the right—exerting downward pressure on the aggregate price level while promoting economic growth and reducing unemployment.

FIGURE 12.8

SHIFTS IN AGGREGATE SUPPLY

An increase in aggregate supply from AS to AS' reduces the equilibrium price level and increases real national output. A decrease in aggregate supply from AS to AS'' increases the equilibrium price level and reduces real national output.

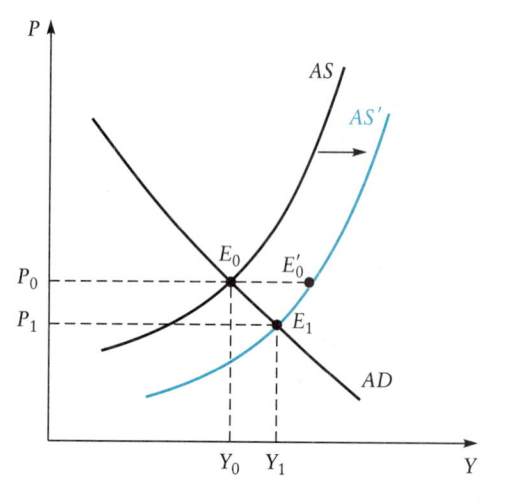

(a) Increase in Aggregate Supply

(b) Decrease in Aggregate Supply

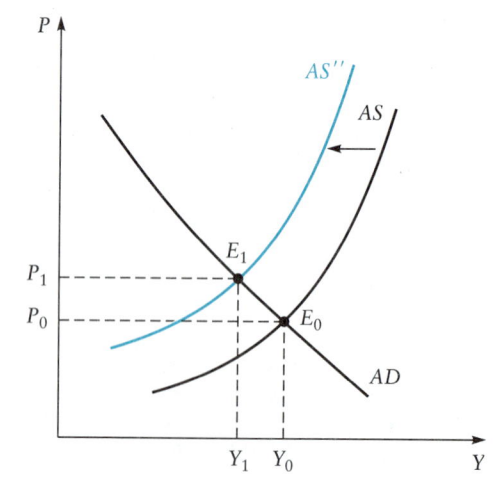

CHAPTER 12   AGGREGATE DEMAND AND AGGREGATE SUPPLY

TABLE 12.1
Stagflation in U.S. Economy: 1974 and 1975

	Percent Change in Real GDP	Unemployent Rate (Percent)	Percent Change in Implicit Price Deflator for GDP
1973	5.2	4.9	6.4
1974	− .6	5.6	8.7
1975	− .8	8.5	9.6

SOURCE: *Econmomic Report of the President 1992* (Washington, DC: U.S. Government Printing Office, 1992), Tables B-2, B-3, B-37.

Conversely, a decrease in aggregate supply (for example, due to an upward shift in the schedule for nominal wages or increased government regulation) pushes up the aggregate price level and unemployment rate. A decrease in supply is illustrated in Figure 12.8 by the leftward or upward shift in the aggregate supply curve. For any aggregate price level the quantity supplied of national output is less—alternatively, for any rate of national output, the aggregate price level is higher. Such upward shifts in the aggregate supply curve occurred in the 1970s with the steep hikes in the price of petroleum, a key input in the production of energy and many commodities, including plastics and fertilizers. The phrase **stagflation** is used to describe the concurrence of *stag*nation, or falling real output (from Y_0 to Y_1) and in*flation* (from P_0 to P_1). For evidence for the stagflation in the U.S. economy in 1974 and 1975 following the oil price shocks beginning in late 1973, see Table 12.1.

With our understanding of the aggregate demand-aggregate supply framework, we can turn to the analysis of business cycles.

BUSINESS CYCLES

With technological progress and growth in the capital stock and labor force, the aggregate supply curve shifts to the right, increasing the productive capacity of a nation. If we define **full employment** as the rate of national unemployment consistent with the underlying population growth and labor force participation rates, the skill composition of the labor force, and the normal rate of utilization of the nation's physical capital stock, then we can observe that the economy is usually not operating at full employment.

Periods of rapid economic growth and declining unemployment (with the economy sometimes operating beyond full employment) alternate with slower, even negative, growth and rising unemployment. Inflation typically alternates with unemployment as the primary concern of the economic policymakers; although, as noted, with supply-side shocks the economy must simultaneously deal with rising inflation and unemployment. In short, the economy moves through *cycles,* with real national output fluctuating around **potential national output,** the rate of national output that the economy could produce if it were operating at full employment. The difference between potential national output and the actual national output is known as the **national output gap.**

The swings in economic activity are so common that a vocabulary exists for the *business cycle,* illustrated in Figure 12.9. The top, or upper turning point,

FIGURE 12.9

BUSINESS CYCLE

The business cycle consists of significant swings in real national output (Y) around a longer-run trend consistent with full employment or potential real national output (Y_f). The difference between Y_f and Y is the real national output gap.

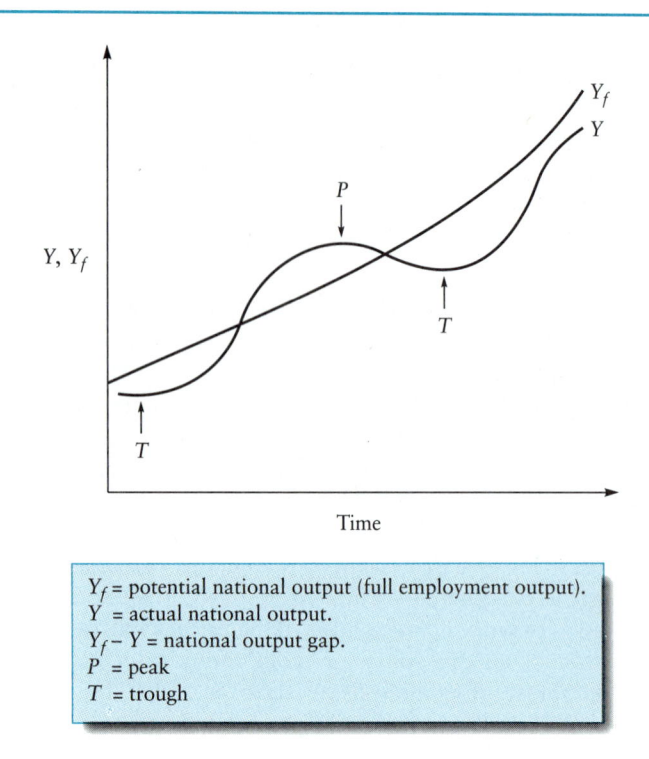

Y_f = potential national output (full employment output).
Y = actual national output.
$Y_f - Y$ = national output gap.
P = peak
T = trough

---

of a business cycle is known as a **peak**. The bottom, or lower turning point, is the **trough**. An **economic downturn** refers to the movement from a peak to a trough. A **recession** is a prolonged decline in the level of economic activity. The last severe recession in the United States began in the summer of 1981 and lasted six quarters (through 1982). The unemployment rate topped 10 percent near the end of that recession. In 1990–1991 the U.S. economy experienced another prolonged, if milder, recession. A **depression** is an unusually severe recession with respect to duration and depth. The effects of the Great Depression (from 1929 into 1933) lasted virtually the entire decade of the 1930s, with the unemployment rate in the United States reaching as high as 25 percent in 1933. An **economic expansion** refers to the movement from a trough to a peak. The longest recorded peacetime expansion for the U.S. economy occurred between the recessions of 1981–1982 and 1990–1991. A **boom** is the term given to a rapid economic expansion.

It is important to emphasize that business cycles vary in length and magnitude. Economists work to develop models that accurately forecast trends in economic activity, but despite significant advances in economic theory, statistics, and computer technology, macroeconomic forecasting remains an exercise beset with uncertainty. Of course, as a social science, economics deals with human behavior, which will never be completely predictable.[8]

---

[8] An *Index of Leading Economic Indicators*, tabulated monthly, is used to forecast turns in the economy. Included among the statistics comprising the index are common stock prices, residential building permits, initial unemployment claims, real growth in the money supply, new orders for consumer goods, and new orders for business plant and equipment.

In Figure 12.10 we chart the annual levels of real GDP for the U.S. economy for 1960 to 1990. In Table 12.2 we list the annual growth rates for real GDP, the unemployment rates, and the inflation rates for the same period. Although the trend for real GDP is clearly upward, the performance of the U.S. economy has been uneven. The decade of the 1960s was characterized by rapid growth—with the U.S. economy operating even beyond full employment (unemployment rates of then under 4 percent) from 1966 through 1969. In 1970 the economic boom was broken with a mild recession. The economy rebounded sharply in 1972 and 1973 before the oil price shocks in late 1973 and the resulting stagflation of 1974–1975. By 1976 the recovery was underway, and the economy picked up steam over the latter half of the 1970s. Then, in late 1979 the U.S. economy began to stall with the second wave of oil price increases and the policy shift of the Federal Reserve to tighter control over the nation's money supply to rein in inflation. The brief recession of 1980 turned out to be only a prelude to the deeper recession of 1981–1982. Seven years of uninterrupted economic growth were broken in mid-1990 when the United States slipped into a recession.

FIGURE 12.10

GROWTH IN REAL GDP OF UNITED STATES: 1960–1990

Plotting the real levels of Gross Domestic Product for the United States over the past three decades shows an upward trend only occasionally interrupted by declines (in 1970, 1974–75, 1980, and 1982).

SOURCE: *Economic Report of the President, 1992,* Table B-2.

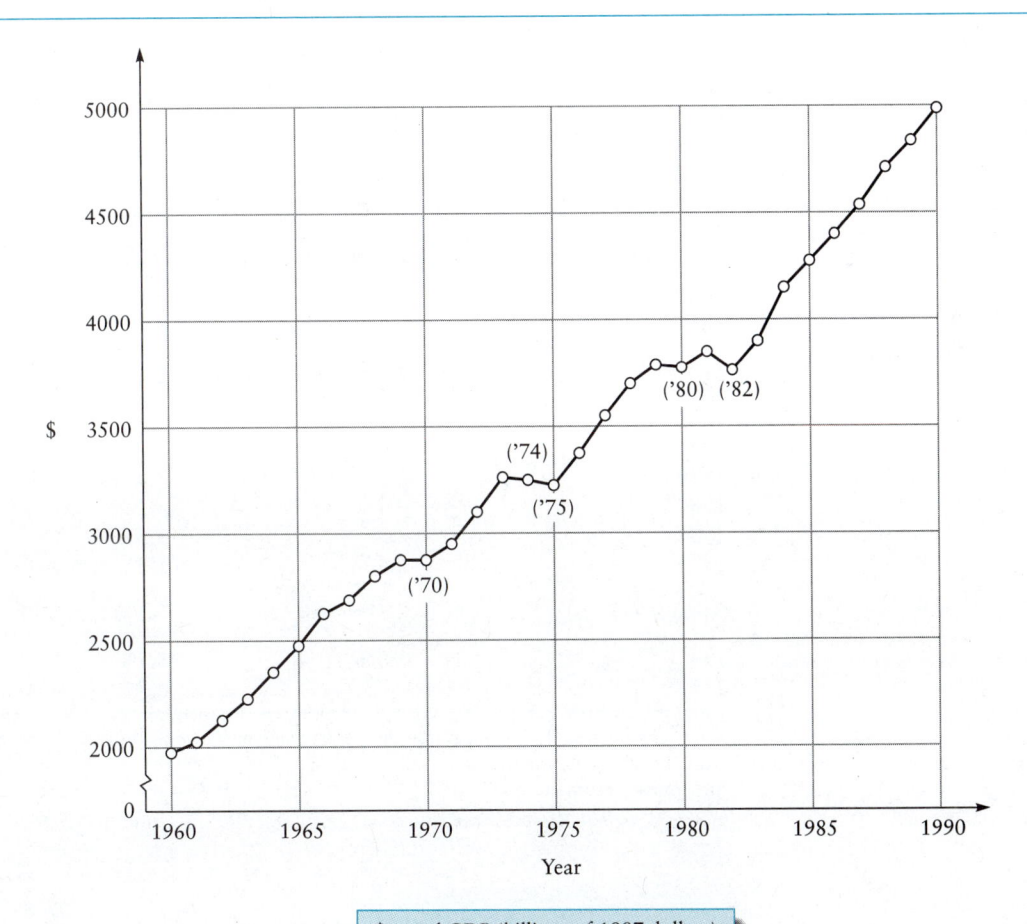

$ = real GDP (billions of 1987 dollars).

TABLE 12.2
Economic Growth and Unemployment and Inflation Rates for the United States: 1960–1990

Year	Growth Rate in Real GDP	Unemployment Rate	Inflation Rate
1960	2.2%	5.5%	1.6%
1961	2.7	6.7	1.2
1962	5.1	5.5	1.9
1963	4.1	5.7	1.5
1964	5.6	5.2	1.8
1965	5.6	4.5	2.5
1966	6.0	3.8	3.5
1967	2.6	3.8	3.1
1968	4.1	3.6	4.6
1969	2.7	3.5	5.0
Average (1960s)	**4.1%**	**4.8%**	**2.7%**
1970	−.0%	4.9%	5.4%
1971	3.1	5.9	5.4
1972	4.8	5.6	4.9
1973	5.2	4.9	6.4
1974	−.6	5.6	8.7
1975	−.8	8.5	9.6
1976	4.9	7.7	6.3
1977	4.5	7.1	6.9
1978	4.8	6.1	7.9
1979	2.5	5.8	8.6
Average (1970s)	**2.8%**	**6.2%**	**7.0%**
1980	−.5%	7.1%	9.5%
1981	1.8	7.6	10.0
1982	−2.2	9.7	6.2
1983	3.9	9.6	4.1
1984	6.2	7.5	4.4
1985	3.2	7.2	3.7
1986	2.9	7.0	2.6
1987	3.1	6.2	3.2
1988	3.9	5.5	3.9
1989	2.5	5.3	4.3
Average (1980s)	**2.5%**	**7.3%**	**5.2%**
1990	1.0%	5.5%	4.2%
1991[a]	−.7	6.7	3.6

NOTES: The inflation rate is measured by the percentage change in the implicit price deflator for Gross Domestic Product.
[a] preliminary estimate.
SOURCE: *Economic Report of the President 1992*, Tables B-2, B-3, and B-37.

FIGURE 12.11

HYPOTHETICAL BUSINESS CYCLE

The business cycle illustrated here begins with an increase in aggregate demand (from AD_0 to AD_1). The economic expansion turns into a boom with a second increase in aggregate demand (to AD_2). Labor supply responds to the higher aggregate price level by demanding higher nominal wages, and the aggregate supply curve shifts back to AS_3. The economy turns down. With the burst in spending exhausted, aggregate demand falls back to a more normal rate (AD_2 to AD_4), which aggravates the economic downturn and induces a recession. Eventually, aggregate supply rises (from AS_3 to AS_5) as a result of capital stock increasing from earlier investments, firms reducing their profit margins, and labor making wage concessions. The economic recovery begins. If consumer and business confidence rebound, then another economic expansion will be underway (AD_4 to AD_6).

P = aggregate price level.
Y = real national output.

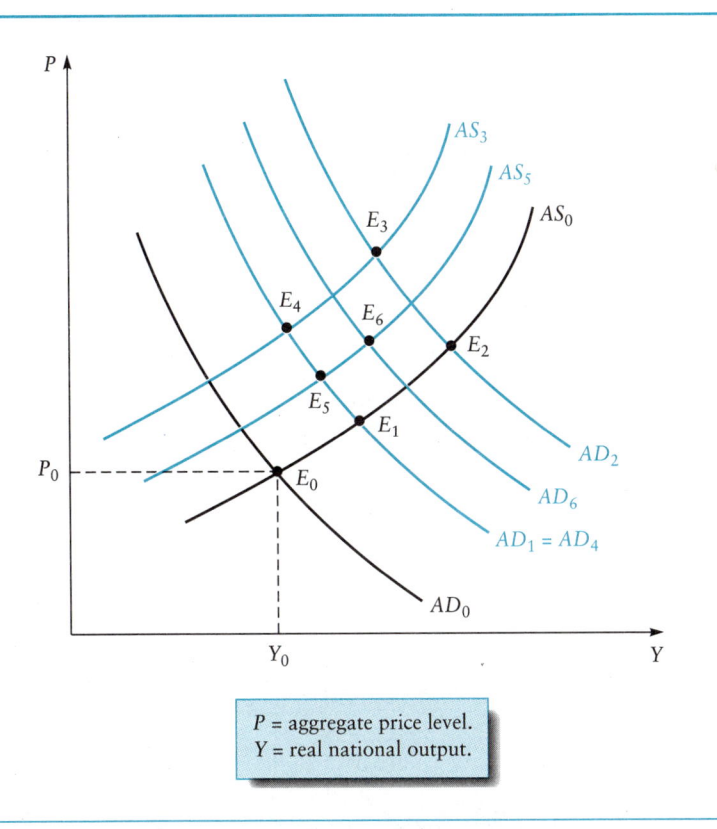

Over the three decades there were significant variations in the key performance measures of the economy. Annual unemployment rates ranged from a low of 3.5 percent (1969) to a high of 9.7 percent (1982). The inflation rate (measured by the percentage change in the implicit price deflator for GDP) ranged from a low of 1.2 percent (1961) to a high of 10.0 percent (1981). The annual growth rate in real GDP ranged from a low of −2.2 percent (1982) to a high of 6.2 percent (1984).

Relative shifts in aggregate demand and aggregate supply account for the variation in unemployment, inflation, and economic growth rates. Consider Figure 12.11, which is used to illustrate the course of a hypothetical business cycle. Suppose the economy begins at E_0 with Y_0 and P_0. An increase in aggregate demand to AD_1 (due perhaps to a rally on Wall Street boosting wealth, or a surge in residential construction because of an increase in the national birth rate) results in a rise in real national output and upward pressure on the aggregate price level. The economy moves along the aggregate supply curve to E_1. With the fall in inventories and the economic expansion, business and consumer confidence may rise, leading to increased spending on plant, equipment, and machinery, residential construction, and consumer durables. The aggregate demand curve again shifts out to AD_2. The economic expansion may turn into a boom. Unemployment falls further, but inflation heats up (see E_2).

In response to the higher prices, workers may demand higher money wages (in fact, some labor may be automatically protected with cost-of-living adjustments). The aggregate supply curve then shifts back to AS_3, which again

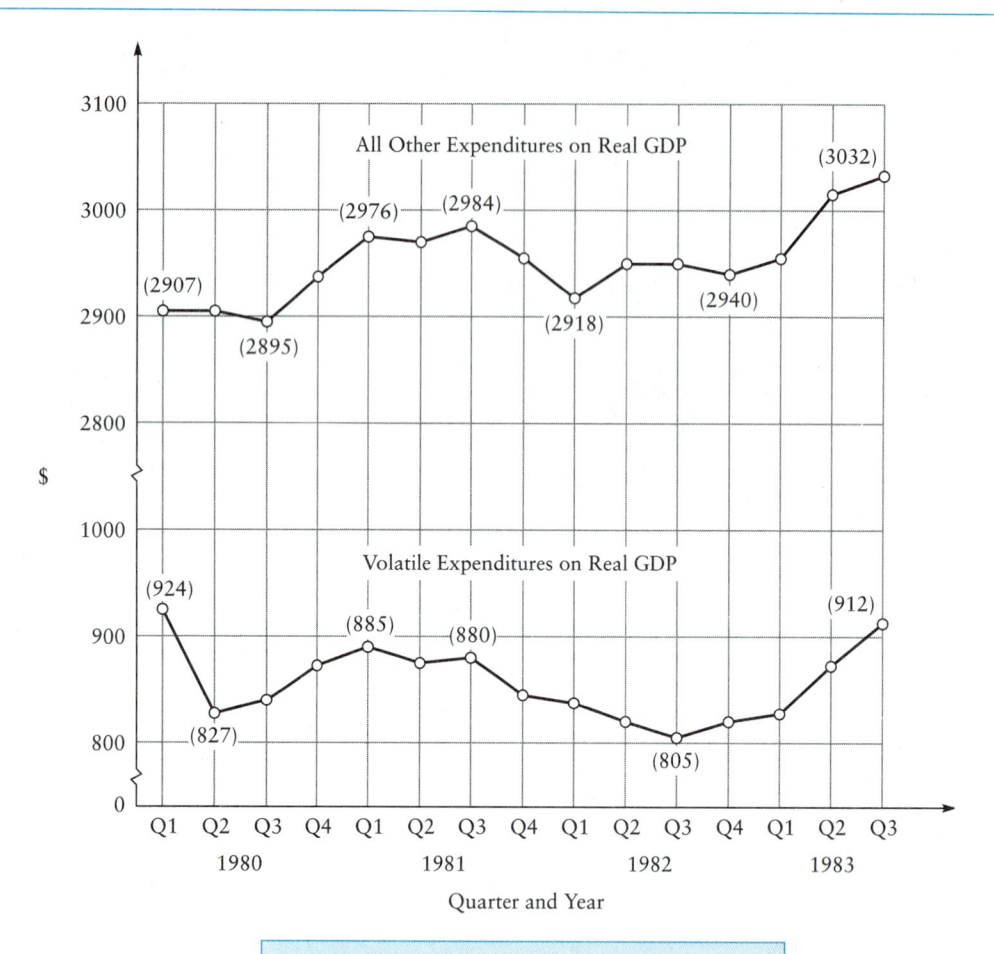

[Graph: Real Growth in Expenditures on GDP from First Quarter of 1980 through Third Quarter of 1983]

All Other Expenditures on Real GDP: (2907), (2895), (2976), (2984), (2918), (2940), (3032)

Volatile Expenditures on Real GDP: (924), (827), (885), (880), (805), (912)

Quarter and Year: Q1–Q3 1980 through Q3 1983

$ = expenditures on real GDP (billions of 1987 dollars).

FIGURE 12.12

REAL GROWTH IN EXPENDITURES ON GDP FROM FIRST QUARTER OF 1980 THROUGH THIRD QUARTER OF 1983

Volatile expenditures on real Gross Domestic Product include personal consumption expenditures on durable goods, business fixed investment, and residential fixed investment. Nonvolatile expenditures are equal to all other expenditures on real Gross Domestic Product.

SOURCE: *Survey of Current Business,* Nov. 1991, Table 2.

pushes up the aggregate price level at the same time that real output declines and unemployment increases. The economic downturn is illustrated by the movement from E_2 to E_3.

By this point households may have exhausted their spending on housing and durables and firms may have completed their investment projects. Moreover, the downturn in the economy may shift the attention of the households and firms to paying off the earlier loans used to make these expenditures. Consequently, aggregate demand falls back to a more normal rate ($AD_4 = AD_1$). The fall in demand and buildup of inventories, however, further contracts the economy, and may even induce a recession. The economy moves back along the aggregate supply curve AS_3 from E_3 to E_4.

Eventually the aggregate supply curve will shift right—as the earlier business investment in new capacity comes on line; or, if the recession is deep enough, firms may lower profit margins and labor may accept wage concessions. A rightward shift in the aggregate supply curve would start the economic recovery (from E_4 to E_5 along AD_4). The increases in real output and employment may, in turn, revive consumer and business confidence. Some households and firms will need to replace worn-out consumer durables and machinery. At this point, an increase in aggregate demand (to AD_6) would enhance the economic recovery. The economy will then come full circle in this business cycle.

From the expansion (E_0 to E_1) to the boom (E_1 to E_2) to the downturn (E_2 to E_3) to the recession (E_3 to E_4), then recovery (E_4 to E_5), and expansion (E_5 to E_6), the cycle may take several years to work through. The types of desired spending most volatile in the course of the business cycle are business and residential fixed investment and consumer durables—expenditures sensitive to credit conditions and dependent upon business and consumer confidence.

In Figure 12.12 we plot these volatile components (in 1987 dollars) against all other expenditures on GDP for the United States economy for a 15-quarter period covering the two recessions in the early 1980s. Although accounting for less than 25 percent of all real expenditures on GDP, the interest- and confidence-sensitive expenditures on consumer durables and business and residential fixed investment contributed greatly to the swings in the business cycle.

For example, from the first to the second quarter of 1980, these volatile expenditures fell by $97 billion, which pulled the U.S. economy into a recession. From the third quarter of 1981 through the third quarter of 1982, the decline in these volatile expenditures of $75 billion exceeded the decline of $35 billion in all other expenditures on GDP. The subsequent rise of $107 billion from the third quarter of 1982 through the third quarter of 1983 surpassed the increase of $83 billion in spending on the steadier components of GDP.

CONCLUDING NOTE

Business cycles appear to be an inevitable characteristic of capitalist economies—for reasons not entirely understood. Since the end of World War II, the United States has experienced nine business cycles, including two record economic expansions. The longest expansion, which covered over 100 months, lasted from February of 1961 to December of 1969 and included the effects from the escalation of the Viet Nam War. The longest peacetime expansion, encompassing more than 90 months, lasted from November 1982 to mid-1990.[9]

Whether policymakers should actively intervene in the economy to moderate the business cycle is an issue of active debate among economists. In the next two chapters we will discuss macroeconomic policies designed to offset the swings in the business cycle and stabilize the economy near full employment. In Chapter 13 the subject is fiscal policy, or the discretionary changes in government expenditures and taxes designed to achieve some macroeconomic objective. In Chapter 14 we turn to monetary policy, or discretionary changes in the money supply engineered by the Federal Reserve.

---

[9] These statistics on the business cycle from the National Bureau of Economic Research appeared in Alfred Malabre, Jr., "Recessions Can Bring Benefits with Pain," *The Wall Street Journal*, November 5, 1990, A1, A5.

KEY TERMS

aggregate demand schedule
aggregate demand curve
aggregate supply schedule
aggregate supply curve
Keynesian range
intermediate range
Classical range
unit cost of labor
stagflation
full employment

potential national output
national output gap
peak
trough
economic downturn
recession
depression
economic expansion
boom

QUESTIONS

1. What are the three most important ideas in this chapter? Discuss why each is important.
2. Assume the economy is initially in equilibrium in the intermediate range of the aggregate supply curve. Discuss the effects on the equilibrium real national output (income), the aggregate price level, the nominal interest rate, and desired real fixed investment expenditures of
   a. an increase in real government purchases of goods and services.
   b. an increase in real autonomous imports of goods and services.
   c. an increase in income tax rates.
   d. an increase in the nominal money supply.
   e. technological progress.
   f. an increase in the nominal wage schedule, i.e., labor demands higher money wages for any quantity of labor supplied.

   Discuss the economic transition to the new equilibrium as a result of these events. You may want to illustrate your answer graphically.
3. Note specific macroeconomic factors that could account for
   a. a rise in the aggregate price level and a fall in the national unemployment rate.
   b. a fall in the aggregate price level and a rise in the national unemployment rate.
   c. a rise in the aggregate price level and a rise in the national unemployment rate.
   d. a fall in the aggregate price level and a fall in the national unemployment rate.

   Explain your answers.

PART

V

MACROECONOMIC POLICY

CHAPTERS

— 13 —
THE CONDUCT OF FISCAL POLICY

— 14 —
THE CONDUCT OF MONETARY POLICY

— 15 —
SUPPLY-SIDE POLICY

— 16 —
UNEMPLOYMENT AND INFLATION:
TRADE-OFFS

CHAPTER

13

THE CONDUCT OF FISCAL POLICY

THE PRIMARY MACROECONOMIC goals for a nation are full employment, price stability, and a healthy rate of economic growth. Attaining these goals is not easy. Consider that not once in the last three decades has the U.S. economy achieved both an unemployment rate of less than 5 percent (which roughly corresponds to full employment) and an inflation rate of under 2 percent (which begins to approximate price stability). The last year the national unemployment rate was below 5 percent was 1973 (at 4.9 percent). The last year the inflation rate (measured by the percentage change in the Implicit Price Deflator for Gross Domestic Product) was less than 2 percent was 1964 (at 1.8 percent). Nevertheless, much of the public and many economists favor an activist role for the federal government in managing aggregate demand to offset major fluctuations in the business cycle.

We can use the aggregate demand-aggregate supply framework to illustrate. See Figure 13.1, where for the given short-run aggregate supply curve, Y_f represents potential or full employment national output. If the economy were operating with an aggregate demand of AD_1, there would be a positive national output gap of $Y_f - Y_1$, with above normal unemployment. If the economy were operating beyond full employment with an aggregate demand of AD_2, the national output gap would be negative, $Y_f - Y_2 < 0$. In this event, inflation would likely become a problem. An aggregate demand equal to AD_f would close the national output gap and yield full employment.[1] Ideally, then, economic policy could be used to maintain aggregate demand at the full employment level of national output.

Many other economists argue that the economy is inherently stable, with a natural tendency toward full employment, and that activist demand-

---

[1] As we will discuss in Chapter 16, there is no unique aggregate price level (or inflation rate) consistent with full employment national output.

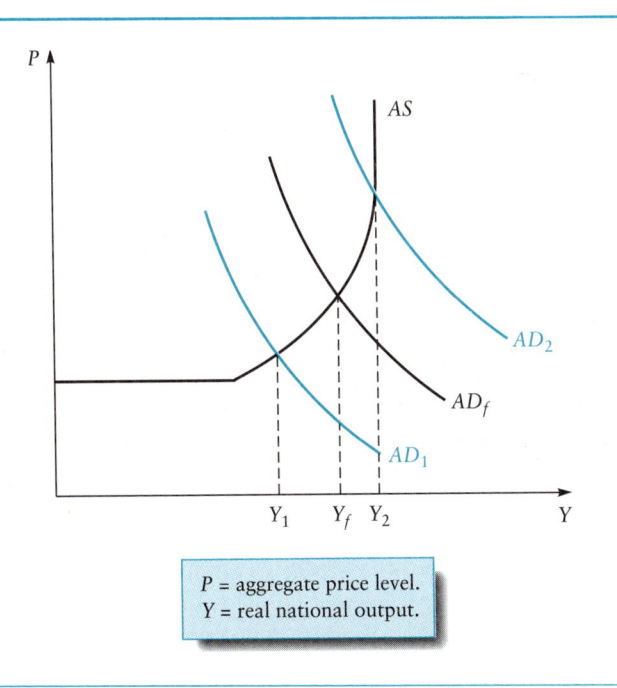

FIGURE 13.1

Aggregate Demand Management and Full Employment

With the given short-run aggregate supply curve AS, the full employment level of real national output is Y_f. If aggregate demand is AD_1, the national output gap is positive, $Y_f - Y_1$. If aggregate demand is AD_2, the national output gap is negative, $Y_f - Y_2$. Only if aggregate demand is AD_f is the national output gap eliminated.

P = aggregate price level.
Y = real national output.

---

management policies of the government are destabilizing. In this and succeeding chapters we will discuss the controversies over macroeconomic policy.

As noted at the end of Chapter 12, there are two basic types of *demand-management* policies. **Fiscal policy,** formulated by the president and Congress, refers to discretionary changes in government purchases, transfers, and taxes that are designed to alter the level or composition of aggregate demand. **Monetary policy,** set by the Federal Reserve, operates through changes in the money supply that in turn affect interest rates and interest-sensitive expenditures. In the present chapter we address fiscal policy.

KEYNES AND DEMAND-MANAGEMENT POLICY IN A DEPRESSED ECONOMY

In the 1930s the British economist John Maynard Keynes sought a solution to the dilemma of an economy stalled well below full employment. He asked, if desired aggregate expenditures were insufficient to purchase the national output consistent with full employment, then what could boost aggregate spending enough to reach full employment? Keynes believed that in a depressed economy expansionary monetary policy would be ineffective. That is, increases in the money supply would do little to increase interest-sensitive expenditures and stimulate aggregate demand. At low levels of national income and prices, the market-clearing interest rate tends to be low. The interest elasticity of money demand, however, tends to be high—due largely to the speculative demand for money. With low interest rates, bond prices are high, and speculative money balances are held in anticipation of eventual declines in bond prices. Therefore, increases in the money supply (for example, with open market purchases of bonds by the Fed) only further drive up bond prices. The interest rate does not have to fall very much to clear the money market since any increase in the money supply is quickly added to speculative balances. In short, when the demand for money is very sensitive to the interest rate, changes in the money supply will have relatively little impact on the equilibrium interest rate.

Second, even if the market interest rate does fall more than marginally when the money supply is increased, desired aggregate expenditures on national output will not be significantly affected according to this view. Firms will not likely invest in new plant and machinery with excess capacity on hand. Households will not take on loans for purchases of homes and consumer durables with unemployment high and income prospects uncertain.

Thus, the combination of the high interest-sensitivity of money demand and the interest-insensitivity of spending on business and residential fixed investment and consumer durables that is characteristic of depressed economies renders monetary policy ineffective in changing the level of aggregate demand. Keynes therefore advocated expansionary fiscal policy—primarily increased government spending—to fill the gap between desired aggregate expenditures and potential national output. Moreover, with the full force of the multiplier effect, the necessary increase in government expenditures would be less than the output gap.

In hindsight the proposed Keynesian remedy may seem obvious. If private spending falls short of full employment output, then public expenditures could pick up the slack. At the time Keynes wrote, however, the conventional wisdom was just the opposite. If it made sense for a household to tighten its budget when its income fell, so, too, it was believed, should government spending be reduced when tax revenues fell. During the early years of the Great Depression, in an attempt to avoid greater budget deficits as tax revenues declined along with national income, the federal government sought to cut expenditures and increase tax rates.[2] In the Simple Keynesian model presented in Chapter 9,

---

[2] The severity of the Great Depression reflected the confluence of a number of factors, including a general overcapacity in agriculture and industry that discouraged fixed investment, a stockmarket crash and widespread banking failures that sharply reduced wealth and consumer spending, a proliferation of international trade barriers that sacrificed productive jobs in export industries, and misguided monetary policy, which, like fiscal policy, was contractionary.

With respect to fiscal policy, the overriding concern was to balance the federal budget. To counter the budget deficits that grew as tax revenues fell with the declines in national income, tax rates were raised and government spending was reduced. The idea that the government should aggressively pump up aggregate demand was not seriously considered, since further budgetary "red ink" was perceived as eroding public confidence in the government. Moreover, the share of government expenditures in national output in the 1930s was much lower than in the post–World War II era—which may have reduced the perceived leverage of government spending to boost the economy. (We should add that the policymakers did not have the benefit of organized national economic statistics to guide their decisionmaking. National income accounting and the systematic measuring of aggregate economic performance were not developed until the 1940s.)

In particular, Keynes's proposed remedy of significantly increasing government spending for the purpose of stimulating aggregate demand was never really tried during the 1930s. The entrance into World War II required the United States to increase government spending substantially. The adoption of Keynesian demand-management economic policies, however, did not occur until the 1960s with the Kennedy and Johnson administrations—some 15 years after Keynes's death. For a good overview of the economics of the Great Depression, see Robert Puth, *American Economic History,* 2d ed. (Chicago: Dryden Press, 1988), 469–484.

reducing government expenditures or increasing tax rates directly reduces aggregate demand and further exacerbates unemployment. Keynes argued on this basis that during a major economic downturn, the federal government should not attempt to balance the budget but rather should increase spending and deliberately run a deficit.

In sum, Keynes and the early Keynesian economists believed that expansionary fiscal policy was required to lift an economy from economic doldrums.[3] To illustrate the fiscal policy options, we return to a discussion of the Simple Keynesian model.

FISCAL POLICY OPTIONS

Recall the key assumptions of the Simple Keynesian model. The economy is assumed to be operating well below full employment on the Keynesian range of the aggregate supply curve. Investment expenditures are assumed to be completely insensitive to the interest rate. Aggregate demand alone determines the level of real national output. We will illustrate the fiscal policy options of the federal government for closing a positive national output gap with a numerical example extending this basic version of the Simple Keynesian model.

Specifically, we modify the tax function to allow for real autonomous net taxes. In Chapter 9 we assumed there were no transfer payments and that all taxes were personal income taxes. Personal income taxes, in turn, were assumed to be proportional to real national income. We now write

$$T = T_0 + tY$$

where $0 < t < 1$, and

T = real net taxes (i.e., real tax revenues less real government transfer payments).
Y = real national income (real national output).
t = marginal rate of taxation.
T_0 = real autonomous net taxes.

That is, real net taxes are directly related to real national income by the **marginal rate of taxation,** t. The autonomous component of real net taxes, T_0, also known as **net lump-sum taxes,** captures the tax revenues and government transfer payments that are independent of the level of real national income. For instance, in the comprehensive tax reform of 1986 in the United States, numerous tax shelters and tax loopholes were closed ($\Delta T_0 > 0$), while tax rates were reduced ($\Delta t < 0$). If, instead, welfare programs were changed so that more individuals qualify for public assistance, then net lump-sum taxes would fall ($\Delta T_0 < 0$).

Writing the tax function in this way will also alter the expression for real disposable personal income (Y_d).

$$Y_d = Y - T = Y - (T_0 + tY)$$
$$= -T_0 + (1 - t)Y$$

---

[3] The converse would hold for an inflationary economy overheating near the Classical range of the aggregate supply curve. To reduce aggregate demand and curb inflation, the federal government should adopt contractionary fiscal policy—cutting government expenditures, raising taxes, and running a budget surplus.

Note, in our model, real personal consumption expenditures (C) and real imports of goods and services (M) are also functions of real disposable personal income. Thus, these two functions will similarly need to be recalculated.

We will see that while each of the fiscal policy options considered will close the output gap, moving the economy to full employment, the implications for the government budget balance and the role of the government in the economy will differ.

Define the government budget balance (GBB) as

$$GBB = T - G$$

where

G = real government purchases of goods and services.

If $T - G < 0$, there is a budget deficit; $T - G = 0$, there is a budget balance; $T - G > 0$, there is a budget surplus.

A budget deficit must be financed. (Later in this chapter we will discuss how the federal government finances a budget deficit.) A budget surplus can be regarded as government saving.

Consider the following model:

$C = 5 + .92Y_d$	Personal consumption expenditures
$I_0 = 45$	Investment expenditures
$G_0 = 105$	Government purchases of goods and services
$X_0 = 35$	Exports of goods and services
$M = 2 + .12Y_d$	Imports of goods and services
$T = -15 + .25Y$	Net taxes
$Y_d = Y - T$	Disposable personal income
$A = C + I + G + X - M$	Desired aggregate expenditures
$A \stackrel{e}{=} Y$	Equilibrium condition

To solve the model we begin with the desired aggregate expenditure schedule. Recall, to derive the desired aggregate expenditure schedule we first need to convert the consumption and import schedules into functions of national income. Here disposable income is

$$Y_d = Y - T = Y - (-15 + .25Y) = 15 + .75Y$$

Substituting the expression for disposable income into the consumption and import schedules gives

$$C = 5 + .92Y_d = 5 + .92(15 + .75Y) = 18.8 + .69Y$$

$$M = 2 + .12Y_d = 2 + .12(15 + .75Y) = 3.8 + .09Y$$

Adding the components of desired aggregate expenditures yields

$$A = C + I + G + X - M$$
$$= 18.8 + .69Y + 45 + 105 + 35 - 3.8 - .09Y$$
$$= 200 + .6Y$$

The desired level of real autonomous expenditures on national output is equal to 200. The marginal propensity to spend on national output is equal to .6. Solving yields an equilibrium level of national output and income ($\bar{Y}_0$) equal to 500.

CHAPTER 13 THE CONDUCT OF FISCAL POLICY

$$A = 200 + .6Y = Y$$

and

$$\bar{Y}_0 = 200/.4Y = 500$$

There is initially a surplus of 5 in the government budget balance.

$$GBB_0 = T - G = -15 + .25(500) - 105 = 5$$

Suppose full employment national output is estimated to be 540 ($Y_f = 540$). The national output gap is equal to 40 ($Y_f - \bar{Y}_0 = 540 - 500 = 40$). Let us consider two basic fiscal policy options available to the president and Congress for closing the output gap. Each of the options will increase aggregate demand by enough to reach full employment output.

Change in Government Spending

First, government spending on national output could be directly increased. To close an output gap of $N, the government would not have to increase expenditures by $N—remember the multiplier effect. An increase in autonomous expenditures on national output of $N induces additional spending, so that the cumulative increase in national output exceeds the $N increase.[4] Recall that the autonomous expenditure multiplier in the Simple Keynesian model is given by

$$K_{A_0} = \frac{1}{1 - a}$$

where a = marginal propensity to spend on national output. Here,

$$K_{A_0} = \frac{1}{1 - .6} = \frac{1}{.4} = 2.5$$

Thus, a $1 increase in autonomous expenditures would ultimately increase national output and income by $2.50. The required increase in autonomous government expenditures, then, to close an output gap of 40 would be $\Delta G_0 = 16$.

$$\Delta G_0 = \frac{Y_f - \bar{Y}_0}{K_{A_0}} = \frac{540 - 500}{2.5} = 16$$

To confirm that an increase in government expenditures of 16 will generate an increase of 40 in national output, the new aggregate expenditure schedule is

$$A' = 200 + 16 + .6Y$$

Solving gives

$$216 + .6Y = Y$$

$$216 = .4Y$$

$$\bar{Y}_1 = 540 = Y_f$$

---

[4] The increase in government purchases is assumed to be spent entirely on national output. Otherwise autonomous imports would also increase by the amount of government spending on imported goods and services.

Will the government budget balance fall by 16 when government spending rises by 16? No, not with taxes being a function of national income. When national income increases with the boost in government expenditures, tax revenues rise. In this example the level of net taxes at the full employment national income is

$$T' = -15 + .25(540) = 120$$

The new budget balance is

$$GBB_1 = T' - G'_0 = 120 - 121 = -1$$

that is, a deficit of 1.

In sum, an increase in government spending of 16 reduces the budget surplus by only 6—since tax revenues rise by 10.

Change in Net Lump-Sum Taxes

Alternatively, the federal government could decrease net lump-sum taxes in order to stimulate the economy. For instance, transfer payments could be increased or tax laws changed to reduce lump-sum taxes ($\Delta T_0 < 0$). To close the output gap of 40 in this example, would the required decrease in net lump-sum taxes be the same as the required increase in government purchases? That is, would a decrease of 16 in net lump-sum taxes (a decrease in lump-sum taxes or an increase in government transfers) also increase equilibrium national output and income by 40? The answer is no.

A portion of the increase in disposable personal income due to the tax cut or transfer payments will be saved. And, unlike the increase in government purchases, which were assumed to be entirely for national output, only part of the increase in consumption expenditures will be spent on national output. Part of the increase in consumption will be for imported goods and services. In this example, with a marginal propensity to consume equal to .92, only 92 cents out of every dollar increase in disposable income will be spent; 8 cents will be saved. A marginal propensity to import equal to .12 means that 12 cents of every dollar increase in disposable income will be spent on imports. Thus, only 80 percent (.92 − .12) of any increase in disposable income, will be spent on national output. Consequently, the required change in net lump-sum taxes must be greater than the required change in government purchases.

The lump-sum tax multiplier is equal to

$$K_{T_0} = \frac{-(c - m)}{1 - a} = -(c - m)K_{A_0}$$

where c and m are the marginal propensities to consume and import out of disposable income, respectively. The lump-sum tax multiplier is negative, since an increase in taxes (a withdrawal of income from the national expenditure stream) reduces national output and income. As long as the marginal propensity to consume national output ($c - m$) is less than 1, the lump-sum tax multiplier will be less (in absolute value) than the autonomous expenditure multiplier.

Here the value of the lump-sum tax multiplier is −2.0.

$$K_{T_0} = \frac{-(.92 - .12)}{1 - .6} = -.8(2.5) = -2.0$$

The required change in net lump-sum taxes is

$$\Delta T_0 = \frac{Y_f - \overline{Y}_0}{K_{T_0}} = \frac{40}{(-2.0)} = -20$$

A decrease of 20 in net lump-sum taxes will increase equilibrium output by 40, thereby closing the gap. (You should confirm this independently.) The new tax schedule is

$$T'' = -15 + (-20) + .25Y = -35 + .25Y$$

Evaluated at the new level of real national income of $Y_f = 540$, net taxes are equal to 100.

$$T'' = -35 + .25(540) = -35 + 135 = 100$$

The new government budget balance is

$$GBB_2 = T'' - G_0 = -5$$

that is, a deficit of 5. Thus, compared to the government expenditure increase, the lump-sum tax cut produces a greater deficit.

The two fiscal policy options differ in another respect. In the case of the rise in government spending, the role of the government in the economy increased—in terms of the share of government purchases in national output (G/Y), and the share of net tax revenues in national income (T/Y). In contrast, with the cut in net lump-sum taxes, the role of the government in the economy decreased. For those primarily concerned with minimizing the increase in the budget deficit, the expansionary fiscal policy option of increasing government purchases would be preferred. For those primarily concerned with minimizing the role of the government in the economy, the tax cut would be preferred.[5]

---

[5] There is a third possibility, the so-called *balanced budget* change in government purchases and net lump-sum taxes. That is, a change of $N in government purchases would be accompanied by a change of $N in net lump-sum taxes. In the Simple Keynesian model, the balanced budget multiplier

$$K_{B_0}$$

is equal to the sum of the autonomous expenditure multiplier

$$K_{A_0}$$

and the lump-sum tax multiplier

$$K_{T_0}$$

Thus,

$$K_{B_0} = K_{A_0} + K_{T_0}$$

Since the two fiscal changes involved have opposite effects on equilibrium national output and income, we would expect a relatively small value for the balanced budget multiplier. In this numerical example,

$$K_{B_0} = 2.5 + (-2.0) = .5$$

That is, for every dollar increase in government spending matched by a dollar increase in net lump-sum taxes, the net multiplier effect is to increase equilibrium national output and income

A variant of the decrease in net lump-sum taxes would be a decrease in the tax rate. The derivation and interpretation of the tax rate multiplier, however, is more complex. It turns out for this example that reducing the marginal tax rate from .25 to .213 will increase spending on national output enough to close the gap of 40.[6] That is, if the net tax function is

$$T''' = -15 + .213Y$$

then the desired aggregate expenditure function becomes

$$A''' = 200 + .63Y$$

Solving yields the full employment level of national output of 540 (approximately). The change in the government budget balance with the tax rate cut is the same as with the decrease in net lump-sum taxes.

---

by 50 cents. It follows that the increases in government purchases and lump-sum taxes required to close a real national output gap of 40 would be equal to 80 (a rather substantial increase).

$$\Delta G_0 = \Delta T_0 = (Y_f - \bar{Y}_0)/K_{B_0} = \frac{540 - 500}{.50} = 80$$

The new level of government spending and new tax function would be

$$G_B = 105 + 80 = 185$$
$$T_B = -15 + 80 + .25Y_f = 65 + .25Y = 65 + .25(540) = 200$$

The new government budget balance would be

$$GBB_B = T_B - G_B = 200 - 185 = 15$$

that is, a surplus of 15. Thus, if expansionary fiscal policy is called for to close a positive national output gap, a balanced budget change in government purchases and net lump-sum taxes would have the most favorable impact on the government budget balance. In this example, the initial government budget surplus actually increases. The balanced budget approach, however, would clearly result in the greatest increase in the role of the government in the economy—here, it would seem, an improbably large increase.

[6] Given the initial equilibrium national income of 540, the .037 reduction in the marginal tax rate translates into an increase of 18.5 in disposable income, which in turn increases consumption expenditures by 17 (i.e., 92 percent of the increase in disposable income) and import expenditures by 2.2 (i.e., 12 percent of the increase in disposable income). The net increase of 14.8 in consumption expenditures on national output can be viewed like an increase in autonomous expenditures that will induce further spending on national output through the multiplier process. The ensuing multiplier process will incorporate the new tax rate. That is, the relevant autonomous expenditure multiplier is

$$K'_{A_0} = \frac{1}{1 - a'} = \frac{1}{[1 - (c - m)(1 - t')]}$$

In this example, the value of the autonomous expenditure multiplier increases from

$$K_{A_0} = \frac{1}{1 - .6} = \frac{1}{[1 - (.92 - .12)(1 - .25)]} = 2.5$$

to

$$K'_{A_0} = \frac{1}{1 - .63} = \frac{1}{[1 - (.92 - .12)(1 - .213)]} = 2.7$$

Consequently, the decrease in the tax rate from .25 to .213 will prompt an initial increase in expenditures on national output of 14.8, which will kick off the multiplier process and ultimately increase national output by the desired 40.

$$(\Delta A_0)(K'_{A_0}) = (14.8)(2.7) = 40$$

$$T''' = -15 + .213(540) = 100$$

$$GBB_3 = T''' - G_0 = 100 - 105 = -5$$

that is, a deficit of 5. Note that a change in the tax rate alters the values of the autonomous expenditure and lump-sum tax multipliers. Here the decrease in the income tax rate raises the marginal propensity to spend on national output and thereby increases the values of the multipliers.

EFFECTIVENESS OF FISCAL POLICY

It might seem from the previous example of the Simple Keynesian model that maintaining the economy at full employment would be a rather straightforward task. Once the gap between the current level of national output and the level consistent with full employment is determined, the required dose of fiscal policy could be found by dividing the output gap by the appropriate multiplier. In this way the fiscal authorities, through discretionary changes in government expenditures and taxes, could manage aggregate demand to stabilize the economy at full employment. Several factors, however, complicate such use of fiscal policy.

Aggregate Supply Constraints

First, fiscal policy is likely to be most effective under the conditions that characterize the Simple Keynesian model. That is, a given change in government spending or net lump-sum taxes will have the greatest impact on national output when the aggregate supply curve is perfectly elastic and investment expenditures are completely insensitive to the interest rate.

As the economy expands, moving to the right and off the Keynesian range of the aggregate supply curve, the values of the autonomous expenditure and lump-sum tax multipliers decline. Diminishing returns to labor set in, short-run capacity constraints become increasingly binding, and the ability of the economy to produce additional output is reduced. Attempts to increase national output to accommodate growth in aggregate demand yield rising inflation. Indeed, in the Classical range of the aggregate supply curve, the autonomous expenditure and lump-sum tax multipliers equal zero—changes in demand affect only the aggregate price level.

Aside from the variation in the values of the multipliers due to the elasticity of supply, a related confounding factor is knowledge of the components of the multipliers. Recall the equations for the multipliers.

$$K_{A_0} = \frac{1}{1 - a}$$

which is the autonomous expenditure multiplier, and

$$K_{T_0} = -(c - m)/(1 - a)$$

which is the lump-sum tax multiplier, where

a = marginal propensity to spend on national output: $a = (c - m)(1 - t)$.
c = marginal propensity to consume.

m = marginal propensity to import.
t = marginal tax rate.

The marginal propensities to consume and import, hence the marginal propensity to spend on national output, are only estimates. While economists continually analyze macroeconomic data in order to develop more accurate estimates for these parameters, the fact remains that the values assumed by the policymakers for the marginal propensities to consume and import are estimates of the true, unknown values. Moreover, the true values may vary over time and with income. For example, over the past four decades the U.S. economy has become more open, that is, more dependent on foreign trade. An increase in the marginal propensity to import (m), ceteris paribus, reduces the values of the autonomous expenditure and net-lump sum tax multipliers.

Interest-Sensitivities and the Monetarist Position

When the analysis of the Simple Keynesian model is realistically extended to incorporate the money market, and when allowance is made for the sensitivity of investment expenditures to the interest rate, predicting the impact of a fiscal policy change on national output becomes even more complicated. To illustrate, consider an expansionary fiscal policy—for example, an increase in government purchases. With the rise in government spending, aggregate demand increases, inventories fall, and real national output expands. The demand for money increases with the rise in real national income and the rise in the aggregate price level (assuming the economy is on the intermediate range of the aggregate supply curve). For a given money supply, the increase in the demand for money pushes up the interest rate. The higher interest rate reduces the quantities demanded of interest-sensitive expenditures such as business and residential investment. In short, the rise in government purchases "crowds out" some private investment.

Macroeconomists known as **monetarists** believe that this *crowding out effect* is significant. That is, a $\$N$ increase in government purchases (or a $\$N$ increase in consumption expenditures arising from a tax cut) will eventually crowd out roughly $\$N$ of private investment expenditures—even if the elasticity of aggregate supply is high. Consequently, monetarists do not believe in the efficacy of demand-management fiscal policy.

To elaborate, monetarists argue that money demand is not very sensitive to the interest rate. The primary motive for holding money balances is for transactions. The quantity of nominal money balances demanded is assumed to be a rather stable proportion of nominal income. On the other hand, monetarists believe that investment expenditures are very responsive to the interest rate and thus the interest elasticities of business and residential fixed investments are high.

In the traditional Keynesian approach, money demand is assumed to be sensitive to the interest rate. (Keynes added speculative demand as a motive for holding money balances.) Moreover, Keynesians do not believe investment spending is much affected by the interest rate. Business and residential fixed investments are viewed as rather volatile components of aggregate demand, dependent more upon expectations and the perceived state of the economy.

Thus, according to Keynesians, demand-management fiscal policy is capable of changing real national output and employment.

In Figure 13.2 the two sets of assumptions are illustrated. The initial levels of the interest rate (i_0) and real fixed investment expenditures (I_0) are the same in the Keynesian (upper panel) and monetarist (lower panel) versions.

Consider again the effects of expansionary fiscal policy. Increases in government purchases (or decreases in net taxes) raise desired aggregate spending on national output and the demand for money—the latter indicated by a rightward shift in the money demand curve from M^d to $M^{d'}$ in Figure 13.2. (Note that the horizontal shifts are equal in both panels.) According to Keynesians, the interest rate would not have to rise much to eliminate the excess demand for money (from i_0 to i'_k). In contrast, for monetarists, the rise in the interest rate needed to clear the money market would be greater (from i_0 to i'_m), since the quantity demanded of money is not very responsive to the interest rate.

For monetarists, the greater rise in the equilibrium interest rate combined with the higher interest elasticity of investment results in a much larger crowding out effect of private investment expenditures. (Compare I'_m with I'_k.) For Keynesians, the crowding-out effect is small. Which view is correct? Empirical tests on the interests elasticities of money demand and investment expenditures have not satisfactorily resolved the controversy.

Nevertheless, we offer the following generalizations. The change in real national output (ΔY) resulting from a given fiscal policy change (ΔG_0 or ΔT_0) will be greater, (1) the further the economy is from full employment (that is, the more elastic aggregate supply is), (2) the more sensitive money demand is to the interest rate, and (3) the less sensitive investment is to the interest rate.

Do not try to memorize these conditions. Understand why they hold. As an exercise, try reformulating the generalizations to indicate when fiscal policy will be the least effective in changing the level of real national output.

Lags in Policymaking

Another difficulty in using demand-management to stabilize the economy concerns *lags,* the unavoidable time lapses in the formulation, implementation, and consequences of a given policy change. Three lags can be identified.

The **recognition lag** refers to the time it takes the policymakers to assemble and analyze the data and to ascertain the condition of the economy. For instance, data on stock prices, interest rates, and exchange rates are continuously available. The rates for unemployment and inflation (measured by the consumer and producer price indices) are available on a monthly basis. Preliminary Gross Domestic Product estimates are calculated on a quarterly basis, and then usually revised in subsequent quarters. In all, it may take several months of data to establish a trend.

The **response lag** refers to the time it takes, once the condition of the economy is determined, to formulate the appropriate policy. For instance, if sharp increases in consumer prices occur for several months in a row, suggesting an emerging problem with inflation, it will require time to fashion the policy response. The president and Congress (the 100 senators and 435 members of the House of Representatives) are jointly responsible for conducting fiscal policy. There may be disagreement not only on the best policy to deal with inflation, but even on the need for any policy response at all. Different

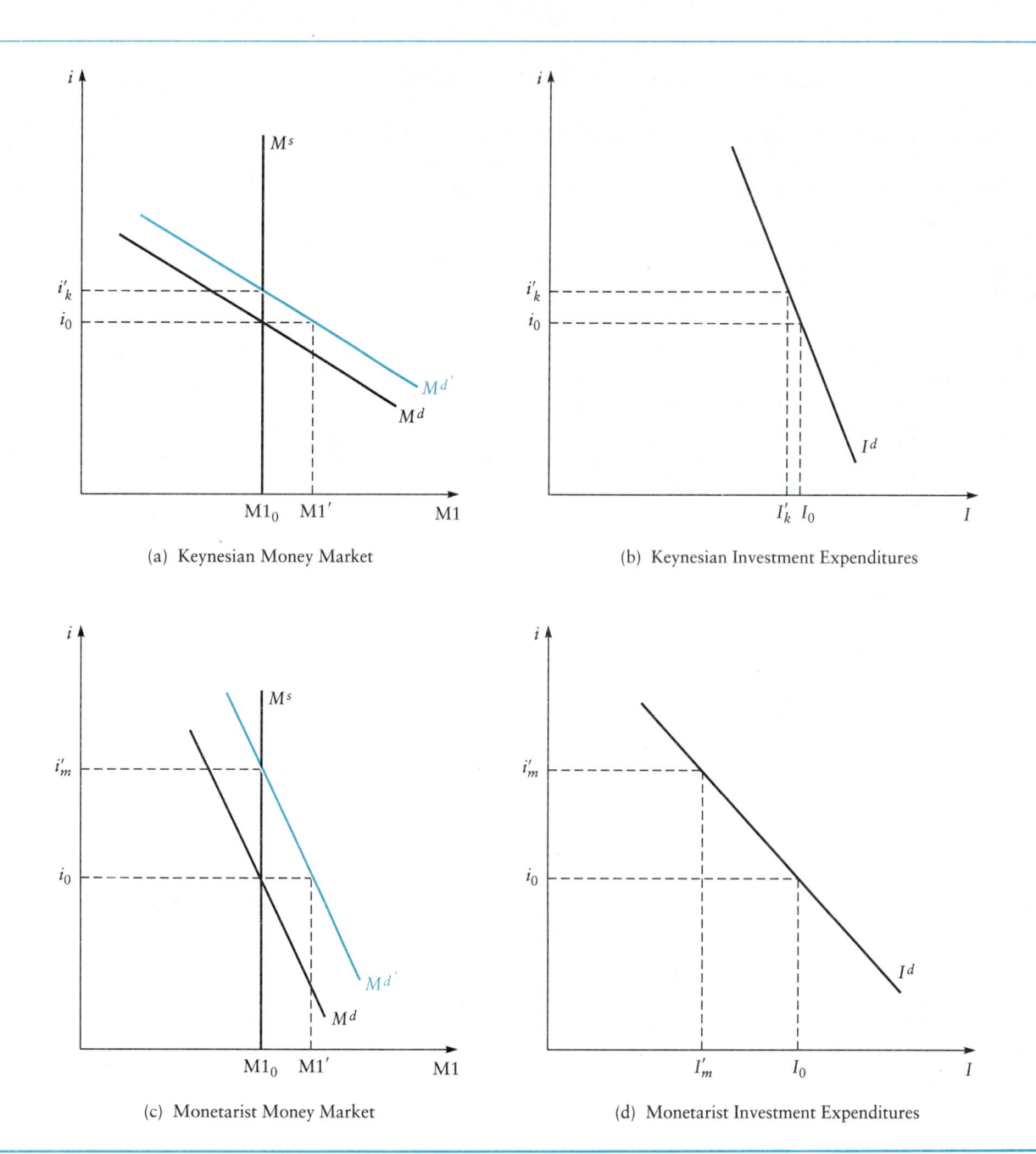

FIGURE 13.2

INTEREST SENSITIVITIES OF MONEY DEMAND AND INVESTMENT EXPENDITURES: EFFECTIVENESS OF FISCAL POLICY

The Keynesian position is that the quantity of nominal money balances demanded is sensitive to the nominal interest rate, while the quantity demanded of real fixed investment is not very sensitive to the nominal interest rate. In contrast, monetarists believe the quantity of nominal money balances demanded is not sensitive to the nominal interest rate, but that the quantity demanded of real fixed investment is very sensitive to the nominal interest rate. Consequently, a given increase in the demand for money will require a greater increase in the equilibrium interest rate to reequilibrate the money market in the monetarist model. Moreover, any increase in the nominal interest rate will decrease the quantity of real fixed investment demanded by a greater extent in the monetarist model.

policymakers have different tolerances for inflation. Even those fiscal policymakers concerned with inflation may refrain from advocating a fiscal policy response, instead relying on the Federal Reserve to tighten monetary policy. If there is a consensus that the rise in inflation does require tighter fiscal policy, then there may be prolonged debate over whether to cut government spending (and in which areas) or to raise taxes (and whose taxes). Recall from the earlier example that a change in government spending and an equivalent change in taxes differ in their implications for the deficit and the role of the government in the economy.

A recent example of the response lag would be the protracted deliberation (and bipartisan gamesmanship before the elections) on the appropriate fiscal policy to address the recession that began in the United States in mid-1990. Two years later, as the summer of 1992 drew to a close, the president and Congress still had not agreed on a fiscal policy package to stimulate the languishing economy. The large federal budget deficits also accounted for much of the fiscal indecisiveness. (Later in this chapter and again in following chapters we will address the causes and consequences of federal budget deficits.)

Finally, after the recognition and response lags, there is the **impact lag**. Once the fiscal policy change is passed—for example, an increase in taxes to trim consumer spending and cool down inflation—it takes time for the macroeconomy to react. An increase in the tax rate will reduce disposable income and consumer spending.[7] The drop in desired aggregate expenditures on national output will result in a buildup of inventories and a cutback in production. The ensuing multiplier effects will unfold over many months. Consider the lags involved: beginning from the point the macroeconomic condition *develops* (an increase in inflation), is *ascertained* (recognition lag), prompts a fiscal policy *change* (response lag), and ultimately is countered with *offsetting changes* in aggregate demand (impact lag). Needless to say, the economy does not stand still for the policymakers. The economy presents a moving target. Thus, by the time the policy change becomes effective, it may no longer be needed—and may even be counterproductive. Suppose that the sharp increase in inflation (as indicated

---

[7] A complicating factor in predicting the effect of an income tax change on aggregate consumption expenditures is suggested by the **permanent income hypothesis**. Briefly, according to this theory, households base their short-run or annual consumption expenditures on an estimate of permanent income. **Permanent income** is real disposable personal income that a household normally expects to receive based on the labor force participation and market skills of the members of the household, earnings from financial wealth (e.g., stocks, bonds, saving accounts) and the income tax and transfer system. Variations in actual real disposable personal income from (the estimates of) permanent income are largely regarded as **transitory income**. The marginal propensity to consume out of transitory income is assumed to be close to zero. Consequently, changes in real disposable personal income not regarded as permanent would have little impact on annual consumption.

The implication for fiscal policy is that households would react differently in the short run to a change in net taxes perceived to be temporary (thus affecting transitory income) than to an identical change in net taxes regarded as permanent. Thus, annual real consumption expenditures may not be as closely related to real disposable personal income as implied by the linear consumption function used in the Simple Keynesian model ($C = C_0 + cY_d$). In particular, given a long-run or permanent marginal propensity to consume of .9, a temporary tax increase of $10 billion may be perceived to reduce permanent income by much less than $10 billion, and may only marginally affect consumption expenditures in the short run. That is, personal consumption expenditures may initially fall by considerably less than $9 billion, with most of the tax increase paid for with reduced personal saving.

by the monthly consumer price indices) were only temporary, and that left alone, the economy would have stabilized. When the contractionary fiscal policy (the increase in the tax rate) takes effect, the economy may be sent into an unwanted downturn. On the other hand, if the economy were truly overheating, then the tax hike would be stabilizing. The importance of accurate forecasts of the economy is readily apparent.

In sum, due to the uncertainty over the magnitude of the multipliers and the inevitable lags in activating policy, most economists acknowledge the inability of fiscal policy to "fine-tune" the economy. That is, attempting to manage aggregate demand so carefully as to eliminate any deviation in real output from full employment output is not feasible. Whether or not demand-management policy should be used to offset major fluctuations in the business cycle, however, garners less consensus. Keynesians believe fiscal policy can be used to stabilize the economy by preventing large swings from full employment. Other economists, including the monetarists, believe the economy is inherently stable and argue against activist demand-management policy.

BUILT-IN STABILIZERS

In fact, the tax and transfer system provides a **built-in stabilizer** for the economy. Recall the formula for the autonomous expenditure multiplier of the Simple Keynesian model.

$$K_{A_0} = \frac{1}{1 - a} = \frac{1}{[1 - (c - m)(1 - t)]}$$

The higher the marginal tax rate, t, the smaller is the autonomous expenditure multiplier. For example, if $c = .9$, $m = .1$, and $t = .3$, the value of the autonomous expenditure multiplier is 2.27.

$$K_{A_0} = \frac{1}{[1 - (.9 - .1)(1 - .3)]} = 2.27$$

If the marginal tax rate is .35, the value of the multiplier falls to 2.08.

$$K'_{A_0} = \frac{1}{[1 - (.9 - .1)(1 - .35)]} = 2.08$$

The implication is that with the higher tax rate, any change in autonomous expenditures will have less of an impact on equilibrium national output—a stabilizing influence. This is not to imply, however, that higher tax rates are necessarily better. In the chapter on supply-side economics we will discuss the incentive structure of the tax system.

The government budget balance moves cyclically with the economy. Return to the linear formulation of the government budget balance:

$$GBB = T - G = T_0 + tY - G_0$$

where

GBB = government budget balance.
T = real net taxes.

T_0 = real net lump-sum taxes.
G_0 = real government purchases of goods and services.

Any change in the government budget balance can be disaggregated as follows:

$$\Delta GBB = \Delta T_0 + t\Delta Y + Y\Delta t - \Delta G_0$$

If the tax rate, net lump-sum taxes, and government purchases are all held constant—that is, $\Delta t = 0$, $\Delta T_0 = 0$, and $\Delta G_0 = 0$—then

$$\Delta GBB = t\Delta Y$$

It follows that in times of economic expansion ($\Delta Y > 0$), the government budget should move toward a surplus ($\Delta GBB > 0$). In practice, not only do tax revenues rise with gains in national income, but government transfers tend to fall as fewer individuals qualify for unemployment compensation and welfare assistance from government entitlement programs. Conversely, with an economic downturn, tax revenues decline, more individuals qualify for government transfers, and budget deficits grow, ceteris paribus. Therefore, even without active demand-management policy, the government budget balance automatically moves to soften the business cycle. The tendency toward a budget surplus during expansions helps keep the economy from overheating. The tendency toward a budget deficit during contractions helps bolster the economy.

Moreover, with a progressive income tax system, this stabilizing influence is enhanced. With a progressive income tax, marginal and average tax rates rise with income. Consequently, with increases in national income, the share of net taxes in national income will rise. With decreases in national income, the share of net taxes will decline. Consider a very simple income tax system with just two tax brackets.

Taxable Income	Tax Rate
under $20,000	10%
$20,000 and over	10% on the first $20,000
	15% on income above $20,000

An individual with a taxable income of $19,000 would pay $1900 in income taxes—a tax rate of 10 percent, .10 = 1900/19000. An individual with a taxable income of $21,000 would pay $2000 in taxes on the first $20,000 of income and $150 in taxes on the next $1000 of income—an average tax rate of 10.2 percent, .102 = 2150/21000. As incomes rise and more individuals move into the higher tax bracket, the average tax rate in the nation increases.

In general, then, under a progressive income tax system, not only the level of tax revenues, but the share of tax revenues in national income, vary directly with national income. Thus, the tendencies for budget surpluses during economic expansions and budget deficits during economic downturns are accentuated.

NATIONAL DEBT AND FEDERAL BUDGET DEFICITS

The gross federal debt, or the **national debt**, represents the total amount that the federal government has borrowed (and not yet repaid) to cover excess expenditures of the past. Every year the federal government runs a budget deficit, the national debt grows. At the end of 1980 the gross federal debt of the United States stood at slightly under $910 billion. A decade later, at the end of 1990, it had increased to more than $3200 billion. The difference is accounted for by the unbroken string of large federal budget deficits.

Many of the state and local governments are required by law to balance their budgets annually. Clearly, the federal government operates under no such restriction, although constitutional amendments requiring balanced federal budgets have been proposed. In this chapter we seek not to explain why the federal debt increased by 250 percent in just one decade. (Adjusting for inflation, the real value of the national debt increased by roughly 125 percent over the 1980s.) That discussion will be saved for Chapter 15, which covers the 1980s and Reaganomics. Here we will review the general consequences of federal budget deficits for the national debt and for the national savings-investment balance.

The United States has had a national debt since the Revolutionary War. In fact, most of the national debt—until the 1980s—had been incurred during wartime. In Table 13.1, the fourfold increase in the national debt between 1940 and 1945 reflects the heavy government spending for World War II.

Whenever the federal government runs a deficit, the U.S. Treasury must borrow the difference. To finance a deficit, the Treasury will print up U.S. Treasury securities (Treasury bills, notes, and bonds) that are then offered for sale. There is a temporary ceiling on the national debt, and the Treasury has the authority to borrow up to this ceiling. When the limit is reached, the U.S. Congress must officially raise the ceiling—otherwise the federal government could spend no more than the current tax receipts. As long as Congress is willing to increase the temporary debt ceiling and as long as there are willing buyers of Treasury securities, the national debt can grow indefinitely. Given the recent inability of the federal government to balance its budget, much less run a surplus, the Congress has no choice but to increase the debt ceiling. (Note: The last surplus in the federal budget was in 1969, when an income surtax was levied.) Given the extremely low default risk in purchasing a U.S. government security, and given that the Treasury will reduce the price of the securities by enough to attract the buyers, there should always be a market for U.S. Treasury securities.

TABLE 13.1

GROSS FEDERAL DEBT: SELECTED YEARS

	Gross Federal Debt (billions of dollars)[a]	Gross Federal Debt as Percentage of Gross Domestic Product
1940	50.7	53%
1945	260.1	123%
1950	256.9	97%
1960	290.5	57%
1970	380.9	39%
1980	908.5	34%
1990	3206.3	59%
1991	3599.0	64%

[a]End of fiscal year.
SOURCE: *Economic Report of the President 1992,* Table B-74.

So, should the size of the national debt be of concern? As illustrated in Table 13.1, the relative size of the national debt, measured by the ratio of the national debt to Gross Domestic Product, steadily decreased during the first three decades following World War II. The large federal budget deficits of the 1980s, however, reversed this favorable trend.

Some observers argue that the national debt, regardless of size, is largely irrelevant, since "we owe it to ourselves." In truth, at the end of 1990, roughly 25 percent of the national debt of $3.2 trillion was held by agencies of the U.S. government. For example, the Social Security Trust Fund may use surplus revenues to purchase U.S. Treasury securities. Another 7 or 8 percent of the national debt is held by the Federal Reserve, acquired through its purchases of U.S. government securities. Some 50 to 55 percent of the national debt is held by domestic investors, including commercial banks and thrift institutions, money market funds, insurance companies, pension funds, state and local treasuries, and directly by private individuals. Only between 12 and 15 percent of the national debt of the United States is held by foreign governments and private foreign investors.

There are, however, three related concerns with the unprecedented surge in the federal budget deficits beginning in the 1980s, a period of peace and economic expansion.

Momentum of the National Debt

The first is the momentum in the national debt for future budget deficits. In 1980 net interest on the national debt was $52.5 billion (8.9 percent of federal government outlays). In 1991 net interest reached $194.5 billion (14.7 percent of federal government outlays) and constituted the third largest expenditure of the federal government, after national defense and social security.[8] In other words, in 1991 one out of every seven dollars of expenditures of the federal government went to meet the interest on the national debt.

Financing Federal Budget Deficits

The second concern is with the financing of the budget deficits. As noted, the U.S. Treasury will sell securities to cover the excess of expenditures over revenues. Financing the deficit increases the supply of securities on the market, depressing the price of the securities and putting upward pressure on market interest rates. (Recall the inverse relationship between the price of bonds and the interest rate.)

For example, suppose the Treasury needs to sell a large amount of one-year Treasury bills (T-bills), each with a face value of $10,000. If the current yield on similar investments is 8 percent, then the current market price of the T-bills would be $9259 (9259 = 10,000/1.08). In order to sell the new T-bills, however, the Treasury may have to accept a lower price, say $9200, which increases the yield to 8.7 percent (.087 = (10,000 − 9200)/9200). In effect the Treasury is competing with other demanders of credit (such as households

---

[8] *Economic Report of the President 1991,* Table B-77; and *Economic Report of the President 1992,* Table B-75.

seeking mortgages and consumer loans and firms seeking to borrow for business expansion). The increase in the market interest rate due to the Treasury's sale of securities (here T-bills) may crowd out private interest-sensitive expenditures. (Recall the earlier discussion of the crowding out effect of expansionary fiscal policy on private investment expenditures. When we consider the financing of the government budget deficits likely to result from the expansionary fiscal policy, this crowding out effect is enhanced.) To the extent gross private domestic investment, especially business fixed investment, is discouraged by the higher interest rates, there will be less capital formation in the private sector, with potentially adverse implications for economic growth.[9] The extent of the crowding out depends on how much the Treasury sale of securities increases the market interest rate and on how sensitive investment expenditures are to the interest rate.

The Federal Reserve can prevent the interest rate from rising when the Treasury finances a deficit by **monetizing the debt.** That is, if the Federal Reserve buys the newly issued Treasury securities at the current market price (in the example above, $9259 for a $10,000 T-bill with a one-year maturity), then there will be no upward pressure on the interest rate. The consequence of monetizing the debt is to increase the money supply. In essence, the Treasury prints up the securities to cover the federal budget deficit, and the Federal Reserve purchases the same, giving the Treasury a check drawn on the Fed. When the Treasury deposits this check in the banking system, reserves increase, and the money supply expands. While no additional output has been produced, there is more money in circulation. More dollars chasing a given amount of national output will be inflationary—unless the economy is well below full employment on the Keynesian range of the aggregate supply curve.

In sum, the two methods of financing the federal deficit differ on the basis of who purchases the Treasury securities. If the securities are purchased by the public, then the primary consequence is a higher interest rate and the crowding out of some private investment expenditures. If the securities are purchased by the Federal Reserve, then the money supply will increase with the attendant potential for inflation.

Budget Deficits and the Macroeconomic Identity

The third concern with federal budget deficits has to do with the national savings-investment balance. Recall from Chapter 8 that the basic macroeconomic identity is:

$$C + I + G + X - M \equiv GDP \equiv C + S + T + R + F$$

where

C = personal consumption expenditures.
I = gross private domestic investment.

---

[9] If the excess expenditures of the government, however, are for physical capital formation (adding to the economic infrastructure, e.g., highways, bridges, airports) or human capital formation (investments in the health, education, and nutrition of the population), then economic growth may be enhanced.

G = government purchases of goods and services.
X = exports of goods and services.
M = imports of goods and services.
GDP = Gross Domestic Product.
S = gross private saving (personal and business).
T = net taxes (tax revenues less government transfer payments).
R = net unilateral transfers to foreigners.
F = net payments of factor income to foreigners.

On the left-hand side of the identity, the allocation of Gross Domestic Product by type of expenditure is illustrated. On the right-hand side is the accounting for the income earned in the production of national output. The income can be accounted for by personal consumption expenditures, private saving, net taxes, net unilateral transfers to foreigners, and net payments of factor income to foreigners.

Rearranging the identity by first subtracting personal consumption expenditures (C) from both sides and then solving for gross private domestic investment (I) yields

$$I + G + X - M = S + T + R + F$$

$$I = S + (T - G) + (M - X + R + F)$$

$$\text{Gross Private Domestic Investment} = \text{Gross Private Saving} + \text{Net Public Saving} + \text{Net Foreign Saving}$$

The sources of funding for *gross private domestic investment* are private saving, net public saving, and net foreign saving. *Private saving* is the sum of personal saving by households and business saving (primarily undistributed corporate profits and capital consumption allowances). *Public saving,* when positive, reflects a net surplus on the overall government budget balance, that is, for all levels of government, federal, state, and local. *Net foreign saving* is indicated by a current account deficit on the nation's balance of payments. (In Chapter 17 we will address the balance of international payments in detail.) Essentially, a current account deficit implies that the nation is consuming more goods and services than it is producing, and borrowing the difference from the rest of the world—hence the net inflow of *foreign saving.*

If the overall deficit in the government budget increases, then to maintain a constant level of gross private domestic investment, the nation either has to cut back on personal consumption (that is, increase personal saving) or incur foreign debt (that is, increase the inflow of net foreign saving). During the 1980s the overall government budget deficits were largely covered by foreign saving or borrowing from the rest of the world. While foreign saving allowed the United States to maintain a higher level of gross private domestic investment than otherwise would have been possible, the nation piled up foreign debt at a record pace.

To illustrate, see Table 13.2, where the national savings-investment balance for the United States in 1990 is given. The net surplus for state and local government budgets was not enough to offset the federal budget deficit, so that overall public saving was negative. Net domestic saving fell short of gross private domestic investment by 82.8 billion dollars. The gap was filled by foreign saving evidenced by the deficit on current account.

TABLE 13.2
NATIONAL SAVINGS-INVESTMENT BALANCE FOR THE UNITED STATES: 1990

I = Gross Private Domestic Investment = 802.6
S = Gross Private Domestic Saving = 859.4
  (personal saving = 206.6)
  (business saving = 652.8)
$T - G$ = Government Budget Balance = −139.6
  (federal budget = −165.3)
  (state and local budget = 25.7)
$M - X + R + F$ = Current Account Deficit = 82.8

$$I = S + (T - G) + (M - X + R + F)$$
$$802.6 = 859.4 + (-139.6) + (82.8)$$
$$802.6 = 802.6$$

NOTE: Figures are in billions of dollars. Totals may not sum exactly due to rounding error.
SOURCE: *Survey of Current Business,* November 1991, Table 5.1.

BALANCED BUDGET AMENDMENT

In the early 1980s, before the succession of large federal budget deficits, a constitutional amendment to balance the federal budget was proposed. Indeed, a theme in Ronald Reagan's 1980 presidential campaign was the need to impose such fiscal responsibility. The thrust of the amendment was that, with only two exceptions, proposed federal government expenditures (purchases of goods and services and transfers) would have to match tax revenues in each year. The two exceptions allowed were in time of war and if three-fifths of both houses of Congress approved an unbalanced budget. In order to prevent balancing the budget by simply raising taxes, the percentage increase in tax revenues of the federal government in any year could not exceed the percentage increase in national income during the previous year.

In August of 1982 the U.S. Senate actually passed a balanced budget amendment by more than the required two-thirds majority. The House of Representatives, however, failed to reach the necessary majority. If the amendment had also passed the House, then to become part of the U.S. Constitution it would have had to be ratified by at least 38 states. At the time there was a parallel movement in many state legislatures for a constitutional convention to consider a balanced budget amendment.

Ironically, as the federal budget deficits hemorrhaged throughout the first half of the 1980s ($128 billion in 1982, $208 billion in 1983, $185 billion in 1984, $212 billion in 1985, and $221 billion in 1986),[10] the enthusiasm for a balanced budget amendment to the constitution waned. Congress did pass the Gramm-Rudman-Hollings Balanced Budget Act in 1985, which legislated a lockstep approach to deficit reduction with the goal of a balanced federal budget by 1991. (In the chapter on supply-side economics and the 1980s we will discuss the Gramm-Rudman-Hollings legislation in more detail.)

---

[10] *Economic Report of the President 1992,* Table B-75.

A constitutional amendment to balance the federal budget evoked sharp debate, although polls indicated that a vast majority of the American public favored such legislation. Proponents argued that only a constitutional amendment could ensure fiscal responsibility. Some observers—on both sides of the issue—questioned whether the U.S. Constitution should be "sullied" by adding an amendment on a controversial economic policy; but the primary economic argument against mandating an annually balanced budget was that fiscal "policy" would become procyclical and destabilizing. The logic for this argument follows.

Recall that in an economic downturn tax revenues fall and transfer payments rise as national income declines. For a given level of government purchases of goods and services, there would be a tendency, then, to run a budget deficit—which would be stabilizing since this automatic fiscal stimulus would bolster disposable income and consumer spending during the economic contraction. If the federal government were required to balance the budget, however, it would have to prevent the deficit either by increasing net taxes (as by a temporary hike in income tax rates or a discretionary rollback in transfer payments), cutting government purchases, or implementing some combination of tax increases and expenditure reductions. The required contractionary fiscal policy would result in a decrease in aggregate demand and would aggravate the economic downturn.

Conversely, if the economy were in a sustained expansion, with national output nearing the Classical range of the aggregate supply curve, the federal government should be able to run a budget surplus. Tax revenues would be rising (even faster than national income if the income tax system were progressive) and government transfers would be falling. This automatic fiscal braking would help prevent the economy from overheating. Yet, if there were an amendment requiring a balanced budget, the federal government would have to prevent the budget surplus by applying fiscal stimulus such as cutting taxes or raising expenditures. The mandated expansionary fiscal policy could thus overheat the economy and set off spiraling inflation.

Accordingly, the required fiscal policy changes under a balanced budget amendment would accentuate, not dampen, the business cycle. It would make more sense for the president and Congress to balance the federal budget over the course of the business cycle. The budget deficits incurred during economic recessions would then be offset by the budget surpluses accumulated during economic expansions. On average, but not necessarily in any one year, the federal budget would be in balance. But can this reasonably be expected? Only twice (1960 and 1969) in the last three decades has the federal government run a budget surplus. Nevertheless, there is historical precedent. In the 14-year period from 1947 through 1960 the federal government ran seven budget surpluses, totaling $30.1 billion, and seven budget deficits, totaling $30.9 billion.[11]

Fiscal responsibility will remain an issue in the 1990s. In 1990 and 1991 the federal budget deficits were $220 billion and $269 billion respectively—and an even larger deficit is expected for 1992.[12] In fact, in June of 1992, despite lobbying from President Bush, the House of Representatives, led by the

---

[11] Ibid., Table B-76.
[12] Ibid., Table B-75.

Democrats, narrowly defeated the most recent attempt to pass a constitutional amendment to balance the federal budget.

CONCLUDING NOTE

As discussed in this chapter, the use of fiscal policy to demand-manage the economy is controversial. Because of the lags involved in policymaking, very few economists would advocate using fiscal policy to fine-tune the economy, that is, to attempt to prevent any deviations in real national output from the full-employment or potential rate of real national output.

Modern-day advocates of Keynes, known as **Neo-Keynesians**, believe that aggregate demand, particularly business and residential fixed investment, is unstable and rather volatile. Consequently, they favor the active use of fiscal policy to offset the major fluctuations of the business cycle: cutting tax rates and stepping up government spending during recessions, and raising tax rates and trimming government spending during inflationary booms. As we will discuss in the next chapter, Neo-Keynesian economists also acknowledge the potential effectiveness of demand-management monetary policy—especially to curb inflation.

Other economists believe that activist fiscal policy is ineffective, and even counterproductive. The monetarist position is that due to the interest rate sensitivity of investment spending and the interest rate insensitivity of money demand, changes in government spending or taxes have little impact on the level of aggregate demand or employment. In subsequent chapters we will illustrate two other groups of macroeconomists (supply-siders in Chapter 15 and New Classicals in Chapter 16), who, for different reasons, oppose demand-management fiscal policy.

In any case, fiscal policy is not the only option for pursuing the macroeconomic goals of full employment, price stability, and economic growth. Monetary policy, carried out by the Federal Reserve, can also be used. In the next chapter we will review the monetary policy options.

KEY TERMS

fiscal policy
monetary policy
marginal rate of taxation
net lump-sum taxes
monetarists
recognition lag
response lag
impact lag

permanent income hypothesis
permanent income
transitory income
built-in stabilizer
national debt
monetizing the debt
neo-Keynesians

QUESTIONS

1. What are the three most important ideas in this chapter? Discuss why each is important.

2. Given the following Simple Keynesian model

$C = 10 + .75Y_d$ Personal consumption expenditures
$I_0 = 105$ Investment expenditures
$G_0 = 190$ Government purchases of goods and services
$X_0 = 50$ Exports of goods and services
$M = 5 + .125Y_d$ Imports of goods and services
$T = -40 + .4Y$ Net taxes
$Y_d = Y - T$ Disposable income
$A = C + I + G + X - M$ Desired aggregate expenditures
$A(Y) \stackrel{e}{=} Y$ Equilibrium condition

  a. Find the equilibrium level of real national income.
  b. Directly calculate (i.e., using the formulas) the
     1. autonomous expenditure multiplier.
     2. lump-sum tax multiplier.
  c. If the full employment level of real national income is $Y_f = 640$, then find the appropriate fiscal policy change to reach Y_f if
     1. the government changes the level of its purchases (G_0).
     2. the government changes the level of net lump-sum taxes (T_0).
     Confirm, by resolving the model, that each of these fiscal policy changes will give an equilibrium real national income of $Y_f = 640$.
  d. Calculate the initial government budget balance. Find the effects on the government budget balance under the two fiscal policy options considered in part "c."
  e. Which policy option increases the role of the government in the economy the most? Explain why. Which policy option reduces the government budget balance the most (i.e., decreases the budget surplus or increases the budget deficit)? Explain why.
3. In the Simple Keynesian model the aggregate price level is assumed to be constant. Discuss why expansionary fiscal policy may not have the full multiplier effect implied by the Simple Keynesian model in the example above.
4. Use the following Simple Keynesian model. In your calculations, round off numbers less than one to three decimal places.

$C = 30 + .8Y_d$ Personal consumption expenditures
$I_0 = 85$ Investment expenditures
$G_0 = 300$ Government purchases of goods and services
$X_0 = 50$ Exports of goods and services
$M = 10 + .05Y_d$ Imports of goods and services
$T = -60 + .334Y$ Net taxes
$Y_d = Y - T$ Disposable income
$A = C + I + G + X - M$ Desired aggregate expenditures
$A \stackrel{e}{=} Y$ Equilibrium condition

  a. Find the equilibrium level of real national income.
  b. Directly calculate (i.e., using the formulas) the
     1. autonomous expenditure multiplier.
     2. lump-sum tax multiplier.

c. If the full employment level of national income is $Y_f = 940$ (i.e., the economy is beyond full employment), find the appropriate fiscal change to reach Y_f if
   1. the government changes the level of its expenditures.
   2. the government changes the level of net lump-sum taxes.
d. Calculate the initial government budget balance. Find the effects on the government budget balance under the two fiscal policy options considered in part "c."
e. Which policy option reduces the role of the government in the economy the most? Explain why. Which policy option improves the government budget balance the most? Explain why.

5. In the Simple Keynesian Model the aggregate price level was assumed to be constant. For a contractionary fiscal policy required to reduce national output and income to the full employment level, this assumption is consistent with the hypothesis of the ratcheting aggregate supply curve (see Chapter 12, Figure 12.7(b)). Discuss why contractionary fiscal policy would not have the full multiplier effects implied by the Simple Keynesian model if the economy initially were on the intermediate range of the aggregate supply curve and the ratcheting effect did not apply.

6. a. Why do you think the American public supports a balanced budget amendment for the federal government?
   b. Why do you think the U.S. Congress has not been able to run a budget surplus for over two decades?
   c. What would you propose to reduce the large federal budget deficit? What would be the economic consequences of your proposal?

CHAPTER

14

THE CONDUCT OF MONETARY POLICY

THE CHAIRMANSHIP OF THE Federal Reserve System is often referred to as the second most powerful position in the U.S. economy, after the presidency. For example, Paul Volcker, Federal Reserve Chairman from 1979 to 1987, is widely credited with wringing double-digit inflation from the U.S. economy in the early 1980s. The repercussions of U.S. monetary policy, now as then, carry well beyond the U.S. economy. Traders on the global financial markets not only respond to actual shifts in U.S. monetary policy, but seek to anticipate the actions of the Federal Reserve.

Monetary policy is the management of the nation's money supply by the Federal Reserve in the pursuit of macroeconomic objectives. The primary macroeconomic objectives of full employment, price stability, and economic growth are shared by fiscal policy; ideally, monetary and fiscal policies should be coordinated. This ideal is not always realized.

Monetary and fiscal policies are independently formulated. Fiscal policy is set by the president and the U.S. Congress. Reaching a consensus on the appropriate fiscal policy is neither quick nor easy. Furthermore, if the president and Congress do fashion a consensus, it usually reflects a lower tolerance for unemployment—consequently a higher tolerance for inflation—than held by the Federal Reserve. (Politicians are loathe to run for reelection when unemployment is high or rising.) In contrast, the 12 voting members of the Federal Open Market Committee (FOMC) of the Federal Reserve periodically convene to chart the nation's monetary policy. While ultimately answerable to Congress and always subject to presidential jawboning, the FOMC operates with considerable autonomy.[1] Moreover, the economic conditions under which fiscal

---

[1] The president's nominees for the Board of Governors must be confirmed by the U.S. Senate. Furthermore, the chair of the Federal Reserve is required to testify before Congress twice a year on monetary policy; and Congress can pass legislation directing the Federal Reserve to give higher priority to certain macroeconomic goals, such as price stability. Clearly, the Federal Reserve is not immune from political pressure.

policy is hypothesized to be most effective in altering aggregate demand are not the same conditions as for monetary policy.

In this chapter we investigate the instruments of monetary policy. As with fiscal policy, there is controversy over the efficacy of using monetary policy to demand-manage the economy. We will review this debate. Finally, we will compare the outcomes from using monetary policy versus fiscal policy to attain a given real national output objective.

INSTRUMENTS OF MONETARY POLICY

From Chapter 11 you should recall that under a fractional reserve banking system, only a portion of the deposits placed in banks must be held as required reserves. Hence, the money supply (measured as M1) is a multiple of the monetary base.

Money Supply = M1 = Currency in Circulation + Checkable Deposits

Monetary Base = MB = Currency in Circulation + Reserves

The Federal Reserve has three primary instruments for changing the level of the money supply: the required reserve ratio, the discount rate, and open market operations. The first two instruments affect the ratio of the money supply to the monetary base. The third, open market operations, directly affects the monetary base. We will discuss each of these instruments.

Changes in the **required reserve ratio** affect the maximum amount of credit that banks can create from a given level of checkable deposits. For example, if the Fed drops the required reserve ratio from 12 percent to 10 percent, then banks need keep $2 less of every $100 of checkable deposits as reserves (that is, as cash in the bank vault or on deposit with the Fed). The banks then have a higher percentage of deposits available for making loans and purchasing government securities. Since reserves do not earn interest for banks, lowering the required reserve ratio increases the potential profitability of banks. In the aggregate, lowering the required reserve ratio allows for a given monetary base to support a greater money supply. The increase in the money supply puts downward pressure on interest rates.

In contrast, an increase in the required reserve ratio means that a higher percentage of deposits must be held back as reserves. The higher reserve requirement reduces the money supply and puts upward pressure on interest rates.

Changing the required reserve ratio is a rather blunt instrument of monetary policy. In particular, banks do not welcome an increase in the required reserve ratio since this withdraws a higher percentage of their deposits to the sidelines as non–income earning assets. On the other hand, lowering the required reserve ratio reduces the degree of control the Fed has over the money supply. It is hardly surprising, then, that this option of monetary policy is not often employed—although in April of 1992 the Federal Reserve did lower the required reserve ratio on checkable deposits from 12 percent to 10 percent.[2]

---

[2] While this drop in the required reserve ratio was welcomed by banks, the boost to profits was expected to be offset by an increase in the premium banks would have to pay in 1992 to the Federal Deposit Insurance Corporation to insure bank deposits.

The second instrument of monetary policy is the **discount rate,** the rate of interest charged by the Fed on loans to member banks. Changes in the discount rate not only affect the cost of being short of reserves, but are a signal to the money market of the Fed's perception of the economy. A decrease in the discount rate reduces the cost of borrowing reserves, which might induce banks to keep fewer excess reserves on hand as precautionary balances.[3] In addition, by decreasing the discount rate, the Fed is suggesting that banks need to lower their interest rates on loans and be more aggressive in extending credit. Conversely, an increase in the discount rate is a signal that a tightening of the money supply is warranted. In this case, banks would likely increase their excess reserve ratios and be more cautious in making loans.

The Fed does reset the discount rate on occasion. The impact of a discount rate change on the money supply, however, may be rather difficult to predict—dependent as it is on the uncertain responses by banks in altering their excess reserve ratios. Furthermore, too frequent changing of the discount rate could diminish its psychological import. In the 12-month period beginning in December of 1990 (when the rate was reduced from 7.0 percent to 6.5 percent), the Fed lowered the discount rate six times, finally, in December of 1991, reaching 3.5 percent, the lowest level in over a quarter of a century. In July of 1992 the Fed went further, dropping the discount rate to 3.0 percent. Typically the Fed will not change the discount rate so often.

The monetary policy option most often relied on by the Fed, **open market operations,** refers to the Fed's purchases and sales of previously issued U.S. government securities (such as U.S. Treasury bills and bonds) in the market where these assets are traded. Through open market operations the Fed directly changes the monetary base.

Recall that in the case of open market purchases the Fed buys previously issued, but yet to mature, government securities and pays for its purchases by writing checks on itself. The sellers of the securities deposit the checks in the banking system. The banks in which the Fed's checks are deposited acquire claims on the Fed. In essence, the Fed has injected reserves into the banking system. The increase in the monetary base equals the amount of the open market purchases. The ultimate increase in the money supply will be a multiple of the increase in the monetary base.

Open market purchases reduce the interest rate. The Fed, in the process of buying the government securities, bids up the market price of the securities, which drives down the market rate of interest—in particular, the federal funds rate. The subsequent expansion of the money supply maintains the downward pressure on the interest rate.

With open market sales, the Fed withdraws reserves from the banking system. The purchasers of the government securities sold by the Fed write checks on their banks. The amounts of the checks are deducted from the accounts of these banks at the district Federal Reserve banks. Thus, the monetary base falls by the amount of the open market sale, maintaining the upward pressure on the rate

---

[3] Recall that banks caught short of required reserves can also borrow from other banks with excess reserves at the federal funds rate or sell off assets from their portfolios (primarily U.S. government securities). If banks do borrow reserves from the Fed at the discount rate, the monetary base is increased by the amount of borrowed reserves.

of interest, pressure that began when the Fed bid down the market price of the government securities.

In sum, reducing the required reserve ratio, reducing the discount rate, and making open market purchases are three options the Fed has available for expansionary monetary policy. The resulting increases in the money supply should exert downward pressure on the market rate of interest. The less expensive credit should, in turn, spur interest-sensitive spending (business and residential fixed investment and consumer durables). Real national output and the aggregate price level will then tend to rise with the increase in aggregate demand.

Raising the required reserve ratio, raising the discount rate, and making open market sales are three options for contractionary monetary policy. The decrease in the money supply should tighten credit. Interest-sensitive expenditures should, in turn, decline. Real national output and the aggregate price level will then tend to fall with the decrease in aggregate demand.

EFFECTIVENESS OF MONETARY POLICY

The conditions under which monetary policy is most effective, that is, where a given change in the money supply produces the greatest change in aggregate demand, differ from those for fiscal policy. Refer again to Figure 13.2 in the previous chapter. Fiscal policy is most effective when the demand for money is interest elastic and desired aggregate expenditures on national output are interest inelastic—conditions characteristic of an economy well below full employment.

Any change in the money supply will affect the equilibrium in the money market. The less sensitive money demand is to the interest rate, the larger the change will be in the interest rate needed to reequilibrate the money market. For a given change in the interest rate, the more interest elastic that desired aggregate expenditures are, the greater the change will be in aggregate demand. Therefore, the less interest-elastic the demand for money is, and the more interest elastic the desired aggregate expenditures are, the greater the effect of a given change in the money supply on aggregate demand.

In Figure 14.1 we illustrate two scenarios. First look at the monetarist assumptions: a low interest elasticity of money demand (thus a steep money demand curve) and a high interest elasticity of desired investment expenditures (thus a flat investment demand curve). Now look at the Keynesian assumptions: a high interest elasticity of money demand (thus a flat money demand curve) and a low interest elasticity of desired investment expenditures (thus a steep investment demand curve).[4]

---

[4] As suggested in the last chapter on fiscal policy, Neo-Keynesian economists—as opposed to the earlier followers of Keynes—do not subscribe to the extreme assumptions illustrated in Figure 14.1. Neo-Keynesians tend to stake out an intermediate position, arguing that (1) money demand does depend significantly on the interest rate, although not necessarily in a highly elastic fashion, and (2) investment expenditures are affected by the level of interest rates, although the primary determinants of business and residential fixed investment are business and consumer confidence and the perceived state of the economy.

Monetarists, on the other hand, also identify a more direct channel for changes in the money supply to affect aggregate demand. Given an equilibrium in the money market, an increase in

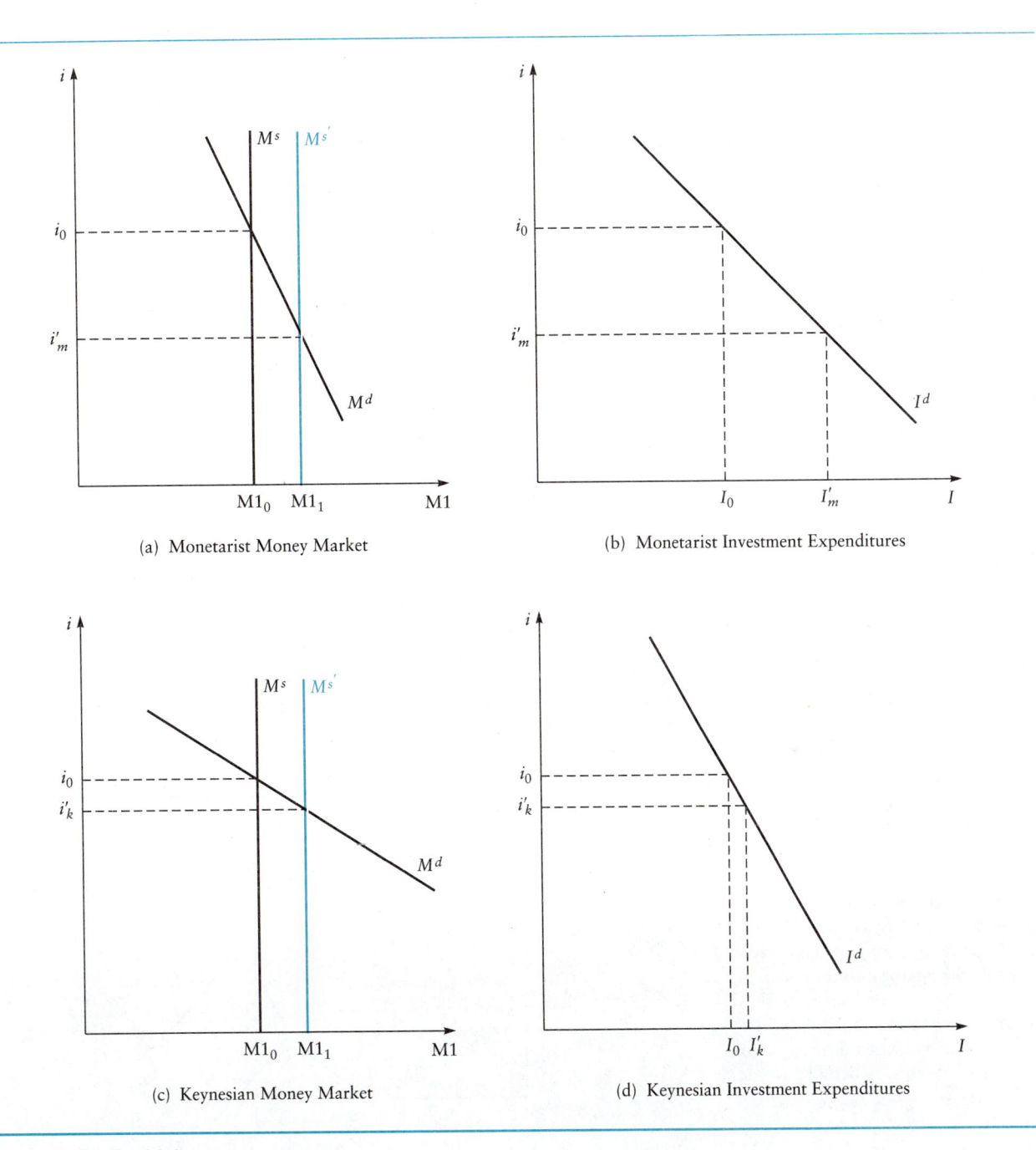

FIGURE 14.1
INTEREST SENSITIVITIES OF MONEY DEMAND AND INVESTMENT EXPENDITURES: EFFECTIVENESS OF MONETARY POLICY

Monetarists believe that the quantity of nominal money balances demanded is not sensitive to the nominal interest rate, while the quantity demanded of real fixed investment is very sensitive to the nominal interest rate. The Keynesian position is just the opposite: money demand is interest-elastic, and desired fixed investment expenditures are interest-inelastic. Consequently, under the monetarist assumptions, a given increase in the money supply will require a greater decrease in the interest rate to reequilibrate the money market. Moreover, in the monetarist model, any decrease in the nominal interest rate will stimulate more fixed investment expenditures.

Comparing the two sets of assumptions illustrated in Figure 14.1, we can see that a given increase in the money supply (from M^s to $M^{s'}$) drives down the equilibrium rate of interest substantially more in the monetarist version (i'_m versus i'_k). Combined with the assumed higher interest sensitivity of desired investment expenditures, the effect of the change in the money supply on aggregate demand is significantly greater in the monetarist model.

The monetarists, despite acknowledging the potency of money supply changes for aggregate demand, do not favor activist monetary policy to demand-manage the economy. Rather it is the Neo-Keynesian economists who argue for the use of demand-management policies—both fiscal and monetary—to offset major swings in the business cycle. Before we discuss the monetarist policy recommendation, we should note the effectiveness of contractionary monetary policy in an inflationary economy.

INFLATION AND CONTRACTIONARY MONETARY POLICY

If the economy were operating in the Classical range of the aggregate supply curve (see Figure 14.2 and the aggregate demand curve AD), then increases in aggregate demand would only fuel inflation. As will be discussed in a later

---

the money supply results in an excess supply of money. To reduce the surplus in money balances, households and firms will increase aggregate expenditures on goods and services. Conversely, from an initial money market equilibrium, a fall in the money supply yields an excess demand for money. Aggregate expenditures on goods and services will then be reduced in order to restore the desired level of money balances.

FIGURE 14.2

ECONOMY IN CLASSICAL RANGE OF AGGREGATE SUPPLY CURVE

Contractionary monetary policy may be especially effective in cooling off an economy operating in the Classical range of the aggregate supply curve. The fall in the money supply pushes up the interest rate, which reduces interest-sensitive expenditures (decreasing aggregate demand from AD to AD').

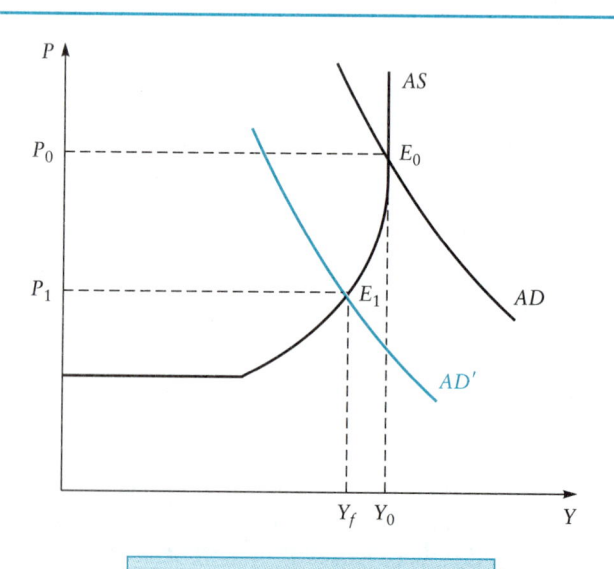

P = aggregate price level.
Y = real national output.
Y_f = full employment national output.

chapter, inflation alters the distribution of income, penalizing those individuals whose nominal incomes fail to keep pace with price increases. Moreover, if unchecked, inflation tends to escalate. Contractionary monetary policy can be effective in reining in an inflationary economy.

For an economy at full employment, the aggregate demand for money is likely to be high—reflecting primarily the transactions balances needed for a high income–high price economy. Consequently, the nominal rate of interest would be elevated, although the real rate of interest need not be.

The real rate of interest (r) is the nominal rate of interest (i) adjusted for inflation (INF). Consider a simple example. Suppose you could borrow $100 for a year at 10 percent interest. At the end of the year you would repay $110, that is, $100(1 + .10)$. If during the year, prices, on average, increase, then the dollars repaid at the end of the year have less purchasing power than the dollars initially borrowed. Specifically, if the actual inflation rate were 6 percent, the purchasing power of the $110 repaid would be $103.77 ($110/1.06). The inflation-adjusted, or real, rate of interest on the $100 loan would be 3.77 percent.

The formula relating the real and nominal rates of interest is

$$r = \frac{1 + i}{1 + INF} - 1$$

where

r = real annual rate of interest.
i = nominal annual rate of interest.
INF = annual rate of inflation.

In this example,

$$r = \frac{1 + .10}{1 + .06} - 1 = 1.0377 - 1 = .0377 = 3.77 \text{ percent}$$

When the rate of inflation is low, a useful approximation for the real rate of interest is the difference between the nominal interest rate and the inflation rate:

$$r \doteq i - INF$$

Here

$$r \doteq .10 - .06 = .04 \doteq .0377$$

Is it possible that the real rate of interest could be negative?

At the time a loan is made, the actual inflation rate over the term of the loan is unknown. Thus, lenders add an inflation premium, based on the expected rate of inflation, to their desired real return in order to preserve the store of value function of their investment. That is,

$$r^e = \frac{1 + i}{1 + INF^e} - 1$$

where

r^e = expected real annual rate of interest.
INF^e = expected annual rate of inflation.
i = nominal annual rate of interest.

It follows that if lenders anticipate an inflation rate of 6 percent, then to achieve an expected real return of 4 percent, the nominal rate of interest should be set for slightly more than 10 percent (10.24 percent, to be exact).

$$r^e = .04 = \frac{1+i}{1.06} - 1$$

Solving for i yields .1024.

As noted, in an inflationary economy, the transactions demand for money would be high. Nominal rates of interest would also be high, making the opportunity cost of holding money balances significant—since cash balances do not earn interest, and the interest rates received, if any, on checkable deposits are usually modest and slow to adjust. With the high interest rates and low bond prices, speculative balances would be at a minimum. Overall, the quantity of nominal money balances demanded may not be very responsive to changes in the interest rate as households and firms try to conserve on M1 balances.

On the other hand, with high interest rates, the cost of financing big-ticket items (consumer durables, business and residential fixed investments) would become more of a factor in the expenditure decision. Consumer durables, capital goods, and real estate usually serve well as stores of value during inflationary times. Consequently, for a given rate of inflation, desired aggregate expenditures may be quite sensitive to changes in the nominal interest rate. For these reasons, contractionary monetary policy may be particularly effective for an economy overheating in the Classical range of the aggregate supply curve.[5]

Return to Figure 14.2 and assume the economy is operating well up in the Classical range of the aggregate supply curve at E_0 with P_0 and $Y_0 > Y_f$, where Y_f corresponds to full employment national output. Suppose the Fed implements contractionary monetary policy in the form of open market sales to reduce the inflationary pressure. The market price of bonds would fall, and the interest rate would rise with the Fed's sale of government securities. Bank reserves and the money supply would contract as the purchasers of the government securities wrote checks on their banks payable to the Fed. The higher interest rates discourage interest-sensitive expenditures. (Note that the use of contractionary monetary policy in an overheating economy increases the real interest rate in two ways—the nominal interest rate rises and the inflation rate falls.) Consequently, aggregate demand falls (the aggregate demand curve shifts left from AD to AD') to restore full employment at Y_f.

MONETARY POLICY AND DEMAND MANAGEMENT

The influence of fiscal policy on aggregate demand can be direct (changes in government purchases) or indirect (changes in net taxes which affect disposable

---

[5] To say that contractionary monetary policy may be very effective in the Classical range of the aggregate supply curve does not imply that contractionary fiscal policy (e.g., a cut in government expenditures or an increase in tax rates) would be ineffective. Even if desired investment expenditures are sensitive to the nominal interest rate while money demand is not, contractionary fiscal policy could moderate aggregate demand and cool off the inflation rate—if the fiscal policymakers would implement such deflationary policies. Over the past two decades, at least, fiscal policymakers generally have been reluctant to raise taxes or cut expenditures—leaving the responsibility of curbing inflation to the monetary authorities.

income and consumption expenditures). The influence of monetary policy on aggregate demand is only indirect (changes in the money supply that affect interest rates and interest-sensitive expenditures).

In this chapter and the last, we suggested that fiscal policy may have a comparative advantage over monetary policy in stimulating an economy mired well below full employment (that is, on the Keynesian range of the aggregate supply curve), and that monetary policy may be relatively effective in cooling off an inflationary economy (that is, one on the Classical range of the aggregate supply curve). On the intermediate range of the aggregate supply curve, both fiscal and monetary policy may be effective in altering the level of aggregate demand. A number of factors, however, complicate attempts to demand-manage the economy with monetary policy.

Lags in Policymaking

As with fiscal policy, the conduct of monetary policy involves lags. The **recognition lag** refers to the time it takes for the Fed to analyze the macroeconomic data and determine the condition of the economy. Because the president and Congress deal with a much broader agenda—from social issues (such as abortion) to national security issues (such as arms control) to foreign policy issues (such as apartheid)—while the Fed can concentrate more on economic policy, the Fed may be more sensitive to the state of the economy and thus more efficient in monitoring economic conditions.

Second, the **response lag,** reflecting the formulation of the appropriate policy, is considerably shorter for monetary policy. As noted earlier, the Federal Open Market Committee (FOMC) meets every six weeks or so to chart monetary policy. Reaching an agreement among the 12 voting members of the FOMC (who are not subject to reelection by the public) is easier than forging a fiscal policy consensus with Congress and the president (who are sensitive to their constituencies).

Although recognition and response lags are shorter for monetary policy than fiscal policy, the **impact lag** is not. While the Fed can change the required reserve ratio and the discount rate and engage in open market operations on very short notice, realizing the intended consequences of the monetary policy on the macroeconomy still takes time. Interest-sensitive expenditures may not respond quickly to a change in interest rates. Moreover, the multiplier process unfolds over an extended period of time.

Nevertheless, considering the three lags involved, monetary policy takes less time to implement and influence aggregate demand than does fiscal policy. It does not follow, though, that monetary policy can be used to fine-tune the economy, that is, to maintain aggregate demand in a narrow range around full employment national output. The lags that exist, particularly the impact lag, are still significant.

Uncertain Multiplier Effects

As with fiscal policy, the values of the multipliers in monetary policy are not known with certainty. Moreover, with monetary policy, there is another multiplier process involved—the money supply multiplier operating through the banking system. For example, the effect of a change in the monetary base on the money supply as measured by M1 cannot be predicted with precision.

The Fed can control the monetary base through open market operations, but the ultimate change in the money supply from a given change in the monetary base depends on the actions of banks (through the excess reserve ratios) and the nonbank public (through the currency-deposit ratios).

Recall from Chapter 11 that

$$\Delta M1 = \frac{1 + cu_d}{rr + er + cu_d} \Delta X$$

where

ΔX = initial change in reserves
   (e.g., from an open market operation by Fed).
rr = required reserve ratio on checkable deposits (set by Fed).
er = excess reserve ratio on checkable deposits
   (determined by banks).
cu_d = currency-deposit ratio (determined by depositors).

As we noted then, the excess reserve ratio and currency-deposit ratio may vary over time and with economic conditions.

The Fed has more leverage in altering the money supply when there are few excess reserves in the system. Consider an open market sale of $10 million worth of U.S. government bonds by the Fed. Assume that the required reserve ratio is 10 percent and that, on average, banks also keep 5 percent of checkable deposits on hand as excess reserves. Refer to the very simplified version of a typical bank's balance sheet as illustrated by First City Bank in Figure 14.3. With $100 million in checkable deposits and $15 million in reserves, First City Bank is just meeting the required reserve ratio and its desired excess reserve ratio. If the purchasers of the U.S. government bonds sold by the Fed write checks for $10 million on their accounts at First City Bank, then First City Bank will be short of reserves. Why?

FIGURE 14.3

EFFECTS OF AN OPEN MARKET SALE: TWO BANK'S BALANCE SHEETS

The loss of $10 million in demand deposits and reserves from First City Bank due to open market sales by the Federal Reserve would require First City Bank to sell $4 million in U.S. government securities to meet the required reserve ratio of 10 percent. Second City Bank, with initially more excess reserves on hand, would not have to sell any U.S. government securities to meet the required reserve ratio of 10 percent with the loss of $10 million in demand deposits and reserves.

First City Bank (in millions of $)

ASSETS		LIABILITIES	
Reserves	15	Demand Deposits	100
	(−10)		(−10)
Govt. Securities	90	Time Deposits	170
Loans	195	Capital Account	30
	300		300

Second City Bank (in millions of $)

ASSETS		LIABILITIES	
Reserves	20	Demand Deposits	100
	(−10)		(−10)
Govt. Securities	90	Time Deposits	170
Loans	190	Capital Account	30
	300		300

The checks for $10 million payable to the Fed reduce First City Bank's liabilities (checkable deposits at First City Bank) and reserves (First City Bank's deposits at the Fed) by $10 million. First City Bank now has $90 million in checkable deposits but only $5 million in reserves. Just to meet the required reserve ratio of 10 percent would require First City Bank to sell $4 million worth of U.S. government securities (or other assets from the bank's portfolio). To meet the desired excess reserve ratio of 5 percent, First City may want to sell an additional $4.5 million in U.S. government securities. If other banks in the system were initially also just meeting the required and desired excess reserve ratios of 10 and 5 percent, respectively, then First City Bank's sale of government securities would set off a chain reaction of further sales and a multiple contraction in the money supply.

On the other hand, if banks in general had surplus reserves—that is, reserves beyond those needed to meet the required reserve ratio of 10 percent and the desired excess reserve ratio of 5 percent—then the contractionary effects on the money supply from the Fed's open market sale of $10 million would be reduced. Return to Figure 14.3 and assume now that the balance sheet for Second City Bank is typical of the average bank in the system. When the depositors of Second City Bank write checks for $10 million, Second City Bank will still have enough reserves to meet the required reserve ratio, and will have to sell only $3.5 million worth of government securities to maintain the desired excess reserve ratio of 5 percent. Thus, the resulting contraction in the money supply will be much less if banks initially hold surplus reserves.

Furthermore, as illustrated earlier in this chapter, the impact of a change in the money supply on aggregate demand depends on the interest elasticities of money demand and desired aggregate expenditures. These elasticities are also not known with certainty and may change with the condition of the economy. Finally, the impact of a given change in aggregate demand on real national output and the aggregate price level depends on the price elasticity of aggregate supply, i.e., the range of the aggregate supply curve on which the economy is operating.

Nevertheless, in the case of contractionary monetary policy, if the open market sales are continued, the Fed will eventually be able to drain the excess reserves from the system and cool off the economy. In the opposite case of expansionary monetary policy, however, the Fed may run into more resistance.

A variant of the adage, "While you can lead a horse to water, you can't make it drink," is the expression, "Pushing on a string," often used to describe the Fed's sometime ineffectiveness in stimulating aggregate demand. In a recession the Fed may be stymied in its efforts to increase the money supply, expand credit, and encourage interest-sensitive expenditures. Banks may be content to hold excess reserves. Consumers and businesses may be reluctant to take out loans, even at reduced interest rates.

As noted, during the recession of 1990–1991, the Fed lowered the discount rate half a dozen times and aggressively pushed down the federal funds rate. Credit remained tight. Banks, perhaps mindful of the overextension of credit in the 1980s, turned more conservative in their lending. Consumers, pessimistic about the economy, and firms, facing worker layoffs and excess capacity, held back in assuming additional debt. Only in the spring of 1992, when interest rates reached levels not seen in 25 years, were there signs—albeit short-lived—of a significant increase in interest-sensitive expenditures, led by residential fixed investment. (We should add that the exercise of expansionary fiscal policy measures during this most recent recession was constrained by the large, and seemingly intractable, federal budget deficits.)

MONETARY POLICY TARGETS

To conduct monetary policy, the Fed needs to select target variables over which it has some control and through which aggregate demand can be affected. The Fed can seek to control the growth rate of a monetary aggregate (for example, M1 or M2) or the level of interest rates (for example, the federal funds rate). Refer to Figure 14.4 for the consequences of these two monetary policy options.

Suppose the Fed sets M1 as the target variable, as shown in the first panel of the figure. Assume, for simplicity, that the Fed targets the level of M1 at $M1_0$ for the period in question. The consequence of targeting the money supply is greater volatility in the interest rate. Money demand will shift with changes in real national income and the aggregate price level. With a stable money supply, the equilibrium interest rate will move directly with money demand. In effect, by setting a monetary aggregate as the target, the Fed "loses control" over interest rates.

Suppose that instead the Fed sets an interest rate target, as shown in the second panel. Pegging the interest rate at i_0 results in greater volatility in the money supply. In effect, the money supply becomes endogenous—shifts in money demand require corresponding shifts in money supply. The Fed "loses control" over the money supply under this option. Stabilizing the nominal interest rate tends to accentuate the swings in the business cycle. In practice, therefore, the Fed tends to set target ranges for the growth rates in the money supply that should, in turn, limit the fluctuations in the interest rates.

FIGURE 14.4
MONETARY POLICY OPTIONS

As shown in the first panel, if the Fed adheres to an M1 target, there will be greater volatility in the nominal interest rate. Disequilibrium in the money market due to shifts in money demand have to be resolved by changes in the nominal interest rate alone. If the Fed adheres to an interest rate target, as shown in the second panel, there will be greater volatility in the money supply. Shifts in money demand must be matched by changes in the money supply.

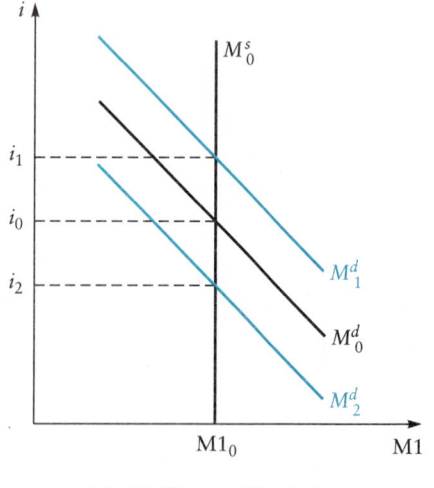

(a) M1 Target: $M1 = M1_0$

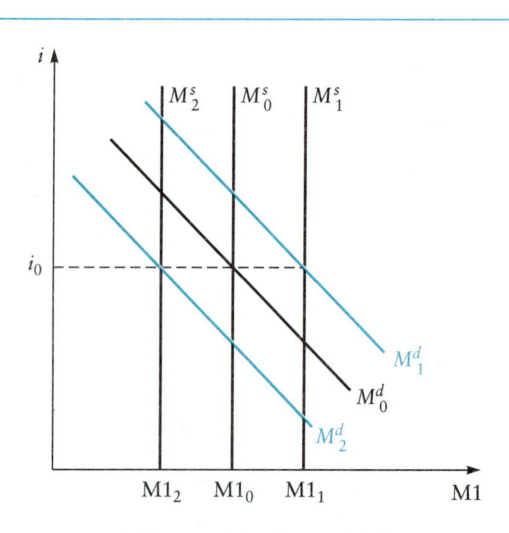

(b) Interest Rate Target: $i = i_0$

Monetarist Monetary Rule

As suggested earlier, the monetarists, despite their contentions that desired aggregate expenditures (in particular, fixed investment and consumer durables) are very sensitive to the interest rate and that money demand is not very sensitive to the interest rate, do not advocate the active use of monetary policy to demand-manage the economy. In part, the monetarist recommendation of nonintervention is based on the aforementioned lags in policymaking. In part, their opposition to demand-management policy reflects a belief in the inherent stability of the economy.

Recall that if the interest elasticity of money demand is low and the interest elasticity of desired aggregate expenditures is high, then changes in autonomous expenditures (e.g., government purchases) have little impact on aggregate demand—hence on national output and employment. The primary determinant of the level of aggregate demand would be the nominal money supply. Frequent changes in the growth rate of the money supply, characteristic of an activist monetary policy, would significantly affect aggregate demand and thus undermine an otherwise stable economy.

The monetarists advocate a **monetary rule:** the Federal Reserve should set a constant growth rate for the money supply equal to the long-run growth rate in real national output (roughly 3 percent annual growth). To understand the reasoning behind the proposed monetary rule, we need to turn to the monetarist hypothesis of money demand. The monetarists believe that the demand for nominal money balances is proportional to nominal income. That is,

$$M^d = kPY$$

where

M^d = quantity of nominal money balances demanded.
P = aggregate price level.
Y = real national income (output).
k = proportion of nominal income (PY) desired to be held as money balances.

The monetarists hold that k is relatively stable, determined by individual payment practices and the available banking instruments (such as checking accounts and saving deposits). A stable k is consistent with the assumption that the rate of interest is not a significant influence on the quantity of nominal money balances demanded. From the equilibrium condition for the money market,

$$M^d \stackrel{e}{=} M^s$$

Thus, we have

$$M^d = kPY = M^s$$

or

$$PY = \frac{1}{k}M^s$$

Let $V = 1/k$. V is defined to be the **income velocity of money,** which is defined as the average number of times a unit of money (for example, a dollar bill) is used to finance expenditures on national output. Thus, we can write

$$PY = VM^s$$

With V assumed to be a constant ($V = V_0$) we have the **simple quantity theory of money.**

$$PY = V_0 M^s$$

The level of nominal national income (PY) is determined by the nominal money supply (M^s). From the simple quantity theory of money, we can show that

$$\frac{\Delta Y}{Y} + \frac{\Delta P}{P} \doteq \frac{\Delta M^s}{M^s}$$

That is, the sum of the percentage change in the real national output (the real growth rate) and the percentage change in the aggregate price level (the inflation rate) approximately equals the percentage change in the nominal money supply.[6] Solving for the rate of inflation, $\Delta P/P$, gives

$$\frac{\Delta P}{P} \doteq \frac{\Delta M^s}{M^s} - \frac{\Delta Y}{Y}$$

According to the monetarists, inflation is essentially a monetary phenomenon. If the nominal money supply grows faster than real output, $\Delta M^s/M^s > \Delta Y/Y$, then, given a stable income velocity of money, the aggregate price level will rise, $\Delta P/P > 0$. Conversely, if the money supply does not grow as fast as real output and income, then the aggregate price level will fall: $\Delta P/P < 0$ when $\Delta M^s/M^s < \Delta Y/Y$.

The monetary rule proposed by the monetarists follows directly: the Fed should set the growth rate in the money supply equal to the long-run or trend growth rate in real output. In other words, allowing for a moderate and steady growth rate in the nominal money supply sufficient to accommodate real growth in national output and income would not be inflationary. In some years real growth in national output would exceed the long-run trend, and there would be deflationary pressure in the economy. In other years real growth in national output would fall short of the long-run trend, and there would be inflationary

---

[6] We begin with the condition derived from the money market equilibrium,

$$PY = VM^s$$

and we assume a constant income velocity of money, ($V = V_0$, $\Delta V = 0$). Allowing for all the sources of change in nominal income (PY) and the effective money supply ($V_0 M^s$), we obtain,

$$P\Delta Y + Y\Delta P = V_0 \Delta M^s$$

Dividing the left-hand side of the equation by PY and the right-hand side by $V_0 M^s$ (which equals PY), gives

$$\frac{P\Delta Y}{PY} + \frac{Y\Delta P}{PY} = \frac{V_0 \Delta M^s}{V_0 M^s}$$

or, rearranging,

$$\frac{\Delta Y}{Y} + \frac{\Delta P}{P} = \frac{\Delta M^s}{M^s}$$

pressure. Over time, or on average, the monetary rule would promote price stability.[7]

In sum, according to the monetarists, the economy is inherently stable, with a tendency toward full employment. Accordingly, policymakers should refrain from activist demand-management of the economy. Discretionary fiscal policy is ineffective due to the high interest elasticity of investment and the low interest elasticity of money demand. Discretionary monetary policy, while capable of significantly affecting aggregate demand, more often than not is destabilizing—due to the lags in policy making and the uncertain multiplier effects.[8] Therefore, the monetary rule that allows for a steady growth rate in the nominal money supply to accommodate the transactions demand for money is recommended.

Neo-Keynesian economists argue that the income velocity of money is not constant, but rather is directly related to the nominal interest rate. The evidence, however, is inconclusive. In Figure 14.5 we plot the income velocities for M1 and M2 (using the left-hand axis) and the interest rate for three-month U.S. Treasury securities (using the right-hand axis) for the U.S. economy for the period from 1960 through 1990. We see that the income velocity of money based on the narrower definition of the money supply (labeled V_1) increases steadily throughout the 1960s and 1970s, then generally declines over the first half of the 1980s, before rising again. Especially after 1980, the movement in this income velocity of money parallels the movement in the short-term interest rate. In contrast, the income velocity of money based on M2 (labeled as V_2) is more or less constant over this 30-year period. This evidence

---

[7] Note, actually it is not necessary for the income velocity of money to be constant, i.e., for $\Delta V = 0$. All that is required is that the growth rate in the income velocity of money be constant, i.e., for $\Delta V/V = v$, where v is a constant. Returning to the equilibrium condition for the money market,

$$PY = VM^s$$

and allowing for all the sources of change in nominal income (PY) and the effective money supply (VM^s), and then dividing through by $PY = VM^s$ and rearranging, gives

$$\frac{P\Delta Y}{PY} + \frac{Y\Delta P}{PY} = \frac{V\Delta M^s}{VM^s} + \frac{M^s \Delta V}{VM^s}$$

$$\frac{\Delta P}{P} \doteq \frac{\Delta M^s}{M^s} + \frac{\Delta V}{V} - \frac{\Delta Y}{Y}$$

Solving for the inflation rate ($\Delta P/P$) yields

$$\frac{\Delta P}{P} \doteq \frac{\Delta M^s}{M^s} + v - \frac{\Delta Y}{Y}$$

While the relationship between the inflation rate and the differential growth rates in the nominal money supply and real output is less clear when the income velocity of money is not constant, the monetary rule can still be applied. With a constant growth rate in the income velocity of money equal to v, price stability ($\Delta P/P = 0$) would require that

$$\frac{\Delta M^s}{M^s} \doteq \frac{\Delta Y}{Y} - v.$$

[8] In Chapter 16 we discuss the monetarist construct of the "natural rate of unemployment," which provides further theoretical justification for the monetarist case against demand-management monetary policy.

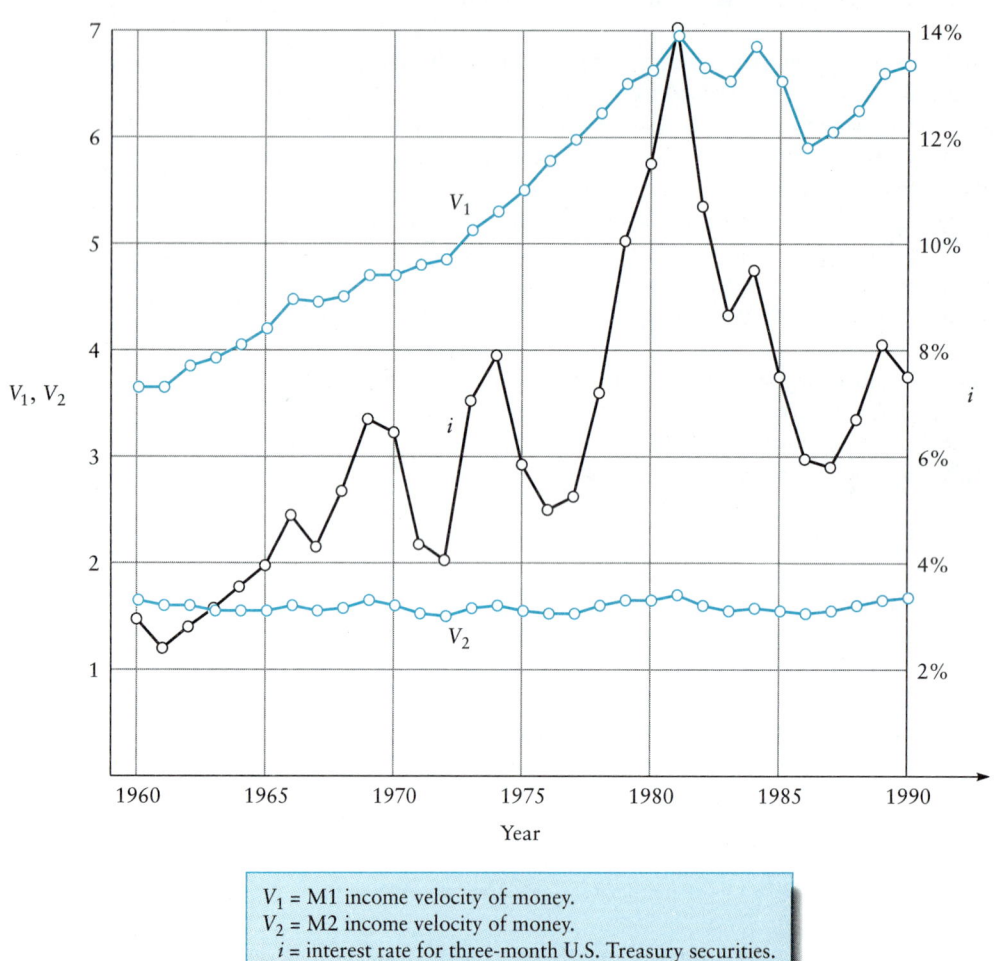

FIGURE 14.5

INCOME VELOCITIES OF MONEY AND NOMINAL INTEREST RATE

From 1960 to 1980, V_1, which is the M1 income velocity of money, steadily increased, consistent with the upward trend in short-term interest rates. Over the 1980s the M1 income velocity of money was more volatile, and more closely paralleled the movement in short-term interest rates, indicated by i. In contrast, V_2, the M2 income velocity of money, was more or less stable over the entire 30-year period.

V_1 is measured as the ratio of nominal Gross Domestic Product to the M1 money supply. V_2 is measured as the ratio of nominal Gross Domestic Product to M2 money supply. The measure of i is the interest rate on three-month U.S. Treasury securities (new issues).

SOURCE: *Economic Report of the President, 1992* (Washington, DC: U.S. Government Printing Office, 1992), Tables B-1, B-65, B-69.

V_1 = M1 income velocity of money.
V_2 = M2 income velocity of money.
i = interest rate for three-month U.S. Treasury securities.

suggests that the Fed may find that a monetary rule based on M2 is easier to implement.

In a study for the Federal Reserve Bank of Cleveland, John Carlson and John McElravey attribute the steady increase in the M1 velocity over the 1960s and 1970s to a combination of the general rise in inflation rates and federal regulations, which restricted the nominal interest rates that banks and thrifts could pay on deposits.[9]

The relative volatility in M1 velocity after 1980 reflects the increased sensitivity of money demand to interest rates. With the deregulation of depository institutions, depositors could take advantage of higher-yielding assets that offered limited check-writing privileges (for example, money market deposit accounts, which are counted in M2, but not M1) and checkable deposits (such as negotiable order of withdrawal, or NOW, accounts). In general, depositors became more sophisticated in the management of money balances. Control of the M1 monetary aggregate by the Federal Reserve, however, became more difficult with the blurring of the distinction between M1 and M2 money balances.

The Fed is not bound by any formulas or set rules, and monitors not only the growth rates of the monetary aggregates, but the variability of interest rates and changes in the inflation rate and real growth rate in the economy. In the late 1980s legislation was proposed in the U.S. Congress to mandate a goal of zero inflation for the Fed. While attaining, much less maintaining, a zero rate of inflation is difficult at best, the legislation reflects the widely shared view of the Fed as the main inflation fighter for the economy.

The call for greater consistency in monetary policy is not surprising. There is, after all, a fairly regular turnover in the membership of the FOMC—with the possibility of a new Federal Reserve chair every four years. In truth, some chairs and FOMCs have been more disposed to activist monetary policy, and others have been more vulnerable to political pressure—especially around election time when there is strong sentiment in Washington, D.C. for a high-employment economy.

COMPARING MONETARY AND FISCAL POLICY

Theoretically, at least according to the Neo-Keynesians, both monetary and fiscal policy could be used to close a given real output gap. The consequences for the composition of aggregate demand, future economic growth, and the federal government's budget balance, however, will differ depending on the policy implemented. To illustrate, assume that the economy is on the intermediate range of the aggregate supply curve, with an equilibrium level of real national output (Y_0) substantially below the potential or full-employment level (Y_f). See point E_0 in Figure 14.6. To close the real output gap of $Y_f - Y_0$, an increase in aggregate demand from AD to AD' would be required. Consider two options.

One, the Federal Reserve could implement expansionary monetary policy by increasing the money supply, perhaps with open market purchases of U.S. government bonds. Refer to Figure 14.7. The increase in the money supply (from M^s to $M^{s'}$) would drive down the market rate of interest, in turn stimulating investment expenditures and aggregate demand. The aggregate demand curve would shift from AD to AD'. Initially the excess demand for goods (represented by the line segment E_0E' at the original aggregate

---
[9] See John Carlson and John McElravey, "Money and Velocity in the 1980s," *Economic Commentary* Federal Reserve Bank of Cleveland, January 15, 1989.

FIGURE 14.6

EXPANSIONARY DEMAND-MANAGEMENT POLICIES TO CLOSE A REAL NATIONAL OUTPUT GAP

To close a real output gap of $Y_f - Y_0$, either expansionary monetary or expansionary fiscal policy could be used to increase aggregate demand (shifting the AD curve to AD' and an intersection with the aggregate supply at Y_f).

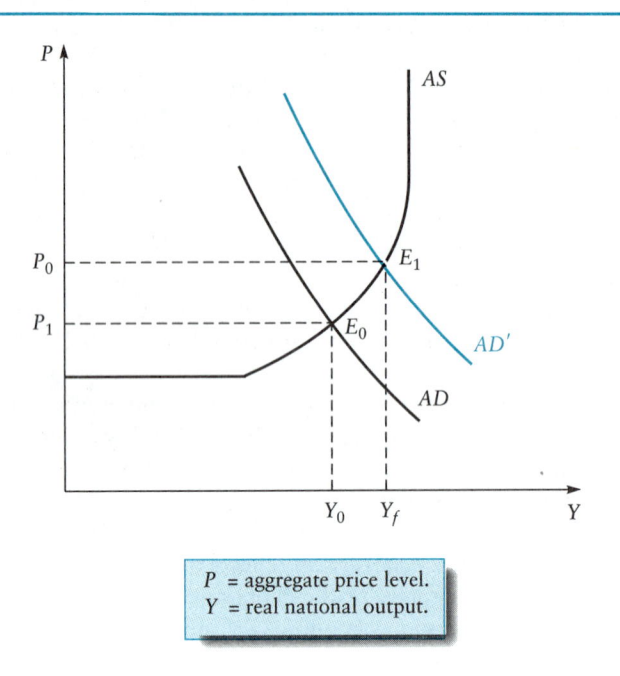

P = aggregate price level.
Y = real national output.

price level) would be met by running down inventories. To replenish the inventories, firms would step up the rate of production. Unit costs of production and the aggregate price level would rise with the expansion of real national output. (See the movement from E_0 to E_1 along the aggregate supply curve.)

The increase in nominal national income (as the aggregate price level rises from P_0 to P_1 and real national output expands from Y_0 to Y_f) increases the demand for money balances. The higher demand for money (from M^d to $M^{d'}$) partially offsets the initial decline in the nominal interest rate from the Fed's increase in the money supply. On net, the consequences of the expansionary monetary policy are an increase in real national output and income (from Y_0 to Y_f), a higher aggregate price level (from P_0 to P_1), a lower nominal interest rate (from i_0 to i_1), and increased real private investment expenditures (from I_0 to I_1).

With expansionary fiscal policy the federal government could increase its purchases of goods and services ($\Delta G_0 > 0$), or reduce net taxes ($\Delta T_0 < 0$ with a drop in net lump-sum taxes, or $\Delta t < 0$, with a cut in income tax rates). Refer to Figure 14.8. In any case, aggregate demand would increase with the fiscal stimulus (from AD to AD'). The excess demand for national output would be met by a running down of inventories and an increase in the quantity of national output produced. The increase in nominal national income would raise the demand for money (from M^d to $M^{d'}$), exerting upward pressure on the nominal interest rate, which would crowd out some private investment expenditures. On net, the consequences of the expansionary fiscal policy would be an increase in real national output and income (from Y_0 to Y_f), a higher aggregate price level (from P_0 to P_1), a higher nominal interest rate (from i_0 to i_1), and a reduced level of real private investment expenditures (from I_0 to I_1).

(a) Money Market

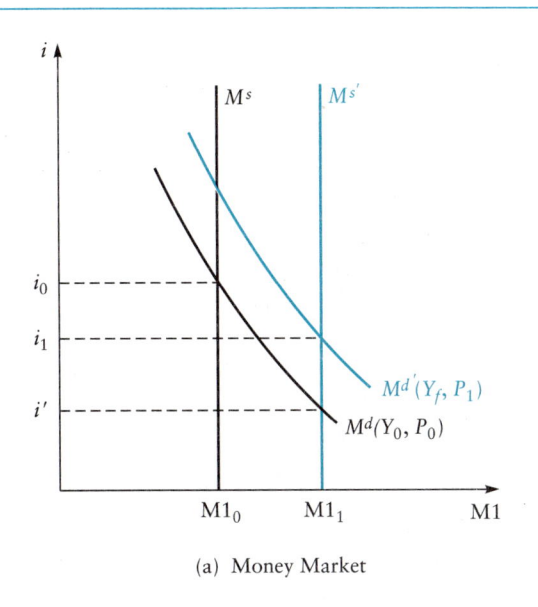

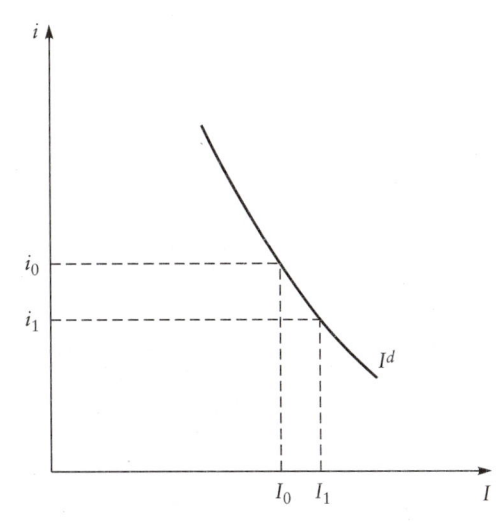

(b) Investment Expenditures

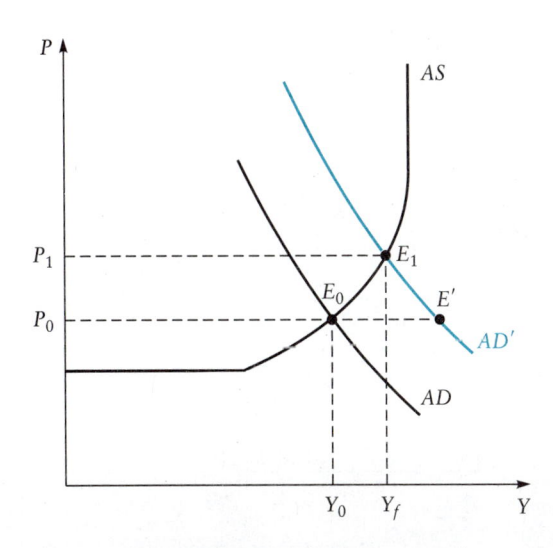

(c) Aggregate Demand–Aggregate Supply

FIGURE 14.7

EXPANSIONARY MONETARY POLICY

Expansionary monetary policy reduces the nominal rate of interest (from i_0 to i_1) and stimulates real fixed investment expenditures (from I_0 to I_1). Real national output increases (from Y_0 to Y_f), the unemployment rate should fall, and the aggregate price level rises (from P_0 to P_1).

In sum, while both expansionary monetary and expansionary fiscal policies would increase real national output, reduce unemployment, and increase the aggregate price level, the consequences for private investment expenditures differ. Expansionary monetary policy drives down the interest rate and stimulates private investment, which adds to the capital stock of the nation. In contrast, expansionary fiscal policy results in a higher nominal interest rate which discourages private investment and capital formation. Unless the fiscal stimulus takes the form of increased spending on the economic infrastructure (as in public investment in highways, dams, and airports) or for human capital

FIGURE 14.8

EXPANSIONARY FISCAL POLICY

Expansionary fiscal policy, in contrast to expansionary monetary policy, results in a higher nominal rate of interest (rising from i_0 to i_1) and a crowding out of real private fixed investment expenditures (from I_0 to I_1). Real national output increases (from Y_0 to Y_f), the unemployment rate should fall, and the aggregate price level rises (from P_0 to P_1).

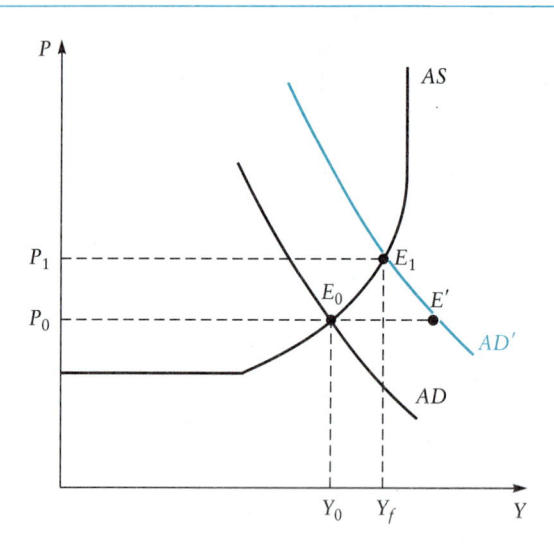

(as in investments in education and health care), then the future growth of the economy may be reduced.[10]

A second difference in the two types of expansionary policies concerns the impact on the federal government's budget balance. Expansionary monetary policy tends to improve the budget balance as tax revenues rise with national

---

[10] Neo-Keynesians discount the crowding out effect of the higher interest rate on private investment expenditures, arguing that as the economy expands, business confidence and profits rise and firms may very well increase investment expenditures—in spite of the higher nominal rates of interest. Moreover, the inflow of foreign saving may moderate the increase in the interest rate needed to restore equilibrium in the money market.

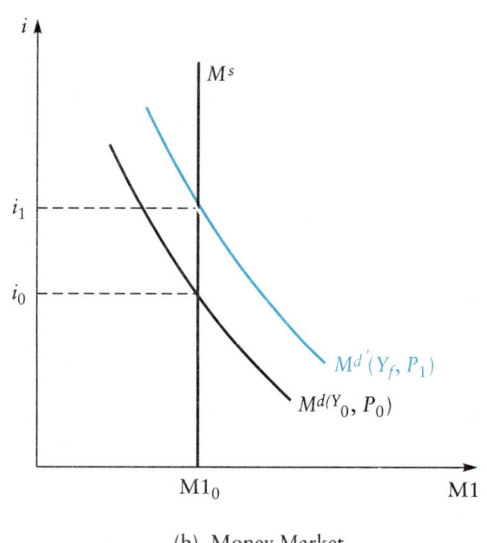

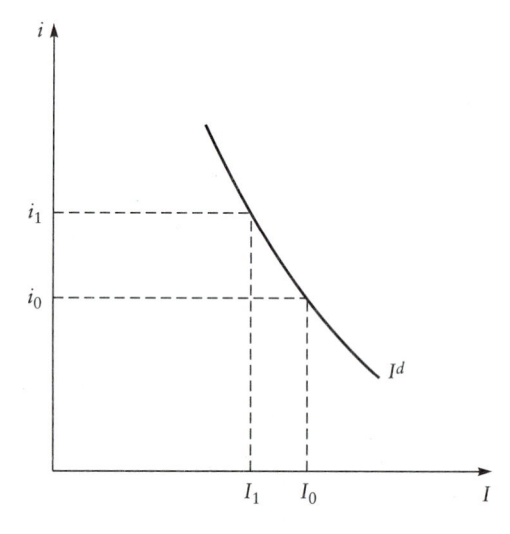

income. Expansionary fiscal policy, on the other hand, tends to reduce the federal budget balance (that is, reduce a budget surplus or add to a budget deficit), since the direct effects of the government expenditure increase or tax decrease dominate the induced rise in tax revenues from the expansion of national income. What would be the differences in the consequences of contractionary monetary versus contractionary fiscal policy?

A point worth mentioning is that fiscal policy is more easily targeted than monetary policy. For instance, government expenditures could be increased more in those regions of the nation where unemployment rates are the highest. Alternatively, tax cuts could be designated for certain income classes or household types (for example, increasing the standard deduction for child dependents). In contrast, the consequences of monetary policy are more diffuse. Changes in the money supply affect the market rate of interest and interest-sensitive expenditures throughout the nation.

Finally, as we noted at the outset of this chapter, ideally monetary and fiscal policies should be coordinated, working in concert toward common objectives. To the extent that monetary and fiscal policies are so aligned, the required doses of each would be moderated. If, however, they are working in opposite directions (for example, expansionary fiscal policy with contractionary monetary policy), then changes in the interest rate and interest-sensitive expenditures would be magnified. The net effects on real national output, employment, and the aggregate price level, however, would depend on the relative strengths of the monetary and fiscal policies.[11]

CONCLUDING NOTE

As noted before, the appropriateness of demand-management policies is a continuing point of debate among economists.[12] In our example where we compared expansionary monetary and fiscal policies, we implicitly assumed that the demand-management policies were successful in eliminating the gap in real national output. In practice, though, due to lags in policymaking and uncertain multiplier effects, demand-management policies rarely work with such precision. Whether this means that all attempts to demand-manage the economy should be avoided is open to question.

The controversy over the efficacy of discretionary monetary and fiscal policies reflects a larger debate over the appropriate role of the federal government in managing the economy. Monetarists are not alone in their advocacy of nonintervention.

---

[11] We should add that in the discussion in the last two chapters about monetary and fiscal policies, we have focused on the internal adjustments of the domestic economy. When we incorporate exchange rates and balance of international payments adjustments, as in Chapters 17 and 18, we may see that, in some cases under fixed exchange rates, it is best for fiscal and monetary policies to work in opposite directions.

[12] Recent evidence on the Keynesian-monetarist controversy over the relative effectiveness of fiscal and monetary policies is presented in a study, "Monetary vs. Fiscal Policy: New Evidence on an Old Debate," by Peter E. Kretzmer, *Economic Review of the Federal Reserve Bank of Kansas City*, Second Quarter (Vol. 77, Number 2): 21–32. Kretzmer's conclusion is "while monetary policy has become less effective over the years, it is still more effective than fiscal policy" (page 25).

Other macro schools, notably the New Classicals and supply-siders also favor a "hands-off" approach. Only the Neo-Keynesians, among the major schools in macroeconomics, favor an active role for the federal government in demand-managing the economy.

In the next chapter we will review supply-side economics, which enjoyed considerable popularity during the Reagan administration. Then in Chapter 16 we will examine the trade-offs between inflation and unemployment in more detail and discuss the contribution of the New Classicals to the ongoing debate over macroeconomic policy. When we extend the analysis in Chapters 17 and 18 to the macroeconomics of international trade and finance, we will see how exchange rates and balance of payments adjustments add another dimension to the conduct of monetary and fiscal policy.

KEY TERMS

required reserve ratio
discount rate
open market operations
recognition lag
response lag

impact lag
monetary rule
income velocity of money
simple quantity theory of money

QUESTIONS

1. What are the three most important ideas in this chapter? Discuss why each is important.
2. Use the following simplified version of First City Bank's Balance Sheet to answers Questions 2 and 3. Assume the required reserve ratio and desired excess reserve ratio are, respectively, 10 percent and 5 percent.

First City Bank (in millions of $)

Assets		Liabilities	
Reserves	30	Demand Deposits	200
Govt. Securities	170	Time Deposits	400
Loans	450	Capital Account	50
	650		650

How many government securities would First City Bank have to sell if
   a. its depositors wrote checks for $20 million to pay for government securities bought from the Fed during open market sales?
   b. the Fed raised the required reserve ratio to 12 percent?
3. What would be the maximum number of new loans that First City Bank could make if
   a. it received $20 million in new demand deposits?
   b. its depositors shifted $20 million from their demand deposits to their time deposits? (Assume there is no required reserve ratio on time deposits.)

4. Illustrate the effects of a contractionary fiscal policy on real national output, the aggregate price level, the nominal interest rate, and desired real fixed investment expenditures—assuming the economy is on the intermediate range of the aggregate supply curve. Describe the economic transition to the new equilibrium levels.
5. In the example of Question 4, we assumed that the nominal money supply is constant. What would be the consequences of the same contractionary fiscal policy if the Federal Reserve had a monetary policy of pegging the interest rate? Would such a policy tend to offset or enhance the effect of fiscal policy on real national output? Explain.
6. Illustrate the effects of a contractionary monetary policy on real national output, the aggregate price level, the nominal interest rate, and desired real fixed investment expenditures—assuming the economy is on the intermediate range of the aggregate supply curve. Describe the economic transition to the new equilibrium.
7. Assume a strong monetarist position: that the aggregate demand for nominal money balances depends only on nominal income. That is, the interest elasticity of money demand equals zero.

$$M^d = kPY \stackrel{e}{=} M^s$$

where

M^d = aggregate quantity of nominal M1 money balances demanded.
k = proportion of nominal national income desired to be held as nominal money balances (assume $k = .2$).
P = aggregate price level.
Y = real national income.
M^s = nominal M1 money supply.

Let the initial values be $Y_0 = 1000$, $P_0 = 1$, and $M_0^s = 200$. Assume that the Fed is following a monetary rule whereby the nominal money supply is targeted to grow at 3 percent a year. Find the implied inflation rate when
a. in the first year the growth rate in real output equals 5 percent.
b. in the second year the growth rate in real output equals 1 percent.
Find the average inflation rate and the average growth rate in real national income for the two-year period.

CHAPTER

15

SUPPLY-SIDE POLICY

SUPPLY-SIDE ECONOMICS refers to a set of policy prescriptions designed to promote rightward shifts in the nation's aggregate supply curve. Recall the factors that are held constant when the aggregate supply curve is drawn: the size and quality of the labor force, the size and quality of the capital stock, the available natural resources, the state of technology, the schedules of factor prices, and government regulations and taxes. Changes in these underlying factors will shift the aggregate supply curve. Supply-side policies attempt to foster noninflationary economic growth by increasing the incentives to work, save, and invest.

Supply-side shocks in the 1970s—in particular, the oil price hikes—renewed interest in supply-side policies. Refer to Figure 15.1 and assume the economy is in equilibrium at E_0 with a rate of real national output of Y_0 and an aggregate price level of P_0. Suppose that sharply higher energy prices shift the aggregate supply curve up (from AS to AS'), so that the aggregate price level associated with any rate of national production is higher. The fall in supply results in stagflation. (See the movement to the new equilibrium, E_1, with a higher aggregate price level and lower real national output.) The economy loses ground on all three macroeconomic goals of price stability, full employment, and economic growth. Attempts to fight the unemployment through expansionary demand-management policies further increase prices. The aggregate price level would rise from P_1 to P_2 with the increase in aggregate demand from AD to AD_2. In contrast, using contractionary demand-management policies to lower prices only aggravates the economic downturn. The decrease in aggregate demand from AD to AD'_2 reduces real national output further (from Y_1 to Y'_2, assuming the aggregate price level is downwardly flexible) and adds to the unemployment. (Note: If the aggregate price level is not downwardly flexible (recall the ratcheting effect of the aggregate supply curve discussed in Chapter 12), then the fall in real national output and rise in unemployment would be even greater. (See point E'_1 where the aggregate demand curve AD'_2 intersects the "ratcheted up" aggregate supply curve P_1E_1AS'.) Clearly, the only good solution

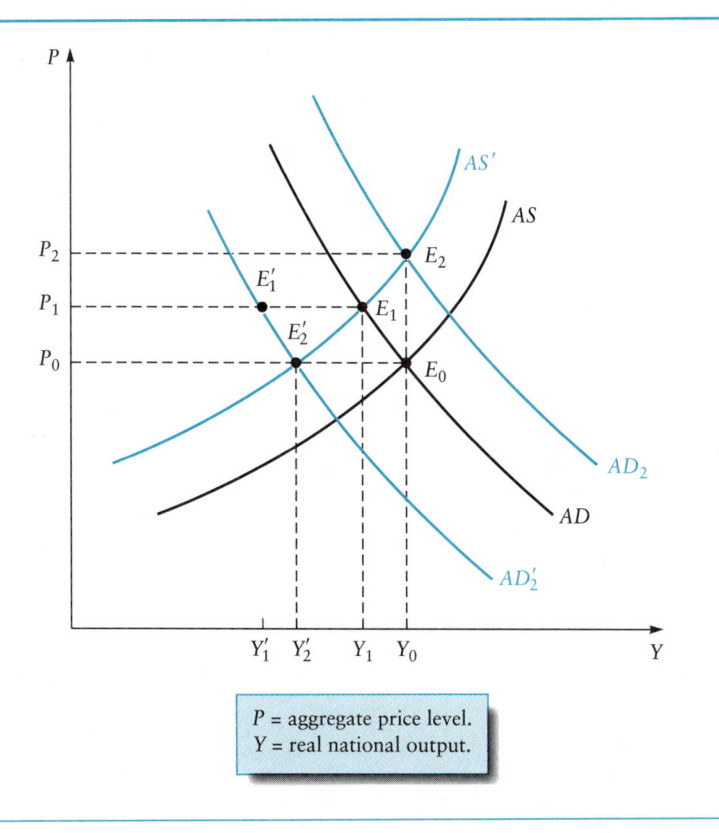

FIGURE 15.1

Supply-Side Shock and Demand-Management Policy

A fall in aggregate supply (from AS to AS′) results in an increase in the aggregate price level (P_0 to P_1) and a decrease in the rate of real national output (from Y_0 to Y_1). Expansionary demand-management policy (AD to AD_2) to restore real national output will fuel the inflation by pushing up the aggregate price level again (P_1 to P_2). Contractionary demand-management policy (AD to AD_2') will deepen the downturn (Y_1 to Y_2') and add to the unemployment.

P = aggregate price level.
Y = real national output.

to a supply-side shock is to have the aggregate supply curve shift back to the right.

Supply-siders view discretionary demand-management policies as erring on the side of overstimulation of the economy, which in turn produces inflation. For reasons discussed later, inflation can undermine the incentives to work, save, and invest.

In fact, in the wake of the first oil price shocks engineered by OPEC in 1973–1974, U.S. policymakers opted to stimulate the economy to counter rising unemployment (shifting the aggregate demand curve from AD to AD_2 in Figure 15.1). While the U.S. economy recovered briskly from the recession, inflationary pressures continued to build over the latter half of the decade. The second wave of oil price increases in 1979 with the Iranian Revolution and the associated panic-buying in the world oil market further fueled inflation. The accelerating inflation in 1979, however, was met with contractionary policies (shifting the aggregate demand from AD to AD_2' in Figure 15.1).

In this chapter we will discuss some of the specific policy recommendations of supply-side economics. A recurring theme is that government "interference" in the economy hinders rightward shifts in the aggregate supply curve and noninflationary real growth. We will also review a recent application of supply-side policies known as **Reaganomics,** the economic policies carried out primarily during the first Reagan administration. We begin with the incentive structure of the tax system.

TAXES AND INCENTIVES

Supply-siders believe that the incentive structure implicit in the tax system is an important determinant in individual decisions on work, saving, and investment.

Labor Supply

The opportunity cost of leisure is the after-tax real wage rate forgone from not working. Up to a point, increases in the after-tax real wage rate will encourage a substitution of work (income) for leisure—the *substitution effect*. If, as might be expected, leisure is a normal good, then a rise in the after-tax real wage rate also tends to increase the quantity of leisure demanded—the *income effect*. A priori, then, the net effect of an increase in the after-tax real wage on the quantity of labor supplied is indeterminate.

To illustrate, consider an individual, for whom the substitution effect predominates over the range of relevant wage rates. That is, the quantity of labor she supplies in each period is a positive function of the expected after-tax real wage rate.

$$l^s = f[\overset{+}{(1 - t_y)(w/P^e)}]$$

where

l^s = quantity of labor hours supplied per period by the individual.
t_y = tax rate on labor income earned.
w = money wage per hour.
P^e = expected price level over the period.

The individual realizes that inflation, or a rise in the aggregate price level, reduces the purchasing power of the money wage received. We assume, however, that the individual, not knowing the actual price level which will prevail over the period, will form an estimate of the price level (P^e). Her expected real wage before taxes is then (w/P^e) and the expected real wage after taxes would be $(1 - t_y)(w/P^e)$.

In Figure 15.2 we sketch the individual's labor supply curve, placing the money wage on the vertical axis and the quantity of labor hours supplied on the horizontal axis.[1] The labor supply curve is drawn holding constant her labor-leisure preferences, the tax rate on labor income, and the expected price level. Changes in any one of these underlying factors would shift the labor supply curve.

If the money wage were w_0, then for the given tax rate on labor income of t_y and expected price level of P^e, she would be willing to supply l_0 hours of work

---

[1] For simplicity, we have drawn the labor supply curves as linear functions of the money wage. More realistically, we might expect that as the number of labor hours supplied by the individual increases in any given period of time, the labor supply curves would become steeper. That is, increasingly higher money wages would be required to compensate the individual for the leisure sacrificed. Beyond some point, the income effect from the higher money wage may dominate the substitution effect, and the labor supply curves will bend backwards, assuming a negative slope for the higher money wages. Moreover, in any period of time there is a maximum number of labor hours any individual could physically work.

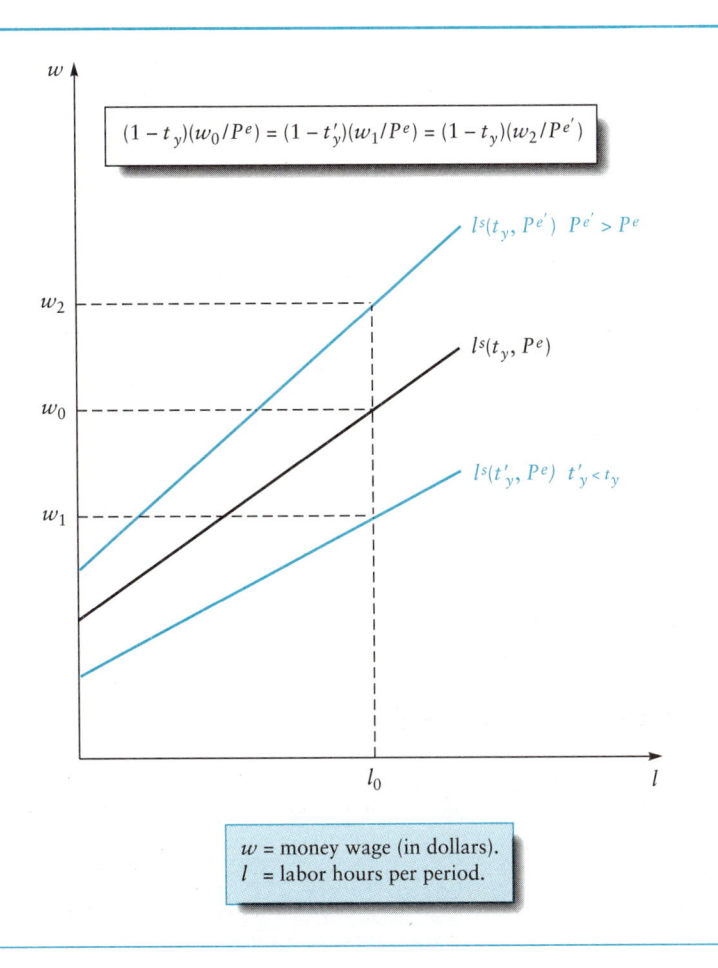

FIGURE 15.2

LABOR SUPPLY CURVES FOR AN INDIVIDUAL

An individual's labor supply curve is drawn holding constant the tax rate on labor income (t_y) and the expected price level (P^e). A decrease in the tax rate on labor income (e.g., $t'_y < t_y$) would increase the quantity of labor supplied at any expected real wage—shifting the labor supply curve to the right. An increase in the expected price level ($P^{e'} > P^e$) would decrease the quantity of labor supplied for any after-tax money wage—shifting the labor supply curve to the left.

w = money wage (in dollars).
l = labor hours per period.

during the period. A decrease in the tax rate ($t'_y < t_y$) would increase the incentive to work for any expected pre-tax real wage, and her labor supply curve would shift to the right. Alternatively, if the tax rate were cut, then for any quantity of labor supplied (for example, l_0), the money wage could be lower ($w_1 < w_0$) and still preserve the same expected after-tax real wage.

$$(1 - t'_y)(w_1/P^e) = (1 - t_y)(w_0/P^e)$$

An increase in the expected price level ($P^{e'} > P^e$), in contrast, would shift the labor supply curve to the left. For any pre-tax money wage, $(1 - t_y)w$, the quantity of labor supplied would decrease. Viewed another way, with an increase in the expected price level, a higher money wage ($w_2 > w_0$) would be required to keep the quantity of labor supplied constant (for example, at l_0).

$$(1 - t_y)(w_2/P^{e'}) = (1 - t_y)(w_0/P^e)$$

A numerical example may help. Suppose the individual's labor supply schedule is given by

$$l^s = -20 + 10(1 - t_y)(w/P^e)$$

FIGURE 15.3

SHIFT IN INDIVIDUAL'S LABOR SUPPLY CURVE FROM CHANGE IN TAX RATE ON LABOR INCOME

A decrease in the tax rate on labor income (from 40 percent to 30 percent) increases the individual's supply of labor.

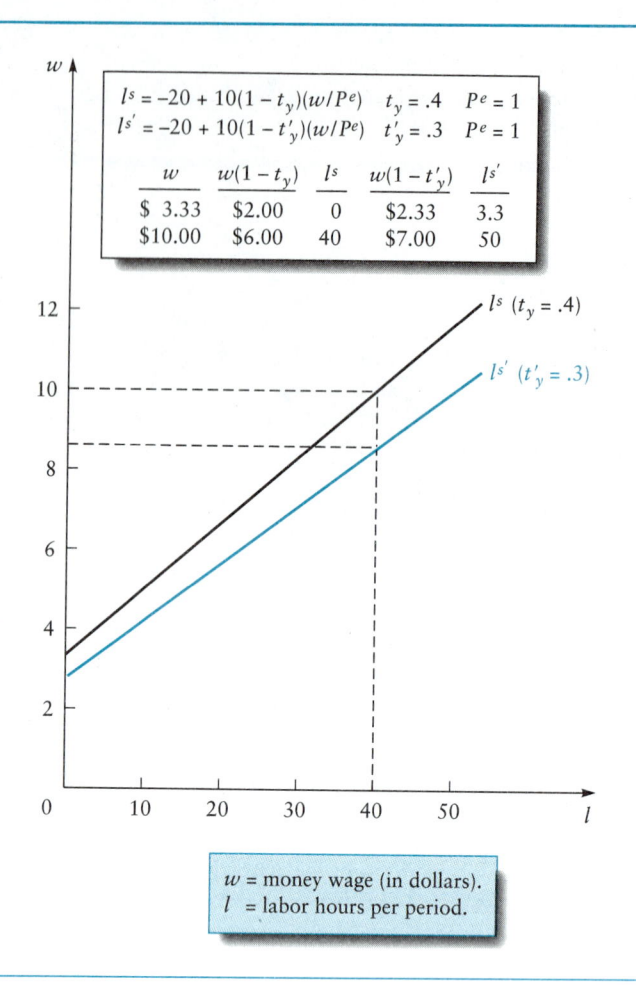

$l^s = -20 + 10(1 - t_y)(w/P^e)$ $t_y = .4$ $P^e = 1$
$l^{s'} = -20 + 10(1 - t'_y)(w/P^e)$ $t'_y = .3$ $P^e = 1$

w	$w(1 - t_y)$	l^s	$w(1 - t'_y)$	$l^{s'}$
$3.33	$2.00	0	$2.33	3.3
$10.00	$6.00	40	$7.00	50

w = money wage (in dollars).
l = labor hours per period.

The quantity of labor hours per week supplied by the individual (l^s) is a linear function of the expected after-tax real wage per hour. If we assume $P^e = 1.0$ and $t_y = .4$, then the labor supply schedule becomes

$$l^s = -20 + 10(1 - .4)(w/1) = -20 + 6w$$

Plotting combinations of the money wage (w) and the quantity of labor supplied (l) gives the labor supply curve (l^s) illustrated in Figure 15.3. We can see that the money wage must be at least $3.33 before she would be willing to supply even the first hour of labor; and that for every increase of $1.00 in the money wage, an additional 6 hours of labor would be supplied.

If the tax rate on labor income were reduced from 40 percent to 30 percent ($t'_y = .3$), the new labor supply schedule would be

$$l^{s'} = -20 + 10(1 - .3)(w/1) = -20 + 7w$$

For a given expected price level ($P^e = 1$), a lower tax rate on labor income earned increases the quantity of labor supplied at each money wage rate. The labor supply curve shifts right. For instance, when the tax rate is 40 percent, the individual in this example is willing to supply 40 hours of labor per week when the money wage is $10.00 an hour. When the tax rate on labor income is 30 percent, the quantity of labor supplied for a money wage of $10.00 an hour is 50 hours per week. Or, if we hold constant the quantity of labor supplied at 40 hours per week, she would require a money wage of $10.00 an hour when the tax rate is $t_y = .4$, but only a money wage of $8.57 an hour when the tax rate is $t'_y = .3$. That is,

$$(1 - .4)10 = (1 - .3)(8.57) = 6$$

The lower tax rate on labor income, by increasing the supply of labor and lowering the money wage that labor would accept for any quantity of labor supplied, reduces the labor cost of producing output. Suppose ten hours of labor are required to assemble a new refrigerator. If refrigerator manufacturers had been paying labor $10.00 an hour (when the tax rate on labor income earned was 40 percent), but could now pay $8.57 an hour (with the tax rate on labor income earned of 30 percent), the labor cost of assembling a refrigerator falls from $100.00 to $85.70.

In general, then, lowering the tax rate on labor income earned increases the incentive to work at any expected pre-tax real wage. In the aggregate for all individuals, the increase in labor supply reduces the money wage and associated labor cost of producing any rate of national output. The rightward shift in labor supply shifts the aggregate supply curve of real national output to the right.

Supply-siders favor not only a cut in the income tax rates to increase the incentive to work, but a revision in the income tax system to neutralize the disincentive effects of inflation. Recall from Chapter 13 on fiscal policy that marginal and average tax rates rise with income under a progressive income tax system. Most income tax systems are based on nominal, not real or inflation-adjusted, incomes. With inflation, even if nominal income before taxes keeps pace with the average increase in prices, an individual's after-tax real income may fall. That is, inflation and nominal income gains may push an individual into a higher tax bracket. This inflation penalty is called **bracket creep**.

To illustrate, consider two tax brackets:

Taxable Income Bracket	Tax Rate
$18,000 to $19,999	15%
$20,000 to $21,999	15% on the first $20,000
	20% on income over $20,000

Suppose an individual is making $19,000 in taxable income. His tax would be $2850 (or 15 percent of $19,000), leaving an after-tax income of $16,150. If the inflation rate is 10 percent, and he receives a raise in nominal income of 10 percent to $20,900, then his before-tax real income is unchanged. Notice, however, that he is pushed into a higher tax bracket. With $20,900 in taxable income, his tax would be $3180 (15 percent of $20,000 plus 20 percent of $900). The after-tax nominal income is $17,720, and deflating by the 10 percent rate of inflation leaves an after-tax real income of $16,109 ($17,720/1.10). Thus, bracket creep has "cost" this individual $41 in real purchasing power.

To eliminate bracket creep, the tax brackets could be indexed to the rate of inflation. Here, with a 10 percent rate of inflation, the new tax brackets would be 10 percent higher.

Original Taxable Income Bracket	New Taxable Income Bracket	Tax Rate
$18,000 to $19,999	$19,800 to $21,999	15%
$20,000 to $21,999	$22,000 to $24,199	15% on the first $22,000 20% on income over $22,000

Now the 10 percent increase in nominal income that just keeps pace with inflation leaves the individual in the same (lower) tax bracket. While indexing the income tax system does eliminate bracket creep, it also reduces the built-in stabilizer quality of the tax system discussed in Chapter 13.

In sum, supply-siders favor both cuts in income tax rates and an income tax system based on real income. Along similar lines, they are generally opposed to transfer payments, which are seen as a disincentive to work and earn income. Also, transfer payments contribute to government deficits, the financing of which leads either to inflation (if the Federal Reserve monetizes the debt) or the crowding out of private investment through higher interest rates. Furthermore, supply-siders argue that transfer payments funded through tax revenues shift income from those with higher saving rates (the taxpayers with higher incomes) to those with lower saving rates (the transfer recipients with lower incomes). As we will see next, supply-siders are also concerned with generating savings for capital formation.

Personal Saving

In addition to tax cuts to increase the supply of labor, supply-siders favor measures to increase the supply of loanable funds—in particular, *household saving*, which takes a number of forms, including time deposits, whole life insurance premiums, and purchases of new issues of stocks and bonds. Increases in household saving lower the market rate of interest, making it less expensive for firms to raise funds for investment. Positive net fixed investment, in turn, adds to the physical capital stock of the economy. Growth in the capital stock, just like increases in labor supply, shifts the aggregate supply curve outward, raising the nation's productive capacity.

Supply-siders believe that one way to increase the national saving rate is to lower taxes on those with a higher propensity to save—the wealthy. Moreover, they view the expected after-tax real return as a primary determinant of household saving. For any given rate of interest, household saving will be encouraged by a decrease in the tax rate on income earned from wealth (such as capital gains, interest, and dividends). Indeed, until recently in the United States, tax rates on income from wealth were lower than tax rates on labor income.

Supply-siders also advocate tax reform. With a tax system based on nominal income, inflation can erode the real after-tax return to saving. Recall from Chapter 14 that the expected real interest rate (r^e) is equal to

$$r^e = \frac{1 + i}{1 + INF^e} - 1$$

where

i = nominal annual rate of interest.
INF^e = expected inflation rate.

When the nominal income from saving is taxed, then the expected after-tax real return is equal to

$$(r^e)^* = \frac{1 + (1 - t_s)i_s}{1 + INF^e} - 1$$

where

$(r^e)^*$ = expected after-tax real annual interest rate on saving.
i_s = before-tax nominal annual interest rate on saving.
t_s = tax rate on income from saving.
$(1 - t_s)i_s$ = after-tax nominal annual interest rate on saving.

Consider the following example of how a rise in expected inflation can reduce the incentive to save for a given before-tax nominal interest rate on saving. Let $i_s = .08$, $t_s = .25$, and $INF^e = .05$. Initially, the expected before-tax real return to saving is 2.86 percent.

$$r_0^e = \frac{1 + i_s}{1 + INF^e} - 1 = \frac{1 + .08}{1 + .05} - 1 = 1.0286 - 1 = .0286$$

The expected after-tax real return to saving, however, is just .95 percent:

$$(r_0^e)^* = \frac{1 + (1 - t_s)i_s}{1 + INF^e} - 1 = \frac{1 + (1 - .25)(.08)}{1 + .05} - 1 = .0095$$

Even if a rise in the expected inflation rate from 5 to 7 percent pushes up the nominal interest rate by enough to maintain the expected before-tax real return to saving at 2.86 percent, the expected after-tax real return to saving will fall. With an inflation rate of 7 percent, the nominal interest rate will have to be 10.06 percent to maintain the expected before-tax real return to saving. That is,

$$r_1^e = \frac{1 + i_s'}{1 + .07} - 1 = .0286 = r_0^e$$

when

$$i_s' = .1006$$

Yet, the new expected after-tax real return to saving falls from .95 percent to .51 percent.

$$(r_1^e)^* = \frac{1 + (1 - t_s)i_s'}{1 + INF^e} - 1 = \frac{1 + (1 - .25)(.1006)}{1 + .07} - 1 = .0051$$

Thus, inflation (actual as well as expected) combined with a tax system based on nominal income reduces the after-tax real return to saving. Supply-siders advocate reform of the tax system so that real returns to saving are taxed. A formula that taxes the actual real return to saving would be

$$r^{**} = (1 - t_s)\left(\frac{1 + i_s}{1 + INF^e} - 1\right)$$

In this example, with an expected inflation rate of 7 percent and a before-tax nominal interest rate of 10.06 percent (yielding an expected before-tax real return of 2.86 percent), the revised expected after-tax real return would be 2.14 percent—the same as when the expected inflation rate is 5 percent and before-tax nominal interest rate is 8 percent.

$$(r_1^e)^{**} = (1 - .25)\left(\frac{1 + .1006}{1 + .07} - 1\right) = .75(.0286) = .0214$$

$$(r_0^e)^{**} = (1 - .25)\left(\frac{1 + .08}{1 + .05} - 1\right) = .75(.0286) = .0214$$

In addition to the dividend and interest income, another motive for saving in the form of stocks and bonds is the potential for a **capital gain,** the profit made when an asset is sold for a higher price than for which it was purchased. Recall from Chapter 10, where the theory of portfolio management was discussed, that the market values of stocks and bonds fluctuate over time—the former with investor perceptions of the profitability of the corporations issuing the stocks and the latter with the market rate of interest. When the capital gains tax is based on the realized nominal capital gains, inflation will erode the after-tax real return to profitable speculative investments. To illustrate, suppose you purchase ten shares of stock in a company for $100 a share at the beginning of the year. If you sell the ten shares of stock for $120 a share at the end of the year, you would realize a capital gain of $200 on your initial investment of $1000 (or a 20 percent nominal return before taxes). If, however, the inflation rate over the year is 5 percent, your before-tax real return falls to 14.3 percent. That is,

$$.143 = \frac{1 + .2}{1 + .05} - 1$$

Assuming a tax rate on capital gains of 25 percent and a tax system based on nominal (not real or inflation-adjusted) capital gains, the after-tax real return on the stock investment is only 9.5 percent. That is,

$$.095 = \frac{1 + (1 - .25)(.2)}{1 + .05} - 1$$

In contrast, if the capital gains tax rate of 25 percent were assessed on the real capital gain, then the after-tax real return on the stock investment would be 10.7 percent. That is,

$$.107 = (1 - .25)\left(\frac{1 + .2}{1 + .05} - 1\right)$$

Therefore, according to supply-siders, to encourage saving in risky ventures (that is, those with the potential for capital gains and losses), the capital gains tax rate should be applied to the real value of the capital gain. Supply-siders would also advocate lower tax rates on capital gains and on the income earned from saving.

Providing greater incentives to savers in order to increase the supply of loanable funds is only part of the supply-side goal of fostering capital formation. The other part is providing greater incentives for business to invest in new plant, equipment, and machinery.

Business Investment

One way to stimulate business investment is with **tax credits.** Under this scheme, firms are allowed to deduct from their taxes a certain percentage of their qualifying fixed investment expenditures. For example, if the investment tax credit is 15 percent, then a firm purchasing a machine for $2000 can subtract $300 from its profits taxes owed at the end of the year. In effect, an investment tax credit subsidizes the purchase price of the capital good.

A second way to encourage business investment is to reduce the tax rate on corporate profits. Corporate profits are subject to *double taxation*—taxed once at the corporate level and a second time at the household level after distribution as dividends. For this reason some argue that the corporate profits tax should be eliminated altogether. Supply-siders would favor at least a reduction in this tax, and failing that, reforms in the tax system to neutralize the adverse effects of inflation.

Specifically, under the current tax laws, firms are allowed to count as costs of production the inventories used up and the loss in the value of the capital stock due to depreciation. The tax values of the depleted inventories and depreciated capital, however, are based on historical costs (that is, the costs initially paid for the inventories and physical capital), not the replacement costs, which would likely be higher due to the intervening inflation. Supply-siders maintain that firms' costs are therefore understated and their profits overstated. As a consequence, firms face a greater profits tax liability than is justified. A simple example will illustrate.

Suppose that the revenues of a firm for the year are $10 million. The total costs, including the original costs of the inventories used in production and depreciated capital, over the year are $8 million. If the profits tax rate is 30 percent, then the firm's profit tax would be $.6 million. Yet, if the firm were allowed to count the replacement costs of the used inventories and depreciated capital, its total costs would be higher, say $8.5 million. Applying the corporate profits tax rate of 30 percent to the revised level of profits of $1.5 million yields a profits tax of $.45 million. The savings on the profits tax (here $.15 million) could be reinvested by the firm in new capital.

Related to business fixed investment and consistent with the theme of limited government involvement in the economy is the supply-side recommendation of reducing government regulation of business. Complying with government regulations—whether for health, safety, or environmental reasons—adds to the firms' costs and may require the use of less profitable methods of production. Moreover, uncertainty about future government regulations may restrain investment expenditures. Firms would be reluctant to invest in new plant and equipment that may later be found to be at variance with government regulations. Supply-siders would also recommend tax breaks for research and development to stimulate technological change and incentives for extractive industries (e.g., mining and drilling) to discover new sources of raw materials.

In sum, supply-side economic policies seek to promote economic growth by encouraging private enterprise through tax and regulatory relief. Providing incentives for work, saving, investment, research and development, and the exploration and recovery of natural resources will increase the nation's productive capacity. Rightward shifts in the aggregate supply curve make possible noninflationary growth in real output and employment.

As noted earlier, supply-siders do not advocate demand-management fiscal policy, which, they argue, tends to result in excessive government spending and large federal budget deficits. Given their recommendations for lower tax rates on income and business profits, they look to a decrease in government expenditures in order to reach a balanced federal budget.

Reducing income tax rates, however, in addition to the intended supply-side effects on labor hours and personal saving rates, will also have demand side effects. For a given level of national income, reducing the income tax rate will increase disposable income and personal consumption expenditures. So, too, investment tax credits and other tax incentives designed to encourage business fixed investment will not only augment the productive capacity of the economy, but increase aggregate demand. Initially, the demand side effects of the tax cuts may dominate, resulting in inflationary real growth.

REAGANOMICS AND THE 1980s

After the booming 1960s, the 1970s witnessed economic turbulence. The international monetary system of adjustable exchange rates, devised after the World War II, collapsed early in the decade, only to be replaced by a "non-system" of mixed exchange rate practices. The stagflation from the supply-side shocks of the oil price hikes depressed business profits and business fixed investment. Increased health, safety, and environmental concerns brought greater government regulation, which further added to the costs of producing the nation's output. National confidence was periodically shaken by political turmoil: Watergate and President Nixon's resignation, the final withdrawal of American troops from Vietnam, and the seizure of the U.S. embassy and hostages in Iran. Even under more favorable conditions, the economy would have been hard-pressed to maintain full employment over the decade, given the entrance of the baby boomers into the work force and the rising female labor force participation rates. As it was, the U.S. economy did create over 20 million jobs during the 1970s for a 25 percent increase in national employment.

By the end of the 1970s the number one economic concern was inflation, which threatened to spiral out of control. President Carter appointed Paul Volcker as Federal Reserve chairman. Volcker set out to rein in inflation with contractionary monetary policy. As expected in a high-income, high-price economy, restricting the growth of the money supply sent interest rates soaring. Consequently, the U.S. economy went into a recession in 1980. In his presidential campaign, Ronald Reagan promised to reduce inflation, restore full employment, and secure healthy economic growth—consistent with the three primary macroeconomic objectives. He proposed to do all this while cutting taxes and stepping up expenditures on national defense (to close the "window of vulnerability" caused by the purported Soviet arms buildup). Reagan also promised to balance the federal budget before the end of his first administration. Federal budget deficits over the last half of the 1970s had averaged 60 billion dollars, or nearly 3 percent of Gross Domestic Product.[2] To pursue these goals, the Reagan administration turned to supply-side economics.

---

[2] *Economic Report of the President 1992* (Washington, DC: U.S. Government Printing Office, 1992), Table B-74.

There were five major thrusts to the Reagan economic program. First were personal income tax reductions. In 1981 personal income tax rates were cut across the board by 23 percent (to be phased in over a three-year period). In addition, the top marginal rate was reduced from 70 percent to 50 percent. The income tax cuts were motivated by the supply-side argument of increasing the incentives to work and also partly by the philosophy of the Reagan administration of reducing the government's control over national income. Some of the more extreme proponents of supply-side economics claimed that cutting the income tax rates would actually increase the income tax revenues collected. This position was popularized by the economist Arthur Laffer. The underlying concept, captured by the **Laffer curve,** is illustrated in Figure 15.4.

The Laffer curve is shaped like a hill. On the vertical axis are the income tax revenues collected by the federal government. On the horizontal axis the average tax rate (the ratio of income taxes to income) is given. Two extreme positions can be readily identified. If the average tax rate were zero percent, then clearly no tax revenues would be collected. On the other hand, if the average tax rate were 100 percent, then no one would have any incentive to work for income. Theoretically, the tax revenues collected would again be zero. Moving to the right from a zero tax rate, initially tax revenues collected would rise with the average tax rate. Beyond some point, however, the disincentive effect of higher tax rates would kick in, and further increases in the tax rates would reduce work effort, reported income, and tax receipts.

Laffer maintained that the U.S. economy was on the downward-sloping portion of the Laffer curve, for example, point A on Laffer curve L in Figure 15.4. If so, then cutting the income tax rates from an average of t_0 to an average of t_1 would increase the tax revenues collected from R_0 to R_1 (moving from

FIGURE 15.4

LAFFER CURVES

The Laffer curve illustrates the hypothesized relationship between income tax revenues collected and the average income tax rate. The more skewed to the left the Laffer curve is, the greater the disincentive effect of taxes on earned income (e.g., L versus L'). A decrease in the average tax rate from t_0 to t_1 using the Laffer curve L would increase income tax receipts (R_0 to R_1). The same decrease in the average tax rate using the Laffer curve L', however, decreases income tax receipts (R_0 to R_1').

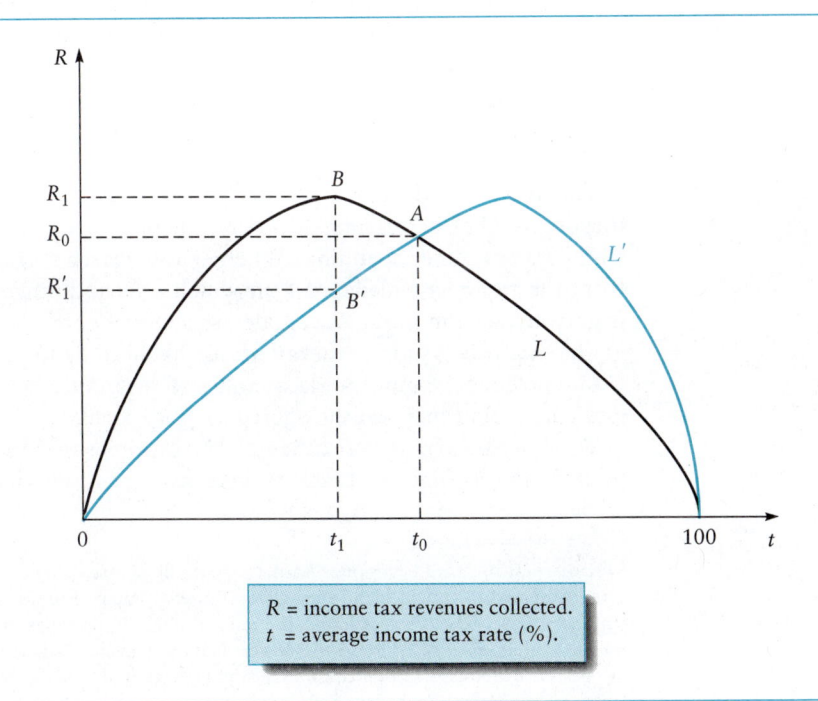

R = income tax revenues collected.
t = average income tax rate (%).

point A to point B on the L curve.) Not only would individuals substitute more labor hours for leisure time, but they might become more honest about declaring their incomes for tax purposes and less prone to seek out tax shelters.

Indeed, tax evasion is a problem for all economies. The **underground economy** refers to the economic activity and income generation that avoids the tax liabilities. Examples abound: the electrician who occasionally insists on being paid in cash so that he need not declare the cash as income earned, the lawyer who offers some legal work to the auto mechanic in exchange for a car tuneup, the babysitter who fails to even file income taxes, as well as all the illegal activities such as drug trade, prostitution, gambling, on which no income is reported. Estimates of the extent of the underground economy in the United States vary, but generally range from 5 to 15 percent of Gross Domestic Product. The lost tax revenues are substantial.

Laffer's contention that income tax revenues would rise with a cut in the tax rates was met with considerable skepticism. Critics, while agreeing on the general principle of the Laffer curve—that at some point high tax rates would become a disincentive to work and declare income—argued that the exact shape of, and the economy's position on, the Laffer curve were unclear. For example, if the Laffer curve were skewed to the right like the curve L' in Figure 15.4, where tax rates were less of a disincentive to work, then a drop in the average tax rate from t_0 to t_1 would decrease tax revenues collected from R_0 to R_1' (from point A to point B').

The empirical evidence on the incentive effect of tax cuts is not conclusive. Most primary workers in households are locked into a 40-hour week, with little flexibility to increase marginally their labor hours, short of moonlighting in a part-time job. The greatest response to lower income tax rates seems to come from second workers in households, who may be enticed into the labor force or better able to increase their working hours when the after-tax wage rate rises. Furthermore, the significance of the *compliance effect*—that is, whether individuals would be more honest in reporting income for tax purposes—is open to question. In any case, while theoretically possible, counting on the income tax cuts to increase tax revenues seems to be stretching the supply-side optimism.[3]

The demand-side consequences of the income tax cuts should not be forgotten. The increase in disposable income from the lower tax rates will stimulate consumer spending. Whether the aggregate price level rises or falls from the tax cuts will depend on which effects dominate—the demand-side (rightward shift in the aggregate demand curve) or supply-side (rightward shift in the aggregate supply curve). In all likelihood, the demand-side stimulus would precede the supply-side stimulus, so that, at least initially, the income-tax rate cuts would increase the aggregate price level.

We should also note here other tax legislation passed during the Reagan years. In 1985 the income tax brackets were *indexed* to eliminate the bracket creep

---

[3] In an article by Marc Levinson, "April 15 Could Be Worse," *Newsweek,* April 13, 1992, 48, it is reported that the tax burden in the United States, compared to other industrialized economies, is relatively light. For example, the ratio of total tax revenues to Gross Domestic Product for the United States of 28 percent is lower than for Canada (34 percent), the United Kingdom (37 percent), Germany (39 percent), France (42 percent), the Netherlands (48 percent) and Sweden (49 percent). Only Japan (26 percent) has a lower tax burden.

caused by inflation. Then, in 1986 a comprehensive tax reform simplified the tax system by eliminating many tax shelters, lowering tax rates, and, in particular, relieving the tax burden on the poor. The taxable income brackets were reduced from over a dozen to basically two—a 15 percent and a 28 percent tax bracket. Collapsing the tax brackets further weakened the built-in stabilizing effect inherent in the progressive income tax system.

The second thrust in the Reagan economic program was to increase physical capital formation. The across-the-board income tax rate cuts, by relieving the tax burden on the wealthy, were also intended to increase the national saving rate. Moreover, the initial tax bill passed in 1981 contained incentives for personal saving in the form of more liberal Individual Retirement Accounts (IRAs). By saving through IRAs, households could shelter income from taxes until retirement. Business taxes were also reduced through the expansion of investment tax credits and accelerated depreciation allowances, which enabled firms to reduce their tax liabilities by writing off the costs of their buildings and capital equipment faster than otherwise warranted.[4]

Relaxed government regulation was the third supply-side policy adopted by the Reagan administration. Funding for, and enforcement by, government regulatory agencies in the areas of health, safety, and the environment were scaled back. The intent was to lower the costs of production (which would help control inflation and make American firms more competitive internationally) and increase business profits (which could be used for reinvestment).

While not a tenet of supply-side economics, a priority of the Reagan administration was to increase substantially the expenditures on national defense. Reagan believed that the United States had slipped dangerously in the arms race with the Soviet Union. Consequently, real expenditures on national defense in the first Reagan administration were more than 20 percent higher than during the preceding Carter administration—$908 billion (1987 dollars), or 5.8 percent of GDP for 1981–1984 versus $743 billion (1987 dollars), or 5.0 percent of GDP for 1977–1980.[5]

The fifth part of the Reagan initiative targeted non-defense spending. In particular, consistent with the supply-side position, Reagan believed that transfer payments were inimical to economic growth. Thus, the overall strategy of Reaganomics entailed tax rate cuts to spur economic growth (and perhaps increase tax revenues), greater defense expenditures to bolster national security, and, to keep the federal budget under control, cutbacks in non-defense spending—especially entitlement programs.

AN ASSESSMENT OF REAGANOMICS

Evaluating the overall impact of any economic policy is difficult. For one, the most valid type of assessment is not possible: to compare the actual history that occurred with the policy in place against the history that would have occurred

---

[4] In the comprehensive tax reform of 1986, some of the earlier supply-side measures were reversed: IRAs were tightened, capital gains were taxed as ordinary income, the investment tax credit and accelerated depreciation allowances were dropped, and taxes on corporations were increased.

[5] *Economic Report of the President 1992*, Table B-2.

had the policy not been in place. Instead, we can only surmise what the performance of the U.S. economy would have been over the 1980s without Reaganomics. Related to this point is the need to evaluate the policy in the context of the economic conditions of the time—in particular, the monetary policy of the Federal Reserve. In general, a policy may be well-informed and appropriate, but undermined by the actions of others or by exogenous events. On the other hand, bad policies may look good when other conditions are favorable. Third, the longer-run consequences of a policy may differ significantly from the short-run impacts. What seems to be sound policy in the present, with the benefit of hindsight may later be regarded as unwise. Fourth, virtually all economic policies will affect the distribution of income, which means that, relatively, some will gain and some will lose. Moreover, different observers will use different weights in evaluating the outcomes associated with the policy. For some, reducing inflation will be the highest priority; for others, full employment or rapid economic growth will be ranked higher. With these provisos in mind, we offer an assessment of Reaganomics.

Let us begin by briefly reviewing the economic conditions in the United States in the early 1980s, and then consider some summary statistics comparing the economic performance during the Reagan administrations with the economic performance during the preceding eight-year period. The fiscal policy package set in motion early in the first Reagan administration was expansionary. The income tax cuts and incentives for business investment, the stepped-up spending on national defense, and the reluctance of Congress to trim non-defense expenditures as much as the president proposed all combined to increase aggregate demand. The supply-side effects on work effort and capital formation were expected to hold down inflation by increasing the productive capacity of the economy.

After the brief recession in early 1980, the Fed relaxed its grip on the money supply and the economy rebounded. Chairman Volcker and the FOMC, however, were not convinced that inflation had been tamed. Indeed, as measured by the Implicit Price Deflator for GDP, the inflation rate in 1980 was 9.5 percent.[6] So, early in 1981 the Fed again imposed tighter monetary policy—and this time the Fed persisted. The combination of expansionary fiscal policy and contractionary monetary policy sent real interest rates up sharply. The annual average for the federal funds rate went from 13.4 percent for 1980 to 16.4 percent for 1981. Business and residential fixed investment fell. The economic downturn spread through the multiplier effect. While the inflation rate dropped from 10.0 percent in 1981 to 6.2 percent in 1982, the nation's unemployment rate rose from 7.6 percent to 9.7 percent.

The recession increased the federal budget deficit. The earlier cuts in the income tax rates, combined with the fall in income from the recession, reduced tax revenues. Transfer payments rose with unemployment as more individuals qualified for assistance. The growth in the federal budget deficits (from $79 billion in 1981 to $128 billion in 1982 and $208 billion in 1983) helped maintain the upward pressure on real interest rates. The high real returns on U.S. assets were attractive to foreign investors, who had to first convert their currencies into U.S. dollars in order to invest in U.S. assets. The resulting

---

[6] Ibid., Tables B-1, B-3, B-37, B-69, B-74.

increase in the demand for dollars boosted the exchange value of the dollar, and the stronger dollar hurt the competitive position of U.S. industry. As the deficits in the U.S. trade balance (net exports of goods and services) increased, protectionist sentiment began to mount in the U.S. Congress.

By the second half of 1982, in the face of the most severe recession since the Great Depression of the 1930s, the Fed relented and began to pump up the money supply.[7] The economy recovered briskly. From a decline of 2.2 percent in 1982, real GDP rose by 3.9 percent in 1983 and another 6.2 percent in 1984. The inflation rate subsided to 4.1 percent in 1983, and while slower to respond, the unemployment rate fell from 9.6 percent in 1983 to 7.5 percent in 1984. In fact, in 1983 the U.S. economy began an economic expansion with only moderate inflation that lasted nearly seven years. In Table 15.1 we present selected statistics that aid in the comparison of the Reagan years (1981–1988) with the previous eight-year period (1973–1980), which actually encompassed three administrations (Nixon, Ford, and Carter).

While aware of the difficulties in making such comparisons, we nevertheless see that the period of Reaganomics was characterized, on average, by slightly

---

[7] Another reason for the Federal Reserve adopting expansionary monetary policy was the international debt crisis, which came to a head in late 1982 when Mexico announced it could no longer meet its external debt obligations. In the course of helping out Mexico, the Federal Reserve expanded the U.S. money supply. In Chapter 19 we will discuss the debt problems of the developing nations.

TABLE 15.1
SELECTED STATISTICS ON THE U.S. ECONOMY: 1973–1980 AND 1981–1988

	1973–1980	1981–1988
Average annual growth rate in real GDP	2.5%	2.9%
Average annual inflation rate (% change in the GDP Implicit Price Deflator)	8.0%	4.8%
Average annual unemployment rate	6.6%	7.5%
Ratio of business fixed investment to GDP	11.9%	12.0%
Ratio of exports of goods and services to GDP	8.7%	8.3%
Ratio of imports of goods and services to GDP	9.2%	10.6%
Ratio of federal government expenditures to GDP	21.6%	23.7%
Ratio of federal government receipts to GDP	19.8%	19.8%
Ratio of federal budget deficits to GDP	1.8%	3.9%
Average annual ratio of personal saving to disposable personal income	7.8%	6.7%
Average weekly hours of work—private sector	36.1	34.9
Average hourly earnings (1982 dollars)—private sector	$8.24	$7.75
Average labor force participation rates: male	78.0%	76.4%
Average labor force participation rates: female	48.1%	54.2%
Real median family income (1990 dollars)	$34,550	$33,700
Percentage of families below poverty level	9.4%	11.3%

NOTE: The ratios of business fixed investment, exports and imports of goods and services, federal government expenditures and receipts, and the federal budget deficit to Gross National Product are based on cumulative totals for the two eight-year periods.

SOURCE: *Economic Report of the President 1992* (Washington, DC: U.S. Government Printing Office, 1992). Tables B1, B2, B3, B24, B28, B30, B34, B42, B77.

higher real growth (2.9 percent versus 2.5 percent) and significantly lower inflation (4.8 percent versus 8.0 percent), but also by higher unemployment (7.5 percent versus 6.6 percent). Part of the explanation for the better performance on growth and inflation would be the contrast between the supply-side shocks of higher oil prices in the 1970s and the general decline in oil prices over the 1980s. Primary credit for the lower inflation, however, should go to the Federal Reserve's contractionary monetary policy. The higher average unemployment in the 1980s is perhaps surprising given the more favorable demographics: the absorption of the baby boomers into the labor force largely took place in the 1970s.

Consider now the specific supply-side targets of increased capital formation and work effort. The share of business fixed investment in GDP (at approximately 12 percent) was virtually the same in both periods. The average personal saving rate was a percentage point lower during the Reagan era (6.7 percent versus 7.8 percent).

It is more difficult to discern the effect on work effort. Average male labor force participation rates fell, while those for females rose. The averages, however, are somewhat misleading. Male labor force participation rates have slowly, but steadily, declined over the last four decades. Female labor force participation rates, in contrast, have steadily increased over the same period. The rate of increase for females did not noticeably pick up in the early 1980s after the cuts in income tax rates—although the recession in 1981–1982 clearly affected labor market conditions. Both the average work week and the average hourly real wage declined in the latter period. Despite an increase in the number of second workers in households, the real median family income fell from an average of $34,550 for 1973–1980 to $33,700 for 1981–1988.

The percentage of families living below the poverty level averaged nearly two points higher during the Reagan administrations. Along with the increase in the average poverty rate, there was a marked increase in inequality in the distribution of income over the 1980s. In particular, lower-income families with children were hit hard by the economic recession of 1981–1982, the increased burden of social security payroll taxes, and the pullback in federal welfare assistance. At the other end of the scale, the upper-income classes benefited significantly from the cuts in income tax rates.

The legacy of Reaganomics is likely to include a fundamental change in the public perception of the economic role of the government. Ideologically, the Reagan administrations will be remembered for stressing private enterprise and limitations on the role of central government. Notwithstanding the ambiguity in the economic record, most observers would agree that the focus of national debate has shifted toward a reduced role for the federal government.

The legacy of Reaganomics will also include the twin debts. The gross federal debt more than doubled during the two Reagan administrations: from $909 billion (34 percent of GDP) at the end of 1980 to $2,601 billion (54 percent of GDP) by the end of 1988.[8] The ratio of federal budget deficits to GDP was more than twice as high during the 1981–1988 period, although the share of federal government receipts in GDP remained steady at 19.8 percent—aided by the increased tax rates for social security. The implication is that the federal deficit

---

[8] *Economic Report of the President 1992*, Table B-74.

problems of the 1980s reflect excessive increases in federal expenditures. The ratio of federal government expenditures to GDP rose from 21.6 percent for 1973–1980 to 23.7 percent for 1981–1988.

During the 1980s the United States piled up foreign debt at a record pace. The erosion of the international competitive position of the United States, largely the result of the sharp appreciation of the dollar over the first half of the decade, can be seen in both the lower ratio of exports to GDP and the higher ratio of imports to GDP. (We will return to the topic of the exchange value of the dollar in the 1980s in Chapter 18.) Nevertheless, the foreign saving (reflected in the U.S. current account deficits) did help finance the federal budget deficits and serve to prop up investment expenditures in the nation.

The massive increases in national debt and foreign debt over the 1980s, indicative of a nation overconsuming, will have to be addressed. Since the federal budget deficits and trade deficits are related (see the discussions in Chapter 13 on fiscal policy and in Chapter 18 on exchange rate systems), tighter fiscal policy seems in order. The Gramm-Rudman-Hollings Balanced Budget Act of 1985 (GRH) was an acknowledgement of the need to rein in government spending. The original goal of GRH was a balanced federal budget in 1991, to be achieved through a phased-in schedule of deficit reductions. As formulated, the legislation required across-the-board cuts in federal expenditures if the submitted budget did not meet the deficit reduction target. Half of the automatic cuts were to come from defense, half from non-defense. Social security payments, interest on the national debt, and selected poverty programs were to be exempt from the expenditure cuts. GRH did not live up to its promise. Creative accounting (such as shifting federal expenditures back and forth between fiscal years), overestimation of future tax receipts with unrealistically optimistic economic forecasts, and the selling of national assets, among other forms of fiscal sidestepping, were employed to lend the appearance of progress on the deficit problem—when, in truth, little progress was being made. The ongoing bailout of the thrifts has added to the fiscal dilemma.

CONCLUDING NOTE

If fiscal policy was expansionary and monetary policy was contractionary in the 1980s, the 1990s may call for a reversal: easier monetary policy and tighter fiscal policy. In fact, the Gramm-Rudman-Hollings mechanism was superseded in 1990 with the Omnibus Budget Reconciliation Act. This attempt at reducing the federal budget deficits involved spending caps on defense and non-defense discretionary programs, "pay-as-you-go" provisions for new entitlement programs, and substantial tax increases, including a new 31 percent marginal tax bracket and increased excise taxes on gasoline, tobacco, alcohol, and air travel. Along with the earlier tax reform of 1986, there were efforts to make the income tax system fairer. The recession of 1990–1991, however, severely hampered the progress in reducing the federal budget deficits. In turn, the large federal budget deficits constrained the exercise of any expansionary fiscal policies to stimulate the economy.

An important lesson from the 1980s may be the need for greater cooperation in policymaking. Coordinating macroeconomic policy is very difficult when there are underlying disagreements on the one level between the administration and Congress over tax and expenditure priorities, and on another level between the resulting fiscal policy package and the monetary policy of the Federal Reserve. This is not to suggest, however, that any one of the three policymakers—the president, Congress, or the Federal Reserve—should become preeminent. Nevertheless, the lack of coordination often produces inconsistencies in the economic policy.

In the next chapter we analyze the trade-off between inflation and unemployment in greater detail. This trade-off, it turns out, may exist only in the short run. The policy implications of the theory of rational expectations will also be discussed.

KEY TERMS

supply-side economics
Reaganomics
bracket creep
capital gain

tax credits
Laffer curve
underground economy

QUESTIONS

1. What are the three most important ideas in this chapter? Discuss why each is important.
2. Consider an individual with a labor supply schedule of

$$l^s = -36 + 15(1 - t_y)(w/P^e)$$

where l^s = quantity of labor hours supplied per week by the individual. (Assume the labor supply curve becomes perfectly inelastic at $l^s = 60$.)

   w = money wage per hour (in dollars).
   t_y = tax rate on labor income.
   P^e = expected price level over the period.

   a. Sketch the labor supply curve, placing w on the vertical axis and l^s on the horizontal axis. Assume that $t_y = .2$ and $P^e = 1.0$.
   b. What would the money wage have to be for this individual to be willing to supply 40 hours of labor per week?
   c. Repeat parts "a" and "b" assuming $t_y = .25$.
   d. Repeat parts "a" and "b" assuming $P^e = 1.2$.
3. Calculate the "inflation penalty," i.e., the additional tax or the loss in real income due to inflation and a tax system based on nominal income for each of the following. Then show how the tax system could be made "inflation-neutral."
   a. An individual's nominal income of $30,000 increases by 5 percent to $31,500, just keeping pace with the 5 percent inflation rate. The tax brackets are

Taxable Income Bracket	Tax Rate
$28,000–$30,000	20%
$30,001–$32,000	20% on the first $30,000
	25% on income between $30,001 and $32,000

    b. The before-tax annual nominal interest rate on saving increases from 6% to 10.1% as the inflation rate increases from 3% to 7%, leaving the before-tax annual real interest rate on saving constant at 2.9 percent. The tax rate on income from saving is 25 percent.

    c. A firm's revenues are $120 million, and the firm's costs, including the original costs of the inventories used and depreciated physical capital, are $105 million. The firm's costs, including the replacement costs of the inventories used and depreciated physical capital, however, are $110 million. The tax rate on corporate profits is 30 percent.

4. Discuss the consequences for real national output, the aggregate price level, the federal budget deficit, and the business cycle of indexing the tax system to inflation such that real income, not nominal income, is taxed.

5. Some critics view Reaganomics as more or less "repackaged Keynesianism." What do you think this means? Discuss.

6. Into the fall of 1992, after two years of economic stagnation, the U.S. economy was still languishing. Consumer confidence was shot. The president and the Congress, humbled by the large and growing federal budget deficits, seemed stymied on the proper fiscal course of action. The Federal Reserve, with numerous cuts, had finally driven the discount rate to 3.0 percent, the lowest level in over a quarter of a century. While inflation appeared to be under control, unemployment rates hovered around 7.5 percent. What economic policies would you recommend in such a situation? Why? Discuss the likely effects of your policy measures on the economy.

CHAPTER 16

UNEMPLOYMENT AND INFLATION: TRADE-OFFS

OFTEN WE HAVE referred to the trade-off between unemployment and inflation. If the economy is operating on the intermediate range of a given aggregate supply curve, then shifts in aggregate demand will manifest this trade-off. An increase in aggregate demand, while reducing unemployment, pushes up the aggregate price level. A decrease in aggregate demand, while lowering the price level, adds to the unemployment rate. In the 1960s, the heyday of Keynesian demand-management policy, the prevailing economic wisdom was that this inverse relationship between unemployment and inflation was relatively stable— in both the short run and long run.

In this chapter we examine the phenomena of unemployment and inflation in greater detail. We begin with the hypothesis of the Phillips curve, which embodies the unemployment-inflation trade-off, at least in the short run. Next we extend the analysis of unemployment from Chapter 7. Then we turn to the causes and consequences of inflation. In the last part of the chapter we discuss the importance of inflationary expectations and the contribution of the New Classical theory of rational expectations to the debate over the efficacy of demand-management policy.

PHILLIPS CURVE

The **Phillips curve** captures the hypothesized inverse relationship between the unemployment and inflation rates.[1] In Figure 16.1 we illustrate a Phillips curve, with the inflation rate on the vertical axis and the unemployment rate on the

---

[1] The Phillips curve is named for the British economist A.W. Phillips, who studied the relationship between the rate of change in money wages and the unemployment rate. The usual presentation of a Phillips curve, however, is with the rate of inflation and the unemployment rate.

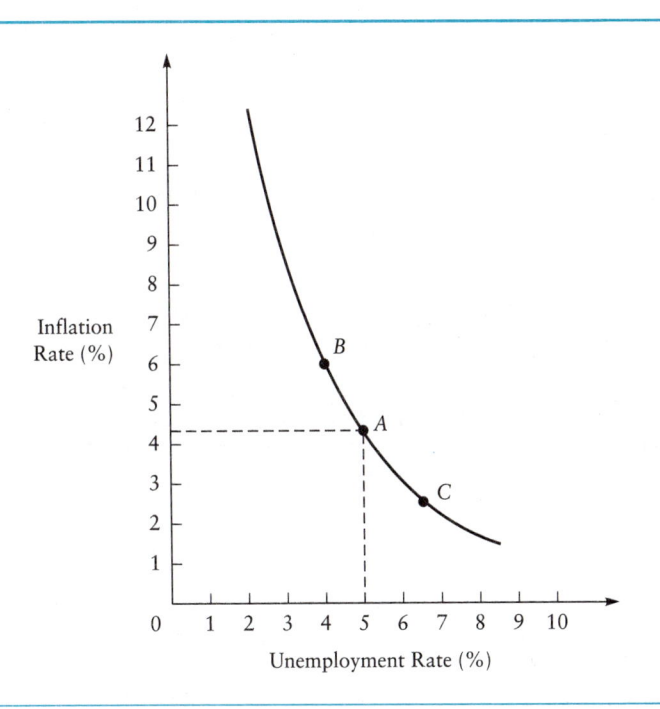

FIGURE 16.1

PHILLIPS CURVE

The Phillips curve illustrates the hypothesized short-run trade-off between the unemployment rate and the inflation rate.

horizontal axis. This Phillips curve is shaped like a hyperbola. Reducing the rate of inflation toward zero becomes increasingly costly in terms of rising unemployment (that is, the Phillips curve flattens out as the unemployment rate increases). Conversely, the cost of reducing unemployment as the unemployment rate approaches zero is accelerating inflation (that is, the Phillips curve becomes steeper as the unemployment rate decreases).

If the Phillips curve were stable, then Keynesians would argue that demand-management policies could be used to target an unemployment-inflation combination (such as point A in Figure 16.1).[2] If the unemployment rate were deemed too high, then a demand stimulus with expansionary monetary or fiscal policy could push the economy up the Phillips curve (for example, in the neighborhood of point B). On the other hand, if the inflation

---

[2] As discussed in Chapter 12, over time, the aggregate supply curve will tend to shift right as a result of technological progress and increases in the quantities and qualities of labor, the physical capital stock, and natural resources. The aggregate demand curve will also shift right over time, as a result of increases in the money supply and in desired autonomous expenditures on national output (e.g., increases in consumption expenditures and residential fixed investment with population growth, in business fixed investment from new and expanding firms, in government services, and in exports from growth in foreign demand). Given an economy normally operating on the intermediate range of the aggregate supply curve, and given a relatively constant growth rate in aggregate supply (as in the case of the long-run average annual growth rate in real national output for the United States of approximately 3 percent), then the growth in aggregate demand will determine the unemployment-inflation trade-off. A relatively rapid growth in aggregate demand (i.e., significantly above 3 percent annually) will tend to yield lower unemployment and higher inflation. Sluggish growth in aggregate demand (i.e., significantly less than 3 percent annually) will tend to produce higher unemployment and lower inflation.

rate were considered too high, then a dose of contractionary monetary or fiscal policy could help pull the economy down the Phillips curve (in the neighborhood of point C). Such was the confidence in demand-management policy in the 1960s. In fact, plotting the inflation and unemployment rates for the U.S. economy for the 1960s does show evidence of a stable Phillips curve (Figure 16.2). As the economy moved beyond full employment in the latter part of the decade—that is, as the unemployment rate dropped below 4 percent—the inflation rate did rise. (Note the points for the years 1965–1969 on the figure.)

Significant decreases in both inflation and unemployment suggest a downward shift in the Phillips curve. Such a shift would be consistent with extraordinary growth in aggregate supply, due perhaps to rapid technological change or large gains in labor productivity. An upward shift in the Phillips curve, indicative of stagflation, would reflect supply-side shocks such as upward shifts in input price schedules or costly government regulations. Changes in expectations of inflation are also an important factor accounting for shifts in the Phillips curve. Later in this chapter we will discuss how expectations of inflation are formed.

In the 1970s there is evidence that the Phillips curve shifted up. See Figure 16.3, where the annual inflation and unemployment rates for the decade are plotted. The cluster of observations for 1970–1973 lie to the northeast of the implied Phillips curve for the 1960s shown in Figure 16.2. (Note: The inflation-unemployment trade-off in the early 1970s was likely distorted by the wage and price controls imposed by the Nixon administration.) A second upward shift in the Phillips curve probably took place in 1974 when the full

FIGURE 16.2

INFLATION AND UNEMPLOYMENT RATES IN THE 1960s

Plotting the annual observations (denoted by 1960, 1961, 1962, etc.) for the inflation and unemployment rates over the decade of the 1960s does suggest the negative relationship embodied in the Phillips curve. As the unemployment rate fell, the inflation rate increased.

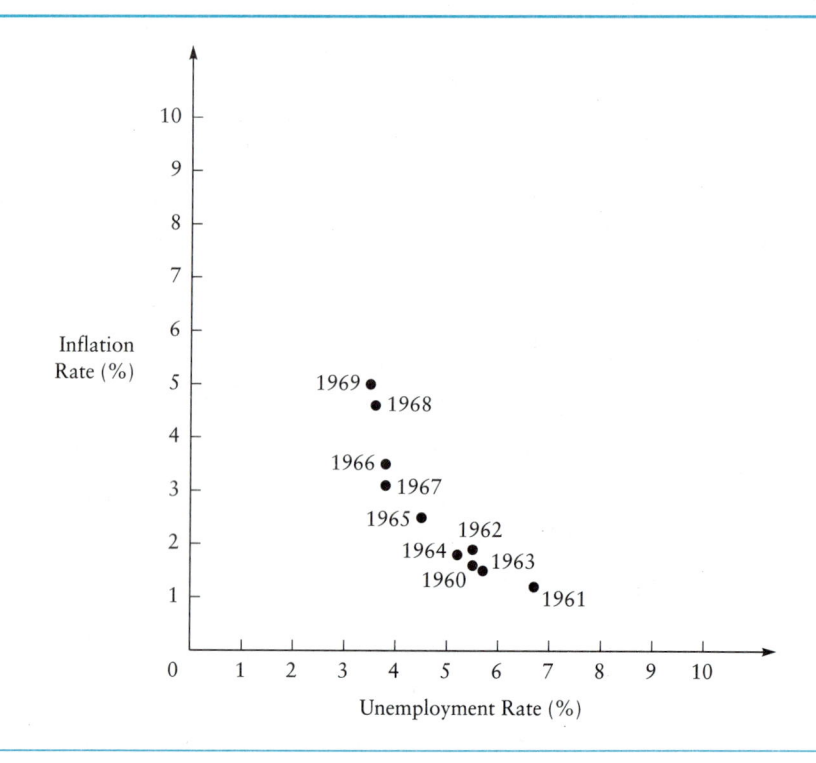

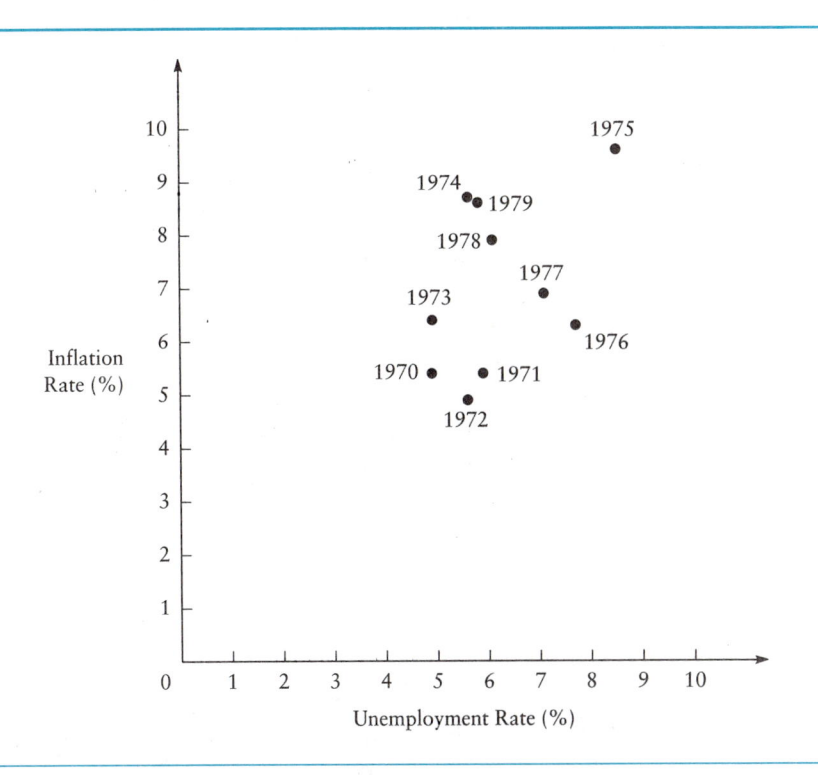

FIGURE 16.3

INFLATION AND UNEMPLOYMENT RATES IN THE 1970s

The stable trade-off between the inflation rate and unemployment rate evidenced in the 1960s seemed to break down in the 1970s. In particular, the oil price shock in 1973–1974 brought stagflation—the concurrence of rising inflation and unemployment—and an upward shift in the Phillips curve.

effects of the oil price hikes were felt. After 1975, a second year of stagflation, the inverse relationship between inflation and unemployment reappears over the remainder of the 1970s.

Another shift in the Phillips curve is evident in the wake of the second round of oil price increases in 1979–1980 and perhaps the consequent ratcheting up of inflationary expectations. See Figure 16.4. The inflation rate increased from 8.6 percent (1979) to 9.5 percent (1980) to 10.0 percent (1981), while the unemployment rate rose from 5.8 percent (1979) to 7.1 percent (1980) to 7.6 percent (1981). A downward shift in the Phillips curve can be discerned consistent with the fall in oil prices and reduced expectations for the inflation rate following the steep recession of 1981–1982. Over the second half of the 1980s we again see signs of an inverse relationship between inflation and unemployment.

In sum, based on the evidence presented here for the U.S. economy over the last three decades, there do appear to be short-run trade-offs between inflation and unemployment consistent with the Phillips curve hypothesis. Significant deviations in aggregate supply from long-run trend growth, however, produce shifts in the Phillips curve. Before we develop further the trade-offs, we should elaborate on the earlier discussions of unemployment and inflation.

UNEMPLOYMENT

As suggested in Chapter 7 when the topic of unemployment was introduced, the national unemployment rate provides only a partial picture of labor market conditions in the economy. Recall, the unemployment rate is defined as the ratio

FIGURE 16.4

INFLATION AND UNEMPLOYMENT RATES IN THE 1980s

The second oil price shock in 1979–1980 led to another upward shift in the Phillips curve in the early 1980s. With the collapse in oil prices and the reduction of inflationary expectations after the severe recession of 1981–1982, which shifted the Phillips curve down, the negative relationship between the inflation and unemployment rates reappeared over the last four years of the decade.

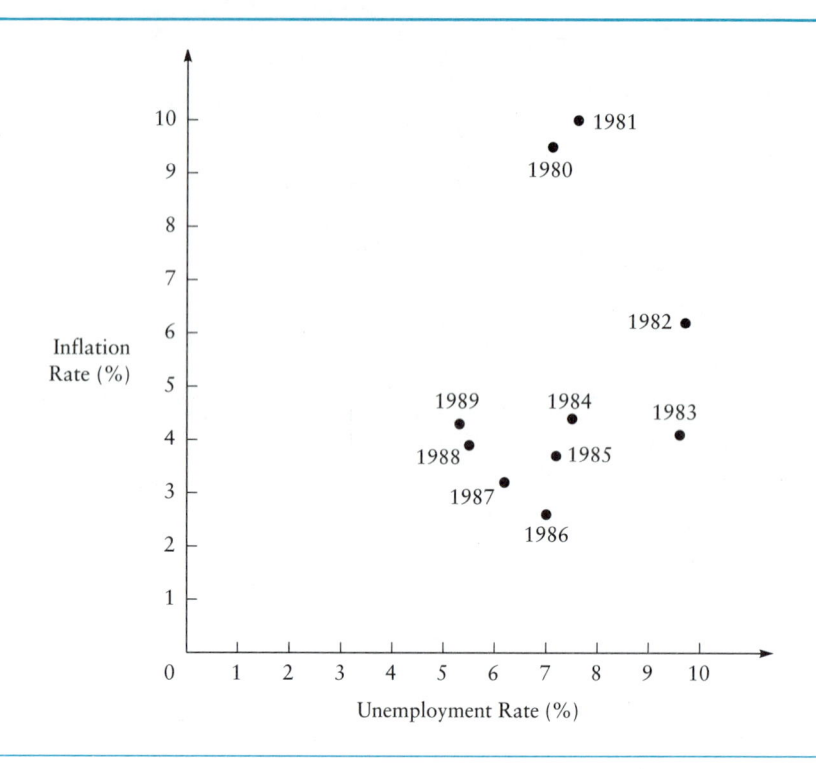

of the unemployed to the labor force (the sum of the unemployed and employed). Officially, unemployment is restricted to include only those individuals sixteen years of age or older who are currently out of work and either actively looking for work, waiting to be recalled after being laid off, or waiting to report to a new job within the month.[3]

Types of Unemployment

The four official statuses of an unemployed individual are (1) one who has voluntarily left a job, (2) one who is initially entering the labor force, (3) one who is reentering the labor force, and (4) one who has lost a job. The annual unemployment rates in the United States for 1990 and 1991 were 5.5 percent and 6.7 percent, respectively (see Table 16.1). Roughly half of the unemployment was due to job losses. Another quarter of the unemployment reflected individuals reentering the labor force. The remaining quarter was divided between job leavers and new entrants to the labor force.

The three major types of unemployment are directly related to these four statuses. **Frictional unemployment** refers to those individuals between jobs—whether new entrants or reentrants to the labor force, or job leavers. Frictional unemployment is inevitable and is the primary reason why full employment is not defined as a zero rate of unemployment. More effective job

---

[3] Recall also from Chapter 7 that "discouraged workers" are not included among the officially unemployed. These individuals, although out of work and willing to work, have ceased actively looking for work.

banks to provide information on the available jobs and required skills would help reduce, though not eliminate, frictional unemployment.

Structural and cyclical unemployment encompass the job losers. **Structural unemployment** is basically due to a mismatching of the skills of the job seekers and the skills required for the job openings. Over time, some industries will be expanding and others will be contracting. The labor released by the contracting industries will not be automatically absorbed by the expanding industries. Retraining and relocation may be necessary. Some structural unemployment is also inevitable in a dynamic economy. Forecasts of the labor skills likely to be in demand in the future and the training of workers in those skills would help reduce structural unemployment.

Cyclical unemployment, which varies inversely with the level of economic activity, accounts for the major fluctuations in the overall unemployment rate. A fall in the demand for national output will reduce the derived demand for labor. Cyclical unemployment will increase. As we discussed in Chapters 13 and

TABLE 16.1

SELECTED STATISTICS ON U.S. EMPLOYMENT AND UNEMPLOYMENT

RECENT UNEMPLOYMENT RATES

	TOTAL	MALES	FEMALES	WHITE	BLACK & OTHER	TEENAGE (16–19 YRS)
1990	5.5%	5.6%	5.4%	4.7%	10.1%	15.5%
1991	6.7	7.0	6.3	6.0	11.1	18.6

UNEMPLOYMENT BY DURATION AND REASON

	MEAN DURATION OF UNEMPLOYMENT (WEEKS)	Job Losers	Job Leavers	Reentrants	New Entrants
1990	12.1	48.3%	14.8%	27.4%	9.5%
1991	13.8	54.7	11.6	24.8	8.9

HISTORICAL TRENDS

	ELIGIBLE POPULATION (MILLIONS)	LABOR FORCE (MILLIONS)	EMPLOYMENT (MILLIONS)	EMPLOYMENT RATE
1960	117.2	69.6	65.8	56.1%
1970	137.1	82.8	78.7	57.4
1980	167.7	106.9	99.3	59.2
1990	188.0	124.8	117.9	62.7

	LABOR FORCE PARTICIPATION RATES — Males	Females	AVERAGE WEEKLY HOURS FOR PRIVATE SECTOR	AVERAGE HOURLY EARNINGS FOR PRIVATE SECTOR (1982 DOLLARS)
1960	83.3%	37.7%	38.6	$6.79
1970	79.7%	43.3	37.1	8.03
1980	77.4%	51.5	35.3	7.78
1990	76.1%	57.5	34.5	7.54

NOTES: *Eligible population* refers to the civilian population aged 16 years or older with the exception of the institutional population, e.g., the armed forces, inmates of prisons, and patients in mental hospitals. The *employment rate* is the ratio of the employed to the eligible population.
SOURCE: *Economic Report of the President 1992* (Washington, DC: U.S. Government Printing Office, 1992) Tables B-30, B-34, B-37, B-42.

14, the use of demand-management fiscal and monetary policies to keep the economy near full employment is recommended by some, but by no means all, economists to counter cyclical unemployment. Alternatively, the government could be the residual employer, absorbing the labor not employed in the private sector. Even fewer economists would favor the government as employer of last resort, due to the high costs and inefficiencies of operating such a program.

In practice it may be difficult to distinguish between structural and cyclical unemployment. During economic recessions the rise in cyclical unemployment—reflecting the general low level of aggregate demand—may force many marginal businesses to close permanently. The released workers may not have the requisite skills for, nor the inclination to relocate to, the jobs that become available when the economy recovers.

Other Dimensions of Unemployment

Perhaps a more indicative measure of employment conditions than the unemployment rate is the **employment rate,** defined as the ratio of the employed to the *eligible population* (that is, the population 16 years of age or more, excluding the *institutional population,* such as the armed forces, inmates in prisons and patients in mental hospitals). Refer again to Table 16.1.

The baby boom generation swelled the labor force in the late 1960s and 1970s. The eligible population in the United States increased by 17 percent over the 1960s and by 22 percent over the 1970s, but by only 13 percent over the 1980s (as the population of ages 16 to 24 years began to decline). In contrast to the national unemployment rate, which fluctuates with the business cycle, the employment rate steadily increased from 56.1 percent in 1960 to 62.7 percent in 1990—a trend that largely reflected the dramatic rise in female labor force participation. From 37.7 percent in 1960, female labor force participation rates increased to 57.5 percent in 1990, a pace far offsetting the decline in male labor force participation rates. Total employment in the United States increased by 52 million (nearly 80 percent) over this 30-year period—an impressive gain.

Other dimensions hidden by the national unemployment rate include the composition of unemployment, the mean duration of unemployment, the average length of the work week, and average hourly earnings. As illustrated by the data in Table 16.1, unemployment rates are relatively high for non-whites and teenagers. In fact, unemployment rates for non-whites have consistently been twice as high as those for whites. This differential may, in part, reflect discrimination—both past and present. Affirmative action laws are intended to redress some of the labor market discrimination faced by minorities. Child development programs like Head Start are designed to ensure that equal opportunities are provided at the earliest ages.

Teenage unemployment is also a widely recognized problem. Typically, unemployment rates for teenagers are three times the national average. For black teenagers, the ratio is closer to 5 to 1. Since teenagers, in general, are less experienced workers, a subminimum wage for teenagers has been offered as a partial solution for teenage unemployment.

The **mean duration of unemployment** (the average number of weeks of continuous unemployment for the unemployed worker) is an interesting statistic that may help capture the severity of the unemployment. Unlike inflation, where the effects are pervasive, the effects of unemployment tend to be concentrated on the small percentage of the nation's families with members out of work. An annual unemployment rate of 5 percent could reflect 5 percent of the labor force being unemployed for the entire year, or 10 percent of the labor force being unemployed for six months, or 20 percent of the labor force with a mean duration of unemployment of three months, and so on. The lower the mean duration of unemployment, the more equally shared is the burden of unemployment.

In times when the unemployment rate is low, the mean duration of unemployment has also been low. For example, in 1990 when the national unemployment rate was 5.5 percent, nearly half of the unemployed (46 percent) were out of work for just five weeks or less; only 10 percent of the unemployed were out of work for six months or more. In 1983 when the post–World War II record of 20 weeks was set for the mean duration of unemployment, the national unemployment rate was 9.6 percent, with a third (33 percent) of the unemployed out of work for five weeks or less, and nearly a quarter (24 percent) out of work for six months or more. An increase in the mean duration of unemployment may be a sign that structural unemployment is rising. From 1990 to 1991, as the economy slipped into a recession and the national unemployment rate rose, the mean duration of unemployment and the proportion of the unemployed accounted for by job losers increased.

Long-term unemployment (six months or more) can have significant psychological, social, and economic effects. Psychologically, the unemployed individual loses self-esteem and maybe even a sense of direction. Financial difficulties mount with the duration of unemployment. Sociologists have found that alcoholism, child abuse, crime, suicide, and homicide rates increase in times of rising unemployment. Economically an unemployed worker's skills atrophy—like an athlete unable to practice. For the nation, the output that could have been produced by the unemployed workers cannot be recovered.

Finally, two other trends in employment in the United States since World War II should be noted. First, there has been a general decline in the average work week. This trend likely reflects several factors—including the increased consumption of leisure as the nation becomes more affluent and the increase in the percentage of households with second workers and part-time jobs. Second, until 1973, real average hourly earnings steadily increased. Since then nominal wage increases, on average, have not kept pace with inflation, and real average hourly wages have fallen. Underlying factors include the increased foreign competition in traditional manufacturing industries with high wage scales (for example, steel and automobiles), the increased share of low-wage and part-time service jobs in the economy (for example, retail sales, restaurants, entertainment, and office workers), and the declining influence of labor unions.

To repeat, there is considerably more to the employment conditions in a nation than is revealed by the national unemployment rate.

INFLATION

In Chapter 7 we discussed the measurement of the inflation rate. In Chapter 15 we illustrated the concern of supply-side economists: how inflation, combined with a tax system based on nominal income, undermines the incentives to work, save, and invest. Now we will address the causes and consequences of inflation.

Causes of Inflation

Inflation has two primary sources. **Demand-pull inflation** is due to excess aggregate demand, meaning that at the prevailing price level, aggregate demand is growing faster than aggregate supply. **Cost-push inflation,** on the other hand, is due to decreases in aggregate supply. In Figure 16.5 the two types of inflation are illustrated.

Assume that the initial equilibrium is given by E_0, and restrict the analysis to the intermediate range of the aggregate supply curves. With demand-pull inflation (produced by the rightward shift in the aggregate demand curve from AD to AD'), the level of real national output increases (from Y_0 to Y'), and the rate of unemployment falls. With cost-push inflation (produced by a leftward shift in the aggregate supply curve from AS to AS''), the level of real national output decreases (from Y_0 to Y''), and the rate of unemployment increases. As drawn in each case, the inflation rate over the period is equal to $(P_1 - P_0)/P_0$, but only with demand-pull inflation is there a trade-off between inflation and unemployment.

FIGURE 16.5

DEMAND-PULL AND COST-PUSH INFLATION

Demand-pull inflation results when aggregate demand increases faster than aggregate supply (e.g., AD to AD' with the given AS). Cost-push inflation results from a decrease (leftward shift) in aggregate supply (e.g., AS to AS'' with the given AD).

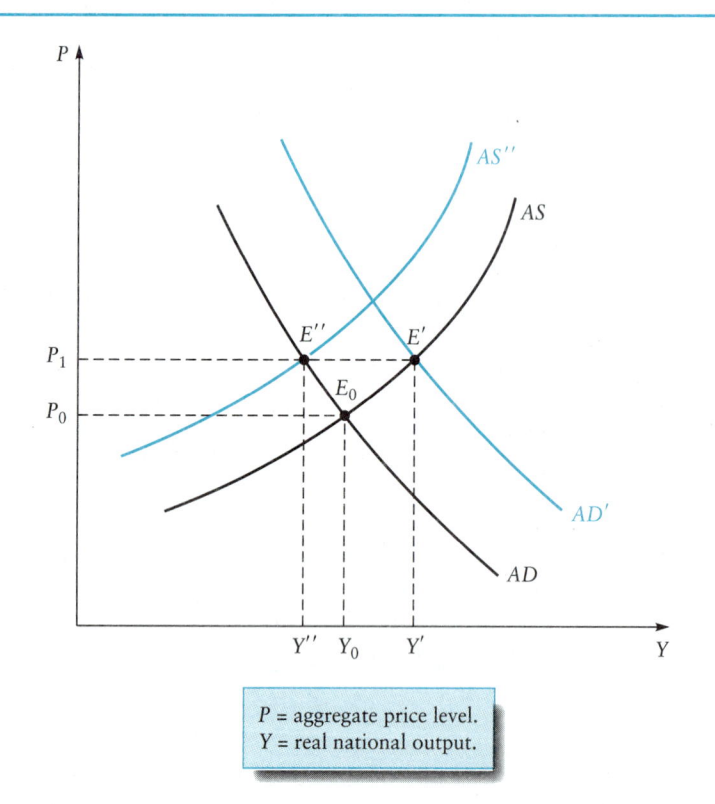

P = aggregate price level.
Y = real national output.

Monetarists attribute the ultimate cause of inflation to excessive growth in the money supply (a specific form of demand-pull inflation). Return to the simple quantity theory of money introduced in Chapter 14:

$$PY = V_0 M^s$$

where

P = aggregate price level.
Y = real national output (income).
V = income velocity of money (the average number of times per period a unit of money is used to finance expenditures on national output).
M^s = nominal money supply (M1 or the sum of currency in circulation and checkable deposits).

Here we make the strong monetarist assumption that the income velocity of money is constant ($V = V_0$). That is, if we assume that the ratio of nominal income to the nominal money supply is essentially stable, then expressing the simple quantity theory of money in dynamic form yields

$$\frac{\Delta P}{P} + \frac{\Delta Y}{Y} \doteq \frac{\Delta M^s}{M^s}$$

(since $\Delta V/V = 0$). Solving for the inflation rate, $\Delta P/P$, gives

$$\frac{\Delta P}{P} \doteq \frac{\Delta M^s}{M^s} - \frac{\Delta Y}{Y}$$

Thus, inflation ($\Delta P/P > 0$) results when the nominal money supply grows faster than real output and income ($\Delta M^s/M^s > \Delta Y/Y$). (Note that the implication for price stability in the face of a supply-side shock and declining real output is a contraction in the money supply. In Figure 16.5, if the economy begins at E' and the aggregate supply curve then falls from AS to AS'', aggregate demand would have to fall (from AD' to AD) with a decrease in the money supply to keep the aggregate price level constant at P_1.)

While this explanation of inflation is perhaps overly simplistic, there is general agreement that the ultimate check on inflation is restraint in the growth of the money supply.

Consequences of Inflation

While the economic consequences of unemployment are direct and concentrated—the loss in labor income for the unemployed workers and their families—the consequences of inflation are more subtle and pervasive. Inflation tends to alter the distribution of income, with the attendant potential for affecting the allocation of resources.

As a way of introduction, consider a simple example of an isolated island economy. Assume that all the adult islanders are fully employed. Cowrie shells serve as money. There are presently 5000 cowrie shells in circulation on the island. Every year during the monsoon season 500 more cowrie shells wash ashore, which serendipitously serves the growing economy's need for additional transactions balances. The new shells are collected and presented to the ruling elders, who disperse them based on the prevailing distribution of wealth. Suppose that one night before the monsoon season a freak storm washes 1000 cowrie shells ashore. What will be the consequences?

If the 1000 shells found the next morning are turned over to the elders for distribution as usual, then money balances will increase by 20 percent. The increase in wealth will prompt a general increase in spending. With the same full employment output of goods and services, however, the increased spending will only drive up prices. The 20 percent increase in cowrie shells in circulation will ultimately increase the cowrie price level by 20 percent. In such circumstances, the increase in the money supply does not affect the distribution of income or the allocation of resources.

Suppose instead that the 1000 cowrie shells washed ashore are found by the "early-risers," a sect among the islanders known for their fondness for fish. The early-risers decide not to share their good fortune with the rest of the population. The shells are not turned over to the elders for general distribution; instead the early-risers add the shells to their own money balances. With their significant increase in wealth, the early-risers step up their spending—especially for fish. The demand for fish increases, bidding up its price. The higher price makes fishing more profitable, so there is an incentive to shift resources into fishing. With full employment on the island, however, increased output for the fishing industry must be at the expense of reduced output in other island industries. Under this scenario, the increase in the money supply alters the distribution of income (in favor of the early-risers) and affects the allocation of resources (toward the fishing industry).

In a more modern economy there are also effects on the distribution of income and the allocation of resources from inflation and deflation. Consider inflation, which reduces the purchasing power of money. Any individual whose nominal income does not increase as fast as the average price level will suffer a loss of real income. For instance, if your nominal income before taxes rises by 3 percent, from $10,000 to $10,300, but inflation is running at 5 percent, then your real, or inflation-adjusted, income falls from $10,000 to $9,810 ($10,300/1.05). If we allow for the possibility of bracket creep due to rising marginal tax rates on nominal income, then real after-tax income would be even less. Workers with money wages fixed in labor contracts are vulnerable to inflation.

Inflation hurts retirees and all others who receive fixed money income flows from earlier investments. During their working years individuals try to build up savings to fund their retirement. Inflation erodes the store-of-value function of the savings. At the price levels prevailing when the savings were accumulated, the expected interest income may have been more than adequate for an individual to live comfortably during retirement. With the intervening inflation the purchasing power of these income flows has been reduced.

Creditors who lend money and underestimate the rate of inflation over the term of the loan lose with inflation. For example, suppose that, anticipating an inflation rate of 5 percent and seeking a real return of 4 percent, an individual makes a one-year $10,000 loan (or buys a $10,000 bond with a one-year maturity) yielding 9.2 percent interest. If the actual inflation rate over the year equals the individual's expected inflation rate, the real return on the loan will be the desired 4 percent:

$$.04 = (1 + .092)/(1.05) - 1$$

If, however, the actual inflation rate exceeds the individual's expected inflation rate, the real return on the loan will be less than the desired 4 percent. Specifically, if the actual inflation rate is 7 percent, then the lender receives $10,920 at the end of the year from the recipient of the loan (the $10,000 of principal and $920 of interest). The $10,920, however, has purchasing power of only $10,206 (10,206 = 10,920/1.07). The real return on the individual's investment is 2.06 percent, or roughly half of the desired return. (Note, if the actual inflation rate exceeded 9.2 percent, the nominal interest rate charged on the loan, then the real return to the lender would be negative.)

In sum, inflation—especially when not fully anticipated—does affect the distribution of income. Inflation tends to penalize those with relatively fixed nominal incomes and creditors who underestimate the rate of price change. The "winners" from inflation would be those with nominal incomes rising faster than the price level and debtors who end up borrowing at reduced rates of real interest. In addition, as discussed in Chapter 15, under a progressive income tax system, the government stands to gain extra tax revenues from the inflation-induced bracket creep. In contrast, *deflation,* or a sustained decrease in the aggregate price level, would have the opposite effects on the distribution of income.

Given that the winners and losers from inflation have different consumption preferences, shifts in the distribution of income from inflation will affect the allocation of resources. Suppose the winners from inflation (debtors, the government, and individuals with fully adjustable incomes) favor travel by air; while those hurt by inflation (creditors, taxpayers, and individuals with relatively fixed nominal incomes) prefer traveling by automobiles. With inflation and the rise in the real incomes of the winners, airlines will enjoy increased demand for their services. Prices and profits in the airline industry (including the suppliers of inputs to the industry) will rise. Automobile producers and their suppliers will experience falling demand, lower prices, and decreased profits. The shift in economic profits will induce a reallocation of resources from the automobile industry to the airline industry. Furthermore, unless the labor released from the contracting automobile industry is readily absorbed into the expanding airline industry, structural unemployment will rise.

Another consequence of inflation for the allocation of resources should be noted. Unless offset by changes in the nominal exchange rate, inflation undermines a nation's international competitiveness. For example, suppose the exchange rate between the U.S. dollar and the Japanese yen is $1 equals 150 yen. Assume that the production cost of a tape cartridge in the United States is $4 and the production cost of a similar tape cartridge in Japan is 630 yen. Ignoring transportation costs and trade barriers (tariffs and quotas), the United States would tend to export cartridges to Japan, since the import price of an American-made cartridge to Japan is 600 yen ($4 times 150 yen per dollar).

If the inflation rate in the United States is 10 percent, while Japan experiences price stability, then the production cost of a tape cartridge in the United States rises to $4.40. Now, under the nominal exchange rate of 150 yen to the dollar, the United States would import cartridges from Japan, since the import price of a Japanese-made cartridge of $4.20 (630 yen divided by 150 yen to the dollar) is less than the domestic price of $4.40. Employment in the U.S. tape cartridge industry would fall. Thus, for a given nominal exchange rate, inflation hurts a nation's export and import-competitive industries, which, in turn, reduces real national output and employment and affects the allocation of resources. (Note: As we will see in Chapter 17, the nominal exchange rate usually does change with the inflation differential, which mitigates the trade balance effect.)

Because the consequences of unanticipated inflation are now widely recognized (lessons learned from the high inflation during the 1970s and early 1980s), individuals are more sensitive to the need to protect the purchasing power of their money incomes. Unions seek automatic cost of living adjustments in their wage contracts. Social security payments are indexed to the rate of inflation. Banks offer adjustable-rate loans where, in return for initially lower rates, the nominal interest rates vary over the term of the loan according to inflation and market conditions.

There are also resource costs associated with inflation:[4]

> It may be impossible to measure how many resources are devoted to protecting individuals and businesses against unexpected price-level changes. What is clear is that such hedging can become more important to firms' survival than other managerial skills. This increases the demand for the specialized financial skills of lawyers, accountants, and economists, and leads some bright young people to make careers in these professions rather than in engineering or production management. Inflation hedging is a diversion of valuable human resources that would be unnecessary if long-run inflation were highly predictable.

The increased sensitivity of economic agents to inflation has implications not only for the allocation of resources, but for the conduct of demand-management policy, as we will see.

NATURAL RATE OF UNEMPLOYMENT

Recall from the discussion of monetary policy in Chapter 14 that monetarists do not favor the use of demand-management monetary policy. The noninterventionist approach of the monetarists reflects not only the inevitable lags in the making and implementation of policy and the uncertain multiplier effects, but also a belief in the inherent stability of the economy. Related to this position is the monetarist concept of the natural rate of unemployment. To develop this concept, we need to discuss the formation of price expectations.

In particular, we return to the familiar framework of aggregate demand-aggregate supply and we cast the discussion in terms of the aggregate price level and real national output rather than the inflation and unemployment rates of the Phillips curve. We will concentrate on how workers (labor supply) form estimates of the aggregate price level (and, by extension, the inflation rate). Since wages constitute the majority of the total factor costs of producing the national output, how labor formulates expectations of the aggregate price level is clearly of interest.

In Chapter 15 we suggested that individuals base the quantity of labor supplied in any given period of time on the expected after-tax real wage rate. That is,

$$l^s = f[(1 - t_y)(w/P^e)]$$

---

[4] Jeffrey Hallman, "Uncertain Inflation and Price Level Rules," *Economic Commentary,* Federal Reserve Bank of Cleveland, January 15, 1992, 3.

where

l^s = quantity of labor hours supplied per period by the individual.
t_y = tax rate on labor income earned.
w = money wage per hour.
P^e = expected price level over the period.

An increase in the expected after-tax real wage (the opportunity cost of leisure) would generally induce individuals to substitute away from leisure and increase the quantity of labor supplied. Summing the labor supply curves of all the potential suppliers of labor gives the aggregate supply curve of labor, illustrated in Figure 16.6.[5] The aggregate labor supply curve is drawn holding constant the size of the population in the labor force years, the labor force participation rates (reflecting the individual labor-leisure trade-offs), the tax rate on labor income, and the expected aggregate price level. Here we focus on the expected price level.

Traditionally, Keynesians and monetarists have assumed that labor supply operates on the basis of **adaptive expectations,** the hypothesis that the expected price level in time period t, that is, P_t^e, is a function of the actual price levels in

---

[5] As discussed in the previous chapter, a higher expected after-tax real wage also allows individuals to purchase more leisure for any quantity of labor supplied (the income effect). Nevertheless, we assume that the substitution effect predominates, so that the aggregate quantity of labor supplied increases with the expected after-tax real wage.

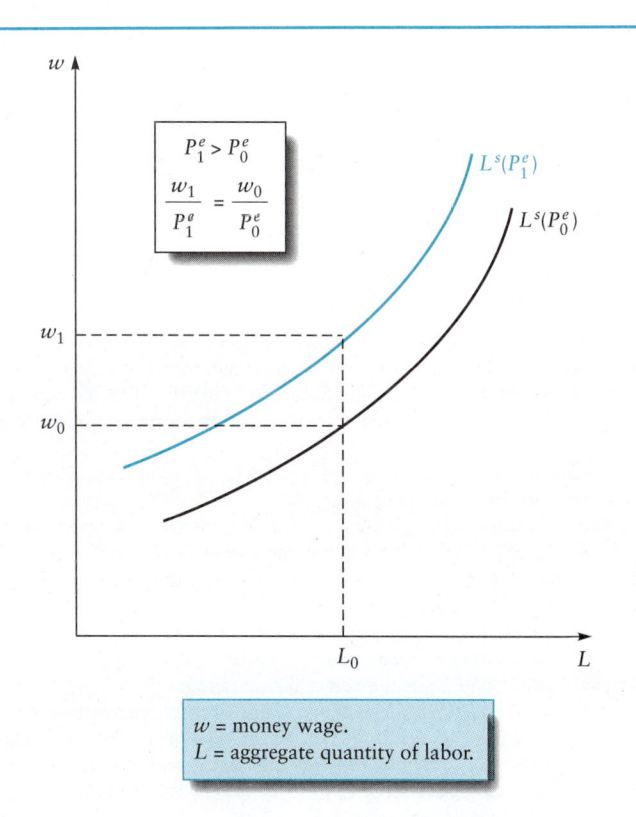

FIGURE 16.6

LABOR SUPPLY AND PRICE EXPECTATIONS

Writing the aggregate quantity of labor supplied as a positive function of the money wage rate, the aggregate labor supply curve is drawn holding constant the size of the population in the labor force years (age 16 and above), the labor force participation rates, the tax rate on labor income, and the expected aggregate price level. In particular, an increase in the expected aggregate price level will shift the labor supply curve upward. The money wage requested for any quantity of labor supplied will rise.

w = money wage.
L = aggregate quantity of labor.

previous periods, P_{t-1}, P_{t-2}, and so on. In the simplest form of adaptive expectations, which we use here, the expected price level in period t is equal to the actual price level of the previous period: $P_t^e = P_{t-1}$. That is, workers, desiring to protect the purchasing power of the money wages received, but not knowing the aggregate price level that will prevail over the period, will simply project forward the price level of the last period.[6] If the hypothesis of adaptive expectations is correct, then the reactions of labor supply to a change in the aggregate price level occur with a lag.[7]

In Figure 16.6, if the expected price level is initially P_0^e, then the labor supply curve is $L^s(P_0^e)$ and the aggregate quantity of labor supplied at the money wage of w_0 is L_0. An increase in the expected price level to P_1^e (due to an increase in the actual price level in the previous period), will shift the labor supply curve back to $L^s(P_1^e)$. A higher money wage will be requested for any quantity of labor supplied in order to maintain the expected real wage. For instance, with the expected price level of P_1^e, the aggregate quantity of labor given by L_0 will be supplied only if the money wage rises to w_1, where

$$\frac{w_1}{P_1^e} = \frac{w_0}{P_0^e}$$

Recall that the aggregate supply curve for national output is drawn holding constant, among other factors, the input price schedules. An increase in the wage schedule, that is, an upward shift in the labor supply curve, due to an increase in the expected price level, will also shift upward the aggregate supply curve for national output. The cost of producing any rate of national output will be higher if the money wage that must be paid for any quantity of labor rises.

We can see now how inflation could be self-perpetuating. If labor expects the aggregate price level to rise, the labor supply curve will shift up, which shifts up the aggregate supply curve and results in cost-push inflation. The ensuing inflation, in turn, may prompt workers to adjust upward again their wage requests, adding a second dose of cost-push inflation. Eventually the cycle will end when an equilibrium is reached where the price level (inflation rate) expected by labor supply equals the actual price level (inflation rate) in the economy.

---

[6] Actually, economists usually conduct the analysis in terms of the expected inflation rate (i.e., the percentage change in the expected price level) rather than the expected price level itself. The substance of our analysis, however, is not affected by using the expected aggregate price level, and further allows us to retain the aggregate demand–aggregate supply graphical orientation.

[7] Under adaptive expectations there is an implied asymmetry of information about the aggregate price level. Employers and the managers of firms, who are setting the prices of the outputs produced, are assumed to react more quickly than employees (labor supply) to changes in the aggregate price level. The hypothesis of adaptive expectations is bolstered to the extent labor supply is locked into money wage contracts and unable to respond quickly to changes in the aggregate price level—even if such changes are known.

Clearly, a key issue is how quickly expectations adapt to changes in the actual price level. At one extreme would be pure *money illusion,* whereby workers are concerned only with nominal incomes and disregard any changes in real incomes due to changes in the aggregate price level. At the other extreme would be *perfect information,* where workers react instantaneously to any change in the aggregate price level and operate on the basis of real incomes. Adaptive expectations fall between these two extremes, depending upon the *reaction lag,* or speed of adjustment to changes in the aggregate price level. Neo-Keynesians believe that the reaction lag is significant.

The **natural rate of unemployment** is the rate of unemployment consistent with equilibrium in the labor market—where the aggregate price level (or inflation rate) expected by labor equals the actual price level (or inflation rate) in the economy. Thus, at the natural rate of unemployment, there would be no tendency for workers to adjust their price expectations. The **natural rate of output** is the rate of real national output consistent with the natural rate of unemployment.

To illustrate, in panel (a) of Figure 16.7 we depict the aggregate labor market. In panel (b) we depict the aggregate demand and aggregate supply curves, where the aggregate supply curve is drawn for the given expected price level underlying the labor supply curve. More relevant to our analysis is the **natural level of employment**. Let us assume the simplest form of adaptive expectations, where the expected price level in any period is equal to the actual price level of the preceding period. If the price level expected by labor supply, P_0^e, is equal to the actual price level, P_0 (given by the intersection of the aggregate demand and aggregate supply curves) then the level of employment, L_0^*, is the natural level of employment. (Note: If $P_0^e = P_0$, then under this form of adaptive expectations, $P_0^e = P_{-1} = P_0$; that is, the aggregate price level is unchanged from the previous period.) In panel (b), given $P_0^e = P_0$, then the level of real national output where the aggregate demand and aggregate supply curves intersect, Y_0^*, is the natural rate of output.

Three points about the natural rate of output should be emphasized. First, the natural rate of output is consistent with any equilibrium aggregate price level.

FIGURE 16.7

NATURAL LEVEL OF EMPLOYMENT AND NATURAL RATE OF OUTPUT

If the expected aggregate price level equals the actual aggregate price level, i.e., if $P_0^e = P_0$, then L_0^* is the natural level of employment, and Y_0^* is the natural rate of output.

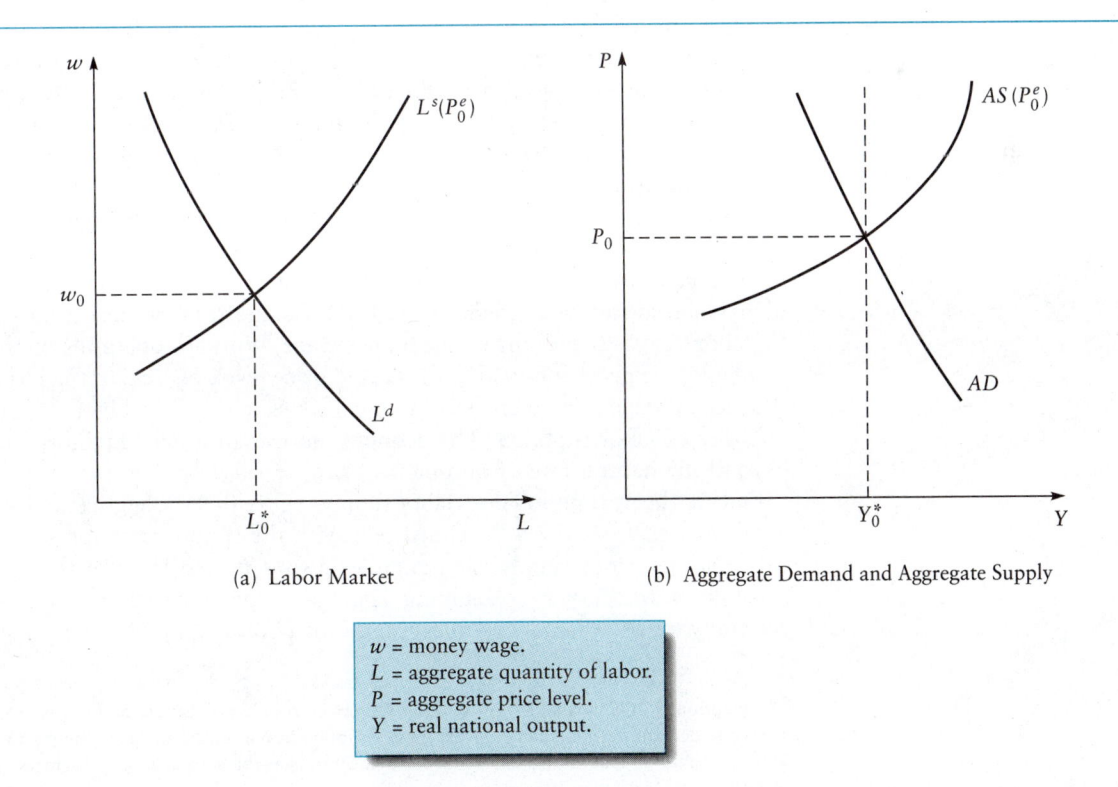

(a) Labor Market

(b) Aggregate Demand and Aggregate Supply

w = money wage.
L = aggregate quantity of labor.
P = aggregate price level.
Y = real national output.

In other words, there is no unique aggregate price level (or inflation rate) for the natural rate of output. Second, when the economy is operating at the natural rate of output, the expected price level underlying the labor supply is equal to the actual price level. Consequently, workers have no reason to adjust their expectations of the price level. Third, the natural rate of output will change over time. In particular, increases in aggregate supply (rightward shifts in the aggregate supply curve) due, for example, to technological progress or increases in the labor force and capital stock, will increase the natural rate of output.

NEUTRALITY OF MONEY HYPOTHESIS

To support their opposition to demand-management monetary policy, monetarists advance the **neutrality of money hypothesis** that, in the long run, changes in the nominal money supply affect only nominal variables such as the aggregate price level and the money wage rate. In other words, real national output and employment are unaffected by changes in the nominal money supply in the long run. By the "long run," monetarists mean the time it takes for workers to adjust completely to an aggregate price level. Thus, long-run equilibrium occurs at the natural rate of output, Y^*, where the expected price level held by labor supply equals the actual price level.

In the short run, however, monetarists acknowledge that changes in the nominal money supply can affect the levels of real national output and employment. In the long run, though, the economy has a tendency to return to the natural rate of output, since workers will continue to adjust their expectations of the aggregate price level (which, in turn, shifts both the labor supply and aggregate supply curves) until the natural rate of output is reached.

To illustrate the neutrality of money hypothesis, refer to Figure 16.8. Assume that the economy is in long-run equilibrium at the natural rate of output, Y_0^*, where $P_0^e = P_0$. An increase in the nominal money supply reduces the interest rate, stimulating interest-sensitive expenditures and shifting the aggregate demand curve to the right (from AD to AD').[8] The excess demand is initially met by running down inventories. As firms step up the rate of production to replace the depleted inventories and accommodate the increase in demand, unit costs of production and the aggregate price level rise. In the labor market the demand for labor increases, pushing up the money wage. Workers, operating on the basis of adaptive expectations and the expected price level, P_0^e, regard the increase in the money wage as an increase in the real wage, and respond by increasing the quantity of labor supplied. The economy moves to a new equilibrium at E_1, beyond the natural rate of output.

Only in the next period does labor supply realize that the aggregate price level has increased from P_0 to P_1. Consistent with the simplest version of adaptive expectations, labor supply then adjusts upward the estimate of the expected price level to $P_1^e = P_1$. Assuming aggregate demand remains at AD', the economy moves to a new equilibrium in this period at E_1'. (The new aggregate

---

[8] As mentioned in Chapter 14 (see footnote 4), monetarists hypothesize a more direct effect on aggregate demand from a change in the money supply. In particular, an excess supply of money spills over into an excess demand for goods and services as the surplus money balances are spent.

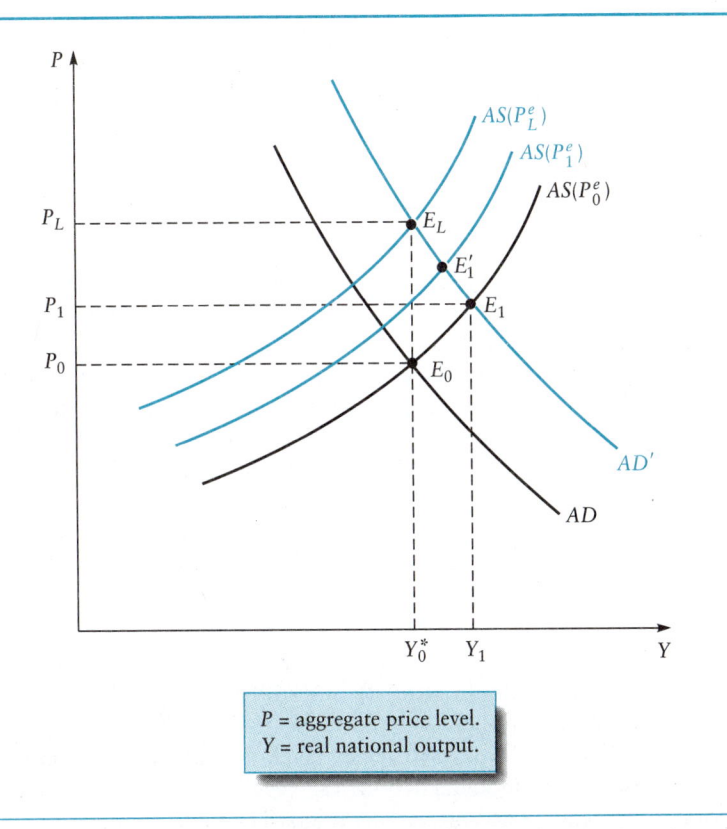

FIGURE 16.8

INFLATION-UNEMPLOYMENT TRADE-OFF: ADAPTIVE EXPECTATIONS

Under the hypothesis of adaptive expectations, an increase in aggregate demand (from AD to AD') will yield the inflation-unemployment trade-off in the short run. That is, the economy will move beyond the natural rate of output (see point E_1). In the long run, however, after labor supply fully adjusts to the demand-pull inflation, the economy will return to the natural rate of output (see point E_L).

P = aggregate price level.
Y = real national output.

---

supply curve $AS(P_1^e)$ cuts the natural rate of output line Y_0^* at P_1.) This equilibrium, however, will not be the long-run equilibrium. As long as the economy is operating at a rate of real national output beyond the natural rate of Y_0^*, workers will continue to underestimate the equilibrium aggregate price level. As workers reformulate their price expectations upward in successive periods, the aggregate supply curve shifts back toward the natural rate of output. Eventually, long-run equilibrium is reached, where the aggregate supply curve $AS(P_L^e)$ intersects the aggregate demand curve AD' at the natural rate of output. See point E_L in Figure 16.8, where $P_L^e = P_L$.

Thus, in the long run—that is, after all the adjustments by labor supply—the increase in the nominal money supply only yields inflation (in particular, a higher aggregate price level and money wage). Neither real national output nor employment increases. In the long run, money is neutral. In the long run, the aggregate supply curve is vertical at the natural rate of output.

As an exercise, reverse this sequence of events. Start out with an initial equilibrium at E_L with $AS(P_L^e)$ and AD' and describe the transition to long-run equilibrium given a decrease in the nominal money supply that reduces aggregate demand from AD' to AD. Note, you will have to assume that money wages and prices are downwardly flexible.

Have the monetarist arguments convinced Keynesian economists of the futility of demand-management? Neo-Keynesians do not dispute that eventually the suppliers of labor will adjust their price expectations in response to changes in aggregate demand. Neo-Keynesians believe, however, that such adjustments on the part of labor supply take considerable time. In particular, given the downward inflexibility in money wages and prices that may exist due to (1) institutional rigidities like minimum wage laws and labor union contracts and (2) the general reluctance of individuals to accept lower money wages and firms to cut prices, decreases in aggregate demand may be met by protracted recessions and high unemployment rates. Neo-Keynesians similarly discount the relevancy of the natural rate of unemployment and the natural rate of output—given the difficulty in ascertaining a long-run equilibrium for the economy with the changing aggregate supply conditions from technological progress and growth in the labor force and capital stock. Thus, while acknowledging the impossibility of fine-tuning the economy within close proximity of full employment, Neo-Keynesians nevertheless still recommend demand-management policies to moderate major swings in the business cycle—swings that are accentuated, Neo-Keynesians believe, by the volatility of private investment expenditures.

RATIONAL EXPECTATIONS

In the 1970s criticisms of the adaptive expectations assumption mounted. Economists known as the **New Classicals** argued that individuals are too sophisticated to rely on simple extrapolation of the past in their formulation of price expectations, but rather will rationally make use of all the economic information available to forecast the price level, paying special attention to the conduct of fiscal and monetary policies. New Classicals referred to this behavioral assumption as **rational expectations.** The theory implies not only that individuals use all the available economic information to formulate expectations of the price level (and inflation rate), but that they have at least an intuitive understanding of macroeconomics. Furthermore, given that the economic information is widely accessible, the hypothesis of rational expectations implies a self-fulfilling convergence of the expectations of the price level to the actual future price level. In other words, it implies that people will not systematically make errors in forecasting the future price level.

The policy implications of rational expectations are interesting. Refer to Figure 16.9 and assume the economy is in equilibrium indicated by point E_0. The aggregate supply curve for national output is drawn conditional upon the price level expected by labor supply. If we assume further that at this initial equilibrium, labor supply has correctly forecast the price level, $P_0^e = P_0$, then the rate of output Y_0^* corresponds to the natural rate of output.

Suppose now that the monetary (or fiscal) authorities decide to stimulate the economy in order to reduce unemployment. If the expansionary policy (the rightward shift in the aggregate demand curve) is anticipated by labor supply, then the increase in aggregate demand will be perceived as inducing demand-pull inflation. Workers would expect the price level to rise ultimately to P_L (that is, $P_L^e = P_L$), where the new aggregate demand curve meets the natural rate of output. Workers will therefore request higher money wages to protect their real wage positions. Thus, if rational expectations hold, the (rightward) shift in aggregate demand will be offset by the (leftward) shift in aggregate supply, and the expansionary policy will not affect the level of real national output or employment. The economy will move directly from the

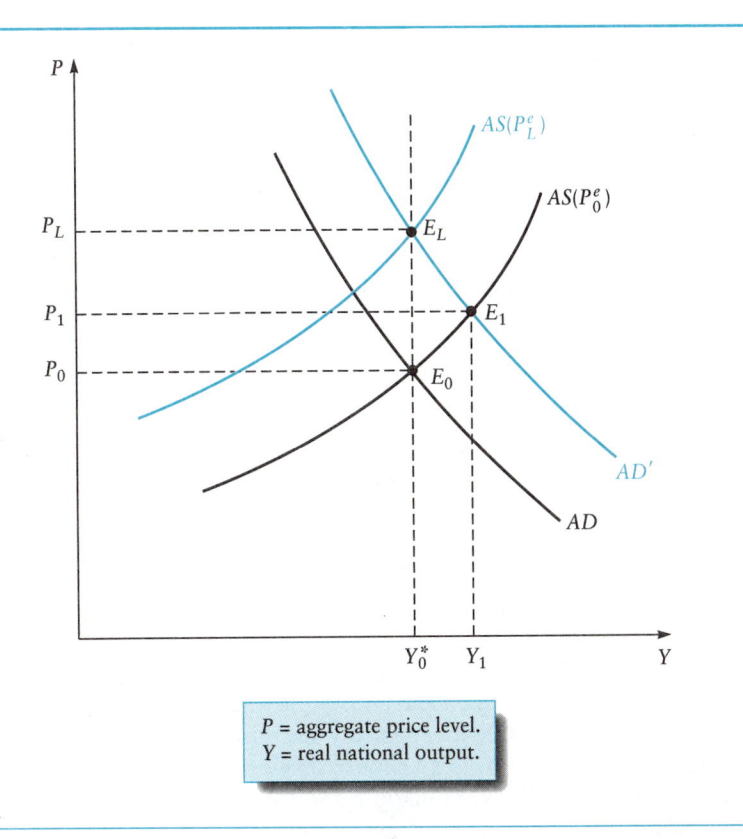

FIGURE 16.9

INFLATION-UNEMPLOYMENT TRADE-OFF: RATIONAL EXPECTATIONS

Under the rational expectations hypothesis, an increase in aggregate demand (from AD to AD') that is anticipated by labor supply will only produce inflation. The economy does not depart from the natural rate of output (Y_0^*) since the aggregate supply curve shifts back, $AS(P_0^e)$ to $AS(P_L^e)$, as the aggregate demand curve shifts out, AD to AD'. If, however, the increase in aggregate demand is not anticipated, then the short run trade-off between unemployment and inflation consistent with the hypothesis of adaptive expectations will be realized (see point E_1).

P = aggregate price level.
Y = real national output.

initial equilibrium E_0 to the new equilibrium E_L. Only inflation will be produced.

In contrast, if the expansionary policy is not anticipated by labor supply, then the increase in aggregate demand will produce the familiar inflation-unemployment trade-off, illustrated earlier under the adaptive expectations assumption. The economy will move from E_0 to E_1 in Figure 16.9. Yet, if rational expectations are assumed, then labor supply will realize in the next period that the aggregate demand has increased (from AD to AD') and will then request the higher money wages. Given the aggregate demand remains at the new level (AD'), the labor supply and aggregate supply curves would then shift back until the equilibrium consistent with the natural rate of output (E_L) is reached.

The essential difference between rational expectations and adaptive expectations is whether labor supply correctly anticipates the change in the price level or whether it simply reacts to the change with a lag. In the absence of unanticipated shocks to the economy, and assuming perfectly flexible wages and prices, under rational expectations there is no trade-off between inflation and unemployment—even in the short run.[9]

---

[9] The name New Classicals, for the proponents of the rational expectations hypothesis, follows from the Classical range of the aggregate supply curve. If rational expectations hold, then, in effect, the aggregate supply curve becomes vertical in the short run.

The hypothesis of rational expectations has been criticized for assuming too much economic literacy on the part of individuals. For instance, does (or can) the average worker assimilate the available economic information into a forecast of the aggregate price level (and inflation rate)? New Classical economists counter that it is not necessary for all individuals to behave this way; what is required is that the key economic agents do. Labor union leaders have access to economists who do formulate expectations of the inflation rate. Moreover, with the proliferation of economic forecasting services and the widely published economic information, more individuals are becoming economically literate. Certainly economic agents are motivated to pay attention to the pronouncements of the economic policymakers. In particular, the testimony of the Federal Reserve Chair before Congress is closely followed for hints on the direction of monetary policy.

The New Classicals join ranks with the monetarists and supply-siders in opposing the activist demand-management policies favored by the Keynesians. Given that the economic information is available and that there is a common understanding of the economy, New Classicals maintain that systematic demand-management policy will be ineffective. With the lags in economic policy, attempts to demand-manage the economy will be anticipated and neutralized by labor supply.

According to the New Classicals, the only way for demand-management policy to affect real national output and employment is by "fooling the public." If, for instance, the president repeatedly promises that there will be no new taxes, and then presides over a tax increase, or if the Federal Reserve Chair expresses grave concern over inflation, and then the Fed adopts expansionary monetary policy, labor supply may not correctly anticipate the economic policies. The problem with fooling the public is that the credibility of the policymakers is undermined. Many economists believe that the recession of 1981–1982 was so severe because the public did not believe the Federal Reserve was serious about reining in inflation. Consequently, workers did not accept wage concessions until well into the economic downturn.

CONCLUDING NOTE

Economists of all stripes acknowledge the important contribution the hypothesis of rational expectations has made to the debate on macroeconomic policy. This is not to suggest, however, that all economists subscribe to the hypothesis. The efficacy of demand-management policy remains a source of controversy. We can see more clearly now why macroeconomists can differ in their policy prescriptions even when they agree on the underlying economic problem.

Among the major schools, Neo-Keynesians stand alone in recommending active demand-management policies. Monetarists believe that the economy is inherently stable, with a tendency toward the natural rate of unemployment; therefore, demand-management policies are not only unnecessary, but potentially destabilizing. Supply-siders favor a very limited role for the government in the economy and maintain that the key to enhancing economic growth is in providing incentives to private enterprise. New Classicals hypothesize that economic agents will anticipate systematic, predictable, or orthodox demand-management policies, thus neutralizing the intended effects on real national output and employment. Yet, unsystematic, unpredictable, or unorthodox demand-management policies, while capable of affecting real national output and employment in the short run, undermine the credibility of the policymakers, making it more difficult for the economy to adjust to future shocks—from either the demand-side or supply-side.

We should not end this chapter with the impression that all macroeconomists can be neatly classified as either Neo-Keynesians, monetarists, supply-siders, or New Classicals. Indeed, many economists take a more eclectic approach, acknowledging the contributions and insights from each of the schools. For example, many would agree that the Keynesian model may be most applicable for an economy operating well below full employment—especially if wages and prices are downwardly inflexible. The monetarist construct of the natural rate of unemployment has provided a theoretical foundation for what is now a consensus against using demand-management policy to fine-tune the economy. The supply-side emphasis on the disincentives to work, save, and invest in an inflationary economy when tax liabilities are based on nominal income is now widely appreciated. And, last, but not least, the New Classical theory of rational expectations gains relevance as information becomes more widely available, individuals become more economically literate, financial markets become more sophisticated, and nations become more economically interdependent.

In the next two chapters we extend the analysis to the macroeconomics of an open economy. As we will see, exchange rates and balance of payments adjustments add another dimension to macroeconomic policy.

KEY TERMS

Phillips curve
frictional unemployment
structural unemployment
cyclical unemployment
employment rate
mean duration of unemployment
demand-pull inflation
cost-push inflation

adaptive expectations
natural rate of unemployment
natural rate of output
natural level of employment
neutrality of money hypothesis
New Classicals
rational expectations

QUESTIONS

1. What are the three most important ideas in this chapter? Discuss why each is important.
2. Discuss the consequences of unanticipated deflation (i.e., an unexpected decrease in the aggregate price level) for each of the following:
   a. individuals working for fixed money wages.
   b. individuals with outstanding loans at fixed nominal interest rates.
3. If you were in charge of negotiating a new one-year labor contract for your co-workers, how would you formulate your money wage request?

Write a short position paper setting out your proposal and the underlying reasoning.
4. Assume the economy is initially in equilibrium at the natural rate of output. Illustrate and discuss the effects of a decrease in the nominal money supply on real national output and the aggregate price level in both the short run (current period) and long run—assuming labor supply is operating on the basis of
   a. adaptive expectations.
   b. rational expectations.
5. Into the fall of 1992, after two years of economic stagnation, the U.S. economy was still languishing. Consumer confidence was shot. The president and the Congress, humbled by the large and growing federal budget deficits, seemed stymied on the appropriate fiscal course of action. The Federal Reserve, with numerous cuts, had finally driven the discount rate to 3.0 percent, the lowest level in over a quarter of a century. While inflation appeared to be under control, unemployment hovered around 7.5 percent. What type of policy would each of the following economists prescribe? Why?
   a. Neo-Keynesian.
   b. monetarist.
   c. supply-sider.
   d. New Classical.

Discuss how each of the policy prescriptions would affect the economy. To which macroeconomic school(s) of thought do you subscribe? Why?

PART
VI

THE INTERNATIONAL ECONOMY

CHAPTERS

— 17 —
BALANCE OF PAYMENTS
AND EXCHANGE RATES

— 18 —
EXCHANGE RATE SYSTEMS

— 19 —
ECONOMIC GROWTH AND
DEVELOPMENT

— 20 —
SOCIALISM AND THE TRANSFORMATION
TO MARKET CAPITALISM

CHAPTER

17

BALANCE OF PAYMENTS AND EXCHANGE RATES

NATIONS HAVE BECOME more economically interdependent in the post–World War II era. For example, the estimated share of exports of goods and services in the combined Gross Domestic Products of the nations of the world increased from one in nine dollars in 1965 to one in five dollars in 1990.[1] Reinforcing this trend toward openness is the movement of the nations of the European Community towards greater economic integration, the adoption of more market-oriented systems by the nations of Eastern Europe and the former Soviet Union, and the signing of the North American Free Trade Agreement (NAFTA) for the United States, Canada, and Mexico.

From the beginning, we have included exports and imports as components of aggregate demand in the modeling of the economy. In the Simple Keynesian model we showed how the magnitude of the multiplier effect was inversely related to the marginal propensity to import. In our exposition of the basic macroeconomic identity, we set forth the relationship between net foreign saving and the net domestic saving. We have yet to develop in detail, however, the macroeconomic consequences of international trade and finance.

Balance of payments accounts and exchange rates reflect the international macroeconomic linkages. In this chapter we address the measurement of the balance of international payments and the determination of exchange rates. We conclude the chapter with a discussion of the consequences of changes in exchange rates.

---

[1] World Bank, *World Development Report 1992*, New York: Oxford University Press, 1992, Table 9.

BALANCE OF PAYMENTS ACCOUNT

International trade allows residents of one nation to exchange goods, services, and assets with residents of other nations. For example, some of the goods and services purchased by U.S. residents are produced abroad (such as imports of French wine and South Korean videocassette recorders, and American tourist expenditures for food, travel, and lodging in India). Assets, too, can be traded internationally. Managers of a U.S. pension fund may want to invest in the Japanese stock market, or a U.S. company may want to purchase a factory in Germany. Because the foreign sellers of these goods, services, and assets usually prefer to receive payment in their own currencies, U.S. buyers must first acquire the necessary foreign currencies. In these situations American residents would exchange U.S. dollars for French francs, Korean won, Indian rupees, Japanese yen, or German marks. Thus, the U.S. demand for foreign goods, services, and assets translates into a demand for foreign currencies.

On the other hand, American goods, services, and assets are purchased by foreign residents, who, in turn, supply foreign currencies and demand U.S. dollars. In short, derived from international trade in goods, services, and assets are *foreign exchange markets,* where the foreign currencies used as mediums of exchange are traded.

Foreign currencies are also used in speculation. Like stocks and bonds, foreign currencies are assets whose exchange values fluctuate with market conditions. Foreign exchange speculators seek to anticipate market trends through purchases of those currencies that are expected to *appreciate* (or increase in value) and sales of those currencies that are expected to *depreciate* (or decline in value).

To keep track of the international transactions, a **balance of payments account (BPA)** is used. A balance of payments account is a summary statement of the economic transactions (exchanges of goods, services, and assets) between residents of one nation and the rest of the world over a specified period of time (usually a calendar year). A simplified version of the U.S. balance of payments account is illustrated in Figure 17.1.

Residents of a nation include individuals, businesses, and government agencies who make the nation their legal domicile. For instance, a subsidiary of a U.S. company (such as IBM) located in Frankfurt, Germany, would be considered a German firm for balance of payments purposes. Conversely, an American college student spending a semester studying in Frankfurt would be considered an American resident.

There are two sides to the balance of payments account. On the left-hand side are **credits,** indicating outflows of value. Credits usually result in inflows of payment for the goods, services, and assets provided to foreign residents. On the right-hand side are **debits,** indicating inflows of value. Debits usually result in outflows of payment for the foreign goods, services, and assets received.[2] In theory, the BPA is recorded in standard, double-entry, bookkeeping form, where each international transaction results in a credit and debit of equal size. That is,

---

[2] We say "usually" result in payment, since in some instances, goods, services, and assets are provided as *unilateral transfers* for which no offsetting payment is made. In other instances, goods, services, and assets are directly exchanged in a form of international barter known as *countertrade.*

FIGURE 17.1

SIMPLIFIED VERSION OF U.S. BALANCE OF PAYMENTS ACCOUNT

Credits	Debits
a) U.S. exports of goods	a') U.S. imports of goods
b) U.S. exports of services	b') U.S. imports of services
c) U.S. investment income receipts	c') U.S. investment income payments
d) Unilateral transfers received	d') Unilateral transfers made
e) U.S. exports of assets (private foreign investment in United States)	e') U.S. imports of assets (U.S. private investment in rest of world
f) Decrease in U.S. official assets (inc. reserve assets)	f') Increase in U.S. official assets (inc. reserve assets)
Increase in foreign official assets in U.S. (inc. reserve assets)	Decrease in foreign official assets in U.S. (inc. reserve assets)
Total Credits	Total Debits

Credits indicate outflows of value (U.S. goods, services, and assets) that usually result in payments by foreigners (nonresidents) → demand for dollars → supply of foreign exchange.

Debits indicate inflows of value (foreign goods, services, and assets) that usually result in payments by U.S. residents → supply of dollars → demand for foreign exchange.

Current Account = Balance of Merchandise Trade $(a - a')$
 + Balance of Invisible Trade $(b - b')$
 + Net Investment Income Receipts $(c - c')$
 + Net Unilateral Transfers Received $(d - d')$

Capital Account = $(e - e')$

Official Settlements Account = $(f - f')$

$$[(a + b + c + d) - (a' + b' + c' + d')] + [e - e'] = [f' - f]$$

Current Account Balance + Capital Account Balance = − Official Settlements Account Balance

for each autonomous transaction (pursued for its perceived benefit) there will be an accommodating transaction (needed for finance or compensation). By accounting definition, total credits must equal total debits on the BPA.

For example, the import of a good (a debit) involves an offsetting payment (a credit) to foreigners. Suppose a U.S. firm imports $10 million worth of sweaters made in England. The British sweater company would expect payment of $10 million worth of British pounds. There are two basic ways for the transaction to be financed. Payment could be made by an electronic transfer or fax from an American bank to a correspondent bank in London, instructing the British bank to transfer $10 million worth of pounds from the American bank's account to the British sweater company. In this case U.S. assets held abroad (pound deposits in the British bank) would fall by the equivalent of $10 million. The American bank would then deduct $10 million from the U.S. firm's account.

Alternatively, the account of a British bank in a bank in New York City could be increased by $10 million. In this case, foreign assets in the United States (dollar deposits in the American bank) would increase by $10 million. The British bank would then add $10 million worth of pounds to the British sweater company's pound account back in London.

This example involves two of the three major subaccounts in the BPA: the current account and the capital account. The third major subaccount is the official settlements account. Each will now be discussed in detail.

Current Account

The **current account** encompasses trade in goods and services, flows of investment income, and net unilateral transfers. **Merchandise trade** involves the international exchange of physical commodities (raw materials, agricultural products, and manufactures). A nation has a merchandise trade surplus when the value of the goods exported exceeds the value of the goods imported. In Figure 17.1, if $a > a'$, then a merchandise trade surplus exists.

In 1990 the United States had a merchandise trade deficit equal to $108 billion. Two product categories accounted for over ninety percent of the net deficit. Imports exceeded exports in "energy products" and "automotive vehicles, parts, and engines" by $52 billion and $50 billion, respectively.[3]

Invisible trade (items b and b') includes trade in services. For example, if a Saudi Arabian firm hires an American tanker to transport oil, U.S. exports of services increase (a credit on the U.S. current account). American tourist expenditures abroad represent imports of services and debit items on the invisible trade balance and current account.

Also included in the current account are investment income flows. If U.S. residents receive interest and dividends from foreign investments, there are inflows of investment income from the rest of the world, which are recorded as credits (under item c) on the current account of the United States BPA. In essence, by making earlier foreign investments (for example, acquiring foreign bank balances or stock in foreign companies), U.S. residents have provided the services of capital to foreigners. The returns on the invested capital are regarded as payment for an export of a factor service. Conversely, U.S. payment of investment income on the assets held by foreigners is a debit item (under item c') on the U.S. current account.

The **balance on goods, services, and investment income** refers to the difference between the credits and debits on the combined balances of merchandise trade, invisible trade, and investment income flows. A surplus is indicated by an excess of credits over debits on line items a, b, and c in Figure 17.1; that is, if $(a + b + c) > (a' + b' + c')$. If the sum of the debits exceed the sum of the credits, or $(a + b + c) < (a' + b' + c')$, then a deficit in the balance of goods, services, and investment income exists.

The final category under the current account is net unilateral transfers. **Unilateral transfers** reflect the movements of goods, services, and assets in one direction, for which no offsetting payment is expected. Examples are foreign aid, private gifts, and remittances of labor income to residents of another country. When the U.S. government provides economic assistance to foreign nations or when U.S. residents contribute to international agencies like UNICEF, debit entries on the U.S. current account under unilateral transfers to the rest of the world result. A Mexican migrant worker in Texas sending part of his labor earnings back to his family in Mexico City is also a unilateral transfer from the United States. Net unilateral transfers refer to the difference between the credit and debit items on the unilateral transfers account ($d - d'$ in Figure 17.1).

To illustrate again the principle of *double-entry bookkeeping*, consider the following. The United States donates $15 million worth of medical supplies to assist earthquake victims in Afghanistan. Consequently, U.S. exports of goods

---

[3] *Survey of Current Business*, December 1991, Table 2.

(medical supplies) increase by $15 million (item *a* on the credit side of the U.S. BPA), and unilateral transfers to the rest of the world increase by $15 million (item *d'* on the debit side of the U.S. BPA).

The **current account balance** refers to the difference between credits and debits in trade in goods and services, investment income flows, and unilateral transfers. If the total value of credits exceeds the total value of debits, that is, if $(a + b + c + d) > (a' + b' + c' + d')$, then a current account surplus exists. For example, a surplus on the current account could mean that over the period in question the nation's provision of goods and services to the rest of the world has exceeded its acquisition of foreign goods and services by more than net payments of investment income and net unilateral transfers made to the rest of the world. Alternatively, a surplus on the current account could mean that the nation's net receipts of investment income and unilateral transfers from the rest of the world have exceeded its deficit in the merchandise and invisible trade balance. A nation with a current account surplus will acquire net claims on the assets of the rest of the world.

Conversely, if total debits exceed credits on the current account, a deficit exists. The rest of the world will acquire net claims on the assets of the economy of a nation with a current account deficit.

For most nations net unilateral transfers are a relatively small portion of the current account, so that the balance on goods, services and investment income largely determines the current account balance. The United States ran a current account deficit of $92 billion in 1990. In Table 17.1 we show the composition of the U.S. current account deficit by trading partner or region. We can see that in 1990 Japan accounted for a third of the total U.S. current account deficit.

Overall, any current account imbalance must be offset by a corresponding imbalance in the rest of the BPA. For the United States, the current account deficit of $92 billion in 1990 was offset by a net surplus of $92 billion on the U.S. capital and official settlements accounts, discussed next.

Capital Account

The **capital account** in the balance of payments encompasses international trade in assets—outside those asset flows of an official nature. On the credit side,

TABLE 17.1
COMPOSITION OF U.S. CURRENT ACCOUNT BALANCE IN 1990
BILATERAL CURRENT ACCOUNT BALANCES (BILLIONS OF DOLLARS)

TRADING PARTNER/REGION	
Japan	−32
Canada	+4
Australia	+7
Western Europe	−2
Eastern Europe	+2
Latin America and other western hemisphere countries	−13
Other countries in Asia and Africa	−61
International Organizations and unallocated	+3
Total U.S. Current Account Balance	−92

SOURCE: *Survey of Current Business,* December 1991, Table 10.

private foreign investment in a nation is equivalent to the private foreign acquisition of assets in the nation—or the export of the nation's assets. Private investment abroad by residents of a nation, or the importation of foreign assets, constitutes the debit items on the capital account.

There are two basic types of foreign investment. **Direct foreign investment** is the acquisition of real assets such as property and significant shares of ownership in foreign enterprises. An example of direct foreign investment in the United States would be the purchase of an automobile assembly plant in Ohio by a Japanese company (such as Honda). Conversely, if an American company acquires ownership of a factory in Mexico, there would be an entry on the debit side of the capital account of the U.S. BPA as U.S. direct investment abroad. In both of these examples, the asset acquired (the factory) does not physically leave the nation; rather, there is a transfer in the ownership of the asset to residents of another nation.

Portfolio investment is the acquisition of foreign financial assets such as stocks (where the investors have less than 10 percent equity in the foreign corporation), bonds, certificates of deposit, and bank balances. It is important to distinguish between the initial acquisition of a foreign asset (an entry on the capital account) and the subsequent flow of income (e.g., interest or dividends) from the investment. For instance, an American insurance company's purchase of $1 million worth of British corporate bonds would be a debit item on the U.S. capital account (under item e', U.S. investment in the rest of the world). Subsequent interest received on the British bonds by the American insurance company, however, would be a credit item on the U.S. current account (under item c, investment income received from the rest of the world).

The net balance between the credits and debits on the current and capital accounts determines the overall condition of a nation's balance of payments. Specifically, a BPA surplus refers to an excess of credits over debits on the two accounts combined. On the other hand, if total debits are greater than total credits on the current and capital accounts, the nation has an overall BPA deficit.

Official Settlements Account

The **official settlements account** in the balance of payments represents asset transactions involving national governments and monetary authorities.[4] Official transactions are accommodating in nature, either financing any net imbalance above the line in the current and capital accounts or undertaken in the conduct of monetary policy. From Figure 17.1,

$$(a + b + c + d + e) - (a' + b' + c' + d' + e') = (f' - f)$$

$$\underset{\text{Current and Capital Accounts}}{\text{Net Surplus on}} = \underset{\text{Settlements Account}}{\text{Net Deficit on Official}}$$

That is, an overall balance of payments surplus must be offset by a deficit in the official settlements account—so that total credits equal total debits in the BPA

---

[4] Official asset transactions are usually included in the overall capital account. For our introduction to balance of payments accounting in this and the following chapter (especially when we compare different exchange rate regimes), it is useful to distinguish the official settlements account.

for the accounting period in question. Conversely, by definition, a balance of payments deficit will be offset by an official settlements account surplus.

Official reserve assets include *foreign exchange* (foreign currencies accepted as international means of payment) and gold held by the monetary authorities (the central banks and Treasuries).[5] Monetary authorities also can hold foreign government bonds—which are official assets, but technically not official reserve assets. Loans from the government of one nation to the government of a second nation are similarly considered as official assets. Credit entries on the U.S. official settlements account indicate either (1) a decrease in U.S. official assets (for example, the sale of official gold, foreign currencies, or foreign government bonds or the repayment of official loans by foreign governments) or (2) an increase in foreign official holdings of U.S. assets (for example, the acquisition of dollar balances in U.S. banks or of U.S. Treasury bonds by foreign monetary authorities).

Debit entries on the U.S. official settlements account refer to increases in U.S. official assets and decreases in foreign official assets in the United States. For instance, if the United States had a balance of payments surplus of $3 billion (perhaps a current account deficit of $8 billion and a capital account surplus of $11 billion), then there would have to be an official settlements account deficit of $3 billion for the accounting period in question. With the overall balance of payments surplus of $3 billion, the U.S. monetary authorities could acquire foreign currencies and foreign government bonds, or foreign monetary authorities could reduce their holdings of U.S. assets.

Sometimes the BPA of a nation is presented in a single column, with credit and debit items indicated by a plus (+) and minus (−), respectively. A simplified version of the BPA for the United States for 1990 is illustrated in Table 17.2.[6] In 1990, the U.S. capital account surplus ($59 billion) did not offset the current account deficit (−$92 billion). Thus, the United States had an overall balance of payments deficit (−$33 billion), which was matched by the official settlements account surplus ($33 billion—with a net increase in foreign official

---

[5] Other official reserve assets are *special drawing rights (SDRs)* and nations' *reserve positions* at the International Monetary Fund (IMF). SDRs are a composite currency created by the IMF and are used primarily as a unit of account. The reserve position of a nation at the IMF is an account that provides access to a pool of foreign currencies. Like gold, SDRs and reserve positions are relatively minor components of international reserves. (Recently, for the United States, SDRs, official gold, and the reserve position at the IMF each accounted for 10 to 15 percent of total U.S. official reserve assets.) The International Monetary Fund will be discussed in the next chapter.

[6] Due to differences in the tabulation of the entries for exports and imports of goods and services and for net unilateral transfers to foreigners, the calculated statistics and the resulting current account balances from the U.S. BPAs and the U.S. national income accounts are not identical. In this text, Tables 8.2 and 8.4 in Chapter 8, Table 13.2 in Chapter 13, and Table 18.1 in Chapter 18 are based on the national income accounts, where the measured U.S. current account balance in 1990 is equal to −$83 billion. Tables 17.1 and 17.2 in this chapter, however, are based on the U.S. BPAs, where the measured U.S. current account balance is equal to −$92 billion.

The differences between the two accounting procedures are technical and include the recording of gold transactions, capital gains and losses of foreign subsidiaries, and transactions with U.S. territories and Puerto Rico. For a detailed account of the discrepancies between the two measurements of the current account balance, see *Survey of Current Business,* December 1991, Table 1 (page 67), and January 1992, Table 4.5 (page 57).

TABLE 17.2
Summary of U.S. International Transactions 1990 (billions of dollars)

Exports of Goods and Services		+653
a) merchandise	+390	
b) services	+133	
c) investment income receipts	+130	
Imports of Goods and Services		−723
a') merchandise	−498	
b') services	−107	
c') investment income payments	−118	
Net Unilateral Transfers	−22	
d − d') unilateral transfers received less unilateral transfers made		
Foreign Assets in U.S., net increase (+)		
e) foreign assets other than official, net		+54
f) foreign official assets, net		+32
g) statistical discrepancy*		+64
U.S. Assets Abroad, net increase (−)		
e') U.S. private assets, net		−59
f') U.S. official assets, net		+1

Merchandise Trade Balance = 390 − 498 = −108
                            (*a*)   (*a'*)

Invisible Trade Balance = 133 − 107 = +26
                    (*b*)   (*b'*)

Net Investment Income Receipts = 130 − 118 = +12
                                (*c*)   (*c'*)

Balance on Goods, Services, and Investment Income = −108 + 26 + 12 = −70

Current Account Balance = −70 + (−22) = −92
                          (*d − d'*)

Capital Account Balance = 54 − 59 + 64 = +59
                      (*e*) (*e'*) (*g*)

Official Settlements Account Balance = 32 − (−1) = +33
                                 (*f*)   (*f'*)

*The statistical discrepancy item reflects omissions and errors in measurement in the various entries of the balance of payments account. The statistical discrepancy is added to the capital account and is equal to the difference between total credits and total debits on the balance of payments.

SOURCE: *Survey of Current Business,* December 1991, Table A (page 60).

assets in the United States of $32 billion plus a net decrease in U.S. official assets of $1 billion).

EXCHANGE RATES AND DEMAND AND SUPPLY OF FOREIGN EXCHANGE

An **exchange rate** is a price; specifically, the price of one currency in terms of units of a second foreign currency. The exchange value of the U.S. dollar can be quoted as the foreign currency price of the dollar or the dollar price of a unit of foreign currency. The exchange quotations are reciprocals. For example, at the end of the day on October 1, 1992, the U.S. dollar–German mark exchange rate was 1.4235 marks to the dollar, or equivalently, one mark equaled $.7025 (roughly 70 cents). At the same time, one British pound exchanged for $1.7335, or the dollar was worth somewhat more than half a pound (.5769 pounds).[7] Note the implied cross-rate between the German mark and the British pound based on the respective dollar quotations: one British pound should exchange for approximately 2.47 German marks: 2.47 = (1.4235)(1.7335).

The exchange value of a currency is determined by the demand and supply of the currency in the foreign exchange market. The international demand for dollars, for instance, arises from the foreign demand for U.S. goods, services, and assets, from speculators betting on the dollar's strength, and from central banks using the dollar for intervention purposes in the foreign exchange market. In order to purchase U.S. goods, services, and assets, residents of other nations must first obtain dollars, the medium of exchange in the United States. Ultimately, the foreign demand for dollars reflects the credit items on the U.S. balance of payments. Moreover, the demand for dollars elicits a supply of foreign exchange, since to purchase dollars, foreign residents must sell their own currencies.[8]

Conversely, the U.S. demand for foreign exchange is derived from the underlying demand for foreign goods, services, and assets, from speculation by U.S. residents in the foreign exchange market betting on the weakening of the dollar, and from intervention by the U.S. Federal Reserve to purchase foreign currencies. Ultimately, the U.S. demand for foreign exchange reflects the debit items on the U.S. BPA. The U.S. demand for foreign currencies brings forth a supply of dollars on the foreign exchange market.

Demand Curve for Foreign Exchange

The quantity demanded of foreign exchange by residents of the United States is inversely related to the dollar price of foreign exchange. As shown in Figure 17.2, the demand curve for foreign exchange is downward-sloping.

Consider the Japanese yen as representative of foreign currencies in general. An increase in the dollar price of yen, known as an **appreciation** of the yen and **depreciation** of the dollar, makes Japanese commodities (goods, services, and assets) more expensive to Americans. Thus, other things being equal, Americans would tend to purchase less from Japan.

To illustrate, suppose the quantity demanded of Japanese-manufactured videocassette recorders (VCRs) is 10,000 units a month when the dollar price of a VCR is $240. If the dollar price rises to $300, assume that the quantity demanded of VCRs declines to 7000 units a month. (The *arc price elasticity* of U.S. demand works out to be equal to −1.6.) Suppose further that the Japanese

---

[7] For the major currencies of the world, the exchange rates fluctuate continuously. The exact quotations at the end of the previous trading day in the foreign exchange market are published daily. These quotations are from *The Wall Street Journal*, October 2, 1992, C13.

[8] The U.S. dollar is a *key currency,* meaning that it is widely accepted as an international means of payment—even for international transactions not involving U.S. residents. Thus, there is another source of demand for dollars arising not from the foreign demand for U.S. goods, services, and assets, speculation, and official intervention, but from the use of the dollar as an international medium of exchange (and perhaps a store of value).

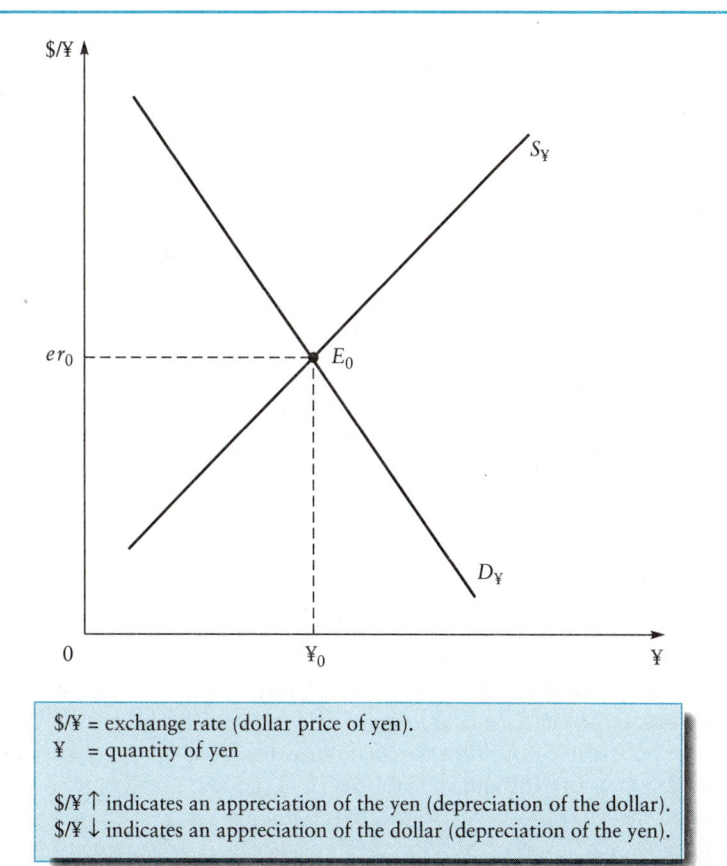

FIGURE 17.2

Equilibrium Exchange Rate between U.S. Dollar and Japanese Yen

The equilibrium U.S. dollar–Japanese yen exchange rate is the exchange rate where the quantity demanded of yen equals the quantity supplied of yen in the foreign exchange market. Graphically the equilibrium exchange rate is found at the intersection of the demand and supply curves of yen.

$/¥ = exchange rate (dollar price of yen).
¥ = quantity of yen

$/¥ ↑ indicates an appreciation of the yen (depreciation of the dollar).
$/¥ ↓ indicates an appreciation of the dollar (depreciation of the yen).

producers stand ready to supply VCRs to the United States for 30,000 yen.[9] If the exchange rate is $.008 = 1.00 yen (or $1.00 = 125 yen), the dollar price of the videocassette recorders is $240 (30,000 yen divided by 125 yen to the dollar), and the corresponding quantity demanded of yen is 300 million yen (30,000 yen times 10,000 VCRs). Total expenditures in dollars equal $2.4 million. If the dollar depreciates to $.010 = 1.00 yen (or $1.00 = 100 yen), the dollar price of a 30,000 yen VCR rises to $300. The quantity demanded of yen falls to 210 million (30,000 yen times 7000 VCRs). Thus, in this example, an increase in the dollar price of yen (from $.008 to $.010 per yen) reduces the quantity demanded of yen (from 300 million to 210 million yen).[10]

---

[9] In this and the following examples in the chapter, we are ignoring transportation costs and trade barriers, which tend to drive a wedge between the foreign supply price and the domestic demand price.

[10] Note that this inverse relationship between the dollar price of yen and the quantity demanded of yen holds regardless of the underlying price elasticities of demand for Japanese goods. Suppose in our example that an increase in the dollar price of Japanese videocassette recorders from $240 to $300 resulted in a decrease in the quantities demanded per month from 10,000 to only 9000 (an arc price elasticity of demand equal to approximately −.5). The quantity demanded of yen would then decrease from 300 million to 270 million yen per month.

Supply Curve of Foreign Exchange

As mentioned, the supply of foreign currencies to the United States reflects the credit items on the U.S. balance of payments. Again we use the Japanese yen as a representative foreign currency. As the dollar price of yen increases, the quantity supplied of yen usually increases. Note the qualifier "usually." Whether or not the appreciation of the yen results in an increase in the quantity supplied of yen depends on the underlying price elasticities of Japanese (foreign) demand for U.S. goods, services, and assets.

Suppose that the quantity demanded of American manufactured drill presses by the Japanese is 5000 per month when the yen price is 6000 yen, and that the quantity demanded rises to 7500 presses per month when the price falls to 4800 yen. (The corresponding arc price elasticity of demand between these two combinations is equal to -1.8.)

If the U.S. manufacturers are willing to supply drill presses for $48 a unit, then, with an exchange rate of $.008 = 1.00$ yen (or $1.00 = 125$ yen), 5000 presses per month would be demanded (at the price 6000 yen, or $48 times 125 yen per dollar). Consequently, the quantity supplied of yen would be 30 million yen (6000 yen times 5000 drill presses). If the yen appreciates to $.010 = 1.00$ yen (or $1.00 = 100$ yen), the new yen price to the Japanese becomes 4800 yen. Then 7500 drill presses would be demanded, and 36 million yen would be supplied (4800 yen times 7500 drill presses). Thus, in this example, an increase in the dollar price of yen (from $.008 to $.010 per yen) increases the quantity supplied of yen (from 30 million to 36 million yen).

In general, when the foreign demand for U.S. goods, services, and assets is price elastic, the supply curve of foreign exchange to the United States is upward-sloping. An appreciation of foreign currencies (depreciation of the dollar) elicits an increase in the quantity supplied of foreign currencies. If the foreign demand for American goods, services, and assets is price inelastic, however, the supply curve of foreign currencies is negatively sloped. Under such conditions, an appreciation of foreign currencies (depreciation of the dollar) results in a decrease in the quantity supplied of foreign currencies.

In the current example, suppose that a decrease in the yen price of drill presses from 6000 to 4800 yen results in an increase in the quantity demanded from 5000 to only 5500 presses (an arc price elasticity of demand of $-.4$). Then an appreciation of the yen from $.008 to $.010 (or a depreciation of the dollar from 125 yen to 100 yen) would, for a given dollar supply price of $48, reduce the quantity supplied of yen from 30 million (6000 yen per press times 5000 presses) to 26.4 million (4800 yen per press times 5500 presses).

In sum, when the foreign demand for American goods, services, and assets is price inelastic, a depreciation of the dollar (appreciation of the foreign currency) results in a decrease in the quantity supplied of foreign currency—since the adverse price effect of the depreciation on total foreign payments dominates the quantity effect of greater sales. In the following analysis, we will assume the "normal" case of an upward-sloping supply schedule for foreign currencies. This, in turn, presumes that the foreign demand for American goods, services, and assets is price elastic, or that domestically produced and foreign-produced goods, services, and assets are perceived to be relatively good substitutes.

Equilibrium Exchange Rate

In Figure 17.2 the demand and supply curves for yen (used to represent foreign exchange in general) to the United States are illustrated. The exchange rate, or the dollar price of yen ($/¥), is measured along the vertical axis. The quantity of yen (¥) exchanged during the period is measured along the horizontal axis. An increase in the dollar price of yen ($/¥ ↑) indicates an appreciation of the yen (and a depreciation of the dollar). A decrease in the dollar price of yen ($/¥ ↓) indicates a depreciation of the yen (and an appreciation of the dollar).

As the yen appreciates, the quantity demanded of yen falls (indicated by a movement up the demand curve from right to left). An appreciation of the yen results in an increase in the quantity supplied (as long as the Japanese demand for U.S. goods, services, and assets is price elastic). An equilibrium exchange rate is one that equilibrates the demand and supply of yen. In Figure 17.2, er_0 is the market equilibrium exchange rate and $¥_0$ is the quantity of yen exchanged by U.S. residents over the period.

As discussed, the U.S. demand for yen is derived from the U.S. demand for Japanese goods, services, and assets and reflects the debit items on the U.S. BPA with respect to Japan. The demand curve for yen ($D_¥$) is drawn holding constant, among other factors

- Real national income in the U.S. (Y_{US}).
- Real national income in Japan (Y_J).
- Relative national price levels (P_{US}/P_J).
- Relative interest rates (i_{US}/i_J).
- U.S. tastes and preferences with respect to Japanese goods, services, and assets.
- The expected dollar-yen exchange rate.
- Foreign exchange intervention by the monetary authorities.

A change in any one of these factors would shift the demand for yen. For example, an increase in the demand for yen (a rightward shift in $D_¥$) could be caused by

- Economic growth in the United States that increases real national income and the demands for normal goods, including imports from Japan ($Y_{US} \uparrow$).
- Economic growth in Japan that might attract U.S. financial capital for direct and portfolio investment in Japan ($Y_J \uparrow$).
- Higher inflation in the United States that, for any exchange rate, makes Japanese goods and services relatively less expensive ($P_{US}/P_J \uparrow$).
- A fall in interest rates in the United States relative to those in Japan, which increases bond prices in the United States compared to Japan and makes Japanese assets more attractive to U.S. investors ($i_{US}/i_J \downarrow$).
- A shift in U.S. tastes and preferences in favor of Japanese goods, services, or assets.
- A change in the expectations of speculators that prompts purchases of yen (and sales of dollars). An expected appreciation of the yen (a rise in the expected future dollar price of yen) would, for any given exchange rate, increase the attractiveness of holding yen.

- U.S. monetary authorities (the Federal Reserve) entering the foreign exchange market to purchase Japanese yen. (In the next chapter we discuss the reasons for official intervention in the foreign exchange market.)

Ceteris paribus, an increase in the demand for yen results in a rise in the dollar price of yen or an appreciation of the yen (depreciation of the dollar). Recall that the counterpart of an increase in the demand for yen is an increase in the supply of dollars to Japan. In order to purchase yen on the foreign exchange market, U.S. residents will sell their dollars.

In Figure 17.3 we distinguish between an increase in the demand for yen and an increase in the quantity demanded of yen. An increase in the demand for yen, illustrated by a rightward shift in the demand curve for yen and reflecting increases in the quantities demanded of yen at all the exchange rates, could be caused by any of the conditions listed earlier—for example, relative inflation in the United States. An increase in the quantity demanded of yen either reflects a movement down a given demand curve for yen from a decrease in the dollar price of yen or, holding constant the exchange rate, a rightward movement between two demand curves for yen in response to an increase in the demand for yen.

The supply of yen to the U.S. reflects the credit items on the U.S. BPA with respect to Japan. The Japanese demand for U.S. goods, services, and assets translates into a demand for dollars and a supply of yen. The supply curve for yen ($S_¥$) is drawn holding constant, among other factors

FIGURE 17.3

INCREASE IN DEMAND FOR FOREIGN EXCHANGE VERSUS INCREASE IN QUANTITY DEMANDED OF FOREIGN EXCHANGE

The shift in the demand curve for yen from $D_¥$ to $D'_¥$ indicates an increase in the demand for yen. The movement from A to B (or A' to B') indicates an increase in the quantity demanded of yen in response to a decrease in the dollar price of yen (an appreciation of the dollar) from er_0 to er_1. The movement from A to A' (or B to B') indicates an increase in the quantity demanded of yen due to an increase in the demand for yen (from $D_¥$ to $D'_¥$).

$/¥ = exchange rate (dollar price of yen).
¥ = quantity of yen

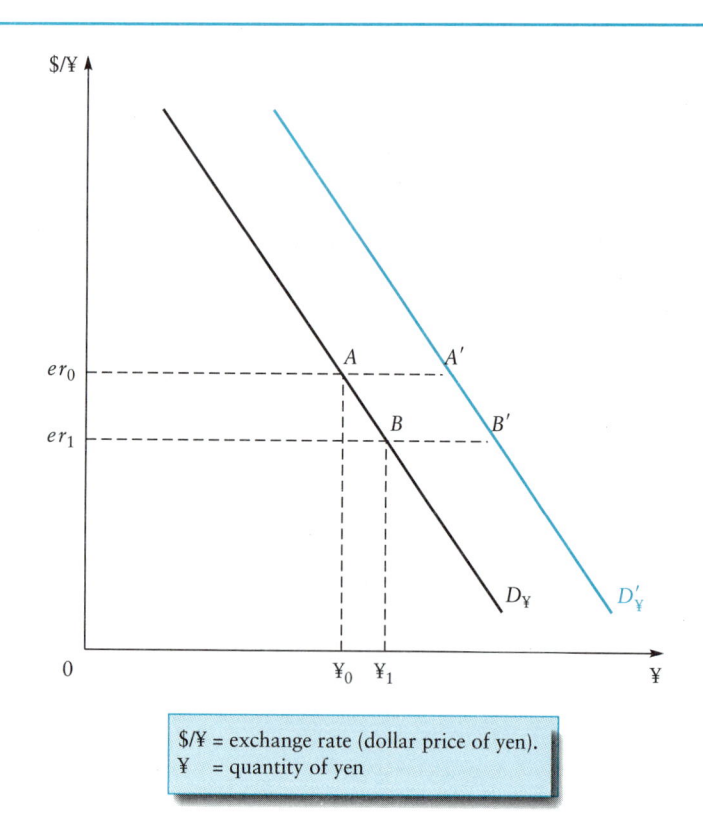

- Real national income in Japan (Y_J).
- Real national income in the U.S. (Y_{US}).
- Relative national price levels (P_{US}/P_J).
- Relative interest rates (i_{US}/i_J).
- Japanese tastes and preferences with respect to U.S. goods, services, and assets.
- The expected dollar-yen exchange rate.
- Foreign exchange intervention by the monetary authorities.

As you can see, basically the same factors underlie the demand and supply curves for yen.

An increase in the supply of yen to the United States (rightward shift in $S_¥$) could be caused by a rise in real income in Japan ($Y_J \uparrow$) or the U.S. ($Y_{US} \uparrow$), lower inflation in the United States compared to Japan ($P_{US}/P_J \downarrow$), a rise in U.S. interest rates or a fall in interest rates in Japan ($i_{US}/i_J \uparrow$), a shift in Japanese tastes and preferences in favor of American commodities, a change in the expectations of speculators favoring the sale of yen for dollars (that is, an expected depreciation in the yen), or official sales of yen on the foreign exchange market by the monetary authorities of either Japan (the Bank of Japan) or the U.S. (Federal Reserve). Ceteris paribus, an increase in the supply of yen (that is, an increase in the quantity supplied of yen at all exchange rates) results in a fall in the dollar price of yen or a depreciation of the yen (appreciation of the dollar).

In Figure 17.4 we illustrate the difference between an increase in the supply of yen and an increase in the quantity supplied of yen. An increase in the supply of yen is reflected by a rightward shift in the supply curve for yen, meaning that the quantity supplied of yen has risen for any exchange rate. For example, an increase in interest rates in the United States or economic growth in the United States, that attracts foreign investment in United States assets in anticipation of capital gains could cause an increase in the supply of yen. An increase in the quantity supplied of yen, in contrast, means either a movement up a given supply curve with an increase in the dollar price of yen or a rightward movement between two supply curves for yen—holding constant the exchange rate—due to an increase in the supply of yen.

CHANGES IN THE EXCHANGE RATE

Building on our understanding of the market for foreign exchange, we turn to a discussion of exchange rate changes. We begin with the determinants of exchange rate changes.

Determinants of Exchange Rate Changes

Using again the Japanese yen to represent foreign exchange in general, we can conclude that an appreciation in the yen (depreciation in the exchange value of the dollar) will be caused by an increase in the demand for yen or a decrease in the supply of yen. On the foreign exchange market, an excess demand for yen is equivalent to an excess supply of dollars. Recall that in the foreign exchange market, the demand for yen (supply of dollars) arises from the debit items on the U.S. BPA. The supply of yen (demand for dollars) arises from the credit items

FIGURE 17.4

INCREASE IN SUPPLY OF FOREIGN EXCHANGE VERSUS INCREASE IN QUANTITY SUPPLIED OF FOREIGN EXCHANGE

The shift in the supply curve of yen from $S_¥$ to $S'_¥$ indicates an increase in the supply of yen. The movement from A to B (or A' to B') indicates an increase in the quantity supplied of yen in response to an increase in the dollar price of yen (a depreciation of the dollar) from er_0 to er_1. The movement from A to A' (or B to B') indicates an increase in the quantity supplied of yen due to an increase in the supply of yen (from $S_¥$ to $S'_¥$).

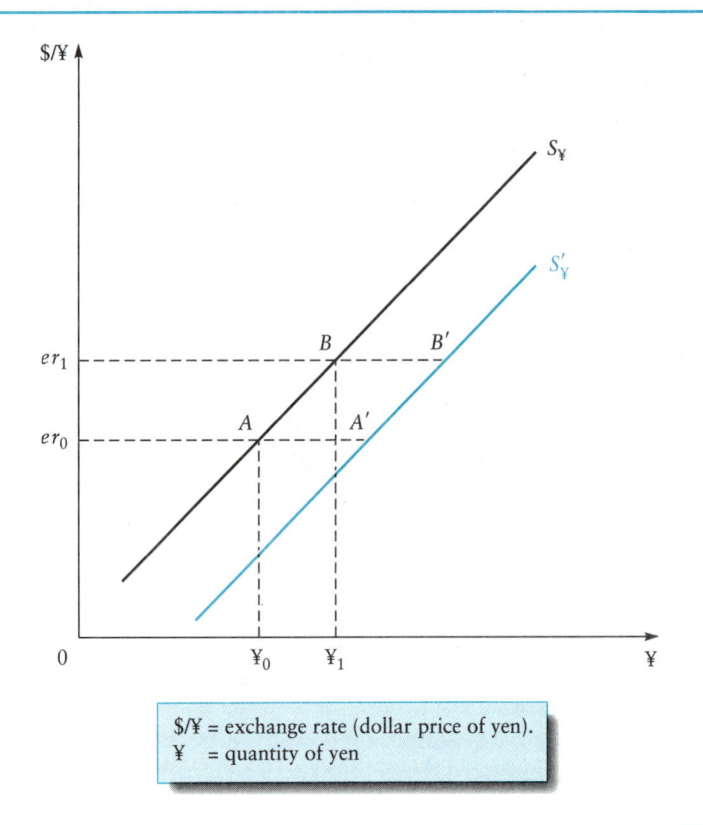

$/¥ = exchange rate (dollar price of yen).
¥ = quantity of yen

on the U.S. BPA. Therefore, an excess demand for yen corresponds to an excess of debits over credits on the current and capital accounts of the U.S. BPA, or a U.S. balance of payments deficit.

To illustrate, refer to Figure 17.5 and assume that at the dollar-yen exchange rate of er_0, the U.S. BPA is initially in equilibrium (the current account balance is exactly offset by the capital account balance). Suppose there is an increase in the demand for yen (for example, increased direct foreign investment by U.S. companies in Japan). The shift in the demand curve for yen (from $D_¥$ to $D'_¥$) creates an excess demand for yen, with upward pressure on the dollar price of yen. The yen appreciates (the dollar depreciates). As the yen rises in value, the quantity demanded of yen declines (from E'_0 to E_1) along the new demand curve. The weaker dollar makes Japanese goods and services more expensive to Americans. In addition, as the yen appreciates, the quantity supplied of yen rises (from E_0 to E_1) along the supply curve $S_¥$. Dollar-denominated U.S. goods and services become less expensive to the Japanese. Ceteris paribus, the yen would continue to appreciate until the foreign exchange market clears with a new equilibrium exchange rate of er_1.

In sum, from an initial balance of payments equilibrium, the increase in the demand for yen (with the increase in U.S. direct investment in Japan) produces a U.S. balance of payments deficit (here the U.S. capital account balance deteriorates). The subsequent depreciation of the dollar, however, works to bring the U.S. balance of payments back into equilibrium (here by improving the current account balance).

Conversely, an appreciation of the dollar is caused by an increase in the supply of yen or a decrease in the demand for yen. A balance of payments surplus (or an excess of credits over debits in the U.S. current and capital accounts) would induce an increase in the exchange value of the dollar until a balance of payments equilibrium is restored.

Consequences of Exchange Rate Changes

A change in the exchange value of a currency, indicative of changes in the underlying demand and supply of the currency in the foreign exchange market, will likely have consequences for real national outputs, employments, and aggregate price levels. For example, a depreciation of the dollar improves the U.S. balance of trade as imports become more expensive to American consumers and U.S. exports become less expensive to foreign consumers.[11] Output and

---

[11] To what extent a given depreciation of the dollar improves the U.S. trade balance depends on the underlying price elasticities of demand and supply for both exports and imports. Moreover, due to lags in the responses of the quantities traded to a change in the exchange rate, there may be a delay of up to two or three years before a depreciation in the dollar significantly improves the U.S. trade balance. In the next chapter we note reasons for the delayed response.

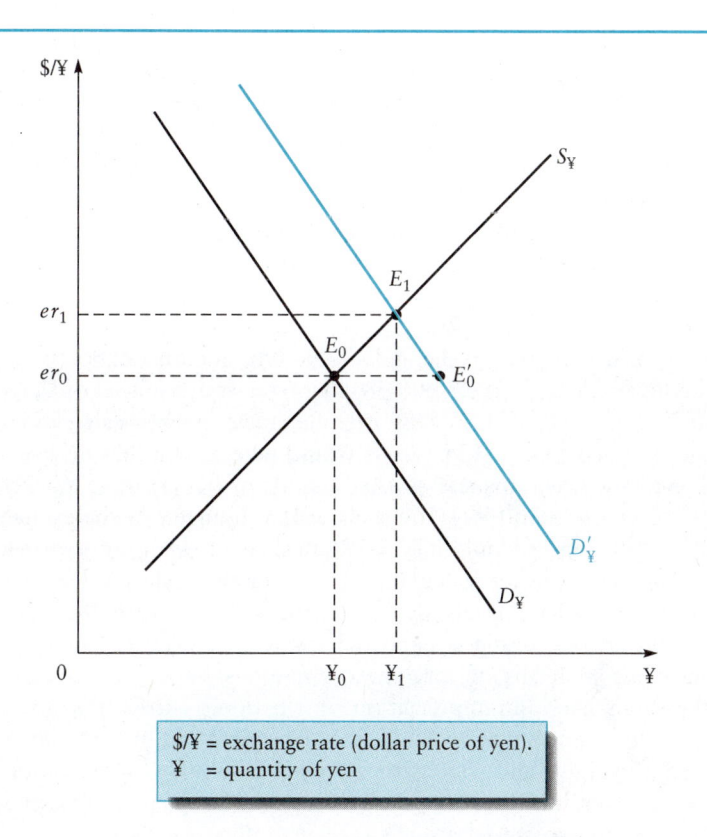

FIGURE 17.5

DEPRECIATION IN DOLLAR FROM INCREASE IN DEMAND FOR YEN

An increase in the demand for yen (from D_Y to D'_Y) results in an excess quantity demanded of yen at the initial equilibrium exchange rate (represented by the line segment $E_0E'_0$). The appreciation of the yen (depreciation in the dollar) from er_0 to er_1 eliminates the excess quantity demanded of yen.

$/¥ = exchange rate (dollar price of yen).
¥ = quantity of yen

employment in the United States would rise—directly with the expanded production of export and import-substitute commodities, and indirectly through the multiplier effect from the increase in aggregate demand. Unless the economy is operating well below full employment on the Keynesian range of the aggregate supply curve, the increase in the rate of real national output produced will exert upward pressure on the aggregate price level. Any increase in the domestic price level, however, will undermine the favorable effect of the depreciation of the dollar on the U.S. trade balance.

Consider the following example. Suppose that the exchange rate is 125 yen to the dollar (that is, $1.00 = 125 yen, or the dollar price of a yen is $.008), and that the U.S. production cost of a bushel of oranges for export is $4.00, and the Japanese production cost of a pocket calculator for export is 750 yen. Ignoring transportation costs and trade barriers, the unit import price to Japan of U.S. oranges would be 500 yen ($4.00 times 125 yen to the dollar). The import price to the United States of a Japanese pocket calculator would then be $6.00 (750 yen divided by 125 yen to the dollar).

If the dollar depreciates to 100 yen (that is, if $1.00 = 100 yen, or the dollar price of a yen rises to $.010), then the yen price of the $4.00 bushel of oranges declines to 400 yen, and the dollar price of a 750 yen Japanese pocket calculator increases to $7.50. Consequently, U.S. exports of oranges to Japan should increase, and U.S. imports of Japanese pocket calculators should decrease. If, however, as the United States increases the production of oranges to export to Japan, the unit cost of producing oranges rises, then the Japanese import price will not fall by the full extent of the depreciation of the dollar. In fact, if the cost of producing a bushel of oranges in the United States increases from $4.00 to $5.00, then the depreciation of the dollar will be entirely neutralized—the import price of a bushel of U.S. oranges to Japan will remain at 500 yen and U.S. exports of oranges to Japan will not increase.

To generalize, the beneficial impact of a depreciation on the trade balance can be offset by higher domestic prices. The closer an economy is to full employment, the more likely a depreciation in the currency, which stimulates the production of export and import-substitute commodities, will generate increases in the aggregate price level.

Moreover, a depreciation in the currency of a nation will reduce the purchasing power or real exchange value of the nation's exports. Return to the earlier example, with the $4.00 production cost of a bushel of U.S. oranges and the 750 yen production cost of a Japanese pocket calculator. At the exchange rate of $1.00 = 125 yen, it would take 1.5 bushels of U.S. oranges to exchange for one Japanese pocket calculator: 1 Japanese pocket calculator = 750 yen = $6.00 = 1.5 bushels of U.S. oranges. At the exchange rate of $1.00 = 100 yen, it would take 1.875 bushels of U.S. oranges to exchange for one Japanese pocket calculator: 1 Japanese pocket calculator = 750 yen = $7.50 = 1.875 bushels of U.S. oranges. Thus, with the depreciated dollar, a bushel of oranges exported by United States, ceteris paribus, commands less in terms of foreign commodities.

On the other hand, an appreciation of a nation's currency would tend to deteriorate the nation's trade balance, putting downward pressure on domestic output, employment, and the aggregate price level. The appreciation of the currency, however, increases the purchasing power of the nation's exports. You should be able to explain why.

CONCLUDING NOTE

The exchange value of a nation's currency is one of the most important prices in an economy—increasingly so with the growing internationalization of economic activity. Changes in an exchange rate not only reflect an underlying disequilibrium in the nation's balance of payments, but affect real national output, employment, the aggregate price level, the allocation of resources (especially for export and import-competitive industries in the nation), and the distribution of income.

In this chapter we have implicitly assumed there were no restrictions on the movement of an exchange rate to a disequilibrium in the balance of payments. How far an exchange rate is allowed to change, however, depends on the exchange rate system in operation. In the next chapter we analyze the major types of exchange rate systems—the essential difference being the degree to which the exchange rate is freely determined by market forces.

KEY TERMS

balance of payments account (BPA)
credits
debits
current account
merchandise trade
invisible trade
balance on goods, services, and investment income
unilateral transfers
current account balance
capital account
direct foreign investment
portfolio investment
official settlements account
official reserve assets
exchange rate
appreciation
depreciation

QUESTIONS

1. What are the three most important ideas in this chapter? Discuss why each is important.
2. Let the British pound *(bp)* represent foreign exchange in general. Discuss how each of the following events, ceteris paribus, would affect the U.S. balance of payments and the U.S. dollar–British pound exchange rate, that is, the dollar price of a British pound ($/*bp*). Illustrate your answer with a graph of the foreign exchange market, and show how the U.S. demand curve for British pounds and the supply curve of British pounds to the U.S. would be affected by
   a. a rise in interest rates in Great Britain.
   b. a rise in the aggregate price level in the United States.
   c. speculators' expectation that the British pound will appreciate relative to the U.S. dollar.
   d. a fall in the level of real national income in the United States.
   e. entrance of the U.S. Federal Reserve into the foreign exchange market to sell British pounds.

3. Let the German mark, the deutsche mark *(dm)*, represent foreign exchange in general. Assume that the demand and supply curves for deutsche marks to the United States are given by

$$Q^d_{dm} = 100 - 150P_{dm}$$

and

$$Q^s_{dm} = -20 + 90P_{dm}$$

where Q^d_{dm} and Q^s_{dm} are the quantities demanded and supplied of deutsche marks in the foreign exchange market (billions of deutsche marks per day) and P_{dm} is the dollar price of a deutsche mark (or the number of dollars required to purchase one deutsche mark).
   a. Find the initial equilibrium exchange rate.
   b. Suppose the U.S. demand for deutsche marks increases to

$$Q^{d'}_{dm} = 124 - 150P_{dm}$$

   Find the new equilibrium exchange rate. What has happened to the dollar?
   c. If a pair of blue jeans manufactured in the United States could be exported to Germany for $20, then find the price to German importers in deutsche marks before and after the change in the dollar–deutsche mark exchange rate.
   d. Suppose that the price elasticity of demand of German consumers for American blue jeans equals −1.5 (that is, assume that a 1 percent increase in the price of a pair of American-made blue jeans decreases the quantity demanded by German consumers by 1.5 percent). Assuming a constant dollar export price of $20 and that initially 100,000 pairs of U.S. blue jeans per month were exported, find the effects of the change in the dollar–deutsche mark exchange rate on the export receipts from U.S. blue jeans sold in Germany—in both dollars and deutsche marks.
   e. If a case of German beer could be exported to the United States for 50 deutsche marks, find the price to American importers in dollars before and after the change in the dollar–deutsche mark exchange rate.
   f. Suppose that the price elasticity of demand of American consumers for German beer is −1.2. Assuming a constant deutsche mark export price of 50 deutsche marks and that initially 100,000 cases of German beer per month were imported, find the effect of the change in the dollar–deutsche mark exchange rate on the U.S. import payments for German beer—in both dollars and deutsche marks.
4. Discuss the consequences of an excess of credits over debits in the current and capital accounts in a nation's balance of payments for
   a. the exchange value of the nation's currency.
   b. the level of real national output.
   c. the aggregate price level in the nation.

CHAPTER
18

Exchange Rate Systems

So far in our study of macroeconomics, we have focused on the **internal balance** of a nation—the attainment of full employment and price stability. We now turn our attention to a nation's **external balance**—the attainment of a balance of payments equilibrium with a stable exchange rate. We will see that just as there is controversy over the efficacy of demand-management policies for achieving the internal balance, there is an ongoing debate over the relative merits of different *exchange rate systems*.

Indeed, one of the most important macroeconomic decisions for a nation is the selection of an exchange rate system. The foreign exchange value of a nation's currency directly affects not only the international competitiveness of the nation's traded goods and services, but also the real growth rate of the nation's output and the nation's inflation and unemployment rates. And, in turn, exchange rates reflect the economic and political conditions across nations.

As we discussed in the last chapter, changes in exchange rates are due to shifts in the underlying demands and supplies of currencies in the foreign exchange market. The extent to which an exchange rate is allowed to change, however, is determined by the system in operation Exchange rates are free to vary without restriction under a **flexible exchange rate** system. In contrast, under a **fixed exchange rate** system there are official exchange values for currencies with only a limited range of fluctuation allowed. There are also hybrid systems. An **adjustable peg** is basically a fixed exchange rate system with provision for changing, or repegging, the official exchange values of the currencies. A **managed float** is basically a flexible exchange rate system with allowance for discretionary intervention in the foreign exchange market by monetary authorities to manage the range of fluctuation in the exchange rates.

Over the past century the United States has operated under three different exchange rate systems: a fixed exchange rate (the gold standard from the late nineteenth century up to the early 1930s); an adjustable peg exchange rate (the Bretton Woods system from the late 1940s to the early 1970s); and a managed float (since the early 1970s).[1] While the degree of official management of the dollar over the last two decades has varied from minimal to active, the United States really has not relinquished complete control over the dollar to market forces—as would be the case under a flexible exchange rate system.

In this chapter we review the "rules of the game" under the flexible, fixed, adjustable, and managed float exchange rate systems. We examine the advantages and disadvantages of flexible exchange rates. In addition, we will discuss the causes and note the consequences of the recent volatility in the exchange value of the U.S. dollar. Over the first half of the 1980s the dollar appreciated by over 50 percent. Over the second half of the decade, it reversed course and plummeted. The elevator ride of the dollar has been a source of both national and international concern—and has fueled the debate over the need for reform in the international monetary system.

FLEXIBLE EXCHANGE RATES

With a perfectly flexible (or freely floating) exchange rate system, market forces alone determine the exchange rates. Consistent with the market mechanism, the exchange rate moves in response to disequilibria between the demand and supply of foreign currencies.

To illustrate, refer to Figure 18.1, where the demand and supply of yen to the United States are depicted. (Note: As in the last chapter, yen is used to represent foreign currencies in general and Japan can be viewed as representative of the rest of the world.) The market equilibrium exchange rate is er_0, and $¥_0$ is the equilibrium quantity of yen exchanged during the period. At this exchange rate the U.S. balance of payments is in equilibrium, meaning that any imbalance in the current account is offset by the capital account.

Suppose that the aggregate price level in the United States rises. The inflation increases the demand for yen ($D_¥$ shifts right to $D'_¥$) and decreases the supply of yen to the United States ($S_¥$ shifts left to $S'_¥$). In both nations there will be a substitution of the less expensive Japanese commodities for American commodities. At the original exchange rate, er_0, there is now an excess quantity demanded of yen (indicated by the line segment FG). The excess demand for yen corresponds to an excess supply of dollars and the emergence of a balance of payments deficit for the United States. The yen will tend to appreciate (the dollar will depreciate) toward er_1, where equilibrium in the balance of payments and foreign exchange market is restored. As the dollar price of yen rises, the quantity demanded of yen falls (from point G to point E_1 along the demand curve $D'_¥$), and the quantity supplied of yen rises (from point F to point E_1 along the supply curve $S'_¥$). That is, as the dollar weakens, dollar prices of yen-denominated Japanese commodities rise, while the yen prices of American-made commodities fall. The exchange rate moves to "correct" the imbalance in the current account caused by the inflation in the United States. Whether the

---

[1] The period from the 1930s through World War II was not defined by any coherent international monetary system. Along with a number of other industrial nations, the United States left the gold standard in the early 1930s. The volume of international trade and investment fell sharply—initially reflecting the economic depression and the rise in protectionism, and later the result of the hostilities and destruction of the war.

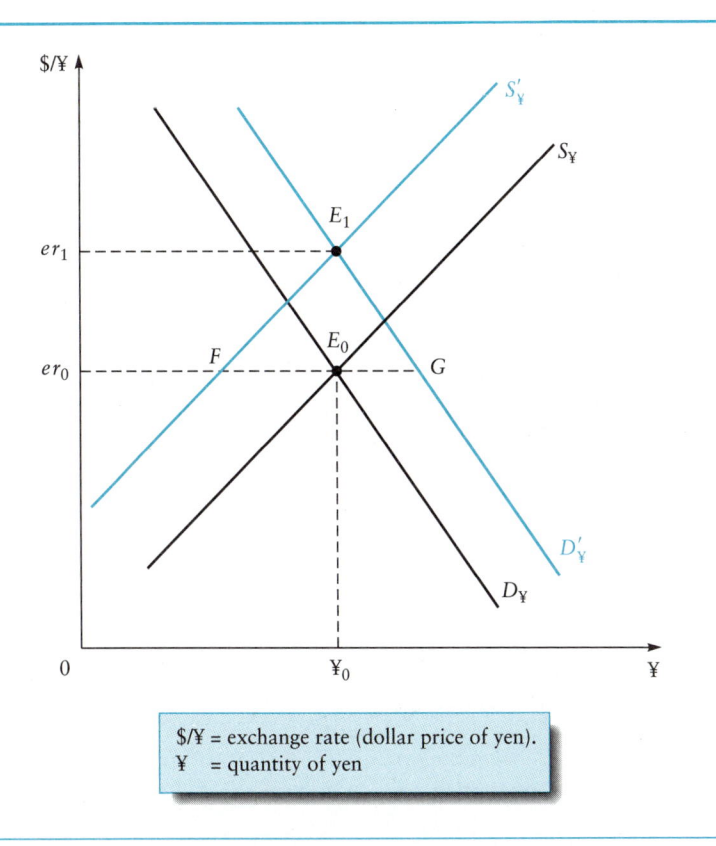

FIGURE 18.1

CONSEQUENCES OF INCREASE IN U.S. AGGREGATE PRICE LEVEL ON EXCHANGE VALUE OF DOLLAR UNDER FLEXIBLE EXCHANGE RATES

An increase in the aggregate price level in the United States, ceteris paribus, would make U.S. goods and services less competitive internationally. The resulting increase in the U.S. demand for foreign exchange (from $D_¥$ to $D'_¥$) and decrease in the supply of foreign exchange to the United States (from $S_¥$ to $S'_¥$) would appreciate the yen (depreciate the dollar) from er_0 to er_1.

equilibrium quantity of yen exchanged rises or falls over the period depends on whether the supply curve or demand curve for yen is more responsive to the U.S. inflation. (Note, in Japan the appreciation of the yen would tend to eliminate the Japanese balance of payments surplus.)

In practice, the changes in the exchange rate may not reestablish the current account balance and balance of payments equilibrium so readily. There is generally a considerable lag between changes in the exchange rate and the response of the trade balance. Usually the shipment of the traded goods occurs well before the subsequent payment in foreign currencies. Previous orders and contracts based on earlier exchange rates still have to be fulfilled. Moreover, it takes time for consumers and producers to adjust to the new relative prices between foreign and domestic commodities brought by changes in the exchange rate.

Consider now a rise in the level of interest rates in the United States due, for example, to an increase in the demand for credit. Again assume that at the exchange rate, er_0, illustrated in Figure 18.2, the U.S. balance of payments is in equilibrium with offsetting imbalances in the current and capital accounts. Ceteris paribus, a rise in U.S. interest rates would make bond prices in the United States fall. There would be a net capital inflow as both domestic and foreign investors, attracted by the higher yields and perhaps the possibility of capital gains if U.S. interest rates fall in the future, turn to U.S. assets. Consequently, the demand curve for yen would shift to the left while the supply curve of yen

FIGURE 18.2

CONSEQUENCES OF INCREASE IN INTEREST RATE IN U.S. ON EXCHANGE VALUE OF DOLLAR UNDER FLEXIBLE EXCHANGE RATES

An increase in the level of interest rates in the United States, ceteris paribus, would make U.S. assets more attractive. Consequently, the net inflow of capital to the United States is shown by the increase in the supply of foreign exchange (from $S_¥$ to $S'_¥$) and the decrease in the demand for foreign exchange (from $D_¥$ to $D'_¥$). The dollar would appreciate (from er_0 to er_1), reflecting the improvement in the U.S. capital account.

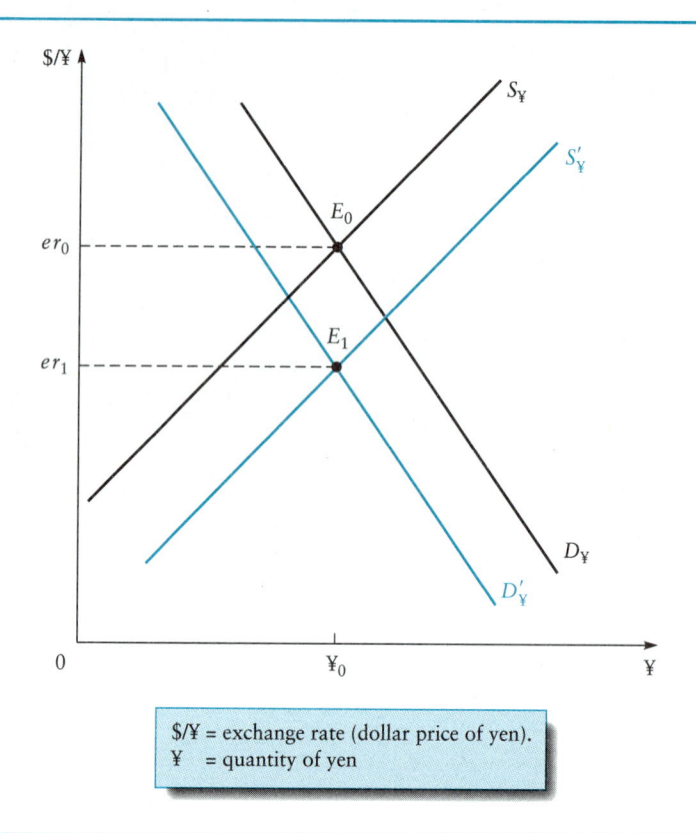

$/¥ = exchange rate (dollar price of yen).
¥ = quantity of yen

would shift to the right. The capital account on the U.S. balance of payments account would improve. The resulting balance of payments surplus would appreciate the dollar (the dollar price of yen falls to er_1 in Figure 18.2). The stronger dollar would eventually affect the U.S. current account, as U.S. exports would become more expensive when expressed in foreign currency prices, and the higher exchange value of the dollar would lower the price of imports to U.S. consumers. As in the previous example, the exchange rate moves to reequilibrate the balance of payments. Here the improvement in the U.S. capital account, due to the higher interest rates in the United States, would be offset by a deterioration in the current account.

Again, in practice, given the significant lags in the adjustment of traded goods, the U.S. balance of payments surplus and the appreciation of the dollar caused by the rise in interest rates in the United States could continue for some time. The capital, or asset, markets tend to clear much faster than markets for goods and services. With the sophistication of international communication networks, literally billions of dollars can be moved electronically from one financial center to another in a matter of minutes in response to a change in interest rates or investor outlook.

Nevertheless, the arguments for a flexible exchange rate system are compelling and parallel the arguments for relying on the market mechanism. By allowing exchange rates to adjust automatically and continuously to reflect changes in demand and supply conditions, disequilibria in balance of payments tend to be corrected. Monetary authorities are spared the need to hold international reserves for the purpose of intervention in the foreign exchange market. Furthermore, since the adjustment of the exchange rate tends to equilibrate the balance of payments, monetary and fiscal policies are freer to focus on internal objectives such as full employment and price stability.

On the other hand, among the disadvantages of a flexible exchange rate system is the danger of excessive fluctuations in exchange rates. Such volatility in exchange rates increases uncertainty and thus may reduce the volume of international trade and investment. Unanticipated exchange rate fluctuations can affect the realized profits from international transactions. For example, importers will want to guard against appreciation in the foreign currencies in which future payments are to be made. Suppose a U.S. importer is considering purchasing 10,000 pocket calculators from a Japanese manufacturer at 1500 yen per calculator, with total payment in yen due in thirty days. At the present exchange rate of $1 equals 125 yen (or $.008 = 1 yen), the U.S. importer would need $120,000 in thirty days to buy the 15 million yen to pay for the 10,000 pocket calculators. If the exchange rate in thirty days is $1 = 120 yen (that is, the yen has appreciated), then $125,000 would be required to purchase the 15 million yen needed for the calculators. On the other hand, if the dollar appreciated over the thirty-day period to, say, $1 = 130 yen, then only $115,385 would be needed to purchase the 15 million yen. The risk of exchange rate fluctuations (especially an appreciation of the yen) may be enough for the U.S. importer to postpone, or even forgo entirely, the foreign order—perhaps turning to a domestic producer of pocket calculators, even if the domestic calculators are more expensive at the present exchange rate.[2]

Similarly, investors in foreign assets who expect to convert the foreign currency proceeds back into their home currency will want to guard against the depreciation of the foreign currencies in which their investments are denominated. Consider an American investor deciding whether to invest $10,000 in a Japanese bond with a one-year maturity and paying 6 percent interest. At the present exchange rate of $1 = 125 yen (or $.008 = 1 yen), it would cost 1.25 million yen to buy the bond. At the end of the year when the bond is redeemed, the American investor would expect to receive 1.325 million yen, or $10,600 after conversion. If, however, the yen depreciates over the year to $1 = 130 yen (or $.0077 = 1 yen), then, when the bond proceeds are converted back into dollars, the 1.325 million yen would be equivalent to only $10,192. In effect,

---

[2] We should note that it is possible to avoid some foreign exchange risks through **forward contracts,** in which traders and investors purchase or sell given amounts of foreign currencies at set prices for delivery at specified dates in the future. Suppose that, in this example, the U.S. importer can enter into a forward contract to purchase 15 million yen for delivery in thirty days at an exchange rate (called the *forward rate*) of $1 = 123 yen. Then in thirty days, the U.S. importer would need $121,951 to buy the 15 million yen to pay the Japanese manufacturer for the 10,000 pocket calculators. While more expensive than the $120,000 required at the current exchange rate, the U.S. importer may prefer the forward contract if either the importer does not presently have the dollars needed to buy the 15 million yen and expects the dollar to depreciate more than to just 123 yen in thirty days, or if the importer desires to retain the use of the dollar balances for thirty days before making payment to the Japanese manufacturer. In any case, such *hedging* to avoid foreign exchange risk adds to the expense of the underlying commercial transaction, since there are costs associated with buying a forward contract.

the return on the bond to the American investor would be less than 2 percent. On the other hand, if the dollar depreciates over the year, the American investor realizes a return of more than the 6 percent earned directly from the Japanese bond.[3]

In the case of investment in physical capital, exchange rate risk may also be an important concern. Business fixed investment is beset by considerable uncertainty anyway. A firm's rate of return on investment in new plant, equipment, and machinery is dependent on, among other factors, the future demand for the firm's output. At the time of the commitment of funds for the investment project, the firm can only anticipate the future demand for its output. For traded goods and services, the projection of demand will depend in part on future exchange rates.

To illustrate, assume that the current exchange rate is $1 = 125 yen. Assume further that firms in the United States can produce microcircuits for a unit cost of $10, and that firms in Japan can produce similar microcircuits for a unit cost of 1500 yen (or $12 at the current exchange rate). Consequently, unless prohibited by transportation costs and trade barriers, microcircuits should be exported from the United States to Japan. Suppose that the U.S. firms, anticipating a stable exchange rate and a continuation of this competitive edge, build additional factories to meet the expected growth in the world demand for microcircuits. If, however, by the time the new factories come on-line, the dollar has appreciated to $1 = 175 yen, then the competitive advantage, ceteris paribus, would have shifted to Japan. For the given unit costs of production, the Japanese firms would now be able to ship microcircuits to the United States for $8.57 (1500 yen divided by 175 yen per dollar). The microcircuit firms in the United States would face excess capacity, with a significantly lower return on the capital invested in the new factories than anticipated.[4]

In sum, while speculators deliberately assume foreign exchange risks, hoping to profit from correctly anticipating exchange rate changes (for example, by buying a currency before it appreciates), international traders in goods and services and international investors generally prefer to avoid the foreign exchange risk. The added uncertainty associated with exchange rate fluctuations, uncertainty that is heightened when exchange rates are volatile, may be enough to discourage some foreign trade and investment—in both financial assets and physical capital. The reduced volumes of trade and investment result in a less efficient allocation of resources. Traders would not as often use the least-cost foreign suppliers of goods and services. Financial investors would hesitate to purchase foreign assets, even when the return to the foreign investment at the current exchange rate is higher. Firms might hold off on fixed investment expenditures until exchange rates become more stable. We will return to this issue later when the experience of the dollar over the last 15 years is discussed. First we need to analyze balance of payments adjustment under a fixed exchange rate system.

---

[3] As discussed in the previous note, the American investor could eliminate the foreign exchange risk by purchasing a forward contract to sell 1.325 million yen in one year at a preset exchange rate. The cost of the forward contract, however, reduces the net return on the foreign bond purchase.

[4] Even with the stronger dollar, the firms in the United States may still be competitive if they are able to reduce their unit cost of production from $10.00 to $8.57. For example, the new factories may embody the latest technologies and thus be more cost efficient.

FIXED EXCHANGE RATES

Under a fixed exchange rate system a nation defines an official value for its currency. Under the **gold standard** that operated before World War I, each nation expressed the value of its currency in terms of gold. The exchange rates, or the **par values,** for the currencies were derived from these gold prices. For example, suppose that the gold prices of the U.S. dollar and British pound (bp) were set for $20 = 1 ounce of gold (or $1 = .05 ounces of gold), and 4 pounds = 1 ounce of gold (or 1 pound = .25 ounces of gold). Then the implied exchange rate between the U.S. dollar and British pound would be $5 = 1 pound (or $1 = .20 pounds).

Around these par values a small range of fluctuation was allowed.[5] If the exchange rates were allowed to fluctuate plus or minus 1 percent around the par value, then the dollar could vary from .198 to .202 pounds, and the pound could vary from $4.95 to $5.05.

It would be the responsibility of the monetary authorities to maintain the official exchange values through intervention in the foreign exchange markets and adjustments in the domestic money supplies. Under the gold standard a nation's money supply was backed by gold. In fact, with a fractional reserve banking system, the money supply would be a multiple of the official gold stock. In theory the monetary authorities stood ready to convert the outstanding domestic currencies into gold at the established gold values. A disequilibrium in the balance of payments would set off official gold flows and initiate automatic adjustments in the money supplies. The changes in the money supplies in turn would induce changes in internal prices, interest rates, and real incomes that would tend to eliminate the initial balance of payments disequilibrium.

Assume the United States and Great Britain are the only two nations in the system. Suppose the United States begins to run a surplus in the balance of payments, due perhaps to lower inflation or higher interest rates in the United States than in Great Britain. The overall excess of credits over debits in the U.S. current and capital accounts would appreciate the dollar with respect to the British pound. Under a fixed exchange rate system, however, once the dollar appreciated to its upper limit (in this example that would be once the dollar reached .202 pounds), gold would have to be sent from Great Britain to the United States. The inflow of gold to the United States would be recorded as a debit entry on the U.S. official settlements account, that is, an increase in official (reserve) assets. (Recall that a surplus in the balance of payments has to be offset by a deficit in the official settlements account.) Conversely, the loss of gold in Great Britain would be recorded as a credit entry on the British official settlements account.

The gold flows, indicative of the balance of payments disequilibrium, would change the money supplies in the two nations. The inflow of official gold would expand the U.S. money supply, driving down interest rates, pushing up prices, and perhaps stimulating real national output and income. The lower interest rates would induce a net outflow of financial capital (resulting in a deterioration in the U.S. capital account). The higher price and income levels would worsen the U.S. current account. Thus, the initial balance of payments surplus for the

---

[5] In practice, the range of fluctuation around the par value was determined by the cost of shipping an ounce of gold between the nations.

United States would be eliminated. Schematically, the economic transition for the United States would be as follows:

U.S. balance of payments surplus → U.S. gain of official gold →
increase in U.S. money supply → decrease in interest rate in United States
→ net capital outflow as American and British investors redirect their saving to the purchase of the lower-priced British assets (U.S. capital account balance deteriorates)
→ increase in interest-sensitive expenditures in the United States (business and residential fixed investment and spending on consumer durables) → increase in aggregate demand in United States → run-down of inventories in United States → increase in rate of production of real national output and increase in aggregate price level in United States
→ increase in real imports of United States as real national income rises
→ increase in real imports of United States and decrease in real exports of United States as U.S. aggregate price level rises (U.S. current account balance deteriorates.)

In Great Britain the adjustment process would be the reverse. The loss of official gold would reduce the money supply, driving up interest rates and pushing down prices and real income. The deflationary process would continue until the balance of payments deficit in Great Britain was eliminated.

In sum, under a fixed exchange rate system, the adjustment mechanism operates not through changes in exchange rates, but through changes in money supplies, domestic prices, interest rates, and real income levels. Under the gold standard, official gold flows between nations, reflecting the balance of payments disequilibrium, set off the adjustment process. According to the "rules of the game," nations with balance of payments surpluses are supposed to expand their money supplies and stimulate their economies. Nations with deficits are supposed to contract their money supplies and deflate their economies. In either case the monetary authorities are expected to accept the discipline imposed by the fixed exchange rate system.

To contrast better with flexible exchange rates, return to the earlier analysis of foreign exchange markets and a more modern-day version of a fixed exchange rate system. Consider again the United States and Great Britain as the two nations operating in the fixed exchange rate system. Assume that initially the balance of payments is in equilibrium at the official exchange rate, er_0, as shown in Figure 18.3. The allowed band of fluctuation around the official exchange rate is indicated by the parallel lines at $\overline{er}$ and $\underline{er}$.

Suppose now the United States economy experiences a rise in real national income (due perhaps to reduced saving rates increasing desired consumption expenditures). The rise in real national income (and the aggregate price level if the United States is operating beyond the Keynesian range of the aggregate supply curve) increases the U.S. demand for British pounds and shifts the demand curve for pounds, D_{bp}, to the right.[6] The excess quantity demanded of pounds at the official exchange rate, represented by the distance E_0E', puts upward pressure on the exchange rate. The dollar begins to depreciate. As the

---

[6] For ease of exposition, we will assume here that the economic growth in the United States does not attract British investors seeking capital gains from purchases of U.S. assets (corporate stocks and real properties). Hence, the supply curve of British pounds is assumed not to shift to the right with the rise in real income in the United States.

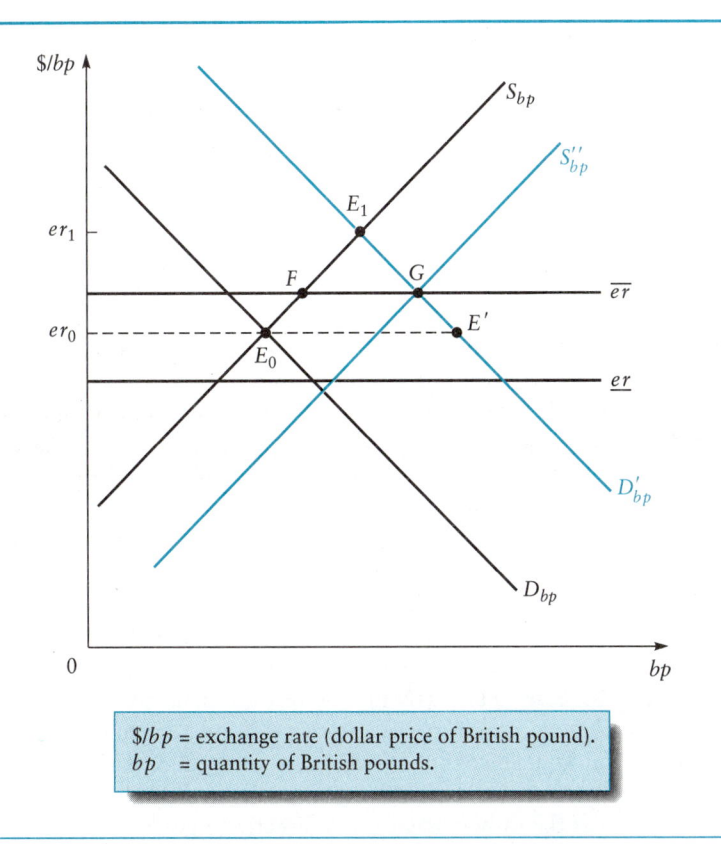

FIGURE 18.3

CONSEQUENCES OF INCREASE IN REAL NATIONAL INCOME IN U.S. ON EXCHANGE VALUE OF DOLLAR UNDER FIXED EXCHANGE RATES

An increase in real national income in the United States would increase the U.S. demand for foreign exchange (from D_{bp} to D'_{bp}). Ceteris paribus, the dollar would tend to depreciate from er_0 to er_1. With a fixed exchange rate, however, the U.S. monetary authorities would have to intervene once the dollar depreciated to the allowed upper limit of $\overline{er}$, and sell off foreign currencies (here British pounds). The official intervention would shift the supply curve of foreign exchange outward (at least by the distance FG, and in this example from S_{bp} to S''_{bp}).

$\$/bp$ = exchange rate (dollar price of British pound).
bp = quantity of British pounds.

value of the dollar nears $\overline{er}$, the upper limit, the monetary authorities must intervene. In this case the U.S. Federal Reserve could meet the market's excess demand for pounds by selling pounds (at least the amount indicated by the distance FG in Figure 18.3) on the foreign exchange market. The Fed's sale of pounds shifts the supply curve of pounds to the right, say, to S''_{bp}. Here the exchange rate is maintained at the upper limit. The sale of pounds by the Fed reduces the U.S. money supply, since the purchasers of the pounds write checks on their deposits in U.S. banks payable to the Fed. As in the case of an open market sale by the Fed, bank reserves fall as the Fed deducts the checks from the banks' accounts at the Fed. The fall in the U.S. money supply should tighten credit in the United States (i_{US} ↑) and modify the increases in real national income (Y_{US} ↓) and prices (P_{US} ↓). These internal adjustments would work toward eliminating the U.S. balance of payments deficit and reversing the depreciation of the dollar caused by the initial rise in real national income. (Recall, an increase in interest rates and decreases in the levels of prices and national income in the United States result in an increase in the supply of pounds (S_{bp} ↑) and a decrease in the demand for pounds (D_{bp} ↓).)

In contrast, under a flexible exchange rate system, the increase in the demand for pounds (with the rise in real national income in the United States) depreciates the dollar to er_1 in Figure 18.3. Ceteris paribus, the deterioration in the U.S. balance of trade and current account due to the induced increase in imports would be eventually offset by the boost to U.S. exports and import substitutes given by the weaker dollar. Balance of payments adjustment under a flexible exchange rate system is continuous and automatic and relies on changes in one price, the exchange rate. Balance of payments adjustment under a fixed exchange rate system not only may require official intervention in the foreign exchange market in the short term, but ultimately relies on changes in the aggregate price levels, interest rates, and real national incomes.

ADJUSTABLE PEG EXCHANGE RATES

Under an adjustable peg exchange rate system there are official exchange rates or par values; however, nations have the option of resetting, or repegging, the official exchange values of their currencies. A **devaluation** is when a nation officially lowers the international exchange value of its currency. A **revaluation** is when a nation officially increases the international exchange value of its currency.

The international monetary system known as *Bretton Woods,* which was established at the end of World War II and prevailed until the early 1970s, was an example of an adjustable peg exchange rate system.[7] In the Bretton Woods system a compromise between the rigid discipline imposed by fixed exchange rates and the potential volatility of flexible exchange rates was sought. The **International Monetary Fund (IMF)** was instituted to administer a code of conduct for exchange rate practices and to facilitate adjustment to balance of payments disequilibria. Since the United States emerged from World War II with the strongest economy, the U.S. dollar was set up as the key currency. In fact, the U.S. dollar was the only currency tied directly to gold—with one ounce of gold equivalent to $35. The U.S. Treasury officially stood ready to convert outstanding dollars to gold at this exchange rate. Other member nations of the IMF expressed their par values in terms of the dollar. From these dollar values, the schedule of exchange rates was derived. For example, if the par values for the British pound and the (then) West German deutsche mark were, respectively, 1 pound = $5.00 (or .2 pounds = $1.00) and 1 mark = $.40 (or 2.5 marks = $1.00), then the exchange rate between the pound and the mark would be 1 pound = (5.00)(2.5) = 12.5 marks (or 1 mark = .08 pounds).

Nations were supposed to maintain the dollar exchange values of their currencies within a narrow range of plus or minus 1 percent around par. Each member nation was assigned a *quota,* or subscription, by the IMF based on the size and openness of the nation's economy. One-quarter of the quota was to be paid in gold. The remainder of the quota was made up of the nation's own currency. The quotas provided a pool of international reserves held by the IMF from which nations experiencing balance of payments deficits and needing to intervene in the foreign exchange market could borrow. This additional source of international reserves enhanced the ability of a nation to support the par value of its currency while undertaking the economic reforms (such as deflation of the

---

[7] Bretton Woods, New Hampshire, was the setting for the 1944 international conference that created the International Monetary Fund. The International Bank for Reconstruction and Development (better known as the World Bank) was also established at this time to facilitate the postwar reconstruction of the industrialized nations and assist the economic development of the less developed nations.

FIGURE 18.4

Consequences of Increase in U.S. Aggregate Price Level on Deutsche Mark–U.S. Dollar Exchange Rate under Adjustable Exchange Rate

An increase in the aggregate price level in the United States, ceteris paribus, would reduce the foreign demand for U.S. dollars (from $D_\$$ to $D'_\$$) and increase the supply of dollars on the foreign exchange market (from $S_\$$ to $S'_\$$). The resulting deficit in the U.S. balance of payments account as the U.S. current account deteriorates would depreciate the dollar. The deutsche mark price of the dollar would fall from er_0 to er_1. Under an adjustable peg exchange rate, foreign monetary authorities, in this case, the German central bank, would have to intervene in the foreign exchange market and buy up enough dollars to maintain the exchange rate within the allowed band of fluctuation. (See the shift in the demand curve for dollars from $D'_\$$ to $D''_\$$.) Under the adjustable peg exchange rate system, another option for Germany would be to revalue the deutsche mark, establishing a new official exchange rate at er_1.

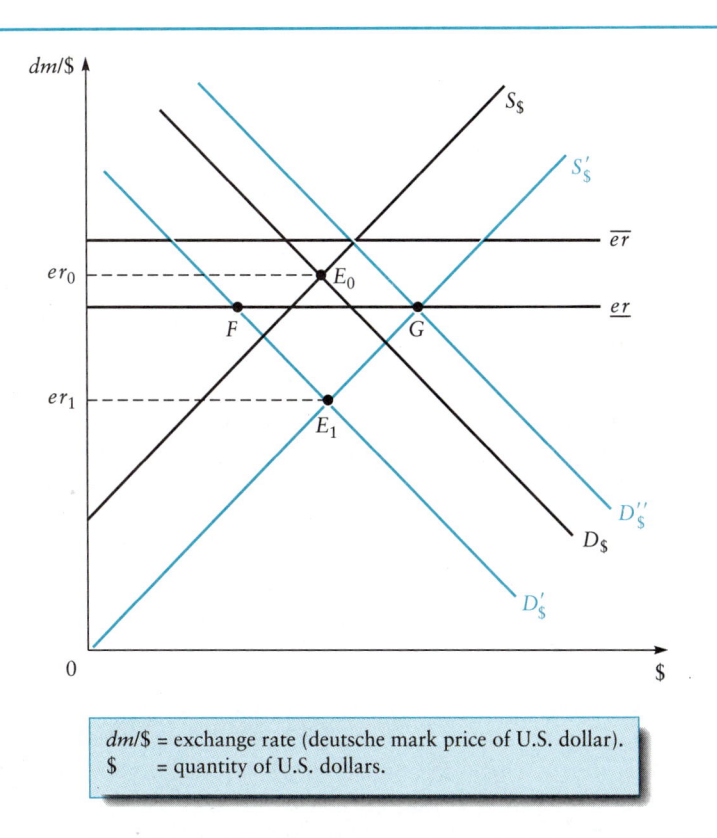

dm/\$ = exchange rate (deutsche mark price of U.S. dollar).
\$ = quantity of U.S. dollars.

domestic economy) necessary to restore equilibrium in the balance of payments.

In addition, in the case of a **fundamental disequilibrium,** or where the balance of payments disequilibrium appeared to be intractable given the par value of its currency, a nation, after consulting with the IMF, could change the official value of its currency. A persistent balance of payments deficit would call for a devaluation. A persistent surplus would call for a revaluation.

Consider the demand and supply of dollars to the West German economy depicted in Figure 18.4.[8] The supply of dollars to West Germany reflects the credit items on the West German balance of payments account (BPA). The demand for dollars by West Germany reflects the debit items on its BPA. The relevant exchange rate is the deutsche mark price of the dollar, that is, $dm/\$$. The BPA of West Germany is assumed to be initially in equilibrium at the par value er_0.

Suppose, due to an increase in the aggregate price level in the United States, the German current account improves. The demand for dollars falls ($D_\$$ shifts

---

[8] Note that we are using West Germany as an example here (instead of the United States) since under the Bretton Woods system all currencies were expressed in terms of the dollar. The dollar was used not only for foreign exchange intervention but as an international means of payment. National monetary authorities other than the Federal Reserve were responsible for maintaining the dollar par values. For historical accuracy, we use West Germany (instead of Germany), since the reunification of Germany did not occur until nearly two decades after the breakdown of the Bretton Woods system.

left) as imports from the United States are now relatively more expensive. The supply of dollars rises ($S_\$$ shifts right) as West German exports become more affordable. With the German balance of payments surplus, the deutsche mark appreciates. When the mark reaches the lower limit, shown by $\overline{er}$ in Figure 18.4, the West German monetary authorities must intervene and soak up the excess quantity supplied of dollars, shown by the distance *FG*.

That is, the balance of payments surplus for West Germany indicates an excess supply of dollars and an excess demand for deutsche marks. The West German monetary authorities, the central bank or Bundesbank, would need to buy up the excess supply of dollars, paying with checks drawn on the central bank. The demand for dollars would shift to the right by the amount of the Bundesbank's dollar purchases to keep the deutsche mark's value within the allowed range of fluctuation (the demand for dollars would have to increase from $D'_\$$ to $D''_\$$, or by the distance *FG*, in Figure 18.4). The intervention in the foreign exchange market by the Bundesbank would be recorded as a debit item on the official settlements account for West Germany—an increase in official reserve assets. Alternatively, the Bundesbank could use the dollars purchased to buy U.S. government securities (such as U.S. Treasury bills). If so, this would still be recorded as a debit entry in the official settlements account as an increase in official assets—but not in official reserve assets.

The checks written by the Bundesbank to pay for the dollars purchased would, when deposited in the German banking system, increase the German money supply. The increase in the money supply would put downward pressure on interest rates and stimulate aggregate demand and national income in West Germany. As the German economy expanded, inflationary pressures could build. Lower interest rates and higher real incomes and prices would work to eliminate the West German balance of payments surplus and shift the demand and supply curves for dollars back toward the initial positions.

The monetary authorities of West Germany, however, might resist the increase in the money supply that results from their official intervention to purchase dollars. If the German economy were near full employment, increases in the money supply could fuel unacceptable rates of inflation. The Bundesbank could neutralize the expansionary effect of the dollar purchases on the money supply with open market sales of bonds. (Recall from Chapter 14 that open market sales are a contractionary monetary policy.) While *sterilizing*, or offsetting, the foreign exchange intervention and leaving the overall money supply unchanged, the open market sales would also prevent the internal adjustments in interest rates, income, and prices in the German economy that work to correct the underlying balance of payments surplus.

Under the Bretton Woods system of the adjustable peg, another option existed. If the higher U.S. inflation were believed to be chronic and the resulting West German balance of payments surpluses believed to reflect a fundamental disequilibrium that could only be corrected with a realignment of the exchange rate, then the deutsche mark could be revalued. In Figure 18.4, the new par value could be set at er_1, with a new band of plus or minus 1 percent allowed. This revaluation of the deutsche mark would offset a generally lower West German inflation rate. Thus, the adjustable peg offered more flexibility than a fixed exchange rate system.

DEMISE OF BRETTON WOODS SYSTEM

Set up in the aftermath of World War II, the Bretton Woods system lasted until the early 1970s. During this period national outputs and international trade grew rapidly. The dollar was widely used as an international medium of exchange and was intended to serve as a store of value. Dollar balances held by foreign monetary authorities could be converted into gold when presented to the U.S. Treasury. The role of the United States in the international monetary system was to provide sufficient liquidity to accommodate the rising volume of trade. By running balance of payments deficits the United States could ensure that the supply of dollars in the foreign exchange market was adequate.

During the 1960s, however, the deficits in the U.S. balance of payments grew—in no small measure due to heavy foreign investment by Americans, especially in Europe. That is, for the United States, the capital account deficits more than offset the current account surpluses. Domestically the U.S. enjoyed a booming economy. Military expenditures required by the Vietnam War and an ambitious antipoverty program at home meant that U.S. fiscal policy was expansionary. For the most part, U.S. monetary policy was accommodating. The overheating of the American economy led to inflation and undermined the nation's competitive position in trade. International confidence in the dollar waned as the increasingly large balance of payments deficits of the United States produced a surplus of dollars on the foreign exchange market. Foreign central banks became reluctant to soak up the excess dollars. France, in particular, periodically presented the U.S. Treasury with surplus dollars for conversion into gold.

Nations with balance of payments surpluses, like West Germany and Japan, were reluctant to revalue their currencies, since to do so would hurt their export industries. The United States could not selectively devalue the dollar against these stronger currencies, since the dollar was the common standard for all the currencies. The United States did not want to devalue the dollar in terms of gold (which would have relieved the pressure on the U.S. official gold stocks), since this would have increased the purchasing power of gold. The major beneficiaries of a higher exchange value for gold would have been the major gold producers, the Soviet Union and South Africa—and the U.S. government was not inclined to favor either of these nations.

In August of 1971, when it had become apparent that the U.S. competitive position had seriously eroded and that the Treasury gold stocks were vastly insufficient to back the outstanding supply of dollars, President Nixon suspended the dollar's convertibility into gold. For all practical purposes this act signaled the end of the Bretton Woods period of adjustable exchange rates.

What followed has been a mixed system, or even a "non-system." A number of European nations have implemented the European Monetary System where, as in the Bretton Woods system, there are fixed but adjustable exchange rates for the members; however, there are no limits to the fluctuation of exchange rates against nonmember nation currencies. Many of the developing nations peg their currencies to the U.S. dollar, French franc, or to some other single currency or to a basket of currencies. Several of the major currencies, including the U.S. dollar and the Japanese yen, float on the foreign exchange market with discretionary intervention by the monetary authorities. In fact, under the current "system," nations have a choice in which type of exchange rate system to adopt.

MANAGED FLOAT

With a managed float, a nation essentially allows the exchange value of its currency to be determined by market forces, but reserves the option of intervening in the foreign exchange market to "manage," or influence, the range of fluctuation in the exchange rate. For example, to offset an unwelcome appreciation of the domestic currency, the monetary authorities could purchase foreign currencies and increase the supply of the domestic currency on the foreign exchange market.

The "rules of the game" are less clear under a system of managed floats. The International Monetary Fund has set forth guidelines for member nations with floating currencies. In the short term, for example, on a daily or weekly basis, nations are supposed to intervene to moderate sharp fluctuations in market exchange rates. Sudden swings in exchange rates often reflect a flurry of speculation set off by political and economic shocks. The foreign exchange market (and financial asset markets in general) reacts quickly to new information—some of which turns out to be unfounded rumor. In such instances of speculative frenzy, monetary authorities may intervene to calm the foreign exchange market. For example, the U.S. monetary authorities moved quickly to support the dollar when President Reagan was shot early in his first term.

In the longer term, for example, on a monthly or quarterly basis, under the IMF guidelines, nations are encouraged to "lean against the wind." That is, monetary authorities should offer some resistance to market trends. In any case, nations should not engage in aggressive manipulation of their currencies. In particular, they are enjoined against practicing **dirty floating,** where the monetary authorities sell their currencies when depreciating in order to gain an unfair competitive advantage in trade.

DEMAND-MANAGEMENT POLICY AND EXTERNAL BALANCE

Recall the three primary macroeconomic objectives of full employment, price stability, and economic growth. In the following discussion on the consequences of aggregate demand-management policies for the external balance, we will assume a managed float exchange rate system.

Expansionary monetary policy, that is, increases in the money supply due to the Federal Reserve's reducing the required reserve ratio or discount rate or engaging in open market purchases, is designed to stimulate aggregate demand through lowering the cost of credit. *Expansionary fiscal policy* enacted by the president and Congress also is designed to stimulate aggregate demand—either through increases in government expenditures or with tax cuts that raise disposable income or business profits and thus increase personal consumption or business investment expenditures.

While both types of expansionary policy tend to increase real national income and the aggregate price level—given the economy is operating in the intermediate region of the aggregate supply curve—the policies differ in their consequences for interest rates. Expansionary monetary policy directly drives down interest rates. In contrast, expansionary fiscal policy has the effect of driving up interest rates—due to the increased demand for money and the need for the Treasury to finance the resulting budget deficit. As a result, the impacts on the balance of payments and exchange rates differ.

By stimulating aggregate demand and putting upward pressure on real national income and the aggregate price level, expansionary demand-management policies initially tend to worsen the current account balance. With higher incomes, expenditures on imported goods and services rise. Higher prices reduce the international competitiveness of a nation's goods and services. The difference comes with the impact on the capital account. Expansionary monetary policy, ceteris paribus, results in a deterioration of the capital account as lower interest rates induce a net outflow of financial capital. Hence, easier monetary policy unambiguously shifts a nation's balance of payments toward a deficit, which depreciates a nation's currency. Expansionary fiscal policy, ceteris paribus, indirectly improves the capital account balance. The higher interest rates attract both foreign and domestic investors. Whether the overall balance of payments improves or not with expansionary fiscal policy depends on the relative shifts in the current and capital account balances.

On the other hand, *contractionary monetary policy* strengthens both the current and capital account balances. *Contractionary fiscal policy* improves the current account but may weaken the capital account, so, a priori, the net effect on the balance of payments is indeterminate.

It is important to consider the repercussions for the balance of payments and exchange rate of policies intended to achieve internal objectives such as lowering the inflation rate or increasing employment. In general, asset markets tend to clear faster than goods and services markets. Given the far greater volume of asset transactions, movements in exchange rates in the short run primarily reflect changes in the capital account balance. With a lag, movements in exchange rates affect the balance of trade (and current account balance), thus the rate of production and level of employment in the nation's export and import competitive industries.

It is also important to realize that increases in the international mobility of financial capital tend to reduce interest rate differentials across nations. For example, if a nation adopts a tighter monetary policy (such as open market sales of government bonds), the subsequent rise in domestic interest rates will be moderated to the extent there are induced inflows of international capital (foreign savings attracted by the lower bond prices). Thus, the degree of international capital mobility will be a factor in assessing the effectiveness of demand-management monetary and fiscal policies.

EXCHANGE VALUE OF DOLLAR AFTER BRETTON WOODS

Since the breakdown of the Bretton Woods system of adjustable exchange rates, the U.S. dollar has floated on the foreign exchange market. The degree of management of the dollar through official intervention in the foreign exchange market has varied with political administrations and economic conditions. While the average exchange values of the dollar in 1975 and 1989 were virtually the same, exchange rates in the post–Bretton Woods era have been far from stable.

The decade of the 1970s was characterized by sharply higher prices for petroleum, which brought stagflation to the economies of oil-importing nations. The first supply-side shock in late 1973, when the world price of petroleum quadrupled, resulted in huge current account surpluses with massive transfers in wealth to the oil-exporting nations. The major industrialized nations adopted expansionary economic policies to deal with the international recession of 1974–1975. The United States, in particular, assumed the role of the "engine of growth" and led the global economic recovery. As illustrated in Figure 18.5, the dollar depreciated over the latter half of the 1970s with the strong rebound of the U.S. economy.

There was another bout of cost-push inflation with the second surge of oil prices in 1979, prompted by the fall of the shah of Iran and panic-buying in the world oil market. This time, however, the major industrialized nations elected to deal with the inflation. Paul Volcker had been appointed as chairman of the Federal Reserve by President Jimmy Carter in 1979. Volcker, determined to arrest the spiraling U.S. inflation, shifted to contractionary monetary policy. The election of Ronald Reagan brought a fiscal mix of supply-side-motivated tax cuts and national security–motivated growth in defense spending. The combination of higher energy prices, tight monetary policy, and expansionary fiscal policy produced sharply higher real interest rates. (The real interest rate on three-year U.S. Treasury Securities increased from −1.7 percent in 1980 to 6.3 percent in 1982. See Table 18.1.) Interest-sensitive industries such as construction, capital goods, and consumer durables were hurt. In the summer of 1981 the U.S. economy went into a deep recession, which lasted through nearly all of 1982.

The U.S. unemployment rates rose during the recession while real national income fell. The federal government budget deficits grew with the declines in net tax revenues. The financing of the deficits by the sale of U.S. Treasury securities boosted the demand for credit. The conservative monetary stance prevented the Federal Reserve from monetizing the debt. Consequently, real interest rates in the United States remained high. The high yields on U.S. assets attracted foreign savings and increased the demand for dollars. From 1980 through 1985 the U.S. dollar appreciated by more than 50 percent. The strong dollar had mixed consequences for the U.S. economy. The increased purchasing power of the dollar, together with the decline in world petroleum prices and the downward pressure on real wages from the depressed labor market conditions, lowered the inflation rate. The competitive position of U.S. industry, however, was undermined by the appreciation of the dollar. The U.S. current account balance moved from a small surplus in 1981 to increasingly large deficits.

The United States did not try to halt the appreciation of the dollar during the first Reagan administration. By 1985, however, the strength of the dollar and the string of current account deficits had convinced the United States that a change in policy was needed. In late 1985 the United States, Great Britain, France, West Germany, and Japan agreed to coordinated intervention in the

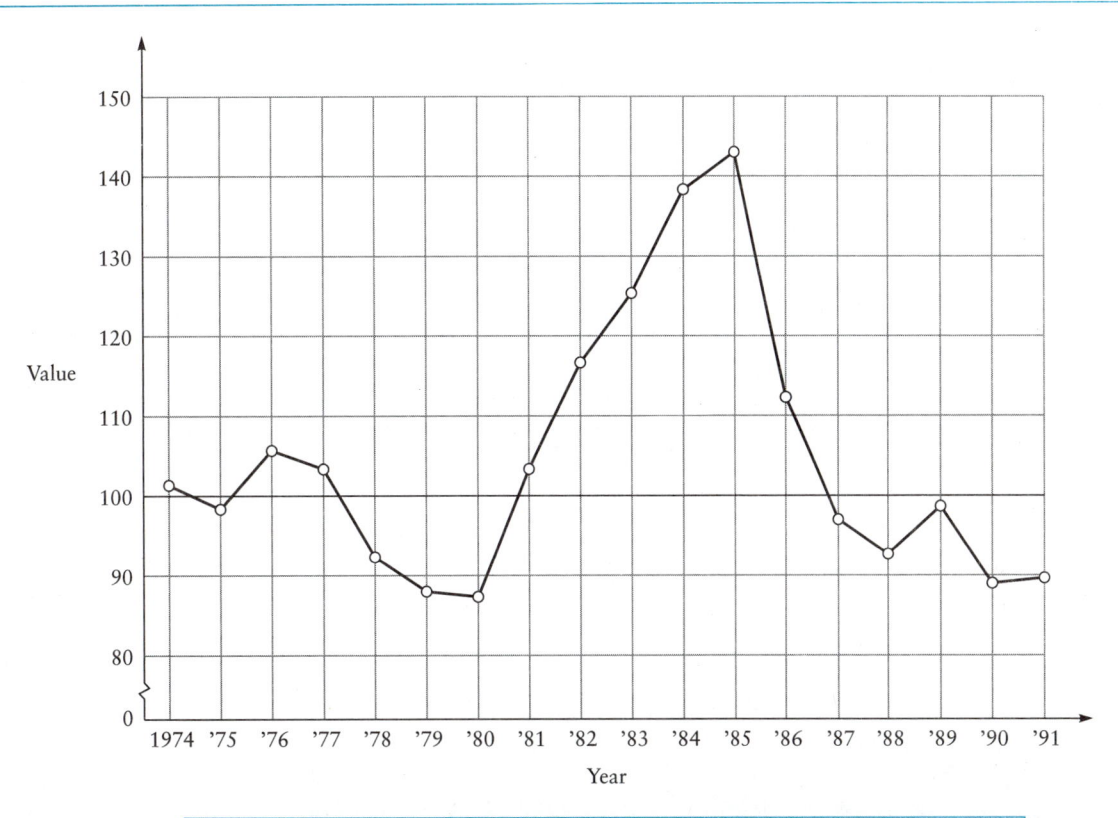

Annual Average–Multilateral Trade Weighted Value of the U.S. Dollar (March 1973 = 100)

Year	Value	Year	Value	Year	Value
1974	101.4	1980	87.4	1986	112.2
1975	98.5	1981	103.4	1987	96.9
1976	105.7	1982	116.6	1988	92.7
1977	103.4	1983	125.3	1989	98.6
1978	92.4	1985	138.2	1990	89.1
1979	88.1	1985	143.0	1991	89.8

Note: The exchange rates of the dollar are weighted averages of exchange rates where the weights are based on international trade with the United States. The reference period is March 1973, where the exchange value of the dollar is set to be 100.

FIGURE 18.5

EXCHANGE VALUE OF U.S. DOLLAR: 1974–1991

SOURCE: *Economic Report of the President 1992*, Table B-107.

---

foreign exchange market to drive down the dollar. The Federal Reserve adopted a more expansionary monetary policy, and real interest rates in the U.S. declined. From 1985 through 1988 the dollar depreciated sharply. The dollar rebounded slightly in 1989, dropped again in 1990, briefly stabilized in 1991, and then sunk to record low levels during 1992.

The roller-coaster ride of the dollar over the decade is illustrated in Figure 18.5. In Table 18.1 we list the real exchange values of the U.S. dollar for the period of 1980 to 1990. Although adjusting the nominal trade-weighted value of the dollar for relative price levels in the United States and abroad gives a better

TABLE 18.1
Real Interest Rates, Exchange Rates, Government Budget Balances, and Current Account Balances for United States: 1980–1990

YEAR	THREE-YEAR U.S. TREASURY SECURITIES YIELD	PERCENT CHANGE IN CONSUMER PRICE INDEX	REAL INTEREST RATE	REAL MULTILATERAL TRADE-WEIGHTED EXCHANGE VALUE OF U.S. DOLLAR
1980	11.6%	13.5%	−1.7%	84.9
1981	14.4	10.3	3.7	100.9
1982	12.9	6.2	6.3	111.8
1983	10.5	3.2	7.1	117.3
1984	11.9	4.3	7.3	128.8
1985	9.6	3.6	5.8	132.4
1986	7.1	1.9	5.1	103.6
1987	7.7	3.6	4.0	90.9
1988	8.3	4.1	4.0	88.2
1989	8.6	4.8	3.6	94.4
1990	8.3	5.4	2.8	86.0

YEAR	GOVERNMENT BUDGET BALANCE (BILLIONS OF DOLLARS) All Levels	Federal	CURRENT ACCOUNT BALANCE (BILLIONS OF DOLLARS)
1980	−35	−60	+12
1981	−30	−59	+10
1982	−109	−136	−2
1983	−140	−180	−35
1984	−109	−167	−94
1985	−125	−181	−118
1986	−147	−201	−141
1987	−112	−152	−155
1988	−98	−137	−118
1989	−83	−124	−96
1990	−140	−165	−83

Notes: The formula used to calculate the Real Interest Rate is:

$$\text{Real Interest Rate} = \frac{1 + \text{Treasury Yield}}{1 + \text{Inflation Rate}} - 1$$

The real exchange values of the dollar are weighted averages of exchange rates, where the weights are based on international trade with the United States. The reference period is March 1973, where the real exchange value of the dollar is set equal to 100. The nominal weighted average exchange rates are adjusted for relative inflation rates for the United States and its trading partners.

SOURCE: *Economic Report of the President 1992,* Tables B-26, B-59, B-69, B-107.

indication of the international price competitiveness of U.S. goods and services, the trends in the exchange value of dollar are little affected.[9]

Despite the depreciation of the dollar over the second half of the 1980s, large deficits in the U.S. current account remained. In fact, reflecting the delayed response of the trade balance to exchange rates, the deficits in the current

---

[9] A drop in the U.S. aggregate price level, relative to the price levels in foreign trading partners, reduces the real exchange value of the dollar for any given nominal exchange rate—thus increasing the international competitiveness of U.S. goods and services.

account increased from 1985 to 1987 as the dollar fell sharply. The persistence of the current account deficits should not be surprising—given the government budget deficits. Recall the discussion from Chapter 13 on the basic macroeconomic identity and the government budget balance. Rearranging the basic macroeconomic identity to solve for the government budget balance (or net public saving) gives

$$(T - G) = (I - S) + (X - M - R - F)$$

Government Budget = Private Domestic + Current Account Balance
    Balance   Investment-Saving   (on the Balance of Payments)
   (all levels)   Balance

As long as the government budget deficits ($T - G < 0$) are not covered by net private domestic saving ($I - S < 0$), then foreign saving will have to make up the difference—and the current account will be in deficit.

As detailed in Table 18.1, the U.S. federal government budget deficits over the 1980s overwhelmed the cumulative state and local government budget surpluses. The sum of the U.S. federal government budget deficits from 1980 through 1990 equaled $1.56 trillion, or more than three times the sum of the total surpluses for the state and local governments of $.43 trillion. Over 70 percent of the total government budget deficit of $1.13 trillion for the period was covered by borrowing from the rest of the world, that is, the deficits on the U.S. current account. From 1980 through 1990, net foreign investment in the United States increased by a total of $.82 trillion; and the United States went from a position as the leading creditor nation of the world to become the leading debtor nation.[10]

Viewed in a more favorable light, the inflow of foreign saving did enable the U.S. economy to sustain higher rates of gross domestic investment over the decade than otherwise would have been possible. The United States used the foreign saving, however, not so much for investment in plant and equipment and for the nation's economic infrastructure (such as the transportation and communication networks) as for consumption. We have made frequent reference in this and other chapters to the net public dissaving manifested by the large federal budget deficits over the decade. It is also true that the share of personal consumption expenditures in Gross Domestic Product increased in the 1980s. The share of Gross Domestic Product accounted for by personal consumption expenditures for the United States over the 1980s was 66.1 percent, compared to 63.9 percent for the 1970s and 63.3 percent for the 1960s.[11]

---

[10] Whether a nation is a net creditor or net debtor with respect to the rest of the world depends on its **net international investment position.** If the value of the nation's foreign assets exceeds the value of the nation's assets held by foreigners, then the nation is a **net creditor.** While it is difficult to assess accurately the value of assets at any point in time (e.g., whether an asset should be valued at the current market value or historical purchase price), there is a general consensus that with the string of current account deficits beginning in 1982, the United States became the nation with the greatest net foreign debt by the end of the decade. With direct foreign investment measured at market value, the net international investment position of the United States went from an estimated +$259 billion at the end of 1982 to an estimated -$361 billion by the end of 1990. (See *Economic Report of the President 1992* (Washington, DC: U.S. Government Printing Office, 1992), Table B-99.)

[11] Calculated from *Economic Report of the President 1992* (Washington, DC: U.S. Government Printing Office, 1992), Table B-1.

Just as there is a built-in momentum from the accumulating interest on the national debt for future federal government budget deficits, so, too, does the rising foreign or external debt perpetuate current account deficits on the nation's balance of payments account. Recall from Chapter 17 that payment of interest on external debt is recorded as a debit item on the current account balance. The way to reduce foreign indebtedness is to generate current account surpluses. The implication for the United States is this: If the 1980s were characterized by the nation "spending beyond its means," then the 1990s may need to be the decade of thrift, with domestic production exceeding domestic expenditures.

Notwithstanding the seemingly intractable federal budget deficits, the United States is making progress in shrinking the current account deficits. In fact, for 1991 the deficit in the U.S. current account is estimated to fall to less than $10 billion. Although roughly half of this improvement is due to the special receipt of some $40 billion in unilateral transfers (cash contributions by foreign governments to the United States for waging the Persian Gulf War with Iraq), the United States did sharply reduce its merchandise trade deficit in 1991. Slower economic growth and lower inflation in the United States than abroad and the weakness of the dollar contributed to the improved trade balance.[12]

CONCLUDING NOTE

Would the United States have been able to run these large federal budget deficits of the past decade if a fixed exchange rate system had been in effect? On the other hand, did the flexibility in exchange rates absorb some of the economic turbulence caused by the supply-side shocks of the 1970s? These are the types of questions that debate over the relative merits of fixed versus flexible exchange rates must address. Since it is not possible to "replay" history under different exchange rate systems, definitive answers are impossible.

The wide swings in the exchange value of the dollar are seen by the proponents of fixed exchange rates as an indictment of flexible exchange rates. The sharp appreciation of the dollar from 1980 to 1985, largely the result of the loose fiscal–tight monetary policy mix of the United States, undermined the nation's international competitiveness. Many of the U.S. export- and import-sensitive sectors still have not completely recovered—even though the exchange value of the dollar has since fallen to levels prevailing at the beginning of the decade. Moreover, as we will discuss in the next chapter, the high real interest rates and strong dollar during the first half of the 1980s added to the debt burden of the less developed nations of the world.

Volatility in exchange rates is viewed by proponents of flexible exchange rates as a symptom, not a cause, of economic instability. Allowing exchange rates to move

---

[12] For a detailed, early account of the U.S. balance of payments for 1991, see Kathryn A. Morisse, "U.S. International Transactions in 1991," *Federal Reserve Bulletin* 78 (May 1992): 313–325. In 1992, however, there were signs that the U.S. current account deficit was again widening.

freely in response to market disequilibria provides another source of economic adjustment. Furthermore, flexible exchange rate advocates question whether any nation today would abide by the monetary discipline imposed by a fixed exchange rate system.

So the debate continues. The adjustable peg exchange rate system of Bretton Woods, which was intended to be a compromise between fixed and flexible exchange rates, broke down in the early 1970s, only to be replaced by a mix of exchange rate practices. In the fall of 1992, in the midst of economic stagnation in western Europe, the European Monetary System showed signs of breaking apart over the comparatively tight monetary policy of Germany. The increased technological sophistication of financial markets and the growing interdependencies of national economies may well dictate the evolution of a new international monetary system. The "rules of the game" for such a new international monetary order are open to speculation.

KEY TERMS

internal balance
external balance
flexible exchange rate
fixed exchange rate
adjustable peg
managed float
forward contracts
gold standard
par values
devaluation
revaluation
fundamental disequilibrium
dirty floating
net international investment position
net creditor

QUESTIONS

1. What are the three most important ideas in this chapter? Discuss why each is important.
2. Let the British pound (*bp*) represent foreign currencies in general. Suppose that the demand and supply schedules for British pounds in the foreign exchange market are

$$Q_{bp}^d = 60 - 20P_{bp}$$

and

$$Q_{bp}^s = -20 + 20P_{bp}$$

where Q_{bp}^d and Q_{bp}^s are the quantities of British pounds demanded and supplied (in billions of pounds per day) in the foreign exchange market, and P_{bp} is the dollar price of a British pound.
   a. Find the market equilibrium exchange rate.
   b. Suppose that comparatively high inflation in the United States shifted the demand and supply curves of British pounds in the foreign exchange market to

$$Q_{bp}^{d'} = 65 - 20P_{bp}$$

and

$$Q^{s'}_{bp} = -25 + 20P_{bp}$$

Find the new market equilibrium exchange rate—assuming a perfectly flexible exchange rate system.

c. Suppose instead that a fixed exchange rate system was in operation, with the official dollar-pound exchange rate ($/*bp*) of $2 = 1 British pound, and with the allowed band of fluctuation of plus or minus 5 percent around this official exchange rate. Explain the obligations of the monetary authorities given the changes in the demand and supply of pounds created by the higher U.S. inflation. Specifically, at what point (or exchange value of the dollar) would the monetary authorities have to intervene in the foreign exchange market and how many British pounds would they have to buy or sell?

d. Discuss the internal macroeconomic adjustments required by the United States under a fixed exchange rate system when there is a relative increase in the U.S. inflation rate.

e. Discuss the additional flexibility provided by an adjustable exchange rate in the case of a relative increase in the U.S. inflation rate.

3. Consider two alternative investments: (a) a $10,000 U.S. Government security with a one-year maturity and paying 8 percent interest, and (b) a 5,000 British pound U.K. government security with a one-year maturity and paying 7 percent interest. Suppose that the current exchange rate is $2 = 1 British pound, and that the exchange rate you expect to prevail in one year when the government securities mature is $2.05 = 1.00 British pound. Assuming that your expectation of the future exchange rate is correct, i.e., in one year the dollar price of a British pound is $2.05, then which security would have the highest return? Why? Which security would you purchase? Why?

4. Discuss the adjustments in the equilibrium level of real national income, the aggregate price level, the interest rate, and the exchange rate for a nation with a balance of payments surplus (i.e., an excess of credits over debits on the current and capital accounts) under
   a. a flexible exchange rate system.
   b. a fixed exchange rate system.

5. Suppose that in addition to having a balance of payments surplus, the nation is operating at full employment. Discuss the policy options under a fixed exchange rate system for dealing with the surplus in the balance of payments and the effects on (and possible conflicts with) the nation's internal balance. How would your analysis differ if the nation were operating with a flexible exchange rate?

6. Compare and contrast an adjustable exchange rate with a managed float. What do you think would have been the difference for the U.S. economy over the 1980s if the United States had been operating with an adjustable exchange rate rather than a managed float?

CHAPTER

19

ECONOMIC GROWTH AND DEVELOPMENT

Reducing poverty is the fundamental objective of economic development.[1]

Despite the vast opportunities created by the technological revolutions of the twentieth century, more than 1 billion people, one-fifth of the world's population, live on less than one dollar a day—a standard of living that Western Europe and the United States attained two hundred years ago.[2]

Poverty exists in all nations. Some nations, however, whether due to historical circumstances, unfavorable climates, deficiencies in natural resources, or misguided economic policies, are much poorer than others. The World Bank offers the following account of a poor subsistence-farmer's household in Ghana, a small nation on the East coast of Africa.

> In Ghana's Savannah region a typical family of seven lives in three one-room huts made from mud bricks, with earthen floors. They have little furniture and no toilet, electricity, or running water. Water is obtained from a stream a fifteen-minute walk away. The family has few possessions, apart from three acres of unirrigated land and one cow, and virtually no savings.
>
> The family raises sorghum, vegetables, and groundnuts on its land. The work is seasonal and physically demanding. At peak periods of tilling, sowing, and harvesting, all family members are involved, including the husband's parents, who are sixty and seventy years old. The soil is very low in quality, but the family lacks access to fertilizer and other modern inputs. Moreover, the region is susceptible

---

[1] World Bank, *World Development Report 1990* (New York: Oxford University Press, 1990), 24.
[2] World Bank, *World Development Report 1991* (New York: Oxford University Press, 1991), 1.

to drought; the rains fail two years out of every five. In addition to her farm work, the wife has to fetch water, collect firewood, and feed the family. The market town where the husband sells their meager cash crops and buys essentials is five miles away and is reached by dirt tracks and an unsealed road that is washed away every time the rains come.

None of the older family members ever attended school, but the eight-year-old son is now in the first grade. The family hopes that he will be able to stay in school, although there is pressure to keep him at home to help with the farm in the busy periods. He and his two younger sisters have never had any vaccinations and have never seen a doctor.[3]

In this chapter we are concerned with the growth and development of "underdeveloped" economies. In the 1950s and 1960s economists stressed capital accumulation and economic growth as the key to economic progress. In the 1970s the emphasis shifted to economic development and to meeting the basic needs of the population. We discuss the role of international trade in economic development—contrasting the import substitution and export expansion strategies. We examine the debt crises of the developing nations in the 1980s, and the shift back in orientation to economic growth and market incentives. We also present the very different perspective on the underdeveloped economies offered by the radical critique. We begin the chapter with an economic classification of countries and an overview of the characteristics of the less developed nations.

COUNTRY CLASSIFICATION

While recognizing that each nation is uniquely defined by the particular mix of geographical, historical, cultural, political, as well as, economic factors, observers, nonetheless, have found it useful to group nations by economic achievement. The basic division is between the **developed countries (DCs)** and the **less developed countries (LDCs)**. The former include the United States, Canada, Australia, New Zealand, Japan, and the nations of western Europe. The LDCs encompass virtually all of Latin America, Asia, and Africa. Because the DCs are primarily in the northern hemisphere, while most of the LDCs are in the Southern hemisphere, the labels "North" and "South" are often used. The DCs have diversified, industrialized economies, high per capita incomes, and low rates of population growth. In general, the LDCs have more agrarian-based economies, low per capita incomes, and high rates of population growth.

This split between the developed and less developed nations, however, is too crude to capture the gradations of economic progress. The World Bank further classifies countries on the basis of per capita Gross National Products: low-income economies (per capita GNPs in 1990 of under $610), lower-middle-income economies (per capita 1990 GNPs between $610 and $2465), upper-middle-income economies (per capita 1990 GNPs greater than $2465 but less than $7620), and high-income economies (per capita GNPs in 1990 greater than $7620). In Table 19.1 we present some summary statistics for these nation

---

[3] World Bank, *World Development Report 1990* (New York: Oxford University Press, 1990), 24.

TABLE 19.1
Selected Statistics on Economic Growth and Development

	LOW-INCOME ECONOMIES			MIDDLE-INCOME ECONOMIES		HIGH-INCOME ECONOMIES (OECD)[a]
	China	India	Other	Lower	Upper	
Population 1990 (millions)	1,134	850	1,075	629	485	777
Population growth (average annual)						
1965–1980	2.2%	2.3%	2.5%	2.4%	2.2%	.8%
1980–1990	1.4%	2.1%	2.6%	2.2%	1.7%	.6%
GNP per capita 1990	$370	$350	$320	$1,530	$3,410	$20,170
GNP per capita growth (average annual)						
1965–1990	5.8%	1.9%	1.7%	1.5%	2.8%	2.4%
Infant mortality rate (1990)[b]	29	92	92	51	45	8
Percent of Females in Secondary School 1989[c]	38%	31%	23%	56%	57%	96%
Percent of Population Urban 1990	56%	27%	27%	52%	71%	77%

NOTES: These statistics are based on weighted averages for the over 100 countries in the designated groups with reported data and with at least one million population by 1990. The weights are population shares.

[a] Here OECD (Organization for Economic Cooperation and Development) includes only Australia, Austria, Belgium, Canada, Denmark, Finland, France, Federal Republic of Germany, Ireland, Italy, Japan, Netherlands, New Zealand, Norway, Spain, Sweden, Switzerland, United Kingdom, and United States.

Greece, Portugal, and Turkey are OECD members but are included with the middle income economies. Other high-income economies, but nonmembers of OECD are Israel, Singapore, Hong Kong, Kuwait, and the United Arab Emirates.

Nonreporting nonmbers of the World Bank, at the time the statistics were tabulated, are Cuba, Democratic People's Republic of Korea, and the former Union of Soviet Socialist Republics.

[b] The infant mortality rate is the number of infants who die before reaching one year of age per thousand live births in a given year.

[c] The secondary school enrollment rate for females is the ratio of females enrolled in secondary school to the female population of secondary school age (generally 12 to 17 years).

SOURCE: Adapted from *World Development Report 1992*. Copyright © 1992 by The International Bank for Reconstruction and Development/The World Bank. Reprinted by permission of Oxford University Press, Inc.

groups. In Table 19.2 we present the same summary statistics for the LDCs grouped by region.

Because of their size, China and India, with respectively one-fifth and one-sixth of the world's population, are usually separated from the other low-income LDCs, which are sometimes referred to as the *Fourth World* and include most of sub-Saharan Africa and the large South Asian nations of Bangladesh, Pakistan, and Indonesia. With some notable exceptions (such as China and Sri Lanka), the low-income nations are characterized by rapid

TABLE 19.2
SELECTED STATISTICS ON ECONOMIC GROWTH AND DEVELOPMENT:
LESS DEVELOPED COUNTRIES BY REGION

	SUB-SAHARAN AFRICA[a]	EAST ASIA, PACIFIC[b]	SOUTH ASIA[c]	MIDDLE EAST, N. AFRICA[d]	EUROPE[e]	LATIN AMERICA, CARIBBEAN[f]
Population 1990 (millions)	495	1,577	1,148	256	200	433
Population growth (average annual)						
1965–1980	2.7%	2.2%	2.4%	2.8%	1.1%	2.5%
1980–1990	3.1%	1.6%	2.2%	3.1%	0.1%	2.1%
GNP per capita 1990	$340	$600	$330	$1,790	$2,400	$2,180
GNP per capita growth (average annual) 1965–1990	.2%	5.3%	1.9%	1.8%	…	1.8%
Infant mortality rate 1990	107	34	93	79	30	48
Percent of Females in Secondary School 1989	14%	42%	27%	45%	70%	55%
Percent of Population Urban 1990	29%	50%	26%	51%	60%	71%

NOTES: These statistics are based on weighted averages for the countries with 1990 populations of at least one million in the designated regions. The weights are population shares.
[a]Sub-Saharan Africa comprises all countries south of the Sahara except South Africa.
[b]East Asia and Pacific comprise all the low-income and middle-income economies of East and Southeast Asia and the Pacific, east of and including China and Thailand.
[c]South Asia comprises Bangladesh, Bhutan, India, Maldives, Myanmar, Nepal, Pakistan, and Sri Lanka.
[d]Middle East and North Africa comprise the low- and middle-income economies of Afghanistan, Algeria, Egypt, Iran, Iraq, Jordan, Lebanon, Libya, Morocco, Oman, Saudi Arabia, Syrian Arab Republic, Tunisia, and Republic of Yemen.
[e]Europe comprises the middle-income European countries of Albania, Bulgaria, Czechoslovakia, Greece, Hungary, Poland, Portugal, Romania, Turkey, and Yugoslavia.
[f]Latin America and Caribbean comprise all American and Caribbean economies south of the United States.
SOURCE: Adapted from *World Development Report 1992*. Copyright © 1992 by The International Bank for Reconstruction and Development/The World Bank. Reprinted by permission of Oxford University Press, Inc.

population growth, modest economic growth, and limited investment in human capital.[4]

---

[4] Another popular classification of nations has been in terms of "worlds." The developing nations (low- and middle-income economies) are the **Third World**; the market-oriented, high-income nations, the **First World**; and the non-market-oriented, socialist nations, the **Second World**. The label **Fourth World** was added to designate the poorest group of nations in the Third World. The events of the last few years, in particular the economic liberalization of the previously non-market-oriented economies of the (former) Soviet Union and Eastern European nations, have blurred the distinctions between the First, Second, and Third Worlds.

Lower-middle-income economies (including several North African nations and most of the Latin American countries) are generally more developed than the low-income economies—as indicated by lower infant mortality rates, higher female secondary school enrollment rates, and greater percentages of the populations in urban areas. The upper-middle-income economies are the most diverse lot, and include, among other nations, South Africa, Hungary, Mexico, the Republic of Korea (South Korea), and Libya. A few of these nations—in particular, the Republic of Korea, Portugal, and Greece—are closing in on the ranks of the high-income economies.

As the World Bank notes, classification by income does not necessarily reflect development status. As we discussed in Chapter 8 on national income accounting, per capita Gross National Product is not always an accurate indicator of the average standard of living within a nation. Recall the problems in using per capita GNP to measure comparative welfare across nations: differences in the distribution of income and the composition of output, omissions and errors in recording economic activity, and the potential for distortion when converting into a common base (such as U.S. dollars) with official exchange rates. Moreover, as we suggested then, there are noneconomic dimensions to the quality of life.

To illustrate, consider the examples of Sri Lanka and Mexico. In 1990 Mexico's per capita GNP ($2490) was more than five times that of Sri Lanka's ($470), yet the infant mortality rate, a more sensitive indicator of the average standard of living, for Sri Lanka (19) was half that for Mexico (39).[5]

Part of the reason may be a history of a more egalitarian distribution of income in Sri Lanka. In Figure 19.1 points for Mexico (for 1977) and Sri Lanka (for 1969–1970 and 1980–1981) are plotted on a **Lorenz curve,** which is a graph that relates the cumulative percentage share of household income to the percentage of households. If the distribution of income is perfectly equal—that is, the bottom 20 percent of the households receive 20 percent of the household income, etc.—then the Lorenz curve would be a 45 degree line from the origin. The more bowed the Lorenz curve is, the less equal the distribution of household income. Data on the distribution of income are not only scarce (these periods for the two countries were the most comparable available) but suspect (the percentage shares should be regarded as rough approximations). Nevertheless, the greater income inequality in Mexico is apparent with a comparison of the Lorenz curves.

Mexico achieved rapid economic growth in the postwar decades of the 1950s, 1960s, and 1970s; however, the benefits of this growth were not widely shared. Sri Lanka adopted a different strategy of development, one emphasizing the basic needs of the population. Thus, while sacrificing some economic growth, Sri Lanka attained relatively high levels of human capital formation in nutrition, health, and education. (Note: To the extent the government provides directly for the basic needs of the population—such as free health care or food subsidies—data on the distribution of household income may understate the economic equity present within the nation.) So, in which nation is the average standard of living higher?

We do not intend to explore this issue in depth here, although, we will add two observations. First, Sri Lanka, with a change to a more conservative

---

[5] *World Development Report 1992,* Tables 1 and 28.

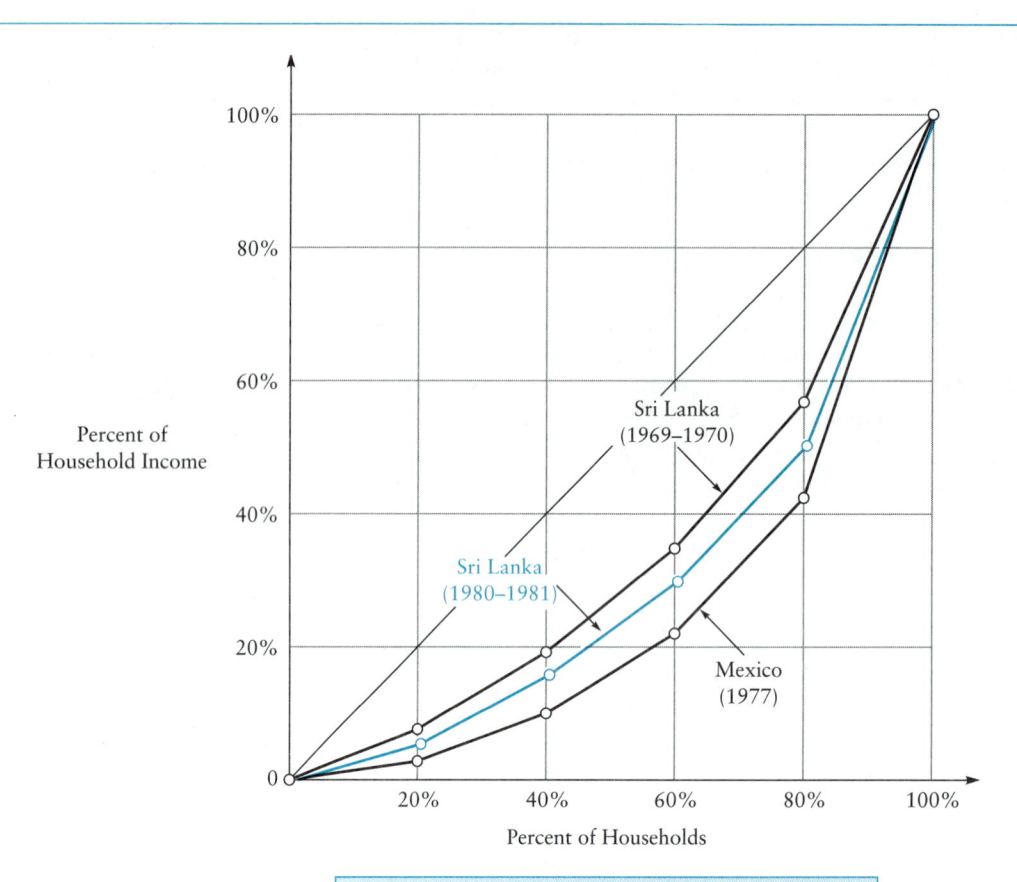

Percent of Households	Percent of Household Income		
	Sri Lanka 1969–1970	Sri Lanka 1980–1981	Mexico 1977
Lowest 20%	7.5%	5.8%	2.9%
2nd Quintile	11.7	10.1	7.0
3rd Quintile	15.7	14.1	12.0
4th Quintile	21.7	20.3	20.4
Highest 20%	43.4	49.8	57.7

FIGURE 19.1

LORENZ CURVES FOR SRI LANKA AND MEXICO

The Lorenz curve illustrates the distribution of income within a nation or society (here the shares of household income). The more the Lorenz curve deviates from the 45 degree line of perfect equality, the more unequal is the distribution of income (e.g., Mexico in 1977 compared to Sri Lanka in 1980–1981 or Sri Lanka in 1969–1970).

SOURCE: *World Development Report 1986*, Table 24; *World Development Report 1989*, Table 30.

government in 1977, shifted from its basic-needs orientation in favor of policies to stimulate economic growth. While Sri Lanka's economic growth rate increased, the distribution of income in the country became less equal. (Compare the two Lorenz curves for Sri Lanka.) The deterioration in the distribution of household income does not necessarily mean that the absolute incomes of the bottom 20 percent of the population declined, though. Economic growth may increase the real incomes of the poorest even as their relative incomes fall. Mexico, flush with oil revenues in the late 1970s, spent the decade of the 1980s coping with a severe external debt crisis. Per capita income fell over the 1980s in Mexico, while rising in Sri Lanka.

Second, noneconomic dimensions of the quality of life are important. For example, in the post–World War II era Mexico has maintained a remarkable degree of political stability—albeit through the dominance of one party. Sri Lanka, in the last two decades, has been torn by ethnic conflict and civil unrest.

This example of Sri Lanka and Mexico suggests that simply comparing per capita GNPs to draw inferences on relative standards of living may be misleading. Moreover, this example suggests that economic growth and economic development are not synonymous.

GROWTH AND DEVELOPMENT

Economic growth refers to quantitative change and is fairly straightforward; it is defined as a sustained increase in per capita output and income. Rightward shifts in the aggregate supply curve, due to increases in the available factors of production and technological change, make economic growth possible. Over the past quarter-century, economic growth rates have varied widely across the LDCs. For example, for the period of 1965 through 1990, the average annual growth rate in real GNP per capita was estimated to be −3.3 percent for Nicaragua, a Central American nation plagued by civil war and political turmoil. Over the same period, the estimated average annual growth rate in real GNP per capita was 7.1 percent for the Republic of Korea, an East Asian NIC (newly industrializing country) aggressively pursuing an export-oriented growth strategy.[6]

Economic development is harder to define and measure; it has a qualitative dimension and involves fundamental structural change—in particular, the transformation of a traditional, agrarian-based economy to a modern, diversified economy. Economic development yields a general and pervasive improvement in the standard of living. Indicators of economic development include reductions in the infant mortality rate, increases in the adult literacy rate, and a rising share of the labor force in industry and modern services.

Economic growth can enhance economic development but, by itself, does not guarantee economic development. Whether growth translates into development depends partly on the social institutions in place and the public policies followed.

GROWTH MODEL APPROACH

The International Bank for Reconstruction and Development, the International Monetary Fund, and the General Agreement on Tariffs and Trade are three international institutions formed in the 1940s to foster economic growth and development, balance of payments adjustment, and international trade, respectively, in the postwar era. Initially the attention of the International Bank for Reconstruction and Development (better known now as the World Bank) was focused on rebuilding the war-devastated economies of Western Europe. The United States assisted in the reconstruction of Europe with the Marshall Plan. The economies of the LDCs were relatively ignored until the mid-1950s, when East-West tensions and the Cold War spilled over into competition for Third World allies.

---

[6] Ibid., Table 1.

The prevailing view was that economic growth in the LDCs was constrained by shortages of capital and technology. Consequently, capital flows and technical assistance in the forms of foreign aid and foreign investment were promoted—as well as internal measures to generate saving and fund physical capital formation in the developing economies.

The LDCs were experiencing population explosions. Death rates were falling sharply, largely due to medical technologies imported from, and financed by, the developed Western nations. Antibiotics and malaria eradication campaigns using the insecticide DDT (to destroy the disease-bearing mosquitoes) were able to reduce mortality rates dramatically—even in the absence of significant economic development in the LDCs. Birth rates remained high, though, set by custom and in accordance with the perceived advantages of having many children in agrarian economies.[7] The rapid population growth translated into labor surplus conditions. Low capital-to-labor ratios in turn translated into low rates of labor productivity and low per capita incomes. Thus, it appeared that economic growth could be stimulated by combining more capital with the existing labor to generate more output. Indeed, to achieve increases in per capita income, growth in national income had to exceed the growth in population.

This economic theory was embodied in simple *growth models*. A distinguishing feature of these models is the emphasis on the production function. To illustrate, we will set up a **fixed coefficients' production function** using two factors, capital and labor, in which we assume there is a constant and inflexible relationship between inputs and output. In particular, no factor substitution is possible. The fixed coefficients' production function can be written as

$$Y = \text{Minimum } (K/v, L/u)$$

where

Y = real national output.
K = capital stock.
L = labor force.
v = fixed capital-output ratio.
u = fixed labor-output ratio.

For example, suppose the capital-output ratio (v) is equal to 5 and the labor-output ratio (u) is equal to 10. To produce one unit of output, then, would require 5 units of capital and 10 units of labor. To produce two units of output would require 10 units of capital and 20 units of labor. Note that the capital-labor ratio is also constant at 1:2 (one unit of capital to two units of labor). As illustrated in Figure 19.2, the isoquants of the fixed coefficients' production function are right-angled. [*Isoquants* represent the combinations of inputs (here the primary factors of production of capital and labor) capable of producing a given level of output.] The only economically efficient point on

---

[7] In agrarian and traditional economies, children are often perceived to be economic assets. They are put to work at an early age, helping out in the fields, tending livestock, and doing chores around the home (including the supervision of younger siblings). The absence of a social security system, combined with an inability to save enough to finance old age, leads parents to depend on their children—especially sons—for old age support. Moreover, with the high rates of infant and child mortality prevalent in developing economies, fertility rates need to be high to ensure the desired one or two surviving sons. Under such conditions, it is not surprising that there is rather limited demand for family planning programs and birth control.

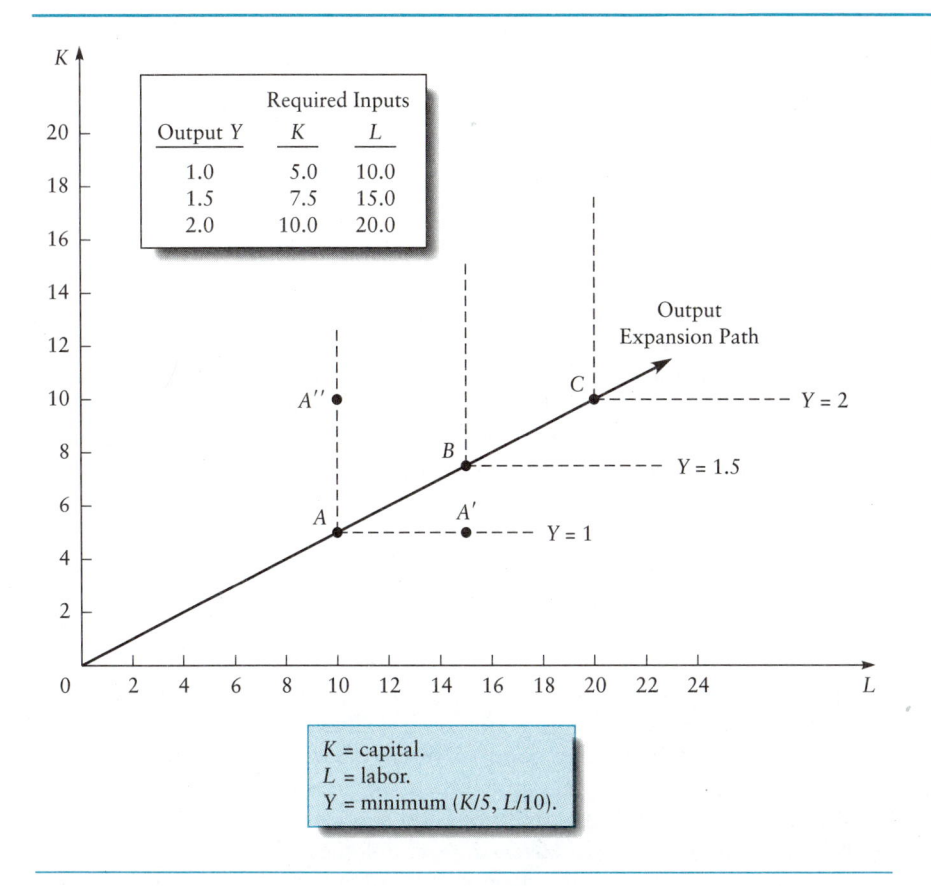

FIGURE 19.2

ISOQUANTS OF FIXED COEFFICIENTS' PRODUCTION FUNCTION

With a fixed coefficients' production function, the relationship between output and inputs is rigid. In this example, to produce n units of output would require $5n$ units of capital (K) and $10n$ units of labor (L).

Output Y	Required Inputs K	L
1.0	5.0	10.0
1.5	7.5	15.0
2.0	10.0	20.0

K = capital.
L = labor.
Y = minimum ($K/5$, $L/10$).

each isoquant is the corner point (for example, point A on isoquant $Y = 1$). The *marginal product of labor* (the additional output produced with another unit of labor) is zero on the horizontal portion of the isoquant (for example, point A' on the isoquant $Y = 1$). Similarly, the *marginal product of capital* (the additional output produced with another unit of capital) is zero on the vertical portion of the isoquant (for example, point A'' on the isoquant $Y = 1$).[8]

For instance, suppose there were 5 units of capital and 15 units of labor available in the economy. Assuming the fixed coefficients' production function that we have set out, what would be the maximum national output? The 5 units of capital could be combined with 10 units of labor to produce one unit of output. On the other hand, 15 units of labor would require 7.5 units of capital to produce 1.5 units of output. Since only 5 units of capital are available, the economy is constrained to producing one unit of output. Five units of labor are unemployed (see point A' on the isoquant $Y = 1$). Capital is the factor constraining economic growth. If the economy had another 2.5 units of capital

---

[8] The assumption of no factor substitution imposed by a fixed coefficients' production function may seem overly restrictive. Nevertheless, this assumption was often made in the early growth models and still is useful for illustrating the constraint on growth imposed by a scarce factor (e.g., capital).

(for instance, from foreign aid or foreign investment), then the 5 units of unemployed labor could be absorbed and another .5 units of output could be produced (see point B on the isoquant $Y = 1.5$).

With the rapid population growth in the developing nations, labor supply was growing much faster than physical capital. Measures to increase domestic capital formation were therefore adopted. Often interest rates were officially set below market equilibrium levels to subsidize business investment. Official exchange rates were overvalued to subsidize imports of capital goods. To increase the domestic saving rate, shifts in the distribution of income were engineered to favor capitalists and the high-income classes with the greater propensities to save. To extract tax revenues indirectly from agriculture, the largest sector, the government set the prices paid to domestic farmers at below market equilibrium levels. The government could then resell the agricultural produce for higher prices, using the proceeds to fund public investment in economic infrastructure (highways, railroads, seaports, and power plants).

In retrospect, some of the policies adopted by developing nations may have been counterproductive. As economic theory would suggest might happen, the artificially low interest rates led to an excess demand for credit. The available credit was allocated to borrowers favored by the government—and not always for the most productive investments. Similarly, the overvaluation of the exchange rate led to an excess demand for foreign exchange. Import licenses were used to allocate the available foreign exchange. Corruption and bribery often influenced the distribution of the licenses, however, and resulted in the importation of luxury consumer goods. Overall, the interest rate and exchange rate policies promoted more capital-intensive production processes than warranted by the labor surplus conditions and modest economic infrastructure in the developing nations. Moreover, the technologies embodied in the capital goods imported were sometimes inappropriate (that is, had a labor-saving bias) for the LDC economies. The low prices paid to farmers discouraged the production of food for the domestic market and increased the dependency of the nation on imported foodstuffs.

BASIC NEEDS APPROACH

By the early 1960s, some economists, notably Theodore Schultz, were arguing that shortages of human capital, as well as physical capital, were constraining economic growth and development. Human capital formation (increases in the quality of the population through education, nutrition, and health care), they pointed out, complements physical capital formation. A modern, industrialized economy requires skilled workers to run the machinery and entrepreneurs to exploit the profitable opportunities. In particular, education was promoted as a key to economic growth. In numerous developing countries, sharply increased expenditures for higher education resulted. On a related front, to reduce the population pressures on schools and the labor markets, family planning programs to reduce fertility rates were recommended.

In the 1970s there was a shift in development orientation. While economic growth, often impressive, had occurred in the LDCs during the 1960s, economic development in many cases seemed to lag behind. Specifically, increases in per capita GNP did not always guarantee the alleviation of poverty. In fact, there was evidence that even in the early stages of economic development, not only did income inequalities widen, but the real incomes of the poorest in the nation declined. The argument was then advanced that if the goal of economic development were to reduce poverty, then the most direct approach would be to provide for the basic needs of the population.

In contrast to the top-down approach of the growth models (physical capital formation increasing national output with the benefits of economic growth filtering down to improve the general standard of living), the **basic needs approach** represents a bottom-up strategy of development. Human capital formation as the foundation of economic development and growth is stressed. The idea is that investing first in the quality of the population will not only directly raise the standard of living, but will increase the intrinsic productivity of labor and thus enhance economic growth. In short, if the credo of the growth model was "grow now and develop later," the credo of the basic needs strategy was "develop now and growth will follow."

The basic needs approach begins by addressing the requirements for a minimally acceptable standard of living: adequate food, clothing, and shelter, and access to clean water, primary health care, and elementary education. While public expenditures might be necessary, especially at the beginning, to ensure that the basic needs of the poor are met, productive employment is seen as the most effective antipoverty program. By using labor-intensive technologies more suitable to the labor-abundant conditions in developing economies, by allowing interest rates to rise to levels consistent with the true scarcity of capital, and by ending the practice of overvaluing the exchange rate, relatively scarce capital would be spread further, and more of the surplus labor could be absorbed into productive employment.

For example, rather than importing a sophisticated power loom that requires only one operator, a developing nation could import (or manufacture domestically) ten hand looms, for the same cost, that would employ ten workers. Raising the interest rate would not only induce saving and increase the quantity of loanable funds supplied, but, by increasing the relative cost of capital, would encourage employers to use more labor-intensive input combinations. Devaluing the domestic currency would boost the nation's exports (especially in labor-intensive commodities) and generate additional employment.

Another change in orientation was the emphasis on rural development. Recall that a policy derived from the growth model's push for capital accumulation in modern industries was the indirect taxation of farmers through the artificially low prices paid for farm output. Moreover, land ownership in many developing countries often was (and still is) highly concentrated.[9] Under such circumstances, small farmers producing basic foodstuffs for the domestic markets have been squeezed not only by the low prices for their output but by the powerful, large landowners who produce more profitable cash crops for export (coffee, tea, bananas, beef) and use their political influence to gain access to the scarce credit. As a consequence, many farmers in developing nations are landless

---

[9] Inequality is particularly notable in Latin America. The World Bank reported that in Latin America "about 1 percent of the population controls more than 50 percent of the land and accounts for almost one-third of agricultural output and more than one-sixth of total GNP." See World Bank, *World Development Report 1986* (New York: Oxford University Press, 1986), 83.

peasants—working as laborers on large estates and as tenant farmers for landlords. Many other families have given up farming, left their rural homes, and joined the multitudes migrating to urban areas.

Basic needs advocates, consistent with their philosophy of expanding economic opportunities, favor land tenure reform, where the large estates (which tend to rely on more capital- and land-intensive methods of production) are broken up and redistributed to small farmers using labor-intensive production techniques. Secure title to land would give the farmers an incentive to invest in improving the quality of the land tilled. Furthermore, letting the market set the prices for the farm output would give farmers an incentive to increase production, as prices rise from their controlled levels. The land tenure reform should be supported by greater access to credit for the small farmers (to purchase fertilizers and other needed farm inputs), public investment in rural infrastructure such as improved roads to markets and irrigation systems, and technical assistance from agricultural extension agents. These measures would increase the productivity and incomes of small farmers (who comprise a large share of the labor forces in many of the developing nations) and might reduce the need to import foodstuffs. Finally, basic needs proponents favor greater investment in rural schools and health clinics in order to increase popular access to these essential services.

There are, however, major questions about the feasibility of the basic needs strategy of development. First, is there a consensus on the basic needs associated with a minimally acceptable standard of living? If primary education is a basic human need, then what about secondary education? Is employment a basic need? Even if there were widespread agreement on just the core basic needs of nutrition, health, water, shelter, and clothing, defining acceptable standards would be difficult. At one extreme, the least expensive diet consistent with the minimum caloric intake for survival could be defined as satisfying the basic need for nutrition. Such a diet, however, is likely to be monotonous and unappetizing. And would basic needs fulfillment in health care be simply innoculation against infectious diseases? Perhaps basic needs standards could be defined not as absolutes, but as a certain percentage of the averages for the nation, in which case, as the economy prospered, the standards would rise.

A second issue concerns the attainment of basic needs goals. Developing nations seldom have the resources to operate substantial *transfer* programs. Nevertheless, the quickest way to ensure access to an adequate diet is with food transfers. (For example, Sri Lanka in the 1960s and 1970s provided its population with heavily subsidized rice.) Income and income-in-kind transfer programs are not only expensive, but run the risk of creating dependencies on the part of the recipient populations. Also, providing universal primary education and even rudimentary health care, while meeting basic needs and enhancing future economic growth, is difficult—especially in the developing nations with young and rapidly growing populations.

Finally, government expenditures for basic needs have opportunity costs. Proponents of the growth model approach would argue that a rapidly expanding economy is the best antipoverty program, that funds spent on directly providing for basic needs would be better spent on physical capital formation, which adds to the productive capacity of the economy.

TRADE AND ECONOMIC DEVELOPMENT

Historically the dynamic process of economic development has been characterized by structural change. Primarily agrarian economies are transformed into diversified, urban-industrial economies. Essential to this process is the establishment of a modern manufacturing base. One of the most important policy decisions for any developing nation is the degree to which economic development and the establishment of a modern manufacturing base will be fostered through international trade.

There are two core strategies. **Import substitution** is an inward-looking strategy that emphasizes switching domestic demand from foreign production (imports) to domestic production. With a reduction in imports, desired aggregate expenditures on national output will increase; and through the multiplier effects, national output, income, and employment will rise. Moreover, to the extent that some imports can be replaced with domestic production, the balance of trade will be improved and scarce foreign exchange conserved.

Export expansion, in contrast, is an outward-looking strategy with an emphasis on directing domestic production towards foreign demand (exports). By increasing exports, desired aggregate expenditures on national output will increase, with the attendant multiplier effects on national income and employment. Rather than reducing imports and conserving foreign exchange, the export expansion strategy seeks to improve the balance of trade through the generation of export revenues.

Import Substitution

The first step in the implementation of an import substitution strategy is the selection of the domestic industries to promote. Typically LDCs have only limited economic infrastructure (that is, underdeveloped transportation systems, communication networks, and public utilities). Their labor forces are generally without much experience in modern manufacturing. Consequently, the industries targeted for import substitution must not only be those where domestic demands are currently being met by imports, but also where the technological requirements and physical capital investments are relatively modest. Examples would be shoes, textiles and apparel, chemical fertilizers, and bicycles.

In the beginning, domestic producers usually are not able to compete with the more experienced and more efficient foreign producers. Therefore, the nation erects import barriers (tariffs and quotas) to allow the domestic **infant industries** to develop in a protected environment. To the extent these industries do thrive in the insulated domestic market, backward linkages through the derived demands for inputs may be generated. Examples of such supplier industries would be manufacturers of looms and sewing machines for textiles and apparel, chemicals for fertilizers, and steel mills and tire manufacturers for bicycle production. Ideally, through "learning by doing," the protected infant industries will mature into efficient international competitors, so that not only can the import protection be removed, but export revenues will be generated.

Export Expansion

In contrast to import substitution, where foreign competition is initially shut off, an export expansion strategy seeks to engage in international competition from the outset. With an abundance of labor, wages should be relatively low, thus developing nations should have a comparative advantage in labor-intensive manufactures. Indeed, regardless of the orientation (import substitution or export expansion), many of the same industries will be involved—shoes, apparel, and textiles, for example. Moreover, the same problem of initially competing with more experienced foreign producers must be confronted.

With export expansion, the selected domestic industries are *subsidized* (including preferential access to credit, tax breaks, and marketing assistance) to enhance their international competitiveness. Multinational corporations often are useful in providing the needed marketing and technical expertise. And, increasingly, multinational corporations are establishing foreign subsidiaries in developing nations for the assembly of manufactured components for goods (such as televisions and personal computers) for which the domestic demands in these nations may be still quite limited.

Important to the success of an export expansion strategy is maintaining a realistic exchange rate. As noted, LDCs often operate with overvalued currencies—that is, the official foreign exchange value of the currency is greater than the market equilibrium value. An overvalued currency acts like a tax on a nation's exports—and a subsidy to its imports. To illustrate, suppose that the market equilibrium exchange rate for the Philippine peso is 1 peso = $.02 (or 50 pesos = $1.00). A pair of shoes produced for 1000 pesos in the Philippines would have an export price of $20. If the official exchange rate were 1 peso = $.025 (or 40 pesos = $1.00), then the pair of shoes with a production cost of 1000 pesos would have an export price of $25. With the overvalued peso, fewer shoes would be exported by the Philippines—and given a price-elastic foreign demand for shoes produced in the Philippines, total dollar receipts from shoe exports would be less with the overvalued peso.

Even if a nation has a comparative advantage in, for example, the production of shoes, and even if the nation operates with a competitive exchange rate, the success of an export expansion strategy still depends on international cooperation. That is, tariffs, quotas, or other trade barriers may restrict the nation's access to foreign markets.

Theoretically there are advantages to an export expansion strategy. Recall from Chapter 4, where the gains from trade and international specialization were illustrated, that free trade and production according to comparative advantages (lower opportunity costs) yield the most efficient allocation of resources. Exposure to market competition requires attention to product quality and cost minimization. Moreover, for a small country, the ability to realize the economies of scale that come with volume production is greater when the production is geared for the world market instead of being limited to serving just domestic demand.

The evidence over the past quarter-century does indicate that developing nations adopting a more outward-looking orientation have achieved more rapid rates of economic growth.[10] The best examples are the East Asian nations of the

---

[10] See, for example, World Bank, "Trade Policy and Industrialization," Chapter 5 in the World Bank's *World Development Report 1987*.

Republic of Korea, Taiwan, Singapore, and Hong Kong—often referred to as the "Four Asian Tigers." Like Japan before them, these nations have pursued a common strategy of outward-looking growth based on the expansion of labor-intensive manufactured exports. Drawing on literate and industrious labor forces (the product of earlier investments in human capital) and guided by comprehensive and ambitious economic policies, the Four Asian Tigers have become world-class competitors in the international marketplace. As their firms gained experience and expertise, these nations upgraded the technological sophistication of their exports. For example, from a reliance on textile and apparel exports in the early 1960s, the Republic of Korea progressed into being a major exporter of simple consumer electronics, steel, automobiles, and computers.[11] We should note that the Republic of Korea's successful export-led development was preceded by a period of import substitution.

Indeed, most developing nations have found it easier to begin with an inward-looking strategy of import substitution. The challenge here is to develop genuine infant industries—effectively weaning domestic producers from protection. Moreover, as noted, the viability of an outward-looking strategy of export expansion crucially depends on access to foreign markets—a factor usually beyond the control of the developing nation.

EMERGENCE OF THE EXTERNAL DEBT PROBLEM

The economic turbulence of the 1970s brought on by the breakdown of the Bretton Woods international monetary system and the oil price shocks made it difficult for most developing nations to pursue a basic needs strategy of development. Still, substantial gains were made in increasing school enrollments and reducing infant mortality. The higher oil prices contributed to growing trade deficits for the oil-importing LDCs; and to finance their development programs, many nations turned to Western banks.

The **recycling of petrodollars** refers to those dollar deposits placed by the oil-exporting nations in Western commercial banks and loaned to the developing nations to cover their increased trade deficits. It made sense for the LDCs to borrow in order to continue the imports of the capital goods, oil, and other intermediate inputs needed to sustain their economic developments. With the increase in global inflation, the real cost of borrowing was low. In addition, the LDCs counted on the continued expansion of the global economy for the growth in export revenues needed to pay off their external debts. Western commercial banks, in turn, flush with the deposits of oil-producing nations, were only too willing to lend to developing nations at higher nominal rates of interest than could be charged in the developed countries.

For the most part, the United States and other developed nations accommodated the first oil price hikes with expansionary economic policies. After the recession of 1974–1975 the international economy recovered fairly briskly. With the second run-up in oil prices in 1979, however, the United States, with Paul Volcker at the helm of the Federal Reserve, adopted a contractionary

---

[11] For an overview of the Republic of Korea's strategy, see Larry Westphal, "Industrial Policy in an Export-Propelled Economy: Lessons from South Korea's Experience," *Journal of Economic Perspectives* 4, no. 3 (Summer 1990): 41–60.

monetary policy to deal with the escalating inflation. As discussed in Chapters 15 and 18, the combination of tight monetary and easy fiscal policy (the Reagan administration's tax cuts and defense spending) sent real interest rates soaring. The effects of the U.S. monetary restraint spread to other developed nations and pushed up interest rates internationally. The developing nations were vulnerable, since in the latter part of the 1970s their loans from commercial banks had increasingly been at variable interest rates tied to the international cost of capital. The rise in interest rates directly increased the interest burden of the LDC debt.

Developing nations were hurt in two other ways. Recall from Chapter 18 how the high real interest rates in the United States attracted foreign capital, which appreciated the U.S. dollar over the first half of the 1980s. Since much of the external debt of the developing nations was denominated in U.S. dollars, the domestic currency burdens of repaying the debt increased with the value of the dollar. Second, the severe recession that began in the United States in mid-1981 spread to the rest of the world. LDC export revenues declined with the fall in incomes and subsequent rise in trade barriers in the developed economies.

As reported by the World Bank, "the total medium- and long-term debt of developing countries rose fourfold in nominal terms, from about $140 billion at the end of 1974 to about $560 billion in 1982. In real terms it more than doubled."[12] While the increase in interest rates, appreciation of the dollar, slowdown in the international economy, and rise in protectionism all contributed to the debt problems, many of the developing countries themselves had exacerbated their situations with economic mismanagement, a proliferation of inefficient state-owned enterprises, and the running of large budget deficits financed by printing money.

The debt crisis became front-page news in August of 1982 when Mexico announced that it could no longer meet the scheduled interest and principal payments on its foreign debt. The possibility that Mexico and other LDCs would default on their debts alarmed the commercial banks. Commercial bank credit to developing economies accordingly dried up, which further heightened the debt predicament of the LDCs.

The threat of default and severe balance of payments difficulties faced by the heavily indebted developing nations forced the International Monetary Fund (IMF) to arrange additional financing.[13] The IMF-sponsored funding, however, was conditional upon the adoption of certain policy reforms. Developing nations receiving IMF assistance had to agree to reduce their budget deficits

---

[12] *World Development Report* 1988, 27.

[13] Recall that the International Monetary Fund was originally charted under the Bretton Woods Agreement of 1944 to regulate the exchange rate practices of the member nations in the international monetary system and to assist (with loans) member nations with large balance of payments deficits. The external debt crisis of the early 1980s increasingly pushed the IMF into a role as economic policy prescriber. In addition, the IMF has been involved in debt renegotiations between commercial banks and LDC borrowers. The World Bank also makes loans to developing nations but under different circumstances. It borrows money on the international capital markets in order to relend to LDCs (at a slightly higher interest rate, but one still lower than could be obtained directly by the nations themselves) for specific projects (e.g., an irrigation system in Kenya, a highway in Ecuador, or an adult literacy program in Bangladesh). Some of the World Bank loans to the poorest countries, however, are on very soft terms, that is, well below the market rate of interest and with lenient repayment schedules. The World Bank is also the leading international center for research on economic development.

(especially by trimming government expenditures), tighten up on the monetary policy, devalue their currencies, free up institutionally set prices, and privatize state-owned enterprises. In a sense this prescription was a shift back to an emphasis on economic growth, but with a reliance on the market mechanism and private enterprise.

Some LDCs, including Mexico, accepted the IMF structural adjustment program and made progress in dealing with their debt by reducing inflation and becoming more internationally competitive. In general, middle-income Latin American countries, with the greatest amount of debt owed to Western commercial banks, slashed imports (including imports of capital goods) in order to generate the current account surpluses needed to meet their debt obligations. Low-income sub-Saharan African nations, with their debt largely owed to other governments and international institutions, continued to struggle with little apparent direction. For these two regions, the 1980s have been called the "lost decade of development." Real per capita incomes fell in many developing nations. More ominous were the declines in investment spending. From 1980 through 1990 the average annual growth rates in real gross domestic investment were -4.3 percent for sub-Saharan African nations and -2.0 percent for Latin American and Caribbean nations.[14] The reduced physical capital formation bodes ill for future economic growth, especially given the rapidly expanding labor forces in these areas.[15]

The Brady Plan (named after U.S. Secretary of the Treasury, Nicholas Brady, who introduced the scheme in the spring of 1989) involved limited debt cancellation to selected countries adopting more market-oriented policies. Western banks have written down some of their LDC loans. Yet, despite the economic tightening and modest debt forgiveness, total LDC external debt significantly increased over the 1980s. By 1990, estimates of the external debt of the developing nations exceeded $1 trillion.

Rightly or wrongly, the IMF has become associated in the developing nations with the bitter medicine their economies are forced to take in dealing with their external debts. Austerity measures implemented by LDC governments (such as devaluations that increase the domestic currency price of imports and cutbacks in food subsidies that raise the cost of living to urban consumers) are not popular and have, on occasion, sparked violence and riots. Consequently, some LDC governments have adopted a more confrontational stance, unilaterally limiting debt repayments and even threatening to renounce part of their external debts. Fears of a *debt cartel*, where a group of the highly indebted nations jointly renounce their external obligations, so far have not materialized. Still, the debt crisis looms over the international economy with no comprehensive solution in sight.

---

[14] *World Development Report 1992*, Table 8.
[15] The developing nations of Europe also fared poorly, with an average annual growth rate in real gross domestic investment of $-.1$ percent for 1980–1990. In contrast, the developing nations of East Asia and South Asia achieved real growth rates of 10.6 percent and 4.6 percent, respectively (the former group dominated by China's extraordinary growth rate in investment of 13.7 percent). (Note that these averages are weighted by the shares of the individual nations in the total population of the region. The average growth rate in investment for the developing nations of the Middle East and North Africa for this period was not available.) In order to raise the capital-labor ratio (and average labor productivity and per capita incomes), the growth rate in the capital stock has to exceed the growth rate in the labor force.

RADICAL SCHOOL'S CRITIQUE

The **radical school** of economic development, grounded in the theories of Karl Marx (to be discussed in the following chapter), maintains that the underdevelopment of the LDCs is largely a consequence of exploitation, past and present, by the capitalist nations (the Western, market-oriented developed economies). Past exploitation occurred, this reasoning goes, when the dominant nations competed for overseas colonies in what are the contemporary developing nations. The colonies were seen as cheap sources of the raw materials needed for the industrialization of the capitalist economies and as new export markets for manufactured goods. The subsequent development of the colonies was biased toward the production of minerals and primary commodities, creating export enclaves with few linkages to the rest of the native economies. Even today, many of the poorer LDCs rely on just a few mineral-based and agricultural products for the bulk of their export earnings.

Upon gaining independence in the post–World War II era, many developing nations were faced with economic and political vacuums since little in the way of indigenous entrepreneurship or civil administration had been nurtured. All too often the political vacuums have been filled by military-controlled governments, with a resultant loss of civil liberties. Multinational corporations have rushed in to fill the economic vacuums. The radical school sees multinational corporations as an extension of neocolonialism—continuing the exploitation of the natural resources of the developing nations, using inappropriate capital-intensive technologies, introducing expensive Western lifestyles, and meddling in the internal politics of the host countries.

According to this school, the present international economic system is designed to promote the interests of the Western capitalist nations. For example, the General Agreement on Tariffs and Trade (GATT) has been successful in reducing tariffs and liberalizing trade in many areas, but not in the areas of greatest importance to the developing nations. Agriculture and labor-intensive products (for example, textiles and apparel), areas in which developing nations are likely to have comparative advantages, are among the most heavily protected in the international economy.[16] Similarly, the IMF and World Bank are characterized as organizations controlled by Western-educated technocrats with a fixation on economic growth and little understanding of the real causes of underdevelopment. Even foreign aid is held to be a form of leverage exercised by capitalist nations. Aid flows, especially bilateral aid between nations, are perceived to reflect more the strategic interests of the donor nations than the economic needs of the recipient nations.

In sum, the radical school sees the exploitation of the masses in developing nations continuing under capitalism, a system based on market incentives and personal profits. Only widespread revolution by workers can overthrow the system and lead to genuine socioeconomic progress.

---

[16] The most recent round of multilateral trade negotiations under GATT sponsorship, the Uruguay Round, was supposed to address some of these issues—in particular, protection in agriculture and labor-intensive manufactures. The Uruguay Round bogged down, however, when the issue of reducing subsidies to agriculture became a sticking point for the developed countries.

AN AGENDA FOR DEVELOPMENT

It should not be surprising that economic development theory and policy are subject to such controversy. The growth model, basic needs, and radical school approaches do not exhaust the different perspectives on economic development. Indeed, this chapter has provided only a brief overview of this complex and important field in economics.

The World Bank has set forth a "market-friendly" strategy of economic development.[17] The key elements of this approach are investments in human capital, competitive domestic markets, macroeconomic stability, and international integration. For their part, the developing nations are urged to continue, as a high priority, their investments in human capital. Ensuring that the education, nutrition, health care, and family planning needs of the populations are met pays off not only in an enhanced quality of life, but in increased labor productivities and greater economic growth.

Competitive domestic markets are to be encouraged according to this strategy. Efficiency in resource allocation dictates that prices be set in competitive markets, not imposed by central authorities. To this end, private enterprise, entrepreneurship, and competition should be fostered. Inefficient state-owned enterprises stifle competition and drain government budgets.

The role of government extends beyond the provision of public goods (for example, national defense, the police, the judicial system, primary and secondary education, and economic infrastructure). Governments also need to establish and enforce the economic rules—including well-defined property rights, and health, safety, and environmental regulations. A capable and efficient civil service is needed to carry out these responsibilities of the government with dispatch.

To secure macroeconomic stability, fiscal and monetary discipline must be exercised. Government budget deficits need to be controlled, and growth in the money supply needs to be sufficiently moderated to keep inflation in check. As discussed in Chapter 16, inflation affects the distribution of income and allocation of resources—and diverts economic activity away from the production of goods and services to speculation and hedging in assets. Moreover, for a given nominal exchange rate, inflation undermines a nation's competitive position.

Ideally, along with *economic liberalization* (increased reliance on private enterprise) and macroeconomic stability would come *political liberalization* (increased reliance on democratic processes) and political stability. Generating self-sustaining economic growth and development is very difficult in the absence of political stability. To give just one example of the cost of political turmoil, we cite the World Bank: "Far and away the most important cause of famine in developing countries in recent years has been not inadequate agricultural output or poverty, but military conflict."[18]

Even in the absence of civil war or external aggression, many developing nations have devoted substantial shares of their government budgets and foreign exchange earnings to military expenditures and arms imports. With the pressing

---

[17] See the "Overview," pages 1–11, in *World Development Report 1991*, for an outline of this strategy.
[18] *World Development Report 1991*, 2.

demands for investments in human capital and economic infrastructure—all the more urgent given the rapid population growth—any military spending in excess of that needed to ensure national security has a very high opportunity cost.

The recommended orientation of development is outward. By pursuing their comparative advantages in production, developing nations should be able to realize efficiency gains through international trade. With the investments in human capital, the emphasis on private enterprise and the market mechanism, and the attainment of economic and political stability, an environment conducive to private investment is created. There will be less of an outflow of domestic financial capital for the purchase of foreign assets, and an increased inflow of foreign capital, including direct foreign investment and the transfer of technology.

For their part, the DCs can enhance the economic progress of the LDCs by further opening their markets to them. Consequently, a high priority of GATT should be to liberalize trade in agriculture and labor-intensive manufactures so that an export expansion strategy of development becomes viable. More and better-targeted economic assistance from the DCs would help the LDCs fund their investments in human capital and economic infrastructure.

While the proposals outlined here should significantly improve the development prospects, progress in the LDCs will still be constrained by their external debt burdens. Additional debt rescheduling, if not debt cancellation, seems inevitable. One promising possibility is debt cancellation for environmental preservation. In those developing areas where rain forests are threatened, species are endangered, and croplands are vulnerable to erosion or desertification, compensation in the form of debt relief might be extended to those governments undertaking measures to protect the environment.

CONCLUDING NOTE

We conclude with the opinion that the socioeconomic progress of the less developed countries should be of great concern to all the inhabitants of planet Earth. The destruction of rain forests and the desertification of farmlands are but two indicators of the combined pressures of poverty and rapid population growth on the environment.

Generally population growth rates are highest in the poorest nations of the world. An annual population growth rate of 2.6 percent (the annual average for the low-income economies, other than China and India, for 1980–1990) translates into a doubling of the population every 27 years. Debt-ridden, and struggling to accommodate their present populations with the basic necessities of life, let alone generate the human and physical capital formation required to improve per capita incomes, developing nations can ill afford continued rapid population growth. Yet, even if all the developing nations were immediately to attain **replacement level fertility** (where a woman, on average, would have two children survive her and her partner), the world's population would still increase over the next half-century by at least half again—from the current 5.5 billion to over 8.25 billion.[19] The World Bank projects that "nearly 95 percent of the increase in the world's labor force during the next twenty-five years will occur in the developing world."[20]

The fact is that very few of the developing nations are near replacement level fertility. Short of an authoritarian birth control policy, as in China, family planning programs alone will not significantly reduce fertility rates.[21] Family planning programs that provide contraceptive services work best in concert with economic development. With declining child mortality rates, increased access to education, and greater economic mobility, parents begin to perceive the advantages to reducing fertility.

The Worldwatch Institute estimates that approximately 1.2 billion people (or more than one in every five persons on earth) were living in absolute poverty at the beginning of the 1990s. Alan Durning of the Institute noted that "the poor are increasingly concentrated in fragile regions where land is least productive and tenure least secure—arid and semiarid lands, mountain slopes, tropical forests, and sprawling shanty-towns around overcrowded cities."[22]

Poverty, rapid population growth, and environmental deterioration are connected in a vicious cycle. How to break this cycle and lift the poorest fifth of humanity from absolute poverty presents one of the major challenges facing the global community.

KEY TERMS

developed countries (DCs)
less developed countries (LDCs)
third world
first world
second world
fourth world
Lorenz curve
economic growth
economic development

fixed coefficients' production function
basic needs approach
import substitution
export expansion
infant industries
recycling of petrodollars
radical school
replacement level fertility
population momentum

---

[19] This phenomenon is due to **population momentum,** or the built-in propensity for growing populations to continue to increase after the onset of replacement level fertility. With a positive rate of population growth, each generation will produce more children than the previous one, hence, more potential parents for the next generation. Even if at some point in the future replacement level fertility is attained, the number of children will continue to increase for some time due to the greater number of parents on hand. Currently all of the developed economies (with the possible exception of Ireland) are below replacement level fertility, yet most are still experiencing modest natural increases. A handful of European nations (e.g., Germany, France, Belgium, Denmark, Hungary) have reached virtually zero population growth.
[20] *World Development Report 1991,* 1.
[21] Some two decades ago the leaders of China saw that China's resource base would not support the predicted future increases in population. Thus, China instituted a policy of one child per family in an attempt to reverse population momentum and ultimately reduce population size.
[22] Alan Durning, "Ending Poverty," *State of the World 1990,* Worldwatch Institute (New York: W. W. Norton & Company, 1990), 146.

QUESTIONS

1. What are the three most important ideas in this chapter? Discuss why each is important.
2. Sketch the Lorenz curves for the two nations based on the following income distribution data (from World Bank, *World Development Report 1992*, Tables 1 and 30). Note that the data on income shares are based on the percentages of income received by the population (not by the households).

   | | PERCENTAGE SHARES OF INCOME | |
PERCENTAGE OF POPULATION	Costa Rica (1986)	Poland (1987)
Lowest 20%	3.3%	9.7%
2nd Quintile	8.3	14.2
3rd Quintile	13.2	18.0
4th Quintile	20.7	20.9
Highest 20%	54.5	35.2

   a. If the income distribution data were based on household shares, why might the Lorenz curves show a lesser degree of inequality in each nation?
   b. The estimated per capita GNPs of these two nations for 1990 are similar: $1900 for Costa Rica and $1690 for Poland—especially when adjustments are made for the higher cost of living in Costa Rica. What could explain the significant difference in the distribution of income between these two nations? (After reading Chapter 20, you may want to return to this question.)

3. Suppose there are three alternative methods for producing a unit of national output (Y).

   | | REQUIRED INPUTS | |
METHOD	Capital (K)	Labor (L)
I	4 units	15 units
II	6 units	12 units
III	8 units	10 units

   a. Assume that the nation Sierra has 72 units of capital and 300 units of labor available for producing its national output. Determine the maximum amount of output Sierra could produce and the method of production used. Which factor would be constraining further increases in output? How much "unemployment" of capital or labor would there be?
   b. Assume that the nation Norte has 132 units of capital and 150 units of labor available for producing its national output. Determine the maximum amount of output Norte could produce and the method of production used. Which factor would be constraining further increases in output? How much "unemployment" of capital or labor would there be?
   c. Can you think of a way to increase the total or combined output of both nations, given the same available resources? Explain and illustrate.

4. Develop a working definition of the "basic needs" of a six-year-old child living in
   a. a high-income developed country.
   b. a low-income less developed country.

   Is there a difference in the definition of "basic needs"? Should there be a difference? Discuss.
5. Discuss whether or not the developed countries should help the less developed countries. If you think that they should, explain how. If you think that they should not, discuss the consequences of failing to help.

CHAPTER

20

SOCIALISM AND THE TRANSFORMATION TO MARKET CAPITALISM

IN THIS CHAPTER we provide a brief description of socialism as a system of economic organization. We begin with the writings of Karl Marx, particularly his critique of capitalism and his promotion of a communist economic system. We then outline two variants of socialism, centralized and decentralized. An overview of the evolution of the Soviet command economy is provided for historical perspective. We conclude the chapter with a discussion of the prospects and problems facing the former republics of the Soviet Union in their transformation toward market capitalism.

MARX AND HIS CRITIQUE OF CAPITALISM

Adam Smith (1723–1790) published his *An Inquiry into the Nature and Causes of the Wealth of Nations* in 1776. He wrote of the virtues of the unregulated capitalist market system, praising the market system's ability to coordinate efficiently the economic decisions of which outputs to produce and which input combinations to use. According to Smith, the "invisible hand" of self-interest would lead to efficient outcomes. Other economic philosophers were not so favorably disposed toward capitalism. Criticizing a system based on self-interest, which generated glaring economic inequalities, reformers such as Robert Owen (1771–1858) and Henri Saint Simon (1760–1825) argued for a tempering of the harsher aspects of the capitalist market system. Each of these reformers had a plan for humanizing the market system.

Karl Marx (1818–1883) concluded that the ideas both of Adam Smith and of the idealistic reformers were misguided. He felt that the static analysis of

Adam Smith and the naive schemes of the reformers alike missed the true essence of capitalism, which he saw as simply one stage of a dynamic and inevitable human progression to socialism and, eventually, to full communism. Thus, for Smith to assert that competitive laissez-faire capitalism was a highly desirable means for organizing an economy seemed to Marx to be an irrelevant conclusion—one that failed to recognize the place of capitalism in the sweep of history. And in contrast to the reformers, Marx did not see the relevance or feasibility of reforming capitalism, since the passage to socialism and then to communism was the only valid hope of the working class. Moreover, Marx could envision neither the capitalist employer nor the state providing reforms to aid the workers.

Marx felt that the private ownership of property gave capitalists the license to exploit the mass of society, that is, the hired workers. To Marx the only productive input was human labor. The fact that the worker was not paid the total value of production (some of it being kept, or expropriated, by the capitalist) meant that the worker was exploited. The belief that all value created in the production process originates with the power of labor is called the **labor theory of value**.[1] The portion of value created by labor but kept by the capitalist (that is, not paid as wages to labor) is called **surplus value**.

Marx felt that the private ownership of property had to be abolished, with society collectively owning all resources, so that the workers would receive the full benefit of their labor. Consequently, **Marxism** (the doctrine based on Marx's writings) is characterized by an aversion to private property and a call for collective ownership of the means of production.

Marx viewed the workings of society in a dynamic sense. His dialectic process envisioned continual changes in technological forces, which in turn produced change in other aspects of society. Associated with this process, Marx viewed societies as passing through stages: primitive, feudal, capitalist, mature capitalist, and socialist, before attaining communism. He had great respect for the power of the capitalist phase, during which great bodies of infrastructure and productive capacity would be built, but he believed that inevitably, because of certain self-destructive features of capitalism, a society would pass into **mature capitalism**, where there would be heightened conflict between the workers and capitalists. Technological progress leading to a greater use of highly productive machines would cause a reduction in the amount of labor used in the production process. Capitalists would increasingly need to exploit those workers who remained employed in order to maintain a given level of profits. Thus, the substitution of capital for labor would lead to reduced wages and increased unemployment. As a result, the mass of the population would be unable to purchase the output of the more productive capitalists. In the ensuing competition for survival among the capitalists, larger capitalists would consume the smaller capitalists, leading to a less competitive economy. Eventually, according to Marx, both technological progress leading to more capital-intensive production (with resulting unemployment of labor) and capitalist greed would cause the breakdown of the system.

---

[1] For a discussion of the origins of the labor theory of value, with reference to the insights of Adam Smith and David Ricardo, as well as the contributions of Karl Marx, see Fernando Vianello, *The New Palgrave: A Dictionary of Economics,* vol. 3, edited by John Eatwell, Murray Milgate, and Peter Newman (London: The Macmillan Press Limited, 1987), 107–113.

Marx did not give a detailed plan for the workings of the socialist and communist systems that would emerge. His description of socialism was one of transition from capitalism to communism. Under socialism, although some income inequality (as a means of motivation) would still exist, private property would be gradually eliminated, and the vestiges of capitalism would be attacked and destroyed. Following this stage, the utopia of full communism would be realized. Self-interest would be replaced by a desire to serve the greater good of society. Work effort would be "from each according to his abilities"; distribution would be "to each according to his needs."

Objective scholars regard Marx as a truly remarkable intellect. Unfortunately, given the political overtones of Marxian analysis, it is difficult to be truly objective when studying Marxian thought. While Marx's labor theory of value is incomplete and logically inconsistent as an economic model, that theory is only one part of Marx's writings. Many of Marx's other insights have proven extraordinary.

Marx highlighted the class nature of production within the capitalist system. Certainly, labor and capitalists represent two different and often competing factions. Moreover, many of Marx's predictions about capitalism have in fact occurred. Within the capitalist countries there has been increased concentration in the ownership of productive assets since the mid-nineteenth century. Exploitation of overseas markets, or imperialism, also foreseen by Marx, did occur, and perhaps still does today.

Arguably, Marx was mistaken in predicting the increased exploitation of the industrial worker; he did not foresee the effective role of labor unions and the democratic state. Contemporary Marxists, however, argue that the exploitation continues with the underclass workers and the unemployed in the industrial economies and with labor in general in the economically less developed nations.

Another area of knowledge in which Marx made a major contribution concerns the existence of business cycles. Marx felt that the periodic booms and busts of capitalism were endemic to the system. In fact he predicted increasingly serious business cycles as capitalism began to self-destruct and collapse. Marx advanced an idea to which John Maynard Keynes later gave respectability, the idea that insufficient purchasing power could lead to reduced production and increased unemployment. According to Marx, as the capitalist employers increasingly exploited workers, the workers would be unable to purchase the increasing output which the capitalists were producing. This was another of the contradictions of capitalism that Marx saw.

In conclusion, Marx provided a rich and insightful critique of capitalism. He did not, however, give a detailed plan for organizing a socialist economy. The task of developing an operational model of socialism fell to Lenin and the organizers of the Russian revolution.

THEORY OF SOCIALISM

Before discussing the economy of the former Soviet Union, it is important to understand how a socialist economy addresses the basic economic questions facing any society. Partially as a result of the Soviet experience, a coherent body of thought concerning socialism has emerged in the twentieth century. There are two broad variants to socialism: a centralized version and a decentralized version.

Centralized Socialism

Within **centralized socialism** significant economic power is vested in a *central planning board (CPB)*. Generally speaking, the CPB decides what output will be produced and how it will be produced. Operating plans are given to each firm or enterprise within the economy. These plans provide the enterprise's output targets (generally expressed in physical units, like tons of steel or pairs of shoes) and allocation of inputs—labor, capital, and intermediate goods—to produce the output. As used in the former Soviet Union, this system is called the **material balance** form of planning. For each commodity and for each input a balance of **sources** and **uses** was kept.

The sources for a product are current production, drawing from inventories, and imports; the uses of a product are for current consumption, production of other commodities, additions to inventories, or export. For a plan to be consistent, sources and uses must be in balance, or equal. Within centralized socialism, prices primarily play an accounting role, not an allocative role; thus the balances must be set and verified administratively for each good. In a market system, sources are simply product supply and uses are product demand. The equality of demand and supply, achieved by a competitive pricing system, automatically equates sources and uses.

There are inefficiencies in the material balance planning process. First, the process takes time. The communication between the planners, the industry managers, and the heads of enterprises is an interactive process that consumes a considerable amount of labor resources. Second, there is a tendency for enterprise managers to over-request and stockpile inputs. Given that the primary indicator of success is meeting an output target, an enterprise manager has an incentive to request more inputs, labor and machinery, than necessary to meet the target. Obviously, these inputs are then not available for other uses. In a market system, where profitability is the goal, a firm would not hoard inputs, since the excess inputs would raise the costs of production and lower the profitability of the enterprise.

A third problem with the emphasis of the material balance approach on output targets is unacceptable product quality. Firms do not have an incentive to provide products of high quality. In a market system, if a product of unacceptable quality cannot be sold, profitability is reduced. In the material balance approach, where output level is the key indicator, there is an incentive to scrimp on product quality in order to save inputs and increase the total volume of output produced. Finally, the material balance approach of command socialism has generally been accompanied by controlled prices that need not (and usually do not) correspond to market-clearing prices. Often prices are set below those that would equate uses (demand) and sources (supply), leading to excess demand. For consumer goods, this excess demand is usually manifested in the form of rationing or waiting in line hoping to be able to purchase the product. Alternatively, if a price is set above the level to equate uses and sources, there will be excess supply and accumulating inventories of unsold goods.

The distribution issue is also addressed by the state in a centralized system. The CPB sets input prices that include wage levels for different types of employment. A household's income would essentially be these labor earnings, although the state can supplement the labor earnings with grants or transfers to the household. In addition, the worker may receive bonus labor income from the firm or enterprise if the enterprise's target is equaled or surpassed. Given that all capital and land resources are owned by the state, there is no income accruing to the household that has been derived from the private use of capital or land. In the absence of this capital income, there will be less wealth inequality, and probably less income inequality, with socialism compared to laissez-faire capitalism.

Growth is also determined by the CPB's allocation of input use and output targets between current consumption and investment. Higher targets for investment goods will result in reduced current consumption but enhanced future production and an outward shifting of the nation's production possibilities boundary. Given this role for the CPB, a centralized socialist economy has wide latitude in promoting economic growth. Unlike a capitalist market system, where the allocation between current consumption and investment is primarily determined by the individual decisions of households and firms, the CPB can mandate the share of current output that will be devoted to investment.

Decentralized Socialism

The functioning of a **decentralized socialist economy** is less clearly defined than that of the centralized socialist model. Usually in discussing decentralized socialism, there is a presumption that the central planning board has less power and that individual economic actors have more power. Further, market prices that equate uses (demand) and sources (supply) often characterize decentralized socialism.

There are several ways in which economic agents can have enhanced economic power. First, firms may be given autonomy to decide on output levels and the associated input mixes. In these cases, firms usually have some objective function that they are maximizing (perhaps the profitability of the firm or the profitability per unit of labor, as in a labor cooperative). Usually the motive for introducing a more decentralized form of socialism is to provide incentives for the economic actors, particularly the firms, to produce increased quantities of quality products.

A second aspect of decentralized socialism vital to the introduction of the profit motive is the use of market-clearing prices. Freely fluctuating prices that replace officially set prices result in a more efficient allocation of resources. For example, if price has been controlled below the market-clearing level, then the introduction of a freely fluctuating price will lead to a price increase and will work to eliminate the prior shortage or excess quantity demanded.

Third, decentralization of economic decision making is often associated with a greater opening of the domestic economy to international trade. Firms may be allowed to export their output or to import needed inputs. Imported consumer goods may be made available. Generally speaking, the free flow of traded goods is most efficient when market-clearing prices are used. If imported goods were sold below their free-trade price, the state would have to assume costly subsidies that would have to be paid in foreign currency, gold, or through foreign loans. Most socialist countries would prefer avoiding these costly subsidies.

In reality, the decentralized socialist economy often becomes a very mixed system. Both controlled and fluctuating prices tend to exist. Central planners often control key or priority industries in which operating plans continue to be used. Domestic shortages of both commodities and foreign exchange tend to result in controls on imports and exports. While small private enterprises in the service sector (such as restaurants) and private ownership of limited quantities of agricultural land may be permitted, the ownership of larger firms will often be maintained by the state.

The introduction of decentralized economic reforms into a centralized socialist system is complicated by the issues discussed here. First, central planners often resist the transfer of responsibility and authority to individual economic units. Second, introducing market-clearing prices, which will usually increase the price to the consumer, is not viewed as politically astute or acceptable. Finally, the privatization of assets, particularly land and capital, is often considered ideologically suspect, in former Marxian societies.

Nevertheless, some countries succeeded in introducing a large degree of decentralized decision making and private-sector activity into their economies. Yugoslavia and Hungary, despite significant differences, were often cited as highly decentralized socialist states. Recently, China, all the Eastern European countries, and the former Soviet Union have been confronting the problems of transforming a command economy from centralized socialism toward a mixed system of decentralized socialism and capitalism.

SOVIET ECONOMY

The Soviet Union was the first nation to organize an economy based on the ideas of Karl Marx. The Soviet experiment with socialism provides valuable historical precedent to evaluate socialism in practice and to study the transformation from socialism toward capitalism.

Historical Perspective

During World War I, in the early part of 1917, Russia was losing badly in its fight against Germany. Staggering Russian casualties and widespread hunger had virtually destroyed popular support for Tsar Nicholas II. Moderate groups persuaded the tsar to abdicate. A provisional government, one committed to pluralistic democracy, assumed power in March 1917. The new government agreed to continue the war effort, fighting on the side of the Allies. The Germans, eager to have peace on their Eastern front, helped Vladimir Lenin, dedicated to a Marxist revolution and an end to Russian involvement in the war, enter Russia. Uniting the hungry and war-weary urban workers, Lenin overthrew the provisional government in October 1917.

Having seized power, Lenin had the responsibility of organizing the world's first socialist economy. He faced two major problems. First, groups loyal to the tsar (the pre-1917 monarchy of Russia) united with others loyal to the provisional government to fight against the newly formed Marxist government. The Civil War, which severely disrupted the economy of Russia, lasted from 1918 until 1921, when the last remnants of opposition were driven from Russia. Lenin's second major problem was more persistent. Marxist ideology, while providing a detailed critique of capitalism, gave only glimpses of how the socialist state would operate.

In the first years of the revolution, Lenin practiced a brand of socialism called **war communism.** The basic feature of this system was a relatively tight control of the economy and a belief that both urban workers and rural peasants needed sensitizing to instill in them the ideals of the socialist state. This led to Lenin's idea of the *dictatorship of the proletariat,* a rather strict, centralized control over economic and political matters. The Lenin government promulgated and enforced strict grain requisitions that the peasants had to deliver for the feeding of urban workers and the Red Army. Little was offered in return to the peasants; there were few industrial or consumer goods to barter for the grain. The peasants became disenchanted with this "revolution," hoarded grain, and in some cases, reduced plantings. With the food situation growing increasingly serious Lenin changed course in 1921, instituting the **New Economic Policy (NEP),** which was, in many respects, a reversion to capitalism.

With the NEP the farmer was permitted to sell quantities of grain at free-market prices. Given the demand for grain and the paucity of consumer goods, the terms of trade became quite favorable to the agricultural sector. Urban workers had to pay higher food prices. Many peasants became relatively prosperous; they were called **kulaks.** The return of capitalist features, particularly in the rural sector, began to cause concern for many of the revolutionary leaders, who felt that the revolution might be compromised by the capitalist tendencies of the peasants. In 1924, before this issue was resolved, Lenin died. By 1929 Stalin had emerged as the undisputed leader of the Union of Soviet Socialist Republics (USSR).

Soviet Economy under Stalin

A great debate concerning industrialization occupied the attention of Soviet political leaders during the mid-1920s. Rightists favored a continuation of the NEP, arguing that peasants' profits would be voluntarily invested and that there would be an economic integration of the agricultural and industrial sectors. In contrast, those on the left, including Leon Trotsky, argued that the peasants could not be trusted to reinvest their profits and spearhead the industrial development of the Soviet Union, and that forced grain requisitions would have to pay for the industrial development of the USSR. Stalin, who was rapidly gaining power, dismissed the leftists as being insensitive to peasant needs. Having vanquished his leftist rivals, however, Stalin then ignored the rightists, who felt that cultivating peasant cooperation was vital.

Many key economic decisions made by Stalin long influenced the Soviet Union, even in its later attempt at economic and political reform. These economic decisions included (1) the collectivization of agriculture, (2) the institution of a rigid system of central planning, (3) the priority given to investment and growth at the expense of consumption, and (4) the varying degrees of tolerance of private markets.

SOVIET AGRICULTURE. Stalin's actions clearly showed a willingness to exploit the rural sector in order to support Soviet industrialization. Rather than paying peasants higher prices to provide grain for urban dwellers, Stalin suppressed the peasants, beginning the collectivization drive. Peasants were forcibly and violently moved into collective agricultural operations. The long-term effects of

Stalin's decisions are difficult to exaggerate. To this day, agriculture in the republics of the former Soviet Union is predominantly collective in organization. Rural living standards are still very low in comparison to urban living standards, and Soviet agriculture is considered, not withstanding climatic disadvantages, inherently inefficient.

There have been three components to Soviet agriculture. The state and collective farms that evolved from Stalin's collectivization drive of the late 1920s accounted for more than 96 percent of the cultivated surface. While there are some differences in size and crops grown, these two systems (the state and collective farms) operate in a similar manner. These farms can be as large as 35,000 acres, with thousands of employees. Both types of farms have been subject to the central planning authority, which targets crop outputs and inputs within the country's central plan. The government pays bonuses for overfulfillment of the annual plan, theoretically providing some incentive for enhanced productivity. In the last 20 years massive amounts of investment have been poured into the agricultural sector to increase output and productivity. While some increase in output occurred, periodic climatic problems coupled with rising grain demands (primarily for increased meat production) resulted in continual grain deficits and the chronic need for grain imports.

The planning process greatly limited the discretion that the farms' managers had to adjust planting and other work decisions to local conditions and events. Moreover, the incentive structure failed to provide sufficient motivation for the farm employee, who perceived that his individual effort had relatively little effect on the farm's production.

The third component of Soviet agriculture was the legal private sector. Each collective and state farm worker had a private plot of about one acre; in the aggregate these private plots accounted for about 4 percent of cultivated Soviet land. Yet, on these plots approximately 30 percent of the value of Soviet output was produced. The farmer was free to sell his output in the competitive, legal market that existed for agricultural products. Many observers claim that the success of the private plots demonstrated the superiority of private, individual farms where economic incentives are the motivating force.

CENTRAL PLANNING. In 1928 the Soviets embarked on their first five-year plan. While the 1986 reform program of Gorbachev questioned this planning process, the Soviets never entirely discarded the idea of the central plan. Using the material-balance approach previously explained, the central planning agency, GOSPLAN, in conjunction with the central political authorities, set broad aggregate economic targets for such items as growth of Gross Domestic Product, investment, defense expenditures, and consumption spending. Also, output targets in key sectors such as steel and other basic inputs were established. Following these decisions, industry managers would receive preliminary targets for required output levels. The managers then would work with the subordinate firms or enterprises to disaggregate the industry targets into planned output levels for individual firms.

The individual firms would in turn give the industry managers an accounting of their input needs—for raw materials, labor, machinery, and intermediate goods. The industry manager totaled the requested inputs and communicated the aggregate input requirements to GOSPLAN. The planning process would culminate with the five-year plan; there would be more detailed annual and monthly operational plans which, in principle, were legally enforceable contracts between the enterprise and the government.

As indicated, the inefficiencies in this planning process are numerous. First, the desires of the planners do not necessarily coincide with those of the population. In the Soviet Union heavy industrial goods and military items received priority at the expense of consumer goods. A second inefficiency concerns the labor and resources devoted to the planning process. Third, motivation to minimize cost and to increase productivity, both on the part of managers and employees, is lacking. This leads to the inefficiency noted earlier, where excess inputs are requested by the firm, a phenomenon called *input hoarding*. Finally, the incentive to produce commodities of acceptable quality is compromised in a system that awards bonuses based solely on the amount of production.

GROWTH AND INVESTMENT VERSUS CONSUMPTION.
Stalin decided that the growth of the economy was the number one priority facing the USSR in the late 1920s. Stalin wanted a country sufficiently strong to protect itself from other countries hostile to the revolution. Two ramifications of this decision are important. First, the desire to industrialize rapidly led to the need to extract significant economic surplus from the rural areas to support a high level of investment—which increased the attractiveness to Stalin of the collectivization drive. The second was the need to rely on a strong centralized planning mechanism to allocate resources to the priority areas, like heavy industry and national defense.

The drive to industrialize and to promote rapid economic growth was highly successful. From the late 1920s through the early 1970s the annual average rate of growth of Gross Domestic Product was estimated to be approximately 6 percent. Such sustained growth is virtually unprecedented for any nation. The expansion of the favored industries and of defense-related production contributed to this aggregate economic growth through the early 1960s; however, growth in consumer goods lagged. Between the early 1960s and early 1980s resources were diverted to consumption goods, increasing living standards, primarily in urban areas.

Economic growth results either from an increase in the quantities of inputs employed (like labor or capital) or from technological progress—an increase in the productivity with which a given quantity of inputs is employed. The Soviets relied primarily on increases in the quantities of inputs used to achieve their impressive growth rates. In particular, during the last 60 years there have been major increases in the quantity of capital used in the production process, reflecting the priority given to investment. In the earlier years the rural sector disproportionately paid for this investment in terms of reduced consumption and lower living standards. Increased utilization of labor, particularly with the greater labor force participation of females, also contributed to economic growth.

The reduction in the rate of economic growth in the Soviet Union during the 1980s reflected the difficulty the country had in further increasing the use of labor and capital. Rising demands by the defense sector, coupled with the need to provide more consumer goods to meet public demands, limited the share of Gross Domestic Product that could be devoted to capital investment. A reduced rate of growth of the population, particularly in the urbanized western republics, including Russia, led to slower growth in the availability of labor. Given the decreased growth rates of both labor and capital, it became increasingly important for the Soviets to look toward economic reforms to stimulate productivity improvements as a source of economic growth.

TOLERANCE OF PRIVATE MARKETS. In addition to the official marketing channels that operate within the planning process and are subject to controlled and fixed prices, there has always been some legal and quasi-legal free-market activity. The legal acceptance of the free market has tended to vary with the disposition of the government at the time. Generally there has been a prohibition, which has been enforced, against private market activity in industrial goods produced through the planning process, illegal drugs, prostitution, and foreign currency. Private market activity in second-hand goods, some consumer services such as plumbing and carpentry, and in agricultural output produced on the private plots, however, was permitted in varying degrees.

POLITICAL AND ECONOMIC INEQUALITY UNDER THE SOVIET SYSTEM. One presumed appeal of socialism is the greater equality of income and the absence of class structure in the society. How well did the Soviet economy do in this respect? In reality, there have been significant political and economic inequalities in contemporary Soviet society. Marx envisioned the disappearance of class concerns and inequality as the culmination of an evolutionary process characterizing the communist stage of the revolution. Within the socialist stage, according to Marx, there still would be some inequality.

Indeed, inequality has existed throughout the history of the USSR. Stalin, in fact, claimed that equality in wages would be an enemy to the socialist revolution. Inequality was necessary and even desirable to motivate the worker as the socialist society was being developed. Following collectivization and the seizing of land from the kulaks, rural living standards declined in comparison to those of urban workers. To this day, rural residents tend, on average, to have lower incomes, to have access to fewer consumer goods, and to have less desirable housing and public amenities than their urban counterparts. This differential in living standards contributed to the desire by the young to leave rural areas and live in urban areas. While rural-to-urban mobility was highly restricted, the better educated and more ambitious were often able to move to urban areas, draining rural areas of scarce talent.

There was inequality within the urban sector as well. Professional people, particularly successful enterprise managers and highly placed party or government officials, were paid considerably more than laborers. Some estimates placed the degree of inequality of labor income (wages, bonuses, and other compensation) as being comparable to that in some Western societies.

In any economic system where the important decisions are made by government and party officials, political power is greatly sought. Higher status and privilege are accorded those with obvious political power. In the Soviet Union these privileges included shopping in special stores for goods not available to the typical Soviet citizen, better health care, and greater opportunity for travel outside the country.

The extent of the inequality found in the Soviet society and its persistence would seem to have violated a presumed tenant of socialism. Yet, the overall degree of income inequality was significantly less in the former Soviet Union than in the United States. The income from private invested capital greatly skews the American income distribution. (A primary source of inequality in the United States is the very unequal distribution of wealth and the derived income from this invested capital.) In the Soviet Union, where most wealth has been collectively owned, this source of inequality, while not completely absent, was less significant.

Gorbachev Reform Process and Demise of the USSR

Soon after becoming the president of the USSR in 1986, Mikhail Gorbachev launched an economic reform program aimed at revitalizing the Soviet economy to enhance economic growth, to increase the availability of consumer goods, to reduce the power of the state in economic decision making, and to integrate the Soviet economy into the global economy. Economic stagnation, a decline in living standards coupled with rising expectations among the population—particularly the young—and a growing gap between Soviet and Western economic performance had created a situation where economic reform was perceived as vital.

The implementation of the Gorbachev program was not effective. Certain reforms were introduced only in selected geographic areas, while other reforms were discussed but not implemented. Not surprisingly, vested interests, particularly the planning bureaucracy and the political leadership, resisted reforms that would reduce their power and importance. Thus, Gorbachev did not succeed in giving individual firms more control over their output and input decisions. And fearing the consequences of unemployment, the government hesitated to promote efficiency measures that would reduce the use of labor. Moreover, continued high levels of defense spending, encouraged by the military, hindered the transfer of resources to needed consumer goods. Finally, consumer resistance to higher prices obstructed any true price reform that might have resulted in market-determined prices.

The political reform and increased openness of *glasnost* were more successful than the economic reform and restructuring of *perestroika*. The 15 individual republics of the former Soviet Union desired a more rapid economic reform program and even greater political autonomy. In the autumn of 1991, the three Baltic republics (Estonia, Latvia, and Lithuania) became independent states. At the end of 1991, the Soviet Union was formally disbanded. Of the 12 remaining republics, all but Georgia have agreed to form a new Commonwealth of Independent States. Russia and Ukraine are the two largest and economically powerful members of this new commonwealth.

Each of the 15 republics, whether within or outside of the new commonwealth, must confront economic problems in their transition from the command socialism of the Soviet Union. In the concluding section of this chapter we discuss some of these problems.

Transition from Command Socialism

To varying degrees, the former command economies of Eastern Europe and the former republics of the USSR face a common set of problems. For each country, however, the ultimate approach to solving the problems of economic transition from the command economy will undoubtedly vary. In a recent article, Richard E. Ericson summarizes these problems:

> Virtually all calls for reform of the Soviet-type economy propose some form of a market-based economic system. The defining elements of such a system include: generally free, market-determined prices; generally independent firms, motivated by economic considerations; a significant, if not predominant, role for non-state property; industrial regulation in the place of industrial planning; generally hard currency; and a modern financial system, including commercial banking, exchanges, and other financial intermediaries. Yet the nature of the existing economic system makes such a program far harder to implement than most reformers seem to realize.[2]

MARKET-DETERMINED PRICES. As previously explained, the Soviet-style command economies tended to have official fixed prices, which, for basic necessities, were set below market-clearing levels. Consequently, there were excess demands, manifested in shortages, long lines, and a diversion of output to the parallel or illegal black market. To illustrate, at the controlled price, P^*, in Figure 20.1, consumers wish to purchase Q^d; producers wish to supply only Q^s. Therefore, there is an excess demand of $Q^d - Q^s$. In the absence of a price control, price would rise to P_0 and output would increase to Q_0. If the supply function is relatively inelastic, then the increase in price will be proportionately greater than the increase in quantity, as shown in the figure. Given the rigidities in the Soviet-type system of production and distribution, output in the short run may not be highly responsive to price increases if there is not a concurrent dismantling of the socialized sectors of the economy.[3] In this case, consumer resistance to a significantly higher price, without a significant increase in quantity, can be expected. Low-income consumers, particularly the elderly on fixed incomes who have been accustomed to receiving an allotment of output at the lower, controlled price, are apt to suffer great hardship with this type of a *price decontrol* program.

Price decontrol can be further complicated if buyers and sellers have expectations that prices will increase sharply in the future. In that case, buyers, trying to hoard output and avoid future price increases, may attempt to increase their purchases of output, shifting outward the demand curve. Note the shift in demand from D to D' in Figure 20.1. Suppliers, withholding output in anticipation of higher prices, may reduce their offerings at each price, shifting in the supply curve. Note the shift in supply from S to S'. The obvious result is a higher equilibrium price, P_1 (both from the demand increase and the supply decrease), with an uncertain impact on quantity.

---

[2] Richard E. Ericson, "The Classical Soviet-Type Economy: Nature of the System and Implications for Reform," *The Journal of Economic Perspectives* 5, no. 4 (Fall 1991): 23.
[3] When a planned output level is set by the state and supplied to the market regardless of price, the supply curve will be vertical, or perfectly inelastic. In such a case, the increase in price will not lead to any increase in output.

FIGURE 20.1

Price Decontrol in a Command Economy

At the controlled price of P^*, consumers demand Q^d; producers supply Q^s. Therefore, there is excess demand of $Q^d - Q^s$. Following price decontrol, price increases to P_0 and quantity transacted increases to Q_0. The extent of the quantity increase, $Q_0 - Q^s$ is determined by the price elasticity of supply. Consumers, anticipating higher prices, might try to purchase increased amounts of output at each price, shifting the demand curve from D to D'. Suppliers, anticipating higher prices, might reduce output at each price, shifting the supply curve from S to S'. In this case, there would be upward pressure on price with an indeterminate impact on the quantity transacted.

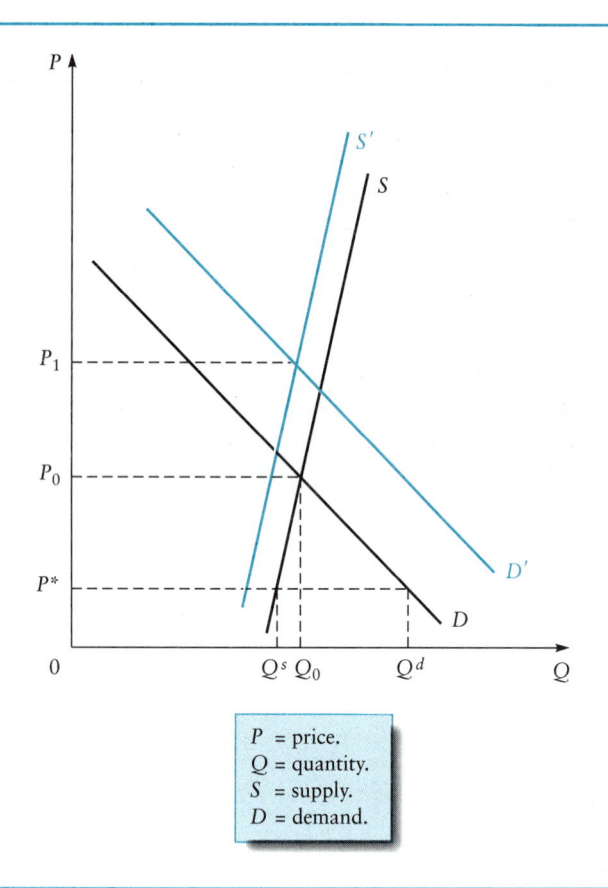

P = price.
Q = quantity.
S = supply.
D = demand.

In summary, price decontrol is complicated by general consumer resistance to higher prices, the impact of higher prices for basic foods and other necessities on the poor and elderly, an uncertain short-run supply response to higher prices, and a tendency for inflationary expectations and panic-buying to bid up current prices.

PRIVATIZING STATES ENTERPRISES. The transition from a command socialist economy to a market capitalist economy requires *privatizing* assets and according property rights to the new owners. This process is very complicated. First, there has not been a strong consensus in all countries as to which assets should be privatized. In certain cases, there has been a desire to continue state ownership of certain industries. Second, there are different methods for privatizing the selected industries and firms. Variants to privatization include selling the firms to workers, selling the firms to the highest bidders—either domestic or foreign—and giving all citizens partial ownership (that is, shares of stock) in the privatized firms. In October 1992, the privatization process began in Russia. Each citizen was given a voucher worth 10,000 rubles (approximately $33 at the time) to be used to bid for shares of ownership in large state enterprises scheduled to be privatized in 1993.

Moreover, privatizing large collective farms in the former Soviet Union will be especially difficult. The organization of the farm and its allocated capital equipment have been based on collectives of many thousands of acres. Such large-scale farming does not lend itself to a simple partitioning of assets among the hundreds of families that often work a collective farm.

Finally, if firms are privatized and operated as profit-maximizing entities, there will be additional economic hardships in the short run. First, in minimizing the cost of producing output, firms will lay off the excess labor that was often assigned to the firms during the period of command socialism. These unemployed individuals are apt to have few resources to survive during the time that it will take to restructure the economy and create new jobs. Moreover, the output produced by these firms is apt to command relatively high prices, generating short-run economic profits for the new owners. Experience suggests that such profits may not be socially acceptable amidst the general austerity during the economic reform. For instance, private cooperatives, encouraged during the Gorbachev reform process, were subject to public resentment when they became relatively profitable. On the other hand, the short-run profits should be the catalyst for the expansion of existing firms and the entry of new firms—reducing prices and increasing outputs—so any government taxation of these profits would reduce the incentive for economic expansion. The actual pace of privatization and sectors to be privatized will no doubt be an ongoing debate within the former command economies.

MONEY AND BANKING. Within the former Soviet Union there was a single currency, the ruble, and a state banking network. Excessive printing of rubles to pay for public sector activity and consumer subsidies led to inflation and an erosion of confidence in the ruble. Residents of the former Soviet Union had ruble balances that were not easily spent given the paucity of consumer goods. In an unpopular decision in 1991, Gorbachev withdrew the 50 and 100 ruble notes from circulation, reducing the wealth of households with savings hoarded in those denominations.

Producers of agricultural goods, with reason, can be hesitant to sell their output for rubles when few consumer goods are available. These producers may prefer holding foodstuffs as a store of value, the price of which may increase, rather than rubles, the value of which may decrease. (Refer again to Figure 20.1, and note the shift in supply from S to S'.) The financial situation is further clouded by individual republics, such as the Ukraine, issuing their own currencies. Economists fear that each republic's having a separate currency will erode financial discipline and contribute to trade barriers among these republics.

The state banking system must be replaced with financial intermediaries which depositors and borrowers trust. By early 1992, many private banks had emerged; these banks, however, are undercapitalized and not experienced in financial intermediation. Moreover, there is no system of government deposit insurance to protect depositors. The development of a credible banking system, so vital to channeling funds from savers to investors, will clearly take several years.

INTERNATIONAL ECONOMIC INTEGRATION. The integration of the former Soviet republics into the international economy involves several related components, including increased trade, a convertible currency, membership in international economic organizations, and a freer flow of foreign investment. Currently, increased trade with the Western economies is hindered both by a lack of purchasing power for the imports from the West and a lack of desired tradable goods produced by the former Soviet states. While there is significant demand for Western goods—foodstuffs, manufacturing, and related services—there is little ability to pay for them. The Russian (Soviet) ruble is not yet fully used as a medium of international exchange. Few exports from the former Soviet territories are in demand in the West; and there is a hesitancy in the West to extend significant credit to the emerging states for the importation of Western goods.

The lack of full convertibility of the ruble also hinders trade and investment flows to former Soviet republics. While the official exchange rate once was as high as $2.00 per ruble (or .5 rubles to the dollar), exchanges of the ruble and the dollar in late 1992 occurred at rates in excess of 400 rubles to the dollar. Given the weak demand for rubles to purchase Russian goods or to invest in the former Soviet Union (and the significant supply of rubles to exchange for foreign currencies), the market value of the ruble against Western currencies will be very low when the ruble formally becomes convertible. Nevertheless, full integration into the world economy will require a convertible currency.

Several of the former republics of the Soviet Union have petitioned for membership in the IMF and World Bank. In April 1992, Russia joined these two organizations, giving it access to the expertise and capital of these bodies.

Finally, joint economic ventures with Western partners are another avenue to acquire Western technology and needed capital. Clearly, a convertible ruble and a sound banking system will facilitate such joint economic endeavors.

CONCLUDING NOTE

Given the political and economic uncertainties in the former Soviet Union and the nations of Eastern Europe, it is impossible to predict the future of the emerging economic reforms. As the events in these nations unfold, we will gain valuable insight into the transition of centralized socialist economies to more decentralized market economies. Difficult issues such as raising consumer prices, reducing the power of the planning bureaucracy, promoting greater global integration of East and West, improving product quality, stimulating work effort without undue income inequality, and reforming agriculture present a challenging agenda for the former command economies. In a real sense, we are witness to an economic experiment of unprecedented scale.

KEY TERMS

labor theory of value
surplus value
Marxism
mature capitalism

centralized socialism
material balance
sources
uses

decentralized socialism
war communism

New Economic Policy
kulaks

QUESTIONS

1. What are the three most important ideas in this chapter? Discuss why each is important.
2. Does the current economic transformation of the former Soviet Union discredit the ideas of Karl Marx? Discuss.
3. Is it possible, within a former command economy, to have meaningful price decontrol without privatization of firms?
4. How could the high-income capitalist market economies effectively aid the former republics of the Soviet Union in their economic transformation? Should this aid be given? Discuss.
5. Do you think socialism (centralized or decentralized) will ever again be considered a viable economic system? Or is it inevitable now that all economies will become capitalist? Discuss.

Glossary

Absolute advantage A lower resource cost of production.
Absolute poverty A household income below a critical minimum level that provides for basic necessities.
Accounting total costs The sum of the firm's total explicit costs; implicit opportunity costs are not included in accounting total costs.
Accounting profits Total revenues minus accounting total costs.
Accounts payable Money owed by a firm; a liability.
Accounts receivable Money owed to a firm for goods or services previously provided; an asset.
Adaptive expectations The hypothesis that economic agents form their expectations of changes in the aggregate price level (inflation rate) on the basis of changes in the aggregate price levels (inflation rates) from earlier periods.
Adjustable peg An exchange rate system similar to a fixed exchange rate but with provision for changing (repegging) the official exchange values of the currencies.
Ad valorem tax A tax of a fixed percentage of the sales price of a commodity.
Aggregate demand curve The graphical representation of an aggregate demand schedule.
Aggregate demand schedule The relationship between the quantity of real national output demanded and the aggregate price level.
Aggregate household income A household's market (factor) income plus any government transfer payments received, minus federal, state, and local income and payroll taxes paid.
Aggregate supply curve The graphical representation of an aggregate supply schedule.

Aggregate supply schedule The relationship between the quantity of real national output supplied and the aggregate price level.
Allocative efficiency A level of production where price and marginal cost are equal; all units of output for which consumers are willing to pay the extra production costs are produced.
Allocative inefficiency A level of production where price and marginal cost are not equal, as in the case of imperfect competition or in the presence of an externality.
Antitrust laws Laws or statutes intended to promote perfect competition and to deter imperfect competition.
Appreciation A rise in the value of an asset. Appreciation of a currency refers to a rise in the international value or an increase in the foreign currency price of the currency.
Assets Possessions or stores of value.
Autonomous consumption The personal consumption expenditures that depend on exogenous factors; in the Simple Keynesian model of national income determination, the personal consumption expenditures that do not depend on disposable personal income.
Autonomous expenditure multiplier The ratio of the change in equilibrium real national income to a change in autonomous expenditures on real national output.
Autonomous imports The imports of goods and services that depend on exogenous factors; in the Simple Keynesian model of national income determination, the imports of goods and services that do not depend on disposable personal income.
Average fixed cost Total fixed costs divided by output.

Average product of labor Output divided by labor.
Average propensity to consume Personal consumption expenditures divided by disposable personal income.
Average propensity to save Personal saving divided by disposable personal income.
Average revenue Total revenues divided by output; equal to price.
Average total cost Total costs divided by output; equals average fixed cost plus average variable cost.
Average variable cost Total variable costs divided by output.

Balance on goods, services, and investment income In the balance of payments account the difference between the credits and debits on merchandise trade, invisible trade, and investment income.
Balance of payments account (BPA) A summary statement of the economic transactions between residents of one nation and the rest of the world over a specified period of time.
Balance sheet A measure of a firm's financial health at a point in time; defined as Assets = Liabilities + Net Worth.
Bank capital The net worth of a bank; equal to the difference between the value of a bank's assets and liabilities.
Barriers to entry Hindrances to new firms entering a market and beginning production.
Basic circular flow of economic activity In a simple economy consisting of households and firms, the flow of factor services from households to firms, who produce final goods and services that are then sold to households. In return is a counterflow of factor payments from firms to households, who use the income for expenditures on the final goods and services produced by firms.
Basic macroeconomic identity The identity relating the expenditures on national output to the disposition of the income generated in the production of the national output.
Basic needs approach A strategy of economic development where the initial emphasis is on providing for the basic needs of the population in food, water, shelter, clothing, primary health care, and education.
Bilateral monopoly Market structure in which there is a single buyer and a single seller.
Black market Any transaction of a commodity for a price above the official price ceiling.
Bond An instrument of debt that promises to repay a certain sum of money with interest at a specified date in the future.
Book value (per share) The current net worth of a firm divided by the number of shares of ownership.

Boom Rapid economic expansion with the economy operating at, or beyond, full employment.
Bracket creep The inflation penalty that occurs when a rise in nominal income proportional to the inflation rate pushes an individual into a higher income tax bracket, reducing the individual's after-tax real income.
Budget constraint For a given set of commodity prices, an equation showing combinations of commodities that just exhaust a given consumer income.
Building and equipment The value of the physical plant owned by a firm; an asset.
Built-in stabilizer Any feature of an economic system that automatically serves to moderate economic fluctuations or trends.
Business inventories The stocks of raw materials, intermediate goods, semi-finished goods, and finished goods held by firms.
Business transfer payments Business contributions to nonprofit organizations and business write-offs of bad debt.

Capital account In a balance of payments account, the subaccount encompassing international trade in assets, with the exception of official assets.
Capital consumption In national income accounting, the estimated loss in value of the nation's physical capital stock.
Capital gain The profit realized when an asset is sold for a higher price than it was purchased.
Capital goods The plant, equipment, and machinery used to produce goods and services.
Cardinal utility The assumption that the level of satisfaction or total utility can be measured in units, often called *utils*.
Cartel An international producers' cooperative; sellers coordinating output decisions to maximize joint economic profits.
Cash The store of value represented by the coins, currency, and checking accounts (demand deposits) that an economic agent possesses.
Centralized socialism The command variant of socialism that relies on a planning board to direct production, allocate inputs, and set prices.
Certificates of deposits Time deposits of minimum denominations.
Ceteris paribus A Latin phrase meaning "other things being equal"; used in partial equilibrium analysis to indicate the isolation of the effects of a change in one of the independent variables in the model.
Change in demand A shift in a demand curve; for each price there is a change in quantity demanded.
Change in quantity demanded Either a movement along a demand curve in response to a change in price,

or for a given price, a movement between two demand curves in response to a change in demand.

Change in quantity supplied Either a movement along a supply curve in response to a change in price, or for a given price, a movement between two supply curves in response to a change in supply.

Change in supply A shift in a supply curve; for each price there is a change in quantity supplied.

Classical monopolist A single seller, typically in the output market.

Classical range The perfectly inelastic (vertical) portion of the aggregate supply curve that corresponds to an economy operating at maximum capacity.

Coase Theorem The thesis that private contracting, without government intervention, can be an efficient remedy for a negative externality.

Coefficient of determination A statistic that measures the percentage of the variation in a dependent variable that is explained by an estimated regression equation.

Coins (or metallic money) Minted money of given denominations.

Command economy An economy where the allocation of resources and the production of goods and services predominantly reflects the decisions of the government or central authorities.

Commodity money An asset that serves as money and has inherent value or utility.

Comparable worth A non-market wage-setting process in which jobs are classified according to criteria such as responsibility and educational requirements.

Comparative advantage A lower opportunity cost of production.

Comparative statics A method of analysis whereby two equilibrium states of a model are compared, with the difference in the equilibrium states due to a change in an exogenous variable in the model.

Compensation of employees The component of national income consisting of payments to, and on behalf of, employees, inclusive of benefits and taxes.

Complementary goods (commodities) Commodities that tend to be consumed jointly; for complements there is an inverse relationship between the price of one commodity and the demand for the other commodity.

Constant-cost industry An industry for which there is no change in input prices as the industry expands or contracts; the long-run market supply curve is horizontal.

Constant costs of production Refers to a situation where the opportunity cost of producing a unit of a commodity does not vary with the rate of production of the commodity.

Consumer durables Consumer goods that are expected to last for several years; examples would include furniture, appliances, and automobiles.

Consumer Price Index (CPI) A price index that measures the changes in the cost of a fixed market basket of goods and services purchased by the average urban household.

Consumer surplus The difference between the price a consumer would willingly pay for a good and the market price of the good.

Consumption possibilities boundary A curve representing the possible combinations of goods and services that could be consumed given the production possibilities boundary and the terms of trade.

Corporate profits The component of national income consisting of the net income (revenues less costs) of corporations before corporate profits taxes are paid.

Corporation A form of business organization where the owners of the firm are stockholders. A private corporation, or *closed corporation* is one where the shares of ownership are not transferred or sold. An *anonymous corporation* is one where shares are sold, typically on a stock exchange.

Cost-push inflation An increase in the aggregate price level due to a decrease in aggregate supply.

Craft unions A labor organization of workers organized according to similar skills, such as electricians.

Credits In a balance of payments account, credits represent outflows of value for which offsetting inflows of payment are usually due. Credits arise from foreign demand for a nation's goods, services, and assets.

Cross-price elasticity of demand A measure of the responsiveness of the demand of one good to a change in the price of another good. A positive value indicates that the goods are substitutes; a negative value indicates that the goods are complements.

Current account In a balance of payments account, the subaccount encompassing merchandise trade, invisible trade, investment income flows, and unilateral transfers.

Current account balance The difference between credits and debits on the current account of the balance of payments account.

Current surplus less subsidies of government enterprises In national income accounting, the profits less the subsidies required to cover the losses of government enterprises.

Cyclical unemployment The unemployment due to deficient aggregate demand.

Debits In a balance of payments account, debits represent inflows of value for which offsetting outflows of payment are usually due. Debits arise from a nation's demand for foreign goods, services, and assets.

Debt The amount of borrowed funds.

Debt financing Borrowing from a commercial bank or the issuing of bonds.

Decentralized socialistic economy An economic system with collective ownership of the means of production, but with a role for markets and individual decision making.

Decreasing-cost industry An industry for which at least one input price falls (rises) as the industry expands (contracts) ceteris paribus; the long-run market supply curve is downward-sloping.

Deflation A decrease in the average level of prices.

Demand curve The graphical representation of a demand schedule.

Demand deposits Funds placed in banks or thrift institutions that can be withdrawn on demand or transferred to other parties by means of a check.

Demanders The potential buyers of a commodity.

Demand-pull inflation An increase in the aggregate price level due to an increase in aggregate demand.

Demand schedule The relationship between the quantity demanded of a commodity and the unit price of a commodity.

Deposit multiplier The ratio of the cumulative change in deposits to an exogenous change in reserves.

Depreciation The estimated value of the capital equipment used up in the production process. Depreciation of a currency refers to a fall in the international value or a decrease in the foreign currency price of the currency.

Depression A severe recession in both depth and duration.

Derived demand The demand for inputs due to the final demand for the output produced with the inputs.

Devaluation A decrease in the official exchange value of a currency.

Developed countries (DCs) The high-income nations of western Europe, North America, Australia, New Zealand, and Japan which have achieved an advanced level of economic development.

Differentiated products Products that, while not identical, satisfy similar needs.

Direct foreign investment The acquisition of real assets, such as property or significant equity in an enterprise, in one nation by residents of another nations.

Dirty floating Aggressive intervention in the foreign exchange market by a monetary authority to depreciate its currency in order to gain a competitive advantage in international trade.

Discount rate The rate of interest the Federal Reserve charges banks on borrowed reserves.

Discouraged workers Individuals 16 years of age or older who are currently out of work and, dispirited by the job prospects, have given up actively looking for employment. Discouraged workers are not counted among the officially unemployed.

Diseconomies of scale The range of production over which total costs increase faster than output; the increasing portion of a firm's long-run average cost curve.

Disposable personal income The personal income of households after taxes are paid and transfers are received.

Dissaving Negative saving; occurs when consumption expenditures exceed income.

Dividends The portion of a firm's accounting profits paid to the owners of the firm.

Economic capacity The output level where a firm's short-run average total cost reaches its minimum.

Economic development The general improvement in the standard of living that accompanies the transformation of an agrarian-based economy into an urban, industrialized economy.

Economic downturn A decline in real national output after a peak in a business cycle.

Economic expansion A sustained increase in real national output after a trough in a business cycle.

Economic growth Sustained increases in per capita output and income.

Economic profits Total revenues minus total costs (including opportunity costs); also defined as accounting profits minus implicit opportunity costs.

Economies of scale The range of production over which output increases faster than total costs; the declining portion of a firm's long-run average cost curve.

Effective competition (workable competition) A market structure with a sufficiently large number of firms producing a sufficiently similar product so that the results of perfect competition are approached.

Efficiency An outcome where it is impossible to enhance the well-being of one individual (or increase the production of one good) without reducing the well-being of another individual (or decreasing the production of another good).

Efficiency wages The payment of a wage above the market-clearing, or equilibrium, wage in order to have a better selection of potential employees, or increase worker loyalty, or deter unionization.

Elasticity The responsiveness of a dependent variable to a change in a related variable. *Arc elasticity* is the percentage change in the value of a dependent variable divided by the percentage change in the value of the related variable. *Point elasticity* is the instantaneous change in the value of a dependent variable for an infinitesimal change in the value of the related variable. *Partial elasticity* is the responsiveness of a dependent variable to a change in one related influence when other related influences are held constant.

Employed The labor market status of working in a job; to be counted as employed in the United States an individual must be at least 16 years of age and presently working—either self-employed, as a paid employee, or as an unpaid family worker of at least 15 hours per week in a family-operated enterprise.

Employment rate The ratio of the employed to the eligible population (the population aged 16 years or older and not in institutions or serving in the armed forces).

Endogenous variable A variable whose value depends on other variables in the model.

Engel's curve A curve showing the relationship between the level of income and the consumption of a good, ceteris paribus.

Entrepreneur The initiator or organizer of the firm, one who assembles the various inputs and directs the production of output.

Equilibrium price A market-clearing price, where the quantity demanded equals the quantity supplied, so there will be no inherent tendency for the price to change.

Equilibrium state A condition in which all the forces in a system are counterbalanced.

Equity A subjective judgement of the fairness or desirability of a distribution of goods or income among individuals.

Excess reserves Any reserves held by a bank in addition to the required reserves.

Exchange rate The price of one currency expressed in units of a second currency.

Exogenous variable An independent variable whose value is assumed to be given or determined by factors outside the model.

Explicit costs Costs or expenses directly incurred by the firm, such as wages and materials.

Export The provision of a good, service, or asset to a resident of another country.

Export expansion An outward-looking strategy of economic development that seeks to stimulate output and employment growth and improve the trade balance by expanding exports.

Exports of goods and services In national income accounting, the component of Gross Domestic Product consisting of expenditures by foreigners.

External balance The simultaneous attainment of a balance of payments equilibrium and a stable exchange rate.

Externality A divergence between the private and public net benefits (benefits less costs) of an action.

Factor markets The markets where the prices and employments of factor services provided by labor, land, raw materials, and financial capital are determined.

Factor-payments approach In national income accounting, the approach to measuring Gross Domestic Product based on the factor incomes generated in the production of national output.

Federal funds rate The rate of interest charged on reserves loaned between banks.

Federal Open Market Committee (FOMC) A committee made up of the 7 members of the Federal Reserve Board of Governors and the presidents of the 12 district Federal Reserve Banks. The FOMC formulates the nation's monetary policy.

Federal Reserve System The central banking system of the United States, consisting of a 7-member Board of Governors and 12 district Federal Reserve Banks across the nation.

Fiat money Money declared by the government to be *legal tender* (acceptable as a means of payment). The intrinsic value of fiat money may be nil, as in the case of paper currency.

Financial capital Money funds available for investment.

Firms One of the three basic economic units of analysis (along with households and the government). The firm is the primary production unit, using factors of production to produce final goods and services.

First-come/first-served A method of allocation of a scarce commodity under a binding price ceiling. Buyers wait in lines for the available supplies of the commodity.

First World A label for the developed countries with predominantly market economies.

Fiscal policy Discretionary changes in government purchases or net taxes intended to achieve some macroeconomic objective.

Fixed coefficients' production function A production function characterized by an inflexible relationship between inputs and output; there are constant returns to scale, but no factor substitution is possible.

Fixed costs Short-run costs that must be paid regardless of the level of output.

Fixed exchange rate An exchange rate system where the official exchange values for currencies are allowed to vary only within narrow bands.

Flexible exchange rate An exchange rate system where the exchange values of currencies are freely determined by market supply and demand.

Flow A variable whose value is defined for a period of time.

Forward contract A contract to buy or sell a specified amount of an asset, such as foreign exchange, at a set price for delivery at a designated date in the future.

Four-firm concentration ratio A measure of market power equal to the sales of the top four firms as a percentage of the total industry sales.

Fourth World A label for the poorest of the less developed countries or the least developed economies.

Frictional unemployment The unemployment reflecting the natural turnover in the labor force due to the new entrants, reentrants, and job leavers searching for employment.

Full-cost pricing In imperfect competition, the firm's setting of a price equal to average total cost plus a profit margin.

Full employment The rate of national unemployment consistent with the underlying population growth and labor force participation rates, the skill composition of the labor force, and the normal rate of utilization of the nation's physical capital stock.

Fundamental disequilibrium Under the Bretton Woods system of adjustable exchange rates, a chronic disequilibrium in the balance of payments of a nation that could only be corrected with a change in the official value of a currency.

Futures markets Markets where contracts to buy and sell commodities or assets at set prices for delivery in the future are traded.

Game theory An analytical framework for interdependent decision making; a player (for example, a firm) has options or strategies where the payoffs depend upon the options or strategies of rival players; useful in analyzing a firm's pricing, output, and advertising decisions.

General Agreement on Tariffs and Trade (GATT) The international organization instituted in 1947 to promote trade liberalization through the reduction of barriers to trade.

Giffen good An inferior good for which the income effect dominates the substitution effect, leading the consumer to purchase more (less) of the good as its price increases (decreases).

Gold standard A fixed exchange rate system where the official or par values of the currencies are denominated in gold.

Government (or central authorities) One of the three basic economic units of analysis (along with households and firms). The government (1) enters the factor markets as a demander of factor services, (2) enters the product markets as a demander of final goods and services and as a provider of public goods and services, (3) collects taxes and makes transfers, and (4) regulates economic activity.

Government purchases of goods and services In national income accounting, the component of Gross Domestic Product consisting of expenditures by the government; includes purchases of final goods and services and the payment of wages to government employees, but excludes government transfer payments and interest on the government debt.

Gross Domestic Product (GDP) The market value of all final goods and services produced in an economy over a year.

Gross National Product (GNP) The market value of all final goods and services produced by residents of a nation over a year. GNP equals Gross Domestic Product plus net factor income received from the rest of the world.

Gross private domestic investment In national income accounting, the component of Gross Domestic Product consisting of the expenditures by firms; the major components of gross private domestic investment are business fixed investment, residential fixed investment, and the change in business inventories.

Herfindahl-Hirschman Index (HHI) A measure of market power equal to the sum of the squared percentage shares of total sales by each firm in the industry.

Households One of the three basic economic units of analysis (along with firms and the government). The household, assumed to be characterized by joint decision making, is the primary consumption unit, allocating income to various expenditures on final goods and services.

Hypothesis A statement expressing a surmised relationship between two variables or events.

Hypothesis of diminishing marginal utility The presumption that additional units of consumption of a commodity provide successively smaller increments of total utility to a consumer.

Immediate run (market period) The time frame during which a firm's output has been produced and cannot be varied.

Impact lag The delay, or time lag, in policymaking between the implementation of a policy and the realization of the policy's intended effects.

Implicit cost An opportunity cost not directly paid; measured by the value of the best alternative use of a resource.

Implicit Price Deflator for GDP A price index equal to the ratio of nominal Gross Domestic Product to real Gross Domestic Product.

Import The receipt of a good, service, or asset from a resident of another country.

Import quota An upper limit, or ceiling, on the quantity of a commodity that can be imported during a period.

Import substitution An inward-looking strategy of economic development that seeks to stimulate output

and employment growth and improve the trade balance by replacing imports with domestic production.
Import tariff A tax on an imported commodity.
Imports of goods and services In national income accounting, the component, consisting of expenditures on foreign goods and services, that is subtracted from Gross Domestic Product.
Incidence The relative burden of a tax; in the case of an excise tax, the proportions of the tax borne by the consumers and producers of the commodity.
Income-consumption curve A curve illustrating the combinations of two goods consumed as income varies, ceteris paribus.
Income effect The response of a consumer to an increase (decrease) in purchasing power which results from a decrease (increase) in the price of a good.
Income elasticity of demand The sensitivity of the demand for a commodity to a change in the average income of the demanders. Ceteris paribus, when the percentage change in quantity demanded is less than the percentage change in income, the good is *income inelastic*. Ceteris paribus, when the percentage change in quantity demanded is greater than the percentage change in income, the good is *income elastic*.
Income statement An accounting measure that indicates the economic performance of a firm over a period of time. Total revenues minus accounting total costs equal accounting profits.
Income tax rate The percentage rate at which income is taxed.
Increasing cost industry An industry for which at least one input price rises (falls) as the industry expands (contracts) ceteris paribus; the long run market supply curve is upward-sloping.
Income velocity of money The average number of times a unit of money is used to pay for expenditures on national output; given by the ratio of nominal Gross Domestic Product to the nominal money supply.
Increasing opportunity cost A rise in the opportunity cost of using resources as more of the resources are committed to a given endeavor.
Indifference curve A curve that represents combinations of two goods providing the same total utility.
Indirect business taxes In national income accounting, the tax receipts on the production and sale of national output. Indirect business taxes include sales and excise taxes and property taxes.
Infant industry In a developing country, an industry that initially needs protection from foreign producers until it can develop into an efficient competitor.
Infant mortality rate The number of deaths to infants under age one, per thousand live births in a year.
Inferior good A commodity with a negative income elasticity of demand; for inferior goods there is an inverse relationship between the average income of the demanders and the demand for the commodity.
Inflation An increase in the average level of prices.
Interest The payment for the use of funds during a time period.
Intermediate goods Goods produced by firms that are incorporated as inputs in the production of other goods—for example, spark plugs in power lawnmowers.
Intermediate range The upward-sloping portion of an aggregate supply curve where increases in the aggregate quantity supplied of real national output are accompanied by increases in the aggregate price level.
Internal balance The simultaneous attainment of full employment and price stability in an economy.
International Monetary Fund (IMF) The international organization founded in 1944 to administer a code of conduct with respect to balance of payments adjustments and exchange rate practices.
International terms of trade The barter exchange rate at which two commodities can be traded internationally.
Inventory The stocks of finished products, semi-finished products, intermediate goods, and raw materials held by a firm.
Invisible trade International trade in services.
Isocost line A line which, for given input prices, shows the combinations of two inputs that represent a given level of total costs.
Isoquant A curve that represents combinations of two inputs that produce a given level of output.

Keynesian cross diagram A graph illustrating the solution to the simple Keynesian model of national income determination; consists of a ray from the origin with a slope equal to 1 and desired aggregate expenditures on real national output plotted against real national output.
Keynesian range The perfectly elastic (horizontal) portion of an aggregate supply curve; corresponds to an economy operating well below full employment.
Kinked demand model A theory that explains the relative price stability often found in oligopoly; a firm assumes that rivals will match price decreases but not match price increases.
Kulaks The relatively prosperous farmers in Russia who were perceived by Stalin to be an obstacle to the development of communism.

Labor force The sum of the employed and unemployed workers in an economy.

Labor theory of value The theory that all value created in the production process originates with the power of labor.

Laffer curve The hypothesized parabolic relationship between income tax revenues collected and the average income tax rate.

Laissez-faire capitalism Market capitalism with minimal government intervention.

Law of demand The hypothesized inverse relationship between the quantity demanded and price of a commodity.

Law (hypothesis) of diminishing returns The hypothesis that in the short run, as the use of a variable input increases, eventually the gain in additional output (the marginal product of the input) will begin to decrease.

Law of supply The hypothesized direct relationship between the quantity supplied and price of a commodity.

Less developed countries (LDCs) The low-income and middle-income nations of Africa, Asia, and Latin America who have yet to achieve a high level of economic development.

Liabilities Obligations or debts.

Limited liability Financial responsibility that is limited to the amount of initial investment; an advantage of a corporation versus other forms of business ownership.

Line of best fit The regression line that best represents the relationship between a dependent variable and independent variable based on a sample of observations.

Liquidity The ease with which an asset can be converted into a medium of exchange without a loss in its value.

Liquidity preference The desire to hold wealth in the form of money balances.

Liquidity preference schedule The relationship between the quantity demanded of money balances and the interest rate.

Long run The time period during which the state of technology is fixed but output can be changed by varying the use of any input.

Long-run expansion path For given input prices, the curve that shows the cost-minimizing input combinations to produce different output levels.

Lorenz curve A graph showing the cumulative shares of household income by the percentages of households.

M1 The most narrow definition of the aggregate money supply; consists of currency in circulation, checkable deposits, and traveler's checks.

M2 A measure of the aggregate money supply equal to the sum of M1 and less liquid assets like savings accounts, small time deposits, money market deposit accounts, and money market mutual funds.

M3 A measure of the aggregate money supply equal to the sum of M2, large time deposits, and other fixed-term money instruments.

Macroeconomics One of the two major branches of economic theory (the other being microeconomics). Macroeconomics deals with the determination of real national output, employment, and the aggregate price level.

Managed float An exchange rate system similar to a flexible exchange rate except that monetary authorities can intervene at their discretion in the foreign exchange market to influence the ranges of fluctuation of the currencies.

Marginal cost The change in total costs per unit change in output.

Marginal factor cost The additional cost of employing another unit of an input.

Marginal product of labor The change in total output per unit change in labor.

Marginal propensity to consume The proportion of any change in disposable personal income used for personal consumption expenditures.

Marginal propensity to import The proportion of any change in disposable personal income used for expenditures on imported goods and services.

Marginal propensity to save The proportion of any change in disposable personal income that is saved.

Marginal propensity to spend The proportion of any change in national income used for expenditures on national output.

Marginal rate of substitution (MRS) The slope of an indifference curve; indicates the rate at which the consumer is willing to substitute one good for another with total utility unchanged.

Marginal rate of taxation The proportion of any change in income to be paid in taxes.

Marginal rate of technical substitution (MRTS) The slope of an isoquant; indicates the rate at which one input can be substituted for another input with total output unchanged.

Marginal revenue The change in total revenues per unit change in output.

Marginal revenue product The additional benefit from employing an input; equal to marginal physical product times marginal revenue.

Marginal utility The change in total utility resulting from a change in the consumption of a given commodity.

Market Any arrangement through which buyers and sellers transact goods, services, or assets.

Market capitalism An economic system in which the means of production are privately owned and used for individual gain. Free, competitive markets accompany capitalism.

Market economy An economy where the allocation of resources and the production of goods and services predominantly reflect the decisions of households and firms.

Market mechanism A system of allocation where the prices and quantities transacted are free to vary according to changes in demand and supply.

Marxism Doctrine based on the writings of Karl Marx; stresses the labor theory of value and the ultimate transformation of capitalism to socialism and then to communism.

Material balance The form of central planning used in the former Soviet Union wherein accounting balances for the sources and uses of each commodity are set.

Materials Intermediate goods used in the production process.

Mature capitalism According to Marxist theory, the advanced phase of capitalism characterized by oligopoly and monopoly and preceding the transition to socialism.

Mean duration of unemployment The average number of weeks of continuous unemployment for unemployed workers.

Medium of exchange An asset that is readily acceptable as payment and thus facilitates transactions in goods and services.

Merchandise trade International trade in physical commodities.

Merit good A good to which all members of the community, regardless of ability to pay, should have access, e.g., primary education.

Microeconomics One of the two major branches of economic theory (the other being macroeconomics). Microeconomics deals with theories of consumer and firm behavior, the determination of prices and outputs in individual markets, and the allocation of resources and distribution of income.

Mixed economic system An economic system combining elements of both capitalism and socialism.

Monetarists Macroeconomists who subscribe to the theory of the natural rate of unemployment and maintain that the key determinant of the level of nominal national income is the nominal money supply.

Monetary base The sum of bank reserves and currency in circulation.

Monetary policy Discretionary changes in the money supply by the Federal Reserve intended to achieve some macroeconomic objective.

Monetary rule A policy advocated by monetarists whereby the Federal Reserve sets the annual growth rate in the money supply equal to the long-run growth rate in real national output.

Monetizing the debt Procedure in which the Federal Reserve purchases U.S. Treasury securities newly issued to finance federal budget deficits.

Money market deposit accounts Funds placed in banks or thrift institutions that earn market interest rates and provide limited check-writing privileges.

Money market mutual funds Funds pooled together by mutual funds and invested in large-denomination certificates of deposit and government securities.

Money substitute An asset that serves as a temporary (but not final) medium of exchange; for example, a credit card.

Monopolistic competition Market structure in which there are many buyers and sellers of a differentiated product.

Monopoly Market structure in which there is a single seller, typically in the output market.

Monopsony Market structure in which there is a single buyer (of either an input or an output).

Most favored nation One of the fundamental principles of the General Agreement on Tariffs and Trade (GATT), indicating that any trade-liberalizing measures between two nations should be extended to all members of GATT.

National debt The total outstanding debt of the federal government; accumulated from the previous federal budget deficits that have not been offset by previous federal budget surpluses.

National income The sum of compensation of employees, proprietors' income, rental income of persons, net interest, and corporate profits. National income is a measure of Gross Domestic Product at factor cost.

National output gap The difference between potential national output and actual national output.

Natural level of employment The level of employment associated with the natural rate of unemployment.

Natural monopoly A situation in which a single firm has economies of scale (decreasing long-run average cost) over a range of output that satisfies market demand.

Natural rate of output The level of real national output corresponding to the natural rate of unemployment.

Natural rate of unemployment The unemployment rate consistent with equilibrium in the labor market, where there is no tendency for workers to alter their price expectations or wage demands.

Negative externality An action where the private net benefits (benefits less costs) exceed the social net benefits; often arises because the social costs of the action are greater than the private costs, as in the case of a paper mill that pollutes.

Neo-Keynesians Modern followers of Keynesian economic theory who believe in active demand-management policies to stabilize the economy near full employment.

Net creditor A nation with a positive net international investment position.

Net factor income In national income accounting, the difference between factor income receipts from the rest of the world and factor income payments to the rest of the world.

Net interest The component of national income consisting of the interest paid by business less the interest earned by business. Consumer interest payments (except on mortgages) and government interest payments are not included in net interest.

Net international investment position The difference between the value of a nation's foreign assets and the value of the nation's assets owned by foreigners.

Net lump-sum taxes Net taxes (taxes less government transfers) that are independent of the level of national income.

Net National Product (NNP) In national income accounting, the value of the nation's output of final goods and services after subtracting the loss in value of the depreciated capital stock. NNP is equal to Gross National Product less capital consumption.

Net private domestic fixed investment Gross private domestic fixed investment (business and residential fixed investment) less capital consumption.

Net private domestic investment Gross private domestic investment less capital consumption.

Net worth The difference between assets (stores of value) and liabilities (debts).

Neutrality of money hypothesis The theory that changes in the nominal money supply affect only nominal variables, such as the aggregate price level and money wages, and do not affect real variables, such as employment and real national output.

New Classicals Macroeconomists who, drawing on the theory of rational expectations, maintain that systematic aggregate demand-management policies will be anticipated and neutralized, thus such policies will have no effect on real national output or employment.

New Economic Policy (NEP) Lenin's 1921–1924 economic program which stressed a return to market forces and private initiative to revitalize the Russian socialist economy.

Nominal GDP Gross Domestic Product measured in current dollars or in the prices prevailing when the goods and services were produced.

Non-price competition The competition between firms for sales using advertising and differences in product quality or service.

Non-satiation The restriction that additional consumption of a good will never lower total utility and that marginal utility will therefore always be nonnegative.

Nontariff barriers to trade Quotas, domestic content legislation, customs regulations, and other non-tariff measures intended to restrict international trade.

Normal goods Commodities with positive income elasticities of demand; there is a direct relationship between the average income of the demanders and the demand for the commodity.

Normative statement A statement expressing an opinion or value judgment.

Official reserve assets The gold, foreign currencies, and special drawing rights owned by the monetary authorities of a nation plus the reserve position of the nation at the International Monetary Fund.

Official settlements account In a balance of payments account, the subaccount that records the acquisitions of official assets by monetary authorities and governments.

Oligopoly Market structure in which there are only a few producers of either a standardized or differentiated product.

Open market operations Purchases or sales by the Federal Reserve of previously issued U.S. government securities.

Opportunity costs The wants not met or possibilities not realized when resources are used for a given purpose; measured by the best alternative use of the same resources.

Orderly marketing arrangements A system of quotas negotiated between countries that serves to limit foreign access to a market.

Ordinal utility The assumption that the consumer is able to rank preferences but cannot measure the actual level of satisfaction or total utility.

Output-expenditure approach In national income accounting, the approach to measuring Gross Domestic Product based on the aggregate expenditures required to purchase the national output produced.

Par values The official exchange values of currencies in a fixed or adjustable peg exchange rate system.

Partial equilibrium analysis An analysis of the effects of a change in an independent variable on a dependent variable while holding constant the levels of the other independent variables.

Partnership A business jointly organized and owned by two or more individuals.

Payment-in-Kind (PIK) A government agricultural program for selected crops whereby farmers agree to plant less of the crops in exchange for like crops released from government storage.

Peak The upper turning point of a business cycle.

Perfect competition The market structure in which there are many relatively small buyers and sellers of a standardized (identical) product.

Permanent income The real disposable personal income expected by a household based on the employment prospects and financial wealth of the members of the household.

Permanent income hypothesis The theory that personal consumption expenditures are determined by permanent income.

Personal consumption expenditures In national income accounting, the component of Gross Domestic Product consisting of the expenditures of households; usually disaggregated into durable goods, nondurable goods, and services.

Personal income Current income received by persons from all sources, including transfer payments.

Personal saving In national income accounting, the residual after subtracting from disposable personal income the following: personal consumption expenditures, interest payments on consumer debt, and net personal transfers to foreigners.

Phillips curve A plot of an inflation rate against the unemployment rate for an economy over time. A Phillips curve is hypothesized to be shaped like a hyperbola, illustrating an inverse relationship between inflation and unemployment rates in the short run.

Physical capital The plant, equipment, and machinery used to produce goods and services.

Planned inventory investment The planned or desired change in business inventories over a period.

Population momentum The built-in potential for rapidly growing populations to continue to increase in size after the onset of replacement level fertility.

Portfolio A collection or arrangement of assets.

Portfolio investment In the balance of payments account, the acquisition of financial assets such as stocks, bonds, and bank balances in one nation by residents of another nation.

Positive externality An action where the social net benefits (benefits less costs) of production exceed the private net benefits, as in the case of the recycling of plastic bottles and aluminum cans.

Positive statement A statement whose validity can be confirmed or tested against evidence.

Potential national output (or full employment output) The rate of real national output that would be produced if the economy were operating at full employment.

Precautionary demand (for money) The demand for money balances, beyond the transactions demand, to cover unforeseen expenditures.

Prediction error The difference between the actual value of a dependent variable and the value of the variable predicted from a regression equation.

Present value The value in current dollars of a future stream of payments; *future values* are discounted by the opportunity cost of capital. *Net present value* is the discounted value of a stream of benefits and costs, useful in analyzing the desirability of an investment.

Price ceiling A maximum price for a commodity above which no transactions can legally take place.

Price floor A minimum price for a commodity below which no transactions can legally take place.

Price of capital The cost per unit of using a capital good (e.g., a machine), consisting of the opportunity cost of invested funds and the depreciation cost of the capital good.

Price-consumption curve A curve showing the combinations of two goods consumed by an individual as the price of one of the goods varies, ceteris paribus.

Price discrimination A pricing strategy practice where a monopolist charges different prices to different groups of consumers for identical output produced at the same cost. With *perfect price discrimination*, each consumer is charged a price equal to the full willingness to pay for a unit of output, with the monopolist capturing all the consumer surplus.

Price elasticity of demand A measure of the responsiveness of the quantity demanded of a commodity to a change in the price of the commodity. When the percentage change in quantity demanded is less in absolute value than the percentage change in price, demand is *price inelastic*. When the percentage change in quantity demanded is greater in absolute value than the percentage change in price, demand is *price elastic*. When the percentage change in quantity demanded is equal in absolute value to the percentage change in price, demand is *unitary elastic*.

Price elasticity of supply A measure of the responsiveness of the quantity supplied of a commodity to a change in the price of the commodity.

Price parity index An index giving the terms of trade in farming; equal to the ratio of the average prices received by farmers (for agricultural output) to the average prices paid by farmers (for agricultural inputs and financing).

Price support A type of price floor whereby the government will purchase any surplus of a designated commodity at the support price.

Price taker An economic actor that accepts price as given and is unable to influence that price, e.g., an individual firm within perfect competition.

Prime rate of interest The rate of interest charged by commercial banks on loans to their best corporate customers.

Producer Price Index (PPI) A price index that measures the changes in a fixed market basket of goods at different stages of production.

Producer surplus The surplus generated by a firm when it sells a unit of output at a price exceeding the marginal cost of production; equals total revenues minus total variable costs.

Producers' cooperative Firms joining together to coordinate their output decisions to maximize joint economic profits.

Product markets The markets where the prices and quantities transacted of final goods and services are determined.

Production function For a given state of technology, the relationship between the inputs used and the maximum outputs of a commodity produced.

Production possibilities boundary A curve representing all the possible combinations of goods and services that could be produced using the available resources fully and efficiently.

Profits The difference between total revenues and total costs.

Proprietors' income The component of national income consisting of the income of unincorporated enterprises (single proprietorships and partnerships).

Pure economic rent A relatively permanent surplus to an input; equal to the difference between the actual payment to the input and the payment that would be required to have the input supplied.

Pure public good A commodity for which the consumption by one individual does not reduce the consumption of others; moreover, it is often difficult to exclude nonpayers from consumption. Public goods (such as national defense) are typically provided by government.

Quantity demanded The total amount of a commodity that buyers are willing to purchase during a given time period.

Quantity supplied The total amount of a commodity that suppliers are willing to sell during a given time period.

Quasi-economic rent A shorter-run surplus to an input; equal to the difference between the actual payment to the input and the payment that would be required to have the input supplied.

Quota rent The difference between the total expenditures of domestic consumers and the total revenues foreign producers would otherwise receive for supplying the quantities under a binding quota on an imported commodity.

Radical school of economic development The Marxist view that the underdevelopment of the less developed countries stems from the past exploitation by the Western capitalist nations and is perpetuated through the current international economic system.

Rational expectations The hypothesis that economic agents form their expectations of changes in the aggregate price level (inflation rate) on the basis of all the available information, especially with respect to the anticipated fiscal and monetary policies.

Rationing A method of allocation for a scarce commodity under a binding price ceiling. The available supplies of the commodity are sold on the basis of a distribution system devised by the central authorities.

Reaganomics In general, the label for the economic policies of the two Reagan administrations (1981–1988); most closely identified with the basic fiscal policy package of tax cuts and increased defense spending of the first Reagan administration (1981–1984).

Real GDP The value of Gross Domestic Product when measured in constant dollars or in the prices prevailing in a base period.

Recession An economic downturn or a decline in real national output for at least two consecutive quarters.

Reciprocity The basis for bilateral trade negotiations under the General Agreement on Tariffs and Trade (GATT). If one nation grants trade concessions to another nation, that second nation should respond with trade concessions to the first nation.

Recognition lag The delay, or time lag, in policymaking between the onset of a problem and the identification of the problem.

Recycling of petrodollars The lending by Western commercial banks of the dollar deposits from the current account surpluses of the oil-exporting nations to less developed countries to finance the increases in their current account deficits from the sharply higher world prices of oil in the 1970s.

Relative income A household's ranking within the distribution of all household incomes.

Rental income The component of national income consisting of the income earned by individuals on rental units and royalties. Also included in rental income is the estimated value of owner-occupied housing.

Replacement level fertility The level of fertility where the average woman has just enough children to replace herself and her partner. If maintained, replacement level fertility will eventually yield zero population growth.

Required reserve ratio The minimum percentage of deposits that a bank must hold as reserves.

Reserves (of a bank) The cash in a bank's vault and the deposits of the bank at a Federal Reserve Bank.

Residential fixed investment The value of new residential construction during a period of time.

Response lag The delay, or time lag, in policymaking between the identification of a problem and the implementation of a policy to address the problem.

Retained earnings The portion of a firm's accounting profits retained for use by the firm.

Returns to scale The consequence for output of a proportionate change in all inputs. With *constant (increasing, decreasing)* returns to scale, a proportionate change in all inputs leads to a change in output of the same (a greater, a smaller) proportion.

Revaluation An increase in the official exchange value of a currency.

Savings accounts Funds placed in banks or thrift institutions that earn interest and on which there may be restrictions on withdrawals.

Scarcity The situation in which, for the given inputs and state of technology, society's production of final goods and services will be less than the total wants of the society.

Scatter diagram A plot of the ordered pairs of sample observations for a dependent variable and an independent variable.

Second World A label for the former command economies of the Soviet Union and Eastern Europe.

Sellers' preference A method of allocation for a scarce commodity under a binding price ceiling. The available supplies of the commodity are sold on the basis of criteria determined by the sellers.

Service The performance of a task.

Shortage An excess quantity demanded.

Short run The time period in which output can only be varied by changing the use of the variable inputs; in the short run at least one input is fixed.

Short-run industry supply For an industry, the horizontal summation of the firms' supply curves, or the summation of the portion of each individual firm's marginal cost curve that rises above its average variable cost curve.

Shut-down price The price of output below which the firm would cease production in the short run, accepting losses equal to total fixed costs. At the shut-down price, total revenues equal total variable costs.

Simple quantity theory of money The hypothesis that, assuming a constant income velocity of money, the level of nominal national income is determined by the nominal money supply.

Single proprietorship A business organized and owned by a single individual.

Socialism An economic system in which the means of production are collectively owned. *Command socialism* refers to an economy directed with central planning. *Market socialism* is more decentralized and combines markets with collective ownership.

Social science A discipline such as economics, psychology, anthropology, or political science that deals with human behavior and social institutions.

Sources The origins for commodities within material balance planning; include production, use of inventories, and imports.

Specific tax A tax of a fixed monetary amount on each unit sold of a commodity.

Speculative demand (for money) The demand for money balances to be in a position to profit from expected changes in the market prices of assets.

Stagflation The concurrence of rising inflation and a rising unemployment rate (or declining rate of real national output).

Standardized product A good for which the output of each seller is identical.

Statistical discrepancy The residual item in national income accounting included in the factor-payments approach to reconcile the estimate for Gross Domestic Product with that from the output-expenditure approach.

Stock A variable whose value is defined at a point in time. Stock also refers to a share of ownership in a corporation giving the owner a proportionate claim to any corporate profits.

Storage scheme A mechanism for stabilizing prices and revenues received by farmers. The excess quantity supplied (demanded) of a commodity on the market at the target price is added to (released from) storage.

Store of value An asset that represents a stock of purchasing power or command over goods and services.

Structural unemployment Unemployment due to a mismatching between the skills possessed by the unemployed and the skills required for the open jobs.

Subsidy A negative tax or other assistance to firms that serves to lower the supply price of a commodity.

Substitute goods (commodities) Commodities that tend to be consumed independently; for substitutes there is a direct relationship between the price of one commodity and the demand for the other.

Substitution effect The reaction of an economic agent to a change in relative prices, purchasing more (less) of a good for which the relative price has fallen (increased).

Sunk cost A cost that has already been paid and is not likely to reoccur, e.g., legal fees to establish a business.

Suppliers The potential sellers of a commodity.

Supply curve The graphical representation of a supply schedule.

Supply schedule The relationship between the quantity supplied of a commodity and the unit price of the commodity.

Supply-side economics The set of policy prescriptions designed to promote economic growth through increases in aggregate supply.

Surplus An excess quantity supplied.

Surplus value According to Marx, the portion of value created by labor in the production process that is kept by the capitalist.

Sustainable economic growth Economic growth (an increase in national output) that does not impair the natural environment.

Target price/deficiency payment scheme A program where the government pays farmers of designated crops the difference between the target price and market-clearing price for each unit of the quantity supplied of the crops.

Tax credit A reduction in taxes owed for qualifying expenditures; for example, an investment tax credit allows a firm to deduct from taxes owed a certain percentage of the purchase price of a qualifying capital good.

Technical efficiency A situation in which the output is produced with a minimum of inputs; that is, no inputs are redundant or wasted.

Theory of contestable markets The theory that with relatively costless entry into an industry, competitive results are apt to be approached regardless of the number of firms in the industry.

Third World A label for the less developed countries.

Time deposits Funds placed in banks or thrift institutions that earn interest and on which there is a fixed maturity before withdrawal.

Token coins Coins where the face value of denomination exceeds the intrinsic value of the metal in the coins.

Total costs The sum of all costs, fixed costs plus variable costs, including all relevant opportunity costs.

Total expenditures The total outlays of buyers on the purchases of a commodity.

Total revenues The total receipts of sellers of a commodity.

Trade unionism The organizing of labor in the pursuit of common goals, such as improved wages and fringe benefits or more secure employment.

Tradition Methods of production, distribution, and consumption established in the past and perpetuated by custom.

Transactions costs Costs associated with the process of exchanging a good, such as search costs by the contracting parties.

Transactions demand (for money) The demand for money balances to serve as a medium of exchange for planned expenditures.

Transfer payments Payments of income or income-in-kind for which no goods are produced nor services rendered in return.

Transitory income The difference between actual real disposable personal income and permanent income.

Traveler's checks Check-like money favored by travelers because they will be reimbursed if the checks are lost and because of the checks' wide acceptance as a means of payment.

Trough The lower turning point of a business cycle.

Underground economy The economic activity and income generation that are underreported or unreported, thus on which no taxes are collected.

Unemployed The labor market status of not working; to be counted as unemployed in the United States, an individual must be at least 16 years of age, currently out of work, and either actively seeking work, waiting to be recalled to a job within a month, or waiting to report to a new job within a month.

Unemployment rate The ratio of the unemployed to the labor force.

Unilateral transfers In balance of payments accounting, the international flows of goods, services, and assets for which no payments are expected.

Unit cost of labor The labor cost of producing a unit of output, given by the ratio of the average cost of labor to the average product of labor.

Unit of account A standardized unit of measurement.

Unplanned inventory investment Unplanned or unwanted changes in business inventories that arise when actual sales differ from expected sales.

Uses The dispositions of goods within material balance planning; includes use for final consumption, production of other commodities, inventories, and exports.

Utility The total satisfaction associated with the consumption of commodities over a given time period.

Value added The difference between the value of a firm's output and the value of the inputs it purchased from other firms.

Value of marginal product Marginal revenue product within a competitive output market; marginal physical product times the market price of output.

Variable costs Short-run costs associated with the use of the variable inputs.

Very long run The time period during which the state of technology and the use of any input may change.

Voluntary export restraint A quota, or ceiling, a country accepts on the quantity of a commodity it will export during a period.

Wages The cost of labor during a time period; the wage rate (price of labor) multiplied by the number of units of labor employed.

War communism The form of centrally directed economy introduced by Lenin following the 1917 Revolution; it lasted until 1921.

World Bank (International Bank for Reconstruction and Development) The international institution formed with the International Monetary Fund in 1944 to assist in (1) the reconstruction of the war-torn economies of Europe and Japan and (2) the economic development of the less developed countries of Asia, Africa, and Latin America.

INDEX

A

Absolute advantage, 36–38
Adaptive expectations, 293–94
Adjustable peg exchange rate systems, 323, 332–34
Aggregate demand
    comparative statics and, 199–203
    curve, 99–101, 188–94
    curve shifts, 192–94
    schedule, 99, 188
Aggregate economic analysis. *See* Macroeconomics
Aggregate supply
    comparative statics and, 199–203
    constraints and fiscal policy, 221–22
    curve, 101–2, 194–99
    curve shifts, 195–99
    schedule, 101, 194
Appreciation, 312
Arc elasticity, 71–72, 79
Assets, official reserve, 310
Autarky, 43
Autonomous consumption, 128
Autonomous expenditure multiplier, 141–45
Autonomous imports, 133
Average propensity to consume, 129
Average propensity to save, 130–31
Average revenue (AR), 74

B

Balanced budget amendment, 232–34
Balanced budget change, 219–20n.5
Balance of payment accounts (BPAs)
    capital account, 308–9
    credits, 305
    current account, 307–8
    current account balance, 308
    debits, 305–6
    net unilateral transfers, 307
    offical settlements account, 309–11
    unilateral transfers, 307
Balance on goods, services, and investment income, 307
Bank capital, 171
Banking system and money supply
    See also Money/money market
    cash withdrawals, 175–78
    commercial banks, 168–71
    deposit expansion, 171–78
    deposit multiplier process, 171–78
    discount rate, 178, 239
    federal funds rate, 178
    Federal Open Market Committee (FOMC), 168, 237
    Federal Reserve System, 167–68
    Federal Reserve System's influence on money supply, 178–82
    loans and excess reserves, 174–75
    loans and required reserves, 172–74
    monetary base, 179
    open market operations, 179, 239–40
    required reserve ratio, 169, 238
    savings and loan crisis, 166–67
Barter, 148
Basic needs approach, 354–56
Bonds, 159–60
Boom, 204
BPAs. *See* Balance of payment accounts
Bracket creep, 265–66, 272–73
Brady, Nicholas, 361
Brady Plan, 361
Bretton Woods, 332, 335–36
Brown, Lester, 121–22
Budget deficits, 12
    balanced budget amendment, 232–34
    financing, 229–30
    macroeconomic identity and, 230–32
    momentum of national debt and future of, 229
    national debt and, 227–32
Built-in stabilizers, 226–27
Business cycles, 203–8
Business inventories, 109–10
Business investment, supply-side economics and, 269–70
Business transfer payments, 115
Buyers. *See* Demand/demanders

C

Capital account
    balance of payments accounts and, 308–9
    commercial banks and, 171
Capital consumption, 115
Capital gains, 268
Capital goods, 10
    in production possibilities boundary example, 25

Capitalism
  competitive, 6
  laissez-faire, 5
  market, 4–5
  Marx and his critique of, 368–70
  mature, 369
  monopoly, 6
Capital stock, in production possibilities boundary example, 25
Carlson, John, 252
Cash withdrawals, 175–78
Central authorities. *See* Government
Centralized socialism, 371–72
Certificates of deposit (CDs), 153
Ceteris paribus, 12–13, 51
Checking accounts, 151–52
Checks, traveler's, 152
Circular flow of economic activity, basic, 4, 10
Classical range of aggregate supply curve, 102, 195
Coefficient of determination, 17n.8
Coins or metallic money, 150
Command economy, 12
Commercial banks
  capital account and, 171
  assets and, 169–71
  excess reserves and, 170
  liabilities and, 169
  required reserve ratio and, 169
  reserves and, 169
  role of, 168–69
Commodities
  complementary, 53
  exports of, 110
  government purchases of, 110
  imports of, 110
  inferior, 52–53
  normal, 52
  substitute, 53
Commodity money, 150
Communism, war, 374
Comparative advantage, 36, 39–40
Comparative statics
  aggregate demand and supply and, 199–203
  changes in market equilibrium and, 65–67
  multiplier effect and, 140–45
Compensation of employees, 113
Competitive capitalism, 6
Complementary commodities, 53
  cross-price elasticity of demand and, 79
Constant costs of production, 37
Consumer Price Index (CPI), 92–97
Consumption
  autonomous, 128
  capital, 115
  expenditures, 131
  function and Simple Keynesian model, 128–29
Consumption possibilities boundary (CPB), international trade and, 42–45
Corporate profits, 114
Cost-push inflation, 288
Costs. *See* Opportunity costs

Credit cards, 152
Credits, balance of payments accounts and, 305
Cross-price elasticity of demand, 79
Current account, 307–8
Current account balance, 308
Current surplus less subsidies of government enterprises, 115
Cyclical unemployment, 285–86

D

Debased money, 150
Debits, balance of payments accounts and, 305
Debt
  cartel, 361
  emergence of external debt problem in less developed countries, 359–61
  national, 227–29
Decentralized socialism, 372–73
Deflation, 91, 291
Demand/demanders
  aggregate, 99–102, 186–209
  change in demand, 53–56
  change in quantity demanded, 54–56
  cross-price elasticity of, 79
  curve, 51
  curve for foreign exchange, 312–13
  defining, 50
  determinants of demand schedule, 52–53
  elasticity examples for, 82–83
  income elasticity of, 80–82
  law of, 51n.1
  price elasticity of, 72–79
  quantity demanded, 51, 54–56
  schedule, 51–56
Demand deposits, 151–52
Demand management
  external balance and, 336–37
  Keynes and, 213–15
  monetary policy and, 244–48
Demand-pull inflation, 288
Deposit multiplier process, 171–78
Depreciation, 312
Depression, 204
  Great, 214n.2
Devaluation, 332
Developed countries (DCs), 346
Direct foreign investment, 309
Dirty floating, 336
Discount rate, 178, 239
Discouraged worker, definition of, 89
Disposable personal income, 14, 116–17
Dissaving, 131
Distribution, 3
Double taxation, 269
Durning, Alan, 365

E

Economic downturn, 204
Economic expansion, 204

Economic growth and development
  agenda for, 363–64
  basic needs approach, 354–56
  country classification, 346–51
  defining economic development, 351
  defining economic growth, 351
  emergence of external debt problem, 359–61
  growth model approach, 351–54
  radical school's critique, 362
  trade and, 357–59
Economic models
  example of developing, 12–19
  extending, 17–19
  individual level, 24–26
  national level, 26–31
Economic Report of the President, 14
Economics
  defining, 2
  as a social science, 8
Economic systems
  efficiency and equity in, 6–7
  market capitalism, 4–5
  mixed, 5–6
  socialism, 5
  tradition, 4
Economy, overview of modern, 9–12
Efficiency in economic systems, 6–7
Elasticity
  arc, 71–72
  cross-price elasticity of demand, 79
  definition of, 71
  examples of demand, 82–83
  income elasticity of demand, 80–82
  measurement of, 71–72
  partial, 72
  point, 71n.1
  price elasticity of demand, 72–79
  price elasticity of supply, 83–84
  of residential demand for electricity, 82
Employed, definition of, 89
Employment
  full, 203
  natural level of, 295
  rate, 286
Endogenous variable, 14
Environmental issues, 196
Equilibrium
  exchange rate, 315–17
  money market, 182–84
  price, 60–61
  quantity, 61
  real national output and aggregate price level, 103–4
Equilibrium state
  comparative statics, 65–67
  defining, 50
  determining price and quantity, 60–65
Equity in economic systems, 6–7
Ericson, Richard E., 379
Excess reserves, commercial banks and, 170
  loans and, 174–75
Exchange rates
  bias of, 120
  changes in, 317–20
  consequences of changes in, 319–20

Exchange rates *(continued)*
  definition of, 311–12
  determinants of changes in, 317–19
  equilibrium, 315–17
  U.S. dollar, 337–42
Exchange rate systems
  adjustable peg, 323, 332–34
  fixed, 323, 329–32
  flexible, 323, 324–28
  managed float, 323, 336
Exogenous variable, 14
Expenditure(s)
  consumption, 131
  interest-sensitive, 187–88, 222–23
  investment, 131–32
  output-expenditure approach, 109–12
  personal consumption, 109
  weights, 92
Export expansion, 357, 358–59
Exports of goods and services, 110
External balance
  definition of, 323
  demand management and, 336–37

F

Factor markets, 10
Factor-payments approach, 113–15
Federal Deposit Insurance Corp. (FDIC), 171
Federal funds rate, 178
Federal Open Market Committee (FOMC), 168, 237
Federal Reserve System
  discount rate, 178, 239
  influence on money supply, 178–82
  monetary base, 179
  open market operations, 179, 239–40
  required reserve ratio, 169, 238
  role of, 167–68
Fiat money, 151
Financial capital, 10n
Firms, role of, 10
First World, 348n.4
Fiscal policy
  aggregate supply constraints and, 221–22
  balanced budget amendment, 232–34
  budget deficits, 227–32
  built-in stabilizers, 226–27
  changes in government spending, 217–18
  changes in net lump-sum taxes, 218–21
  compared with monetary policy, 253–57
  definition of, 213
  effectiveness of, 221–26
  interest-sensitive expenditures and, 222–23
  Keynes and demand-management, 213–15
  lags in, 223–26
  national debt, 227–29
  options, 215–21
Fixed coefficients' production function, 352
Fixed exchange rate systems, 323, 329–32

Flexible exchange rate systems, 323, 324–28
Flow, production of goods and, 27–28
Foreign exchange
  See also Exchange rates
  demand curve for, 312–13
  markets, 305
  supply curve of, 314
Foreign investment, methods of, 309
Foreign saving, 231
Forward contracts, 327n.2
Fourth World, 347, 348n.4
Frictional unemployment, 284–85
Fundamental disequilibrium, 333

G

GDP. *See* Gross Domestic Product
General Agreement on Tariffs and Trade (GATT), 351, 362
General Theory of Employment, Interest and Money, The (Keynes), 186
Glasnost, 378
GNP. *See* Gross National Product
Gold standard, 329
Goods and services. *See* Commodities
Gorbachev, Mikhail, 378
GOSPLAN, 375–76
Government
  outlays, 110
  purchases of goods and services, 110
  economic role of, 10–12
  transfers, 110
Gramm-Rudman-Hollings Balanced Budget Act (1985), 232
Gresham's Law, 150
Gross Domestic Product (GDP)
  business inventories, 109–10
  capital consumption, 115
  defining, 107
  exports of goods and services, 110
  factor-payments approach, 113–15
  government purchases of goods and services, 110
  gross private domestic investment, 109
  Implicit Price Deflator for, 96n.8, 99
  imports of goods and services, 110
  measurement of, 109–15
  nominal versus real, 98–99
  output-expenditure approach, 109–12
  personal consumption expenditures, 109
Gross National Product (GNP)
  compared to Gross Domestic Product, 113
  problems with using with country classification, 349
  welfare and, 119–22
Gross private domestic investment, 109
Growth, 4
Growth model approach, 351–54

H

Households, role of, 9–10

Hypothesis testing, 13–17

I

Impact lag, 225–26, 245
Implicit Price Deflator for Gross Domestic Product, 96n.8, 99
Imports
  autonomous, 133
  of goods and services, 110
  marginal propensity to import, 133
Import substitution, 357
Income
  disposable personal, 14, 116–17
  effect, 262
  permanent, 225n.7
  personal, 116
  proprietors', 113
  rental, 113–14
  transitory, 225n.7
Income elastic, 81
Income elasticity of demand
  definition of, 80
  formula for, 80
  income elastic, 81
  income inelastic, 81
Income inelastic, 81
Income tax rate, 131
Income transfers, 11
Income velocity of money, 249–50
Indirect business taxes, 114
Individual Retirement Accounts (IRAs), 273
Infant industries, 359
Infant mortality rate, 121
Inferior commodities, 52–53
Inflation
  causes of, 288–89
  consequences of, 289–92
  Consumer Price Index used to measure, 92–97
  contractionary monetary policy and, 242–44
  cost-push, 288
  demand-pull, 288
  Implicit Price Deflator for Gross Domestic Product, 96n.8
  Phillips curve, 280–83
  Producer Price Index, 96n.8
  rate, 88, 91–97
In-kind transfers, 11
Inquiry into the Nature and Causes of the Wealth of Nations, An (Smith), 5, 368
Interest-sensitive expenditures, 187–88
  fiscal policy and, 222–23
Intermediate goods, 10
Intermediate range, 102, 194–95
Internal balance, 323
International Bank for Reconstruction and Development (IBRD). *See* World Bank
International Monetary Fund (IMF), 332, 333, 351, 360, 382
International terms of trade, 40–41
International trade
  See also Balance of payment accounts

absolute advantage, 36–38
comparative advantage, 36, 39–40
consumption and production possibilities boundaries, 42–45
determining the gains from trade, 40–41
opportunity costs and absolute advantage, 37–38
opportunity costs and comparative advantage, 39–40
International transfers, 110
Inventory investment, planned and unplanned, 132
Investment
    expenditures, 131–32
    methods of foreign, 309
Invisible trade, 307

K

Keynes, John Maynard, 102n.14, 186–87, 370
    demand-management and, 213–15
Keynesian cross diagram, 135–37
Keynesian range, 102, 194
    See also Simple Keynesian model
Kulaks, 374

L

Labor
    supply and supply-side economics, 262–66
    theory of value, 369
    unit cost of, 197
Labor force and unemployment rate, 89
Laffer, Arthur, 271–72
Laffer curve, 271–72
Lags in policymaking, 223–26, 245
Laissez-faire capitalism, 5
LDCs. *See* Less developed countries
Lenin, Vladimir, 5, 373–74
Less developed countries (LDCs)
    agenda for development in, 363–64
    basic needs approach, 354–56
    characteristics of, 346–51
    countries considered, 346
    economic growth in, 351
    emergence of external debt problem, 359–61
    export expansion, 357, 358–59
    growth model approach, 351–54
    radical school's critique, 362
    trade and economic development, 357–59
Line of best fit, 15n
Liquidity, money and, 149
    schedule, 161–62
Liquidity preference, 161–63
Lorenz curve, 349

M

McElravey, John, 252

Macroeconomics
    aggregate demand and supply, 99–102
    basic identity, 117–19
    budget deficits and, 230–32
    difference between microeconomics and, 88
    equilibrium real national output and aggregate price level, 104–5
    growth rate in real national ouput, 88, 98–99
    inflation rate, 88, 91–97
    unemployment rate, 88, 89–91
Managed float exchange rate systems, 323, 336
Marginal propensity to consume, 129
Marginal propensity to import, 133
Marginal propensity to save, 131
Marginal propensity to spend, 134
Marginal rate of taxation, 215
Marginal revenue (MR)
    defining, 74
    relationship between price and, 76–77
Market(s)
    See also Equilibrium state
    basket, 92
    capitalism, 4–5
    definition of, 50
    economy, 12
    foreign exchange, 305
    mechanism, 63
    self-regulating, 62
    types of, 50
Marshall, Alfred, 51n.2
Marx, Karl, 5, 362
    capitalism and, 368–70
Marxism, 369
Material balance form of planning, 371
Mature capitalism, 369
Mean duration of unemployment, 286–87
Medium of exchange, 148–49
Merchandise trade, 307
Microeconomics, difference between macroeconomics and, 88
Mixed economic system, 5–6
M1, 152
Monetarists, 222–23, 240n.4, 242
    monetary rule, 249–53
    neutrality of money hypothesis, 296–98
Monetary base, 179
Monetary policy
    compared with fiscal policy, 253–57
    definition of, 213, 237
    demand management and, 244–48
    effectiveness of, 240–42
    inflation and contractionary, 242–44
    instruments of, 238–40
    lags in, 245
    monetarist monetary rule, 249–53
    multiplier effects in, 245–48
    targets, 248–53
Monetizing debt, 230
Money/money market
    See also Banking system and money supply
    aggregate measures of, 152–53
    certificates of deposit (CDs), 153

coins or metallic, 150
    commodity, 150
    debased, 150
    demand deposits/checking accounts, 151–52
    deposit accounts (MMDAs), 153
    equilibrium, 182–84
    fiat, 151
    functions of, 148–50
    income velocity of, 249–50
    liquidity of, 149
    liquidity preference, 161–63
    medium of exchange, 148–49
    mutual funds (MMMFs), 153
    paper currency, 151
    portfolio management, 158–60
    sandwich coins, 150
    savings accounts, 153
    simple quantity theory of, 250
    store of value, 149
    substitute, 152
    time deposits, 153
    token coins, 150
    traveler's checks, 152
    unit of account, 149
Money demand, determinants of
    precautionary demand, 158
    speculative demand, 158
    transactions demand, 154–58
Money supply. *See* Banking system and money supply
Monopoly capitalism, 6
M3, 153
M2, 153
Multiplier effect
    autonomous expenditure multiplier, 141–45
    comparative statics and, 140–45
    in monetary policy, 245–48

N

National debt, 227–29
National income, factors that make up, 113–15
National income accounting
    definition of, 107
    disposable personal income, 116–17
    measurement of Gross Domestic Product, 109–15
    Net National Product, 116
    net private domestic fixed investment, 116
    net private domestic investment, 116
    value added, 108–9
National income determination. *See* Simple Keynesian model
National output gap, 203
Natural level of employment, 295
Natural rate of output, 295–96
Natural rate of unemployment, 292–96
Neo-Keynesians, 234, 240n.4, 242
Net creditor nation, 341n.10
Net factor income, 113
Net foreign saving, 119
Net interest, 114

Net international investment position, 341n.10
Net lump-sum taxes, 215, 218–21
Net National Product (NNP), 116
Net private domestic fixed investment, 116
Net private domestic investment, 116
Net unilateral transfers, 307
Neutrality of money hypothesis, 296–98
New Classicals, 298–300
New Economic Policy (NEP), 374
Normal commodities, 52
Normative statement, example of, 13
North American Free Trade Agreement (NAFTA), 304

O

Official reserve assets, 310
Offical settlements account, 309–11
Omnibus Budget Reconciliation Act (1990), 277
Open market operations, 179, 239–40
Opportunity costs, 23
    absolute advantage and international trade and, 37–38
    comparative advantage and international trade and, 39–40
    production possibilities boundary and, 30–31
Output
    national output gap, 203
    natural rate of, 295–96
    potential national, 203
Output-expenditure approach, 109–12
Output selection, defining, 3
Owen, Robert, 368

P

Paper currency, 151
Partial elasticity, 72
Partial equilibrium analysis, 12
Par values, 329
Peak in business cycle, 204
Perestroika, 378
Permanent income, 225n.7
Permanent income hypothesis, 225n.7
Personal consumption expenditures, 109
Personal income, 116
Personal saving, 117
    supply-side economics and, 266–68
Phillips, A. W., 280n.1
Phillips curve, 280–83
Physical capital, 10, 206
Planned inventory investment, 132
Point elasticity, 71n.1
Population momentum, 365n.19
Portfolio
    definition of, 158
    investment, 309
    management, 158–60
Positive statement, example of, 13
Potential national output, 203
Precautionary demand for money, 158
Prediction error, 16n

Price elasticity of demand
    along a linear demand schedule, 75–76
    average revenue, 74
    definition of, 72
    formula for, 73
    marginal revenue, 74
    price elastic, 73
    relationship between marginal revenue and price, 76–77
    total revenues and, 77–79
    unitary price inelastic, 73
Price elasticity of supply, 83–84
Price inelastic, 73
Producer Price Index (PPI), 96n.8
Production
    constant costs of, 37
    technique, 3
Production possibilities boundary (PPB)
    individual level, 24–26
    international trade and, 42–45
    national level, 26–31
    opportunity costs and, 30–31
Product markets, 10
Profits
    corporate, 114
    defined, 10
Proprietors' income, 113
Purchasing power, 51

Q

Quantity demanded, 51, 54–56
Quantity supplied, 56–57, 58–59
Quantity transacted, 51

R

Radical school of economic development, 362
Ratcheting effect, 201
Rational expectations, 298–300
Reaganomics
    assessment of, 273–77
    definition of, 261
    description of, 270–73
Real value, 13
Recession, 204
Recognition lag, 223, 245
Recycling of petrodollars, 359
Regression analysis, 14–16
Regulation, Reaganomics and, 273
Rental income of persons, 113–14
Replacement level fertility, 364–65
Required reserve ratio, 169, 238
Reserves, commerical banks and, 169
    excess, 170
    loans and excess, 174–75
    loans and required, 172–74
Residential fixed investment, 13
Resource allocations
    implications of present, 31–33
    individual level, 24–26
    national level, 26–31
    opportunity costs and, 30–31
Response lag, 223, 225, 245

Revaluation, 332
Ricardo, David, 36n

S

Sandwich coins, 150
Savings accounts, 153
Scarcity, 2–3
    production possibilities boundary models depicting, 24–31
Scatter diagram, use of, 14
Schultz, Theodore, 354
Second World, 348n.4
Sellers. *See* Supply/suppliers
Simon, Henri Saint, 368
Simple Keynesian model
    See also Aggregate demand; Aggregate supply
    components of desired aggregate expenditures, 127–33
    consumption expenditures, 131
    consumption function, 128–31
    fiscal policy options and, 215–21
    investment expenditures, 131–32
    Keynesian cross diagram, 135–37
    numerical example for, 137–40
    reasons for using, 126–27
    solving, 133–40
Simple quantity theory of money, 250
Smith, Adam, 5, 36n, 368
Socialism, 5
    centralized, 371–72
    decentralized, 372–73
    Marx and his critique of capitalism, 368–70
    political and economic inequalities, 377–78
    theory of, 370–73
Sources for a product, balance of, 371
Soviet Union
    Gorbachev reform process and demise of the Soviet Union, 378
    material balance form of planning, 371
    sources and uses for a product, balance of, 371
Soviet Union economy
    central planning, 375–76
    collectivization of agriculture, 374–75
    growth and investment versus consumption, 376–77
    historical perspective, 373–74
    New Economic Policy, 374
    political and economic inequalities, 377–78
    Stalin and, 374–78
    tolerance of private markets, 377
    war communism, 374
Soviet Union economy, future of
    Gorbachev reform process and demise of the Soviet Union, 378
    international economic integration, 381–82
    price decontrol programs, 379–80
    privatizing states enterprises, 380–81
    problems with currency and banking, 381

transition from command socialism, 379–82
Speculative demand for money, 158
Stagflation, 203
Stalin, Joseph, 5
    Soviet economy under, 374–78
Statistical discrepancy, 115
Stock, production of goods and, 27–28
Store of value, 149
Structural unemployment, 285
Substitute commodities, 53
    cross-price elasticity of demand and, 79
Substitution effect, 262
Supply/suppliers
    aggregate, 99–102, 186–209
    change in quantity supplied, 58–59
    change in supply, 58–59
    curve, 57, 58
    curve for foreign exchange, 314
    defining, 50
    determinants of supply schedule, 58
    law of, 57n.5
    price elasticity of, 83–84
    quantity supplied, 56–57, 58–59
    schedule, 56–59
Supply-side economics
    business investment, 269–70
    definition/description of, 260–61
    labor supply, 262–66
    personal saving, 266–68
    taxes and incentives, 262–70
Surplus less subsidies of government enterprises, current, 115
Surplus value, 369

T

Tax credits, 269–70
Taxes and incentives, supply-side economics and, 262–70
Third World, 348n.4
Time deposits, 153
Token coins, 150
Total expenditures (TE), 61, 74
Total revenues (TR), 61–62, 74
    price elasticity of demand and, 77–79
Trade
    economic growth and development and, 357–59
    invisible, 307
    merchandise, 307
Tradition economic system, 4
Transactions demand, 154–58
Transfer payments, 11, 115
Transfers
    government, 110
    international, 110
Transitory income, 225n.7
Traveler's checks, 152
Trotsky, Leon, 374
Trough of business cycle, 204

U

Underground economy, 272
Unemployed, definition of, 89
Unemployment
    cyclical, 285–86
    frictional, 284–85
    mean duration of, 286–87
    natural rate of, 292–96
    other dimensions of, 286–87
    Phillips curve, 280–83
    rate, 88, 89–91, 283–84
    structural, 285
    types of, 284–86
Unilateral transfers, 307
Unitary price inelastic, 73
Unit cost of labor, 197
U.S. dollar, exchange value of, 337–42
Unit of account, 149
Unplanned inventory investment, 132
Uruguay Round, 362n.16
Uses for a product, balance of, 371

V

Value added, 108–9
Volcker, Paul, 237, 270, 338

W

Walras, Leon, 51n.2
War communism, 374
World Bank, 332n.7
    creation of, 351
    former Soviet republics and, 382
    less developed countries and, 345, 346, 349
    loans, 360n.13
    market-friendly strategy, 363
Worldwatch Institute, 365